D0397141

Possible Lives

Books by Mike Rose

WRITER'S BLOCK:
THE COGNITIVE DIMENSION

WHEN A WRITER CAN'T WRITE:
STUDIES IN WRITER'S BLOCK AND OTHER
COMPOSING PROCESS PROBLEMS

PERSPECTIVES ON LITERACY
(*Edited with Eugene Kintgen and Barry Kroll*)

CRITICAL STRATEGIES FOR ACADEMIC
THINKING AND WRITING
(*with Malcolm Kiniry*)

LIVES ON THE BOUNDARY:
THE STRUGGLES AND ACHIEVEMENTS
OF AMERICA'S UNDERPREPARED

POSSIBLE LIVES:
THE PROMISE OF PUBLIC EDUCATION
IN AMERICA

MIKE ROSE

Possible Lives

THE PROMISE
OF
PUBLIC EDUCATION
IN AMERICA

HOUGHTON MIFFLIN COMPANY
BOSTON • NEW YORK
1995

Library of Congress Cataloging-in-Publication Data

Rose, Mike.
Possible lives : the promise of public education in America / Mike Rose.
p. cm.
Includes bibliographical references.
ISBN 0-395-74546-2
1. Public schools — United States — Case Studies. I. Title
LA217.2.B7 1995 95-30461
371'.01'0973—dc20 CIP

Printed in the United States of America

Book design by Robert Overholtzer

MP 10 9 8 7 6 5 4 3 2 1

For information about this and other Houghton Mifflin trade and reference books and multimedia products, visit The Bookstore at Houghton Mifflin on the World Wide Web at http://www.hmco.com/trade/.

This book is for the teachers and children who daily create the promise of public education

---

And, as always and to come, it is for
the memory of my father, Tommy Rose,
for my mother, Rose Meraglio Rose,
and for my stepfather, Bill Newby

Love and work

Contents

Possible Lives

Introduction

DURING A TIME when so many are condemning public schools — and public institutions in general — I have been traveling across the country, visiting classrooms in which the promise of public education is being powerfully realized. These are classrooms judged to be good and decent places by those closest to them — parents, principals, teachers, students — classrooms in big cities and small towns, preschool through twelfth grade, places that embody the hope for a free and educated society that has, at its best, driven this extraordinary American experiment from the beginning.

We seem to be rapidly losing that hope. Our national discussion about public schools is despairing and dismissive, and it is shutting down our civic imagination. I visited schools for three and a half years, and what struck me early on — and began to define my journey — was how rarely the kind of intellectual and social richness I was finding was reflected in the public sphere.

We have instead a strange mix of apocalyptic vignettes — violent classrooms, incompetent teachers, students who think Latin is spoken in Latin America — and devastating statistics: declines in SAT scores and embarrassing cross-national comparisons. We hear — daily, it seems — that our students don't measure up, either to their predecessors in the United States or to their peers in other countries, and that, as a result, our position in the global economy is in danger. We are told, by politicians, by pundits, that our cultural values, indeed our very way of life is threatened. We are offered, by both entertainment and news media, depictions of schools as mediocre places, where students are vacuous and teachers are not so bright; or as violent and chaotic places, places where order has fled and civility has been lost. It's hard to imagine anything good in all this.

Though researchers have for some time challenged the simplicity of these representations — reports from the Rand Corporation and the Sandia National Laboratories, for example, dispute the much-broadcasted declines in student achievement — their challenges rarely enter our public discourse in any significant way. We seem beguiled by a rhetoric of decline, this ready store of commonplaces about how awful our schools have become. "America's schools are the least successful in the Western world," declare the authors of a book on the global economy. "Face it, the public schools have failed," a bureau chief for a national news magazine tells me, offhandedly. "The kids in the Los Angeles Unified School District are garbage," a talk-radio host exclaims.

There are many dangers in the use of such language. It blinds us to the complex lives lived out in the classroom. It pre-empts careful analysis of one of the nation's most significant democratic projects. And it engenders a mood of cynicism and retrenchment, preparing the public mind for extreme responses: increased layers of testing and control, denial of new resources — even the assertion that money doesn't affect a school's performance — and the curative effects of free market forces via vouchers and privatization. What has been seen historically as a grand republican venture is beginning to be characterized as a failed social experiment, noble in intention but moribund now, perhaps headed toward extinction. So, increasing numbers of people who can afford to don't even consider public schools as an option for their children, and increasingly we speak, all of us, about the schools as being in decline. This is what is happening to our public discussion of education, to our collective vision of the schools.

But if you would travel with me to those classrooms in Baltimore or Kentucky or Chicago or LA, sit and watch those teachers work, listen in as students reason through a problem, walk around the neighborhoods to see what the schools provide — then the importance of public education and the limits of our portraits of it would become clear. To be sure, the visitor traveling through our nation's schools would find burned-out teachers, lost students, boredom, violence, inertia. But if our understanding of schooling and the conception we have of what's possible emerge primarily from these findings, then what we can imagine for public education will be terribly narrow and impoverished.

If, for example, we try to organize schools and create curriculum based on an assumption of failure and decay, then we make school life a punitive experience. If we think about education largely in relation to our economic competitiveness, then we lose sight of the fact that school has to be about more than economy. If we determine success primarily in terms of test scores, then we ignore the social, moral, and aesthetic dimensions of teaching and learning — and, as well, we'll miss those considerable intellectual achievements which aren't easily quantifiable. If we judge one school according to the success of another, we could well diminish the particular ways the first school serves its community. In fact, a despairing vision will keep us from fully understanding the *tragedies* in our schools, will reduce their complexity, their human intricacy. We will miss the courage that sometimes accompanies failure, the new directions that can emerge from burn-out, the desire that pulses in even the most depressed schools and communities.

Why are we thinking about our schools in such limited and limiting ways? To begin with, the way we perceive problems in schools is profoundly affected by our concerns about broad social conditions that exist well beyond the schoolhouse door. Since the mid-nineteenth century, that period when we began the standardization of the "common" elementary school and the development of the high school, most major periods of national concern about education — and the reform movements that have emerged from them — have coincided with periods of social and economic disruption, and in some ways have been responses to them. As historians David Tyack and Larry Cuban put it, "Americans have translated their cultural anxieties and hopes into dramatic demands for educational reform." The last fifteen years have seen conflict and uncertainty about economic competitiveness, changing demographics and national identity, and our position in the world order. These anxieties shape our perception of the schools — our schools have placed "our very future as a Nation and a people" at risk, states the most prominent of 1980s' reform documents — and manifest themselves in the sweeping but one-dimensional remedies we pose as a corrective, the remedies of siege and devastation.

There are other reasons for our limited perception; some are long-standing, others more immediate, all are interrelated. Though the teacher has been a respected figure in some communities, as a nation we have had little regard for teaching. It has been low-pay, low-status work, devalued as "women's work," judged to have limited intellectual content. In addition, we have little appreciation for the richness and mystery of "everyday cognition," for the small, commonplace intellectual challenges and achievements of the school day. It is also true that through most of this century our society has been in the grip of narrow conceptions of intellectual development and academic achievement; we operate with inadequate, even damaging notions of what it means to be "excellent." For all the hope we place in what school will do for our children — and we have always placed great hope in the benefits of education — we have a tendency to diminish the day-to-day practice of schooling. This has been especially true for our intellectual elite. Few discussions of schooling in policy papers, in legislation, in the endless flow of books by nonteachers telling us how to make it right, few of these discussions take us in close to teaching and learning. They tend to work at a high level of generality and opinion, thereby relying more easily on one-dimensional portrayals of the classroom. Class and race bias play into all this, keeping us from seeing the good in poor schools and orienting us toward stereotype and sweeping condemnation — and this distortion will get worse as public schools increasingly become the domain of the working classes, immigrants, and minorities. Contributing as well to our disillusion with the schools is a general loss of faith in public institutions and an idealization of the private sphere and the free market. Finally, these tendencies have been skillfully manipulated during the last decade by legislators, policy analysts, and entrepreneurs who want to restrict funding to public education, subject it to market forces, and, ultimately, privatize it.

I have written this book to help us think in a different way.

In doing so, I am not trying to ignore the obvious misery in our schools nor the limitations of too many of those who teach in and manage them. Nor have I disregarded the complaints of those whose schools are failing them; they have a strong voice in this book. This is not a call to abandon the critical perspective a citizenry should have when it surveys its institutions. What I am suggesting is that we lack a public critical language adequate to the task. We need a different kind of critique, one that does not minimize the inadequacies of curriculum and instruction, the rigidity of school structure, or the "savage inequalities" of funding, but that simultaneously opens discursive space for inspired teaching, for courage, for achievement against odds, for successful struggle, for the insight and connection that occur continually in public school classrooms around the country. Without a multiplicity of such moments, criticism becomes one-dimensional, misses too much, is harsh, brittle, the humanity drained from it.

Public education demands a capacious critique, one that encourages both dissent and invention, fury and hope. Public education is bountiful, crowded, messy, contradictory, exuberant, tragic, frustrating, and remarkable. We need an expanded vocabulary, adequate to both the daily joy and daily sorrow of our public schools. And we are in desperate need of rich, detailed images of possibility. In the stories that follow, I try to provide some of those images. What begins to shape itself in our minds as we witness good work being done in the South Side of Chicago; in an auditorium just off the freeway in Monterey Park, on the east side of the LA Basin; in a computer lab in Floyd County, Kentucky; in a border town; in a one-room schoolhouse; on the second floor of a market on North Avenue in Baltimore? *Possible Lives* is part inquiry, part meditation, a tour and a discovery, an opportunity to reimagine ourselves through the particulars of people's lives, an attempt to envision the possible from the best of the present.

I planned this journey with a map and a telephone. I highlighted the country's major regions — the industrial Northeast, the deep South, the Southwest, and so on — and began calling people I had come to know through previous research and writing, people who were in the middle of good work, people who knew schools: teachers, principals, superintendents and other administrators in district, state, or regional offices, analysts in policy centers, college faculty who taught teachers, parents and community activists involved in education reform. What's going on in your area, I asked, that seems promising? What do other teachers talk about when they're excited? Who do parents hold in esteem? I tended to focus on the classroom because it is the fundamental unit of the school, a kind of miniature public space, the place where any discussion of educational effectiveness — or reform — would have to be grounded.

These calls led to further calls. To other agencies, teachers, parents, following up on the lead about the school outside of town, or the interesting program in the center of the city, or the new teacher in the next building, the one who has her students talking excitedly about literature or physics or the urban environment. I was trying to tap into the folk wisdom of good teaching — following leads, pursuing the excitement of local perception, getting a sense of the programs and people who engendered respect, sparked hope.

I was blessed with hospitable guides. People walked me around town, took me to community functions, asked me to join them at their favorite restaurant or bar. Usually, I stayed in the homes of teachers or others who were involved with the schools — and this led to conversation over dinner or around the TV, a quick trip to the market or dry cleaner's or mechanic's, daily rides into school . . . all sources of insight into the history of the community, its norms and politics, and its schools.

Once I was inside a school, a teacher would take me across the hall to see a colleague's room bright with student work. Or students I got to know in one class would introduce me to students in another — and that would broaden my understanding of teaching and learning. So it was not uncommon that my plans were disrupted by something new and interesting, and I'd grab a sandwich from the cafeteria and go to visit another teacher or sit with a new group of students, trying to get as good a sense as I could of what was compelling here, what worked.

Schools are nested in complex, often volatile social and political environments, and my trip often coincided with a felicitous shift in policy or a crisis of finances or institutional identity. So another dimension of public education presented itself, and I would change the scope of my inquiry to try to understand the larger forces that encourage or limit good work in our schools.

During these visits, I certainly heard about, and in some cases met, mediocre teachers or teachers who were downright awful: people who were not comfortable in a classroom or were poorly educated or lacked compassion and a sense of possibility or were tired, shut down, marking time, cynical. But one of the significant things about the journey — surprising, given the prevalence of negative press on our nation's public school teachers — was the number of hardworking, competent teachers I met and, among them, those who were outstanding, inspired. I met many more good people than I could include in my study.

A word, then, on how I selected the people I introduce here. I wanted to offer in *Possible Lives* a fair representation of grade level, teaching style, and subject area. And I wanted a demographic balance — among urban center, medium-sized city, small town, and country outpost. The exception to this rule of balance was that in many cases I chose schools that served large numbers of poor and working-class students, since these are usually the kinds of schools at the center of public concern. It was also important to me to spend as much time as possible with someone I selected. The strength of large-scale surveys is that they can sample broadly; the weakness is that detail gets lost. As I've indicated already, and as I hope will be justified as the book progresses, I wanted to get in close to teaching and learning. Therein, I believed, lay the particulars of the potential of public education. In some cases, as with the chapter on the Los Angeles Basin that opens the book, the sweep of my inquiry meant that I could spend only a day or two with a given teacher. Most of the time, though, I spent one to two weeks in each classroom I observed. These various criteria — grade level, subject area, demographics, location, and concerns about method — limit the number of people who move through *Possible Lives.* And because the focus of the study was the teacher and the classroom, I did not include the counselor, the nurse, the psychologist, the college adviser — people essential to school life, working with astounding numbers of students (a counselor case load of seven hundred is not unusual), responding to a wide range of academic and personal needs and problems. Yet, I was still able to observe or interview more than sixty teachers and twenty-five administrators and a wealth of students, parents, and people from the communities I visited.

Classrooms are powerful places. They can be the sites of numbing boredom and degradation or of growth and connection. In my own educational history, I have known them as both. I grew up in a working-class neighborhood in South-Central Los Angeles, and from my elementary grades well into high school accumulated a spotty academic record and a lot of years of hazy, flat disaffection. The schools I attended were not so great, and I was dreamy, unengaged, fearful of things I didn't understand. But I was fortunate. Later in high school and during my first bumpy years at a small college, I met some teachers who had a lasting influence on the direction of my life. And since the age of twenty-four, I have been making my living in the classroom.

I must admit that I have strong feelings about classrooms. I like them, feel at home in them. I like the banter, the crayons and pencils and scratching of pens, the smell of watercolors and acrylics, the quiet of concentration, the bustle of students thinking something through. The classroom is the place of my life's work, the long haul, layered with emotion and memory. It doesn't take much to call forth the wisps of childhood alienation and loneliness — the pages of a worn textbook, a kid's slumping posture, the whiff of disinfectant — or sometimes, in rapid shift, feelings of delicate hope and admiration for a teacher's or student's courage, quickness, humanity. Some of the most significant encounters of my late adolescence and young adulthood took place in classrooms, and it was in classrooms that I appropriated powerful bodies of knowledge and methods of inquiry. As I moved from student to teacher, I came of age in these rooms, realizing things about my own abilities and limits, my talent and fragility, the interplay of understanding and uncertainty that defines teaching, the sheer hard human work of it. I have been privy to remarkable moments, spent untold hours with people — from elementary school children to adults in literacy programs — as they acquired knowledge and new skill, played with ideas and struggled to understand, reached tentatively across divides, felt the grounded satisfaction of achievement, raged against history and moved toward clarity and resolve. A democracy, I believe, cannot leave the conditions for such experience to chance — or, for that matter, to the vagaries of political climate and market forces, for as Walter Lippmann observed, "the market is, humanly speaking, a ruthless sovereign." A society that defines itself as free and open is obligated to create and sustain the public space for this kind of education to occur across the full, broad sweep of its citizenry.

Our journey begins in Los Angeles and the surrounding LA Basin. The movement of the chapter forecasts the movement of the book, traveling through region and community, finding good work in a range of places, arising out of specific histories and cultural conditions, abundant and varied. The LA chapter presents a number of classrooms in relatively quick succession, for I want at the outset to render the complexity of public education in urban America, the overwhelming needs of these schools condemned and abandoned by so many, yet the many kinds of teaching and learning achieved within them. Subsequent chapters proceed at a different pace, but the scheme is the same: a series of portraits of classrooms, each good on its own terms, yet part of a larger social fabric.

I also want to introduce during our time in Los Angeles some of the themes that will re-emerge as we continue the journey: the relation of classroom to community and learning to identity; the nature of a teacher's knowledge and the social and moral dimensions of that knowledge; the role of the teacher as culture broker, boundary mediator; the intricate mix of courage, hope, and thoughtfulness among our nation's youth and the threats to and misrepresentations of those riches; the grounding of the public school in local economy, politics, and social structure; the joy of intellectual work and the role of public institutions in fostering it. We will encounter as well the educational issues that were much in the news as I traveled through the LA Basin and across the country — school restructuring, standards and testing, multiculturalism, and the like — for they have become part of the sociopolitical terrain of schooling. Many treatments of them, unfortunately, tend toward the polemical or the sensational. They will emerge here in the more nuanced contexts of classrooms and the teacher-student encounter.

From Los Angeles I travel south to Calexico, California, a small city on the Mexican border that reveals some of the educational possibilities of bicultural life in the United States and presents, as well, an occasion to reflect on teacher education and development. The third stop in the journey, a long arc cross country from the base of California to the Chesapeake Bay, takes us along North Avenue in inner-city Baltimore, where science, reading, writing, and the African-American experience intersect in a first-grade classroom. Then a six-hundred-mile angle west and a little north to Chicago, the industrial Midwest. We'll make our way through a number of schools, observing, as we will throughout the journey, a range of teaching styles and classroom events, from an advanced placement class analyzing *As I Lay Dying* to a group of sixth-graders putting their day in order. All this takes place in the midst of chaotic school politics and a movement to reform the way schools are structured and governed. It is this reform impulse that takes me back across the Northeast to New York City, to interview nine first-year principals trying to create a new kind of public high school in the largest school system in the nation. There is much said about school reform these days, but we hear infrequently from the people struggling to make it work. We will get close to the day-to-day human reality of social change.

From New York, I fly south and west into one of the early frontiers of the Republic, the Commonwealth of Kentucky. We'll hear from young teachers about to begin their careers, the dreams and uncertainties that consume them, and then travel into the Eastern Coal Field to watch two veteran teachers work through their own uncertainty as they forge an American studies curriculum around independent research projects and computer technology. Farther south to Mississippi, via commuter plane and Greyhound bus to Tupelo, Hattiesburg, Jackson, and a series of small towns in the Delta, where physics, algebra, and the humanities provide the opportunity to consider race, gender, sexual orientation, and school prayer. From Mississippi in sharp angle over the Great Plains, into Western Montana, to a one-room schoolhouse near the ghost town of Polaris in Beaverhead County. The country school, the foundation of public education in rural America. From Polaris we travel to an experimental preschool in Missoula that integrates children with and without disabilities, providing them, at a young age, the opportunity to live across the boundaries of ability. Straight south, then, over the Rockies, to Tucson for a summer enrichment program at the University of Arizona, one example of the many ways colleges and universities — and other public and private institutions — can contribute to the public schools. Here students from the Navajo and Hopi reservations study Greek tragedy, Native American literature, and contemporary novels, writing, in the process, their own defining stories and poetry and plays.

Together, the chapters form an anthology of educational possibility, a series of occasions to think about the future of our public schools. So, though the chapters offer a number of portraits of good teachers, there is no single profile of the Good Teacher; though they offer a number of accounts of skilled practice, I recommend no final list of good practices, no curricular framework or set of instructional guidelines. Such profiles and lists have value: they can suggest direction and generate discussion. But they also have a tendency to be stripped of context, to become rigid prescriptions, at times reduced to slogan or commodity. As we move from classroom to classroom, along the packed hallways of the big city school, along the highway beyond the city, I hope not so much for prescription as for an opening up of the way we think and talk about public schools. What we come to know, we know by settling in, staying a while, watching and listening. There may be no uniform road signs on this journey, but there are rest stops, places to take stock, to reflect on the slowly developing landscape of decency and achievement, to try to leave behind the reductive charts and the stultifying, dismissive language, and ponder the intricate mix of mind and heart that defines the classroom.

The journey comes to a temporary stop in Chapter Ten; there I will try to pull some thoughts together. For all their variety, what do the classrooms share? How did they develop? What threatens them? How can we begin to talk about public schools so that we simultaneously capture their failures and articulate their potential? The kind of talk that comes from thoughtful work and leads to thoughtful action. As the chapter ends, the journey begins again, both across and inward, for public education is ongoing, unfinished, as the democratic state is ongoing, continually trying to realize its promise. "I refer," wrote Walt Whitman, "to a Democracy that is yet unborn"; these classrooms offer a collective public space in which America is being created.

1

Los Angeles and the LA Basin

I BEGAN THIS JOURNEY with the city I know best. I grew up in South-Central Los Angeles, near the site of our first visit, in Watts, came of age absorbing the enticing mythologies of the other cities and neighborhoods in the surrounding Basin, places I would pass through as an adolescent, then as a young man, by bus, by car, on foot, getting closer, coming to understand. My first teaching job was with children east of downtown Los Angeles, beyond East LA in El Monte, one of the communities that developed as people from the East Side moved farther east. Then I taught adults, returning Vietnam veterans, just south of downtown, by a strip of small factories that had seen better days. Los Angeles is a difficult, contradictory place, dizzying, seductive, full of longing, a place of misery and opportunity, evident in its history, revealed in its schools.

The LA Basin is 16,200 square miles, bounded by the Pacific Ocean on the west, the Santa Monica Mountains on the north, and the San Gabriel Mountains on the east. Beginning with the parceling and selling of its vast Mexican *ranchos* in the mid-nineteenth century and continuing with the subsequent building of railway, roadway, and huge-scale water diversion projects, the Basin has been the site of unparalleled development. It has gone through cycles of agriculture, commerce, oil, industry, and real estate; annexation and suburbanization; defense, entertainment, high tech, and international finance. Urban theorist Mike Davis calls LA "the most permanent boom town in American history." This development has been driven and shaped by migrants and immigrants — ROOM FOR MILLIONS trumpets an early promotion for Southern California. "No other city in the U.S.," writes historian George Sánchez, "[has] attracted so many people so consistently for so long." And with this immigration and settlement have come intolerance and residential segregation, leading Carey McWilliams half a century ago to define LA as "an archipelago of ethnic, cultural, racial, and socioeconomic islands." As a result of this history, the Basin contains an extraordinary range of communities: from affluent beach cities on the west — Santa Monica, Playa del Rey, Manhattan Beach, Palos Verdes Estates — to older, once-genteel suburbs like Pasadena, along the northeastern rim of the mountains, to richly Latino East Los Angeles and the residential sprawl east of it — Montebello, Monterey Park, Alhambra — to an old industrial corridor that runs south and southeast twenty miles from the freight yards in downtown LA through Vernon, Bell, South Gate, and Watts to the harbors in San Pedro and Long Beach.

Each of these communities has felt the effects of a recent restructuring of the economy that has, in wild fluctuations, transformed the social and fiscal terrain of Southern California — some communities accumulating great wealth; many others sliding into further decline. And most communities have felt the effects of the astounding, not unrelated, wave of demographic changes taking place over the past twenty years: immigrants from Armenia, Cambodia, China, Colombia, El Salvador, Iran, Korea, Mexico, the Philippines, Russia, Thailand, and Vietnam settling where forebears had settled, creating communities within communities (a Little Armenia, a Little Teheran, Koreatown), creating the largest pool of cheap nonunionized labor in any city in the United States, forming a linguistic and cultural mix that has affected every institution in the Basin: social services, the churches, the schools. There are over ninety languages spoken by the students in the Los Angeles Unified School District.

Reticulated through the communities in the Basin — arteries in the body, mineral veins in rock are common metaphors — is a giant crisscrossing system of freeways, 722 miles of freeway that connect downtown LA to the outlying ports in San Pedro and Long Beach, the western shore to the eastern mountains, suburb to central city, tract houses to industry. These freeways will take us to communities in the center, east, and west of the Basin, visiting classrooms in seven schools located in four school districts — Los Angeles Unified, Alhambra, Pasadena, Santa Monica — spending most time in the massive Los Angeles Unified School District: 650 schools covering 700 square miles with a population of 640,000 children. The teachers we will meet have chosen to work within a system of public education that sometimes encourages their work, sometimes mires, even resists it; yet across a range of subject areas, in a variety of ways, they foster growth and learning by pressing against the limits of the possible. They share a dissatisfaction with the status quo, share a desire to challenge the ways our schools tend to define ability and achievement, establish the curriculum, and respond to the social order. The teachers who populate subsequent chapters of

Possible Lives mount their challenges, as well. Good teaching, I've come to believe, is almost defined by its tendency to push on the borders of things. It is especially fitting that such work gets done in the classrooms of Los Angeles — a city that so disrupts traditional definitions of our national profile and character, a city "conflictual and kaleidoscopic," masking its contradictions, and its cruelty to so many, behind a heritage of manufactured images, a flurry of promotions. A CLIMATE FOR HEALTH AND WEALTH, continues that early advertisement, WITHOUT CYCLONES OR BLIZZARDS. "The Great Gatsby of American cities," says one observer about Los Angeles; "the most mediated town in America," writes another.

We'll start south of downtown Los Angeles, close to the geographical center of the Basin, in Watts. During the first decades of this century, Watts was a semirural junction for the Pacific Electric Railway, Henry Huntington's "Red Car," the largest urban electric railroad system in the nation. Every Red Car traveler from agricultural and beach cities to the west and south rode through Watts en route to Los Angeles. The area became a mixed-race community of Germans, Blacks, Jews, Japanese, Mexicans, and Italians — Simon Rodia, who in 1921 began his ornate and airy construction of steel, mortar, tile, glass, and shell known as the Watts Towers, was an Italian immigrant. In the late 1930s and the 1940s burgeoning manufacturing industries generated a sizable migration of Blacks from the South and from Texas. Because most real estate in Los Angeles was barred to them by race-restrictive covenants, they settled in the Central and South-Central regions of the city, a settlement that was further concentrated in Watts by the building of public housing. LA's heavy industries — aircraft and defense, automotive (for a time, LA's auto production was second only to Detroit's), steel, rubber, metal plating — provided steady, if dirty and dangerous, work for the rapidly growing population of Watts and for a range of blue-collar communities that surrounded the industrial corridor. I remember riding buses full of workmen in oil- and soot-stained denim.

Though Watts began to feel the social effects of overcrowding and inadequate infrastructure, it became a center of African-American life and culture. But as the factories began closing in the 1960s and 1970s, the community, and others like it in the corridor, lost its economic base, and experienced a devastating rise in unemployment and crime, and underwent dramatic shifts in demographics. (In the last fifteen years, through immigration from Mexico and Central America, Watts has become a community that is 43 percent Latino.) There has been little reinvestment in Watts and similiar communities — they are very poor now, palm tree ghettoes — and the few jobs that remain tend to be low-skilled and low-paying. In the last twenty years, unemployment has risen by 50 percent; in 1990, the average household income in Watts was $12,700.

Watts. Since the summer of 1965, the name conjures up images of fire and violence. Given what Angelenos read in the paper or see on television, it is hard to imagine Watts as anything other than a site of drive-by shootings, street crime, squalid projects. Few people other than residents would think of going through there. To get to Watts, you would take the Harbor Freeway, heading south out of downtown LA toward the harbors in San Pedro, and exit to the east at Century Boulevard. You would pass Cathy's Nails and Red's Mini-mart and Pete's Burgers, a gas station, a coin laundry, a liquor store, a place to cash checks, some apartment buildings, and a lot of people on the street. At the corner of Century and Success Avenue, a green metal sign announces WATTS. Some of the side streets you might take would reveal abandoned houses, bars on windows, old couches rotting in vacant lots. But other streets have well-kept single-family homes, trimmed lawns, flower beds. If you got back onto Century Boulevard, continued east to Compton Avenue, and took a right turn, you'd soon find Edwin Markham Intermediate School, a good school sustained by the cohesive forces in the community, by those people who, as one resident said, "try to do the right thing, are ordinary, decent folks."

There are graffiti on several of Markham's bungalows and on the windows of the snack bar. Classrooms sometimes get vandalized. But when you walk into the main courtyard, you'll find a wide stretch of deep green grass, palm and pine trees, azaleas. In the principal's office are a number of trophies for "school beautification" and for academic pentathlon victories. (In 1990, Markham was one of two LA schools designated a California Distinguished School.) Outside the office is a bulletin board that displays certificates for achievement. *Laureates of the Week* it announces. Each certificate bears a student's name *for attendance and academic performance at Markham Middle School.* Two girls coast by on their bikes. "Hey," one says to the other, "did you see? Latisha made the honor roll."

It was three in the afternoon in Room 56, and Yvonne Divans Hutchinson had just kicked off her shoes and was stretching out, spent, releasing the day. She began reflecting on her long local history.

"I grew up here, over in the projects, and went to school in the neighborhood, went to this school, in fact. And I can remember some teachers saying awful things to us. I remember one in particular who told us that we should be glad he came to Watts, because no one wanted to teach here. We were always confronted with attitudes like that. Well, I took umbrage at that comment. I had wanted to be a teacher for as long as I could remember, and on that day, I decided that not only was I going to be a teacher, but I was going to teach at *this* school because we needed teachers who *believed* in us."

She was about eight when her parents moved to Los Angeles from Arkansas and settled in Exposition Park, an area close to the LA Coliseum. She remembers a rooming house, her sister and brother and her sleeping in one bed. And she remembers her mother's excitement when they were finally able to move into the projects called Imperial Courts: "We're going to have a house all our own!" That was in 1954. Yvonne remembers roller-skating around the neighborhood, over to the library on Grandee. She recalls walking to school along the tracks of the Red Car, playing in the courtyard of the Watts Towers, going to the Largo Theater for thirty-five cents. She entered Edwin Markham Junior High School when it opened and was in the first graduating class, in 1958. She returned to teach in 1966 and has been there ever since.

"I've been a mentor teacher and the department chair, and I've had teachers tell me, 'This class can't think; they can't do the work; I can't find anything they can do.' And I'm astounded. You can look at a child and see that brightness, that eagerness. People who come to the classroom with preconceived notions about the kids don't give them a chance. It angers me and saddens me."

Room 56 was brick and dry wall, painted light mustard, some water stains along the baseboards. A long sign over one of the blackboards read: NOTHING IS MORE IMPORTANT THAN YOUR EDUCATION. A life-sized cut-out of Bill Cosby on the back door said the same thing. A table in the back of the class was filled with autobiographies, stood upright on display: Ernesto Galarza's *Barrio Boy,* Dick Gregory's *Nigger, The Autobiography of Malcolm X,* Elie Wiesel's *Night,* Russell Baker's *Growing Up.* Along the chalk tray of the blackboard was a range of novels and stories, many of them autobiographical in content: Amy Tan's *The Kitchen God's Wife,* Maya Angelou's *I Know Why the Caged Bird Sings,* John Knowles's *A Separate Peace,* Sandra Cisnero's *The House on Mango Street.* One of the themes in the district guidelines for ninth grade is "understanding ourselves," and Yvonne had selected books that, for the most part, reflected the backgrounds of her students.

"I had a young Hispanic man tell me last year that he couldn't carry books because he was a homeboy — he didn't want to be a schoolboy. A lot of boys want to be cool, so they'll put their books in their lockers when they go to class. A lot of African-American boys will carry Pee-Chee folders because they can roll them up and put them in their coat pockets or jam them down the back of their pants. So I give notice on the first day of school that for my class you have to have a notebook that can't be folded up. A lot of our kids, the boys especially, identify with the streets; they want to be cool. They don't want to look like nerds. But I like to tell them [laughs], 'The nerds shall inherit the Earth!' [pause] It *is* serious, though. The whole idea of being identified as a tough guy yet also doing well in school is a real dilemma for young Black men — in this neighborhood especially. We have people who are scholarly types, and when they leave the school, they go to the projects and have to prove themselves. It's really difficult."

All around the classroom, student writing and student art was on display. To the right of Yvonne's desk was Mariah Legans's drawing of four very different women, sort of middle-school Cubist in style, colorful, striking: an oblong face, a full, round face, blue spiked hair, tight black hair, tiny eyes, big eyes, a smile, a frown, a nose ring. "We are all individuals," she had written under it. "We don't look alike, we don't dress the same way, but we are all humans living on the same earth. So we need to learn to get along and respect each other."

On the bulletin board by the door was a cluster of four-by-six index cards, arrayed against orange, yellow, and blue art paper. These were done in class, responses to the books the students were reading. Yvonne had asked them to select a passage that grabbed them, draw it as best they could in pencil or pen, and comment on it.

Yardenna Aaron rendered a moment from the early pages of Malcolm X's autobiography:

> The scene depicted is when the police took Mrs. Little to the hospital to see and identify her dead husband. She was very hysterical. My drawing represents my idea and Malcolm's about her. The atmosphere when she entered the room containing the dead bodies. I think the policemen were laughing when she saw her husband. I believe that having no compassion in a case like this is a sin. The police were probably happy that he was killed because he was a strong man and taught Negroes about themselves.

Evonne Santiago had this to say about page 45 of *The House on Mango Street:*

> This nun has made Esperanza embarrassed of where she lived. This reminds me of myself. I always hated where I lived (in New Jersey) because everyone in my Catholic school had beautiful houses and my house was in a bad neighborhood and had rats and roaches.

Alejandra Mendoza, who was still mastering written English, wrote about a scene in Elie Wiesel's *Night:*

> My drawing represents the German throwing the kids up in the air and killing them with a machine gun. The reason the German killed them

is because the kids are Jewish. It reminds me of LA because every day there's a kid dying by violence.

Yvonne continued. "Teachers will say either 'We can't lower our standards' or 'This poor child is reading below grade level, so I'll need a third- or fourth-grade book.' But what you need to do is find a way to make that eighth-grade book *accessible.* You have to respect the child . . . I used to give a speech to new teachers in which I began by enumerating all the adjectives used to describe our kids: *slow, poor, impoverished, deprived, oppressed.* We get so busy looking at children in terms of labels that we fail to look for the *potential* — and to demand that kids live up to that potential. I tell these teachers, 'Do not think that because a child cannot read a text, he cannot read *you.*' Children can tell right off those people who believe in them and those who patronize them. They can tell once they come into the room — as if there's a smell in the air — they can tell right away if this teacher means business or if this teacher is, as they say, *jive.* They rise to whatever expectations are set. They rise or fail to rise. And when they rise, they can sometimes rise to great heights."

And so it was in this room on that day that Michallene Hooper read a draft of a profile of her friend Jennifer:

> "Nothing is more important than my education," declared Jennifer Rene McKnight, ninth-grader of Markham Intermediate School, who thinks very highly of her education. She plans on getting a scholarship for college and becoming a worker in the medical field. . . . This tall, slim, dark-skinned 14-year-old was born and raised in Los Angeles and has always been for helping her fellow Los Angelenos and influencing them to do the same. . . . Once while she was [stranded in the rain] a boy of her age with an umbrella offered to walk her home. "And after that," explained Jennifer, "I have never doubted the abilities of my neighbors. There's no telling what these good people are capable of or are going to do."

And it was in this room that the class held what Yvonne called a Quaker reading of Maya Angelou's inaugural poem, "On the Pulse of Morning." Each student selected some lines that spoke to him or her and read them, in sequence, into a tape recorder, creating a class reading, a new rendering:

> Across the wall of the world,
> A River sings a beautiful song. It says
> Come, rest here by my side . . .

So say the Asian, the Hispanic, the Jew
The African, the Native American, the Sioux . . .

I, the Rock, I, the River, I, the Tree
I am yours — your passages have been paid.

And it was in this room that Evonne Santiago — the girl who, in reading *The House on Mango Street,* recalled her old house in New Jersey — it was Evonne who explained to the class what she thought Maya Angelou's poem meant:

She tells us our faults so we can see what to do with our country, she's telling us how to make it a better country . . .

The rock means strength. And the river — you know how a river goes through the land and picks up different water, well, that's like different cultures. And the tree is America — that can grow big and strong . . .

She's asking all these people — the Asian, the Hispanic, the African American — she's asking them to come under the tree, to let their dream grow. And she writes it for the inauguration because the president, he has to lead the country, he has great influence. If we grow today, we will be strong tomorrow . . .

And all day long in this room, in every class — just as she did every day here in this room — Yvonne Divans Hutchinson demonstrated, encouraged, celebrated, and guided students through an active and critical reading process that undercut the common perception that reading simply involved the decoding of words, that print had single, basic meanings that students had to decipher quietly and store away. She had students write in a "Reading Journal" a dialogue between themselves and the author of whatever book they were currently reading, "agreeing, disagreeing, sympathizing, questioning — engaging the *ideas* in the pages." Before distributing an essay on courage, she asked her students to talk about a movie or television show in which people acted courageously, and from those examples try to explain what courage meant — all this to raise to critical consciousness their own definitions of courage. She had been involved in the development of a new statewide proficiency exam — one that encourages students to offer interpretations of texts — and she handed out a draft of the scoring guide and urged her students to analyze it. And Mariah Legans, whose Cubist plea for tolerance decorated the wall behind Yvonne's desk, said that "when they say *literal* they mean that you just write down what you got from the reading, but when they say *thoughtful* they mean you put some interpretation in it." And Michallene Hooper, the author of the personality profile, explained that when they ask for *implications,* they're referring to those times "when you read something, and it won't just come right out and say what it meant, but kind of suggests it." And from there the class began to discuss what it meant to read critically.

And in this room, at the end of the day, Rahsaan Thorpe took a moment to look at his paper that Yvonne had on yet another display, a response to a quotation about the value of interracial friendships. It began:

> I recall from ages 8 to 12, I was in close relation to other races. I grew up in a house-apartment, and during my time living there many neighbors came and went. Until one Christmas Eve a family moved in next door to me. The next morning I looked outside and there was a [Salvadoran] boy sitting alone playing. I saw him and decided to make conversation, and ever since that day, we have been friends . . .

And from there, Rahsaan and the others went out to 104 Street or to Compton Avenue, some leaving for surrounding communities, some walking home, holding their words clean and tight.

II

DIRECTLY EAST OF WATTS, about four miles, across turf boundaries kids from Watts rarely used to cross, lies Bell, a city of 34,000, another of the blue-collar communities that had grown with the development of LA's once robust industry. I came the long way, driving south out of downtown, picking up the Long Beach Freeway, passing over expansive freight yards, dark factories, storage tanks, and tract houses. Huge power grids ran alongside the freeway; graffiti were on the railroad bridges and the exit signs; and, to the west, the dry LA River. I took the off ramp at Florence Avenue, headed west, passing over the river, and in a few minutes saw a small brick wall displaying the raised metal outline of a bell. WELCOME TO BELL. The smog was thick, the air still and hot. Bell High School sits in the middle of the southern residential edge of the city. I found a parking space under the full trees on Flora Avenue between two customized Toyotas — lowered, miniature mag wheels, many layers of maroon, lustrous. LA car culture. A tricked-out VW Beetle drove by, tinted windows, boom box throbbing, and took a sharp turn into a gated driveway. A kid ran from within the school yard and scrambled, hand over hand, up the chain links, half rolling, half vaulting over the top, leaping down to the pavement. He got into the VW, and it sped off.

Not too far inside that gate Ed Murphy and Larry Stone were teaching their classes in video production, using the old drama room that Ed, over the years, had converted into a studio. Both men were English teachers who have developed their expertise by trial and error. Ed started twenty-two years ago with Super-8 technology and, through donations, grants, and personal expense, has built a classy video production facility; Larry joined in about five years ago as the student demand for the courses continued to grow. Now the students' one-minute public service announcements (about smoking, drugs, rape, gangs) and their video essays (usually three- to four-minute arrangements of images set to popular or original music) regularly win local and state contests. Students enroll in the classes now because they hear so much about them in the school yard. Herbert Aparicio, a senior who has contributed original music to a number of videos, said this: "I started seeing these big changes in my friends. They were starting to get more responsible. These guys! A big change — real quick. I thought, 'What's the big deal here?' So I went to Mr. Murphy and said, 'Do you need help with music?' And he said, 'Yeah, sure.' And I said, 'Well, I'd love to try.'"

Central to Ed's success, and to Larry Stone's, is the fact that they have fostered a culture of achievement, one that includes both college-bound students and students who are sleepwalking through the rest of the curriculum. Ed begins each term with technical instruction — how to use the camera, basic shots, fundamentals of script writing — and uses as illustration videos from his growing library of student work. He then divides the class into groups and turns them loose to develop and execute their projects. From that point until the end of the term, most of his instruction takes place through individual and small group conferences. So, on any given day, you would find Ed up at his desk going over a script with a student while other students were coming in and out with video equipment, or working on scripts at the computer terminals, or surveying the video encyclopedia for just the right images, or whirring through footage at the editing machines. There would be a constant but shifting blend of voices — English, Spanish, street talk, laughter — the beeps and tones of electronic equipment, scuffles behind the stage where scripts were being rehearsed, and music — Metallica, Doctor Dre, Chicano rapper Kid Frost — as students tried to synchronize images with a lyric and a beat.

Driving it all is a demand for quality and originality — generated by the collective student work, both past and present. So student projects get shown in "premieres" and are celebrated continually. During the first of my visits, Ed premiered two recently completed videos. In the first, a sixty-second instructional video, a soft-spoken, bespectacled boy named Frank had dubbed a lesson on amphibians onto a clip from a Teenage Mutant Ninja Turtles cartoon. To match the new dialogue with the cavorting turtles, Frank had worked and reworked his script, finding different ways to phrase things, running the tape over and over again — more than twenty times, Mr. Murphy said — to create the right fit between word and image. So when Raphael turns to Donatello, nose to nose, he asks "Did you know there are many kinds of amphibians?" And when the four muscle-bound mutants dive into water, they are asked by a fifth character if they found amphibians there. Finally, as the cartoon closes, the turtles turn to the screen and in farewell say, "So remember, dudes, when you think amphibious, think land and water."

The second video, a video essay, done by two girls in Larry Stone's class was entitled "Civil Wars" (after the Guns 'n' Roses song "Civil War"), and it took Melanie Alvarenga and Leonor Martinez two months to produce. A visitor from a public television station said it was one of the most professional pieces of student work he had ever seen. The video opened with the scene from *Cool Hand Luke* where Strother Martin knocks Paul Newman into a ditch and, looking down at him, says, "What we have here is failure to communicate." Then "Civil War" fades in and the screen delivers a series of images of battlefields, candlelight vigils, cross burnings, hooded Klansmen, mourners, demagogic speeches, the Vietnam War Memorial, hospital corridors lined with bodies, an autopsy — all paced to the urgent rhythm of the song, the images moving in slow motion or staccato or real time, their shift each to the other enhanced by computer graphics: wipes and fades and a frame folding into a box and tumbling out of sight. The words BOSNIA, EL SALVADOR, KUWAIT, VIETNAM flash in red across the screen; at the end we freeze on IF THIS WAS OUR PAST, LET'S NOT MAKE IT OUR FUTURE.

"It's really powerful," Helen Salcedo said as she walked over to an editing machine. "We don't get a chance in other classes to show our work like this. I like watching other people's stuff. You can make comparisons with what you're doing, and you can learn that way."

Leticia Lopez sat at another editing machine trying to tighten her video essay on rape. "I learned a lot about rape doing this," she explained. "Other students have done videos on rape, but I wanted to do one from a woman's perspective. I wanted it to be different. I didn't want to do a video that was violent; I think that's tasteless. I wanted to get my message across in a different way, so I have the camera follow this young lady through her day — there are no explicit scenes — and at the end the camera zooms in on a pamphlet about rape that's sitting on her coffee table. Would you like to see it?"

Ed had gone across the room to check on Jesse Barrios, who was leaning over a table, looking at a script, tapping his pencil, running his free hand through his orange hair; he wore a nose ring and an oversized jean jacket that smelled of tobacco. He was stuck. Using footage shot by another student, he was trying to create a documentary on a local artist. As he viewed the film, and then viewed it again, he became interested in the painter's involvement with her Mexican heritage. He wanted to do more with that, and was trying to figure out how he could use his film in this new thematic context. And how he could make it interesting. "I don't want it to be just a talking head. Maybe background music —

something Latin — maybe fresh angles, maybe computer graphics . . . I don't know. I might have to go back and shoot again, but I'd like to see if I can do something with what I have." As one of seven children, Ed would later tell me, Jesse had to work just about full-time, so he often had to do a lot with a little. "He never liked school," Ed explained, "never thought of himself as someone who could do much. But now he's beginning to see he has potential, and he's tying some hopes to this work."

After Jesse, I spent time with Juan Jauregui and Frank Santos.

Juan was the most prolific of Ed's students, producing eight public service announcements. He had a distinctive style, and his topics were disturbing: AIDS from shared needles, gang violence, death from smoking, alcohol, and drugs. And his images came at you quickly, sharply, but rhythmic, skillfully timed: gangsters, guns, cocaine; hooded chess players, fingers splayed, caressing a rook, a bishop; car grills and tires, chain link and concrete; graveyards; lost, anguished faces. Harsh, but flowing somehow through eerie music or driving guitar or rap.

Frank's style, on the other hand, was playful, celebratory. He came to the United States four years ago from Mexico, took courses in English as a second language, and moved into the standard curriculum as an LEP (limited English proficiency) student. He still spoke an unsure English, but, Ed said, was "probably the most technically adept student" he had ever had. "He learned it all so quickly, and now he virtually lives here; morning, lunch, he's just here." I saw two of Frank's projects. In the first, young and old Mexicans dance in a local club to Banda Machos's "Casimira": cowboy hats, bandannas, women in jeans and ruffled dresses, the images up close, receding, modulated to the catchy syncopation and back beat of this music, called *banda.* In his manipulation of the images, Frank conveyed the joy of the dance that accompanies *banda, la quebradita* or "the little break": elbows pumping, shoulders dipping, a young woman, chin up, lips pursed, flashing her eyes at the camera, while around the dance a multicolored frame shimmers — *¡Orale!* (all right!), *¡Arre!* (giddy-up!) — with bright encouragement. The second was a brief animated French lesson, in which a boy lies on his bed while his mother berates him for not doing his homework. "If you do not do your homework (*Si tu ne fais ton devoir*)," she says, "you are not going to find a job (*tu ne vas pas trouvé de job*)." The boy remains immobile, grumpy: *"Je ne désire pas trouvé de job!"* — I don't want to find a job! The futile exchange continues — you won't be able to get married (so what?), have a family (so?) — until Mom adds the clincher: then you must not fall in love and can't kiss the girls. *Ooh la la,* the cartoon boy says, springing from bed and doing a half-dance to his desk. "I can't talk to you anymore, because I have homework to do!"

And at the end of the day, I got a chance to sit and talk with Melanie and Leonor, who made "Civil Wars." Melanie was from El Salvador, Leonor from Colombia, both seniors who had met in tenth-grade geometry and who had collaborated on two other videos. They had spent two months on "Civil Wars," trying to get it right, despairing, coming back again. They were good friends, close, effective partners, and they occasionally completed each other's sentences:

> There were times when we felt like quitting. And it wasn't until Mr. Stone pushed us — he said, "Girls, you have to do this." And we were procrastinating. We got so tired looking for the *right* shots. I mean, *shots* — we had plenty of them. But looking for the right one, well . . . then Mr. Stone would say, "It'll work out, I believe in you." We don't like to do simple work. We like to get into what we're doing. Quality work is what we like — that's what we're all about.

Melanie had applied to college, wanting to major in film. Leonor was a single mother who had to stay close to home and make an immediate, practical choice: she would most likely go to nearby East Los Angeles Community College and train to be a physician's assistant. A number of Ed and Larry's students lived with limits. (Seventy-five percent of the students at Bell were from families categorized as "low income.") Some of these young people had had their sights set on college for a while, but a number were not in the college track at all — weren't oriented that way, weren't interested, had, in all kinds of ways, been scared or barred from it. The video classes provided one of the few opportunities for such a range of students to work together and see what each could do. And it was often the student who was less successful by traditional standards who excelled. Some visitors might find a class like Ed Murphy's too unstructured, too loud; might worry, too, about the focus of so much student work on drugs, gangs, violence. And Ed has tried to get his students to reflect critically on this focus — does it inadvertently feed stereotypes about communities like Bell? — but with little result. What seemed undeniable, though, was that the students were engaged, had a sense of importance, worked within a tradition of recognized student achievement, and gave expression to deeply held concerns. Melanie lost her father in the Salvadoran civil war and saw people killed in front of her house. And as a secondary result of the work, some students who had never imagined themselves in college began to see possibilities. It was not uncommon for Ed and Larry's students to gear themselves up for the local community college or for California State University at Los Angeles, just back up the Long Beach Freeway, four miles northeast.

III

IT WAS EARLY IN THE MORNING, the sky beginning to lighten, when Carlos Jiménez and I passed East Los Angeles Community College on our way to Garfield High School, close to the eastern boundary of East Los Angeles. The sun was coming up, breaking through the clouds, light gray and pearl, shining on beige stucco houses, small Spanish arches. Carlos's mother had taught at Garfield, and he's taught there for eleven years. The school was built in 1925, originally serving a predominantly Anglo and immigrant Jewish, Armenian, and Japanese population, but since World War II the surrounding community has become more Mexican in character and has been relatively stable; it is not uncommon for families to remain in the area for two generations, unusual in highly mobile Los Angeles. As the demographers would put it, it is a blue-collar community with a low transiency rate. One indicator of this residential stability is that Garfield, whose constituency is overwhelmingly Latino, needs to provide English-as-a-second-language instruction for only about 15 percent of its student body. Many schools outside of East LA have a higher Latino immigrant population.

Garfield High School was the location for the movie *Stand and Deliver,* the tribute to calculus teacher Jaime Escalante, but though Carlos respected Escalante's work (Escalante is no longer there), he bristled at the film's portrayal of the school as a place that did not believe in the potential of its students. There was a time when the school was in terrible shape, had one of the highest drop-out rates in the city, but student and community activism in the late 1960s contributed to change in general conditions. And during the mid-seventies, before Escalante's tenure, a core of dedicated teachers (John Bennett, Dennis Campagna, Tom Woessner) began building a rigorous advanced placement program, made up of courses, like those depicted in *Stand and Deliver,* which prepare students for tests that secure college credit. For some time, John Bennett has been preparing successful teams for the city's Academic Decathlon competition. "It's a decent school, and the kids are so damned nice," Carlos said en route. "There are the problems that come with poverty — kids are absent, some run away from home, and there is some gang activity — but by and large we don't have too many problems. Some LA schools have it a lot harder." One thing going for Garfield is that it is connected to its community. The annual football game with crosstown rival Roosevelt (another famous East LA school, but farther west, closer to the LA River and the downtown Civic Center) draws twenty-five thousand people. As one young local explained to me, "You look at the band and the parade — you can see that Garfield is real together. The people there are united."

Carlos would get to Garfield about seven — the time we arrived —

and that would give him an hour to arrange his day. He taught U.S. history, two sections of advanced placement history, a course in Mexican-American history, and he coached field events and sprints for the track team. Because there had been so few materials available, he wrote the book he uses for the Mexican-American history course, sitting at his kitchen table, a pile of library books before him, typing units on Cortés or the Mexican Revolution or the Zoot Suit Riots onto duplicating stencils and distributing them to this class the next day. The materials have been revised and published as a textbook. His interest in athletics went back to his own career as a high school and college sprinter and triple-jumper, and he has developed his coaching skills in a series of sports clinics. He was a methodical teacher, relying on detailed notes, working from an outline of events displayed via an overhead projector, giving frequent quizzes, and assigning lots of writing. He would leave school about five, except on those days when there was a track meet; then it would be closer to seven-thirty or eight.

Along the entire south wall of Carlos's classroom was a series of pictures and texts that represented the sweep of Mexican and Mexican-American history: from a drawings of three Aztec warriors looking at an eagle with a snake in its beak to Hernán Cortés to Miguel Hildalgo and the Grito de Dolores, calling for "freedom and justice for the common man." Then came a picture-list of the Mexican presidents, drawings of Benito Juaréz and Emiliano Zapata, a poster for Luis Valdez's *Zoot Suit,* another poster of Cesar Chavez, the cover from Richard Vasquez's novel *Chicano,* a photograph of one of the murals that decorate the walls in East LA — a strong female figure in the style of Diego Rivera harvesting the fields: brown, orange, gold, and blue. At the very end of the pictorial time line was a poster for the Garfield-Roosevelt football game, the two team captains shaking hands, "a winning tradition."

Following Carlos through his day, I got to hear lectures on the Texas Revolt and the short-lived Lone Star Republic, on the Spanish-American War and the debates within the United States between the Internationalists and the Anti-Imperialism League, on the major battles of World War II — Guadalcanal, Anzio, Iwo Jima — watching an old film, watching the faces of the students as the camera focused on the young faces of dead soldiers, listening to a girl beside me, her hand to her mouth, whisper "No." I sat through homeroom ("Good morning, Bulldogs . . ." the public address system blared) and a conference period during which Carlos dealt with a boy who had been kicked out of his house. I sat in as Carlos and another advanced placement teacher brought their classes together for an academic decathlon-style competition. I watched Carlos coach his pole vaulters. And through the day, I got to talk with his students. Here are three vignettes, drawn from my notes. I'll begin with interviews with Ana Gaytan — a junior who was in Carlos's homeroom, had elected one of his sections of advanced placement history, and ran the two-mile for the track team — and Eddie Torres, a senior in Carlos's Mexican-American history class who was in the process of sending out applications for college.

Ana was about five foot two, slim, stood with her back straight, held her books to her chest. She talked about the way Carlos's room made her feel: "comfortable" and "at home." "Spanish was the first language I spoke and wrote," she explained, "and it feels good to see it reflected here. Sometimes during homeroom I'll turn around and just start reading the things on the wall — you know, about the Aztecs or about Father Hidalgo — and it makes me want to know more about it." Eddie — hint of a mustache, neat in T-shirt and jeans, opening a big binder he carried instead of a book bag — explained further as he looked for his homework. "If you grow up in East LA, all you hear are negative things. The movies, negative. The news, negative. The newspapers, negative. But, you know, this room is something *positive.* As you walk around the room, you say, 'Hey, we're somebody!' So that's why I took the Mexican-American history course. I wanted to know who we are."

Ana was interested in working with children — she volunteered at a nearby center for handicapped children — and hoped someday to be a pediatrician. Her days were very full, helping at home, attending a church group, school, homework, track practice. Her father was a lithographer and was going to night school to improve his English, but the family always tried to have dinner together. After dinner, she would clean up, then take a shower to jolt herself awake for her homework. When we spoke, she had just finished a paper for her English class on the emptiness of the character Daisy in *The Great Gatsby.* "Over the years," she said, "you just learn to set a schedule for yourself."

Eddie had more recently found his way. "Many of my friends have dropped out." He shrugged. "The hope, the self-esteem, was not there." He used to take general courses, and according to Carlos, his writing was not up to par. But he got tired of the "worksheets and busy work" and wanted classes where "you could give your own opinion — discuss and debate" — courses that "would help me in the future." He wanted to go away to college, to see new things. "Sometimes we Mexicans stay too tied to the family, but I think we need to gain new experience also." So he elected Carlos's Mexican-American history and advanced placement courses in history and Spanish. "I wanted to feel the pressure of the tough courses," he explained. "I wanted to know what that was like."

Once a week during lunch, Carlos and the man he called his mentor, Tom Woessner — one of the people who built the advanced placement program at Garfield — would bring together their four sections of AP history for a small-scale academic decathlon. Here's how it worked. Each week, two students from each section occupy the "hot seats," representing their respective classes. Over the course of a term, all the students would participate. On the day of my visit, about twenty or thirty spectators packed into the room, sitting on bookcases, leaning against the blackboard. Carlos stood by the overhead that was projecting a score sheet onto the screen, a column for each of the four sections. Tom sat on a stool on the other side of the projector, one foot on the floor. They took turns posing questions and judging answers and keeping score.

"OK," Tom announced with a flourish, "this is round two. We will repeat questions only once. Here goes." He adjusted his glasses and read. "The British attempt to prevent continued warfare between the Colonists and the Indians of the Ohio Valley was called the ——— ?" The students in the hot seats leaned forward quickly and scribbled a response. Carlos collected the slips of paper, read from one of them the correct answer (The Proclamation Line, 1763), and recorded the score on the illuminated transparency: Jimenez, Section 3: 2 correct; Jimenez, Section 4: 1; Woessner, Section 3: 1; Woessner, Section 4: 2. Then Carlos stepped forward, walking in front of the projector as he spoke: "As the colonies start organizing resistance against the British, during the early days of the struggle for independence, something known as the Committees of Correspondence were established. What Boston-based organization was responsible for organizing those Committees of Correspondence?" Answers were scribbled and Tom collected the slips of paper. And as he was reading them, grease pencil in hand poised over the transparency, Carlos asked, "The correct answer, of course, would be?" And a chorus of voices responded: "The Sons of Liberty."

The two men traded off like this through the half-hour period, Tom eating crackers as he read and wrote, Carlos taking big bites out of a cafeteria sandwich when Tom had the floor. They asked about the Maysville Veto, the Sumner Brooks Affair, the *Federalist Papers*, Samuel Gompers, transcendentalism, and the Pullman Car Company railroad strike. They were formal, repeated the questions only once, and allowed little time between them. The students, in turn, were focused and responded quickly; even the observers, except for occasional groans and chatter, were quiet and attentive. Yet for all the machinery of academic challenge, the room felt comfortable. Tom and Carlos lightened things up with little comments and quips ("Whew! That was a hard one," or "Close only counts in dancing"), and the students seemed to feel free to challenge their teachers when they didn't give full credit for an answer. The two men were creating an environment in which their students could develop confidence and skill in the contests of high-powered academics.

When the bell rang, the students in the hot seats scrambled to the projector, where Tom was tallying their scores. Who won? This time it was Jiménez, Section 3.

Out, then, to the athletic field at the end of the day. Carlos was at the runway for the pole vault, surrounded by four boys. Groups of athletes were situated at various places on the field: the high-jump pit, the long jump, the shot put, and discus ring. Sprinters were trying out the blocks under the giant Garfield Bulldog at the edge of the track by the bleachers. Quarter-milers were running the curves, leaning in, three-quarter speed, their shoes making a gritty splashing sound as they hit the track's decomposed granite. Carlos was working with two new vaulters, having them walk, then run through their approach, asking them to "visualize what you're supposed to do." Once they got to a certain point on the runway, there were six steps they had to hit with precision — and Carlos was yelling out the numbers in a quick, rhythmic count. One, two, three, four (the pole moving out in front of the belly), five, six — and the plant into the box and propulsion. They would have their first meet with Bell High School in just two weeks, and there was work to do. Carlos asked questions about technique: "Where should the pole be in relation to your body when you count five?" "Where's your left hand supposed to be at take-off?" He tried to get the young vaulters to think about the steps in the process: "Rick, explain to me in your own words what you're supposed to do." And he suggested things they could do to help them get a better sense of their bodies rotating through space: "I'd like you to take a broom tonight, lie on your bed, and imagine yourself making the turn." ("The hard part," he explained to me, "is turning while the pole is still propelling you. You need confidence, because you can't see where you're going.")

The female distance runners were doing laps on the grass just inside the track, and every few minutes they would come by in fluid stride, breathing rhythmically, concentrating, their hair pulled back in ponytails, lifting in the light breeze. Ana was among them. "The experience of being part of something," she told me, "is beautiful. Like family. I wanted to do something different, do something out of the ordinary. I guess it's a feeling you have inside that makes you want to run."

Carlos would spend most of this day coaching his new vaulters, repeating the drills, the steps in the approach to the box. By the end of practice, they were clearing modest heights. "It'll come," he said to one of the vaulters as the boy was putting on his sweats. "It's early in the season." "It's early in the season," the boy repeated, pulling his leg behind him, stretching, cooling down. Carlos came over and sat down on the grass. "I love this. Coaching enables me to get close to these kids." His veteran vaulter Eddie Ayala walked to the end of the runway — now he could take a few practice vaults himself. Carlos watched him. Eddie was shaking himself loose, focusing his concentration on the crossbar. I asked Carlos whether he saw any connections between coaching and teaching. He thought for a moment. "You know," he said, turning to me, "in both cases you're always asking yourself, 'What can they do now?' and you're matching that against the place where you want them to end up." The sun was casting longer shadows on the grass; the team was taking down equipment, stacking hurdles, walking to the clubhouse. The air was crisp. Eddie began his approach, his lean, muscled legs striding down the runway, every step precise, planting the pole, up into the air, rotating at the torso, thin now in the sun, arms thrown back over the crossbar.

IV

MOTHER JONES, turn-of-the-century organizer for the United Mine Workers, was energetically pacing the stage at Mark Keppel High School, about four miles northeast of Garfield, pacing and banging two tin pans, raising holy hell. (This was a tactic she and other women had used to scare scabs away and embolden striking miners.) "No matter what your fight," she hollered, pans over her head, ready for clatter, "no matter what, don't be ladylike!" And she whacked the pans together, smiling, and, in full stride, walked off the stage.

Before her appearance, Abigail Adams, wife of President John Adams and an early advocate for women's rights, had informed the packed auditorium that she was "part of your past" and asked the audience to learn "something of your lost history." And then came a procession of compelling American women — Sojourner Truth, Anna Carroll, Susan B. Anthony, Emma Goldman, and Lily Chan among them — some found in history textbooks, some not, all seeking public voice amid this convocation of young people, all appealing for inclusion and social justice. The play was Gloria Goldsmith's *Womanspeak,* and social sciences teacher Janeane Vigliotti thought it would be a good way for students to celebrate Women's History Month and, in the process, learn some history by participating in its re-creation. About six weeks earlier, she sent out a flier to the other social sciences teachers asking whether there would be interest. Drama experience wasn't necessary, just a willingness to put in the time. When the first meeting came, her room filled with young women, many of whom had never acted before. Issues of women's history may not have been the primary draw for all the volunteers, but Janeane had hit a nerve. As one sophomore put it, "There's all these activities on campus, but this was the only one for girls, and I thought, 'Hey, I'd like that!'"

Between that first meeting and the production of *Womanspeak*, the students met about ten times, sometimes with the drama coach, Gail MacCartney, whose help Janeane enlisted, sometimes on their own. They rehearsed their lines and went to the library to research their characters. "How could I play Abigail Adams," Claudia Coronel asked me, "if I didn't know about her?" "It was obvious to me," said Amy Tien, "that I just had to learn about Eleanor Roosevelt." Some of the students liked what they found, admiring, as one girl put it, "the strength, the dedication" of the women; others were upset by the history they uncovered, by the lines they had to speak. All this, Janeane observed, affected some of them deeply. "In some cases, I think it stirred their ideas about what it means to be a woman."

Tina Ly played Anna Carroll, a member of mid-nineteenth-century Washington high society who did strategic military and legal research for President Lincoln's cabinet. She was never given credit for these contributions and, as portrayed in the play, was ambivalent, even conciliatory about her situation. Tina understood. "She was real indecisive, she was, but I still admire her. Think of everything she had to face! Someone like Susan B. Anthony would be really disappointed in Anna. But I think I understand." The students ended up forging connections with their characters in a number of ways. Claudia became excited when she found a portrait of her character, Abigail Adams, and asked her mother, who was a seamstress, to copy the lace-collar dress in the faded plate. Vanessa Sun got a big, tittering kick out of playing the bold free-love advocate Victoria Woodhull, and Teresa Ngo delivered with gusto Emma Goldman's line "I am an anarchist of the spirit!" Sara Meeker, a fiery, in-your-face Susan B. Anthony, had acted before, and loved her character's "strong, powerful voice. So many women's parts are soft-spoken — these little, meek, ordinary parts. I like having that loud voice. My height is sometimes a disadvantage, and with that voice, I could make myself bigger." Sara's sister Mari, a first-time actress, responded to "the closeness and support" of working on the project. And she admired Mother Jones's "ambition and determination." "I'm very headstrong, like she was," Mari explained, "and I put a lot of energy into playing her. Doing what she did after everything she went through — she's remarkable!"

A particularly powerful match between student and character came with Martha Figueroa's portrayal of Adelita, a woman who joined forces with Pancho Villa. "She was an actual historical figure," Martha said, "who then became a character in stories and songs." Janeane pursued

Martha for this role because she was "such a good thinker — and so passionate." At first Martha resisted: "I thought, Oh no! not me — I've never acted. But I began thinking, 'Well, it *is* a woman's play,' and then found out more about Adelita. And that did it. I researched her, how she dressed, how she moved. One picture I found, I even *look* like her! I talked to my father about her — he's from Jalisco, and he knew all about her . . . there are so many stories about Adelita." Martha threw herself into the role, keeping her nervousness at bay as best she could. "I know I just couldn't play Martha; I had to play Adelita, *be* Adelita. This would probably be the only time the people at Keppel would ever see Adelita, so I had to get it right."

Janeane Vigliotti struggled to find ways to make history come alive, to breathe life into the social sciences. She wanted her students to understand that history was shaped, and rendered, by living people, that they were participants in history, "were connected to it — to people in the past who thought like them." And she wanted them to develop a perspective on human agency that would encourage them to become shapers of history themselves. Many of her students, reflecting the composition of the wider community around the school, were first- or second-generation Mexican American or Asian American (predominantly Chinese American), so the history of Abigail Adams and Anna Carroll would not seem to be their history. Their history would more precisely be reflected in accounts of immigration, of the dynamics of ethnic identity in the United States, of social and economic developments in California. But, of course, the lives of Abigail Adams and the others reflect trends in the history of the country that their parents or grandparents had chosen to make their own. And, more immediately, Janeane's students recognized in those earlier figures familiar conflicts or dissatisfactions or anger. Many of them have been pulled between women's roles in traditional families and the possible roles they were beginning to imagine for themselves; they knew the complicated, sometimes repressive, sexual politics of their adolescent Latino or Asian community; they felt the desire to be heard, to be masterful, to, as one girl put it, "make a life for myself." All this went to the heart of Janeane's pedagogy. Teaching social science at its best meant assisting students in making connections across time and place, both seeking common humanity and coming to understand broad historical and political forces. From such a position, students could act, could do, could move forward in the difficult times in which they lived.

And, she believed, there couldn't be a much better place to practice such pedagogy than Mark Keppel High School, located right on the border between Alhambra and Monterey Park, six miles east of East LA, about three hundred feet off the freeway that would eventually take you out of LA County to the "Inland Empire" of San Bernardino. Keppel, a WPA school, was the only public high school available to the citizens of Monterey Park, from which it drew the majority of its students.

Monterey Park is a city of sixty-three thousand and, from the time of its incorporation in 1916 to the present, it has reflected many of the kinds of demographic shifts and tensions that characterize the cities in the LA Basin. From 1916 to World War II, the population and power base of Monterey Park was overwhelmingly White and Christian. And the city had a reactionary strain, was a site of robust Ku Klux Klan activity. After the war and into the 1950s, a large population of Jews moved east out of the neighborhoods around downtown Los Angeles, liberalizing the political climate; soon after, newer Mexican, Chinese, and especially Japanese families began settling in Monterey Park, expanding the diversity of the city. In the mid-to-late-1960s, Mexican Americans seeking suburban housing arrived in large numbers from East LA and by 1980 were the largest ethnic group in the city, where they established a Latino power base. About this time, immigrants began arriving from Hong Kong and Taiwan, some bringing considerable resources with them, and by 1986, Asian Americans, not Latinos, were the largest ethnic group in Monterey Park. Within that group, the new Chinese outnumbered the older Japanese by three to one. The city had a Chinese-American mayor (the only female Chinese-American mayor in the United States) and was the only city in the nation with an Asian majority.

Although there has been a tradition of coalition building in the city's postwar history, Monterey Park, as one could imagine, has been a site of social and political conflict. The White population has steadily decreased, from 85 percent in 1960 to 15 percent in 1986, but they have continued to hold positions of power. The Latino population, while forming some alliances with Chinese-American leaders, resisted the erosion of their power base. And older, established families of all backgrounds — Anglo, Mexican, Japanese — resented the influx of so many newcomers. These dynamics have led to some odd political coalitions; for example, there were second-generation Mexican Americans and Japanese Americans supporting an English-only initiative proposed by a recent conservative Anglo mayor. Monterey Park, then, like so many communities in the LA Basin, was a pressure point for a number of social forces: immigration, within-county migration, White flight, local economic restructuring and land development, national and international politics (the curtailing of aid to cities under Reagan and Bush, the upcoming takeover of Hong Kong by mainland China), forces local and global, all of which heightened ethnic conflict, and all of which played themselves out among the students of Mark Keppel High School.

The population at Keppel is about 30 percent Latino, 65 percent Asian, and 4 percent White. Generally, the students lived in peace, and there were a number of interethnic friendships and not infrequent interethnic dating. But sometimes the community's tensions erupted on the campus, as they did a month or so before the production of *Womanspeak.* It began with a fight between members of rival gangs in the community — the Asian Boys and the older Lomas — then another fight, and word traveled that some boys were coming to school with weapons. The fights polarized many of the students, leading them to choose sides by race, and some interracial couples were confronted and threatened. The principal put the school on alert.

Janeane felt that teachers had an important role to play in times like this, and had been preparing herself for some time, becoming an applied social scientist. Since 1985, she had been involved with the Brotherhood-Sisterhood project of the National Conference (formerly the National Conference of Christians and Jews), a series of workshops and summer camps that help students confront, often with great pain, their stereotypes about race, gender, and sexual orientation. And since 1989, she had been participating in the peer-counseling program of her fellow social sciences teacher Maria Manetta, a program in which students took a year-long class in communication and counseling and then, through a referral system involving both the social sciences teacher and the school psychologist, were hooked up with students who wanted to talk, usually about depression or family conflicts.

So when things got hot, teachers like Janeane responded. They stayed out in the yard during lunch, talking to students, being visible, cooling things out. They devoted class time to discussions of campus problems, working them into the curriculum when possible, helping students see connections to other conflicts in literature or history. They opened up their rooms, early in the morning, late in the day, to talk or just to let a kid come in and sit and think — a safe place, a place where anyone, with whatever fury or fear, could find comfort. And as that student looked around, there was information everywhere. A sign by the door read "Gay/Lesbian? Confused? Want to talk? Confidential. See Ms. Vigliotti." A rack by the window contained pamphlets with referrals for teen pregnancy, substance abuse, violence in the home, and teenage depression. Bulletin boards rich with a different kind of information covered the walls. One was a collage of pictures of Fannie Lou Hamer, Dr. King, Emma Goldman, the Chicana activist Magdalena Mora, Barbara Jordan. "Inclusive History," it read, "Good for Everyone." The question that drove Janeane and like-minded teachers at Keppel was this: How, in a time of community conflict, can you create the occasion for people to talk, to be heard, to come together?

Russell Lee-Sung, the director of bands, sat in the far corner of Building M-2 by the parking lot, one of those old portable structures, creaky, a little thin, two concrete steps leading to the door. There was a small stage with three ascending rows of folding metal chairs; gold and silver tubas were upright in their stands; two xylophones and a Ludwig bass drum sat just on the other side of the open door. Members of the jazz band began wandering in. Russell grew up in this neighborhood and went to Mark Keppel. His father, he told me, was originally from El Paso and is of mixed Mexican and Chinese ancestry. His mother is Chinese. He embodied the two ethnic groups vying for power in Monterey Park.

"I use music as the attraction, but I think my biggest impact is in trying to help my students be good people. Music has a tendency to draw people together. The band is composed of many cultures, and we try to support each other. And since I'm both Chinese and Mexican myself, I suppose I provide a good role model.

"When I was a student here, the community was still primarily Hispanic. The Asian population was maybe 30 percent at that time — that would have been in the late '70s. Now those numbers have changed significantly, and it's a source of the tension here. Quite frankly, I'm surprised things haven't exploded earlier. It's a situation a lot of communities in Southern California have faced or are going to face.

"But you have to understand that the hostility comes not only from conflict between races, but from conflicts at home. Some of our students don't have any way to express those conflicts; some are really lost. Just growing up as teenagers in Southern California, these kids are dealing with tremendous cultural conflicts. Their parents come from the old country, yet the kids live in the middle of American values and moral codes. Some of us teachers here try to help them put things in perspective, help them understand where their parents are coming from. You know, 'This is what your parents are thinking, and they're doing this because they love you.' And sometimes their perceptions change. Sometimes they begin to understand both sides."

Two girls rolled a piano past us to the stage. A boy was running scales on his trombone; a trumpeter did the same, but out of phase. Other musicians were testing their horns — bleats, blasts, sounding like a parody of progressive jazz. A long-haired boy rushed in late, plugged in his bass guitar, and started playing soft notes. The band was one of the few occasions in school where a range of students — those of modest means and the well-to-do, college bound and otherwise, Asian, Latino, Anglo — could, as Russell put it, "come together around a common goal."

The band had a show tomorrow night, and this would be their last rehearsal. On the chalkboard was a list that moved from ballads to Dixieland: "Forever" and "Red House" to "When the Saints Go Marching In." Russell walked to the front of the stage. He spoke for a few minutes about the mix of music and the way it would build to the Dixieland crescendo. He talked about timing, about one song leading to the other. The musicians settled in. Russell answered a few questions; then a girl who had been sitting on a stool to his side got up and shook her arms and hands. Russell counted — "a-one, two, three, OK" — and the band eased into "Smoke Gets in Your Eyes," a boy rising for a saxophone solo, the girl, her fingers to her throat, reaching for a note, the room full of music, unsteady, not right yet, Russell watching, listening, the singer closing her eyes, trying again. "They have to step out there," Russell had said. "I keep telling them that they can't be afraid. Music is all about taking risks."

V CONTINUE NORTH from Monterey Park about six winding miles to the foothills of the San Gabriel mountains, and you'll enter Pasadena, located along the northeast rim of the LA Basin. It is linked to downtown Los Angeles by the first freeway built in California, the Arroyo Seco Parkway, a six-mile route built by the WPA and opened in 1940. Though Pasadena is now a middle-class community, it has a history of privilege. Founded in 1874 on the site of an old *rancho* by settlers from Indiana ("The California Colony of Indiana"), Pasadena would quickly develop from what John Muir called "an aristocratic little colony" of orange and lemon orchards, exotic gardens, and learned societies into a booming resort for people of means looking to ease the chill of Boston or Chicago. It hosted the Rose Parade (the first in 1890) and, from 1916, when football replaced chariot racing in the festivities, the Rose Bowl. The city was one of the wealthiest in California until its tourism was devastated by the Great Depression. It was saved — as were a number of other Southern California cities — by World War II, for a local polytechnic institute had developed into Cal Tech, a hub for the region's aerospace and electronics industries. To this day, a large number of residents have undergraduate and graduate degrees and hold managerial and professional positions. Until recently, the power base of the city was exclusively White. Though Mexican and Chinese immigrants were present from the first days of the settlement — employed primarily as field hands — and African Americans migrated in to fill jobs as hotel domestics and chauffeurs (developing eventually a small but active middle class), all non-Whites were strictly segregated in housing, schools, and medical facilities. Such patterns of segregation — restrictive covenants, separate schools — could be found in most Southern California suburbs.

In the last two decades, the demographic mix of Pasadena's citizenry has changed considerably. As the population increased (from 113,000 in 1970 to 132,000 in 1990), the White majority became a minority. The number of African Americans decreased slightly, as well. The Asian population expanded, and the Latino population has increased significantly (from 21,772 in 1980 to 35,912 in 1990), reflecting trends evident throughout Southern California. But the ethnic shifts in the Southland have been marked not only in Latino and Asian numbers. There is a growing Armenian population in Pasadena, migrating in from their point of entry in East Hollywood and Glendale. The 250,000 Armenians in Los Angeles County form the largest concentration outside their homeland.

Pasadena High School graduated its first class in 1890, moved and rebuilt two times to accommodate the city's boom cycles, and opened the doors of its newest campus in 1960. The large, well-equipped facility (it has two swimming pools) served a White middle- and upper-middle-class constituency until 1970, when the courts judged Pasadena to be in violation of school desegregation laws, and busing was mandated. The demographic changes, combined with busing and massive White flight to private schools, have yielded a current ethnic composition of 38 percent Hispanic, 32 percent African American, 25 percent Caucasian (many of whom are Armenian), and about 5 percent Asian. But these percentages do not tell the full story of Pasadena High School. Within the demographer's broad categories, there are forty-two nationalities represented on campus and thirty-eight languages spoken. And since the early 1970s, there has been a shift in class: PHS has the largest number of low-income students in the Pasadena school district, many of whom live in foster homes and/or public housing projects. A lot of these young people see little meaning in school, are regularly truant, are getting in trouble with the law, show all the signs of dropping out.

These problems have absorbed Principal Judy Codding. How, she wondered, could she develop services and programs that would "give our students hope that school can do something for them." One thing she did was establish two academies — one in Graphic Arts and one in Visual Arts and Design — small programs within the school that each enroll 100 to 150 students and attempt an integration of vocational and academic coursework. Such career-academic programs, which have been gaining national attention, can be little more than deceptive tracks away from college and toward low-level employment. But if they are carried out with integrity, they can provide an engaging curriculum, a feeling of specialness, and an expansion of opportunity. Ruby, a junior in the Graphic Arts Academy, saw it like this: the program will enable her to do two things she really wants to do — she wants to go to college, but she has to get a job to support herself. When she graduates, she figures, she'll be able to do both. To ensure that students like Ruby will be able to achieve such goals, Principal Codding has secured mentors and internships from the local printing industry, arranged for students to take courses during their senior year at nearby Pasadena City College, and established agreements so that coursework will be given credit at California State University at Los Angeles.

When I visited it, the Graphic Arts Academy was in its second experimental year. Students entered as sophomores and took some courses in the regular curriculum — a foreign language or physical education or an art elective — but the majority of their courses were taken with academy faculty, teachers chosen because of their skill in the classroom and their interest in creating an interdisciplinary curriculum. There were five: Ellen Abraham and Kirk Odegard taught humanities, Elaine Mirkin taught biology and mathematics, Mary Tsotsis handled chemistry, and Mark Hall was head of the Graphic Arts Lab. They met every week, and conferred on the fly, to develop ways to integrate their curricula: How can you teach humanities or chemistry with an orientation toward graphic arts? What kind of projects can bring the disciplines together in fruitful ways? So, for example, early in their first term, sophomores wrote a haiku or limerick or quatrain in humanities, made their own paper in the Graphic Arts Lab — and tested its weight and thickness and determined its gloss and texture — and made the ink they used to letter their verse in chemistry, testing its reflective density, opacity, and absorbency. At the heart of the academy was one critical question: How is graphic arts a science, an art, and a language?

I was standing by the Heidelberg computerized printing press in the Graphic Arts Lab with Alena Bayramyan, a sophomore who, with her parents, had emigrated from Armenia. "This program is so special," she said. "The teachers don't want you to get a low grade. They really care about you. It's like we're a family." Alena was petite and full of feeling, and she had taken it on herself to walk me around the lab. It was a big room, white brick walls, lots of windows covered with blinds to regulate the light, a gray linoleum floor. Student-made signs with bright safety warnings were everywhere: DON'T RUN, KEEP HANDS AND LOOSE CLOTHING AWAY FROM ALL MACHINES, DO NOT THROW OBJECTS, and, by the door to the teacher's small office, DON'T MESS WITH MR. HALL! Alena had started us off at the entrance, where students were sitting at computers composing and formating text for their projects. Between the terminals were backpacks, bookbags, jackets and sweaters piled in small heaps, folders full of paper, a couple of dictionaries. Next came four "light tables," tables with opaque glass tops illuminated from below. Students were bent over the soft glow, laying out their negatives, using T-squares and triangles to get the images just right. Then came a long sink with curled negatives hanging from a string overhead, and then the darkroom — its red warning light on. "I'm just learning all of this," Alena said. "I can't wait to get really proficient at it."

Once past the darkroom, we paused at the electrostatic plate maker, a kind of high-intensity photocopying machine that created a plastic "plate" from the texts the students had made. "You have to be careful," Alena explained, "if you make it too hot, it'll burn." From there we passed the paper cutter, where two Armenian boys looked up long enough to tease Alena. "Don't you know," one said to me, "she's an illegal alien!" Alena rolled her eyes and sighed as if to say "How pathetic" and shot something back in Armenian — and we continued on to the Heidelberg printer.

On this day, the academy students were making business cards. Some had a personal slant, the student's name and phone number inscribed under or around a cartoon with a simple exhortation to call, to use the number, to dial and see what happens. Others were for a family business, an auto shop or wrecking yard or shoe repair. Dimple and Lynita, best friends, were over at the computers formating their cards, giving each other a little friendly grief, moving, occasionally, to the hip-hop tape playing low on a portable recorder, Lynita now and then executing a gliding dance step. Three or four boys were in close over the light tables, their cheeks and foreheads illuminated a gentle gold, touching up scratches on their negatives with a fine brush — no talking here — or concentrating on a precise cut with an Exacto knife, squinting, biting a lip. The Graphic Arts Academy, according to its position paper, stressed "the central importance of learning how to learn, how to reason, and how to investigate complex issues that require collaboration, personal responsibility, and a tolerance for uncertainty." Two girls traded off at the darkroom. Over by the plate maker, Truc Pham was showing Jack Zabounian how to fuse an electrostatic plate without overheating it. And here at the printing press, the instructor, Mark Hall, stood back as Anthony Willis, a gifted cartoonist, was explaining to a sophomore named Davida how to run the machine. Alena, my guide, stepped to the back of the whirring printer, where sheets of business cards were flapping into a tray. "Hey, Davida," Alena asked, slipping a sheet quickly from the pile, "why did this corner come out so light?" "Oh," Davida answered, "that's 'cause the printer is still loading with ink — right, Anthony?" Anthony nodded and showed her how to adjust a knob on the side of the machine. Mr. Hall watched, arms folded across his lab coat. "Hey, Alena, see," Davida said, grabbing a new sheet. "Look at this — it's darker." Alena's eyes brightened. "Oh, OK, I got it!" "Tell me what just became clear to you, Alena," Mr. Hall said. A few feet away, a Lebanese-Armenian boy named Pierre (there are Lebanese, Egyptian, Iranian, Turkish, and Soviet Armenians in Los Angeles) was standing over the electrostatic plate maker, hesitating. "Hey, Mr. Hall," he called out, "I forgot — do I put this transparency face up or face down?" Mr. Hall looked up from the Heidelberg press. "Where's the light coming from, Pierre?" "Oh, yeah," Pierre said quickly, "yeah, yeah, OK, face down." The bell for lunch rang, and Alena and Davida and Anthony and Pierre and Jack Zabounian and Truc Pham kept working. Across the room, Dimple and Lynita walked over to the printer to get hard copies of their texts, and Lynita started picking, slowly, through the piles of clothing for her jacket, keeping an eye on the printer. Mr. Hall leaned over and tapped my shoulder. "I just love it," he said softly, "when the bell rings and nobody moves."

Mark Hall, thirty-one, six-one, a big man with glasses, both irreverent and sentimental, worked in the printing industry until three years ago, when he decided to become a teacher. "I just found that what I enjoyed most about the work I was doing was training new people. You know, we would hustle, push hard to get out advertising inserts — that's what we printed — and it hit me one day: So what if someone didn't get their Kmart ad? Who would care? They'd just miss that week's lining for their cat box. I wanted to work with someone or something that would matter to people, would make a difference in their lives, so I began to think about teaching. What I guess I like most about this program is that it gives kids a reason to come to school — and once they're here and with it, you have a better shot at everything else."

A few hundred feet south of the Graphic Arts Lab, the chemistry teacher Mary Tsotsis was preparing a class of academy sophomores to conduct experiments on polar and nonpolar materials. For a long time, Mary had been interested in developing ways to integrate the teaching of science and art, and the Graphic Arts Academy provided her the opportunity. She would select a procedure or problem in graphic arts and then focus on the chemistry involved, both concepts and techniques.

She began this day by reviewing for the class the defining characteristics of polarity and nonpolarity (the absence or presence of free electrons), and then asked why they, as future graphic artists, need to know "whether polar materials and nonpolar materials can mix." Billy, a sharp kid who could be a teacher's bad day, answered, "Because we'll be using lots of different materials when we make plates." He slid down in his chair, continuing, "We'll hafta know what'll mix, or we'll mess up." Mary nodded. She was formal, serious, dressed meticulously. "Yes," she said in slightly accented English — she was of Greek heritage — "you would mess up."

She asked the students to go to the small laboratory in the back of the room and begin the experiments. Along a wood counter was a row of neatly labeled polar materials (salt, water-based ink, hydrochloric acid, water, and water-based pigment) and a row of nonpolar materials: carbon tetrachloride, ink solvent, oil, and oil-based pigment — in this case, crayon shavings. Some of these would be found in a print shop; others were commonplace, thrown in to complicate the experiment. There was a tray of beakers behind the materials and, alongside the tray, a cabinet and a sink and draining rack filled with clean test tubes. In front of all this were several Formica-covered tables on which Mary's students began laying out large sheets of white paper. The sheets were lined with dark grids. Along the top and down the left side, the students had written the names of the polar materials — NaCl, water-based ink, HCl — and nonpolar materials, CCl_4, ink solvent, and so on. (Some boys wrote these names in the stylized tagger script you'd usually see in graffiti.) As the students began systematically mixing one material with another (a polar with a polar, a nonpolar with a polar), they were to place a drop of each mix in the appropriate square on the grid, thereby illustrating at a glance if a solution had resulted — a nice blot on white — or a bad mix — little clumps of salt or crayon or unblended streaks and stains. A graphic representation of data. Mary would put these sheets on the wall, and later — as the class created further displays of basic concepts and experimental results — they would be stored in a set of bulging portfolios of student work.

Around the room, the students were washing test tubes, holding them up to the windows for the glint of sunlight, checking for a bad rinse; mixing salt and water to prepare one of their polar materials; shaving more crayons, thin slivers of magenta and violet and black, to replenish their store of nonpolar oil-based pigment; cautiously filling droppers with hydrochloric acid or carbon tetrachloride or ink solvent; stirring solutions with glass rods — *tink, tink, tink* — squinting to see the results. There was chatter and school-yard news and crude flirtation and rebuff, lots of questions of Mrs. Tsotsis and of one another, and an occasional line from a song, sung under breath during the washing and stirring. And Mary Tsotsis walked from student to student, asking what they were doing and why and what they were finding out.

I had been with the academy students in other classes and walked around the school yard at lunchtime. Some of them would probably do well in a traditional academic program. Others would have a hard time of it, would get discouraged, and possibly not see the point of it all. And still others — four or five boys — would most likely end up in a continuation school . . . or worse. In the yard they challenged each other, pushing the verbal limits, and in some of their classes they jockeyed continually for the funny line, a desperate impulsivity, not laughing at one another's jokes, but elbowing for the delinquent limelight. A few boys bore so much anger, such a charged resistance to any authority, that the air seemed to pop when a teacher walked by their desks, trying in vain to cool them out.

But here in chemistry and in Mark Hall's Graphic Arts Lab, the work seemed to focus these students' energies and, at times, virtually demanded collaboration rather than street-culture combativeness. So while you certainly heard young people insulting each other, or, on the other hand, saw them congregating in small groups by gender or ethnicity or neighborhood affiliation, you also saw interaction around joint problems or projects, shared needs. Many of the tasks in Mary's or Mark's classes were hard to do alone, and because of the mix of backgrounds and interests and skill, some students would simply be more adept at the technology, some better artists, some in possession of a sharper eye, some quicker to grasp concepts behind procedures. Working together made sense. "You know," Mark had said to me, "sometimes I think the really big benefit of this program is social. It would be hard to prove — how would I get stats on such a thing — but I see some remarkable things happening with my students." By bringing together young people who would traditionally be in separate academic tracks and by integrating applied vocational and college-oriented curricula, the Graphic Arts Academy was creating an institutional and instructional space that encouraged the formation of a microsociety that valued both hand and brain.

But over the brief history of the academy's existence, the creation of that space had proven to be a challenge of the first order. To begin with, nowhere in their professional education are teachers taught how to work together, jointly solve problems, develop mutual curricula; teaching is defined as a highly individualized pursuit. The isolation is reinforced by the rigid borders our colleges and universities establish between disciplines; for all the current talk in higher education about "interdisciplinarity," chemists rarely interact with physicists, let alone social scientists or humanists. This conceptual insularity is, of course, passed on to those who will eventually move into the schools. Add to the problem society's class-laden distinction between manual work and mental work, demonstrated in school by the fierce gulf between vocational education and college preparation. (John Dewey called this distinction "the most deep-seated antithesis . . . in educational history.") And to all this, add one further complication: the linkages that Principal Judy Codding established with industry, with Pasadena City College, with Cal State LA — connections that will assist academy students as they move beyond high school, but that affect here and now the curriculum Mark and

Mary and the others must develop for them. "We make a lot of mistakes," Mark told me. "It's not like we have the time to sit back and think all this through, troubleshoot it. We have to create it and teach it at the same time. You just hope it goes right."

And some things did go right. On a shelf by Mark Hall's office in the Graphic Arts Lab was a neat row of hand-bound books with multicolored cloth covers. The students had been reading Sandra Cisneros's *The House on Mango Street* in their humanities class, and they were asked to write a series of vignettes — following Cisneros's episodic style — about their name, their house, their neighbors, the language(s) they spoke, their first job, and so on. They were to write their own *Mango Street.* Since this structure allowed for a lot of variation, it occurred to the biology teacher that students could incorporate brief chapters on science that would thematically play off the autobiographical vignettes. So if you paged through, for example, Dimple's and Lynita's books, you'd find a chapter called "Tears" (about the death of a grandmother) followed by a brief chapter on the lacrimal glands, and a summary of genetics following a chapter on the family. Dimple's chapter on her name was accompanied by a definition of *dimple.* Lynita's chapter called "Me" was paired with an illustration of the human brain. The whole project took about three weeks, and at the end, the students had to plan, measure, illustrate, cut, lay out, and bind the book in the Graphic Arts Lab. When the teachers first came up with the idea, they were unsure about it. Could the students pull it off? Could it be sufficiently interdisciplinary? But once they introduced the project, it began to take shape, the students further developing it. Mark remembered the last few days, watching the students going from biologist to humanities teacher to graphic artist for help, working with them after school to get the binding right, driving Dimple and Lynita to the bus stop as the sky was turning deep blue.

VI

IT WAS THE EMERGING BLUE OF MORNING, the moon still in the sky, and the traffic was slowing already, heading out of Pasadena toward the downtown interchange, the high-rises and towers of the city softened deceptively in this light. Just beyond downtown, the I-10, the most traveled freeway in the nation, intersects traffic and heads west across the Basin. The drive would take you through the once-affluent Wilshire corridor, the "Miracle Mile," through mid-city Los Angeles, past La Brea, past Fairfax, past Robertson Boulevard, past Westwood, toward the edge of the mesa that, a century before, had been recorded as Santa Monica, right above the expansive shoreline of the Pacific Ocean. Franklin Elementary School sits on the corner of Montana Avenue and Twenty-third Street, close to the original northeast boundary of Santa

Monica, close to the exclusive Brentwood Country Club, cooler by the shore.

It was the hundredth day of school in Brown Cow's classroom, which was actually two classrooms and three primary grades combined — the door between them permanently open — kindergarten, first, and second grades brought together and team-taught by Anne Brown and Abby Cowan, who, in the three years of this partnership, had become Brown Cow. The children, together for their three primary years, said that they were in the Brown Cow class, that they, themselves, were Brown Cows. One Hundred Days. A milestone in primary school, so there would be all kinds of activities involving the number 100. The mother of one of the children brought in a piece of fabric printed with a hundred brown cows, fairly realistic cows, but for the red-and-white life jackets each wore. Mrs. Brown had all sixty-one children around her, leading them as they counted off: fif-teen, six-teen, seven-teen. Ms. Cowan was quickly laying out the materials for the next lesson, hustling through the two rooms. Along the south wall were rows of mimeographed sheets done in anticipation of this hundredth day of school, blanks in sentences which the children filled in. "I can eat 100 *grapes,*" Yuki's claimed. "I can hold 100 *coins.* I can play *games* 100 times." Joey's made different claims. He could *blink* 100 times, but not eat 100 *beans.* Matthew could *flush the toilet* (he'd whispered this to Mrs. Brown before writing it) 100 times, but certainly not eat 100 *Brussels sprouts.* Who could? And Chris, he couldn't, no way, hold 100 *worms.* Eighty-five . . . eighty-six . . . eighty-seven. Mrs. Brown was approaching the last row, touching each cow in turn, but remaining silent, the chorus of high voices rising even higher in anticipation. Crescendo. The century mark. "Wow," said one boy in front, "it really is a hundred." "Not all the children can count to a hundred on their own," Abby said to me, whizzing by, "but those who can't are guided along by those who can."

The idea of "mixed age" or "ungraded" primary classrooms gained some national popularity in the late 1950s and sixties, then faded; it is once again being discussed as part of school reform. (The Kentucky legislature, for example, recently mandated ungraded primaries.) The pleasant, productive chaos of Rooms 13 and 14 at Franklin Elementary belied the boldness of Anne and Abby's experiment, for what they were doing challenged one of the most widespread practices in elementary education: setting cognitive and linguistic benchmarks for children's development. "Children just don't learn to read or write or count or compute at the same time," Abby said in exasperation. "There's all kinds of normal variation. Some kids don't really start reading until the second grade, and they go on to become fluent readers." Yet the anxiety that can be generated when a child doesn't hit one of these arbitrary benchmarks — especially among some affluent parents who attach great significance to such measures — is considerable and can lead to a range of remedial interventions, some more harmful than helpful. The Brown Cow classroom was attempting a revision of that way of thinking about children's growth.

By the time the children had finished their cow inventory and had had their say about it, Abby had finished setting up the room for the next math lesson. The students would break into two groups. Those who were more advanced mathematically went with Mrs. Brown, and the rest went with Ms. Cowan. This was to be a lesson in counting and grouping by tens. The children had white mats (and the mats Ms. Cowan used had grids on them, clearly marking ten spaces for an added visual clue) and sacks of small objects they had brought in the day before. They were to count out ten piles of ten. And they began.

Walking through the two rooms, you saw children dumping onto the floor paper clips, beans, buttons, canceled stamps, leaves, balloons, pennies, dog biscuits, and packets of Sweet 'n' Low. One girl, rising from a squat, stepped in the middle of another's mat; a boy fumbled his bag of pennies (the splash of coins); two dog biscuits were crunched with a misstep into the rug. But the children got at it, counting, sorting, piling — lots of chatter, to themselves and to others. I sat and watched Abby. She was all over the floor, on her haunches, kneeling, turning quickly on her knees, stretching backward, extending her line of sight. "Count those out, Joey." "Good, Melissa." "Watch, Sebastian, what happens when I do this." "Mantas, show Brittany what you just did." It is remarkable, this ability that good primary teachers have: to take in a room in a glance, to assess in a heartbeat, to, with a word or two, provide feedback, make a connection, pull a child into a task. While the majority of Brown Cow's children were native speakers of English, there were also Eddie and Mantas, making the transition from their native Lithuanian (there has been in LA a significant increase of immigrants from the Baltics, the Ukraine, and Russia), Yuki (and her sister Yuko), whose English was limited when they entered the class, and a fair number of students whose first language was Farsi or Spanish. So Abby and Anne made a conscious effort to get native-born children to help Mantas and the others — and to get Mantas and company to use their new language to explain things to whomever was close by.

In Anne's half of the shared classroom, children were making their piles of ten with little trouble, but there would be more for them to do. One of the benefits of the ungraded primary is that students who were excelling in a subject could be encouraged to go beyond kindergarten or first-grade guidelines. Mrs. Brown had written eight problems on the board, to be solved with the help of the students' "manipulatives," their pennies and stamps and leaves.

1) 20	2) 60	3) How many 5s in 200?
+30	+90	

And so on. "How can we do two hundred when we only have one hundred?" Jeremy asked. "Good question," said Mrs. Brown. "What do you think?" All the Brown Cow children took districtwide achievement tests, so standard measures of learning — and accountability — were in place. But Anne and Abby have also been trying to develop a different kind of report card, one that would reflect the way their class worked. "What's it really mean to say that a kid is doing math at first- or second-grade level?" Anne asked rhetorically. "That's awfully vague . . . and not very helpful. What we want to do is provide a description of each child's strengths and weaknesses. And since we get to know the kids so well over three years, we should be able to do that with precision."

When the bell finally rang for physical education — a twenty-five minute break when the children would be out in the yard — Anne and Abby started setting up for yet another lesson involving the number 100, this one to combine arithmetic and language arts. The teachers distributed old newspapers on the tables in the two rooms, then scissors, glue, and large pieces of art paper: yellow, blue, green, magenta. As they did this, they reviewed the morning. How did the lessons work out? Who was doing well? Who needed help? How might Anne better integrate the math problems with the use of the manipulatives? How can Abby do more with her children? They also talked about a boy who might be ready to move into the more proficient math group, such movement being central to this mixed-age grouping.

The bell rang, and soon there was the flap and chatter of the children's return. Ms. Cowan and Mrs. Brown gathered them around and began explaining the lesson with the newspapers. The children would work in assigned groups of eight — the Yellow Group, Green Group, Magenta Group. These were mixed age and ability groups so that the younger children would learn from the older. (Earlier, I had seen Abby pair a second-grader with a kindergartner to read a book; there were lots of possibilities for such peer tutorials in this room.) The students were to find a hundred words that at least one person in their group could read. "Yikes," said a boy. "One hundred words you know, and cut them out, and paste them." Then the teachers would put the final products on display. Mrs. Brown explained the assignment one more time, and off they went, the girl in the flowered pants, the boy in the Raiders jacket, the girl with the oversized sweatshirt. Anne and Abby moved from table to table, organizing, demonstrating, cajoling. "Ms. Cowan," Lisa said, touching Abby's arm, "I can't read yet." "You know what, sweetheart?" Abby replied, kneeling down. "You're starting to; you can read some. Look." And she pointed to some words on a page of advertisements, and Lisa read them: *and, the, to, Muppet.* Then Lisa wiggled her fingers awkwardly into a pair of scissors and started cutting, *Muppet* first, then *and,* then *to.*

A focused pandemonium spread over the room: kids wrangling for pages with big print, singing the words out as they cut them, pounding them onto art paper, reading loudly, and more loudly, the words they knew, discovering them amid a growing jumble of newsprint. *You, book, tax, four, down, Clinton, dream, deal, warranty, house, Von's, blowout, celebration, doctor, banker, slashing, champagne* ("Hey, I found the word *champagne*"), *Cocoa Puffs, matinee, guarantee.* Cut and crumpled paper piled up on the floor, the children kicking through it as they moved around the tables for yet more words: *silk, tennis, Vietnam* (Abby: "Do you know why that word is important?" The little girl in flowered pants: "There was a war there"), *sale, love, dress, book, need.* A girl came up to Anne with the word *squash* stuck to the tip of her finger. A boy thumped his new word onto green paper. Abby helped a child read *need. Neeeed.* And all around the room, words not known, words cut away, fluttered to the floor.

VII

DRIVING THE RESIDENTIAL STREETS south out of Santa Monica, you see the scenes spliced into so many movies and television shows: stucco, palm trees, agave, bougainvillaea, lawn sprinklers, joggers. I took a left turn at Wilshire Boulevard, passing Princeton, Harvard, Yale, and Berkeley avenues, past a small sign that announced CITY OF LOS ANGELES, east in the thick traffic along a mix of buildings from the 1940s and fifties and sleek new high-rises and minimalls, passing men's shops and video stores, sushi bars and software outlets. Viva la Pasta, Cellular Palace, El Capote Mexican Restaurant. Then a right turn on Barrington Avenue, past the Barrington Plaza, and up alongside University High School. Uni High is close to the Federal Building, the Veterans Administration, UCLA, the Westside financial hub at Westwood and Wilshire (the busiest intersection in Los Angeles) — all told, some of the most expensive land in the Basin.

It is the oldest high school in West Los Angeles. Built in 1924, originally Warren G. Harding High School, Uni changed its name to forgo association with the corruption then being revealed about President Harding's administration and to underscore its key role as a feeder school to the University of California, to nearby UCLA in particular. For some time, the school has had a distinguished academic reputation; as an enticement, some real estate ads mention that property is in the Uni High district. It is a beautiful campus, twenty-five acres, terraced and rich with shrubbery and flowers: rose beds, birds of paradise, carob trees, Canary Island pine. Two natural springs run through it. The administration building — the site of the original cornerstone — is red brick with large windows, cream-colored wood frames. A jacaranda in full bloom is right outside the entrance, thousands of light purple buds spread in a loose circle on the lawn at the base of the tree.

There was the smell of honeysuckle in the dim vestibule outside the principal's office; lettered neatly on the door's frosted glass, a sign:

PRINCIPAL
MR. MOSCOWITZ

Inside, the sun streamed through open windows across a wide desk and a vintage Columbia Dictaphone. There were old pennants and photographs on the wall: the severe Angus Cavanaugh, an early principal; a student named Tom Dixon, big smile, "Winner of Popularity Contest, 1933"; a nameless yell leader, a megaphone with the letters WGHHS lying across his bent knee. Warren G. Harding High School.

"I brought Rick Takagaki here," Jack Moscowitz explained, "to shake things up. He's a stimulant, a catalyst, an irritant. He'll say outlandish things if he has to — and that will get students to question him . . . and argue back." He suggested that I talk to other teachers about Takagaki, and I did. Bonnie Williams, whose room was across the hall from Rick's, started to call him a maverick but caught herself. "No, that's too mild a word. He's irreverent, even sacrilegious. Whatever it takes to get kids to think."

Rick Takagaki was about five-seven, thin, wiry, in his late forties, and as he taught, he moved quickly from a stool behind his desk to a chair in front of it to an open semicircle surrounded by students. He moved in spurts and stutter-steps, and when he paused to write on the chalkboard, he kept his left leg extended behind him, his right knee bent inward, ready to pivot back around his desk to the center of the class, challenging the students, tweaking them, assuming a range of voices, saying whatever it took. He began his first economics class on the day of my visit by adopting the persona of Adam Smith and arguing for pure *laissez-faire* capitalism. "There should be minimal regulation of factories," he stormed. "On his own, the owner will make factories safe. Why? Because it will make workers happy, and that's conducive to high productivity." He stopped, raising a finger, fixing the class with a stare. "That's enlightened self-interest." "How about moral obligation?" a student asked skeptically. "Mr. Chin," Takagaki-Smith shot back, "morality is not the issue. Let the marketplace resolve it."

Economics is a high school requirement in the Los Angeles Unified School District, so, in any class you'd observe, no matter how well conceived, you'd find some students who were sullen, or whispering, or daydreaming — a million miles away. "It's always a challenge," Rick explained to me. "To the degree a course is required across the board, like economics or U.S. government, you'll get students who would rather not be there. But I continually try to bring them into the discussion, take a gamble — and I know when to back off." Most courses were structured around a textbook and taught basic concepts: capital formation, supply and demand, elasticity, inflation, and so on. Rick covered these terms, but did so in a course that was a hybrid of comparative economics and economic philosophy, using handouts, articles, and newspaper clippings to lead his students to analyze the century's major systems: capitalism, scientific socialism, and the various Hegelian syntheses that have developed in our time. Some students who were concerned about grades wanted a more traditional course, a straightforward microeconomics syllabus. But Rick worried that such a course would lack a critical edge.

Takagaki was now fulminating against the U.S. Postal Service. "Inefficient! Always in the red!" And he began arguing for privatization. "Hold on," said Scott from the side of the room. (Scott looked like the actor Giancarlo Esposito and had just been accepted to West Point.) "All people couldn't afford that. Thirty-two cents gets your mail out. If it takes longer than Federal Express, well, then that's an efficiency problem — and you can figure out how to remedy that." Rick rocked on the balls of his feet. "There's only one way to solve inefficiency, my man, and that's through competition." Anna, dressed gangbanger-chic, in baggy pants, oversized X-LARGE pullover shirt, sunglasses, sized Rick up and, head back, said, "Yeah, but, like, what happens if the business collapses? And businesses *do* collapse, Tak. Look at LA, huh? Who's going to provide the service then?" "Good thinking, Girl Wonder," Rick conceded, and turned on his heel to begin another disquisition, this one on the evils of subsidization.

"One of the most important things about Rick Takagaki," Principal Moscowitz had said, "is that he holds students accountable for their opinions. He challenges them, prods them, but out of respect for what they're capable of doing." He told me a story. It seemed that several years ago, some students in an advanced placement government class challenged a penalty Rick gave for a late assignment. OK, he said, fair enough. Since this is a class in government, let's put the issue to the courts. He asked them to set up a trial. He would be the defendant. There would be three judges (two picked by the students, one by Rick), prosecuting and defense attorneys, witnesses. The students had to learn court procedure and rules of evidence, set up the date and time of the trial, subpoena witnesses. Mr. Moscowitz himself was called to testify.

After extensive argument, the judges decided that, while Mr. Takagaki had the right to grade as he saw fit and to deduct points for late assignments, in the case under consideration there were mitigating circumstances. The students were not guilty. Rick rescinded the penalty.

Rick had abandoned the voice of Adam Smith and was now pacing the room as John Maynard Keynes, talking in somber tones about factors of production. "What," he asked, "are the secondary effects of failed industry? What happens when a factory closes down?" "There are a lot of 'em," Amanda ventured, her legs stretched out in front of her, her heels tapping the floor. "Say it's automotive. It closes. It affects the rubber plant, steel, glass, uh, the people who make covering for the seats." "All right. OK," Rick said, leaning back against the chair in front of his desk. "And what else happens?" José, who, during preclass banter about prom tuxedos, identified himself as "the Kmart Poster Boy," noted that when a factory closes, the surrounding economy suffers, too. "Workers can't buy groceries; they don't go out to lunch; they don't buy a new TV . . ." Rick got pensive, rubbed his chin, and wondered out loud about converting such industries, retooling. "What about our local defense plants?" he asked. "Couldn't we save them by turning them to commercial production?" "I don't know about that," Amaury said, pulling himself up quickly from a slump. "I was reading that orders are down for commercial aircraft, too. Retool? Retool for what?" He leaned across his desk toward Rick, worked-up, the words coming quickly. "I've been thinking about this, Tak. We haven't been able to see how basically weak our economy is, because . . . well, we've been in a state of war, sort of. The cold war has created a kind of wartime economy, so to speak. We've been artificially geared toward defense. People don't know otherwise. They don't know how to think about the economy in different ways." "Jeez . . . all *right,*" Rick said, shifting to a voice that sounded like Cheech Marin's. "Stu-pen-dous," and he held out his hand, palm open, as if presenting Amaury to the class.

Rick typically spent his lunch break in his room, leaving the door open for anyone who wanted to talk, hang out, or just have a place to eat alone. During my visit, several groups came together and dispersed, following an easy rhythm of food and talk. Over by the filing cabinets, a group of Asian students — Chinese, Japanese, Korean, Filipino — ate lunch from plastic containers and gossiped and laughed. "Hey, Mr. Takagaki," one girl asked Rick as he walked by, "did you know that when Chinese people go on a diet, they eat with one chopstick?" Next to them, four boys — one African American, three White (two with long 1960s hair) — reviewed the Lakers' game ("Did you see that airball?"), the movie *Sliver* ("William Baldwin is *so* lame"), and Uni's chocolate fundraising drive (lame as well) — and then made plans for a basketball game later that day. A group from Rick's AP government class (students accepted at places like Yale and Brown) sat and stood around him by his desk, discussing the legality of a district proposal to conduct random weapons searches; reading and ridiculing a flier advertising Mace: "Stops drunks and psychotics . . ."; challenging Rick on books he'd recommended ("You know, Tak," said a boy in a Thelonius Monk T-shirt, "*Demian* was impossible"); and teasing one another about the prom: dates, clothes, hair, ride. Some of this was addressed to Rick, some to each other, Rick moving in and out, listening, laughing, throwing it back, pushing on them about probable cause, reading lists, and the amount of money they were going to spend on the prom. Toward the end of the break, a girl came in and motioned Rick to the door. She looked upset and asked to talk to him about something another teacher had said to her. He pulled two chairs into a corner, out of earshot, and listened, nodding.

I took the opportunity to talk with Ayal Goury, one of the guys who had been dissecting *Sliver*. Brown hair, thin, cut-offs, Keds, he was planning to go to Hebrew University in Jerusalem to study social science. "Tak doesn't realize the influence he has on people," Ayal said. "I had been thinking of going to NYU and majoring in business, but Tak's classes made me realize I needed to go experience things. Learn more about human behavior. I guess he got me to look at life in a different way. To take a step back, you know, and think and do the right thing. I mean, it's gotta be about more than getting a great stock deal and buying a car — that's ridiculous."

What was it that made Rick Takagaki a teacher of such influence? There were, of course, the qualities that Jack Moscowitz and Bonnie Williams described: he's stimulating, cynically irreverent, and has a quick, sparring style. From what I could tell, the role playing was effective, too. In addition to assuming roles himself, Rick encouraged his students to do the same: "Imagine you're the CEO of a large corporation." "Imagine you're the owner of a home in East LA, and you're losing it to a redevelopment project." All this opened up the discursive possibilities in the room. Some of the students seemed to have a lot of fun with it.

The many voices Rick assumed contributed to his appeal. In addition to the stern diction of Adam Smith and John Maynard Keynes (or, at other times in the semester, Marx and Lenin and Castro), he spoke in a number of styles, some from popular culture, some from the neighborhoods he had come to know. Rick grew up with second-generation *Nisei* parents in the racially mixed Crenshaw District, went to predominantly African-American elementary and junior high schools, and attended the very diverse LA High. He was at home across a range of cultures, and that familiarity revealed itself in his phonology and gesture. A hip-hop Socrates. What gets lost in most discussions of multiculturalism and education — from the right and the left — is the potential for joy in diversity: cultural gestures and practices counterpointing each other, mixing, sliding about in a vibrant social space. For its first several decades, University High School was almost exclusively White and Protestant. But as Japanese settled on nearby Sawtelle Boulevard in the mid-1930s — many opening nurseries on the then-spacious land — and as Jews migrated west from earlier settlements around downtown LA and then the Wilshire-Fairfax district, the ethnic composition of the high school began to change. It changed again in the mid-1970s as mandated integration brought students in from other sections of the city, parents as far away as Huntington Park and South Gate (in the old industrial corridor, near Watts and Bell) having learned about the school's reputation. The mix, of course, has led to problems, given the broader ethnic conflicts in Los Angeles, but Uni remains a civil place, and Rick in his classroom tried to create a comfortable, at times comic, environment, where ethnic differences not only were respected but played out and played with.

But the heart of Rick's influence, I think, was his belief in each student's moral agency. For all the linguistic jabbing and hip cynicism, he conveyed admiration for his students' ability to make decisions, to come to reasoned judgment, to take a stand. Among the posters around the room, on prominent display was the photograph of the lone Chinese student stopping a row of tanks on Tiananmen Square.

"I was trained to believe," Rick told me as we drove down Sawtelle Boulevard, headed for home, "that you need to reach every student, every minute. Yet what you come to realize is that in the broad sweep of their lives, you're little more than a speck of sand . . ." He was tired; the classroom persona fading. He was more the Rick Takagaki his friends knew outside school, contemplative, soft-spoken. "If you can keep both of these things in your mind at the same time," he continued, "then . . . then you'll be a good teacher."

VIII

BIG CITY PUBLIC EDUCATION is often conducted in the midst of crisis. Financial crisis, management and personnel crisis, board-union-superintendent crisis, broader political crises that affect the schools. While I was visiting classrooms in Los Angeles, the Los Angeles Unified School District was being threatened by a proposal that would have resulted in its breakup into a series of smaller districts. It was a volatile proposal, in tension with a long history of segregation and what Jonathan Kozol calls the "savage inequalities" of public school funding. For a while, it consumed the city. (A *Los Angeles Times* education reporter told me that she was able to cover few other issues because she was spending 80 percent of her time on the story.) To get a feel for the complex political dynamics behind the proposal — and for the dynamics of much of urban school politics — we can head east from Uni High about a mile down Wilshire Boulevard to the Avenue of the Stars in Century City.

In the Century Room of the Century Plaza Hotel, there was a conference in progress on the breakup of LAUSD. The proposal was originally conceived by White middle-class residents and legislators from the west side of the San Fernando Valley — over the Santa Monica Mountains, northwest of the LA Basin but part of the sprawling County of Los Angeles. However, it soon gained support from other constituencies in the huge district. Though its point of origin marked it in the eyes of many as a move to protect Anglo privilege, the issue was complicated by the dissatisfaction felt by many poor and minority parents themselves with LAUSD: schools were in disrepair, test scores were low, some teachers were ill-prepared, insensitive, or burned-out. A further complication was that the proposal was put forth at a time when many school reformers were calling for local control of schools — and though local control does not necessarily require multiple small districts, the advocates of breakup played skillfully to the reform agenda. The proposal also came just when California was in its worst financial shape since the Great Depression: state support for public education — constrained by "taxpayer revolt" and conservative governors — had fallen to forty-first in the nation; 50 percent of LAUSD students came from families that lived below the poverty line; LA was a site of civil unrest, tension among ethnic groups and significant White flight from public education; LA class size was the largest in the nation; LA teachers had been dealt a pay cut of 10 percent (bitterly negotiated down from 12 percent); a school reform and restructuring proposal (called LEARN) brokered by the business community was momentarily hitting rough political waters; and the upcoming state elections would include a (finally unsuccessful) voucher measure to convert public funds to private schools. Things were awful for LAUSD.

So legislators, school board members, administrators, a few teachers, the press, and the architects of the breakup proposal were invited by a private foundation to the Century Room, where they sat for a long day around tables arranged in a large open square. Influential state senators and city councilpersons, the president of the Board of Education, the presidents of both the state and local teachers' unions all took turns at the microphones placed at the tables amid name cards, coffee cups, notepads, and frosted pitchers tinkling with ice water. A reporter from the alternative press whispered to me, "If the ceiling fell in right now, it'd change the nature of school politics in Los Angeles." As the morning moved into the afternoon, the proponents for breakup argued for local control, efficiency, trimming bureaucracy, and "the ability to manage our own resources." The opponents contended that multiple districts would mean more, not less, bureaucracy, that size brings with it political clout, that inner city schools will suffer, that "the breakup proposal is not a solution to our problems but only poses as one." The debate included charges of racism and privilege and countercharges of mismanagement and incompetence, and included, as well, the sparks of evident personal antagonisms.

Only one pair of speakers, Ray Reisler and Paul Cummins, both from the private sector, directly questioned the very grounds of the debate itself, the issue of breakup, pro *or* con. They pointed out that the proposal was consuming an enormous amount of political energy, that it had become a media *idée fixe,* a powerbroker obsession that distracted everyone from the true central issue crippling public education in Los Angeles: funding. If ever common cause was necessary, they argued, now was the time: the business community, the teachers' union, the school board, community activists, and local politicians had to come together around funding. "The crisis in our schools is not structural; it is spiritual," Cummins challenged. "This unwillingness to support children comes from an inexcusable failure of political will."

Other speakers also raised the issue of funding, momentarily slipping out of the confines of the debate to talk about this fundamental problem. "We're in an exercise in denial," said Leticia Quezada, president of the school board. "The schools need more money." "School is the common ground on which we should all be meeting," pleaded city councilperson, Rita Walters. "We've got to learn to live together." Other fundamental issues emerged. City councilperson Mike Hernandez noted that "we bus to avoid integrating our housing," underscoring the fact that we continually ask our schools to do what we can't seem to do in the other domains of our society. And school board member Mark Slavkin, who would go on to become president, said: "There is more good in this district than ever gets talked about — and it gets lost in these discussions. We have crafted around public schools so many layers of control. It's sexy to media, but how do we break out of this system and start talking about how to make life better in classrooms?" But the idea of breakup had so gripped the city, played off so many fears and old injuries and past conflicts, that the proposal seemed impossible to abandon. The participants were webbed within it, the brokerage of power masquerading as educational reform.

There were a few teachers present at the conference, and one student, an earnest young man from an inner-city high school. Toward the end of the day, there was a chance for them to speak. The student, Rubin Green, gave testimony to a special liberal studies program he was in called *Humanitas* and told of his own rise from terrible to solid grades. "My teachers gave me the feeling I could succeed." The moderator asked him whether the issue of the breakup of LAUSD would matter to students. "There's nothing being presented here today," he said pointedly, "that would be meaningful to them." Then one of the teachers spoke, a high school history teacher named George Woods. "The breakup," he said, in exasperation, "is a political decision, not an educational decision. Next time, let's talk about education rather than politics." The last word came from a businessman from another city, here as an observer. "The politics," he said simply, "are eating you up."

IX

WHAT OTHER VOICES might have been heard in that conference room in Century City? Voices that Rubin Green would have found familiar, that those teachers would have recognized? There would most likely be the voice of a teacher from the inner city — often the first stop in an urban teacher's career. There would be someone talking about violence, gangs and violence, for though everyone denounces it, gang life — in all its brutality and desperation and crazy-tragic stylized rebellion (*"la vida loca,"* Chicano gang members call it) — has gripped the imagination of Los Angeles. And there would be a voice in another language — for LAUSD alone has almost ninety thousand students who have been in the United States less than three years, and few come speaking English. Let us end, then, with three speakers, finding them back where we began, back east on the I-10, then south toward the center of the LA Basin, back to Edwin Markham Intermediate School.

I met with the first, a thirteen-year-old English-as-a-second-language student named Claudia, in the office of Lourdes Parvizshahi, Markham's Coordinator of Bilingual Education. It was a small and efficient office — posters, books, filing cabinets — with a constantly ringing phone and a door that endured many taps, many rattles, many loud knocks: questions about schedules and classes, teachers needing to confer, requests to translate. There were about six hundred students at Markham designated as having limited proficiency in English, and of that number, approximately four hundred were recent immigrants, virtually all of whom needed ESL courses. These are not unusual numbers in LA city schools. Coordinating the students' schedules, working out their placement, troubleshooting, giving counsel and advice, trying to solve more problems than possible — all this kept Lourdes moving with the composure of an emergency room surgeon.

Claudia sat in a chair of metal and blue plastic with her feet on the rung; a full round face, open, a gentle demeanor, a soft voice. She could comprehend some English and was beginning to speak it — we could exchange basic information, tentatively, on our own — but we needed Lourdes to act as our interpreter. This account, then, is conveyed mostly through Lourdes, who stood beside Claudia, her left hand touching the back of the chair, just the tips of her fingers. She was Claudia's age when she came from Mexico to the United States. So I would talk and Claudia would talk — Lourdes our interlocutor — and Claudia would look back at me as the translation came, understanding some of the English, smiling or nodding or raising her eyebrows and giving me a knowing look when I smiled or laughed or nodded in agreement with something she said.

Claudia was born in the United States, but her parents separated when she was very young, so her mother moved back to Tijuana and eventually remarried. Several years ago, her mother decided that Claudia would "be much better off" growing up in the United States, and would learn English better than if she studied it in Mexico. So she sent the girl to live with her godmother in National City, a town about five miles south of San Diego. There, Claudia had a good year in school, but the living arrangements didn't work out, and she moved back to Mexico. Here she was again in the United States, three months now, living with her mother, aunt, and grandmother over on 113th Street. She "likes the environment a lot"; there were other relatives who lived close by, and "they give lots of advice."

Her education in Tijuana prepared her well — Mexican schooling is more demanding than many in the United States imagine — and after a few weeks at Markham, she felt she hadn't been placed in the right level, so she came to Lourdes, asking for algebra, science, and more advanced ESL. Now she thought she was doing well in school.

Claudia wanted to be a writer. She started writing when she was eight. Her stepfather in Tijuana had many books around — *Don Quixote, Ben Hur* — and she read them "and started getting ideas and put them into writing." She was trying to write a novel now, but her aunt said the noise of the old typewriter bothered her. (At this point, Claudia's eyes teared up — she waved her hand in front of her face, trying to fan away the emotion — and Lourdes took time out to arrange for Claudia to stay after school and use one of Markham's typewriters.) Claudia went on to describe her composing process. She'll get "many different ideas on many different topics," then begins a routine of culling and selecting. "No, this is no good. No, no, this one is not good enough either. Oh, this is interesting!" And then she starts jotting down her ideas.

Claudia was also interested in science. During her year in National

City, she had a science teacher who "taught us all about protons, electrons, and neutrons" and would tutor students after school and, as well, give them advice about any problems they might be having. It was this teacher who got her excited about science.

She would continue taking her content courses in Spanish for now, and as she advanced in English as a second language, she would make the transition to what is called sheltered English. She was hoping to finish high school and follow a career in science or in writing. She liked both and realized she could wait a while before making her choice.

Veronica was lean and energetic, a tomboyish thirteen, shiny brown skin, long curly hair pulled back and flowing over her shoulders. Her parents were both immigrants, her mother Afro-Cuban, her father Mexican. She grew up "all over South Central" and spoke with a blend of Chicano and Black rhythms and inflections. (Her mixed heritage had, at times, been a source of trouble, "'cause I'm Black but I talk Spanish, so some Black girls used to jack me for my rings and pull my hair.") She lived in a tough housing project over on Ninety-seventh Street called Jordan Downs with her mother, a brother who was twelve, and a fifteen-year-old sister. She also had a twenty-one-year-old sister who was married and wanted to enroll in a community college, and a twenty-three-year-old brother who used to be in a gang but had gone straight and worked in a minimum-wage service job. Veronica's mother supported her children through public assistance; she volunteered at Markham, partly, Veronica believed, "so she can check up on me."

Veronica was wearing black tennis shoes, white jeans, and a white T-shirt, covered with a radiant picture of the Virgin of Guadeloupe. Though Veronica had a bit of a lisp and was classified as a limited-English-proficiency student, she was an enthusiastic conversationalist, eager to talk, thoughtful, seemed to like the give-and-take. We didn't begin by talking about gangs — I asked her about school and her friends and her interests — but she turned our talk quickly to gang life and pursued the topic vigorously, leaning into the table, shoulders hunched, clasping her hands between her legs, halting for a word occasionally, muttering, "How you say?" but shaking her head, giggling the barrier away, her voice strong, seemingly driven to say it all the way through.

"I want to be like a nurse or a teacher or a police officer. I want to help people. I want to help kids so they won't be on drugs. Little kids. I know a lot of guys, a lot of girls, they're into drugs. And a lot of girls get pregnant. At thirteen years old! That's hard for them. They're too small for that. They can't handle it. It's bad for them.

"I see a lot of little kids try to gangbang, and I don't want my nephews or my little brother to gangbang. The gangs be killing a lot of people right now — little kids, sometimes. They killed two of my uncles, and I don't want that to happen again. Kids think if they gangbang, they can do everything. They think, 'My homeboys will back me up.' They think they bad, but if you get them alone, you know they scared.

"I want to grow up and be something in my life. 'Cause my brother, you know, he's got two babies right now, and he don't got nothing for his life. He, like, he don't get paid a lot. I feel sorry for him — he's got two kids and everything and he's trying to do something with his life now. But, but, it's too late.

"My dad, he used to gangbang. He's in jail now. And all my uncles are in jail, too. So, I know. And I see my friends gangbang. I say, 'Noooo! You're gonna gangbang, too? You won't have no future or nothing.' I don't want that to happen in my life. I want to have my own family someday. I could help my family and my mom. But if I gangbang, if I get pregnant, how could I give anything to my mom? I don't want my life to be sorry. I want to feel proud for myself.

"It is hard. It *is* hard. Everybody's gangbanging. Everybody's looking all bad. But my brother says to me, 'Don't you see my life — how it is?' He don't even let me dress like a gangbanger. He talks to me. He says, 'Don't you do it. Your life's gonna be dumb. That's dumb for you.' He be telling me like that, and I be thinking, 'Yeah, it's dumb.' And it *is* dumb. Because in a gang, what am I gonna do? Only get killed, get jumped, or use drugs. You know, that's what happens in a gang. [Slowly] I should know. I should know."

Jolly Enciso's sixth-grade classroom was located in the bungalows on the edge of Markham's campus, looking out across an athletic field to 108th Street on the south and, on the east, to an empty lot and the train tracks along Grandee. Unlike the center of campus, it was a little ragged here: the weathering of the less sturdy bungalows, a web of cracks in the concrete, the lot thick with weeds. Freight trains came by blasting their loud whistles, though not with the regularity of days past, when industry was thriving. From the landing outside Jolly's room, you could see the tallest of the Watts Towers, rising almost a hundred feet into the blue sky. "*Nuestro Pueblo,*" Simon Rodia had called his construction. "Our Town."

Inside, Jolly's room was tight and colorful — low ceiling, the desks close, full bookcases, a pile of student folders, a fern, a map, art supplies, a mound of pillows, a broom, stools, a rack of costumes for plays, stacks of hats, and, along the walls, cast lists and storyboards for the play *The Reluctant Dragon*. By her desk, a blue and yellow bulletin board was crammed with overlapping snapshots of her family and her students, past and present: kids hanging onto a firetruck, carousing on field trips, posing in costumes, looking serious in cap and gown.

Jolly sat at one of her students' desks. She had thick black hair, white blouse and tie, and a strong, emphatic voice, her mouth holding the shape of a word for a moment after it was spoken. She had worked in a law firm and in the music industry before entering teaching. When she decided she wanted to teach in LAUSD, she went to observe at Markham. She sat in on classes for a week — and knew this was the place for her. That was eight years ago. For the last two years, she's been the school's union representative. And lately she has been working on staff development.

"I'm trying to develop a training program for new teachers coming to Markham. Most teachers being recruited by Los Angeles will be sent into neighborhoods like ours. They'll have all the energy and creativity they'll need, but they'll be coming into a world that's very new to them. I'll tell you, there are still days when *I* forget the dangers in our children's environment — and it just takes a flash to realize 'Oh my God, we are still in the inner city no matter what I do.' One day, I had the door open and there, right there on 108th Street, two carloads of guys started shooting at each other. I watched as the PE teachers and about three hundred sixth-graders hit the deck outside on the grass, hit the deck flat out, scared. And stupidly, naïvely, I'm standing at the open door because I'm astonished. When I turned around, there were my kids, flat on the ground, covering themselves. Then, in a matter of minutes, they were back up at their desks, as if nothing had happened.

"It was in the second year of my teaching, and I had this A student, Carlos, who, thank God, is in college now and doing wonderfully well. So Carlos comes in and doesn't have his homework. This worried me — it wasn't like him. On my way home, I stopped at his house over by Imperial Courts. I find the address and knock on the door. 'Excuse me, does the So-and-so family live here?' 'Oh, yeah, yeah,' this guy says, 'in the back.' So I go to the house behind. 'Hi, are the So-and-sos here?' 'Oh, yeah, in the back.' Well, they lived in the garage. Seven children. Carlos was the oldest. His mother was expecting. They all slept on a beat-up vinyl couch. Their bathroom was just a makeshift thing, no door. The kids' stuff was in boxes. And here is Miss Teacher in her little cream-colored suit talking to Carlos's mother about Carlos not doing his homework. Come to find out the electricity had gone out, and they were afraid to use candles, for fear of fire . . . But, you know, you look at it another way, I *had* to worry about his homework. And this is what I tell new teachers. Know your students' limitations, but don't lower your standards. These kids, no matter what, they'll meet 'em.

"I certainly get discouraged. I'm discouraged as hell right now about the district. But what keeps me going are the children who walk through that door. They're the difference. They're eager. They're capable. Sure, there's a challenge to reach the drug baby, the special ed child who's mainstreamed, the second-language speaker, so you work at it. And the kids keep coming back. Ready to start over. Ready to try again. They don't even know how strong they are. These kids. That's the reality here. Ten-, eleven-year-old kids. As a teacher, you do what you can to make their lives comfortable and learning fun and interesting. And you try to challenge them. Sometimes I think the teacher is a teacher — and a mother, father, psychologist, nurse, and cafeteria worker. It takes energy. It takes organization. And it takes *desire.* And that's where my *fight* is these days: for better quality teachers and for the politicians, the public to see what must be done here."

A final image: As I was walking to the parking lot after lunch, I saw Jolly in the distance, twenty to thirty yards away, out on the basketball courts. The bell had rung, so students were moving in big crowds back to classrooms, running and walking. A small cluster around Jolly was breaking up more slowly. I could hear her saying something to them; fragments of her voice were drifting toward me. She was holding a boy, her arms locked around him, her legs braced as he tried to pull away. She hugged him, restraining him, protecting him. Then, as though she were going to talk to him — everyone else had gone now — she lowered her chin, resting it on the top of his head, and I could see now that he was sobbing.

2

Calexico, California

I DROVE out of Los Angeles on the 405, two hours or so, curving through San Diego, close to the Mexican border, heading east onto Highway 8, where the road narrowed from four lanes to two. I passed an abandoned government kiosk, various twists of scrap metal, and a thousand configurations of rock and brush, and began the slow descent onto the desert floor of the Imperial Valley. There were signs for — but no sight of — Lake Moreno, Kitchen Creek Road, the Tecate Divide, Manzanita, Jacumba, and Ocotillo. The sky was clear, deep blue, and the sun played off the rockface in the distance. I was the only car on the road. The air was warm and dry. In the distance: ROAD 98. The road that takes you along the border to Calexico.

Calexico is an American city that speaks two languages, a truly bicultural city. Border culture. Of the 21,000 residents, most are of Mexican ancestry, and the majority of Anglos speak so-so–to–fluent Spanish. This whole area of the Imperial Valley was converted from desert to arable land through water diverted from the Colorado River. The project began just after the turn of the century. Calexico was the surveying camp on the Mexican border — the name blends *Cal*ifornia and M*exico* — and in 1908 was incorporated as a city. A few of the early buildings still stand on First Street, just this side of Mexicali.

Though many families in Calexico are poor — income is low and seasonal — and the school district is always scrambling for funds, the elementary schools exceeded the Imperial County average on recent statewide tests of language arts, mathematics, and science, and the high schools have the lowest dropout rate of any predominantly Latino school district in California. In fact, they are 9 percentage points below the statewide average for *all* schools. A significant number of graduates go on to two- and four-year colleges. One explanation has to do with the unanimity of goals between district administration and school board.

Another with an effective bilingual education program. And a third has to do with the way teacher education develops out of respect for local history.

The Imperial Valley Campus of San Diego State University took up one square block of land six short blocks from the Mexican border. It was located on the site of the old Calexico High School, which had been boarded up and broken into for a long time. The campus retained three original, though refurbished, buildings — archways, white stucco, tile roofs — and had built a few classrooms and brought in some portable structures for administration, student services, and faculty offices. There were plans in the works for a complete reconstruction, but for over twenty-five years this small satellite campus, with its patchwork of buildings and bungalows, has served as the only means for Valley residents to get a four-year degree. Walking down Seventh Street, you came upon it like a park or a historical preserve, nestled between houses and parked cars and an occasional delivery van. Maybe you'd hear the buzz of a lawn mower. Little more.

Students at the campus would usually begin their work at IVC, Imperial Valley College, a two-year school about twelve miles north of Calexico, right up Highway 111, and transfer over to complete degrees in humanities or social science. They majored in liberal studies or Latin-American studies, English or Spanish or criminal justice administration, psychology or history, to prepare themselves for careers in business or law enforcement or education. Many hoped to teach. They were a serious student body — numbering four to five hundred in any given year — and they came to school in order to lead a better life here in the Valley. Most worked, and night classes were popular. Hardly anyone hung out. So unless you walked across campus right at those times when classes were starting up or winding down — noon, say, or four or seven or ten — you might, in fact, think the place *was* a historical monument. There would be the shade and rustle of Mexican fan palms and date palms and eucalyptus, and you might stop to hear the birds chirping in the trees and cooing in the red tile. As you made your way toward the north side of the campus — it's a short walk — you'd begin to hear faint music from behind the closed doors of the service bungalows: the hectic advertisements of Mexican *rocanrol* stations or trumpets and guitars or the lyrics of North American oldies — "Angel Baby" or "Blue Velvet." A little farther, over toward the plywood and corrugated metal, and you'd come upon the faculty offices, faded and baking in the sun.

Evangelina Bustamante Jones sat in front of gray metal bookcases wedged tight against her brief office wall. The shelves were crammed with books on the teaching of writing, bilingual education, reading, and teacher education — her responsibilities here. Student papers and projects from semesters past were boxed or bundled or rolled up and stacked precariously on shelves or placed safely in a corner on the floor. Newspaper clippings about former students — weddings and awards — were taped to the wall. "It's such a small community," she said, leaning forward and loosely folding her hands on the desk, "that you kinda keep track of everyone."

We had just come from visiting a student teacher she was supervising — teaching over in Heber, a little agricultural town about three miles northwest of Calexico. Anthony Heber was one of the early developers of the Imperial Valley — many of the cities in the Valley and the streets within them were named after developers and civil engineers — and the town that bore his name had twenty-five hundred people, two schools, and a lot of cattle that listlessly regarded you as you drove in. The air was heavy and fecund. "You don't notice it," a local told me, "until you leave. Then when you return, it's, well, it's the smell of home." Lori, the young teacher, was born in Heber and wrote in the journal Evangelina asked her to keep, "I am so happy and so lucky to be working in this school where I grew up."

"She's really good," Evangelina continued. "She's very creative, very responsible, and she's empathetic. She may not stay in Heber, but it's important for her to be there now." Evangelina absentmindedly touched a streak of silver in her hair. "You know, some of the teachers Lori had as a little girl are still there — and her principal, too. They give her a lot of support." A pause here. "And in the eyes of her old neighbors. Imagine! 'Look at Lori. She's come back.' *La Maestra*."

Education was highly valued in places like Heber and Calexico, as it was generally in Mexican culture. Teachers were respected, and school was seen as a place where children could learn the skills that would enable them to do better than their parents had done. This support of education played out, however, amid a complex of forces. Many of the families in the Valley were very poor — 35 percent of the residents lived below the poverty line — and sometimes had to make decisions between work and school. As Evangelina put it, "Poverty forces you to parcel out your human resources." So some children would be selected to pursue their education, and others sent out to make money. "I was the oldest and had to work," one man explained, "but my brother was able to go to college." Traditional beliefs about gender factored into these decisions, but not in the unilateral way commonly portrayed. Some families still believed that girls don't need schooling as much as boys do, but I also heard from a number of professional women that it was their working-class fathers who urged them toward achievement. Such achievement could, though, conflict with other beliefs about family cohesiveness and a woman's role in maintaining it — and this could become a source of awful tension if a college-bound woman decided to leave the area to pursue her education. The local San Diego State campus made higher education possible for women who could not easily leave the Valley.

A mild breeze stirred the trees by Evangelina's louvered window. A parrot somewhere outside started whistling. "Do you ever see yourself in these young teachers you supervise?" I asked. "Oh, yes." She laughed. "Except they're a lot better put together than I was!" Evangelina Jones had been teaching for twenty-two years. Middle school, third grade, sixth grade, continuation high school — the works. A few years back, the college asked her to help with their teacher-education courses and to develop a program for those students who came to the campus needing extra work with their writing. So now she's a college professor. She thought back. "My first year of teaching, I cried all the time. My methods classes didn't teach me one damned thing. And I didn't have a mentor in the school. I was isolated, and I didn't have very good techniques, *and* I didn't know how to manage my class." She smiled, her dark eyes could move quickly from the squint of pain to tender reflectiveness to a fixed gaze of conviction. "If you don't get support, you die a little every day."

Dying a little every day. We talked further about mentoring and apprenticeship, about what powerful ways they were to develop skill. "But they're so hard to get." She tapped her folded hands on the desk for emphasis. "I knew I wanted to be a teacher since I was a young girl. I had this dream. I was so idealistic — but the reality was another story. If you don't have other teachers to go to for advice, or just to cry on their shoulder on Friday afternoon, this job will eat you up." We talked a bit more about the kinds of knowledge good teachers develop. Then I told her about a friend of mine, an esteemed professor of education who took some time off to teach elementary school. He failed miserably. The kids wouldn't listen to him; some of his lessons fell flat; he had trouble translating his ideas into practice. Evangelina chuckled sympathetically. "Hey, I can still remember what *that* felt like!" Somebody walking by whistled to the parrot. The parrot squawked and whistled back.

Evangelina was determined that the prospective teachers in her charge would have a better time of it than she had: better techniques, more support. Her teaching-methods courses may not have done much for her, but she was trying her best to make worthwhile the ones she taught. One student teacher told me that Mrs. Jones's courses were very helpful. "She just knows so much. After all, she's been there."

Students in general are not enthusiastic about methods courses. "It's a tradition to hate them," Evangelina observed. But they're not crazy about more theoretical offerings either, seeing them as obscure and irrelevant. An increasing number of teacher educators agree, bemoaning the trivial, unreflective nature of methods courses, the gulf between educational research and teacher practice, and the humdrum, technocratic nature of so much of a student teacher's life.

What Evangelina tried to do was illustrate theory, ground it in practice. She knew how desperately these new teachers would need effective strategies and approaches — things to do when entering the schoolhouse door on Monday morning. She also believed that a good teacher knew these things, so to speak, from the inside, had done them, had developed a knowledge of doing. "How can you teach something," one student teacher asked me, "that you haven't experienced?" As for theory: "How," Evangelina mused, "can you reflect on what you do and justify what you do without it?" Evangelina struggled to create this amalgam of theory and practice. In her opinion, she had a long way to go — "I'm supposed to be the expert; I don't *feel* like an expert" — but the teachers moving through her classes and out into the schools disagreed. "She's an inspiration to me!" that student teacher exclaimed.

Later that day, I visited the Teaching of Reading, taught by Evangelina in Room A-3, the old Music Room. Two nicked speakers hung above the blackboard and over the last row of seats; some simple spotlights were nailed to the ceiling, like those outdoor lights you'd find in someone's back yard. The door was open, and the sky outside was deep blue, the birds still streaking and dipping from tree to tree. It was five to the hour, and the students were drifting in. The youngest looked to be in their early twenties; many more, though, were older, mid-twenties to mid-thirties. They carried backpacks and briefcases and soft drinks, candy bars, and bags of chips — for most were coming straight from work. Except for two, they all went to Imperial Valley College, either right out of high school or after getting a family under way. They all seemed to know each other. The warm hum of chatter began, a free mix of Spanish and English — a question about jobs, a wisp of gossip — and life rose up in the Music Room.

Evangelina walked in right at the hour, and a few students came up to meet her at the podium. They needed a reading or had questions. One held a paper for her to sign, and she leaned forward and crooked her neck to read it. That settled, she took a determined step forward, as though in a fencing move, and asked the class to break up into groups of four. Those sitting along the back by the windows or scattered out to the side had to get up, hoisting backpacks and briefcases. Others simply yanked on the edges of their school desks and executed a half or quarter turn, never leaving their seats. "I want you," she said, "to show each other your modern fairy tales. Enjoy them . . . tell each other how wonderful they are . . . then take fifteen or twenty minutes and write an evaluation of one of them." A mock groan came from two men in the back. Evangelina smiled. "I know. I'm cruel. That's me. *Asi soy.*"

A week earlier, Evangelina had explained "story grammar," the notion from cognitive psychology that common stories, like fairy tales, share certain structural features — their plots unfold in predictable ways — and this predictability helps readers comprehend them. Evangelina had asked her students to determine the "grammar" of a favorite fairy tale and to use that grammar to compose a contemporary variation. The assignment, she hoped, would encourage a practical understanding of the theoretical concept of story grammar and would, to boot, provide an exercise adaptable to the classroom.

The students exchanged their fairy tales, and read, laughing, offering pats on the back. In one story, a young Aladdino found a Coke bottle instead of a lantern in a polluted river in Mexicali, the rapidly industrializing city just across the border, and made various wishes to end poverty and hunger and war. In another, Little Red Riding Hood emerged as Rosita, who, on her way to her grandmother's house, was assailed by the fearsome wolf, El Lobo. But the author, unwilling to stick with the grammar of the original tale, concluded with redemption, not revenge. In the contemporary setting of this tale, the woodsman was a construction worker who reasoned with rather than dismembered El Lobo, getting him to release Rosita, change his ways, and pursue a degree in business administration.

Each group in its own time made the shift to evaluation, growing silent, trying to find the right words. People thought hard, bent over their notebooks, making rhythmic movements with a foot or hand. Concentration. From the middle of the room came a noise that sounded a little like a brush on a snare drum, but with more scrape to it: a woman was hot on the trail of an idea, writing, erasing quickly, then writing again, her thin bracelets grazing the top of her desk.

II

THE STREETS IN CALEXICO were calm and lightly traveled. At the end of the day, there was a predictable jam at Imperial, the main drag to the border, as Mexicali workers crossed back over *la linea,* the line. Birch Street, too, got a little hectic where it met State Highway 111. But otherwise traffic was blissfully light; you'd barely hear the honking of a horn. Every morning, though, Monday to Friday, there would suddenly develop this convergence of cars and trucks on usually quiet streets around the city, those where the district's elementary schools were located — like Encinas, running north and south, just a few blocks away from the college. It would be quick and fleeting, a vehicular whirl of wind: parents and aunts and older brothers dropping off the young ones, pulling in and out of white zones, double parking, stacking up, blinkers on. But no horns. They'd holler and wave to each other, neighbors and bloodlines, generation to generation.

Evangelina recommended I visit the school on Encinas, Dool Elementary — named after another of those early developers. "There's a teacher there you should see," she said. "Elena Castro. She has a good reputation in the district. She teaches bilingual third grade and has mentored a lot of our students. She's a pistol. You'll like her, I think. And, besides, Dool is right down the street." While in Calexico I stayed with an old college roommate, Matt Contreras, now a superior court judge. When I mentioned that I'd be visiting Dool, he laughed and told me a story. He had to transfer to Dool when he was entering the fourth grade, and he was worried. "You'll come in with me, right?" he nervously asked his father. His father mumbled something, apparently not taking this request seriously — after all, the young Matias was an assured and athletic kid. Why worry? "No, I mean it, Dad. You'll walk in there with me, OK?" It seems that Dool had a reputation as a tough school. It was on the wrong side of town. Matt laughed again. *"La Dool!"*

I called Elena Castro. Not long after, I watched the cars on Encinas cluster and pull away, kids running across the sidewalk with books and lunch pails. It was a small, clean school, white and industrial tan, green lawn, on the poor side, but kept up. I turned up the walkway hearing the unsteady bleat of a trombone from the cafeteria, and entered a stream of children coming in from the curb. Other groups gathered around the tree in front of the gate or just inside at the tables by the dissonant cafeteria, talking and bouncing and laughing. The main office was so full that the door was held half open by kids clumped against the jamb. Then came four or five rows of classrooms, some portable buildings — the library and the Writing Center, both the results of grants and donations — and the expanse of asphalt and grass that loudly signified the freedom of the playground. Kids were shooting baskets with a mix of awkwardness and grace, playing tether ball and foursquare and hopscotch, and running every which way on the broad stretch of lawn. Walking among them, ignored and intermittently jostled, I felt the unbridled joy of physical play. I thought about Matt and wanted, right then and there, to call him up and tell him about this. *La Dool*. I don't know how the school looked and felt then — especially to a fourth-grader — but it had the cast of decency to it now. Who knows? It was nice to believe that a school could take a turn for the better.

I found Elena out in the field, two or three kids around her. She handed me the key to her room and said they'd be in shortly. "Make yourself at home," she called after me; then the children pulled her back in. From our earlier conversation I knew that she structured her curriculum around general themes that the students themselves had a hand in selecting. The various subject areas — language arts and science, for example — were integrated and the students studied them in contexts that were interesting to them. The theme they were currently working on was sea life. Evangelina had alerted me that Elena's room itself would knock me out. "Stimulus-rich" was the term she used. I found Room 42 and opened the door. Evangelina was right: the place was vibrant. The walls, the blackboard, even the sliding doors on the cabinets were covered with charts and posters: "Ocean Wonders" and "Milagros del Mar." Blue, orange, and red fabrics formed a backdrop for the copious display of children's art and writing. Books were stacked and leaning everywhere; a sign with coral drawn around it said, "You don't have to read every day, just on the days you eat!" Across the ceiling, clothesline was crisscrossed, and cut-and-pasted drawings of fish dangled — the Crayola butterfly fish, the newsprint manta ray — seeming to swim in the breeze that came in behind me. I thought of Ariel's song in *The Tempest.* This tan room had undergone a sea change. An ocean of color and language. Spanish and English. The shark, *el tiburon,* and *la anguila,* the eel, and the jellyfish, *el aguamar.* The bell rang and I took a few steps inside, into a surround of print and art-paper water.

The children filed in, hot and antsy from play, and headed for the long rectangular tables in the middle of the room on which their chairs were stacked. Clatter and clang and the chairs came down. The flush of the school yard was starting to fade, but not quite, and while the children reached for their books, there was a jibe in Spanish and a questionable tug and nudge. One boy wore a sweatshirt that said MOTOCROSS POWER; another boy had ATTACK FORCE on the heels of frayed sneakers. There were two Beverly Hills 90210 T-shirts, and a pullover from the Salt Lake City Zoo, and an old rugby shirt, and some simple checks and stripes. The boys wore jeans and cords, mostly, and the girls had on pastel jeans and stretch pants and cotton dresses. One girl's dress puffed out at the shoulders; another dress had three ribbons down the front, white against a background of pink and blue verbena.

Elena Castro moved to the front of the room and, while the children did some work at their tables, quickly took roll. Everyone was present. Then she tallied those who would be eating in the cafeteria and had the children stand for the Pledge of Allegiance. Mrs. Castro's voice was strong and precise — "and to the Republic for which it stands" — but tempered by a throaty quality, a lounge singer's rasp, consequential, melodious. These classroom preliminaries were handled with brisk efficiency. Then, in a softening of demeanor, Mrs. Castro said it was time for a story and reached for a chair close to the blackboard. The children got up from their tables and gathered around her. I grabbed a little chair from one of the tables and moved in closer to the half-circle of children. The book was about deep-sea divers. It looked as if it had some years on it. Elena began. She read in English, then translated into Spanish or asked a bilingual child to "explain to us what's happening here." During these moments, she would turn the book around to face the children, using the illustrations as guides to comprehension, tracing the tentacles on the octopus, *tentaculos del pulpo,* and the broad curving wing of the manta ray. She encouraged interaction through comments and questions — "Carlos, you're working on the manta ray, *verdad¿*" or "Why is salt left when the water dries on the boat?" — and the students would respond, sometimes adding observations of their own. At one point, a bubbly girl named Irianna noted that the divers' suits are *soooo* old, Miss Castro, and later Andres, sharp-featured and handsome, observed, in Spanish, that a sinking ship looked like the *Titanic.* Elena acknowledged these and other comments, weaving them into the story when possible, sometimes laughing with the children — a low and easy *heh heh heh* — and continued, the children sitting rapt, legs crossed, elbows on knees, toying with their fingers or cradling their chins. One girl, Arely, reached up as Mrs. Castro read and traced with her finger the octopus on the cover, cocking her head and watching her teacher's eyes widen as the divers went down toward the ocean floor.

Mrs. Castro finished the book at nine o'clock straight-up, folded it in her lap, and called for the first rotation. The children uncrossed their legs and, in springing extensions and ungainly turns, stood up and headed for their stations. What happened from that point on was a study in the way an environment can be organized to foster learning. Though Mrs. Castro usually opened her class with some sort of group activity — a reading or a math lesson, perhaps a discussion of current events — a fair amount of the work the students did was accomplished individually or in small groups. There were eight stations. Starting at the door, and moving counterclockwise, there was the Listening Station (two old-time tape recorders and ear sets on a small table by the door), the Publishing Center (a computer and printer with large, occasionally wobbly script, covers and plastic spines, and a binding machine), and the Writer's Table (actually four small tables pushed together to make one uneven square). Then came the front of the room and the blackboards. Next, the Reader's Corner (shelves crammed with books leaning every which way, a big rocker, a worn red Persian rug), a Math Station and a Research Station, where volumes from two different encyclopedias had been interleaved to create an almost complete set. Then the Teacher's Workshop, where Mrs. Castro did a good deal of her close work with the children. This placed you at the back wall, covered with information about fish, just behind the teacher's desk, which Elena used mostly for the stacking of papers. A red felt apple lay knocked over. "I ♥ my teacher" was printed across it; a green smiling worm curled out and up its side. A few more steps and you have returned to the door and the Art Station, where blue and orange and yellow watercolors had left little ribbons of stain on the tile.

To provide sequence and structure to their day, and to receive close instruction from Mrs. Castro, the students shifted, every half hour or so, from one major task — and one station — to another. They moved in groups or "rotations." Depending on the task, the groups might be composed only of English-speakers or of Spanish-speakers — for example, for writing instruction. Or they might be mixed, combined with fluently bilingual kids (Elena called them "brokers"), the children conversing back and forth, helping each other with a math lesson on sets and sorting. There was a good deal of fluidity here, though Elena, who was meticulous in her organization and record keeping, seemed to be on top of the activity. A visit to the classroom, then, might yield one group of children bent over stories in progress at the Writer's Table — with one of the students, brow furrowed, editing a story on the computer at the Publishing Station. A second group might be working on mathematics, one or two receiving audiotaped guidance at the Listening Station. A third group might be sitting around Mrs. Castro at the kidney-shaped Teacher's Workshop, doing research on the particular sea creatures that caught their fancy. Elena Castro controlled the clock and moved the children through the range of activities, but within these activities, children were free to follow their interests and take responsibility for completing their work in the way they thought best.

Before returning to Mrs. Castro, who was now setting her book back on its shelf, a word on how the curriculum was developed. Although the children helped determine the organizing themes, Elena gave them a sense of how this would work by beginning the year with a unit of her own choosing but of relevance to them, the Imperial Valley. (In a blue basket by the computer, I saw a stack of booklets the students had written collaboratively on the histories of the towns of their birth: Mexicali, Calexico, Brawley, Holtville, Heber.) After studying the Valley for a month, the students voted on the topics they'd want to study through the year. These topics became the conceptual skeleton of the curriculum. A list of them was taped to the door:

Themes We Will Study
Temas Que Estudiaremos

Earth
La Tierra

Sealife
Animales Marinos

Energy
Energia

Pollution
Contaminacion

Cultures
Culturas

And so on. As a particular month progressed, then, the books Elena Castro begged, borrowed from the library, salvaged, and bought from her own pocket would change somewhat, as would the charts and posters and plentiful work of the children that adorned the walls and hung in the air. There was much that was stable, of course — from the multiplication chart to the computer to that incomplete encyclopedia — but this was a classroom always in a state of orderly evolution, structured and unpredictable.

Mrs. Castro walked back to the corner by her desk, the Teacher's Workshop. She wore a black jacket, silver bracelets, a bright blue dress, and heels. She was about five foot two, and moved quickly — though she could stop on a dime to listen to a child's question, seeming to block out everything else. Andres headed her off and asked if he could take the book about the divers home that night: *"Maestra, me puedo llevar el libro a la casa, por favor?"* Sure he could, she said, touching his shoulder, complimenting him for giving the English book a try. Then she settled in at her workshop to help the nine students gathering around her with their marine research.

The students had in front of them booklets Mrs. Castro made to guide their inquiry. Each booklet had four sections: What You Know, What Do You Want to Know?, Bibliography, and Research Notes. Across the top of each section swam a line of sketched fish, each about to gobble the other — a cartoon food chain. Mrs. Castro took a booklet, creased it open, and turned it toward the children, the top of the cover resting on her shoulder. She began slowly turning the pages, explaining the purpose of each section: How you listed all the things you already knew about your puffer fish or manta ray or great white shark. How, on page two, you listed all the things you want to know, what you're curious about, what puzzles you. ("For example, Alex, you wanted to know how the jellyfish eats. You'd put that question here.") Next came the Bibliography, and bubbly Irianna, who had just recently begun acquiring English, leaned across the table and said that was where you put the books you read. "Very good, *mija,*" said Mrs. Castro — using the common term of endearment, "my daughter" — and Irianna smiled in a dimpled way that brought her chin to her chest. Then Elena Castro turned to the final section, Research Notes, and talked a little about how important research was in helping us to learn about the world. "I'm always looking things up — in my dictionary, in my encyclopedia, at the library. *Ay,* we learn a *lot* that way." She paused here and drew herself up in the chair for emphasis. "In fact, when you boys and girls do research, I learn so much." She looked at Irianna. "Yesterday, Irianna showed me something she found on the starfish. Do you want to read it to us, Irianna? It's so interesting!" And Irianna lit up, reached for her book, and read to the group about the eye at the end of each arm of the starfish.

When Irianna finished, Mrs. Castro reached to the center of the table, where she had piled two stacks of books on marine life. On mysteries of the sea, on dolphins and sharks and killer whales, the F volume of an old encyclopedia, a book on coral, and one on the octopus. Books and books, the dirt of innumerable fingers ground into the covers. Books she sorted out like a giant deck of cards. "Alex, here's something on the jellyfish . . . and, let's see, Irianna, look at this, another book on the starfish . . . and, hey, Arely, we're in luck, here's the W volume of the encyclopedia — see if your walrus is in it." As the kids flipped through the books, she showed them how to use a table of contents and an index — and some got this and some didn't yet — and then she gave what brief assistance she could when a book was beyond the third-grade reading level. The children started writing in their Research Notes.

Alex got up and came over to look at the charts on the cabinet doors behind Mrs. Castro's desk. I followed his gaze. On the door closest to me, closed at an angle, off its runners, layers of sea life descended from the barracuda to the mid-level octopus to the sea urchin and deep-sea angler. The door next to that displayed the "Whale Wall Chart" where the hundred-foot blue whale swam past the fifty-foot humpback whale, which curled toward the fifteen-foot narwhal. The blue whale "is believed to be the largest animal that ever lived." The humpback whale emits a low-pitched moaning "song" that can last up to thirty minutes. One of the teeth in the male narwhal develops into a long spiral tusk. On the next door, opened slightly, revealing bags of cookies, was a chart of "Ocean Wonders": the flying fish and the oarfish with its long dorsal fin and the weird luminescent snake dragonfish. And — the jellyfish! Bingo. Alex stopped and folded his booklet, trying to steady it on his forearm, writing irregularly, looking back and forth from chart to page.

Maria, tall for her age and pretty, untangled her feet from her chair and walked over to the Research Station. She sat down and looked up at the wall over the encyclopedias. There was a large hand-drawn sketch of fish anatomy, something I hadn't noticed yet — I'd be discovering new things each day I was here — and Maria settled her chin in her cupped palms and studied a bit longer: heart/*corazon,* aorta/*aorta,* gills/*agallas,* fins/*aleta.* I let myself drift, thinking how rich this was, half-listening to Elena and the students at the Teacher's Workshop. I thought about how radically this classroom clashed with so many of our stock representations of school: monochromatic, trivial, regimented, dull. To the side of the children at the Teacher's Workshop was a broad stretch of wall Mrs. Castro had covered with swirling blue-violet fabric. "Creatures of the Sea" was printed above it. Over the week it would become populated, like a slow-motion nature film, with drawings that had cartoon-like blurbs above them, first-person accounts of what it's like to be a squid or an electric eel or a puffer fish. A few were already done. Arely's skillfully rendered walrus said, through its big tusks and whiskers:

> I am a walrus. I live in the ocean and I eat fish. I am brown and I have big teeth called tusks. I like to be in the ocean and swim a lot. I also live on the land.

On a little table under the display sat a cluster of objects, material for postlunch show and tell: a stuffed, fuzzy dolphin with "Sea World" scripted on its belly, a few pieces of coral, and a construction of four frogs, about six inches high, playing guitars and trumpets — frog mariachis? — made entirely out of seashells. Fat seashell bodies, thin seashell lips, tiny spiral seashell horns. It's a lot of fun under the sea.

III

JUST TO THE SOUTH of the San Diego State Campus is a little park called Rockwood Plaza. If you took a turn out of the snug metal doors of the Rodney Auditorium and cross Rockwood Plaza, you would be at the border in about five or ten minutes. Maybe a little longer in the dead heat of summer. Brief as it is, the walk would provide the beginnings of a sketch of Calexico's history. Rodney Auditorium, built in 1927, was part of the city's first high school. Rockwood Plaza, like Rockwood Street, which you would soon cross, was named after

Charles Robinson Rockwood, the chief engineer of the first project to irrigate the Valley. This area used to be the more prosperous part of the city: it held the old homes of middle-class Anglos and Mexican Americans. To the east — where Dool Elementary is now — there was poorer housing and the new arrivals from Mexico. To the west, across the Southern Pacific railroad tracks, there was once an agricultural shanty town called *La Garra* — a colloquialism meaning "the rag" — where Mexican immigrants settled in the early part of the century.

You could walk straight to the border along Heber — the town northwest of Calexico named after the early developer — or you could veer diagonally, crossing Heffernan (Dr. W. T. Heffernan was one of Rockwood's financiers) and pass by the Hotel De Anza, with its Spanish arches and mission-style cupola. Juan Bautista de Anza was the first Spaniard to cross the desert in search of a land route to the coast. (He would continue northward and found the city of San Francisco in 1776.) My friend Héctor Calderón, a native Calexican, now a professor at UCLA, has childhood memories of being dressed in buckskin and feathers and marching in the Calexico Desert Cavalcade, a pageant re-enacting De Anza's journey to bring, as the late 1930s' promotional literature put it, "God and civilization to the Southwest." The Cocopah Indians, who, in fact, did not wear feathers or buckskin, but who, I assume, Héctor was dressed to represent, served as guides for De Anza and, over a hundred years later, worked on the Valley's irrigation project. During World War I they were declared aliens and exiled to Mexico. Few of them survived.

From the De Anza you would continue south through one more block of modest houses, quiet, sunny, and upon crossing Third Street, hit the energetic business district, which extended, in full commercial tilt, right up against the chain-link fence that marked this particular stretch of the two-thousand-mile border. These few blocks have been the site of Calexico's buying and selling for over sixty years. Walking along First Street, with its weathered shops and storefronts, you would slip in with shoppers from both sides of the border, moving among rows of boxes, jammed and folded, tilted full view toward the street, piled with boots and shoes and slippers, purses, thongs, socks, sandals, bundles of bright fabric, spools of ribbon, of thread, T-shirts with Bart Simpson, the UCLA logo, Michael Jordan, Madonna. "Cash and Carry." Soon, without any fanfare, you would come upon an opening in the fence and a simple concrete walkway. You could, if you wished, cross the line and shop in Mexicali. People have been going back and forth for a long time.

Most of the people I met in Calexico had relatives living in Mexicali, and Calexicans frequently crossed the border to visit them or to shop or dine or secure professional services. For many years, Mexicali's agricultural and industrial laborers have been traveling daily through Calexico, and you could see them cashing checks on First Street, dusty from a day's work in the fields. The arrival of foreign assembly plants, *maquiladoras,* in Mexicali has brought more women into the work force, and some of their meager but steady wages are spent in Calexico. In fact, Calexico's merchants are dependent on shoppers from Mexicali — Kress, Inc.'s most profitable store in the nation is on Second Street — and Calexico's economy wrenches with changes in the peso. "When Mexicali sneezes," a saying goes, "Calexico catches a cold."

Originally a labor camp, then a cow town, Calexico, by the late 1920s, had become an established border city with the extensive agricultural base those early developers had envisioned. It is not surprising, then, that the city's old local histories lavishly celebrate the "courage," "ingenuity," and "pioneering spirit" of Rockwood, Heber and the other engineers and businessmen who founded Calexico. They had, in fact, pulled off an extraordinary technical achievement: turning a desert into lush farmland. Like the writers of those histories, the entire leadership of Calexico was Anglo and would remain so well into the 1950s. Though there was a significant number, eventually a majority, of Mexican Americans in Calexico, the city fathers — and the historians — chose to enhance the city's history through a romanticized portrait of the Spanish past, rather than the Spanish-Indian, Mestizo past and present. Witness the Desert Cavalcade, the Hotel De Anza, and the architecture of the old buildings on the San Diego State campus. Mexican Americans had limited influence: the city council, the judiciary, the police force, the teachers were all White. Classes in the schools were, in effect, segregated, as they were throughout the Southwest, by race.

Change began in the mid to late 1950s. Both Héctor Calderón and Matt Contreras, the judge who acted as my guide through the Imperial Valley, recall the beginnings of Chicano political activity via activist groups that brought Mexican-American families together for a dance, a barbecue, and some grass-roots organizing. In addition, the Viva Kennedy campaign in 1960 mobilized the vote, and the farm workers' movement, which developed a major power base in the Valley, got poor people involved in the political process. Early affirmative action programs gave Mexican-American youth a greater sense of the possible and led to the recruitment of high school students into higher education and subsequent jobs in law enforcement, education, and business. Matt still remembers the strange pride he felt when, in the late 1950s, Rollie Carillo was appointed the first Mexican-American mayor of Calexico.

"Extra!" "Extra!" announced the newspaper banners pinned to the wall way up above the sink where Art Station paints ran pink and orange in the draining water. "Extra! Read All About It!" Tuesday through Friday, right after the Pledge of Allegiance, Elena Castro's students reported on current events in their neighborhood, in the city, county, or state, in the United States, or in the world. They followed a schedule posted on a free patch of wall over the Art Station, their names listed by day — Arely on Tuesday, Carlos on Thursday — monolingual and bilingual speakers mixed on any given day, holding the floor together.

This was one of the ways Elena connected her classroom to the flow of events in the community and beyond. During the week before their presentation, students would be on the lookout for news stories that interested them — from print media, TV or radio, or from the elaborate oral networks of friends and family. Then they would fill out sheets available in a large envelope pinned to that wall beneath the headlines, indicating the focus of the story — city, state, world — and its source: newspaper, radio, and so on. Then they answered journalism's central questions: who (*quien*), what (*que*), when (*cuando*), where (*donde*), why (*por qué*), how (*como*). Finally, they considered how the event affected their lives. When their day of the week arrived, each would read aloud their responses and answer questions posed by fellow students or by Mrs. Castro. There was a lot of interchange between Spanish and English, with Elena acting as facilitator. The schedule was posted on the wall, but by the time of my visit, the students pretty much knew who was up when, and they came forward in the morning to talk about the news, to field questions, to think on their feet about the world beyond themselves.

Sometimes the news was very local. Carlos reported on his aunt being mugged on the streets of Mexicali; Andres's grandmother visited from Heber, and his headline read: *La Visita de la Abuela de Heber.* Elena and the others would then listen to the "where," "why," and "how" of these events and proceed to ask their questions: "Is she OK, Carlos?" and "Why do you think such things happen?" and, for Andres, "*¿Que pasa en la casa cuando visita su abuela?*" or "What happens in your house when your grandmother visits?" City news came primarily from the region's newspapers: the *Calexico Chronicle,* the *Imperial Valley Press, La Voz de la Frontera,* and *El Mexicano* — the last two printed in Mexicali but sold as well in Calexico — or from the local radio stations, KQVO down Highway 111 or XEAO and XED, *La Grande,* across the border. Ricardo reported on the pesticides used in agriculture and the way they can hurt us; Arely told everyone about the fair that was then in progress; Maria said that the school board was trying to get more money so that there could be more aides in schools, and "that would be good for all of us."

State news and beyond tended to come from television: *President Clinton Visits Europe* or *People From Haiti Turned Back To Their Home.* Irianna told the class about AIDS: that people all over the world were dying every day, that it made her very sad because it was hard to find a medicine to cure them. Veronica reported on "the hole in the ozone layer": that it came from spray cans, that we can get skin cancer because of it, and that we can help by not using stuff that comes in spray cans. Jorge reported on smog in *"las grandes ciuadades como Los Angeles y Mexicali,"* explaining that it comes from *"el humo del las fabricas y el humo de los automoviles,"* and observed that it affects everyone, causing much illness, *"muchas enfermedades."*

Elena would be sitting against the board, behind the presenter, leaning in occasionally to ask one of her bilingual "brokers" to rephrase and comment, or to add some information that would place a presentation in context, or she would pick up on a child's question or add one of her own. So, during the report on Haitian refugees, she pulled down the map and pointed out the island, then asked the students whether they thought the United States should turn the people away or let them in. (Let them in was the consensus.) During the discussion of the ozone layer, she asked the class to brainstorm on what they could do to curtail the use of aerosol cans. During the presentation about the school board, she explained what a school board was and how people got elected to it. Then she would slide down a little in her chair, feet together, hands folded, attentive as the next child came forward to engage the news.

Elena Castro moved with her family to Calexico in 1959, just as the power base in the city was beginning its slow shift toward the Mexican-American majority. She entered kindergarten in 1961, a monolingual speaker of Spanish, six or seven years before the advent of bilingual education in the Imperial Valley. (The first bilingual program in modern American public schools was launched in Dade County, Florida, in 1963. Lyndon Johnson signed the Bilingual Education Act in January 1968, and Calexico's first experimental programs were started up in late 1969.) Elena struggled through kindergarten and first grade, not catching on, confused, reprimanded. "She's not trying," the first-grade teacher told her mother through an interpreter. "She doesn't know how to pay attention. She has no discipline." Elena remembers being made to stand outside the classroom; she remembers a particular look in the teacher's eyes. Once, she was trying to shape a plaster handprint, one of those curios kids make for Mother's Day or Christmas, and she was having a hard time of it. She didn't understand the instructions and moved her hand, blurring the mold. The teacher took the mold away and threw it in the trash can, fed up with her intransigence. By sheer luck, Elena's second-grade teacher was a Mexican-American woman, one of the few beginning to enter the teaching force, and though, at that time, the use of Spanish in the schools was forbidden, the woman encouraged Elena and explained lessons to her in her native tongue. Elena credits her with saving her academic life.

When Elena Castro talked about bilingual education, then, she spoke with an authority grounded in the beginnings of her own history in the classroom, a history that developed out of the multilayered history of the border town that became her home. These are histories of power and language, of emerging participation. Participation. One of the things you noticed, you *felt,* right away when you sat in Elena's classroom was the excitement of young minds working. Many of her students came from poor families; a fair number were the children of migrant workers and laborers — people who have very hard lives and little or no opportunity to learn English. In schools across the Southwest, such children often sat silent, uncomprehending, withdrawn — lost to the possibility of the classroom. Like Elena years before. But in Room 42 in Dool Elementary, Andres and Jorge and Irianna and the others were alive, caught up in the flow of words and images and numbers.

On an overhead projector, Elena was reviewing the telling of time. There was a clock on the transparency with no hands; she drew in one, then the other. "What time is it, class, *que hora es?*" The children responded quickly. She erased with a small cloth and drew in a new hour, then a new minute hand. A number of the students answered at once, "Ten-twelve." "Aw, Miss Castro," someone pleaded, "make 'em harder." "OK, OK." She laughed, and wrote 3:15 on the bottom of the transparency, asking Jorge to come forward to draw in the hands. *"Por favor, Jorge, dibuje quince despues de las tres."* Jorge sprang to his feet, tripping a little on Carlos who was lodged in close. He took the grease pencil from Mrs. Castro and quickly executed the answer. Then came the hands waving for the next round. "Pick me!" "Oooooh, let me, Miss Castro!" *"Permite me, Maestra."* The eager voices. The sharp eyes.

After a halting but auspicious start in the late 1960s and early-to-mid 1970s, bilingual education evolved both as a philosophy and a set of methods, always controversial, marked by both incompetence and dogged brilliance, conceptual confusion and real insight into the dynamics of culture and schooling — evolved through a combination of legal decision and legislation into a powerful pedagogy, only to be undermined during the Reagan presidency. Now, lobbying groups like English Only and U.S. English present the most organized opposition to bilingual education, arguing that it will contribute to ghettoization, divisiveness, or, in the worst-case scenario, a balkanized America. The charges stir deep fears in the United States, playing as they do to anti-immigrant and anti-Latino sentiments, but, in one way, they are curious, for there is a long, if neglected, history of bilingualism in our country.

Though English became the dominant language in the colonies, many languages were spoken — German, Dutch, French, Swedish, Polish, and various Indian languages among them — and it was common for pre-Revolutionary War colonials, from indentured servants to the elite, to be fluent in several tongues. It was common, too, for official documents to be published in more than one language. The Articles of Confederation, for example, were printed in German as well as English. By the late seventeenth century, German colonials had opened private schools in Philadelphia in which their native language was the medium of instruction, and throughout the eighteenth century other linguistic minorities developed such schools. With the emergence of comprehensive public education in the nineteenth century, groups with sufficient political clout lobbied for monolingual or bilingual instruction in their local schools, and though such instruction was, at times, contested by other ethnic and religious groups (for example, the Irish versus the French in Massachusetts), it was often granted, primarily to keep students in the newly developing public school system. So, German-language instruction was conducted in public schools in Cincinnati, Cleveland, Baltimore, Saint Louis, Chicago, and San Francisco; French in Louisiana, three counties in Wisconsin, and San Francisco; Spanish in New Mexico. To be sure, such instruction was opposed before our time by policymakers wary of foreign influence, but the most significant force threatening our nation's linguistic diversity was a potent early twentieth-century nativism fueled by increasing Central and Southern European immigration and, finally, the advent of World War I. It was not until those 1960s' experiments in Dade County — urged by a powerful Cuban-American constituency — that bilingual education re-emerged in our country as an educational program of any consequence.

The primary concerns raised by U.S. English, English Only, and similar groups are that bilingual education retards the learning of English and the entrance of non-English-speaking children into the social and institutional flow of American life and that it encourages linguistic and social isolation and divisiveness. To be sure, there are bilingual programs that are poorly conceived and poorly taught — though their limitation, ironically, tends to be their focus on rudimentary functional English in lieu of educationally rich bilingual curricula. And a small number of Latino cultural nationalists in the past have tried to incorporate bilingual education into a separatist political agenda. But when you sit in Elena Castro's classroom, it's hard to believe that what you're seeing will lead to exclusion and separatism.

There were, of course, scuffles and cheap shots in Room 42, the nasty, personal injuries children inflict on one another. But, overall, this was a cohesive class. You saw children working together in groups, helping each other, listening while the other spoke, and the one Anglo child was right in the thick of it all. There did not seem to be a pronounced separation of children who could speak English and Spanish from those who were monolingual — though in Calexico itself there was some friction between established Mexican-American families and poorer new arrivals. In Room 42 there was much translating and other cross-linguistic exchange. The children's native Spanish was appreciated and utilized, and the use of English encouraged and guided. Both were used to communicate, solve problems, learn things, reflect on intellectual work, and make connections to the world outside. There was a belief here, as in other effective bilingual classrooms I've seen, in the power of participation, a belief that engagement in the classroom will lead to rich cognitive and linguistic development, extending outward to the world beyond. "Extra! Read All About It!" The children in Room 42 were becoming civic beings.

It occurred to me after a day or two in Calexico that the city could be imagined as an English Only nightmare. Walking down Heber or Rockwood or Heffernan, spending a few minutes outside Dool Elementary, or shopping on Second Street, you would be likely to hear Spanish more than English. Most of the signs in the business district were in Spanish and English, but sometimes just in Spanish. *"Ahorre comprando con nosotros,"* it said above the Pronto Market, located at Calle Primera y Heffernan. If you entered a ma-and-pa restaurant with a local, the owner might well greet you in Spanish. Your friend would probably order for you.

But when you went to pay your bill at that restaurant, you'd see eight-by-ten color photographs of John Kennedy and Ronald Reagan behind the cash register. Those parents chatting outside Dool Elementary were more than likely bilingual, choosing — as ethnic groups in America have always chosen — to speak their native tongue in informal or private situations. (In this regard, it's interesting to note that in 1911 a federal commission worried that the new immigrants — Italians and Central Europeans, characterized now as model assimilationists — were not learning English quickly enough.) And those parents who spoke only Spanish encouraged their children to learn English, for, as one mother struggled to explain to me, "it will help them get ahead." If you visited English composition courses at Imperial Valley College, or at the San Diego State campus, you would meet young people like Izela, who worked with children in a Mexicali school, or Claudina, who wanted to get a degree in business — both fluently bilingual, working hard after work to master the conventions of written English.

Though infused with Spanish language and Mexican culture, Calexico defied, in its complexity, the kinds of political and social generalizations that are made about such communities. Attitudes toward English ranged from intimidation and resentment to admiration and a desire for fluency. There was a strong Mexican work ethic fused with an American "can do" attitude. There was despair and weariness, alcohol and violence, and a fierce commitment to the possibility of a better life: "Take care of yourself and work hard," was one old man's philosophy. "I never could have owned a home like this in Mexico," said another. There was provincialism, yet there was respect for those who went away to acquire specialized knowledge and brought it back to the community. There were communitarian bonds and a deep commitment to family, yet a strong individualist ethic as well, a belief that, as one woman explained: "You have to show what you can do. You can't be one of so many. You have to stand out." There was talk of solidarity, of *la raza,* and there were class conflicts. There were a wide range of reactions to historical inequities and racism: from fury to denial, with many believing that they could effect change by entering professional and managerial and service ranks and doing things differently. (I heard this especially from people hoping to become teachers.) There was cynicism about politics and pride in citizenship — with many old timers having voted in every election. The power base had changed: all the above played itself out on a Mexican-American political landscape marked by infighting and compromise. The Spanish language was no longer denigrated; the Mestizo heritage honored. But you knew the moment you came back across the border from Mexicali that you were in a city in the United States. It was hard to explain why; something you felt, the movement of the people on the street, the look of things. "You know," one civic leader explained to me, "if you stood up in a council meeting and proposed that we become part of Mexicali, you'd get hooted out of the room."

Rafael Jacinto picked at the crease in his gray flannel slacks, worn, the crease ironed in — he picked as if to say "See what I mean?" He was leaning against a desk in the Music Room, where he and his wife had just completed another session of Evangelina Jones's course in the teaching of reading. Stacked on shelves behind him, warped and dusty, was a library of old record albums — Ralph Marterie, Blossom Dearie, Broadway hits, *Songs of Ireland* — left from another time in the Music Room at the San Diego State University Imperial Valley campus. He looked from his trousers up to me — *see what I mean?* — explaining how this decision to go back to school had limited the hours he can work, how he and his wife have to spend so many hours studying, so he wears these old pants, and this windbreaker, staying up late, tired, the crease carefully ironed in once the kids have gone to bed.

He was telling me the story of his decision. It was made in 1985. He was working in the fields, packing cauliflower. It was past midnight, and he was driving through the desert. Late, tired, those little hallucinatory wisps flitting in from the periphery of the beams of his headlights. "I started thinking about my life. What I had achieved so far. What I would probably achieve in the future. And just like that" — he snapped his fingers — "just like *that,* I knew I had to make a change." When he went home, he woke up his wife and told her what he wanted to do. He asked her to join him, and they began taking high school equivalency classes at the local adult school. They applied for citizenship and enrolled in ESL classes at Imperial Valley College. Five years later, with associate arts degrees in hand, they entered San Diego State. They have both passed the difficult English composition proficiency exam. Last semester, each got a 3.0. They want to become teachers.

Guadalupe Jacinto, who had been outside in the warm evening talking to Evangelina, walked in and took a seat beside Rafael. She was polite, engaging, full of thoughts that she expressed slowly, measuring her expression, conscious of her spoken English, but gaining fluency and fervor as she spoke. She was born in Mexicali, married Rafael at sixteen, had four children — one of whom Evangelina taught when she was still at the elementary school. "My father always wanted me to go to school," she explained, "but . . ." She shrugged and smiled. "She's very smart," Rafael said softly. "The English is very hard," she said, leaning forward, "but we work on it together. We study together." She looked simultaneously weary and poised, in the evening, a warm breeze, dark outside. They have about two more years to go for the bachelor's degree. Then certification. "It's like you're in a dream," she said. "I can't believe it sometimes." There was exhaustion in her voice — as though every word of English came with oppressive weight — but anticipation, too. To be a teacher. Pride and disbelief. "San Diego State University," Rafael said, pausing on each word, melodious, a Spanish lilt to his English.

IV

ELENA CASTRO usually ate lunch in her classroom. Other teachers would drop by for a minute or two or for the duration of a quick meal. There were three regulars, the school's three first-year teachers. They were there most of the time. Carmen Santos was twenty-five and taught first grade. She had a serious, almost studious, demeanor that registered in her gaze and in the slight pursing of her lips. Thin, about five-two, full brown hair; one of her friends called her Carmencita. Veronica Zwart, whose mother was Mexican and father Dutch, taught third grade next door to Elena. She was thirty, five-seven or -eight, angular face, high cheekbones. Jessie Carillo, twenty-five, taught a combined fourth-fifth class in the very room where she was once a fifth-grade student. Jessie's eyes were round, big, and she had a quick smile. When she asked her students to write, she wrote along with them, raising her hand, as they did, when she wanted to read her paper.

The teachers sat at the Writer's Table, spreading sandwiches or burritos or microwaved leftovers out on paper towels grabbed from the sink by the Art Station. There were chips and colas and fruit juice from the cafeteria. Carrot sticks or a salad or soup for the dieters. Pencils. A stray crayon. Like Elena, the three new teachers were all born in the Valley, were all bilingual, and all graduated from the SDSU campus, where they either took courses from or were supervised by Evangelina Jones — Evangelina, who one late afternoon told me, "Your first real teaching job is crucial. It forms you. If you're lucky, you'll find a place that will nurture you and teach you things. It'll shape the kind of teacher you'll become."

On the days I was observing Elena's class, she would ask me to join her and the others for lunch. The group had a casual warmth to it, low-key and inviting. Sometimes they would talk about a shopping expedition to San Diego, two hours west, or exchange local gossip — stopping to explain to me the context of a story — or discuss a union issue, for Elena was Dool's representative. But they also talked a lot about teaching. They talked about particular students or lessons or about upcoming statewide tests and how to prepare for them. And they swapped materials: books, wall displays, the advertisements they found in their mailboxes. So in the easy flow of conversation a lot of advice drifted around the table. Although Elena was by far the most experienced teacher there, the mentor, it didn't show in her bearing. "She's willing to share everything," Jessie told me one day. "She's very knowledgeable, but, you know, she doesn't brainwash you. She definitely has her opinions; she'll say, 'This is what I think,' but then she asks *you* to talk." Isolated in their rooms, young teachers easily get overwhelmed by their notions of success and experiences of failure. Elena's table created a common space for them, familiar, set in shared history, alternately light and serious. And hopeful — I got the sense that competence was taken for granted here. "When I first started," Veronica explained, "I'd go home feeling hopeless. But, now, well, now I'm excited." If one of the young teachers came in defeated, the setback was assumed to be momentary, a problem to be solved. And sometimes a request for direct intervention arose from the problem, a request that seemed natural, part of the give-and-take. That's the way it was when Carmen asked Elena to visit her class and help her with Felipe.

Carmen had her first-graders around her at the front of the room, all singing along to a well-worn record by children's musicians Greg and Steve:

> The world is a rainbow
> With many kinds of people
> And when we work together
> It's such a sight to see.
> The world is beautiful when
> we live in har-mo-ny.

As they sang, the children waved their hands back and forth in the air, sweeping the sky with the curve of the rainbow. Carmen swept the sky as well, rocking her head, a little grin on her face, into it, but with a hint of amusement. Her room was set up like Elena's with a range of work stations — *Estación de Escuchar,* the Listening Station, *Estación de Arte,* the Art Station, and so on — and the walls were filled with print, and overhead hung colorful samples of the children's work.

After the song and a quick stretch — "reach beyond the rainbow, higher, higher" — Carmen began the rotations. Small groups of students went to the *Estación de ABC* and the Listening Station. A larger group went to the Writer's Table where some would be setting down the words of their first stories while others would be dictating more elaborate stories to the aide Carmen had that morning: leaning over the table, stringing events together excitedly with "and . . . and . . . and then . . ." And still others would be joining Carmen at the Teacher's Workshop to continue to learn to read in Spanish. On a shelf behind Carmen sat a short stack of books: *Los Animales de Don Vincencio, Azulin Visita a Mexico,* and a book about a kite, *El Papalote.* Alongside them was a large book, bound in art paper, entitled *Mi Extraterrestre.* I quietly pulled it out. It was a collection of student drawings accompanied by Carmen's neat script; from what I could tell, students had to imagine what their own private extraterrestrial might be like. The creatures they conjured up had multiple legs and heads, long ears, fangs, huge purple hands, big red eyes — lots of them. In English and in Spanish the children described ETs that would knock things down and "spin around to get to the earth" and attend a birthday party and fly to the mall.

Right at the second rotation, Elena came in. The children knew her;

she had visited before, so there was no uneasiness. She walked over to the table where students were writing in their journals — the idea here being that they would write, as best they could, about something that happened to them, and then the teacher or an aide would respond, thus demonstrating to the children that writing did things, was interactive. Elena worked with two or three children, then moved next to Felipe. Carmen drifted over.

"Felipe," Elena said, "can I write in the journal with you?"

"Yes."

"What would you like to write about?"

Silence.

"Did you go to the fair last weekend?"

A big "Yes."

"What did you see?"

And Felipe began to write — slowly, awkwardly — while Elena helped him along. "Saw. Sawww. What letter makes that *www* sound, *mijo?*"

Eventually Felipe wrote, "I went to the fair and saw a bull."

"Felipe, what else did you see?" Felipe fell silent again.

Elena took a different tack. "Felipe, did you eat anything at the fair?"

An enthusiastic "I ate corndogs!"

"Ay!" exclaimed Elena. "Write about that!"

And so it went. After Felipe produced another sentence or two, Elena said to him, "I'm going to respond to you now, OK?" Under Felipe's sentences she began to write — reading out loud what she was writing — "I went to the fair last year, but I'm not going this year." She paused and looked at him, all serious. "Do you know why, Felipe?"

"No, *Maestra.*"

Here she picked up the pen again, talking as she wrote, "Because I ate tooooo many corndogs!"

She laughed her throaty *heh-heh-heh* and turned back to Felipe, who was grinning in skeptical pleasure.

They finished up and, as the aide continued to work with the journals, Elena took Carmen out of earshot and said, "He just needs a little more. Three or four days of intensive work. Then leave him be. But, now, be persistent." Carmen listened, nodding. "Be persistent," she said under her breath and walked Elena to the door. Then she went back and sat with Felipe.

Eddie Hernandez taught kindergarten on the south end of Dool, a couple of hundred feet from Elena, Veronica, and the rest. He had been teaching for ten years; Elena Castro was his master teacher. Now he's known throughout the district and serves as a master teacher for others.

Eddie was born in Calexico — one of a family of ten — went to Imperial Valley College, then to the San Diego State campus up the street. In fact, his kindergartners play on a grassy enclosure that was once the site of his grandmother's house; where there used to be a tool shed and a garden, there were now swings and a slide and a burro and parrot, both saddled, ready to ride, on iron poles rising out of the ground.

Evangelina had sent a lot of students to Eddie, and based on their reports and her own observation, she described him this way: "Eddie is the epitome of the master teacher. He shows trainees how to think about teaching. He expects a lot from his class, and at the end of every week he sits down with his student teacher and thinks out loud about how things went, or about new things that cropped up, or about what he had to modify to help So-and-so understand a concept. It's really something, you know, because Eddie looks so effortless, but really he's always thinking, and the new teacher gets to see how that works."

The philosophy guiding Eddie's classroom — and guiding the way Elena, Carmen, and the others ran their classes — was called "whole language." Proponents of whole language believe that teachers should create environments in which students are immersed in language and are given numerous opportunities to use it: talking, reading, writing, and taking chances with print, telling a story, responding to a reading, writing with and to others, compiling information on topics of personal interest. To be sure, work on discrete skills was done in the whole language classrooms at Dool — Eddie and Elena, for example, helped kids sound out words phonetically — but, as Elena explained, such work was done "in the service of something bigger," was done as children were trying to write stories or pursue the narrative line in a book. So a new teacher in Eddie's room would learn this philosophy and the range of approaches that came with it. A way to think about the teaching of language and a set of beliefs about what students can do under the right conditions.

One of the first things that struck visitors to Eddie's class was how sophisticated it seemed, how much academic work the kids were doing. There were ditties, of course, and snacks, and happy faces everywhere — and half the time the stars Eddie gave the kids ended up on forearms or foreheads, rather than on the fronts of shirts and blouses. But in addition to practicing the formation of letters, the children were trying to write stories; along with learning the ABC's, they were being guided through simple narratives and giving their opinions about them. Spanish and English was all around them — as in Elena's room — and they were expected to try to solve problems with words. Eddie had covered one section of his west wall with samples of print that the children would recognize from their home environment: there was a box of

Lucky Charms and a label from Campbell's Sopa de Pollo and a package of Blue Bonnet and other food and household products. So when, one morning, a little girl was writing a story and got stuck on the word *blue,* Eddie turned her around and asked her to find the word on the display. She did, and copied it down. "See?" he said to the intern who was there that day. "There's all kinds of ways they can learn to spell. The whole idea is to get them to think, to look around at the language that surrounds them and use it."

One day I asked Carmen, Jessie, and Veronica to speculate on the ideal training program for elementary school teachers. "They'd put you in the schools earlier — observing, tutoring, something to get you around kids sooner." "It would be more hands-on." "Reading books alone doesn't do it. Books can't tell you what to actually expect in the classroom." The training would involve a lot of role playing and simulation, for "it's important to go through what the kids go through." Who should conduct this training? "People who have been in the classroom, who have a lot of techniques." Evangelina Jones and Elena Castro were cited as exemplars, as was Eddie Hernandez and a woman named Jane Carpenter, a local teacher who had developed a training program in children's literature for the district. The topic of in-service workshops came up several times, and the young teachers made it clear that they were *not* talking about the typical one-day presentation, usually given by an outside consultant. What they had in mind was an ongoing series — like Carpenter's — where teachers could come, learn some things, try them, and come back, discuss the results, fine-tune, modify, or abandon what they tried, and learn more. This sort of training, said Carmen, Veronica, and Jessie, especially should be in place during a teacher's first few years in the classroom. "So what is it," I asked, "that makes people like Evangelina, Elena, and Eddie so good?" The answers: "They know so many things to do." "They make learning fun." "They have a great relationship with their kids." "They care."

Probably because of the demands of their immediate situation and the early phase of their own growth as teachers, Carmen, Veronica, and Jessie focused their discussion on practice. This made sense. No matter how well they might master a teacher-ed class, or how high they might score on a test, or how skillfully they could talk about teaching in the abstract, they still had to walk into a room full of children five days a week and *do* things, engage in an extraordinarily complex activity fraught with the uncertain and conditional. Developing effective ways to generate and guide discussion, provide feedback on reading and writing, put together a test, even take roll and collect homework — procedures and routines, big and small — these and a formidable number of other activities would determine their success or failure as classroom teachers. And central to that success, and to their sense of themselves as competent teachers and decent human beings, were the ways they could find to manage the classroom and to connect with the children in it. The social dimension of teaching. How could they foster relationships with the children that were caring yet professional, that would enable them to manage the room and touch individual lives? No wonder they admired Elena's warmly attentive but efficient classroom style.

What was interesting to me, and it took a while to grasp it, was the degree to which these concerns about practice and relationships, while certainly emerging from immediate needs, were also reflecting deeply held values and beliefs about children and learning. At first, I wondered — because I didn't hear much specifically about it — I wondered about the importance for these young teachers of the conceptual or moral dimensions of teaching. Did they see themselves primarily as technicians, caring technicians, but technicians nonetheless? Or was there more? What I came to appreciate was that their concerns about practice were embedded in wide-ranging moral imperatives. Take, for example, the talk about "caring."

When Carmen and company praised Elena's "care," they were referring not only to their mentor's affection for kids — though that was part of it — but more so to Elena's absolute regard for children, her unfaltering belief in their potential. "Caring" had as much to do with faith and cognition as with feeling. All children, no matter what their background, had the capacity to learn. And this belief brought with it a responsibility: it was the teacher's intellectual challenge to come to understand what must be done to tap that potential. All this was so basic a tenet of these teachers' beliefs about their work that most of the time it went unsaid. It was simply acted upon. Thus the need for skill, techniques, smart practice. When Felipe wasn't writing, Carmen went to Elena for help in eliciting a story — for Felipe's capacity to produce written language was not in question.

Every time interns watched Elena teach, they saw these beliefs in action, in even the most commonplace encounters — for it's often in the asides, the offhand questions, the microlessons that a teacher's most basic attitudes toward students are revealed. Carlos had written a shaggy dog story. Elena was slowly scrolling up the computer screen, praising the story as she read. Once done, about to move onto the next child, she tapped a key, taking the story back to a line at the beginning in which Carlos described the dog as a "troublemaker." "You know, Carlos," she reflected, "I found myself wondering what Penny did that caused so much trouble?" "She tips over garbage cans," he said. "Good. Anything else?" Carlos giggled. "What?" she asked. "What is it?" "She makes messes!" Elena laughed. "Put that in, too, Carlos. That way your reader will *really* know what you mean by trouble." Another time, Elena was reading to the class in Spanish the story of a marvelous garden, and she came across a description of a beet that was six inches wide. She paused for a moment and reached across the desk for a ruler, handing it to Arely. "*Mija,* show us how big that beet was." Arely counted four, five, six on the ruler. "Whoa!" said Alex. "Big, huh?" And yet another time, Elena was working with a group of students on their marine research when Alex walked over from the Writer's Table to get her attention: he needed a definition of *admire.* She looked up, defined it, and, as he was walking away, called to him and asked if he admired the farmer in a story they had read that morning. He turned back and thought for a moment: "No." No he didn't, thereby applying the new definition to a familiar character. She was masterful at extending a child's knowledge at every turn of the classroom day.

This affirmation of potential was deeply egalitarian. It did not stratify children by some assessment of their readiness or ability or by judgments based on their background or record. It assumed ability and curiosity; learning, in this belief system, became an entitlement. In Elena's words, "You can't deny anybody the opportunity to learn. That's their right." Bilingual education gained special meaning in this context. There is a long history in California schools, and Southwestern schools in general, of Mexican culture, language, and intelligence being deprecated. (Mexican children, one representative educator wrote in 1920, "are primarily interested in action and emotion, but grow listless under purely mental effort.") The profound limits on the quality of education that stemmed from such practice and perception made all the more understandable the commitment of these Calexico teachers to bilingual education. Bilingual education was not just a method; it was an affirmation of cultural and linguistic worth, an affirmation of the mind of a people. It fit into a broader faith that, as Evangelina said before her Teaching of Reading class one afternoon, "all children have minds and souls and have the ability to participate fully in the society, and education is a way to achieve that."

These egalitarian beliefs, from what I could tell, had multiple origins and played out in life and work in complicated ways.

There was a civic base to the teaching of Elena and her colleagues. They took seriously their nation's best promise, held to it against that same nation's abuses of equality. There were pictures of Washington and Lincoln in their classrooms, the flag, the Pledge of Allegiance — icons and credos placed against those forces which have created barriers to the growth of children like the ones in Calexico. Teaching was a means of effecting social change. "Any child can learn," said Carmen. "Any child. They have to be given a fair chance."

On a more personal level, each teacher spoke about a teacher of her own who validated her intellectual worth, who demonstrated to her the power of having someone believe in a student's ability. For Carmen, it was a Mrs. Self; for Jessie, a Mrs. Hems, someone "who gave me the incentive to try my best." Also of critical importance was that Elena, Carmen, and the others shared a history and a community. They knew the families of the kids they taught, knew the streets they lived on and the cultural pathways open or closed to them. This familiarity, of course, widened their sphere of influence — as Jessie said, it's easy to "see a kid on the street and tell him to come by" — but on a deeper level, where heart and instruction intersect, they identified with the children they taught. As Evangelina explained, "When you see that third-grader, you're seeing yourself. You think, 'If someone had done this for me when I was in third grade, how much better my education would have been.'" This was an identification that had significant pedagogical consequences.

Though the teachers certainly had strong community bonds — and in their professional lives they overcame the isolation of the classroom by working together and by involving themselves in unions and educational lobbies — though these bonds were strong, Carmen and the others defied easy ideological distinctions by also putting great weight on individual responsibility. They believed that if one was self-reliant and worked hard, one would succeed. "It's a big thing here to be a teacher," Evangelina explained, "and it's achievable." There seemed to be few illusions about the effects structured social inequalities could have on this success. "You have to work twice as hard," as Elena put it. Because of race and class, it would be a difficult life; all the more reason to develop a resilient inner core. Their family histories were histories of hard work, and they respected those histories, derived from them a personal mythology of strength and endurance. In turn, they have worked hard to enter a profession and develop a sense of institutional efficacy. They believed they could make a difference and pushed themselves to do so.

Given this blend of egalitarianism and individualism, it was no surprise that they had high expectations for their students. This was surely true for Elena. The majority of the children I saw in Room 42 had entered in September with the designation "low achiever" or, in some cases, "slow learner." Elena's response was to assume that they had developed some unproductive habits and were sabotaging their own intelligence. "The first two weeks, it was difficult," she explained one noontime when we were all sitting around the Writer's Table. "I'd put them here to write — and they'd fool around. It took them a while to figure it out, it took time, with me talking to them. 'This is *your* education,' I'd say. 'It's your responsibility. I'm here to support you, but you have to do the work.'" It was warm that day, Elena's sleeves rolled up, the paper fish hanging motionless. She spoke emphatically, with a nod or an exclamation or a quick laugh, her finger tapping the table, her hand slicing the air. "I had to keep some in at recess to finish the work. I had to talk to them. But then . . . look at them now. They're bright kids. They're not underachievers; they're not slow. They were just used to doing what they could get by with." Her room was constructed on work and opportunity. "You can't say 'I can't' in this classroom. You have to try." And that cut both ways.

If you believe so firmly in the potential of all your students, you have few ready explanations for their failure. The first line of scrutiny is oneself. "What you do is not necessarily good for everyone," Elena would say. "You have to try different things. You have to ask yourself, 'What can I change that will work for a child who's not learning?'" When a student was not doing well, Elena would assume she was failing and put herself through a rigorous self-assessment. "Why am I not teaching him," she would ask, her record book open, the child's work spread out in front of her.

Elena's sense of the role of the teacher fit with my own, but spending time with her helped me understand the tension inherent in such a position, the power and the limits of individual force of mind.

Roberto was a sweet, quiet boy who seemed to understand his classwork, would do it when Elena was assisting him, but would just not complete it on his own. "I don't know what to do to get him motivated," she said. "I tried structuring things more, and I tried letting him pursue whatever he wanted. He's a smart boy — I'm doing something wrong. What am I missing?" One day when Elena was sitting with Roberto, encouraging him to write a little more on a story, he suddenly started crying. His mother had left home, and he was sent to stay with his grandmother. He missed his mother terribly and was afraid that his grandmother, who was ailing, would die and leave him alone. How could he concentrate, Elena thought, when his very security was threatened? This was beyond anything she could influence. It was telling, though, that Elena didn't entirely let up. She told him he could talk to her anytime he felt sad, and that she would ease off a little — on him, I suspect, more than herself — but that "they both had a responsibility to teach and learn," and that the best thing he could do was to learn what he could so he would someday be able to take care of himself. "We both have to try," she said, holding him, wanting to make for him, as best she could, her classroom a place of love and learning. In Elena's mind, the consequences for Roberto's future of his not learning to read and write and compute were too great to ignore, even in sorrow.

Among the teachers I got to know in Calexico, the response to hardship was a firm resolve to try harder. On the day of my visit to Carmen's classroom, a San Diego newspaper ran a story on the social and economic problems plaguing the California Latino community and the impact those problems were having on education. She and I talked about the article. "You know, Carmen," I finally said, "some would say that teachers like you are battling insurmountable odds." "The problems *are* big ones," she answered, "and they make me very angry. But everybody's got a job to do. The problems are not going to stop me from teaching."

All this was what it meant to care.

V

I SAT IN THE BOOTH across from Emily Palacio in the large, bright coffee shop of Hollie's Fiesta Motel. There were a few businessmen around us — insurance agents, merchants — and some of the mechanics from the Pep Boys down the street. From our window we could see the traffic lining up on Imperial, eight blocks from the border, and it felt good to settle into the thick Naugahyde cushions in the quiet dining room. Emily was the director of Curriculum Development for the Calexico Unified School District, and she was going to take me to a meeting of the school board. We had some time to kill, dallying with Pepsis, and at one point I asked her to talk about the classrooms I had been visiting, to give me the perspective from the district office. "You have to understand," she said, "the number of things that had to be put in place so that those teachers you saw can flourish." Emily's posture and movement suggested an athletic deliberateness — the result, I would learn, of a back injury — but her strong, almost formal, bearing was counterpointed by a friendly directness.

"Bilingual education," she continued, "is a good example. When I first started teaching, in 1969, we still weren't allowed to use Spanish in the classroom. And, to be honest, when we got our first bilingual ed money, I wasn't sure it would work. There was resistance from some of the Mexican parents too — it's really important to them that their kids learn English — and, well, I was skeptical." She paused, twirling the wrapper from her straw around her fingers. "But then I started reading some research that impressed me, and I looked closely at our kids who were being taught to read in Spanish — and paradoxically they were learning English better than those we moved into English early. I knew then what we had to do." She smoothed out the wrapper and started over. "Nothing came easy. We convinced the parents to let us try things, but got a lot of resistance from some teachers who were monolingual and from some of the city leaders in Calexico. We had to work very hard. It was a struggle. But the leadership was changing here, and slowly, slowly things turned around."

As we continued to talk, me asking her about her own history as well as the more recent history of the district, I heard the same affirmations of potential I had heard from the teachers — "we just don't believe that our kids can't succeed" — spoken from the same kind of personal base. "My father stressed that his children would get an education so that we could help our people." And I heard, as well, a broad linguistic range put to the service of those beliefs. In our time in the restaurant, and during a subsequent visit to her office, I listened as Emily spoke both informal and highly educated Spanish and English, shifted into policy-speak on the phone to the state capital, and adopted the language of educational research — she had done graduate work at Claremont — when talking to a reporter. I would sit back, thinking about the ways in which that fluency affected the classrooms in which Elena, Carmen, Veronica, and the others did their work.

Emily was right: even the most individually brilliant teaching takes place in a historical and political context. There was so much that had to be achieved: the changes in Calexico's power base; the federal-level policy and legislation involving bilingual education, affirmative action, and increased support for education and the resulting availability of loans and scholarships for economically disadvantaged students; the movement of bilingual teachers, both Latino and Anglo, into the work force; new blood in administration; a decent working relationship between the school board and administration (this was recent — a not-so-old joke had it that in Calexico there were three superintendents, the one who just left, the one here now, and the one on the way); the documented successes the schools were having and the sense of pride and purpose this evidence gave to the community about its schools. Hard-won achievements that made further achievement possible.

Emily and I haggled a little over who would pay the bill. We split it, and headed for the offices of the Calexico Unified School District, down Highway 98 to Andrade Avenue on the outskirts of town. I followed Emily's car, the sun low in the sky. Driving through the city, away from the center of things, I thought more about what Emily said, about all the lines of history and power that intersect in one classroom — or circles, concentric circles moving inward from the activism of a previous era, the pain and optimism that made a good classroom possible. Emily's blinker came on, and I turned with a bounce onto Andrade. Palm trees. Open fields. The district office.

The meeting opened with a greeting by the two student representatives on the school board — Lorena and Lizette, both from Calexico High — and proceeded to presentations of awards for Student of the Month. The meeting was taking place right at the time of a regional science fair, so a display of some of the work of Calexico students came next. One young woman told us about studying the reproductive cycle of the whitefly, an insect that had devastated crops in the Valley. A young man explained a research project on the relation between hormone levels in cows and the production of milk. The members of the board sat back while the students spoke. Their posture seemed to say: This is our reason for being.

Then Roberto Morales, the board member with the longest tenure, thanked the students and turned the board toward its administrative agenda. After a number of items dealing with planning and budget came new business: the head of the Chamber of Commerce wanted to honor the schools by putting a photo of the district office on the cover of a promotional brochure. More business. Then another board member, Refugio Gonzales, the director of the University of California Agricultural Extension in the Valley, steered the meeting on a different course. The national meeting of the Mexican-American Legal Defense and Education Fund, MALDEF, was to take place soon, and he wondered whether someone from the board could present data on Calexico's success. "There is so much press about Hispanic failure, I'd like to let people know that there are programs in which Hispanic students are doing well."

On the side of the meeting room, along the west wall, were two architectural models of the schools the district was planning to build. One, a middle school, was going to be named in honor of Willie Moreno, one of the 1960s' activists who worked hard to get Mexican Americans elected to Calexico's school board and city council. I thought about his legacy — evident in this board room — and about the growing importance of the achievements of Calexico's students. The community was inspired by its students, and it was this feeling of hope that made possible effective school governance: the effect of hope on structure and function, the way it can open political space and foster common cause.

But as Willie Moreno certainly knew, the alliances and commitments necessary for progress are tenuous. Previous boards and administrations had been at each other's throats — superintendents kept coming and going — and though that relationship has, during the last few years, been amicable, there were some conflicts brewing between the teachers' union and the administration over benefits. The conflict was potentially volatile, because California was in the middle of a financial crisis, and school budgets were being cut. Could the differences be worked through? On another front, would the long-standing friction between older Calexicans and new arrivals from Mexico worsen and be reflected in school politics? Or would personal rivalries among the city's power brokers erupt into crippling disputes? For now, this was only worrisome speculation; there was broad-based support for the schools and for new ideas. Alex, Arely, Carlos, Irianna, and the others were having an influence on school governance beyond what they knew, and what happened in this room over the next span of years would, in turn, have a profound influence on them.

Down the hall after the board meeting into the superintendent's office. Roberto Moreno (no relation to Willie) spoke easily, steadily. A tall, muscular man, quietly enthusiastic, sweeping his hair away from his eyes. He was born and raised in Calexico and married his high school sweetheart, who was now a counselor at a neighboring high school. As a teacher or administrator, he had been in the district for more than twenty years, except for some time at Stanford to do graduate work. He still looked young.

"We're not in a position," he was saying, "we don't have the resources to invent — it takes a lot of money to develop curriculum from scratch . . . we just can't do that. But we're great at implementing the good things that we find. We might have to beg, borrow, or steal it, but we can apply a good idea. And the board is supportive of innovation and risk.

"We've got some great teachers," he continued, rocking back in an old swivel chair. "A few of them are brilliant. But more so, it's a bunch of ordinary people rising to the occasion, ordinary people doing outstanding work. Our goal is to create the conditions for that to happen." He brought the chair forward, his elbows resting on his knees. "They're always on the lookout, and so are we. Something good appears, and we ask, 'What's this program about? What are the underlying concepts? Can we make it work for us?' Then" — he laughed — "then we try to find the funds to do it."

I had met the person who scouts for those funds, Mary Camacho, director of State and Federal Projects. The district couldn't survive without such assistance, and Mary was compiling an impressive record of securing it from government agencies, industry, and private foundations. Originally a home economics teacher at the high school, she had become an assistant principal, then moved into the district office, where she learned about grantsmanship. "I was told to try things," she said. "A lot of us here are home-grown. We might go away to school, but some come back, and we develop here. I just learned from a lot of people who were generous with their time. This is the kind of place where, if you have an idea, you're encouraged to pursue it."

One of the ideas that had been stirring excitement in the district office originated several years ago with an enterprising middle school English teacher, Gretchen Laue. Gretchen wanted to turn the summer session at her school into a lab school, a place where teachers could learn new methods and students would benefit from an enriched language arts curriculum. She applied for and received a grant from the state, and the project proved a local success. This past year, Roberto suggested to Emily Palacio that they apply Gretchen's idea to summer school for all the district's elementary grades. Get them early. "Be inventive," Roberto told Emily, so Emily decided to reconceive summer school for elementary students in Calexico's public schools.

Summer school had typically been remedial in nature, instruction in basics for kids who weren't doing well or for the children of new arrivals from Mexicali. But Emily didn't want it to be remedial; she wanted it to be an academy, a lab school for teachers and a site of enrichment for students. And she wanted to affect a number of subjects: math, language arts, music, and art. School restructuring that was not merely organizational but involved a new way of thinking about what children could do.

She developed a plan. There would be four expert teachers hired as coaches for each of the subjects. They would conduct workshops for the teachers, visit their classes, do demonstration lessons with their students, and consult with them. According to one pattern, the coach would conduct a lesson before a teacher's class; the teacher would do a follow-up lesson and then a third related lesson, with the coach observing and providing feedback. The new approaches would become part of the teachers' repertoires and, Emily hoped, would be carried over into the regular academic year, thereby extending the benefits of the experiment. Eddie Hernandez was hired as the art coach, and Evangelina Bustamente Jones was brought in to supervise language arts. One of the teachers, it turned out, was Jessie Carillo.

The program took place in the summer after my visit, and Evangelina told me about it by phone.

The language arts curriculum emphasized poetry, revising and editing, and various methods of collaboration. There were thirty teachers involved and about 850 students. From what Evangelina could tell, it was a big success, and Emily, Mary, and Roberto were thinking about funding for next year. The children wrote poetry, letters, and stories in Spanish, English, or both, and composed responses to each other's work. At the end of the program, the students in each class selected the writing they liked best, and it was displayed as part of a celebration that extended across several schools. They were given forms on which they could respond to the work of other children that struck them. "Your writing made me feel ———" was one item on the form; "I'd like to know more about ———" was another. These forms were then returned to the original author.

Evangelina read to me some pieces she had copied down. There were metaphors by first-graders, written as they were encouraged to let their imaginations play over a bowl of popcorn: "Popcorn tastes like haunted candy" and "Popcorn looks like crumpled flowers." There were majestic descriptions of fireworks — Fourth of July fare — produced by fifth-graders: "Under attack, neon fireballs turn with rays curving around them" and "Different colors of fluorescent confetti fall to the ground." And there was this reflection written by a third-grader as she listened to a recording of flute music:

> I was in the ocean and there were lots of leaves and trees.
> I was on a rock on the water. I was singing and touching
> the water by myself and I felt like the world barely started.

3

Baltimore, Maryland

I IMAGINED the tree frog wondering about these kneeling bipeds. Hunched down, hunkered down, faces right up against the glass of his classroom home. "I want some crickets," he might have thought, giving them a dull and sullen look. "Just give me the damned crickets." He didn't move — contemptuous, stolid, the color of the surrounding rocks and dead leaves, looking back at Mrs. Terry's curious first-graders with eyes half closed.

Stephanie Terry's students, thirty of them, were all African American, as was Mrs. Terry, and all lived close by Duke Ellington Primary School in Baltimore's inner city. Stephanie, in her early forties, wore her hair in elaborate braids, had a round, gentle face and a serious lingering gaze. She and her students, half of them boys and half girls, were in the middle of a science lesson on the tree frog, its eating habits and its ability to change skin color in response to the environment. They were about to feed it. But first Mrs. Terry wanted them to look very closely at the frog and its surroundings. "What do you see?" she asked. "Oh, oh, Miss Terry," Frank ventured, twisting around on his knees, "He's real gray now." "Yes, he is, isn't he?" Mrs. Terry said slowly, as if deep in thought. "How could that be?" "Because," Shereese said, looking up from the opposite side of the case, her beaded braids dangling, "he's in with the leaves and the rocks and they're all gray, too." "Hmmm, interesting. Yes. What do we call that ability to change colors?" Frank again, dimples, high forehead, eyes wide: "Ka-ka-meal-e-yon!" "All right. Very good, Frank." Mrs. Terry replied, pausing to let the word settle in the air. Then, "Boys and girls, what else do you see?" "Miss Terry," said Leon, brow furrowed, "the crickets, they're all gone." "No, no," piped up Shereese. "There's one under the cup. Look." And she pointed, tapping, while Leon and the rest of the group scooted around on knees and elbows to get a better look. Mrs. Terry leaned forward in her tiny chair. And there it was. A dead cricket, on its side, under a tilted dish of water. "Why won't he eat it, Miss Terry?" Leon asked, a trace of concern still in his voice. "Ain't he hungry no more?"

"That's a very good question, Leon. I wonder if anyone has any ideas. Let's assume the frog is hungry. After all, it's time to feed him, right?" A chorus of "uh-huh" and "right" and "yeah" and lots of nodding heads. "Well, then . . . " Rachel, who was not in the group of five immediately surrounding the case, asked tentatively from the wider circle where she, I, and the others sat, "Is it . . . maybe he only eats alive crickets?" Mrs. Terry nodded. "What do you think of that, class?" Some murmurings, and Dondi, a picture of Malcolm X and the word *study* on his T-shirt, asked how the frog could tell whether the cricket was dead or "just ain't moving cause he's scared." Mrs. Terry thought that was another good question and began to explain how the frog's eye and brain are set up such that he'll strike only at something moving. "In fact," she continued, "a frog could starve to death if we fed him only dead insects!" Almost all the eyes in the room were on Mrs. Terry now. Amazed. Disbelieving. Everyone's eyes but Leon's, who was still down on hands and knees looking at the frog, waiting for a clue. The frog looked back, impassive, waiting for crickets.

The crickets for that day's feeding were in a jar on the science table against the wall by the sink. The wall was covered with information, in big print, on the aquatic snail, the frog, the newt, the hermit crab, the praying mantis, the blackworm, and the tadpole — all the creatures Mrs. Terry kept in her class to pique curiosity and sharpen the eye. On the floor was a case with hermit crabs, the space for Mr. Frog's home (temporarily relocated to the center of the room), a fish tank with newts, a spotted frog, and a tiny African frog. Right by the science table was a box of books, a few scattered out on the rug: *Backyard Hunter: The Praying Mantis, Snails and Slugs, Pond Life, A House for Hermit Crab, The Tadpole and the Frog.*

The table itself was small and cluttered with the remnants of experiments past, the messiness of good science. There was a cluster of acorns and orange and yellow gourds, the head of a big sunflower, a bird's nest, some stray twigs, the corpse of a newt — carefully laid out on cardboard and labeled — five or six small magnifying glasses, several Audubon Pocket Guides, and a pile of crisp maple leaves.

Mrs. Terry walked over and picked up the pickle jar that held three lively crickets. She selected three students who hadn't yet had a chance to observe the frog closely. There was big excitement, but contained somehow, giddy seriousness. Shaquente went first, extending her thumb and forefinger into the jar like pincers, her face set somewhere between a smile and a grimace. She missed, oops, then missed again, the students around her watching, twitching their arms and shoulders with each of her failed attempts. Mrs. Terry suggested that she tilt the jar a little more, and when she did one cricket hopped up the side. She nabbed it, pressing its wings to its body. Mrs. Terry opened the lid of the case, and Shaquente gingerly dropped the cricket in and got down close to watch. The frog stirred, finally, dislodging itself from the leaves and rock. The cricket crawled around, over an old potato, over a twig, a rock, and the frog came off its hind legs in a flash and engulfed it in one swallow. The class squealed. A minute or so more, and the second cricket met its fate. The third somehow escaped the frog's field of vision and got a momentary reprieve. The frog went back to its niche and settled in. The students were against the case again. The frog closed its eyes.

Over the next few days, Stephanie's students performed experiments. Rachel wanted to see what would happen if Mrs. Terry put a bright color next to Mr. Frog. Would his skin change again? So Stephanie cut a three-inch-square piece of yellow art paper and placed it inside the case, close to the frog's corner. When the class looked again later in the day, nothing had happened.

"Why do you think the frog didn't turn yellow?" Mrs. Terry asked.

"Maybe the frog has to see the paper," Rachel said, raising a delicate hand.

"Do you think if we put the paper where he could see it, it would make a difference?"

"Let's try it, Miss Terry," suggested Frank in a half-bounce.

Stephanie reached carefully into the case, picked up the paper, and slid it along the glass, into the frog's field of vision.

The next morning, no change. The paper had become moist and dried with a warp. That's all.

"Miss Terry," Dondi offered, "maybe . . . maybe, he has to be *on* it."

"Hmm, that's interesting, Dondi. Let's see. Stephanie tried to slide the paper in as close to the frog as possible, a little under the stones and leaves. The frog stirred, but didn't hop away.

When the class looked again, just before lunch, there was no change.

"Why isn't anything happening?" Shaquente asked, disappointed.

"Well," said Mrs. Terry, "sometimes you have to wait. An important part of science is learning how to wait." Then she asked them to take out their journals and write about the experiment with the yellow paper.

For Stephanie Terry, doing science meant waiting and watching — and writing about what you saw. In fact, writing about Mr. Frog — or the newt or the hermit crab — fostered, she believed, a reflective cast of mind. And having Mr. Frog and the newts and the other creatures to write about fired up the kids to put pencil to paper, to practice print's difficult technology. Science and writing. C. P. Snow's two cultures merging in a primary school in inner-city Baltimore.

Three or four days after the unsuccessful experiment with the frog and the yellow paper, Stephanie read to the students a book called *A House for Hermit Crab.* Hermit crabs inhabit empty mollusk shells, and as they grow, they leave old shells to find bigger ones. In this story, we accompany a cheery hermit crab in its search for a more spacious home. Over the year, Mrs. Terry's students had seen this behavior. The case containing the five crabs held thirteen shells of various sizes, and more than once students noticed that a shell had been abandoned and a new one suddenly animated. But as Stephanie read *A House for Hermit Crab,* she raised broader questions about where the creatures lived, and this led to an eager query from Kenneth about where you'd find hermit crabs. "Well," said Mrs. Terry, "let's see if we can figure that out."

She brought the case with the hermit crabs to the center of the room, took them out, and placed them on the rug. One scuttled away from the group, antennae waving; another moved in a brief half-circle; three stayed put. While this was going on, Mrs. Terry took two plastic tubes from the cupboard above the sink and filled one with cold water from the tap. "Watch the hermit crabs closely," she said, "while I go to the kitchen. Be ready to tell me what you saw." She went down the hall to get warm water from the women who prepared the children's lunches. Then she put both tubs side by side and asked five students, one by one, to put each of the crabs in the cold water. *Plop, plop, plop.* "What happened?" asked Mrs. Terry. "They don't move," said Kenneth. "They stay inside," added Miko.

Mrs. Terry gave the crabs a bit longer, then asked five other students to transfer the crabs to the second tub. They did, and within seconds the crabs started to stir. "Ooooo" from the class. Before long, the crabs were really moving, antennae dipping, legs scratching every which way at the plastic, two of the crabs even crawling over each other. "OK," said Mrs. Terry. "What happens in this water?" An excited chorus: "They're moving." "They're walking all over." "They like it." "They're happy like the crab in the book." "Well," said Mrs. Terry, standing up, placing her hands on the small of her back, and having a little stretch. "What does this suggest about where they like to live?"

That night the students wrote about the experiment, and the next day they took turns standing before the class and reading their reports.

Miko, whose skin was dark and lustrous, and whom Stephanie called "our scientist," went first: "I saw the hermit crab walking when it was in the warm water, but when it was in the cold water it was not walking. It likes to live in warm water."

Then Romarise took the floor, holding his paper way out in his right hand, his left hand in the pocket of his overalls: "(1) I observed two legs in the back of the shell. (2) I observed that some of the crabs changes its shell. (3) When the hermit crabs went into the cold water, they walked slow. (4) When the hermit crabs went into the warm water, they walked faster." One by one, the rest of the students read their observations, halting at times over their invented spellings, sometimes losing track and repeating themselves, but, in soft voice or loud, with a quiet sense of assurance or an unsteady eagerness, reporting on the behavior of the hermit crabs that lived against the east wall of their classroom.

The frog and the hermit crab and all of the other creatures in Mrs. Terry's class live in multiple domains: they live in their aquatic or blue gravel or leafy habitats; they live in books; they live in the children's discussion of them — "science talk," Stephanie called it — and, subsequently, they live in the writing that emerges from talk and observation. They live in ear and eye, in narrative, in fantasy. Think of Stephanie Terry's curriculum, then, as the overlay of domains usually separated.

One day Kenneth told a story about fishing with his grandfather. Catfish was the catch, and Kenneth dwelled on the details of their whiskers and their gutted innards — to the delight of the boys and the repulsion of the girls. *Oooo. Ugggh.* "That was a real good story," said Leon. That afternoon, Stephanie dug out one of the district's basal readers and read "New Friends for Catfish." In the story, a catfish is ridiculed by a seal and a turtle because he looks funny — a fish with whiskers! — and, in an escalation of nastiness, Seal and Turtle bully their way onto the sunken ship that is Catfish's home. But when Seal gets stuck in a porthole, Catfish swims back to save him, causing a change of heart in the malicious duo, and the last panel of the story shows Seal, Turtle, and Catfish, in pirate hats and striped bandannas, frolicking together on the deck of Catfish's home.

After getting the class's reaction to "New Friends for Catfish," Mrs. Terry recalled Kenneth's story from the morning. What did the class think of these two catfish stories together? As the boys and girls began making their comparisons, Stephanie reached over for an easel that held a large sketch pad. "Kenneth's Story" she wrote on one side of the page. "New Friends for Catfish," she wrote on the other, and drew a line down the middle. "OK," she said. "Let's start thinking about the differences between these two stories. What should I put here?"

"Miss Terry, Miss Terry," Frank volunteered. "Kenneth ate his catfishes, but nobody ate Catfish." "Good," said Stephanie, and she listed the difference. "Kenneth examined the catfish," Rachel then noted, recalling Kenneth's talk about those innards, "but nobody did that to Catfish." And over the next ten minutes, the students observed that Kenneth's story involved thirteen catfish, while "New Friends for Catfish" was about one, and that Kenneth and his grandfather cut off the catfish's whiskers, but Seal and Turtle did not cut off Catfish's whiskers. And so the list grew.

A few days later, Mrs. Terry read a story called "The Magic Fish." A poor fisherman catches but tosses back a magic fish, which, in turn, grants him a wish. The fisherman's wife, though, is greedy and makes the fisherman return to the sea over and over, asking for greater and greater wealth, finally breaking the magic fish's patience with a request to be "queen of the sun and the moon and the stars." When she finished the story, Mrs. Terry dragged her easel over and, on a fresh sheet of paper, drew a big Venn diagram. The Venn diagram is a simple logician's tool, two partly overlapping circles that illustrate shared properties — those listed within the area of overlap — and properties not held in common, those within each circle's unshared space. Over the circle on the left, Stephanie wrote "New Friends for Catfish," and over the circle on the right, "The Magic Fish."

The children, already familiar with the use of the diagram, started in. They noted shared properties: there was one fish in each story; the magic fish lived in water and so did Catfish; each story had a not-so-nice character. They noted differences: the fisherman had to go back to the sea, while Catfish had to go back to his boat; the fisherman's wife wanted to be in charge of the sun and the moon and the stars, while Seal and Turtle wanted to be in charge of Catfish's home. The children continued — Catfish is a catfish and the magic fish looks like a goldfish — and Mrs. Terry's neat script crammed against the borders of the circles. Kenneth's adventure with catfish had led to a comparison with a story in a basal reader, which led to a logical analysis with a further story: critical thinking emerging from personal experience, logic from fiction — all boundaries crossed in the service of the development of free-ranging thought.

"She just walked into the kitchen and asked me if I had anything to make a circle, so I gave her the coffee can," Rachel's mother told me as she opened the large sheet of paper with the two overlapping circles. Over one side of the homemade Venn diagram was "Harriet Tubman," over the other was "Sojourner Truth," the subjects of two books Rachel had checked out of the school's small library. "Both were slaves," she had printed with a little waver to the letters. "Both earned their freedom." For distinctive properties, she noted that Tubman was born in the South, while Sojourner Truth was born in New York; she noted that Tubman died at ninety-three, but that Sojourner Truth didn't know exactly when she was born. What Stephanie Terry had set in motion,

Rachel continued, crossing the line, using in her home what she had learned in school, incorporating an academic tool into a personal exploration of African-American history.

II

EVERY MORNING Rachel Ortiz's mother walked her to school. They walked past old brick row houses, some of them boarded up, condemned, or burned out. They avoided the corner where lost men stood around the porch of a dilapidated crack house. They walked with purpose and in the presence of Jehovah, talking about home, about church, about school. Duke Ellington Primary School, P.S. 117, occupied the second story of a long brick building on the west 800 block of North Avenue, near the Pennsylvania Avenue intersection of the Old West Side. The Old West Side was once the locus of vibrant small businesses, professional offices, an art scene, and jazz clubs, but deindustrialization, fractious and discriminatory city politics, and middle-class flight — the forces devastating so many of our cities — have left the area poor and dangerous.

Duke Ellington housed prekindergarten, kindergarten, and first grade. The first floor was a market — hand-lettered signs advertising neck bones and chitterlings and money orders were spread across the wall facing the street — and Rachel and her classmates reached the school by ascending concrete stairs at the rear of the building. At the base of the stairs was a sign reading DRUG FREE SCHOOL ZONE. On the landing another sign warned ATTACK DOGS LOOSE IN THIS AREA FROM DARK TO DAWN, a German shepherd, teeth bared, lunging from the rusted script. To the west and just behind the school was an asphalt area belonging to an adjacent apartment complex; it served as a playground for Duke Ellington. There was a hopscotch grid, worn from missteps, a diagram for a volleyball court — but no poles, no net — and a basketball backboard with the hoop torn away. When the teachers used the area, they avoided those places where broken glass from the night before lay scattered in the snow.

But once Rachel and the other children walked through the pitted metal doors of P.S. 117 and into the lobby, a different world opened up — and you were struck by it right away, felt it almost before your eyes could register the particulars: a feeling of warmth and invitation. The wall to one side of the lobby was an abstract mosaic of Duke Ellington's band, a geometric splash of African color: radiant diamonds, zigzagging swirls of triangles, bright saxophones and drums. The wall to the other side had a row of photographs of Ellington and company, black-and-white, neatly spaced, precise. Straight ahead were some small ferns and bromeliads, an American flag, a glass case displaying the children's art, and a long sign in bold computer script announcing DUKE

ELLINGTON IS A SCHOOL THAT READS. The place was immaculate, and you were usually greeted at the door by Mrs. Thompson, who worked with parent volunteers, or by one of those volunteers, like Mrs. Ortiz.

"The school encourages parent involvement," Mrs. Ortiz told me. "At first, some parents may feel intimidated, but we really try to bring them in." Moving through this school, turning right or left from the lobby to one row of classrooms or another — separated by partitions rather than walls — you'd see mothers helping teachers prepare art materials, putting children's work on display, or reading a story to a small group of kids. It was all this you were sensing when you stepped into the lobby. On the way to Duke Ellington, you occasionally saw a window in those row houses that had a lamp lit behind lace curtains or some flowers on a table. The school gave you the same feeling. It was a good place to be.

Her students would start appearing in Mrs. Terry's room fifteen or twenty minutes before class officially began. The parents often lingered, talking to Mrs. Terry about their kids while the children put their coats and boots in the crowded wooden cabinets along the south wall. Then they would find a book, or take out their journals and write, or check out the creatures in tanks and cases amid the science paraphernalia. "I want our classroom to be an interesting place," Stephanie told me when I first arrived. "I want it to be a place where children *want* to come . . . and where *I* want to come, too." She spent a lot of her time and money to make it a place that children enjoyed.

There was a table full of math games, the whole array of science materials and displays — and, of course, the African frog, tree frog, hermit crab, and all their associates. Alongside them were three reading carrels stacked with books: from *Green Eggs and Ham* and *Curious George* to fairy tales recast with Black characters — *Jamiko and the Beanstalk*, for example — to books on Native Americans, *Buffalo Woman* and *The People Shall Continue.* At the front of the room, Stephanie's blackboard looked like a paper mosaic: word lists, which the children consulted when writing in their journals; alphabet strings; work from the previous day, taped up for the children to examine; and checklists of the books the children were borrowing overnight. Past the next corner was the half wall of shelves separating Mrs. Terry's room from the first-grade classroom. The shelves were packed with district-issue basal readers, writing paper, art paper, scratch paper, scissors, glue, pencils, and crayons. Along the top shelf, Mrs. Terry had opened up for display a row of alphabet books: Lucille Clifton's *The Black ABC's; The Yucky Reptile Alphabet Book* (B is for *boa,* G is for *gila monster*); *The Calypso Alphabet* (C is for *Carib,* Y is for *yam*); Dr. Seuss's *ABC's;* and Margaret Musgrove's Caldecott winner, *Ashanti to Zulu.*

From the point where the full wall began again, all the way around to the edge of the wooden coat cabinets, Mrs. Terry had fashioned a big comfortable corner. There was a piano, scratched and dinged from years of service, several large pillows and corduroy backrests, a piñata shaped and colored like a rainbow, a box of books, mostly on prominent African Americans, a tape recorder with a box of tapes — airy instrumentals, gospel, and peace songs by Pete Seeger and Holly Near — and a wall display, decorated with colorful kente cloth that featured snapshots and sketches of African peoples: Egypt, Mali, Zaire, Mozambique. "We Are Beautiful People" it read across the top. Mrs. Terry and the children spent a lot of time in this corner: she read stories here, the children read their stories here (a little chair was labeled "Author's Chair"), they listened to music here, they shared experiences — like Kenneth's catfish expedition — here. And if a student wanted to be alone, spreading out a math game or leaning against a pillow to thumb through a book, this was a choice spot. There were no open windows in Duke Ellington — temperature was centrally regulated — but right behind the piano were two translucent, partly covered windows, and warm light suffused the pillows and rug.

Every morning Mrs. Terry would begin class by sitting on the rug by the piano and gathering the children around her in a full circle. With thirty students, the circle — the Morning Unity Circle, she called it — extended out past the coat cabinets and close to the math games and science displays. Mrs. Terry and her students would close their eyes and take a few deep breaths. Though there was the sound of the children in the class next door or a little late movement in the hall, the room would get very quiet. A calming, pleasant silence. Then Mrs. Terry, in a hushed voice, would begin reciting some variation of the following, and the children, softly, would recite along with her:

> I am a special person.
> My teacher knows I'm special.
> I can do great things.
> I shall do great things.
> I will learn all that I can to become all that I can.

Another pause, the children sitting cross-legged, eyes closed, one or two taking a peek or squirming into a more comfortable position, but meditative, serious. Then Mrs. Terry would say something like, "Let's think about all the good work we're going to do today," and lead the children in a further recitation:

> I will become a better writer.
> I will become a better thinker.
> I will really be ready for school today.

The children would turn to those next to them and say, "Good morning, I'm glad you're here today," and shake hands — lots of smiles and giggles, a few exaggerated pumps of the arm — and either go to their desks or gather in closer around Mrs. Terry to do science or share experiences or hear a story.

One of the books Stephanie read during my visit was *Amazing Grace.* The title character was an African-American girl who loved good stories and enthusiastically acted them out: she became Joan of Arc, Hiawatha, the West African trickster, Anansi the Spider. So when Grace's school announced a production of *Peter Pan,* who else but Grace was expected to try out for the lead? But her desire was crushed. "Peter Pan's a boy," announced one child; "Peter Pan isn't Black," proclaimed another. Fortunately for Grace, the two strong women in her life came to the rescue. Her mother said a girl *can* be Peter Pan. Her grandmother, incensed, said Grace could be anything she wanted to be, and took her to see the Black ballerina Rosalie Wilkins in *Romeo and Juliet.* That did it. All weekend Grace, enraptured, leaped and twirled around the house, and when the auditions came, everyone agreed that only Grace had the moves to be Peter Pan.

The children loved *Amazing Grace.* Romarise was up on his haunches beside Mrs. Terry as she read, peering over her arm at the illustrations. Both Kenneth, of catfish fame, and Rachel thought it was unfair of the other children to tell Grace she couldn't be Peter Pan. And Miko, the class scientist, pointed out that Grace practiced very hard, and that was why she got the part. In Miko's line of sight, on the wall just to the side of Mrs. Terry, were photographs of two Black NASA astronauts, Dr. Mae Jemison and Dr. Guion Bluford, Jr. Underneath the photographs was the crammed box of books that held the stories of Sojourner Truth, Frederick Douglass, Ida Wells, Paul Robeson, Thurgood Marshall, Dr. King, Malcolm X, and Rosa Parks. And on display or tucked away on the shelves and in the carrels and piled on the floor were folktales and alphabet guides and serious books about science and lyrical books about words — books written by Black Americans. Books and books. Evidence of achievement was all around the room. Not contested; no polemic; present in the deed. Present in what the children accomplished each day, present in the history of accomplishment that was part of the surround.

Right at the entrance to Stephanie's room was a sign:

> Each child is sent into this world with
> a unique message to share . . . a new song to
> sing . . . a personal act of love to bestow.
>
> Welcome to Grade 1.
> I'm glad you're here.

There was no other way to think about yourself:

I can do great things
I will do great things

Stephanie Terry taught, by paradoxical logic, at the intersection of hope and despair. There were a host of probabilities that could lead one to believe that the academic future of her students would not be bright: the danger and seduction of the streets, the limited resources her students' families have for education, the overt restrictions and hidden injuries of class bias and racism. Yet Stephanie knew how profound was the desire in some of those row houses for achievement — knew from the inside the African-American legacy of self-help and self-improvement. She knew in her bones the brilliance of her people and believed, in the deepest way, in the promise of their children.

Stephanie assumed, therefore, that her students could "do better than many people expect them to," that "if you put good stuff in front of them, wonderful things will happen." She was always on the lookout for materials and techniques to interest and challenge them. Sometimes she drew on their immediate experience, sometimes on the legacies of their culture. But sometimes she called on more distant resources. Take, for instance, those Venn diagrams. About four years ago, Stephanie visited a "very exclusive private school" and watched a first-grade teacher skillfully use the diagram to enhance the way her students thought about the books they were reading. "I'd like to try some of that," she thought. "My kids might not be able to read as well, but they're just as verbal." Stephanie's science curriculum provided another illustration. Two years ago she joined a National Science Foundation project aimed at integrating science into the elementary school curriculum. Most of the participants came from schools different from Duke Ellington; several even expressed skepticism as to whether students from such schools could benefit from the project. Stephanie had no doubt, and by the following year her science curriculum was captivating Romarise, Miko, and the others. It was not uncommon, then, for Stephanie to move across educational boundaries, seeing what was done in more privileged settings, and asking herself how she could bring it to the children who came, full of energy, into her room each day.

Stephanie Terry grew up in a family that celebrated children. "Our house was always full of neighborhood kids. Every night, it seemed, there was an extra face at the dinner table, and my parents just made it known how lovely it was to have us . . . to have all of us around them." She and I were sitting in small chairs in the corner by the piano, right alongside the Author's Chair and a big box of books. "Kids came first, and as I grew older, I guess I never forgot that. It just felt very natural to be around a lot of young people . . . to enjoy them and support them." Stephanie was wearing a full purple dress, a swatch of kente cloth around her long, braided hair, and earrings from which crescent moons dangled. It was late afternoon, but there was still a soft light on things. A few pencils and some crumpled papers were scattered around us. The debris of thought. "Maybe," she said, "maybe that's why I always wanted to be a teacher. I've wanted to be a teacher for as long as I can remember."

She attended public schools in the city of her birth, York, Pennsylvania, then went to nearby Lock Haven State College (now a university) to major in teacher education. Since graduating, twenty-one years ago, she has taught in York, then in Trenton, New Jersey, then in Baltimore, where she has lived since 1977. About six years into her career, while still in Trenton, she was selected to participate in the planning of an experimental school, one that involved teachers in the development of curriculum and the structuring of the school day. The project gave her, at a young age, a sense of intellectual daring — she came to see teaching as an ongoing experiment, as inquiry. Once in Baltimore, she had the opportunity to participate in further educational experiments, one of which combined "regular" students with the "gifted and talented" — with the result that half of the regular students tested as gifted and talented, and reshaped their academic careers. This convinced her that "if your expectations were high and you put the right things in place in the classroom, a lot was possible." For some time, then, Stephanie Terry has pushed on limits, has taken risks — "stepping outside the district curriculum," she called it — has been instrumental in challenging assumptions about what poor, usually poor and Black, children can do. She shrugged her shoulders and brought her hands together as a cup. "I guess some see me as a bit of a renegade. But what else can I do?"

If Stephanie ventured beyond protocol, though, she did so with a quiet step. She spoke softly, deliberately, and as she talked about her students, she looked at you often, holding connection. She was intent on making herself understood: pulling out a piece of student writing to illustrate a point, telling a story, stopping momentarily to reflect on what she had just said, a slight lilt to her voice as she questioned herself, then starting off on a different tack. She was both focused and even-tempered, seeming to speak from some deep self-knowledge and a bedrock sense of peace. As Mrs. Ortiz put it, "Stephanie just seems to have a special quality."

"How does such a strong advocate," I asked her, "stay so calm?" She laughed, disavowing any hedge on serenity. But as we talked further through the afternoon, those translucent windows turning dark blue, the conversation taking casual and unexpected turns, Stephanie revealed three sources of her strength. There was, of course, her family. "My parents gave us a powerful sense that we were valuable, that we could accomplish whatever we set our mind to." Then, during the 1960s, she, like so many Black Americans of her generation, began to read the history of Africa and African Americans, and that reading sparked a lifelong cultural and spiritual quest. That night, in fact, she was going to a rehearsal of an *a cappella* group she and three other women had formed called Rafiki Na Dada, Swahili for Friends and Sisters. The members included, beside Stephanie, a physician, an epidemiologist, and a lawyer, and they sang what Stephanie called songs of the African Diaspora: from South African freedom songs, to gospel, to rhythm and blues à la Marvin Gaye and the Pointer Sisters. "I think that when some folks hear about such an African-centered focus," Stephanie mused, "they think of White-hating, because that's what makes it into the papers. But I don't see it that way [she paused on each word] not at all. I see it as positive. I'm interested in positive things . . . you know, like contributions to culture, family and spiritual values, respect for each other and for the earth."

And there was a third source of strength for Stephanie Terry. Meditation. For six or seven years, she had been a member of a study group organized to "read and talk about the intellectual dimension of Christianity and other religions." Though Stephanie's own religious affiliation was with the Heritage, United Church of Christ, she found something compelling in the meditation techniques of Eastern religions. And, in line with her experimental bent, she had wondered whether a kind of secularized meditation could assist her teaching. "A way, maybe, to begin the day with some sense of unifying, some focus . . . a sense that we've all come together for the same purpose." Thus was born the Morning Unity Circle.

Stephanie Terry lived and taught, then, out of the flux of the stable and the exploratory. "It's important for me to have my base as an African-American woman — and it's solid and steady — but I also have to be able to move out to find things for me and my classroom. I can't separate things into all sorts of compartments." To place her culture and personal history at the center was not to wall off movement. "With a solid base, you can travel far and wide. That's what I want to impart to my kids." In Stephanie's eyes, the center made movement possible. In life and work. Center. Movement. One enabling the other.

III

STEPHANIE HAD RESISTED FOR SOME TIME various district mandates to have fixed and precise time slots for her subjects — math from 8:35 to 9:15; reading from 9:20 to 10:05 — and had finally paid enough dues and had accumulated enough success to negotiate her own way. She believed that students needed to cross disciplinary lines to be afforded interesting problems — writing about science, for example. And she also believed that a teacher needed to have the freedom to seize opportunities for learning that arose unpredictably — like following Kenneth's catfish story with "New Friends for Catfish" — even if that meant spending twice as long on a subject as was recommended, and making adjustments elsewhere in the day. This discomfort with rigid disciplinary boundaries explained why she did not organize her classroom by stations — an art station, science station, reading station — through which the children passed sequentially. To her way of thinking, such an arrangement would signal a separation of what should be joined together.

Certainly there was structure to Stephanie's day. Some activities were fixed — the Morning Unity Circle, for example — and because of tutorials and enrichment programs, like art and music, additional time slots were firmly set. Freer movement came in the other spaces. But if you mapped out everything that Stephanie did over a week or two, you would find a structure. All the subject areas got covered, but not in linear, segmented fashion; it was more the structure of weave, of overlap and intersection — a structure emerging from the dictates of learning and curiosity.

Two questions come to mind when considering such a structure: How did Stephanie evaluate her students' work and, with so much going on in her classroom, how did she maintain order?

Evaluation came naturally from the multiple events of the day. The children were always *doing* something — writing, reading aloud, reasoning their way through a problem — so Stephanie observed a stream of academic activity. And she watched closely. People visited often, but she rarely took time out for a back-of-the-classroom conversation; she stayed in the middle of things, taking it all in. She confirmed or revised her observations with the thick folder of student work she kept for each child: full of writing, art, math homework, and the like. On request, she could give you a detailed account of a child's strengths and what she called that child's "challenges."

As for order, Stephanie Terry's classroom was one of the most orderly I had ever seen — I never once heard her raise her voice, never saw her shame a child or grab a forearm in anger. As her student Rachel observed one day, "She doesn't fuss a lot." In the education literature, discussions of classroom management are usually found in places separate from curriculum, but it seemed to me that the order in Stephanie's classroom emerged precisely out of the curriculum she had created and the sense it gave the students that what they were doing was important. "They come to know," she explained, "that this is the place where they do good work, and that they won't get as much done — they won't get to do science, for example — if they don't get along, if everything is chaotic." When she could, Stephanie tried to begin this socialization early. Every so often, she would visit the kindergarten classes and note the particularly rambunctious children — and invite them to visit her room after school. She'd show them the frogs and newts, the books, the stories her children wrote. This, she would explain, is what they could look forward to. She created an intellectual environment in which it was just more fulfilling, even more fun, to behave.

But first-graders come to school with a lot on their minds and a twitch in their developing muscles. I would not want it to seem that Stephanie's room was stilled of this energy. There was exuberance here and funny transgression, sputtering K'POWS and the pointed taunt. Frank bouncing in his chair, lunch on the horizon, ready to fidget out of his skin; Shaquente leveling a street barb in the hallway; Leon, lost in dreams of Power Wheels, leaning, leaning, then tumbling backward to the floor; Michael informing me that his sidekick Antonio eats boogers. The first decade of life. When it seemed to Stephanie that intervention was needed — when a child was clearly disturbing another or drifting too far from the task at hand — she quietly took that young person aside and had a talk. Her voice would be soft and direct, and she often touched the child while she spoke. She was "kind but firm," as one aide put it, and she always appealed to the child's value and self-esteem: "You have important things to do," she might say. "You're special and you have a good mind."

This whole approach to classroom management couldn't help having an effect on social relations. One of the first things I noticed was the consideration Stephanie's students had for one another. Kenneth was trying to get through a cluster of kids to hang his coat: "'Scuse me," he said as he put one hand forward. "'Scuse me, please." Dondi was helping Michael tie his shoes; Leon was getting a pencil for Shereese. When it came time for the science lesson, I was struck by the ease with which children would give up their privileged places by the tree frog's home to allow others to see. "The children learn about the possibilities of the room," Stephanie noted, "and about the value of one another."

The work the children did, then, fostered a particular attitude toward self and a kind of cooperative interaction. Just as Stephanie blurred the lines between subject areas, she encouraged both individual responsibility and respect for others. "Where did we get the idea," she said, "that these are separate ways of being?" To talk about Stephanie's classroom at times seemed to require the ability to talk about many things at once: individuality and collaboration, personal experience and analytical distance, music and language, reading and writing. One of the places where all these potentially separate strands came together was the Author's Chair.

The Author's Chair might have come from an inexpensive set of kitchen furniture, if it weren't so small — housekeeping drilled and pressed in miniature. Steel tubing, blue-green speckled plastic seat and back rest. A sign, curled at the edges, was taped across the top: AUTHOR'S CHAIR. At least once a week, each student in Stephanie's class had the opportunity to sit in it and read something he or she had written, the rest of the class listening and responding. The students looked forward to the readings, letting out a moan when, for some reason, a scheduled session had to be canceled, or an athletic *"yesssss"* — hitting that *s* with brio — when Mrs. Terry announced that it was time for the authors to come forward.

Jamika's trip to the Author's Chair was typical. Jamika's parents were devout Jehovah's Witnesses, so it was not uncommon for Jamika to write on religious themes. She was small and serious and had the full cheeks that relatives yearn to pinch. Just before Jamika started to read, she inched forward on the chair so that her feet were steady on the ground:

> Saturday and Sunday I went to a Assembly. I ate breakfast in the Assembly's cafeteria. They gave me a chicken sandwich. I took my food home. When I was in the Assembly in the Auditorium I took off my shoes because my mother said I could. Lots of Brothers gave lots of talks. People got on the stage.

When she finished, she looked over the top of her paper, anticipating questions. "That was a good story," said Shaquente. "Thank you," replied Jamika, glancing at Mrs. Terry and smiling. "You gave a lot of details," said Leon from the back, standing up to be heard. "Thank you," Jamika said again. "Why did you take your sandwich home?" asked Frank, alert to the advent of lunch. "Because I wasn't hungry," explained Jamika. "Well, uh, maybe you could say that, too," he offered. "If you decide to say something more about your sandwich" — Mrs. Terry tapped her lip with her index finger, as if in thought — "where would you put it?" "I could put it where I say 'I took my food home,'" answered Jamika. "I could say, 'I took my food home because I wasn't hungry.'" "OK," replied her teacher. "Think about it."

Kenneth was next, shooting his hand up in the air, waving it, pressing his cheek against his arm. "Wa . . . what did the people do on the stage?" Stephanie waited a moment, then added that she was curious about that, too. Jamika set the paper on her lap. "They talked about the ministry, and they told stories from the scripture and . . ." — a pause here, looking at Mrs. Terry again — "and that's what I remember." "Well, Jamika," said Mrs. Terry, "I think your readers would like to know that," and leaned over to provide a quick assist to Jamika, who was fishing a pencil out of the pocket of her dress.

When Stephanie first introduced me to the children some days earlier, she told them I was a teacher and an author. "We're going to have an author staying with us for a while." "Ooooo, Miss Terry," Dondi offered, waving his hand, "we're authors too!" You couldn't be in Stephanie Terry's classroom for long before the children walked up to you, their dog-eared journals folded back, asking whether you'd like to hear a story. They saw themselves as writers. And, thanks to Mrs. Terry's feedback and the experience of the Author's Chair, a number of them were becoming reflective about their prose. Ciera came up to me — hair in cornrows, pretty, a little coy — and read me a description of her rings: "I have four rings. One has a whitish stone. One has a red stone. One is gold, one silver." She finished and looked up. I complimented her, and she said "Thank you," but then she paused, pursing her lips, and said, "I think I need more ideas, huh?" "Like what else?" I asked. Again a pause. "Maybe how I *got* the rings?" "Now that's a good idea," I said. She turned on her heel and ran off, still holding her paper in both hands. Six or seven minutes later and she came back, a big smile on her face. "OK," she said, "this is better." She read her original description and then her new sentences: "My mother got me the rings. She got two at Kmart and two at Sears."

Not too long ago, it was assumed that children couldn't learn to write until they had learned to read. It was — and in many classrooms still is — assumed that a critical awareness of one's writing and the impulse to revise should not be expected or encouraged until the later elementary grades. And in many settings it is assumed that the most effective language arts curriculum for poor kids, inner city or rural or immigrant, is one that starts with the alphabet, phonics, and lists of simple words, presented in sequence, learned through drills and packaged games, and builds slowly toward the reading of primer prose. Stephanie Terry's classroom challenged those assumptions.

Writing and reading were taught as related processes and were developed apace. Children did receive instruction in letter recognition and principles of phonics, both from Stephanie and from the school's reading teacher, Carol Hicks. Carol was, by her own description, "a traditionalist," who worked with Stephanie in her classroom and, together with Stephanie, planned supplemental instruction for those children "who may fall through the cracks." But while the students were learning about letter-sound correspondences, they were also learning to brainstorm, consider an audience, reflect on their writing, add detail, and revise. The development of these complex processes was not put on hold until more discrete language skills were perfected. So Ciera spelled "stone" as *ston* and "Sears" as *Sers,* and Jamika, who was the most proficient speller in the class, wrote *Sauterday* and *cafetereia* and *chiken.* Errors like these would gradually disappear as Ciera and Jamika read more and wrote more, as Stephanie and Carol gave them feedback on their work, as they received more direct instruction — from Stephanie, from Carol, from an aide — in phonics and spelling. Meanwhile, they were using language in full, rich ways to tell the stories they wanted to tell.

"It's all part of it," Stephanie had said to me. "Everything contributes to the writing. The animals, the books, the music, the things on the wall, the African themes and images — it all feeds into their journals. And the activities. They need lots of opportunities to talk, to hear good books, to ask questions, to share experiences with classmates, to help each other, to read the things they've written." So any given reading at the Author's Chair may grow from a number of sources, all part of the classroom environment.

There were, of course, the books. Each day, Stephanie read at least one book to the class: fairy tale or folktale, a story about children, biography, history, an account of other cultures, an explanation of the biology or ecology of the creatures living along the wall of the classroom. In any given month, then, the children might hear a tale set in the African rain forest, a linguistic romp by Dr. Seuss, an explanation of the Navajo cosmology, information on the newt or hermit crab, the life of Harriet Tubman or Rosa Parks, a story about a magic fish or a spirited girl or a trickster spider. A wide range of genres.

The children could check out any of the books overnight. In the front of the room, taped to the blackboard, was a long sign-out sheet, and at the end of each day, those children who wanted a book would line up and write in the title and their initials. This usually went surprisingly fast; the kids were used to the procedure. When they came in the next morning, they would, along with hanging their coats and other routines, put a check by their name and indicate, in one of three columns, whether the book was "easy," "just right," or "a challenge." Stephanie could thereby tell a lot at a glance. And the children had the chance to be with books. Reading them for a first or second or third time, or just looking at the illustrations — words and pictures feeding their imagination.

There was music. Some was instrumental — drums, harps, guitars, and birdsong to accompany that rain forest tale, for example. But most involved language play and storytelling: Taj Mahal's "Shake Sugaree," Sweet Honey in the Rock's "All for Freedom," "Yoruba Children's Tales," and a collection called "Peace Is the World Smiling." Picking up on the lyrics of the peace songs, Kenneth started one of his entries with "My Earth give us Love and Peace. You got to love the Earth just like you love your friends."

There were the creatures and all the print surrounding them. Words referring to their anatomies — *claw, antenna, gill* — to their habitats and birth cycles — which the children had observed — words about how to care for them ("In our room, we feed praying mantis nymphs apple bits"), and words on the ecological functions they served: "aquatic snails keep our aquarium clean." The language, for the most part, came from the children themselves — with a spelling assist from Mrs. Terry. (It was not uncommon to see children leave their desks to copy from the walls the correct spelling of a difficult word.) And there was all that talk, "science talk," the language of close observation that led to the creation of the children's own explanatory texts.

Another kind of generative talk was the daily recounting of the children's experience: fishing expeditions, trips to the zoo, church services, birthday parties, visits to relatives, neighborhood journeys with "best, very best" friends. These accounts were taken seriously as contributions to the linguistic environment. Children's oral stories were celebrated, analyzed, incorporated into discussions of written stories, and considered for further elaboration. And occasionally one student's story would find its way into another student's composing.

If the books and animals and the rest provided a multilayered content for the children's writing, the journals themselves offered the occasion to learn about the process. Each month, Stephanie passed out homemade stapled booklets filled with lined paper. The children wrote every day, sometimes on an assigned topic, more often on a topic of their choosing — but not infrequently with some kind of guiding principle that arose from other classroom work. If, for example, Stephanie had read a book that was especially rich in description, she might ask the children to try to "add lots of detail" to their own writing. And as Stephanie or an aide circulated around the room, they would give on-the-spot instruction in spelling or encourage a student to be a little more descriptive or point out an unhelpful repetition. All of this, of course, set the stage for revision.

Such work was done on the fly, but once or twice a week Stephanie drew from everything she saw to present a more formal demonstration of the composing process. Resting on an easel in the front of the room, right by the blackboard, was a three-foot-high version of a journal. On the front was Stephanie's self-portrait in crayon, braids twisting into the air. *Mrs. Terry's Journal,* it said across the top. With felt pen in hand, she would model how to get started and how to revise, and would provide opportunity for children to apply their editing skills. "Last week I went to the Baltimore Aquarium," she might say in mock consternation, "but, uh, but I don't know what to say about it." And the children would jump in: "Did you go alone?" "What fish did you see first?" "Did you have fun?" These were the kinds of questions they heard when they were in the Author's Chair. Then Stephanie would start writing, making many simple errors — "on sunday i wnt to the aquarium" — and a chorus of her students would happily edit her writing: "Miss Terry, you need to start with a capital." "Miss Terry, there's a *e* between the *w* and the *n.*" "Miss Terry, oooh, you didn't put a period at the end." As she proceeded, she repeated herself or put sentences out of logical sequence, and that would lead to discussion of broader revisions — as would a question like: "What else would you as a reader like to know about my trip?" With time, these questions and operations, and an awareness of the linguistic contexts that give rise to them, would gradually work their way into the children's composing process.

The journals encouraged another kind of work. At the table close to the door, Romarise leaned over and asked Kevin how to spell *night.* Kevin thought for a moment, then wrote *n-i-g-h-t* across the top of his page. A few minutes later, Kevin turned to Shereese. "Hey, Shereese, do you know how to spell *Friday?*" Shereese ticked off the letters, and Kevin wrote it out and thanked her. At another table Rachel had gotten up with her journal in her hand and was guiding Shaquente toward the comfortable section of rug and pillows by the piano. They settled in, and Rachel read to Shaquente her thoughts on the biography of Sojourner Truth that had been capturing her interest for the past week or so. Stephanie encouraged her students to work with one another: to write about each other's experiences, to help with spelling and punctuation, to share stories and elicit peer reactions. Individual writing, in her eyes, was enhanced by a community of writers.

It was all this that made possible Ciera's and Jamika's and Romarise's performances at the Author's Chair.

Another way to consider how Stephanie Terry's students grew as writers would be to look at their work over time, getting a sense of how growth happens in a curriculum of such sweep and embrace. I'll present two students: Kevin, whose writing would place him somewhere in the upper half, maybe third of this classroom's achievements, and Rachel, who, despite some trouble with spelling and mechanics, was one of the most accomplished writers in the class.

Kevin was one of four or five boys who, in another setting, might have been labeled a "behavior problem." He had large, soulful eyes and was usually pretty low-key, but he could easily slip from a task and turn his pencil into an imaginary airplane zipping noisily over his desk or surreptitiously pester the child sitting next to him. About once a day I would see Stephanie sitting with him, head to head, reminding him of the importance of his work, of the importance of his very presence here among the children. And he would usually calm down and get to it, writing a story, or helping other kids spell — for he was a decent speller — or finding a book to take home with him later that day.

The first few entries in Kevin's journal, those for early September, were simply his attempts to copy words he saw on the science displays:

newtafricanfrog
tadgole bloodwormS *Sept. 9*

He had good control of his letters, though he ran words together and hadn't yet mastered capitalization. He also occasionally miscopied — as you can see with *tadgole* for *tadpole.*

About a month later, in early October, Kevin was still copying words but was getting them from all around the room and rearranging them. He was also making his first attempts to guess at the spelling of words he couldn't find on the walls:

Beautiful simWnPeat
The Right crab mhTsnu
Thing hermit crabs Rainbow *Oct. 7*

Beautiful came from the "We Are Beautiful People" display, *hermit crabs* from the science area across the room, *Rainbow* from above the reading carrels, and *The Right* and *Thing* from the title of Spike Lee's movie, which Stephanie had spelled out in red and blue art paper letters over the sink by the science materials. He may or may not have been trying to tell a story with them. But by late October he was attempting to write stories like all the ones he was hearing and was relying solely on his own attempted spellings. The first line of one read:

thet's Info. psw. wIgto psw *Oct. 28*

What's interesting about these entries — which look a little like a print-out from a haywire computer — is that they could be seen as a step backward, since there are no recognizable words here at all. Yet Kevin was experimenting with phonetic strings to try to communicate, experimentation that would, within a month, begin to yield simple written stories:

> Ie wint too The zooo.
> wif mi fe mly.
> wif mi murr. *Nov. 22*

"I went to the zoo, with my family, with my mother." Kevin was getting the idea about word boundaries and punctuation, and his phonetic guesses were much improved. Here he used his developing skill to take a shot at creating a story common in the primary grades: the visit to an exciting place.

Over the next few months, Kevin's writing took a big leap forward. Here's another zoo story:

> I can go to the zoo with you
> but you can,t go to day with
> me Can i go now not yet
> you can go at the zoo at day
> With me you can to the zoo
> with me now. *Jan. 16*

His printing was quite good by now, word boundaries were under control, and he was developing a repertoire of simple words. What caught my attention, though, was the experimentation with story structure. There were several voices at work here, possibly a result of all the dialogue Kevin was hearing in the books Stephanie read to the class. Kevin seemed to be using the basic frame of his zoo story to try out some new linguistic maneuvers.

By the time of my visit in March, six months after his first entry, Kevin had gained greater control over sentence boundaries and punctuation and was taking more adventurous chances with his vocabulary. And along with these skills, he was developing a sense of narrative:

> On friday we went on a trip. And it was
> fun at the trip. And we saw a man with
> firer. And he got a beloon and he bust
> the beloon. *March 9*

Stephanie's next move with Kevin would be to encourage more of the nice detail in those last two sentences — fire and bursting balloons — and to help him develop other kinds of experiences, from inside or outside the classroom, into material for his journal.

Rachel looked delicate — thin arms and legs — but, during gym, had a quick, pumping sprint, and, though usually reserved, could match anyone's squeal when the tree frog zapped an unlucky cricket. She was not the most technically proficient writer in the class — Jamika would spell words like *sorrow* and *dwelling* for her — but she was the most inventive. She read all the time and wrote in a variety of settings and for a variety of purposes. She wrote copious entries in her journal, which she frequently took home with her; she copied out long stretches of books she liked; she took notes on church services in a little pad her mother had given her; and there was that Venn diagram on Harriet Tubman and Sojourner Truth. Rachel used writing to render experience and tell stories, to record and relish other people's prose, to keep track of speech, to conduct logical analyses.

The first entries in Rachel's journal showed some basic proficiency and an occasional touch, but it would have been hard to predict her future work from them. Take, for example, this passage:

> The FRogsdo not go
> rib rib rib and we ~~jump~~
> Did not see thoe jump *Sept. 20*

Rachel had a sense of word boundaries and could spell some simple words. But it was interesting to see the way she used her writing to record an observation with a critical thrust: frogs do not make a *rib-it, rib-it* sound as kids are led to believe.

About three weeks later, Rachel began constructing basic narratives on her experiences:

> Me an my fin India are walling
> at the prak and I get sug
> by a bee an we ran hm *Oct. 8*

Though Rachel had some trouble with spelling, increasingly she took chances in order to get her experience on paper: *fin* for *friend, walling* for *walking, prak* for *park,* and *sug* for *stung.* Stephanie would sometimes respond right on the journal page; here she wrote, "Oh no! What did you do then?" The question would urge Rachel to tell more, to extend the narrative she had written.

Rachel's reading and writing were developing together, and about a week after the bee-sting story there was an entry in her journal, pages and pages long, that recorded her favorite Dr. Seuss book:

> I am gon to tellw you
> The story By Dr. Seuss

it is Green Eggs and
Ham. that-Sam-I am
that-Sam-I am I do not
like that-Sam-I am do you
like Green Eggs
and Ham . . . *Oct. 14*

The entry continued, Rachel seeming to enjoy writing the rhythmic words, making them her own. About a month later, there was another long entry. This time, though, Rachel tried to recount rather than copy stories, and, in an intriguing move, blended two in unlikely unison. The first was from Margaret Musgrove's alphabet book *Ashanti to Zulu,* which Stephanie had read to the class.

A. is for the ashot
people . . . the hoozl
people was running
after The ashot
people when The
ashot people got
to a river . . .

The retelling went on for a while; then, on the same line, Rachel picked up *Green Eggs and Ham* once again:

people could not
get them . . . Green
Eggs and ham By
Dr. Seuss . . . that Sam-
I-am that Sam-
I am *Nov. 18–19*

The shift to Dr. Seuss continued to the end of the entry. I didn't get a chance to talk to Rachel about this, but she seemed to be playing with two stories she liked, connecting them in her own retelling.

Over the next two months, Rachel would gain better control of mechanics, sentence boundaries, punctuation, capitalization — and her spelling would improve.

I love my brother and my sister.
I love my mother and my father
they are apart of my family and
I love them all the same. If they

make me mad I will stil love them
beacus I know they did not meen
it. When somebody dose something
to you it doesn't mean do it
back. *Jan. 17*

Through January and February, Rachel's entries were fairly straightforward, less experimental as she gained control over conventions. She tended to use her writing now to address a range of topics and to reflect on her own interests and on her developing competence:

I love all kinds of book.
I love Green eggs and ham.
I love Cinderella and Rapunzel.
Piggies. It don't matter what
book it is. It is so fun to read all
kinds of books.
I can read. I am somebody.
I am me. *Feb. 24*

Roughly two weeks later, Rachel began a longer piece in the computer lab about the funeral of a family friend. Stephanie encouraged her to revise it, and she did so. Her phonetic guesses were improving, and she was beginning to catch and correct her own mistakes. The paper proved to be her most ambitious piece of writing to date:

On saterday I went to the
froonrol of Manerva Homes. It was
sad to look at her. She had
six girls and one boy. My
family crid. When the froonrol
was omost over we got to see
her and I kissed her. She was
like a grandmother to me and
my brother and sister. I loved
her so much. She helped my
mother knit and everyday we
went to see her. She was in the
housbidol taking some pilse and
deid in her sleep. We had
he froonarol at the kingdom
hall. We sanged song 15 and
that says can you see with

your minds eye people are
dwelling togather. Sorrow has
pass no need to weep or fear.
sing out with joy of heart
you too can have a part.
Man and beast living in peace
cause no harm to each other.
Food will be there all will
share in what our God pervids. *March 11*

Rachel was doing some fascinating things here. She told the story of the funeral and of her feelings about the passing of Mrs. Homes, and, relying on the notes she took, she incorporated the psalm into her written text. Her earlier practice of copying favorite passages was being put to a rhetorical purpose, and she was using the notes she had taken in one setting to embellish a piece of writing being done in another.

Kevin and Rachel and the rest of the students kept their current journals at their desks; journals from earlier months were filed in a large box by the piano. So you could sit on the rug before class or after the children had gone home and flip back through the dog-eared pages, thin in places from vigorous erasure, and watch the print becoming more stable, the stories getting longer. Soon you would find places where something wonderful was going on: an experiment in narration, a new understanding of form, an unexpected increase in the kinds of words attempted. And you might, as I did, lay the journals down month by month and stretch out to get a longer view, no longer seeing the particular letters and erasures, but a flow of language, words and effort over time, the development of possible lives.

IV

THROUGH A MIX OF hard work, ingenuity, and local support, Stephanie Terry was able to put into play in her classroom an innovative and personally meaningful philosophy of education. She has managed to finesse a number of the strictures that characterize public education in urban America. Twice during my visit, though, I saw her beliefs and methods clash headlong with district realities. In one case, involving citywide assessment tests, the clash led to a reflective discontent, from which came a fruitful compromise. In the other — involving the referral of one of her students to special education — Stephanie remained stymied, fixed in an unsolvable dilemma.

All teachers who move outside a standard curriculum must determine how to deal with the proficiency and achievement tests mandated by the agencies that govern their working lives. They have little or no control over the format and content of these tests, and it's not unusual for the tests to be at odds with their own curriculum and objectives. One such test was on the horizon for Stephanie. It would be multiple choice in format and would deal with the particulars of language ability — the use of synonyms, for example. Now Stephanie's students, to be sure, were learning about synonyms as they read stories, wrote and revised, and conducted their logical analyses, but Stephanie did not teach synonyms specifically in the focused way that would lead more directly to multiple-choice assessment. She did not have lessons on "the synonym," for example, nor did she use workbook sheets or judge language competence with objective tests. Such an approach, she felt, would drain the vitality from language arts and would send some reductive messages to her students about the value and use of written language.

Yet the tests were coming up, and the children's performance on them could have an effect on their academic future. Furthermore, they would face such tests all the way into adulthood and would have to develop skill at taking them and some savvy about them. Stephanie had long talks about all this with Carol, the reading teacher, who, though she also questioned the value of the tests, could work with them. And several times Stephanie and I tried to think through an effective compromise. She was alternately angry, pensive, curious, and resourceful. After some thought, she arrived at a solution.

She began one afternoon with a lesson at the board, all thirty children gathered around her. Just before lunch, she had read them a hilarious book called *The True Story of the Three Little Pigs,* an account of the classic tale from the wolf's point of view. "Today," she wrote on the board, "the big, bad wolf told his side of the story." Then she slowly underlined the word *big.* "Class," she said, "I've got a problem. I'd like to write this sentence over — you know, the way we sometimes write sentences over" [nods from the children here], "but I don't want to use the word *big* again." Her voice rose quizzically. "Can you help me by thinking of another word that means the same thing?" You bet. Dondi offered "large"; Leon suggested "giant"; Shereese weighed in with "huge." "OK," Stephanie said, "thanks." A pause, finger to lip, puzzlement. "But I've got another problem. What if I don't want to use the word *told,* what word could I use instead?" "Said," whispered Miko. "How about 'stated,'" suggested Romarise.

Stephanie worked on another sentence. "When we use a word that means the same thing as another word, that word is called a synonym, a syn-o-nym." The class followed suit: "syn-o-nym." "Why," she asked, "why would we want to think of ways to describe something with different words? You know, instead of saying 'this was big' and 'this was big' and 'this was big,' too. Why try to find other words that mean the same thing as *big*?" "Miss Terry, Miss Terry!" said Frank, waving his hand. "To keep it from getting boring."

The lesson took about twenty-five minutes. Over the next few weeks, Stephanie would use two or three similar blocks of time to work on synonyms and other such language skills. She would explain the strange test that the children were going to take: "This test is to enable people who aren't in this class to see how much you know about words." She would acquaint the children with the format of the test. For example, she'd write out:

mad
a. happy
b. boy
c. green
d. angry

Then she would ask the children why "happy" or "green" isn't a synonym for "mad." "Discount the silly answers," she'd then advise. "There will always be a silly answer. Discount it right away, just the way you did just now." And she would try to spark reflection on the process: "How do you know how one word can mean the same thing as another? Think a minute. Think about what goes on in your mind."

In addition to this formal treatment, Stephanie would take a moment here and there during the day to anchor the lessons in the ongoing work the children were doing. When she held out that pickle jar of crickets for the tree frog, she asked quickly for a synonym for *jar*. "Container," said Rachel, looking up from the glass case. While she was reading the story of a great African king, she stopped, pondered the word *great*, and got a stream of synonyms: "excellent," "fantastic," "wonderful," "stupendous," "perfect," "marvelous" . . . this last one repeated by Shereese in a mock British accent: "mah-va-lous."

In this way, the students began to gear up for the district test, receiving instruction on some language concepts and on test format, and doing some drills on the fly — but drill energized by the flow of fuller language work. Occasionally, Stephanie pushed beyond the requirements of the test by getting the students to consider this business of synonymity itself, laying the groundwork for them to make discriminations among words that might, in a general way, be similar. She was writing in her oversized journal, the one on the easel by the board, when she stopped and asked the gathered students for a synonym for *walk*. "Stomp," said Kevin, and Stephanie thought about that for a moment and then asked Kevin to stomp around the room. Surprised, he did, and with mounting relish — to the pleasure of the group. Stomp, stomp, stomp. "Hmmm, Kevin," asked Stephanie. "Were you doing the same thing as when you walk?" "No," said Kevin. "I guess that means," continued Stephanie, "that though those two words are kind of alike, they're not really the same." Shaquente offered *skip*. "Well, 'skip,' let's try that. Shaquente, would you skip around the room?" And Shaquente got up, smiling, and proceeded to skip back to the piano, arms swinging. "This ain't walkin'," she observed, giggling, halfway through the journey. "Well, I guess not," answered Stephanie. "Any other ideas? This isn't so easy, is it?" "Maybe *step*," said Rachel. And, of course, Stephanie had Rachel step around the room and asked the class what they thought. They said, yes, *step* sure looks like a synonym for *walk*. "Let's think about this," said Stephanie. And Romarise did. "A lot of words," he said, "can sorta mean the same thing . . . but, ah, they won't all work the same, will they?"

A disproportionately high number of African-American boys get placed in special education; they are diagnosed as behavior disordered, mildly retarded, or, most frequently, learning disabled. Some educators see this as the unfortunate result of social and familial disruption, the medical complications that attend poverty, and the problems many nonmainstream children have adapting to the routines of school. Through its focused curriculum and small student-teacher ratio, special education, these educators believe, will enable such children to receive the particular care they need and develop their skills.

But there are other educators who see the situation differently. While admitting that some children — thanks to the number of committed teachers in special education — may benefit from such placement, they point out that, overall, many children who enter special education rarely move back out. They continue to do poorly, falling progressively behind their peers, and, all too frequently, drop out of school. There are a number of reasons for this dreary record, the critics believe, and some of the most troubling ones can be found in the assumptions central to the special education enterprise itself, especially where the diagnosis of learning disability is concerned. While there is some acknowledgment of social dynamics and emotional distress, a good deal of learning disability assessment, curriculum, and pedagogy assumes, with limited empirical support, that a child's problems have to do with hard-to-detail dysfunctions in perception and cognition, minor neurological defects within the child that cause flawed linguistic processing, erratic attention span, and the like. These assumptions lead to a curriculum that breaks the complex down to the simple, concentrates on bits and pieces of subject matter, and relies on drill and repetition. Such a curriculum, the critics say, doesn't engage students and it traps them in a limited course of study. And the assumptions behind the curriculum, and the way they play out in the culture of the school, serve to stigmatize children, leading others and, worse, themselves to define them as odd, handicapped, or strange. That so many African-American boys should be delivered to such a future becomes, then, an act of scholastic ghettoization.

But what does a teacher like Stephanie do, someone with strong beliefs about teaching and learning and a commitment to the advancement — no, the celebration — of Black people? What does she do when she must acknowledge that one or more of the students in her class might have no other option in the current system but to be placed in special ed? For therein lies the problem: the only way for children, other than those with the resources of the privileged, to receive special care and one-to-one attention is to enter special education, with all its assumptive baggage and potential to isolate. Stephanie was friends with some special education teachers and admired their dedication. But she also knew how few children, Black children especially, ever left that track. She could not be the agent who sent an African-American child to that fate. Yet, there was Herman.

Herman was slim, agile, and had an appealing, open face. He smiled a lot, mugged it up, whoop-whooped like Arsenio Hall. He was disruptive, but never in an aggressive way. He would nudge into a line or tug at the other children's work, trying to see what to do — almost, it seemed, trying to get into the swing of things. Angela McNair, the aide who worked with him, told me that he often came to school hungry and tired. During one of Stephanie's lessons on synonyms, I looked around to see him falling forward from a kneel, his eyes closed, Shereese catching him and shaking him awake. In this class of considerate kids, he was, before long, avoided. "Herman don't wash," one child whispered to me. "Herman can't write," said another.

Herman could spell his name, but little else. He could copy words from the walls and board into his journal if you asked him to, but didn't seem to do much of that on his own. Mostly he produced random strings of letters, some ill-formed and off-center. He didn't do any better in math, and he couldn't read. What he could do was observe the other children — and try to mimic their performance. He would wave his hand during math and give an answer, right or wrong, that another student had just given. He would bend over his journal, scribbling away while Shereese or Kevin were hot on a story, looking up occasionally and smiling, pretending to write a story too, wanting to exhibit competence, wanting to belong.

It struck me one day that the way this desire to belong manifested itself had, ironically, become one of Herman's biggest barriers to attaining competence. The class was out on the asphalt playground — it had been raining for two days, and the kids were feeling cooped up — when Stephanie organized a tag race. She had the children arrange themselves into five lines. The front runner in each would run to the fence, touch it, run back, and tag the next child in line, who would repeat the sprint to the fence, and so on. When Herman came forth and was tagged, he just stood there, smiling nervously, looking around for the runner in the next line to take off, waiting to mimic his neighbor. The kids in his line howled. I ran up alongside him, tugged his coat sleeve, and said, "Herman, *you* run, like this," and paced him for about a quarter of the distance before I peeled away. He stumbled, ran hesitantly, then took off, breath steaming, and locked into the idea of the race.

An hour or so later, I accompanied Herman to Angela McNair's tutorial. Angela was one of the aides funded by federal money, and among her duties was the responsibility for conducting tutorials with Herman and two other children who were more recent arrivals to Stephanie's class. She did this two or three times a week, depending on her schedule. She conducted close, fundamental work with words and numbers: basic word recognition (*cat, boy, saw*), simple sentence reading (*The boy saw the cat*), and beginning arithmetic — counting, the number line, simple addition and subtraction. The kind of thing that would be done in special ed. Angela was street smart and caring, and kept the kids on task and praised them generously. Herman did pretty well with her, particularly when she could get him to focus on his own work and not look to the other children for cues. I told her about the incident on the playground, and she suggested that I slide down the table with him and do some arithmetic.

Herman went for this. Ever since my first day in Stephanie's class, Herman had been hugging me, asking me to read to him, or just rushing into my legs, grabbing on, and looking up, smiling. Stephanie noticed and asked me to spend time with him, reading and helping him with his letters. When we first scooted down the bench, I asked him to work with the number line — adding 6 to 2, deciding if 8 was greater than 2, that sort of thing. He had a hard time of it, getting jumpy, looking with a grim smile over his shoulder to the other kids, his usual strategy failing him. I put my arm around his shoulder and turned him toward me. "Herman," I said, holding his gaze, "you can do this. *You* can do this. Just stick with me and look at what's in front of you and go slow. I'll help you." And so we started. Simple stuff. But Herman watched and concentrated — and he could do it. He counted along. He could say which number was bigger. When he got something right, he smiled broadly, not that sad smile of his, but one that was steady and full. At the end, I complimented him, and he turned to me and, with unusual seriousness, said, "See, I don't have my brain turned off."

Later that day, once the children had gone home, I told all this to Stephanie, and she listened, nodding, somber as I'd seen her. "I know," she said, closing her eyes, rubbing her forehead with her fingertips. "I know he can do it. If from the start he could have been in here and had that kind of close work every day . . ." Herman had entered first grade late, and he did not come in knowing what many of the other children knew. Furthermore, he came in with needs far greater, far more urgent than the need to master cognitive skills — the need I would feel in his embrace. Maybe he came in with his mimetic strategy already developed or maybe he developed it in Mrs. Terry's classroom, but I suspect that as he saw kids doing things he couldn't do, he became anxious and tried to mimic the surface features of competence. His problems were not in neurological fiber. He required social services and tutoring. With those, he could possibly find his way in a room like Stephanie's.

Stephanie wanted to hold Herman back for another year. (Though in a city where a third of the kids fail by the third grade, this option was not without problems of its own.) She wondered out loud whether she could work with him during the summer — though these days her summers were pledged to her daughter. Herman was getting some valuable things by being in a class like hers: he responded to the images of Black people; he liked to hear stories; he was captivated by the frogs and newts and hermit crabs. And if she had had the time, she could have turned his powers of observation to scientific ends. But she couldn't kid herself. She knew how far behind he was. She could see that the close, skills-oriented tutoring he received from Angela worked. But could she be the person who sent him forth with the tens of thousands of other African-American children into special ed? We sat together talking through the evening, going from school to a coffee shop. She was uncharacteristically agitated. There was no satisfying answer. She was alone, finally, with a decision that would tear her either way she went.

> We'll learn a lot while we are here.
> And some of us will shed a tear.
> But we will try to do our best.
> To prove to you, we'll stand the test . . .

Every Friday, Duke Ellington had an assembly. All three hundred of the prekindergartners, kindergartners, and first-graders would gather in the large open area by the cafeteria. There would be songs, a few recitals, a math puzzler posed by a first-grader, and a list of weekly accomplishments read by the school's principal, Barbara Grier: the rooms with perfect attendance, students who had won achievement awards. Applause and much praise. One Friday I attended, a group of kindergartners recited Christina Rossetti's "Who Has Seen the Wind." They came out wearing big, floppy hats and spoke the lines in unison, chests out, heads back:

Who has seen the wind?
Neither I nor you;
But when the leaves hang trembling
The wind is passing through . . .

On hitting the poem's last couplet, they whipped off their hats, which, I then realized, represented bushy treetops, and took a full, dramatic bow:

But when the trees bow down their heads
The wind is passing by.

The pianist followed with the school anthem — the words were set to the tune of "O Tannenbaum" — and a wave of voices sang along, straining, but holding to the melody. Angela, Stephanie, and I stood behind a large group of students and sang with them:

Duke Ellington, Duke El-ling-ton
Our school is num-ber one.

The children were kneeling or sitting on mats; Frank's voice was loudest, the others rising and falling, eager and unsteady. Herman was leaning back, propping himself against one of my shins, Shereese was against the other:

. . . we will try to do our best,
To prove to you, we'll stand the test.

There was a good deal of emphasis at Duke Ellington on achievement and on rewarding children for it. The assemblies were public celebrations of academic prowess, and over the year all the children from all the classes would participate. Day by day, all around the school, you would find the children's work on display: by the entrance, along the hallways, outside the classrooms. Stories, lists of books, drawings, art paper constructions, trophies, and plaques. The reputation Stephanie enjoyed in the school was related to that achievement. Mrs. Peck was an aide who had been at Duke Ellington since it opened in 1973. "Stephanie's kids learn what they've got to learn," she told me, nodding in approval. "She makes them feel good about themselves." Starting outside Stephanie's room, a bookworm wiggled along the top of the wall and extended all the way down the corridor and around the corner over the top of the kitchen. He had a grin on his face and wore a puffy bow tie. His body was constructed of little circular segments, and on each segment there was written the title of a book read by one of Mrs. Terry's students. A sign by his head said: "Help our bookworm grow and grow. Pick a good book to read and enjoy." The cafeteria manager, Betty Lee, laughed. "Isn't that something?" she said, looking up, "I don't know where that thing's gonna end!"

You didn't have to be at Duke Ellington long to understand how important this achievement was. The student body was virtually 100 percent African American, a reflection of the de facto segregation in the city of Baltimore, segregation that has always carried with it brutal economic consequences. In 1920 the Maryland public school system's expenditure per child was $36.03 for Whites and $13.20 for Blacks; in 1990 the average Baltimore city classroom, which is predominantly African American, had $40,000 to $50,000 less to spend on its children than a classroom in predominantly White Baltimore County. In its way, therefore, P.S. 117 became another site of struggle and hope in the long, powerful history of Black life in America. Learning to read and write and do science was important not only for Frank's or Rachel's or Romarise's future, but important, as well, because it represented what a people could achieve in the face of oppression. A verse in the school song went:

Our reading scores will never fall.
We'll grow up always standing tall.

That sounds like pretty dull business for a rousing anthem, until you consider it along with another song the children sang:

Sing a song full of the faith
that the dark past has taught us.
Sing a song full of the hope that
the present has brought us.

One of the things Stephanie did with her classroom was to open its doors wide, to extend it to the neighborhood beyond. Parents lingered in the morning to talk, would stop by during their lunch break — a father in overalls settling into a tiny chair — to check up on a child's progress.

They often volunteered to help out: to drive the kids to a field trip, file the children's work, or decorate the room. Stephanie had what she called a "parents' journal," and in it parents could record their impressions of their children's development, or ask questions about how a child should be doing homework, or offer suggestions. Stephanie also encouraged them to contribute their observations to the language of the classroom — and in doing this was, in her way, extending Duke Ellington's celebration of achievement to them, honoring the achievement of their lives and their hopes for their children.

During Black History Month, for example, she asked them if they would like to contribute to a class journal she and the students would be creating. "Will you, too, be a part of this celebration by writing or by illustrating 'What Black History Month means to me.'" She got responses like these:

> Black History means a very great deal to me. To know and to remember all the famous Blacks who have made a difference in this world gives me the strength and the courage to be the best I can be.
>
> Black History Month is a time to pay tribute to all of the famous Black Americans who made a difference [and] to acknowledge the fact that the struggle is not over and [to] have our ancestors before us as role models to help us better deal with the situations of today.

And from Rachel's mother, this poetic vignette:

Child: Sojourner Truth? I've heard that name.
What did she do to earn her fame?
Langston Hughes? Haven't got a clue.
First Black doctor? You say Charles Drew?
Harriet Tubman? A courageous woman.
Garret Morgan, the first stop light.
You mean our people actually lit up the night?
Lawyers, doctors, aviators, musicians?
Nurses, scientists, explorers, mathematicians?!
Even entertainers like
Cosby and Aretha queen of soul?
Wow! All my people . . . I didn't know.

Parent: Sit right here child, next to me
As I unlock the door to your Black History.

Not all the parents responded, of course, and not all were so articulate and inventive. But some of them were enrolled in high school equivalency courses or were going to community college, and some read extensively as part of religious observance or in tandem with personal educational journeys. And they wanted to put their thoughts forward, to enter Mrs. Terry's celebration and join their voices with their children's voices.

Stephanie often talked about the building of *community,* a word used frequently these days — frequently and loosely. But the more time I spent with Stephanie, the more involved I understood her use of the word to be. There was, of course, her school's position in the neighborhood. And there were the personal links Stephanie had formed with the custodians, cafeteria workers, aides, and other teachers, which affected the way her children were perceived and treated. There was her classroom, a civil place. But there was more to it: when Stephanie used the word *community,* she was not simply referring to a location or to a web of social arrangements, but to a goal, something in process, something to be achieved.

Stephanie was trying to create a place where Black life could flourish. Where the glory of one's history was in the bookshelves, on the walls. Where learning was fun and purposeful and spanned a broad range of activity and discipline. A place from which Black children could move forth, strong, open, curious.

"That's my basic question." Stephanie was saying. "What do I have to do to help my children see themselves as a community of writers?" It was a question that nagged at her — trying to specify, to gain precision. "How do I . . . how does anybody create the conditions for that sense of community to develop? That's what I want to research, to explore."

"I'm curious about that, too," said Joe from the other end of the table. "I'd ask the same question about the international students I teach."

"I would think," observed Padma, jotting a note to herself, "that the answer lies in all those things you *do* do. All of it."

"Yes, OK," said Stephanie, leaning over to catch Padma's eye, "but how do I describe the process to someone who's not in my classroom. How do I help them to see how to do it, too?"

Joe Bellino, Padma Krishnan, Stephanie, and five other Baltimore-area teachers sat around a makeshift table in front of the science displays. They had been meeting like this twice a month . . . or once every month . . . or whenever they could to talk about their teaching and the questions that arose from it. As Stephanie put it, "The group provides a way to enter conversations beyond those possible in the teacher's lounge." In addition to Stephanie, Joe, and Padma, there were, around the table, Sandy Scott, wryly called Dr. Scott by her colleagues here because of her resonant voice and magisterial presence; Arthur Seidel, intense, speculative, who went by "Otts," a regional nickname for Arthur; Diane Mitchell, Diane Laverne Thomas Mitchell, who was consumed with questions about the human dimension of computer-assisted instruction; there was entrepreneurial Jacki Rone, who had established a mentoring program with local businesses; and Pam Morgan, who was the chair of the English division of a local middle school. The history of their meetings was, in a way, a case study in the building of a sense of community.

These eight teachers worked in different schools with different levels of students — Padma in kindergarten, Sandy Scott in middle school, Joe in high school — levels infrequently represented around the same table. They worked with different constituencies — special education, standard classroom, honors, African American, White working class, immigrant Cambodian, Haitian, and Salvadoran — and, though all were interested in language development, they ranged in expertise from English to mathematics. Their own backgrounds and cultural affinities varied — Padma was born in India, Joe and Otts were European American, Stephanie, Sandy, Diane, Jacki, and Pam were African American — and their personal passions and commitments were all over the map. Yet all of them cared deeply about the urban public school and felt a strong need to test their own ideas and find out what others were doing. It was these "mutual concerns," as Dr. Scott called them, that first brought the teachers together.

But all those differences were potentially divisive. From what I was told, the group spent a long time getting to know and trust each other. How would Joe's work with immigrant students intersect with Stephanie's? How would Padma's kindergarten-level perspective jibe with Otts's high school concerns? How would a mixed-race group work harmoniously in these awful times? There were hot moments — moments of fragmentation and suspicion — and temptations to retreat to one's own turf, but the group, engaged by their commitment to the urban school, came to terms with their differences, and in some cases learned powerful things from them. As I sat there among Sandy and Joe and the rest, I was struck by their sense of cohesion, by their ease and focused intelligence and mutual respect.

Two people in the group were representatives of local teacher-education institutions: Elyse Eidman-Aadahl from the Maryland Writing Project, housed at Towson State, just north of Baltimore, and Lisa Delpit, from Morgan State, a historically Black college in the northeast quadrant of the city. It was through Elyse and Lisa, and the avenues their institutions provided, that the teachers began, a year or so ago, to bring their questions and their expertise beyond their own borders. They met with teachers in other districts; they spoke at conferences in Boston, in Philadelphia; they got to talk with people who were trying to explore the same issues that absorbed them. "Teachers don't normally get the opportunity to do this," Stephanie told me later. "These opportunities allow people like me the luxury to dream, to take risks." Her voice became more cadenced, emphatic. "I just have the sense that I'm not out there struggling alone. Other teachers should have this opportunity. You can't teach alone."

I imagined Stephanie at one of those gatherings. She was trying to find words to describe her curriculum and the mood it engendered. She talked about the children's work and the parents and Duke Ellington — pushing, questioning what it might mean to have a community of writers. She wanted others to see, to say, yes, this is possible, yes. The tree frog, the Venn diagrams, the zoo stories, *Amazing Grace,* the Morning Circle. The bookworm, inching along, heads for the far corner of the cafeteria, toward the door. The children's work is moving beyond itself. An exemplar and an offering. "Welcome to grade one," I could hear Stephanie saying to some new audience. "Yes, welcome. I'm glad you're here."

4

Chicago, Illinois

I THE STEPS to the old Victorian houses were covered with leaves, the sidewalks too. As I stepped off the curb, my foot sank with a soft crackle into a street thick with leaves. Elm and maple. And the cars, all the cars, were speckled, as if from the indiscriminate fling of a house painter's brush, with the small gold, oval leaves of the tree called black locust. Hyde Park. On the South Side of Chicago by the lake, six miles southeast of the downtown financial district, the Loop. The houses were two and three stories high — turrets, bay windows, leaded glass — and the yards were punctuated with clusters of late-blooming roses and bright yellow marigolds. There was more modest housing, too, subsidized, neat two-story, brick and wood. And there were a few sites of construction. FINANCED BY MID TOWN BANK, a sign read. INVOLVED FROM THE GROUND UP. It was the week before Halloween, jack-o'-lanterns and frenetic skeletons in the windows — the sun full and warm on my face, softening the chill. Kenwood Academy was only three or four blocks away, to the east, on Blackstone Avenue near Fiftieth Street, three quarters of a mile from the University of Chicago, close, as well, to a vast stretch of South Side ghettoes. Hyde Park was one of the few integrated neighborhoods in what some call the most segregated city in the nation. "Rather than race," Studs Terkel wrote in *Division Street: America*, "class is the factor here."

Most people were off at work by now, kids at school. There was the occasional slam of a back door, a car starting up in the distance. As far down the street as I could see, the trees extended and crisscrossed, layered, canopied, leaves casting shadows on other leaves, a dappling of light and shadow. The leaves were red, some almost purple, and gold, gold. I passed a park, empty now, where an older woman sat on a bench, alone. She wore layers of clothes — frayed sweaters and a loose coat — and she was talking vigorously to no one: "I say, I say, 'I *am* somebody.'"

Close, now, to Blackstone, I turned the corner, the wind catching me, sharp as I inhaled. School buses passed, their exhaust acrid in the chill. WARNING, a sign announced, SAFE SCHOOL ZONE. Then I heard the *slap, slap, slap.* I wasn't sure what it was, but it got louder as I walked north — and then I saw the flagpole of Kenwood Academy. Silver against the clear, blue sky, the flag fluttering, the cable extending nearly the full length of the pole, slapping hard in the wind off the lake.

"I was completely confused," said Alastair. "I could understand some of the characters a little. But it was like I needed a key, a view." "I was confused utterly . . . until I got to the very end," added Raina. Brian smiled, "I never thought I could enjoy something so difficult . . . and so horrible." It was the first day of the two weeks that Steve Gilbert's advanced placement English class would be devoting to William Faulkner's *As I Lay Dying.* Steve assigned the novel with some trepidation, a grisly, tragicomic story told by a number of different characters, with no organizing narrative voice. It is a very hard book. Would the students be able to engage it, Steve had wondered. Would it just be baffling? So, when the initial comments about confusion began to shift — he would later tell me — he felt not only relief, but a rush of excitement.

"Did you like, in any way," he asked the class, "that experience of not knowing exactly what was going on?"

Qisha leaned into the small circle of desks — there were only eight students in the class — and began her quick, glancing articulation. "At the beginning I was lost; then I stopped. I realized I couldn't read this book like the others — and I went back and read slowly. Then I started getting it. I thought Faulkner was having a lot of fun with the reader. I liked it. It's like you get all these different people's views of themselves. And you see the way that . . . that people say one thing but think another. It's kinda . . . unlike *Fathers and Children* or *Brave New World,* it doesn't really seem like fiction. I mean, we know *Fathers and Children* is a story — someone tells it to us — but this is more like real life."

It was at this moment that Steve felt that rush.

"My objective for the first day," Steve explained later as we sat in his office, reviewing my notes on the class, "was to raise the question of how we know things. And the way we know things in fiction is through a narrator. When you come into this novel, you soon realize that there is no one who, as Alastair said, will give you a key. The excitement of the novel, I think, comes from the lack of equilibrium that we feel from constantly having what we know undercut. And it was Qisha who laid the groundwork to talk about that. She's a very powerful reader. She began answering my question before I asked it."

Steve Gilbert had been at Kenwood Academy since 1981, and had been teaching for thirteen years before that. His primary duties were now administrative: he coordinated a Gifted and Talented Magnet Program that enabled children from around the city — about ninety per year — to complete their last two years of elementary school (the district has very few junior high or middle schools) in an accelerated course of study at Kenwood, and then enter the school's regular student body at the ninth grade. The program resulted in a greater racial and class mix than would otherwise be likely. Though Hyde Park itself is integrated, a number of residents, White and Black, send their children to private schools; furthermore, much of the area surrounding Kenwood Academy — other than Hyde Park — is poor and segregated. The Seventh- and Eighth-Grade Program that Steve coordinated drew in a mix of students that was about a third White, a third African American, and a third Latino and Asian. Just under a third of Kenwood's eighteen hundred students entered the school via that route. Some of the students in AP English came through the program.

So Steve spent a good deal of time recruiting — talking at length to parents and children, devising the children's schedules, and monitoring their progress. He recruited for the entire school as well, for there were several ways by which Chicago parents could send their kids to school outside their neighborhoods. He was constantly on the move, typing a hurried memo with a forward tilt of the head, as though he were looking over the top of his glasses, returning phone calls lined up on his answering machine, checking records and verifying grades, sitting with parents, consulting with faculty. Then, as the clock ticked toward the minute of his class, he would grab his briefcase and rush out, with a slight sideways bend — Steve was a tall man, six foot one or two — out the door and down the hall.

Things were even more hectic than usual during my visit, because the Chicago school district was caught in a severe, politically intractable budget crisis. It was throwing the schools into turmoil. I had come to Chicago to observe Steve Gilbert's racially mixed advanced placement class, one of interest to me, for historically AP courses have been, de facto, pretty segregated offerings. But as the crisis wore on, and as its progress revealed more and more about the nature of public schooling in this city, I would be drawn as well to other classes, other schools, and all became part of my perception of teaching and learning in Chicago. I'll present some of that journey as we accompany Steve and his students in their exploration of *As I Lay Dying* — shuttling between his classroom and others — for connections emerged, resonances in the voices I heard, relations between Faulkner's epistemology and the way life in school gets defined in America. And always present, as shadow or stage, was the economic and political reality of the Chicago public schools.

An entire generation of Chicago's children has come of age in an atmosphere of public school crisis: budget shortfalls, charges of bureaucratic incompetence and corruption, stalemate between the board of education and the teachers' union and between the city and state. There have been nine teachers' strikes in eighteen years. It is a system that, in one observer's words, "is in near-fatal collapse." Here is a sketch of the current disaster.

The district, after trying to balance its budget with an early retirement program that fell short, came to the school year with a deficit of $300 million. Because of past deficits, the state legislature long ago passed a law mandating that the Chicago schools must have a balanced budget before they could open. At the last minute, the board tried a further cost-cutting move to reduce staff: they trimmed the number of periods in the school day, lengthened each new period, and increased class size. This sent schools scrambling to reorganize their day and somehow compensate for lost personnel. (Steve's program, for example, was threatened, and he had to fight bitterly to save it.) And, in a desperate pre-emptive strike, the board sought an injunction by a federal district judge, appealing to desegregation law, arguing that the schools can't be integrated if they're not open. The judge complied. A series of such court orders has kept the schools in session through October.

During the month, the board and the teachers' union finally agreed on a contract — the teachers had gone to work without one — and as part of the agreement, the board was to borrow $110 million from the teachers' pension fund to help run the schools. But the legislature in the state capital at Springfield, two hundred miles to the south, refused to agree to the contract and the borrowing plan. So the 411,000 students in the Chicago public school district lurched forward week to week on the force of the federal court orders. The people I talked to downstate were fed up with the district in Chicago. "Why can't those people get their act together?" one exclaimed. A state representative from the south wrote in the *Champaign-Urbana News-Gazette* that Chicago children were "being shortchanged by an inefficient system that relies on a bloated bureaucracy and perks . . . and 'featherbedding' work rules." Other social dynamics were playing out, both downstate and in the suburbs and small cities around Chicago. A letter writer from an affluent city to the north complained in the *Chicago Tribune* of "the virtual enslavement of those who work for a living," of taxpayers being "soaked [to] provide . . . Rolls-Royce physical plant[s] and lavish pay scales . . . to placate the minority population." He concluded by suggesting that Chicago secede from Illinois to become the fifty-first state.

So when that clock inched up on sixth period, Steve would grab his briefcase with a feeling of pleasure, ready to engage, for fifty minutes, in a different kind of intensity: textual and immediate and human.

Advanced placement courses of the sort Steve was teaching were created in the mid-1950s, as an experiment among a small number of elite colleges and secondary schools whereby "able and ambitious students" could take college-level courses and through examination gain college credit while still in high school. The program gained full momentum in 1957 with the launching of Sputnik, and as it evolved — a daunting 360,000 students took AP exams in 1991 — it has encouraged the development of challenging curricula in most of the schools that participate (nearly 50 percent of the nation's high schools) and has enabled more than two and a half million students to accelerate through their lower division course of study. There are some problems with AP, however. The original architects of advanced placement tended to take a conservative view of their disciplines and were anxious that subject-matter integrity not be compromised as colleges gave up control of disciplinary standards. Though more recent staff at the College Board and the Educational Testing Service — the overseers and administrators of the program — have worked to expand the AP guidelines and exams, there is still a traditionalist bent to the program, and it places constraints on what teachers can do. For the clear bottom line is that they have to prepare their students for the test.

Steve's extensive teaching experience included honors and AP English, but this current assignment came to him suddenly, when the regular AP teacher retired about a month before school opened. He reworked that teacher's reading list as best he could on short notice, but it was still, as he put it, "very much a University of Chicago canon." He planned to revise the entire course over the summer, keeping its rigor, but making it more inclusive and giving it a more coherent and critical focus. Here, then, is the reading list that Alastair, Qisha, and the rest were working from when I arrived at Kenwood — a list Steve continued to amend through the year.

Ivan Turgenev	*Fathers and Children*
Aldous Huxley	*Brave New World*
William Faulkner	*As I Lay Dying*
Toni Morrison	*Sula*
Joseph Conrad	*Heart of Darkness*
Chinua Achebe	*Things Fall Apart*
Franz Kafka	*The Metamorphosis*
James Joyce	"The Dead"
Richard Wright	*Native Son*

Henry James	*Portrait of a Lady*
Maxine Hong Kingston	"No Name Woman" (from *Woman Warrior*)
Sophocles	*Oedipus Rex* and *Antigone*
William Shakespeare	*Merchant of Venice, King Lear* (or *Twelfth Night*), *Hamlet*
Friedrich Dürrenmatt	*The Visit*
Tom Stoppard	*Rosencrantz and Guildenstern Are Dead*

There was also a selection of poetry, some of which Steve would choose by consulting old AP exams: Wordsworth, Keats, Hopkins. After covering each work, students wrote in-class papers, preparing them for the demands of the exam. They also had to write a research paper. Then there would be a final project that, after all the strictures of advanced placement preparation, would encourage a throwing-off of fetters, a free-ranging, creative response. Students were in some way to address the basic existential question, to express their sense of the meaning of life. They had to incorporate three or more of the works they read, but could write poetry or fiction or drama, produce a video, or work in oil or charcoal or collage or ceramic. Steve hoped this would provide an alternative way for his students to integrate the reading and establish a personal connection to it.

Before I arrived, the class had read *Fathers and Children* and *Brave New World,* two books with an omniscient narrator and traditional narrative structure. *As I Lay Dying* provided a radical jolt. It was published in 1930, drafted, Faulkner claimed, in six weeks while he worked nights at the University of Mississippi power plant, written, when the furnaces permitted, on the bottom of an overturned wheelbarrow. The novel consists of fifty-nine vignettes told by fifteen characters, most of them poor rural Southern Whites, some of whom speak in a direct and uncomplicated manner — though in regional dialect — while others speak in a mix of direct address, recollection, reverie, and stream-of-consciousness.

The story is this — though it by no means emerges this readily. Addie Bundren is dying and has asked her husband, Anse, to bury her in Jefferson, her place of birth, some forty miles away. She has also asked that her oldest child, Cash, a carpenter, build her a proper coffin, and that he build it outside her window, in her line of sight, so that she can be sure of its quality. Once Addie dies, the journey to Jefferson begins — Addie's coffin resting unsteadily in the Bundrens' old wagon — only to be disrupted by a washed-out bridge, where the coffin is almost lost, and a barn fire that nearly incinerates it. The journey provides multiple revelations (and takes so long that Addie's body begins to decompose), and by the time the family reaches the graveyard, we realize that many of the family had their own private motives for accompanying Addie to Jefferson.

Addie had five children. Cash, the carpenter, takes a craftsman's pride in building his mother's coffin, and is compassionate in a reserved, literal-minded way. Trying to save the coffin in the flooding river en route to Jefferson, he breaks his leg, and, with bones held roughly in place by a makeshift and mutilating cement cast, rattles along in silent pain atop the box he has built for his mother. Darl is keenly observant and introspective. Though he and Cash share some feelings, we gradually discover that two of the three other siblings, Jewel and Dewey Dell, hate him. He is the most frequent speaker and, at times, seems to be telepathic, becoming almost a central narrator. At the end, however, he is declared insane for torching the barn in which his mother's body was temporarily stored. Jewel, the third son, is physical and harsh, but in truth is fiercely devoted to his mother and speaks of her in a language of violence and protection. Dewey Dell, the only daughter, about seventeen, describes things in a sensual and enticing way, but is not wordly wise and is secretly pregnant. Vardaman, a child, is retarded and prone to simplified and confused associations. Fearing his mother is suffocating in the coffin, he drills holes in the top and into his dead mother's face. Because Addie died on the same day he caught and killed a huge fish, he gradually comes to believe — in a moment that sent Steve's class over the top — that "my mother is a fish."

"I like," Qisha was saying, "the way people aren't what they seem to be."

"Can you give us an example?" Steve asked.

"You take Darl," Qisha continued. "He seems to be the only one who has a lot to say, and we kind of come to rely on him, and then he's declared insane!"

"Qisha," Steve said, "given the point you're making, this would be a good time to return to something you said earlier. You said that *As I Lay Dying* was not like a traditional narrative, was more like real life. Can you say more about that?"

"Well," she answered, "there isn't somebody in your life telling you what to think, someone to organize what you see, what you hear. And, like that, this book just gives you the pieces of thought."

Steve glanced from Qisha to the rest of the class, panning the circle. "One thing we do all the time," he said, "is tell each other stories. We organize experience into narratives. So if we don't have a single story, if we have a series of stories, how do we determine truth?"

Ayana, quiet up till then, looked over at Steve, touching her glasses. "We compare the stories, try to determine accuracy that way."

"OK," said Steve. "Let's find a good example." And he began flipping through his copy of the novel — which was heavily annotated — and read contradictory selections from Darl, from Cora, a sanctimonious neighbor, and from Jewel himself on the topic of Jewel's feelings for his mother. "Now," said Steve, "how do we come to the truth about Jewel?"

"What Cora says, that's just hearsay," Ayana continued. "She's a busybody. But Darl, he was there."

"Was he?" asked Steve. "Or are we getting his perception?"

Ayana pondered that. "No, actually, he sees Jewel through his eyes — and he has a funny relationship with Jewel."

Steve came to class knowing that, at some point in the day, he would go to the board and ask the class to list all the things they thought they knew, the events they felt sure of. And at that moment, when Ayana was pushing on the provisional nature of so much in the novel, he uncurled himself from the desk and palmed a piece of chalk.

"Let's make a list of what we think we know," he said, turning to the board to become the students' scribe.

"Well," said Brian, "we know Addie died." Steve wrote "Addie died."

"Dewey Dell is pregnant," ventured Tequia, speaking for the first time.

"They're taking Addie to Jefferson to bury her," Raina said. But, as Steve was writing, Qisha interjected: "Wait, isn't that a difficult question — I mean, what do you mean, 'What do we know?' Do you mean what people tell us or what we finally think happened? I mean, people have different reasons for taking Addie to Jefferson — so what each one would *know* is different."

"Absolutely right," said Steve, appreciating Qisha's tough-mindedness. "Good point. So maybe the best we can do is continue this list provisionally, listing what *we* think we know." The class continued: Addie's body is decomposing; Cash breaks his leg; Addie's body has holes in it; Darl sets fire to the barn. Steve was keeping a watchful eye on the clock, and just before the bell, he held up his hand, palm outward, and said, "OK, nice going, class. I'd like us to test these 'knowings' over the next two weeks."

And as the bell rang and everyone was wedging books into stuffed backpacks, Brian laughed and asked, "Yeah, but does anyone know why Darl set the barn on fire?"

II IF YOU WALKED from Steve Gilbert's class down the hallway and up one flight of stairs — jostling in the stairway among shoulders, knapsacks, thick padded jackets — then took a left turn, walked forty more feet and took a right, you'd be at Room 208, where Bonnie Tarta, Kenwood's immensely popular history teacher, was handing out to her honors section of tenth-grade U.S. history a list of the first ten amendments to the Constitution, the Bill of Rights.

Bonnie's classroom was a fairly traditional place. The chairs were lined up in neat rows, and Bonnie moved methodically from podium to blackboard. But there was ample room in her lectures for exchanges with students: a range of questions of fact and review, and "what if" questions, and thought experiments, and requests for opinion. And there was laughter and, occasionally, some mid-decibel jiving among a group of boys who sat in the middle of the room and among a smaller group of girls who sat in the front by the door. An easygoing seriousness. The walls were decorated with posters depicting suffragists, striking coal miners, and civil rights marchers; World War II factory workers; scenes of old Chicago; a map of the United States; and prints of Edward Hopper's *Nighthawks* and Archibald Motley's *Nightlife*. Except for a metal heating vent along the baseboard, the entire south wall was glass, so the room was warm with light. You could look out onto a small courtyard and watch the wind stir the branches of gold rustling leaves. Bonnie Tarta was in her mid-forties, with gentle eyes, thin face, wire-rim glasses, short curly gray hair tapered at the neck. She would laugh often with the class, a shy chuckle, dipping her head. The people in Steve Gilbert's class, most of whom had taken a course from her a year or two before, said she was "wonderful," "a great teacher," "really, really great." "She actually listens to students," said one. "She treats her students equally," said another.

The first four or five weeks of U.S. history covered the foundations of the nation's democracy: the articles of the Constitution, the establishment and roles of the three branches of government, and the Bill of Rights and other amendments. During my stay, Bonnie was focusing on the dynamics among the branches, checks and balances, and, particularly, the protection of the individual against the power of the state. A fair amount of discussion, then, dealt with protected rights, with the process of amending the Constitution, and with the judiciary — and the last was of no small interest to the students, since a federal district judge was keeping the Chicago schools in session.

Bonnie presented information and then invited discussion, which she wove in with the lesson of the day. Here is a typical moment, one that developed after Bonnie had handed out copies of the Bill of Rights and was discussing the First Amendment. Though a good number of students talked on any given day, on this day, five were especially vocal.

Bonnie: Is there absolute freedom of speech?

Dwayne: No, there's certain things you can't say on television or the radio.

Agatha: Speech can go too far. Like with hate groups.

Bonnie: But hate groups *do* have freedom of speech, don't they? Neo-Nazis can distribute leaflets, talk on the radio.

Gloria: But if you say certain kinds of things about people, about their race or their beliefs, that can cause a lot of trouble.

Bonnie: But even that might be protected.

Charmaine: OK, but certain things you might say would go against other parts of the Constitution.

Mario: [Aside, to Dwayne] Let 'em know, Charmaine!

Bonnie: Hmmm. Interesting point, Charmaine. Let's say a guy is standing on the street corner yelling obscenities about the President. Is that protected?

Mario: Yes.

Bonnie: Now let's say that same guy is in front of the White House agitating people.

Mario: Whooo. Yeah, I think, still.

Bonnie: Any circumstances where his speech wouldn't be protected?

Agatha: There'd have to be. Like, when, what do they say, you can't yell 'fire' in a theater.

Bonnie: OK, so your freedom can't jeopardize public safety or infringe on another's rights. And, also, as Charmaine pointed out, there may be conflicts with other Constitutional guarantees. A lot of this comes down to the problem of conflicting rights.

A few days later, Bonnie was engaging the class in one of her thought experiments. She asked them to imagine that they had the power to amend the Constitution. What would they do? "I think," Charmaine said, "that we should amend the Constitution to ensure education for everyone. Make it a federal responsibility. 'Cause the way it is now, it isn't working." Charmaine's suggestion hit a nerve. Some students voiced approval, but Mario pointed out that there would be a conflict, because the states would not want to give up their power. Yes, but Charmaine's plan might be more effective, said Dwayne. That led the class to speculate on the possibility that the states could keep some power, but the federal government would impose guarantees. After all, one student said, it's a federal judge who's keeping us open now.

It was a time in Chicago of strong opinion about the schools, and everyone I spoke to, especially those with kids in the public schools, had something to say. ("We're feeling frustrated and ripped-off," one mother lamented.) As I listened to Charmaine and the others, I began to wonder about *their* thoughts on the current crisis. Here they were, learning about the foundations of their government at a time when their education was being threatened by a breakdown in governance, and they were in school because a judge at the federal level intervened in the local collapse. I talked with Bonnie and was able to interview, over the week, the five students who had caught my eye a few days before.

Each was fifteen, and all but Agatha were African American. Mario was a local, born in Cook County Hospital, wiry, muscular; played football and basketball; spoke with ease and charm — the kind of kid who would be at home in a variety of settings. Dwayne was soft-spoken, had a round face, gentle eyes, a little arch to his eyebrows. He wore a Toronto T-shirt at a time when the Canadian team was playing the White Sox for the division title. Gloria spoke with punch and assurance, looked older than her years, dressed stylishly in slacks and dresses, snazzy, gold designs on purple. Agatha, whose parents were Polish immigrants — Chicago historically has had a large Polish population — came from the North Side, across the city; she wore a vest and a tuxedo-style shirt with jeans. She was, in Bonnie's words, "earnest and thoughtful." Charmaine spoke quickly and with a political and analytical bent. She was neat in jeans and white blouse, serious, an A student, and lived by the defunct steel mills in South Chicago.

Mario Kidd

Originally most schools in Chicago were on a nine-period day — and they had to go to a seven-period day at the last minute. And we didn't know what classes were going to be cut. That messed up a lot of people. I mean, for me personally, I lost typing. I want to be a computer programmer, so I have to learn how to type. Now I have to wait till next year to take typing. Still, we're lucky. Four teachers went through our programs for four straight days and reworked everybody's schedule. Every student. Eighteen hundred students! But there's a lot of schools that don't have schedules. The students have to go sit in the auditorium every day and wait. So a lot of kids just say "forget it" and don't come to school. Hang out on the streets. Get into mischief. And one thing leads to another.

See, Chicago schools must have a balanced budget to operate. No other school system in the state has to have that. Back before we were born — or right after, '79, or '80 — the board's budget was a disaster and there was a big strike, and the state made the agreement that for the Chicago schools to be open, they must always have a balanced budget. Now that agreement has come back to haunt us. It's a trip.

There's the north of the state and downstate, and a lot of times the state, the rest of the state really seems to dislike Chicago. When they try to pass legislation that will affect Chicago, downstate won't go for it. They ask what they will get out of it — though the whole state would be getting money from taxes. Chicago wanted to get a riverboat casino — and some of that money would be earmarked to go to the schools — but the Legislature said organized crime would come. But the fact is [laughs], it's *already* here. I mean, this is Chicago! See what I'm saying? Everyone's got their own priorities, and no one wants to compromise. There's a lot of screaming and yelling down at Springfield, and everybody's drawing sides, you know. I'll tell you, if it wasn't for this judge, I doubt the schools would be open today.

My question is this: Who are these people — the board, the state — they already have their education. It's hard watching the news every night, wondering, "Will I be going to school in the morning?" You feel like they really don't care. Don't nobody care. Like they forgot about the kids who have got to go to school, 411,000 kids. They keep saying "We're the future." But if we're not going to get educated, what does that say for the future of the city?

Dwayne Hamilton

Here in Chicago we've got a situation where there's not enough money to keep the schools running. So far, the schools have been running on a federal judge's decision. I think that maybe if the schools would close, it would put more pressure on the board, the teachers' union, and the state to get something done. But, then, if *nothing* gets done [pause, exasperated laugh], then I think a lot of people would try to transfer to somewhere else, if they could.

It makes me mad because you don't know if you're going to be in school or not. And if they close, they'll be closed for a long time. This is, like, every year. Last year this happened — and it just barely got resolved. And when something gets done, it's strictly short-term.

For whatever reason, the teachers' union and the board don't get along. They're not going to give an inch, either way. I don't know if that's ever going to resolve. And the legislators downstate seem slow to get anything done. I don't know if it's that they have no interest in Chicago, in kids going to school, or what. When they saw that the schools would be open another ten days, it seems like they stopped talking. It's like "We've got ten more days — let's do something on the ninth day." They're not coming close to resolving it. Every year it's like this. Every year.

Gloria Valentine

I've been in Chicago for seven years, and just about every school year there's a budget crisis and the threat of a strike. Now if every single year they know they don't have the money, I don't understand why this problem doesn't get solved. I mean, if the money is not there, they *know* it's not there — why don't they work on it before we come back to school?

Last year, they were going to cut out all extracurricular activities, but FootLocker donated money for us to have our programs. Now, this year, they're borrowing from the teachers' pension fund. But every year, the board says they don't have the money, so what makes the teachers think that they're going to be able to get that pension money when they decide to retire? The way it was coming down made the teachers look like the bad people, because they didn't want to risk their pension. But for the first four or five weeks of school they were working without a contract — and they came to work anyway. I have no idea why everything is so unstable. We have schools that are raggedy. We have schools that are closed down. Classes are getting larger. The teachers are being cut back. They're playing Russian roulette with our future.

Agatha Sajewicz

I don't know what the solution to this mess will be. I mean, they're borrowing from the teachers' *pension* fund! The whole problem is money, money, money — they're not really thinking about the students. It makes me feel cheated. I mean, if this schedule stays as it is, I'm going to have to drop my German class to take art — yeah, art — because we need an art credit to go to college. And I really wanted this German class.

It's just not right. There's always a threat, an overhanging dark cloud above us. Everybody's supposed to work together in order to keep us in school. We're the ones who should be wanting out of school [laughs], but instead, we're begging to be let in! I mean, a judge has to come in and force the issue. It's very strange. Like everything's reversed. I mean, who are the leaders here?

My parents are really angry at the system. Sometimes they say that if they could afford it, they'd send me to a private school. If the Chicago public schools don't provide us with our education, what's going to happen to the future? Everything, everything that happens amounts and accumulates to a greater sum in the end. Our geometry teacher was talking about chaos theory, about how every little thing results in some other effect. So I was thinking how, if we have a shutdown, it could discourage some students, and some of those could get into trouble, and that could have an effect on the future of Chicago kids, this generation.

Charmaine Williams

We have a federal district judge in Chicago who is keeping the schools open through desegregation laws. If the schools are closed, then they can't comply with the law — I mean, students can't be mixing if they're not able to go to school. That's real flimsy, but it's keeping the schools open.

I've been thinking that if the schools were located in richer neighborhoods or had a majority of White students, they would look at this as a major problem and get it fixed sooner. But because it's primarily a minority school system, they don't seem to think it's as great a problem. I mean, it's evident in other things that go on. Like, my uncle, he lives in a neighborhood that's mainly White, and it's a very nice neighborhood. Well, they call the city about a problem — like they may call about the streets — and it gets taken care of. Now, we had some buildings burn down around my house; a couple of old stores caught fire. So a few days later, my mother called about this because she knows kids play around there, and she didn't want anybody to get hurt. So she calls and asks if the buildings could be torn down or boarded up or something. Well, she had to make five phone calls, and it took months and months. It just takes so long to get anything done in our neighborhoods. And so I'm thinking that it's the same problem with the schools. It's evident in every other aspect of government [rushed, with emotion]. Everyone is important. They shouldn't treat people differently because of their race or the neighborhood they live in. I mean, things wouldn't look so crappy where we live if there weren't burned buildings all around, if the streets weren't all torn up, full of potholes and everything.

I think a teacher has one of the most important jobs in the United States — educating students so they can be of some significance in the future — and they're treating teachers like their jobs aren't worth anything. They pay basketball players so much more, and how are *they* helping people?

I realize there's things going on that I don't understand, I don't know much about all the legal stuff, but it makes me feel like me and the other students aren't worth enough for them to sit down and say: "We have to get this solved. No matter what, we're going to compromise and come up with a solution." It gets so frustrating, you think, "Well, I'll go to a private school and get away from the problem." But that's not the answer. You can't do that. You can't run away from it. What we need to do is speak out. Say "this is important!" No one has the right to keep people from getting the best education they can, from trying to make the best of themselves.

Bonnie's students were on to things that would be hard to learn from a survey of how the branches of government function in the abstract: the history of distrust between labor and management; the often unproductive tensions of party politics; the play of regional rivalry and the mutual incomprehension of people, urban and rural; the influence of class and race in governance and the delivery of services; and the fierce protection of privilege. What they knew as well was that teaching and learning in the Chicago public schools had to somehow go on in the midst of all this. It was always there, and placed profound limits on the possible.

III STEVE THOUGHT HIS CLASS had done very well with the overall structure of *As I Lay Dying* and had spoken beautifully about the problem of knowledge, how we come to know what we know in the book. Now it was time to push further, the close, careful work of literary analysis. Over the next week, Steve would have his class examine the novel's individual characters.

"Faulkner doesn't tell us how to read these characters," he explained just before class. "It requires a careful accumulation of data to help us understand these people. And without a narrator to guide you — just like in 'real life,' as Qisha said — there's just so much material! You have to carefully assemble that material in your mind in order to make any kind of intelligent judgment. I want my students to understand texts in a way that will allow them to be thoughtful readers, people who can discuss literature thoughtfully. I don't want them to have a vague, sloppy sense of a text. I want their understanding to be grounded in details."

One technique he used to get the class to consider the motives and perceptions of the characters in *As I Lay Dying* was to have them read as a unit all the sections told by a single character. So, for Wednesday, they were to have read all of Cash's sections; for Thursday, all of Dewey Dell's. For though "the placement of the sections is very important in this novel, let's see what happens when we look at a single character this way."

Cash speaks in five of the fifty-nine sections. In the first, he provides a list of the reasons he beveled each of the planks of the coffin: "There is more surface for the nails to grip," "It makes a neater job," and the like. In the second and third sections, which are brief, he voices protestations and warnings about the need for Addie's coffin to be balanced in the wagon. (And, in fact, the coffin will dump into the swollen river, and Cash will break his leg in the accident, so for much of the journey he will ride atop Addie's coffin in silent pain, mumbling, when conscious, that the injury "don't bother none.") But in his last two sections, which come at the end of the book, he speaks at length. He articulates the values of order and craft evident in his earlier behavior: "Folks seems to get away from the olden right teaching that says to drive the nails down and trim the edges well . . . It's better to build a tight chicken coop than a shoddy court house." And he gives us the account of Darl's capture and removal to an asylum for burning the barn where his mother's coffin had been stored. Although he cannot justify the destruction of the barn — he believes too much in order and craft for that — he also "ain't so sho that ere a man has the right to say what is crazy and what ain't."

Steve began with Tequia, whom he had characterized to me as shy, not vocal in class, but "very sharp, someone you would like to know."

"Tequia, what did you first notice about Cash?"

"He seemed real mechanical to me," she said. "I didn't feel like I really knew him."

"His carpentry," ventured Aisha, "is like a focus that keeps him from being crazy like some of the others. Concentrating on the carpentry, trying to bevel all those boards, that keeps him steady."

Raina looked across to Tequia. "Is he so mechanical after all? 'Compassionate' may not be the word, but he's something like compassionate."

Tequia didn't respond, but Qisha did. "I think he's too cut-off, too clear-cut, too stingy with his emotions. He's so 'not-there.'"

"I don't know," wondered Ayana, looking out at the class. "By the end of the book he seemed wiser to me than the others. Everyone else in the book seemed 'out there' — but he seemed, finally, to be kind of wise. Building the coffin was something he could *do.*"

"Doesn't he put his passion," asked Alastair, "*into* the building of the coffin?"

"I think it's important," said Aisha, glancing up at Steve, tapping the book solidly with her finger, "to show different reactions to death — and Cash's is one of them."

"Qisha," Steve said, seizing the moment, "if we believe what Aisha just said, then aren't we obliged to try to understand the *language* of Cash's reaction —"

At that moment, the public address system came on with an announcement about the day's abbreviated schedule. Steve sighed in exasperation, cut off before he could finish the point.

As soon as the announcement ended, Chris spoke: "I thought he was very passionate in the building of the coffin. I thought it was moving, building that box. I like that."

Chris's response helped Steve shake off his irritation. "You know," he said, "in all those early chapters, we hear Cash sawing in the background — it's like the novel's background music. What's he do with the planks, Chris, once he's beveled them?"

Chris: Brings them up to the window to show Addie.

Steve: Why?

Chris: To show his love.

Then another public address interruption about the abbreviated schedule.

Steve picked up again, moving quickly. "We've been reading all of Cash's sections together as a strategy to help us understand him, but the *placement* of the sections in this book is important, too. What distinguishes the last two longer sections from the first three?"

Brian: He says a lot more. This is where we find out about Darl being declared insane.

Steve: Why is he talking more? Any ideas?

Brian: Maybe because Darl is taken away?

Alastair: He kind of takes Darl's place?

Steve: And what does he think about Darl?

Aisha: He questions anybody's right to say someone's insane.

Steve: OK. And what fact finally makes Cash judge Darl?

Tequia: Burning the man's barn.

Steve: Find the passage, Tequia.

Tequia flipped through the book running her finger down the pages. "'Ain't nothing justifies the deliberate destruction of what a man has built.'"

Steve: Excellent. What really matters to Cash, what is of fundamental value to him?

Raina: Doing something right and carefully — like building the coffin. He's saying it's better to do something right than do it shoddy.

Aisha: To put your heart into it.

"I really love Cash," Steve said to me later that day. "I think he's an example of why *As I Lay Dying* is so interesting. Since we don't know the characters through a central narrator, we have to come to understand them ourselves. I mean, the awkwardness with which Cash reveals his feeling for his mother, the inarticulateness — there's something sweet and vulnerable about that. And the way he rides along in that damned bumpy wagon, you know, with his leg broken, the bones rubbing, passing out. And what's he say? 'It don't bother none.' He's so willing to erase himself, to *not* be a problem, though when you read carefully, you see he's in agony. Though I don't think I'm anything like Cash, I understand him, I can relate to him very much."

We then spoke briefly about Dewey Dell, the character the students would be discussing the following day. "I think some of the characters are more complex than the class sees yet. I'd like them to see that those characters are much more dimensional than they might have originally thought. I didn't get to make the point I wanted to about Cash's language. Maybe I can with Dewey Dell. Her motives are complex, I think, and she understands the consequences of her pregnancy. It's cruel, the way she's sent out into the world on her own. And at the end, when she realizes nothing will change — you can only imagine how she must feel. Now, Ayana said something very interesting to me the other day as we were breaking up. She said she thought Dewey Dell was 'just plain ignorant' and 'a slut.' If she'll agree, that might be a good place to begin the discussion tomorrow."

Dewey Dell speaks directly to us four times in *As I Lay Dying,* and while some of what she says is readily comprehensible, some of it is opaque and associational. What is clear is that she is pregnant by a neighboring farm boy named Lafe, is eager to go to Jefferson with the coffin so that she can get an abortion there, and, once there, is duped by an unscrupulous drug-store clerk named MacGowan and has intercourse with him, believing, initially, that it is a "cure." Murkier are Dewey Dell's motives. Though some of the language she uses is highly sensual — she feels a cow's breath "in a sweet, hot blast, through my dress, against my hot nakedness" — she also talks in a near-poetic language of the void, darkness, aloneness, and the longing for connection.

As the students were coming in, Steve took Ayana aside and asked whether she would mind repeating for the class her judgment about Dewey Dell. She said she wouldn't. So when class began, Steve turned to her, and she expressed in no uncertain terms her feelings about Dewey Dell's behavior.

Alastair responded quickly. "But in some ways, she didn't know better. I mean, she was raised with boys . . ."

Ayana shot back, "I don't buy it."

"She was naïve," Qisha said, "I don't think you should fault her."

Ayana: "Look, all her language goes back to sensual things. How naïve do you think she is?"

Tequia, sitting right alongside Ayana, started tapping Ayana's arm with her fingertips, "But that doesn't mean that's all she is."

From across the circle, Raina agreed with Ayana. "I thought she was pretty shallow. I mean, the scene with MacGowan in the drug store! My sister's a sex-ed counselor, and Dewey Dell reminds me of the girls she tells me about who think you won't get pregnant if you take a shower."

Tequia stuck to her position. "I don't think she was shallow. She didn't have any women figures in her life. Her mom certainly didn't seem to do much for her."

But Raina continued. "MacGowan's combing his hair, saying, 'Oh, come on back here for a special abortion,' and she, being such a ditz, she goes along with it."

"I just don't understand her," Ayana said finally, folding her arms.

Steve listened, then began to speak, picking his words carefully. "One thing that I personally believe is that it's very important to hear, listen closely to the language spoken by minority characters — and in this book, Dewey Dell is a kind of outsider. We have to be careful because it's very easy to define such characters — and such people in our lives — by the language of the dominant culture, of White, heterosexual male culture. We can't measure their language by that language. So let's look closely at what Dewey Dell says."

He then began a close reading of some of Dewey Dell's passages that showed the longing that drove her sexuality, zeroing in on those strange associations and moments of inarticulateness that are central to Dewey Dell's consciousness. The students read along, some looking up occasionally, surprise on their faces. Raina would later tell me that the reading shocked her and initiated a re-evaluation of Dewey Dell. ("Maybe Dewey Dell wasn't what I thought," she said to her friend Aisha the next day over lunch.) This led her to make some comparisons with Denver in Toni Morrison's *Beloved,* a character in the book she was reading for her term paper, a young woman who was also "pushed aside."

When Steve finished, Raina was the first to speak, her hand to her forehead. "Gee, I don't think I saw that at all."

"I think there's more reason for her having sex," Aisha suggested, "than just horniness — she wants a connection, to alleviate loneliness."

Steve turned to Ayana. "I know you wouldn't necessarily want to defend her, Ayana, but just as an exercise, would you try to give us a perception of the world *through* Dewey Dell's eyes?"

Ayana smiled and exhaled and leaned forward. "Well," she said tentatively, "I wouldn't want her life; there's all these people around her, yet she's alone. And I think she gets very confused — sometimes her thoughts are a jumble." Then, looking at Steve, talking with more certitude, "Look, I still don't like her character. I think she should take more control over her life." Slower, then: "But I can see why she doesn't . . . or maybe can't."

"OK," Steve said, looking from Ayana to Aisha to the rest of the class. "If you can accept Aisha's contention that Dewey Dell has sex to feel less alone, and if you can accept, at least provisionally, Ayana's hypothetical reconception of Dewey Dell, then, however else you judge her, she was at least trying to forge some connection. If you buy that, doesn't it affect your reading of Dewey Dell?"

After class, Steve reflected on the discussion. "I've been very impressed with them. This material is *so* hard. It's understandable that they would miss some of the detail in Dewey Dell. The sexual behavior is clear, but so much that surrounds it is inarticulate.

"In some ways, Dewey Dell is not *that* distant from them, from any high school student. I think her *vocabulary* is distant, yes, but the urge to escape our isolation is not uncommon. I think that what *is* uncommon for them, thank God, is that none of them would be left out there so alone. First of all, they're extraordinarily articulate. Also, they have much more support around them. I think there may be some kids here at Kenwood who might be closer to Dewey Dell. But these students are very sophisticated, and *if* one of the girls found herself in Dewey Dell's position, somebody would be there for her. And there's something else. They have a very strong sense of personal power in their lives — you can hear that in Ayana's judgment.

"I thought that what Ayana said would be an important place to begin. Because if you read Dewey Dell unsympathetically, then she is not too bright and is simply looking for sex. But I wanted the class to see what can happen when you become more sympathetic to vocabularies that aren't your own.

"Somewhere Toni Morrison says that all language is dominated by majority meanings or codes — I'm paraphrasing here — and that when we read, we're assuming these meanings. What she tries to do is to get us to see that there are other meanings. I think many students judge people on the basis of these dominant codes, these meanings. Even when you have students who are politically and racially aware — like some of the students in the class — they are still under the shadow of these codes. I think one thing a teacher can do is to help them listen to unusual vocabulary with more sensitive ears. I don't believe that only about literature [laughs]; I feel that way about life."

IV

IN THE HISTORY of Chicago public schools, a teachers' strike was not an uncommon event. But a strike in 1987 occurred during, and helped to shape, an unusual historical moment. For a decade there had been increasing documentation of the district's financial mismanagement and of the schools' poor performance. A study in the mid-1980s, for example, claimed that 75 percent of the freshmen entering Chicago public high schools were reading below national norms. This played out against a legacy of state underfunding: though 80 percent of the bilingual children and more than 50 percent of the poorest children in Illinois were attending Chicago public schools, those schools operated on less money per pupil than did schools in the suburban districts to the north and west of the city. Over the years, business had tried to intervene in traditional ways — consulting, adopting a school — and had been unsuccessful. And parents and activist teachers were frustrated in their attempts to influence what they saw as an unresponsive system. When the strike was not resolved — locked as it was in labor-management enmity and the city's intractable politics — it set the stage for the frustrated constituencies of parents, education activists, community groups, and business leaders to come together in an unlikely coalition, eventually forming the Alliance for Better Chicago Schools. The alliance drafted successful legislation that called for a radical decentralization of governance, giving more power to each of the 542 school sites in the district. Many decisions would now be made by a local school council consisting of parents, community members, teachers, and the principal — a remarkable move away from central bureaucracy and toward community control. In the judgment of historian Michael Katz, it was "the swiftest, most dramatic structural reform of any urban school system since the middle decades of the nineteenth century."

Some local school councils have been active and successful, some have not made much difference, and some have been rendered ineffective by infighting and racial discord. As Bill Ayers, a University of Illinois professor of education who chaired the Alliance for Better Chicago Schools, put it, "The Chicago school reform movement is a powerful experiment in democracy. Like every experiment in democracy, this one is full of contention and conflict, uncertainty and unevenness." And the decentralization reforms were not connected to any fundamental structural reform in the way the state funds schools, so fiscal inequity remains pretty much unchanged. As the current crisis illustrates, the terrible financial condition of the district is also unchanged, and attempts by the board to respond to it can throw individual schools into chaos. But alongside or within — it's hard to arrive at the right metaphor here — the dreary history of crisis, there has been created an activist, community-based, experimental force in the Chicago public schools. One effect has been the willingness at some schools — possibly as many as a third — to try new things, to think in new ways about teaching. Many of those reform-minded schools are following a national trend and scaling down schooling through the creation of small programs or academies within large schools. Bill Ayers has tried to foster such school-within-school experimentation by setting up, with funding from private foundations, an advocacy and advisory unit called the Small Schools Workshop. Pat Ford, an educator and community activist, co-directed the Small Schools Workshop, and during my visit, I got to spend a day riding the reform circuit with her.

Programs like those at Kenwood — Gifted and Talented magnet programs, advanced placement courses — emerged as part of an earlier national reform movement that focused on the needs of high-achieving students. One justification for such programs was that they would set a high standard of instruction for the school that housed them, but, in fact, many programs remain exclusive and separate, have had little effect on school culture at large, and tend, as educational researcher Jeannie Oakes puts it, to let the rest of the curriculum off the hook. What we desperately need is to bring to a broader range of children the kind of quality instruction and the respect for student ability that one finds in selective programs. This is what drove Pat Ford.

Pat grew up in Cabrini Green on the North Side of Chicago, one of the toughest housing projects in the city. "It *was* Cabrini," she said, her long, expressive fingers lifting off the steering wheel, "but it was home too — folks looked out for each other, you know, delivering messages, watching kids." Her mother had come to Chicago from Birmingham, part of the Great Migration northward of one and a half million Southern Blacks; her father was from Dayton, Ohio. She came of age in the projects, attending the local elementary school until the seventh grade, when she had the opportunity to go to a magnet school, then to Whitney Young High School, a school on the West Side that, in its special programs, is not unlike Kenwood Academy. When she was twelve, she began receiving tutoring at CYCLE, a community youth program based in Cabrini. At thirteen, she became a tutor herself, and through high school and college she would continue to tutor and supervise in the program, until Bill hired her a year ago. "I learned what I know," she said, "working in Cabrini Green."

In the time I spent with her, Pat committed to finding a few hundred dollars so that teachers could take their students on a field trip; conferred with a reading teacher about her school's attempt to remodel its curriculum; thought through with two other teachers at two other schools the possibilities of starting small academies, one of which would focus on health care; worried that a principal was not delegating enough responsibility to her teachers; worried, too, that teachers were jumping on the small-schools bandwagon without considering all the planning that would be necessary — and worried, therefore, that some of their efforts would fail from limited forethought. We visited schools that were thriving, schools that were holding it together, and schools that were in disarray. We talked with teachers who were on fire with a new idea and teachers treading water. We saw skillful work, and we saw the effects of underfunding and retrenchment. It was a full day. Here are four moments from it, four vignettes of hope and uncertainty in the reform counterforce in the Chicago public schools.

We began the day at Dyett Middle School at Fifty-first and Martin Luther King Drive, about eight blocks southwest of Kenwood Academy. One of the few middle schools in Chicago, Dyett was a fairly new building, metal and smoked black glass — the sun glinting off it as we drove up — located in the middle of tree-lined Washington Park. Dyett's eight hundred students were almost all African American, drawn largely from a wide stretch of the South Side ghetto. The principal, Yvonne Minor, an aggressive, forward-looking administrator, had, in the spirit of the reform movement, reorganized her faculty to set the conditions for team-teaching and the collaborative development of curricula and special programs. Last year, when the Chicago Teachers' Union issued a call for proposals to set up schools-within-schools (each grant for $1000), three young teachers who had formed a team at Dyett applied and won. So Stephanie Clark, Kim Day, and Diana Shulla were able to begin planning a new program six months in advance of the coming school year — the kind of time, Pat thought, that was absolutely necessary for such an experiment to have any chance of success. Eventually, Stephanie would leave to take a principalship at a private school, but Kim and Diana continued, and were now in the fifth week of Perspectives, an academy within Dyett that had as its general goals the enhancing of perspectives by which children consider global and local events, relations with others, personal development, and the world of work. The curriculum integrated math, science, and computers and had a strong focus on writing and the humanities. The students were sixth-graders, Black and Latino, and were of "mixed ability," were recruited, Kim would later explain, "on the strength of the parents' and kids' commitment, not on standardized test scores or past report cards."

When Pat and I walked into Kim and Diana's classroom, the students were engaged in "silent reading," that period at the beginning of the day when they read newspapers, magazines, or books of their choice. First Diana, then Kim came over to quietly greet us and invite us in to sit and read. Pat grabbed the *New York Times* and went to a table with three children, her long braids dangling over newsprint. I sat in the back by a case full of books and looked around. The children were sitting three to five at a table, the tables taking up about three quarters of the room in front of me. They were all reading, newspapers spread out, novels propped open; they wore maroon polo shirts with a circular logo *Perspectives.*

The room was neat and orderly, warm with earth tones and pastels. Close by me, under large posters of Martin Luther King and Malcolm X, was a work area that Kim and Diana had fashioned with scavenged furniture: a futon, some fat pillows — gray and rose — an old overstuffed chair, and a large oval rug, green and cream. Books were stacked all around and newspapers sat in irregular piles. The walls were filled with pictures of young people from around the globe, newspaper clippings, student writing, a huge map of the world, a poster for Latino Horizons, and a long, narrow poster of Michael Jordan, arms way, way out, one hand palming a basketball. By the map, letters running diagonally down the wall spelled out A DISCIPLINED LIFE, and around it signs on bright art paper read: "Seek wisdom," "Accept only quality work from yourself," "Hope, dream, and set goals."

Silent reading time was followed by Advisory, a period during which the class took care of its business, discussed problems, and tried to reach resolution on issues of mutual concern. (Many schools-within-schools are trying to replace the old homeroom — with its custodial air and listlessness and squawky public address system — with a period that would encourage serious discussion of problems and issues.) "Good morning, friends," said Diana, walking to the front of the room, pushing up the sleeves of her black suit jacket. "Some of you have been talking to us about problems with the new bus schedule. So let's talk about transportation." It seemed that a new driver and a change in schedule was getting kids home late, and the driver was not yet familiar with all the stops. Six or seven children spoke, and Kim and Diana listened intently. "Boy," said Kim finally, "it sounds like things are getting really confusing." "It's a different schedule," added Diana. "We've told the office about it, but you have to talk directly to the driver and let him know where you need to be dropped off." "Yes," Kim interjected, "maybe you can give him advice." At this point, several children raised their hands. "Talk to me," said Diana, moving in close to them.

The students in Perspectives were encouraged to read as many books as they could each month — during silent reading time and at home — and the next order of business for Diana and Kim was to explain the procedure for the short conferences they wanted to have with the children about these books. Basically, the children would talk with Kim or Diana one at a time about the books, what they liked about them, didn't like so well, points of connection or difference between the experiences rendered in the books and their own experience. "We want you to set your goals high," Kim said. "What do you think is possible?" asked Diana, taking the nod from Kim. "Two books, maybe three in a month? Maybe four?" Back, then, to Kim: "Take a moment and think about a reasonable goal for yourself."

Then came the questions: "Can you change your goal?" "What if I'm reading a book now, can that count?" "Can we read books in Spanish?" "If we want to read a book, and we don't have it, can we get it from the public library?" Kim or Diana answered each in turn — "yes" to all — then the questions got more complex. "What if you're reading a book that's too hard for you?" "That's an excellent question," said Diana and shot a mischievous glance at Kim. "Ms. Day, would you like to answer that question?" So Kim took the volley and sparked a discussion about how the children could tell if a book is too hard. They had some thoughts: "You have trouble understanding it." "You don't know the words." Kim said that those sounded like good indicators, and that, as the term progressed, they would all talk more about what made certain books hard to read. Diana asked if she could pose a different question. "Give me some examples of books you think might be too *easy* for you." Lots of students had responses: *Cat in the Hat, Beauty and the Beast, Little Red Riding Hood, Aladdin, Winnie the Pooh.* Glancing at the clock, Diana said, "We'll talk more about why these books seem easy to you now. That's interesting to think about, too."

Kim and Diana thanked the Perspectives students for a good session and spent the last few minutes listening to individual boys and girls summarize the discussion about the bus schedule and the reading conferences — even an announcement for their parents about a "coffee sip," turning routine information distribution into an occasion for instruction. It was the most productive use of homeroom time I'd ever seen — respectful, instructive, and engaging — and it nicely illustrated how broad changes at the institutional level can yield micro-level effects in the classroom, can affect the minute-by-minute nature of the simplest interaction. Pat pointed out how all the pieces had been in place for Perspectives to work: the support of Dyett's administration, some development money, however meager, ample planning time, and teachers with energy and a vision of the kind of classroom they desire. Later I spoke with some of Kim and Diana's students about Perspectives, which they referred to as their school. "This isn't a gang school," one said. "It's not a violent school. They teach you how to speak and write." "Students learn here," said another. "You'll feel at home here," added a third. "They don't make fun of you if you mess up."

After Dyett, Pat and I drove farther south to Sheridan, a huge, overcrowded elementary school near the corner of Commercial and Eighty-ninth, in that area of the city known as South Chicago. Sheridan's population was approximately 60 percent Latino and 40 percent African American, and at seventeen hundred students — with the number rising — it was way too packed to work effectively with small children. A number of teachers were trying to respond to the anonymity, the blurring of individual student need, by starting small academies, though things were still at an early stage of development. The principal had reorganized the building, clustering teachers with like-minded interests adjacent to one another. Some groups had begun planning, so Sheridan's long, concrete block corridors held colorful signs and banners announcing the Early Literacy Academy, the Bilingual Academy, and the Fine Arts Academy. The Fine Arts Academy was in the basement — paint peeling, pipes and heating vents crisscrossing overhead — close to the double doors of the school auditorium, and we were heading there to find Lena Linnear, the driving force behind the fledgling academy.

Pat had been spending extra time with Lena and her colleagues. Unlike those working in the Bilingual Academy or the Early Literacy Academy, they did not share a methodology or history of work with similar students and therefore had no immediate cohesiveness. This was not going to be easy. But Lena had begun to think through how an academy for fine arts might work by experimenting with her recently completed summer school class. Because it is often geared toward remediation, summer school can be a humdrum experience, for teachers and students alike, so Lena tried giving her course a fine arts focus. And as a final project, the children had to write and produce a play. The results gave her great hope. "I am so excited," Lena said when we met in her classroom. "I'm really being stretched, trying to bring all of us together, but I'm learning so much." Lena was an upbeat woman, and when she talked, she tended to tap her desk or pat her leg for emphasis. "I am *so* excited." She was beginning to imagine a new way to teach, to shape instruction, and the possibilities thrilled her.

Lena took us around the corner close to the auditorium to see some of the materials the children had designed for the play, which were still on display. There was a jovial wooden wagon, light blue with fat red wheels and big oval windows cut out of the sides. Along the sides were lavender, yellow, coral, and red high-rise buildings, all with the white-tipped waves of Lake Michigan cresting behind them. *Chicago Tour Bus* was scripted over the top. Along the walls were some striking posters, about four feet high, used as stage decoration, bright acrylics, the rich colors of a Jacob Lawrence palette. One showed children at the zoo: a giraffe whose neck was arched across the whole middle of the panel, big white eyes, a goofy smile; a stately zebra; a tentative antelope; a hot pink panther; a royal blue monkey hanging by its tail. In the right bottom corner, brown and magenta-faced children stood waving behind a sign that said *Chicago's Zoos.* In another poster, orange and blue fish and a bright green turtle swam amid bubbles and starfish and stringy ocean flora while, in a nice play with perspective, eager children on the other side of the fish looked into the aquarium, hands pressed against glass you could only imagine, the blue fish reflected in the lenses of a bespectacled, smiling boy.

It was clever, beautiful work. Pat told me she was keeping her fingers crossed. She had seen other enchanting experiments, exciting first trials that didn't generate broader consensus and find an institutional niche. A year from now, would this be noted as the first stage of a program, or remembered as a wonderful, fading success?

Sheridan fed into nearby Bowen High School, three or four blocks away, one of the oldest secondary schools in the city. With its massive stretch of dark red brick, its large unornamented windows, and its towering smokestack, it looked like a Rust Belt factory. South Chicago, close to the Indiana border, was part of the once-robust industrial sector that extended all the way to the steel mills in Gary. South Chicago had been defined by steel. U.S. Steel, Wisconsin Steel, Republic Steel. But where U.S. Steel once employed thousands of locals, there was now a vast vacant lot, weeds, broken glass, a few busted shacks. Wisconsin Steel was closed also. And Republic (now LTV) produced on a reduced schedule, and was tearing down some of its buildings. The area was terribly depressed. There were still some nice houses around the school, but just a few blocks east, beyond Commercial Avenue, were dilapidated houses and storefronts — burned, boarded up, a tangle of fallen beams, cables, and chunks of concrete. Liquor stores with gates across the front remained open. This was the area referred to by Charmaine Williams, the politically astute U.S. history student at Kenwood. Over the years, Bowen's population had shrunk from forty-one hundred to fifteen hundred students.

There was an experiment going on within Bowen that Pat was trying to encourage. The faculty had developed a small academy, forty-six ninth-graders, that aimed to prepare students to enter college and pursue a career in teaching. The academy had stirred the interest of both parents and students because it provided a sheltered environment and guided young people toward a profession. But a short while into its first year, it was already in trouble. The political and fiscal turmoil of the district and the resulting budget cuts had forced the staff to drop an advisory period during which teachers would have been able to work with individual students, to do away with the teachers' common planning time, necessary to maintain the coordinated teacher preparation curriculum, and, of all things, to cut a seminar in education.

We met Joann Podkul, a veteran teacher who was a central figure in the Teacher Prep Academy, and Maria Moreno, an intern for Teachers for Chicago, a program for people from other professions who want to enter teaching. (Maria was homecoming queen at Bowen and a student of Joann's. She had gone to college, had become a banker, and now was returning to Bowen to teach math.) We sat over trays of greens and corn and fish fillets and Jell-O and listened as the two teachers voiced their frustration.

"We're doing catch-as-catch-can with an originally thoughtful program," Joann said. Maria tapped the table, her fingers stained with mimeo ink, her nail polish chipped. "As much as we're trying, we keep getting set back." Joann smiled wearily, running both hands through her hair. "We have to do in seven periods what we had planned to do in nine. We're trying to help our students learn how to learn, and we're trying to integrate education and English and social studies and math, but . . ." "It's disillusioning," Maria said, completing Joann's thought. "But we're trying." "Look" — Joann leaned forward, a spark — "bottom line: our kids come to school with big needs for safety, so it takes a lot of support just to get them ready to learn. In the old days, a kid could drop out of high school and get a good job in the mills. Could send his kids to college. But no more." She lightly tapped her fork on her tray. "This is a program that had wide support among the faculty." People who didn't teach in the academy — a shop teacher, a special ed teacher, people "who didn't get paid a dime" for their involvement — had helped plan it and continued to stand behind it. But the academy, like the neighborhood around Bowen, was being wrenched by forces beyond its control. "It's just that we need to know," Joann said finally, "that we're doing something to help these kids survive."

Our final stop was across town from Bowen in a Latino section of Chicago called Little Village. *Carnecerias, discotecas, supermercados,* La Azteca Hardware Store, Los 3 Rosas Bar, Cancun Food & Liquor. Little Village was home to many of those — and to the parents and grandparents of those — who, as early as the 1920s, were coming north from Mexico and Central America and west from New York and the Caribbean beyond to work in the railroads, mills, and stockyards. Spry Elementary School was another large K–8 school, weathered stone, PUBLIC SCHOOL etched with minimal ornamentation high above the front entrance. As we walked toward the building, Pat explained that the current principal, Carlos Azcoitia, had been brought in by the local school council on the rush of school reform, not without some controversy and the play of race politics, and was now seen as a principal who had made a difference. He fostered productive relations with the community, and Spry enjoyed wide support. As one local activist put it, "He's entrepreneurial, fanatical, hard-working, and he knows how to access the city." Pat had to check in with Carlos about an academy planned for next year that would focus on Mexican arts and culture and was aligned with the nearby Mexican Fine Arts Museum. It turned out that Carlos was at a meeting at the central office, but the few minutes we spent trying to track him down provided their own revelations.

The foyer in Spry led quickly to a wide flight of stairs, shiny black, wrought-iron filigree between the steps ascending to the main floor. The ceiling was high, the walls cream-colored, and the window frames and doors were dark wood. A soft light suffused — like a sepia memory of an old school — but at the top of the stairs, above a receptionist seated outside the main office, a bright, unfurled *Bienvenidos* greeted us. Up and down the long hall other banners stretched, in Spanish and English: *Children of Today . . . Leaders of Tomorrow, ¡Ganas!* [desire], and alongside orange and black pumpkins and witches, *Feliz Dia de las*

Brujas. Carlos had brought in artists from the community to work with the children, and as Pat and I walked the halls we saw murals depicting the transformation of technology — giant cogs blending into railroad tracks blending into computer terminals — and the neighborhood: automobiles, little stores, a hip-hop nation fashion shop, Spry School, and, in the middle of it all, a fantastic rocket ship hovering in midair. Yellow, red, green, brown, blue. Immaculate. The floors shiny. The filigreed steps and old wood restored; the walls, the spirit vitalized.

It was clear that a lot of people took care of this place. When we finally met up with Ms. Cavey, the assistant principal, who knew the whereabouts of Carlos, I commented on the look of things. "Do me a favor," she said, "would you tell that to the chief engineer?" And so, heading back to the front door, Pat and I detoured through the cellar to find Wayne Winters, a bespectacled man in his mid-fifties. He received our compliments with little affect, and then asked if we had a minute. "Let me show you something." He led us through a corridor and through some double doors into the boiler room. The hidden engine of the school. The place was well lit and spotless, the floors freshly mopped, the corners tidy; even the flues and water pipes overhead were brushed clean. In the middle of the room sat the immense heating system, bright as a trucker's rig. Wayne was standing by us, his arms folded.

If our visit with the Perspectives sixth-graders at the beginning of the day had crystallized for me the immediate possibility of school reform in Chicago, this huge piece of machinery, like the stairway and the hallways here at Spry, represented the possibilities of material change, building — or rebuilding — the school from the community in, from the ground up. "You can have a clean building," Pat reflected as we pulled out of the parking lot, "but to have a colorful, inviting environment, that's more work. A lot of people, inside and outside the school, have to feel part of it. But it takes time. It all takes so much time."

V

SINCE STEVE GILBERT'S CLASS was justified, institutionally and fiscally, by the Advanced Placement Program and the test that certified successful completion of it, he kept the exam in mind when considering the books his students would read. "There are certain kinds of texts, *As I Lay Dying* is one, *Sula* is another," he explained, "that lend themselves to a great number of questions. There are a lot of different ways into them. And there's a 'free response' question for which you can use any text that applies. So I try to choose works that have many possibilities." A large proportion of the writing he assigned was of the type that would prepare his students for the exam: timed, in-class essays on a central theme or issue. Steve would prime the class for this task by devoting the day before to a class discussion that helped them articulate and focus their thoughts, a warm-up for the actual writing.

All this was not without its conflicts. As Steve put it: "I don't just want to teach to the AP test, yet that is the purpose of the class. And many of the readers of the exam will be fairly traditional in their orientation to texts." Yet Steve's approach to the books, the orientation on reading and language he tried to foster in the class, didn't always lead to neat themes and understandings. A book like *As I Lay Dying* resisted, in its basic epistemology, such ready expression. But Steve worked fruitfully from the center of the contradiction: urging toward precision, pushing continually on what students were able to say. This provided some of the most intellectually challenging and rewarding time in the class. As Steve put it, "I think it's useful for students to see how they can explore and build on an idea that emerges in discussion." And this attempt to articulate distributed itself across the class, each utterance contributing to further expression.

This movement toward articulation is nicely illustrated in some moments from the last day's discussion of *As I Lay Dying.* But to make sense of them, you'll need to know a bit more about the novel's central figure, Addie Bundren, who, ironically, holds language in the lowest regard, but who, in her single monologue, two-thirds of the way through the book, offers her history in painful clarity.

Before marrying Anse, Addie had been a schoolteacher who lived in silent despair — "The reason for living," her father used to say, "was to get ready to stay dead a long time" — hating the children she taught, feeling alone among them, feeling alive and recognized only when she beat them. "When the switch fell, I could feel it upon my flesh . . . and I would think . . . Now you are aware of me! Now I am something in your secret and selfish life!" She married Anse in a futile attempt to rend her isolation.

In fierce and sexualized language — she talks of her desire for her "aloneness" to be "violated" — Addie explains how the birth of her first son, Cash, gave only momentary relief from her silent misery, realizing finally the meaninglessness of words like *love* and *motherhood.* She felt tricked into having her next son, Darl, and took "revenge" on Anse by making him promise that when she died, he would take her all the way back to Jefferson, her place of birth. (In one of the central ironies in the book, we find out at the very end that Anse went on the journey not only to bury Addie but also to get a new wife.) Still seeking a violation of her terrible aloneness, Addie has an affair with a minister, the most violating of acts, one beyond words and in violation of the Word, the minister "coming swift and secret to me in the woods dressed in sin." Jewel, her favorite son, her jewel, is the offspring of this encounter, and, significantly, his speech is fierce and violent. Addie hid "nothing," "tried to deceive no one," and has two more children by Anse to compensate for the affair: Dewey Dell, who also seeks a physical answer to her isolation, and Vardaman, who is retarded. Then, she says, "I could get ready to die."

Steve began by asking for someone to "indicate what he or she thinks a central theme might be."

Brian: Truths are subjective.

Steve: OK, how would you support that theme?

Brian took a moment, started to page through the book, looked up, and laughed. "Ah, let me get back to you on that."

Ayana: How about the fact that Darl and Anse give us different versions of certain events?

Qisha: Also, there's the different reasons they're going to Jefferson.

Steve: Fine. Now let me ask you this. Is there a better way to summarize those examples than saying "Truths are subjective?"

Alastair: Everyone has their own version of truth.

Brian: People perceive reality differently.

Steve: OK, not bad. Let's come back to that. Any other themes?

Alastair: It strikes me how religion is depicted in the book. I mean, there's Addie and the minister; when Cash broke his leg the first time, he fell off a church; some of the townspeople talk piously but are hypocritical.

Steve: That sounds promising. There's also Addie's belief about deception . . .

Alastair: I'm not sure that's religious.

Steve: All right, good point. Ethics, maybe. Can anyone see a theme developing?

Alastair: Some of the people who act religious aren't religious at all.

Steve noticed that Tequia wanted to speak. He also knew she was a religious person. "Tequia" he said, "I want to bring you into this discussion. Any thoughts?"

Tequia: Well, Cash is faithful to carpentry.

Steve: What's he say about carpentry?

Ayana: Regardless of the materials you have, you should do it well.

Tequia: It's a kind of philosophy.

Steve: Who is the most famous carpenter we know?

Aisha: Jesus.

Tequia: Some of the other characters don't realize it, but for Cash, carpentry might be a kind of religion.

Steve: So different characters might express religious feelings in different ways? Fine. Other themes, people?

Qisha: How about "Blood relatives don't guarantee love."

Aisha: There might be a simpler way to say that.

Steve: Give it a try, Aisha.

Aisha: I'm not good at this.

Steve: That's OK; try it.

Aisha: Love is tainted by obligation?

Steve: That's very interesting. Can you say more?

Aisha: [pausing, looking for words] All the characters in the novel seem to classify their love . . . uh . . . I don't know.

Steve: I think you're on to something.

Qisha: That there is no simple way to define love or emotion in general . . . I mean, usually you can only do certain things to be thought of as love.

Steve: Going back to Aisha's word classify — is it easy to classify or categorize the emotions in this novel?

Qisha, Brian, Aisha, Raina: No.

Steve: [looking at Brian] Remember you were talking about truth being subjective?

Brian: Yes.

Steve: Well, another way to talk about that might be to say that there aren't easy slots or categories for truth or, for that fact, for emotions. Some of the characters may feel and express something that could generally be called love, but it wouldn't fit traditional definitions of love. It's a wide spectrum.

Qisha: It's as though emotions between family members don't follow guidelines.

Steve: OK, but push yourself, Qisha — guidelines is not the best word there.

Chris: How about "Emotions can be defined with different vocabularies?"

Steve: That's promising. How about what Brian was working with?

Brian: Appearance is not really reality?

Aisha: This is really clichéd, but, "Nothing is the way it seems."

Steve: What's wrong with that?

Aisha: It's too broad, I think.

Tequia: Maybe "It's impossible to know other people's reality."

Chris: "It's impossible to know the entire truth about someone's life."

Steve: I think we're developing some major themes, and they all seem to deal with the subjectivity of knowing, of truth, with appearance versus reality . . . That was wonderful. [Turning to me] Wasn't that just wonderful?

And the bell rang.

VI

IT WAS EARLY IN THE MORNING, first period in Sarah Howard's tenth-grade social studies class, the smell of the custodian's disinfectant still in the air, harshly sweet, like a blend of bubble gum and detergent. The students weren't all here yet, ten or so, a few more drifting in to the third-floor classroom at William R. Harper High School, about six miles southwest of Kenwood Academy. Darnell was fiddling with the chart he had made, an illustration of his lineage in the form of a family tree, stalling on the side of the room, by the old wood cabinet, the glass panels gone. The fluorescent light overhead flickered on and off. The bell rang. "OK, Darnell," said Ms. Howard, sitting with her students in a half-circle of desks. Up and down the center of the hardwood floor were dark, scored ovals, like thick burns in the worn wood, the places that once anchored student desks. Darnell placed the bottom edge of his chart in the chalk tray, leaning it back against the board, carefully, carefully, carefully, taking a moment longer. Then he turned three quarters of the way toward the class, hand in pocket, a stray shirt tail loose, and began to read the family anecdote that was to accompany the family tree. He looked at the paper as he read, intently but seemingly without focus, swaying, uncomfortable as hell, reading in a barely audible voice about both his father and mother attending this school and something further about his father going to the Police Academy. The other students couldn't understand him. His classmate Nakesha asked him to read his paper one more time.

I would see Darnell again a half hour later in Michelle Smith's geometry class, right across the hall. He was sitting in the back of the room, just before class started, joking easily with his teacher and another student about the number of people expected at the homecoming dance. "If a survey would be taken," he proclaimed with oratorical flourish, "the figures would be truly astronomical."

William Rainey Harper Senior High School, named after the first president of the University of Chicago, one of the architects of the modern research university, was located close to the color line that Richard Wright described in *Native Son,* the street separating the Black Belt from White neighborhoods farther west. That line, though it had drifted some, was still very real; two years back the Ku Klux Klan held rallies in nearby Marquette Park. Harper was virtually all African American, a fact not without historical irony, for William R. Harper was a eugenicist who believed in the inferiority of the Black race. The surrounding neighborhood, called Englewood, was poor and, in the opinion of students like Tequia at Kenwood, was "one of the toughest neighborhoods in Chicago." It had the fourth highest crime rate in the city. Harper had a bad reputation. It was the kind of school, like so many schools in urban America, that was pretty much ignored by the city's power brokers, wasn't feted or supported or selected in any significant way — except, perhaps, to be featured in a report on the decay of the inner city: poor physical plant, low test scores, kids in trouble. But even those reports tend to miss the complex truths about schools like this, the not-easily-defined nature of the abilities and desires of the young people in them, the tenuous but vibrant possibilities in students, faculty, and community that, with the right support, under the right conditions, can flourish in unexpected ways.

I was visiting Harper through the Small Schools Workshop. Sarah Howard and four colleagues, along with Darnell and about 130 other students, were involved in a school-within-a-school called COMETS. COMETS was the acronym for Communication, Education, and Technology for Success, and, in addition to social studies, geometry, and English, offered courses in science and computer science. This was the program's first year. It was about five weeks old, and its creators were trying, in the midst of the crisis in the Chicago public schools, to fashion a comprehensive and integrated course of study for a segment of Harper's sophomore class. Bill Ayers would drop me off at Harper early in the morning to spend time with them.

Most of the houses around the school were modest wood frame and brick structures lined up along streets with small lawns and trees. Some needed paint desperately, some had broken windows and slats missing from the siding, and some were boarded up. But many were kept in decent condition. One empty lot had been converted into a garden by the Hopewell Church; another lot had been cleared, and, in the back, sat a large mulch pile. Two or three people were out raking leaves. Several blocks were set off with big hand-lettered signs like the following:

Welcome to the 6600 S. Wood Street Block
No loitering
No ballplaying
No speeding
No repairing or washing cars in front
No drugs
Please help us keep our block clean
We call Police

"You can see the evidence," Bill Ayers pointed out, "of the struggle against urban decay." A few blocks away, things were in much worse shape.

Harper was a neighborhood school, no magnet programs. The main building, a four-story rectangular structure, tan brick and unadorned windows, was built in 1917 as a grammar school. Perhaps, one teacher noted, that's why the blackboards were so low. Along with its additions, built in 1972, and parking lot, the school covered the block of Wood Avenue between Sixty-fifth and Sixty-sixth streets. It had a plain grassy courtyard in front, a few shrubs, a low iron fence. It looked like a school . . . or a hospital . . . or some sort of municipal building. You entered through metal detectors, the kind you see in airports, and it's possible that you would be further checked with a hand-held device, as was one girl I saw who, because of an emergency, had to get to the main office before school officially opened.

If you were in Harper that early, you would see that one of the stairwells was sealed off with a large metal gate until just before school opened. A grid was locked permanently around a ladder leading up to the roof. "Everything's restricted," a teacher told me, "even the auditorium; it's always locked." The floors and walls were clean — potentially volatile graffiti was removed quickly. The hallways, painted a kind of peach-orange, like peach sherbet, were long and wide, with high ceilings. There was a broad central stairwell that led beyond the main floor.

Sarah Howard taught social studies and Michelle Smith taught geometry, two flights up those stairs, on the third floor. Right next door, in Room 300, Kris Sieloff taught English. All three were born in Chicago. Kris came of age in a White working-class neighborhood just west of Englewood; Sarah was raised on the North Side; and Michelle grew up in the Black West Side, in a neighborhood she described as being similar to Englewood. All three were products of Chicago public high schools, and all three were still in their twenties.

One thing Kris and Sarah were trying to achieve was an integration of social studies and English around common themes. They had begun the year with the theme of origins. Sarah did a series of lessons on Native Americans — studying the geography, economy, and social structure of the Chippewa, Seminole, Sioux, Navajo, and several other Indian nations — and Kris had brought in, at her own expense, a poet named Eddie Two Rivers, who spoke about his people's origin myths, discussed his personal history as a Chippewa, and read some of his poetry. (He told Kris it was one of the best receptions he'd ever had.) During the time of my visit, Sarah and Kris were making a gradual shift from Native American origins to the origins of African peoples in America. The family tree assignment (the one that gave Darnell such a rough time) was meant to get students reflecting on their personal and familial histories as African Americans before turning to the African Diaspora. And Kris was having the students in COMETS read Alice Walker's "Everyday Use," a short story that, in a comic way, raises some pointed issues about discovering and honoring one's heritage.

The students were to have read "Everyday Use" for class, but Kris was quickly discovering that about half of them had not. She had planned a discussion analyzing the way Walker describes her characters and the ideas the writer conveys through those descriptions. So much for that. "Goddammit," Kris thought, "what now?" She had a cohort of girls for whom, as she put it, "learning had become part of their social life and their identity." They had read the story. Some of her quiet boys had read it. Some hadn't. Then there were James and Demetrius. Both were big guys, both looked way older than sixteen, and both were immensely appealing, in a bad-boy sort of way. Each generated a swirl of social energy around himself, a kind of force field that, in a millisecond, could capture the attention and intelligence of a classroom. They had not read "Everyday Use."

Kris hesitated for a moment, then forged ahead. She slapped the chalk dust from her jeans and asked the class to copy some questions about "Everyday Use" she had written on the board.

"I lost my pen," moaned James.

"Hey," rejoined Demetrius from across the room, "I'm selling pens for a nickel."

Kris walked over and handed James a pencil, eraser first. He leaned into his notebook, bouncing his knee, singing to himself and to the two or three girls within earshot:

> Why must I be like that?
> The dog chases the cat . . .

Finally, one girl shot him a glance and said, "Shut up!"

Meanwhile, Demetrius was asking Ms. Sieloff, in his big, boomy, smiley voice, "We gotta copy that?"

"Yes," she answered with little affect.

"What a drag," he offered, and settled in, sort of.

The narrator in "Everyday Use" is a rural Southern Black woman with two daughters: Maggie, who is shy and ungainly and lives with her mother, and Dee, who is confident, beautiful, and, disenchanted with her origins, has gone away to college. The central dramatic moment in the story occurs when Dee returns home for a visit. To her mother's and sister's amazement, she has taken an African name and has developed great interest in the most humble of her mother's household fixtures, desiring to do something "artistic" with them. What she most covets are her grandmother's old quilts, complaining that Maggie is "backward enough to put them to everyday use." In a moment of epiphany, the mother-narrator realizes that the quilts must go to Maggie, and Dee leaves in a huff, complaining that her mother doesn't understand her heritage.

Kris turned to the board and wrote *Dee* on one side and *Maggie* on the other. She explained to the class that, for starters, she wanted them to describe the qualities of the two sisters Alice Walker had created. As she was talking, she saw James tapping his pencil, bouncing his head, looking around. In an inspired flash of affection and strategy, she called on him.

"James, my man, I'd like you to be the secretary."

"What?" James yelped, as though she had asked him to parade in diapers.

"Hey!" Demetrius yelled. "I'll do it!"

So Demetrius went to the board, the force field swirling like the luminous arcs in bad sci-fi toward the chart Ms. Sieloff had drawn.

And the discussion began.

"Dee, she just wants everything for herself," said one girl. "Spoiled," Demetrius wrote in the *Dee* column, summarizing the comment. "Maggie don't show off; she don't talk much, neither," said a boy over at the side. "Humble," Demetrius wrote under *Maggie*. Though he hadn't read the story, James picked up the gist of "Everyday Use" and tried to edge into the discussion, taking the floor now and then. And Kris let him. Demetrius continued as scribe, halfway calm, spelling carefully, popping off occasionally — a jab or a retort, chin out — but doing a proficient job of summarizing and recording the descriptions of the daughters, Maggie and Dee.

COMETS was off to a bumpy start. The principal who had supported its development — and who, conceivably, would have provided some organizational protection for it — had been invited to participate in a regional program to develop future superintendents. Furthermore, the person in charge of scheduling had placed a number of students in the program who had not requested it, who, to boot, were among the more disruptive kids in the school. And while the COMETS teachers did not want to exclude anybody because of test scores or past grades, they did require that students and parents select the program, buy into it. So the presence of so many kids who were, at best, indifferent to COMETS had a powerful negative influence on the culture of achievement the teachers were trying to nurture. As the new principal found his way at Harper, he would champion the program. But for now . . . "To not have the support of your administration," Michelle said, "is murder."

There was also animosity on the part of some teachers and staff toward COMETS. There were teachers who refered to Sarah Howard and company as the Seven Dwarfs and the Brat Pack, and one of the counselors, Kris and Michelle found out, was telling students that COMETS was a program for "dumb kids." This sort of internal bickering is a common development in school reform efforts, and the COMETS teachers (they realized with hindsight) had not done the day-to-day political work among the faculty that could have softened it. Such work would have been beneficial, for the suspicion and resentment were more than an irritant. One very real outcome of the friction was an unwillingness on the part of some faculty to lend the kind of simple material support that can help a colleague get through a day. When Nancy Kusler, the science teacher, requested some test tubes from her department, she was told that, since she was a member of COMETS, they couldn't help her.

But, there were few resources available any place for the COMETS teachers. The program received $9000 from philanthropists, but that went to buy computers. There were no other funds, and Harper was pitifully broke. Sarah taught social studies without maps, atlases, or reference books. Michelle had to lend out protractors and calculators and collect them at the end of class. Kris needed paperback books. Speaking on the urban public school crisis, former Secretary of Education Lauro Cavazos once said that "money is clearly not the answer." It was hard to believe that, sitting in Harper's classrooms. Sarah, Michelle, and Kris, as do so many teachers, became informal agents in their district's economy by paying for materials out of their own pockets.

And, finally, the chaos across the Chicago public schools took its toll. It threw the first few weeks of COMETS completely off balance. Students didn't know if they would be coming to school the next day or not — and, as Kris explained, "The first few weeks of school are crucial, because they set a tone and a pattern." Also, when the board cut the school day from nine periods to seven, it rendered unusable a schedule Sarah had created that gave COMETS students several long periods in the day so that they could work on projects, get help with research and writing, and, in general, get the most out of their teachers' attempts to integrate curriculum — like the reading and discussion the poet Eddie Two Rivers provided.

Reflecting on the first five weeks of COMETS, Bill Ayers said that "the time those teachers should have been able to put into an original program went into struggling against obstacles." Lack of administrative support, contentious social dynamics, exhausted resources, unstable political and institutional context. But they moved on. "They're doing a heck of a job," Pat Ford observed, "if they can just hang in."

"Yes," said Michelle Smith, "yes, we *do* have work to do today." A few moans. "And y'all have a lot of homework tonight." "Oh, man," a boy near me said in halfhearted protest. "So, let's go!" The little noises of retrieval: notebooks, folders, pencils. Soft chatter. Shifting posture in seats. "Shannon, my young gentleman," Michelle said, tapping a ring on her desk, "I'd like you to sit up here where I can see you." Slow movement on Shannon's part, for the benefit of peers. "C'mon, darlin'," Michelle intoned, head tilted, hand on hip, "humor me." Shannon, tall in football jersey, sauntered up to the first row. "Thank you, Shannon. I feel much better." Shannon fluctuated between a smirk and a smile, the left side of his mouth rising into his cheek. He stretched out his long legs and fiddled with his notebook. The class settled in. "OK, people. Good morning. Let's go."

Taped to the board on the side of the room were two sheets of paper, one pink, one blue. Together, they listed fifty angles the students were to draw using a protractor, developing their proficiency with one of the geometer's basic tools.

45° 89° 139° 147° 179°

Michelle turned to the board and went over the assignment. She later told me that her goal for the year was to help the COMETS students develop adequate proficiency to solve both practical problems (of the sort, for example, a carpenter faces) and to do basic proofs. Some of her students had entered the tenth grade unable to use the fractional measurements on a ruler — "reality slapped me in the face," she said — so she had to fill in a lot of basic work, some of which she coordinated with the science teacher.

Michelle then handed out a further assignment sheet, one requiring students to apply their developing knowledge of angles and to reflect on the subject's personal relevance.

> Look around the classroom and find as many items as you can that have angles.
> Name as many body parts as you can that move in angles.
> Is it possible for your knee to form a 120 degree angle?
> Name as many careers as you can that involve using angles. Explain why people in each career would need to know about angles.
> What career are you interested in for yourself?
> Does your career choice involve angles, and, if so, in what way?

"Though we've got a lot of catching up to do," Michelle told me, "I don't want the course to be just remedial. I don't believe in that. Even a kid who can't use a ruler can do some mathematical things. I want them to think, to apply what they're learning."

Finally, Michelle distributed simple plastic protractors, the kind found in the school supply section of a market or drug store: five and a half inches long, "multipurpose," serving as a protractor, a ruler, and a template for circles and triangles and French curves.

The assignment would extend over the next two or three days.

Michelle rolled back thc billowy sleeves of her blouse and walked to the overhead projector at the front of the room. She began a brief demonstration on how to use the protractor: how to position it on the page, how to fix a reference point (which would become the vertex of the angle), how to find the proper degree of angle along the inscribed half circle in the middle of the protractor, how to mark it, and how to draw the two rays of the angle, connecting them at the vertex.

"Give me a number," she asked the class.

"One forty-five," said Shannon, looking up at the illuminated screen.

"Good. I like that," said Michelle, and proceeded to illustrate how to use the protractor to draw a 145° angle.

"Shannon, is this angle acute or obtuse?"

"Obtuse."

"Thank you."

After the demonstration, the class began to draft the angles, some moving quickly down the list on the board, others working slowly, hesitantly. Some students worked together. In the back of the room, one boy helped another. "Look," he was saying, "it's hard but it's easy." A boy knelt alongside a girl's desk, the two of them shifting the protractor across the page. Michelle walked around the room, tutoring, listening in, rallying on. "Anybody else need my help?" she'd ask and a hand would go up. "I'm on my way," she'd say, rocking back on her lead foot, then walking with a slight forward lean, determined.

Several students who could draft the angles readily had looked ahead to the sheet of application problems, so Michelle took them to her desk and was having them bend their knees and elbows and fingers, eyeballing the resulting angles. Then the students moved off around the room, scribbling notes about the angles of desks, an old filing cabinet, windows and door jambs, the intersection of walls, the immobile hands on the dead clock.

You can't be in a class like this for long without being drawn in, so while Michelle was tutoring, I did the same. Even after Michelle's demonstration, Shannon was still having a little trouble with the protractor. He'd never used one like this before and didn't quite see "where to put the abscissa," how to locate the angle on the page among the curves and lines and little holes of the plastic protractor. I plotted one angle for him, and he caught on quickly. We talked a moment longer, and I asked him about the class. "Miss Smith, she's a good teacher," he said, tapping the protractor emphatically on the desk. "Why is that?" I asked. "Because," he replied, "she's teaching us how to do things we couldn't do before."

Though the teachers in COMETS had to expend considerable energy dealing with day-to-day crises — with kids in trouble and kids losing control, with the myriad small assaults of an unfriendly school environment, and with the financial and operational chaos of the Chicago public schools — though they lived in the eye of an institutional hurricane ("frantic" was how Kris described most of her days), these teachers were working to develop a thoughtful and ambitious curriculum for an academically heterogeneous, inner-city population. Students in COMETS had to discuss and orally present and write something every day. They had to do research (though with minimal resources), and plan and execute projects. And, when their teachers were able to create the conditions for it, they were encouraged to make connections across disciplines and with their own backgrounds and ambitions. Some of these students, maybe 20 to 25 percent, came into COMETS with a history of school achievement. These were young people for whom, as Kris put it, learning was part of their social lives and their identities — though even with them, many of them, there was a decidedly practical bent to learning. It was a way to advance in life, and schoolwork was measured against that criterion.

But for most of these students, COMETS was more challenging than anything they had encountered in their careers at underfunded schools with undemanding curricula. They were being asked to revise their definition of school — and, in some ways, to redefine themselves. Some of them met the challenge. Though they complained, they knew something unusual was going on here, and, even with the gaps and ruptures in their knowledge and skill, they tried. Others attempted to glide, wheedle, and bluff their way through, and you would see Michelle or Kris or Sarah talking to them out of earshot, hand on a shoulder, trying doggedly to pull them in. And some students resisted most of the way, didn't do the work, were tardy, missed class often, were on the path to dropping out of school.

As is true of many student populations in the nation's inner cities, there was a complex range of variables affecting what the COMETS students did in school, a complexity rarely captured in media reports and legislative position papers on our urban schools. Some students came from two-parent households, some from single-parent and extended family households, some lived with grandparents or aunts or foster parents. Any of these arrangements could be stable and nurturing or unstable, abusive, at times violent. What they had in common was that they were most likely poor, or at best holding tight on to a working-class income. A family disaster — a serious injury, a death, the loss of a job — could permanently destabilize the most solid of these households.

Some students were born into such disrupted living conditions — so bereft of nurture and guidance — that they had never developed a healthy sense of self and sustaining social and cultural values. But many grew up absorbing strong core values from one or more sources: church, racial pride, a family history of struggle and achievement, those values often labeled middle class or mainstream American: individualism, self-reliance, the work ethic. Some young people, though, experienced these values as alien and oppressive, for reasons ranging from unorthodox aspirations to religious skepticism to conflicts with traditional gender roles.

Some students had developed keen interests in sports or fashion or music or crafts or books, or political and racial concerns, or things mechanical or scientific. Others had never found a consuming, and possibly redemptive, passion. Some had early school experiences that encouraged skill and fostered imagination; others had an awful time. Many had profoundly limited knowledge of science, literature, history, and mathematics. Some — more than school critics think — saw school as a safe if uncompelling place. And some associated it with humiliation.

What all the students shared was that they lived amid extraordinary violence — a recent Justice Department survey indicates that twelve-to-seventeen-year-olds are the most common victims of violent crime in the United States — and these young people had to learn to deal with it. Some had family or mentors to help them; others desperately sought protective connection. Being threatened and shoved was inevitable, but the majority of students had developed shrewd ways to avoid serious confrontation — ranging from the logistics of the walk home to the crafting of a streetwise persona. And the student who wanted to be schoolwise and streetwise had to shift among a complex range of public selves. And some students sought refuge from violence in violence.

Gangs. Some boys and, increasingly, girls will tell you that broken families or alcohol- and drug-addicted parents or the longing for some kind of solidarity brought them into gang life. But kids from intact families, churchgoing families — all the demographer's indices of stability — those kids, too, can succumb to the allure of the streets. Surrounded by America's passion for glamorous violence, they feel the flat, unremitting boredom and humiliation of poverty, see the continual reminders of racial and class raw deals. ("The contrast is so stark," Pat Ford said of living in Cabrini Green. "You can *walk* from the projects to the incredible wealth of the Gold Coast.") All this generates a force stronger than can be imagined by anyone who grew up outside of communities like Englewood, a force driving you toward potency at any price, identity and excitement and fast money. As a student of mine who had watched members of her family enter "the crazy life" once put it, "It's a quick way of becoming somebody."

Pregnancy also presents a way to become somebody. Many girls from the inner city (but certainly not only from the inner city) get pregnant out of a volatile mix of desire, ignorance of means of prevention, pressure from partners, defiance. But an equally important factor involves the desperate quest for identity, the quest for love and meaning and the status of motherhood. "This is somebody who needs me," one teenage mother said, "someone who loves me and is mine."

The hurt and disappointment some of these young people carry, the longing and confusion, can quickly wrench out of control. So they strike out, in fury or desperation; like Addie in *As I Lay Dying,* they seem to be saying, "Be aware of me!" And as they strike out, the damage they cause slaps back at them. There's further retaliation and insult from the institution or the street — and this builds, cycles, and is made more volatile by alcohol and drugs. It's no wonder that when you talk to some kids who are always in trouble, you sense that they're barely holding spirit and flesh together, that their skin is about to fly off their bones.

These are some, but not all, of the factors influencing the performance of the tenth-graders enrolled in the program called COMETS at William Rainey Harper Senior High School.

Here are some moments from COMETS that further reveal its complication.

> The students in Sarah Howard's social studies class were discussing an article on the misuse by sports teams of Native American names and symbols: the Redmen, the Braves, and so on.
>
> Ms. Howard: Well, what about the Seminoles, would that be different?
>
> Lashandra: It could be, maybe, because that's the name of a tribe, but the other names are things they call Indians, somebody's stereotype.
>
> Ms. Howard: That's a good observation. But can you think of a reason why someone might take offense at Seminoles?
>
> Lashandra: Well, most other sports teams are named after animals. It could seem like a Seminole is like a mascot.
>
> Darnell: It also makes it sound like Indians are only warriors.
>
> Ms. Howard: Interesting, Darnell. What did Eddie Two Rivers wear? What did he have on?
>
> Nakesha: Jeans, a shirt, some jewelry.
>
> Ms. Howard: Did he fit the stereotype of an Indian?

Nakesha: No.

Ms. Howard: What is the image of the Native American we get on TV?

Darnell: They're wild and crazy.

Ms. Howard: And of Black people?

Darnell: Fight, jump high, kill, sing.

Carla was intently calculating the complements and supplements of the angles she had drafted. She was a striking girl, a face Kris described as "angelic." Carla looked to be about eight months pregnant. It was her second child. She was "serious" her teachers said, "no nonsense." She wore a nose stud, a tiny jewel. She sat by the windows, a few seats away from the others, looking back and forth from protractor to scratch paper to page, pencil moving down the column of angles. "Those eyes," Kris said, "are sharp."

Kris was sitting with a girl off to the side of the room, trying to find out why she, a competent enough reader, would always come to class without having read the assignments for the day — like Alice Walker's "Everyday Use."

"But Miss Sieloff," the girl finally said, "I'm just not into it."

Sarah had all the charts the students had made of their family trees laid out on a table by the wall. I was looking through them, finding some impressive pieces of work. Lashandra had sketched and colored a large leafy tree with a fat trunk. Carefully inscribed along the fissures of the bark were the names of grandparents and great-grandparents; the branches were thick with aunts, uncles, and cousins. Shannon, obsessed with football these days, turned a goal post into a chart of his lineage. "The Football Field of Family," he titled it. Nakesha had drawn an elaborately reticulated landscape of what looked like a series of analytic decision trees. I called her over to congratulate her and ask her about the trees, wondering if she had adapted the idea from her computer class. "What's wrong?" she asked as she walked over. "Did I mess up?"

It was Michelle's homeroom period. She sat at her desk, signing forms for students, talking seriously to one or two, doing a little quick tutoring. I sat at the back, reading the top of the gouged wooden desk: *Kathy 'n Big Tone, Phonky, Cisco G., Lady Love.* There was a beeper number and the word *Smoke* written in ornate script. The six-pointed star of the Gangster Disciples, the most powerful gang in Chicago, was scratched into all the desk tops I could see.

The public address system came on.

"Good morning students and staff . . ."

"The minimum skills proficiency exam is being given today in Room 498 . . ."

"Homecoming tickets are on sale today and tomorrow . . ."

A boy sitting by me, glasses, very baggy pants, was assiduously completing a list of math problems. Three girls in the far corner were talking and giggling into their hands. Two boys behind me were trying to fix a Walkman and were talking softly about a football game. Around the room, students were doing homework or doodling or resting their heads in the bend of their elbows.

"Orientation for the Big Brother, Big Sister Program will be at . . ."

"Please have a good day . . ."

Students hung out in Sarah's, Michelle's, and Kris's rooms between classes, during breaks. A husky senior, thick forearms, glasses, well-spoken, came into Room 300 looking for Kris. He was fidgety, kind of excited. One of his other teachers was encouraging him to try out for the academic decathlon team, and he wanted Kris's advice. He trusted her. Kris lit up and encouraged him. "Do you think it'll take up a lot of time," he asked with a worried laugh. "You'll have some control over that," Kris assured him. "It's just that you'd be great. You got what it takes." He looked at me, the visitor. I imagined him the scholar-athlete — this big, articulate guy. I encouraged him, too. "Well," he said, tapping his fist against the edge of his binder, "I'll think about it; it might be interesting." He thanked us both and rushed off to class. Later that day, Kris confided that he was a long-time member of the Gangster Disciples and carried a lot of authority on the streets around Harper. He had also, in the last year or so, become an A student. So she and the teacher who recommended the academic decathlon were trying, in every way that presented itself, to encourage his burgeoning interest in school.

Kris Sieloff's classroom looked out from the third floor onto Wood Avenue. It was the end of the day, and she was putting things in order, her thoughts drifting. One window was about half open, and the sound came suddenly. Not the loud bang or the threatening crack you'd imagine, but more like a sound from a cartoon: the rapid *pop pop pop pop* of an automatic weapon. "That's not what I think it is," she flashed, setting down a handful of student papers. Then, just as quickly, "Yes it is!" She stood stock still, numb, looking toward the half-open window. Then she ran into the hallway, thinking, "Thank God they've all gone home. Have they?"

Michelle's students were busy drafting angles when Nakesha, who was sitting close to the door, a heating vent above her, began to cough. Then a girl next to her. Then another. Michelle looked up from a tutorial, her nose in the air. Was it the smell of overheated electrical wires? Of turpentine? "You smell it, Miss Smith?" Nakesha asked. "Yes, I do," said Michelle, and began opening windows, then walked into the hall to check out there. Was it a solvent? Dangerous? She was getting ready to move the class out to the hall when it dispelled, and everyone gradually got back to work.

Kris stopped by Robert's desk to congratulate him on his good contributions to the discussion of "Everyday Use." "You're doing pretty well, Robert," she said, sitting down next to him, getting at eye level. "I'm proud of you. You could do really well this term." Robert nodded. "Yeah, I know. I'm tryin'. I am." As Kris got up and walked away, she ran her hand over his shoulder. He leaned back into the essay he was writing.

A few weeks later, Kris told me that Robert was kicked out of Harper for fighting. He had gotten into trouble in the ninth grade, but up until now, six or seven weeks into the semester, he had been watching himself, holding things together. Then something happened. He was being transferred to another school.

Michelle's room was once a science demonstration classroom — thus those old school desks bolted to the floor — so extending across roughly three quarters of the front, right before the chalkboards, was a low platform and a long lab table. At different times during the day, Michelle would sit there tutoring. I would occasionally sit there, too, on the end, catching a quick minute with Michelle or collecting my thoughts or scribbling a reminder to myself.

It was near the end of one of my mornings at Harper, when I retired to the lab table to write some notes. The class was quiet, some students working in groups, everyone calculating the complements and supplements of the angles they had drafted or working on the word problems requiring them to apply their knowledge of angles. "We need to capture the energy they put into other things," Michelle had said to me, "and focus it here. It's sometimes very hard for them to see beyond the streets." I looked out at Darnell, Shannon, Nakesha, and the rest, feeling, suddenly, strongly the power of what the teachers in COMETS were attempting to do, the terrible history of neglect they were trying to counter, the destructive forces — from street, from state — they were contending with now. Little that they or any group of teachers could do would compensate directly for the legacy of racism and the evils of class that had affected the students sitting in those battered desks. But what they were doing was converting the classroom into a place where a young person in Englewood could find meaning, develop identity, actualize the yearning to be somebody. Some of their students already knew the classroom that way, and COMETS could provide the occasion for them to push beyond what they could already do, to take safe risks, to experiment without the fear that they would "mess up" and lose what they've gained. For those students who had not known the classroom to be a particularly compelling place, COMETS could become transformative. For some, it seemed possible. They had an awfully long way to go, had been deprived of opportunity for too long or had resisted it to protect or assert themselves. But now some of these young people were taking the chance.

Earlier in the hour, I had been tutoring a boy named Dion. He was having trouble calculating the complement of an angle (the number that, when added to an angle, will yield 180°), and we kept at it until that look came into his eyes. He hadn't understood the concept underlying the calculations, and was just going through motions he knew were rote and empty. Then he saw it. I stayed with him until he did a few more, then got up to leave. He grabbed my forearm. "Thanks," he said, looking right at me. "Really, thanks a lot." Comprehension. The spark of understanding. The feeling that you know what you're doing. The conditions for such an experience, that moment of insight, abound in everyday life — and the streets certainly provide opportunity for them. Could the classroom? Watching the students in third-period geometry, knowing how far behind they were, all that limited them, I was struck by the magnitude of the risk they were taking. And I was struck, too, by the delicacy of their achievement, by all that could happen to destabilize it.

That night I phoned Michelle to check some facts. I told her about that sense of uncertainty, the apprehension. "It's as if they're walking a tightrope," I said. "And they feel it," Michelle responded quickly, "They're very aware of it. Imagine what that feels like." Then she became reflective. "You know, these kids have to learn at a young age to wear a mask. The mask is the only thing that protects them from going crazy. If they take it off in front of the wrong person, they'll pay for it. But when you see them drop it, the way Dion did with you, when they feel safe enough to take it off . . . well, it's just so important to hear them."

VII

SITTING WITH STEVE GILBERT in his office, the end of the day, the phone quiet, his briefcase leaning against the legs of an empty chair. "As a teacher," he was saying, "I want people to have their voice respected, and I want to help people arrive at a sense of their value and worth. One of the reasons the whole politics of education is so upsetting to me is that there's this assumption — and you hear it explicitly or indirectly all the time — that the students who inhabit urban public schools are a kind of debris. I think my class offers a refutation of that judgment.

"When you teach, the young people with whom you work are, in a profound sense, your co-workers, your colleagues. They become very important to you. A number of students I've taught are extraordinary people. You'd be lucky to have one of them as your child. You'd be thankful to have such an extraordinary person as *your* child.

"It's easy to dismiss a class like mine because it's an advanced placement class. But the regular English class I taught last year had some equally remarkable students in it. There was this one young man who saw himself primarily as an athlete but also wanted very much to succeed in the class. He was perceptive in his reading. And he worked very hard on his writing, very hard. By the end of the year, he was doing excellent work. To know the kids I regularly come in contact with is to know a group of people who truly deserve the best we can offer them.

"You continually hear talk about our country's founding values, but the truth is that realizing those values requires a great deal of effort. We say we believe in democratic institutions, but, as a citizenry, we aren't willing to commit ourselves to a literate population. The politics of the school system basically shows that people aren't committed to either these children or to the institutions that should be making democracy work."

In a corner of the second floor of Kenwood's library, out of the way, at a table by shelf after shelf of fiction, I talked, one by one, with some of the students who had completed *As I Lay Dying.*

Qisha

It was remarkable to find out that Faulkner wrote this while he was at work! Things come across so deep — how could he have written it in a boiler room? I think he was testing the limits of what he could get people to believe, of what a character can do. I think it's great literature. Faulkner's being very spiritual, in a way; he's saying that we can't take things literally. I mean, everyone assumes a father will work hard, that a mother will love her children. This goes against the expectation, makes the reader see things in a very different way. Maybe reading it will make someone more open-minded. If I'd written it, I'd be so proud.

Alastair

I definitely appreciate the book more. The first time through, I found myself asking, "What the hell is this?" It seemed so jumbled. I do appreciate it more — but I still don't like it, didn't enjoy reading it. It's an incredibly difficult book to wrestle with. It's like having somebody's thoughts thrown at you and trying to make something out of them.

But it is an interesting and pretty challenging way to go about writing a book. I guess I kind of like the idea. I mean, on a TV show when a character's thinking, it's all in clear sentences. But that's not the way people think. They think in fragments and little stems of ideas. As Qisha said in class, the book's realistic about the way people think, and trying to deal with somebody's raw thoughts in real primitive form is extremely difficult. I mean, can people themselves even understand all that goes on within themselves? We have so many conflicting thoughts. At a certain level we understand ourselves, but I don't think we can truly . . . completely see what's, how, we're made up, composed.

Aisha

In all honesty, I put off reading *As I Lay Dying* until the last possible minute. Then I tried to speed through it! [Laughs.] When I read, if I don't understand something, I'll just skip over the entire paragraph. So there I was, skipping in and out. Whoa! It was *confusing.*

But now I like it. I like it a lot. You know, I didn't like *Brave New World.* It was, it was kind of science-fictiony, and I don't like science fiction. I *did* like Turgenev. It reminded me of a Jane Austen, Charles Dickens kind of book — that era. I like that kind of fiction. There were so many tense relationships between everyone, an unspoken tension. The way people would phrase things — like everyone's walking on eggs — they would allude to something but never come out and say it. I liked the tensions between generations and between the sexes.

And *this* book. As we worked on it in class, I liked it more and more. There was so much. If you pick any random paragraph, that, in itself, is a story. You have to infer things — like with Dewey Dell. Every section was like a little mystery in itself. There's just so many different aspects to the characters' personalities. I don't like books where the characters are like caricatures. You know what I mean? These are real people with real problems and doubts. And I really liked the fact that Darl had this kind of omniscient, this telepathic quality. I thought that was a *very* interesting thing to have in a rural Southern character. You know, you'd usually think in terms of simple-minded farmers. You wouldn't think of them as extraordinary people.

Chris

When I started reading *As I Lay Dying,* I have to admit I wasn't enjoying it — I was doing it as an assignment. It's something I would have never read on my own. I mean, I really didn't know what was going on. Now, I understand it infinitely better — though I still don't think I understand the total theme of the book as well as I did with *Fathers and Children* and *Brave New World.* I have an idea [laughs], but I think there's a lot more to it.

I think what we do in class is great, how we hear everybody's views. It's just that when I first read the book, I didn't have *any* views. I felt I didn't have anything to contribute, except for random facts about plot or something. I like to uncover things for myself, feel that sense of accomplishment. That didn't happen with *As I Lay Dying.* The book didn't excite me, never blew me away. You kind of trudge along, and then you finish it. It hasn't changed the way I think or given me a new perspective. It's like I almost feel a little cheated.

I'm reading *Crime and Punishment* now for my term paper. It's a hard book too, but I almost instantly understood what was going on; I was already asking questions. And now I'm reading criticism — and these people are coming up with some of the same themes I was arriving at. I felt a sense of accomplishment — I've actually figured out some things about the book. I think it's the best book I've ever read. When I pick it up, it's very hard to put down. I just love that book.

Raina

Once I started writing about *As I Lay Dying,* I realized I understood the book better than I thought. When I write, I try to find support for my ideas, and as I do, I begin to make connections.

I like a book like this. It makes the reading exciting — like discovering who the characters are by what the other characters think. You have to piece things together, like a puzzle. I'd like to read it again in a year. That's important. I read *Beloved* last year and didn't like it. Mr. Gilbert happened to see me carrying it around. He said it was his favorite book. He said something about a part of the book — and I thought, "Wow, I didn't think of it that way." It made me want to reread it.

He's a difficult and strict teacher — if you're not there right on time, he wants to know where you were. And he's very demanding. In honors classes, you usually get As or high Bs. I've gotten lower grades from him on papers than I've gotten from most anybody else. But he works with you, goes over the papers, gives you his home phone number. He really extends himself, takes it to the personal level.

When Steve Gilbert talked about his love of literature — about his feelings for a character in *As I Lay Dying* or his thoughts about a work of literary criticism he was reading — he often referred to something a student had said or imagined how a scene or an idea might play out in class. "You know, all the things Raina mentioned she liked about Cash are the things I like about him, too." Or: "*As I Lay Dying* is clearly a text *about* reading, and these are some of the best readers at Kenwood; but the difficulty comes, I think, in getting them to *read* their reading." Or, simply: "God, I can't wait to see what they'll make of this!"

There was no doubt that Steve's excellence as a teacher was grounded in his knowledge of literature. He read widely in fiction, drama, poetry, and literary criticism, contemporary criticism particularly — deconstruction, reader response, and a range of work in feminism and cultural studies. But there was a telling, and I think unusual, quality to his disciplinary expertise: he would talk about fictional characters as though they were acquaintances, real people for whom he had feelings, with whom he had disagreements and points of identification or curiosity. He "loved" Cash; he felt Dewey Dell's situation was "unbelievably sad"; he thought Jewel, the violent son, was an "extremely moving character." Steve was schooled in contemporary literary theory, but I never heard in him a trace of the ironic detachment, or the postmodern skepticism present in the work of some who write from those theoretical positions. He took literary characters more seriously than any literary scholar I know. Steve talked about literature more like an actor or director . . . or a fellow writer.

But his deep appreciation — it wouldn't be inaccurate to call it a passion — extended continually beyond his own encounters with literature. It embraced his students, his "co-workers." This was important, I thought, given the values of the places that produce disciplinary specialists for our schools — academic departments in colleges and universities. You could read the modern history of those departments as a history of increased specialization and a gradual move away from concerns about pedagogy, teacher training, or the novice's acquisition of disciplinary knowledge. (These concerns would be appropriated by the teachers' colleges and schools of education coming into being during the first three decades of this century.) As departments of English evolved, little consideration was given to the development of the ability to read and appreciate literature, to the cognitive, aesthetic, or moral dimensions of the encounter between young people and literary texts. But Steve Gilbert fused literary study with concerns about the growth of the people he taught. His was an affectionate, engaged aesthetic. "Getting kids enthusiastic about language and writing," he said, "is just pure fun for me."

It was, though, a pretty serious kind of fun. Steve demanded a high level of intellectual work. He began class the moment the minute hand hit its mark and did not let up until the bell rang. The dialogue around the text moved quickly, demanding an alert focus — students commented to me about how fast the fifty-minute period went by — and Steve asked questions and made connections methodically and apace. He had a good sense of what his students knew and could do, and he was gifted at nudging them beyond where they were, helping them extend what they could say, the connections they could make. "He really does a good job of coaxing our thinking along," Alastair told me, "pushing our thinking to its limits, really bringing out our best interpretive abilities." And when things were in high gear, the room was charged with the intensity of people thinking hard and well.

There was a tension here, however, and both the students and Steve were aware of it. When there was a short day or a lot of material to cover (and of the nine days I spent in the class, three were attenuated because of crisis scheduling or a fire drill), Steve had a tendency to slip from diligent Socratic questioner to a lecturer who asked questions. The students could tell the difference, and told me they were less enthusiastic about those sessions. Steve knew the difference well and berated himself when, as he put it, he "leaped into the breach and talked too damned much." "If I hadn't said that right there," he'd think later, reflecting on a comment he had made, "if I hadn't come in so soon, maybe they would have come to the idea on their own." It was what he disliked most about his teaching.

Steve was exceedingly demanding of himself. He listened carefully when a student spoke, tilting his head, concentrating, nodding, asking a clarifying question. (Aisha noted that "sometimes when Mr. Gilbert is looking at you, it kind of puts pressure on you; you're put on the spot.") Steve could recall what his students had said days earlier and use it to foster connections, to seek clarification, appropriating the history of their discussion to frame the present analytical moment. He insisted on his own precision — you could see him monitoring his expression, pausing, rephrasing, seeking precise articulation. He seemed, at times, driven toward precision, not letting anything loose, from himself or others, pass easily, pondering it, seeking clarity. Occasionally, it made him a little contentious. "I don't want this to be a touchy-feely experience," he said of the class. "I want it to be serious; I'm very critical of sloppiness in thought and writing." It struck me after a few days with him that there was an ethical base to this meticulous care with language.

A concern for social justice — as well as a love of literature and a regard for young people — drove Steve's work in the classroom. His concerns were long-standing. He had been involved in the civil rights movement and followed the debates within the gay community on gay rights and identity. Recently, he had been influenced by his reading in philosophy and cultural criticism. That work asserts that language is central to the way we construct our social reality, and that the various definitions, categories, judgments we bring to bear on our everyday world are not absolute, fixed, or true in some basic or transcendent way, but arise from shifting social forces and can serve to legitimate existing social inequities and biases. Thus, it becomes critical to explore the language we receive as members of a social order and to be relentless in examining the way we use it — recall Steve's desire to push on the class's early judgments of Dewey Dell, and to get them to consider her language on its own terms. "I'm sure," he observed, "that my commitment to respecting 'effaced' voices, 'erased' voices is related to my own identity as a gay person. But I would like to think that it's not only because of that, that there are other social and ethical reasons for my beliefs." A long stretch from one of our late-afternoon discussions picks up these issues.

"I think it's perfectly all right for Ayana and Dewey Dell never to be friendly, never to like each other. But if Ayana can *listen* to Dewey Dell and judge her from a position of understanding, from inside her language . . . well, that's something. If we can do that as a society, then we will move a great deal. That's a crucial issue for me: How can we come to recognize that there is not this one, single, absolute norm that we *all* fail to live up to? Years ago when I was teaching a seventh-grade class, we read *Catcher in the Rye.* There's this scene where Holden Caulfield goes back to see his old teacher, Mr. Antolini — do you remember it? Holden stays there and wakes in the middle of the night to find Mr. Antolini looking at him and patting his head. Holden panics, thinks the guy is coming on to him — and my students laughed. Well, this was an important moment, I thought, one of those 'teachable' moments. I mean, the students could hardly speak the word *gay,* and, finally [laughs], I almost had to force them to utter it. So we talked about Holden's reaction and Holden's judgment — which is the *only* judgment we're given. We don't get to hear Mr. Antolini's thoughts or speech directly, only through Holden.

"Well, I went through this whole thing about how you can't choose your prejudices, that if you find racist perceptions unacceptable, then all prejudicial ways of thinking are unacceptable. Otherwise, there's no moral ground to stand on."

These concerns about bias and fairness extended beyond language and perception to the structure of advanced placement itself. It had been the practice at Kenwood (as it is in many schools) to place a number of restrictions on entrance to AP, and though that practice did not result in a racially segregated class this time around (nor in a strict socioeconomic barrier, for several in the class came from families of modest means), it *did* limit the group to just eight students. "I simply don't believe in an eight-person class," Steve grumbled, and now that control of AP would be passing to him, he planned to open it up and recruit among the student body. "In my experience, when students select challenging classes, they tend, after a little time, to choose appropriately and work up to the level of expectation. And the results can be wonderful. A richer mix of backgrounds, of experiences, and points of view."

Finally, fundamentally, Steve's work in the classroom gave his life meaning. "I think one way I can exercise my concerns about society is by working in very small stages with my students. I mean, if, at the end of my life, there are five hundred people who see the world differently because of the work I've done . . . Well, I'd be very happy about that."

So Steve continues, day after day, urging critical reflection, careful mental work, articulation. There is a potential contradiction in all this. The deconstructive, poststructuralist literary theory he incorporates into his teaching — a theory that insists on the fluidity, the instability of language — could be seen as undercutting the possibility of precise expression. But Steve worked productively from the contradiction: pushing for articulation in an unstable discursive universe, believing in the value of the process, guiding, urging students *through* the process, creating the occasion for them to question what they know, extend what they can articulate — one utterance leading to another to another. The result is a challenging, at times generatively unsettling, set of expectations.

One day, the class was struggling to figure out the details of Darl's past. Brian zeroed in on an allusive, difficult passage and, taking a chance, wondered if Darl had been taken away to an asylum before. Further analysis revealed a more plausible reading of the passage — Darl had been conscripted — but Brian's interpretation proved to be a key moment in the discussion, freeing up a paralyzed inquiry. Later in the day Steve had a lot to say about it.

"Risking an idea is very important. Stretching yourself means getting it wrong sometimes. One of the ways the education system has betrayed the learning process is that we have told students that being successful means being successful all the time. But, in fact, being successful means being *wrong* lots of times — but sticking with it, struggling with it. One of the reasons I assign books like *As I Lay Dying* is that they almost demand an uncertain reading, less sure-footed, riskier — you have to continue to struggle to find ground you can stand on. That's the kind of thing I think is very important, that struggle. The analytical process involves going down roads that lead nowhere. Students think that being wrong is bad, but being wrong is better than saying nothing. It's better to come up with a tentative analysis that you or others can revise later. Brian came up with an important first reading that made subsequent readings possible. That's very risky for these students, who are used to getting everything 'correct,' used to getting A's. But I admire the way they take that risk. I hope I encourage it, make it possible. I was very impressed with them today. I think that kind of work is what the class should be about, taking that risk."

VIII SPEAKING TO AN ORGANIZATION of business leaders in the fall of 1987, Secretary of Education William Bennett declared the Chicago public schools the worst in the nation. "If [Chicago] is not the last," he said, "I don't know who is." It was a devastating proclamation — one, I'm sure, a number of people would have lined up to confirm. But the more time I spend in education, the more uneasy I become with such sweeping judgments, such dismissive summation. Though language like this catches the public's attention, it doesn't lead us to think deeply about the problems in our schools. As a person trained in the humanities, the secretary could have helped us understand how the terrible condition of the Chicago schools came to be. He could have probed the history of the district, for it is a revealing and not atypical history of corruption and neglect. Virtually since their beginnings, in the mid-nineteenth century, the Chicago schools have been compromised by graft and patronage. In 1921, for example, the school board charged almost $9 million to unitemized "incidentals"; in the mid-1930s, $370,000 more was spent annually on supervising, heating, and cleaning schools — all patronage jobs and contracts — than on educating children. And, though it was the furious growth of the city that put unmanageable pressure on the schools, Chicago's business interests, the driving force behind that growth, historically did little to assist the schools and often undercut attempts to provide them with more resources.

Or, coming at it another way, the secretary might have considered the degree to which the district's problems were shaped and exacerbated by political, economic, and social conditions outside the schools. He might have reflected on the degree to which the humane, creative, growth-fostering forces within the schools were blunted by those conditions. How they have been blunted and sabotaged by the intractable nature of urban politics; by the economic and social collapse of entire communities; by the unproductive way that labor-management relations have developed, by the very application of the labor-management model to schools; by race and class bias, the demographic breach of the Brown decision, and the vicious protection of privilege. All the conditions that Bonnie Tarta's tenth-graders saw so clearly, conditions that do not exist in Chicago alone, that devastate public schools in Los Angeles, New York, Baltimore — in so many of our cities. If Chicago was to be singled out, it should have been singled out as an emblem.

What the secretary might have assailed was the way our nation's public schools — this remarkable, if flawed and incomplete, experiment in democracy — are being so threatened. As the nation's highest education officer, he might have voiced moral outrage, called out across the history and future of the Republic. He might have asked what he could do to support the forces of democracy, of learning and human growth, of respect for the potential of young people. "What might I do," he could have asked, "to help the public see more clearly the complexity, to hear the many voices. What resources do you need? How can I lobby for you?"

It's a speech that many would have liked to hear. Here's Bonnie Tarta, the U.S. history teacher from Kenwood:

"I've been in the system a long time, twenty-three years, and I've gone through, oh, I don't know, ten to twelve strikes, up and down, thinking every year in the middle of August whether we're going to start in September. And it's getting to the point [softly] where I'm losing the will to do it. You get the feedback from the public, from the local government, from the federal level, that we're imbeciles, that the schools are filled with kids who aren't teachable and teachers who don't teach. It's sad.

"We desperately need young, fresh teachers, but there's no way to keep young teachers in the system because they just cut 'em right out. At Kenwood, twenty-four positions were cut this year. We had something like eighteen people retire, and we have a new principal, all gung-ho with lots of new ideas. This was such an opportunity — and she had lined up all these young people coming in from other fields. And all these positions were closed down. All they keep doing is dropping teachers, putting more kids in classes, cutting our programs — where's the reform? Under these conditions reform means nothing . . . what do you mean, 'reform'?"

Bonnie's question brings into focus a fundamental contradiction in Chicago school reform. The hope driving the decentralizing of authority from the main bureaucracy to local school councils was that school-site decision-making and the greater participation of the community in those decisions would make schools more responsive to the needs of the children. Unfortunately, the majority of Chicago schools and their local councils — for a range of social and political reasons — have not yet been able to change in any significant way, though a recent study estimated that 20 to 30 percent of the schools have moved toward democratic governance and revitalized instruction. Our journey with Pat Ford took us through some of those schools. And Kenwood Academy, with its dynamic new principal, Beverly LaCoste, and a newly elected local school council was on its way. Yet an immense drag on reform, even in places making big change, is funding. When money is as unstable as it is in Chicago, schools are thrown into chaos. It is cases like this that lead some observers of urban school reform to be skeptical of site-based management. Without adequate control over funding, they contend, there is only the appearance of redistributed power; the local school is free to make choices, yes, but within a pinched or shifting fiscal space. "Where's the reform?"

I think there is an answer to Bonnie's question — an answer of sorts, a paradoxical, incomplete answer — and in trying to articulate it, I don't want to soften the anger in her lament. I want to hold it tight.

What struck me during my stay in Chicago, and continues to impress me as I get in close to classrooms in the nation's most troubled urban school districts, is the way good work continues — tentative, risky, but ongoing, threatened but tenacious. It is something you can't see from afar, might miss in aggregate data or in the policy survey — and certainly in the quick sweep of the news camera. It has many configurations, different expressions, some just shaping themselves. It is a change in what we think children are capable of achieving in school. All children. The run-of-the-mill kid, the poor kid, the kid who can't speak so well, the kid sitting at the back of the room, the kid who's just doing OK. At its best, reform in Chicago involves not only a restructuring of governance arrangements, but, as well, what educator Asa Hilliard calls a "deep restructuring" of beliefs about what chidren can do.

We have a tendency in American education to classify our students in ways that have significant consequences for how they're taught and what they'll learn. We believe that students who are deemed "bright" or "gifted" must be challenged and stimulated, pushed to the limits of their capacity — and we define that capacity generously. Bless those students like Qisha, Alastair, Aisha, and the rest who blossom under such attention. Their achievement is dazzling. The sad thing is that we do not think as rigorously, as creatively, with the same generosity of intellect about the rest. And this defect in imagination easily plays off an antidemocratic strain in the American character, a desire to keep the really good things — in this case, superior education — for the few. An issue of instructional delivery takes a quick and ugly shift to the politics of privilege.

What I saw in Chicago was a complication of such easy definitions and distinctions, a recognition here and there that what we thought we knew and had under instructional control was far more involved. More tragic. More promising. As chaotic as things were, there was a mood that encouraged a rethinking of the classroom, as new teachers came of age, influenced by the moment; as veteran teachers felt free to play out their visions.

It might be expected that a discussion that included students like those in Steve Gilbert's AP English and students like those in COMETS would end up comparing them in some way. To be sure, there could be many comparisons, some enlightening, some unkind. If nothing else, considering Steve's students underscores how cheated the students in COMETS have been. But the more time I spent shuttling back and forth, thinking about all that their teachers shared — the creation of a respectful classroom space, the urging toward risk, toward expression, the desire that their students be heard — and the more time I spent with those young people, the harder became neat distinction and separation. Their needs and their voices began to play off each other. Perhaps they should not be contrasted, but blended polyphonically, entered in all their intricacy into the public conversation. There is the assumption, Steve said, that the students who inhabit urban public schools are a kind of debris. I thought of that talk show host in Los Angeles who referred to the kids in LA's schools as "garbage." Can we now call up Bonnie Tarta's anger?

What should infuriate us is that the intellectual work of *all* these students was so threatened — by public perception, by cuts, by chaos, by violence, by what an editor of the *Chicago Tribune* called "an extraordinary combination of greed, racism, political cowardice, and public apathy."

As I rode in the back of a cab en route from Harper to Kenwood, the driver, a big man named Willie talking about his two kids, I thought of Darnell, Qisha, Alastair. The wind hissed through a crack in the side of the window, the trees were sparer now, red, brown. Lashandra, Raina, James and Demetrius, Ayana, Tequia, Brian and Chris, Shannon and Aisha. New York City principal Deborah Meier once said that good schools, good educational programs, don't just die off; they're murdered. The anger comes, finally, because all these manifestations of possibility are so threatened. The secretary of education should have wept over that.

5

New York, New York

I FRANKLIN K. LANE HIGH SCHOOL, on the border between Brooklyn and Queens, a WPA building completed in 1938, was an imposing and magnificent structure in the Federal style: three-story-high columns above the main entrance, a domed tower rising the height of three stories beyond that into the sky. The school building is to America, a school planner proclaimed a decade earlier, what the cathedral was to the Middle Ages. Lane served a student body of four thousand, was, in the fashion of its time, a "comprehensive" high school with a boys' gymnasium and a girls' gymnasium, an auditorium, a library, an art gallery, rooms for student clubs, a boys' corrective training room and a girls' corrective training room, studios, typing rooms, a music room, rooms for a hierarchy of administrators, an impressive range of lecture rooms and laboratories for a widely differentiated curriculum — even a homemaking apartment, with a fully furnished living room, bedroom, and kitchen. Schools like this were meant to be both monuments to the Republic — "temples . . . of a practical civic brotherhood" that school planner called them — and educational factories, embedded in an elaborate bureaucracy, responding on an efficient grand scale to the stunning diversity of an immense urban population.

Architectural style has changed, of course, and contemporary school planners use a less elevated language to describe their buildings, but some of the notions that drove the construction of Franklin K. Lane High School still influence public school construction today — differentiation of function, economies of scale — ways of thinking born of the development and operation of industry, the reigning model for school planning through the first half of our century. But one of the ironies of institutional life is that one era's enthusiastic solution to social and economic challenges can become another era's intractable problem.

There is a dynamic, multiconstituent reform movement in New York City — in other large cities as well — that calls for us to think about schools, high schools especially, in a very different way. This new generation of educators believes that the problems endemic to large urban districts — low achievement, high drop-out rates, disciplinary mayhem — are, in part, a byproduct of the typical high school's size and structure. Claiming that the standard comprehensive high school loses kids, fosters anonymity, isolates teachers, and keeps decision-making in the hands of a few, and citing studies suggesting that small size is positively related to student retention and achievement, these reformers urge us to make schools smaller. They want to increase the opportunity to know children and their families, to attenuate the distance between teacher, child, and community; they want to bring decisions about school organization and curriculum closer to the people who do the work; they want to reduce the physical and personal scale of education. Small schools, they admit, might limit the range of offerings — the value of the comprehensive high school is its array of courses and services — but that could be overcome somewhat through a flexible use of space and coordination with neighboring schools and service agencies. Furthermore, they ask, isn't it worth sacrificing a huge auditorium or a separate music room if you can keep kids in school? This rethinking of scale and function was about to be realized in more than thirty experimental high schools, and I came to New York City in the summer before they opened to talk to some of the people who would be directing them.

There is a long history of educational reform in New York City, emerging both from within the public school establishment and outside it. There were attempts, through the early settlement houses, to respond to the needs of immigrants; there was the progressive education movement, prominent at Columbia Teachers College from the 1920s through the 1940s; and there were the experiments during the 1960s and 1970s with open education, free schools, and street academies. The basic concerns of those earlier movements can be found, in varied incarnations, in the work of the current reformers: addressing the needs of immigrants and the urban poor, employing the classroom as a laboratory for democracy, involving students as active agents in their own learning, connecting school to community, and treating education as a vehicle for social change. But there were two more immediate and overlapping influences, which affected many of the current reformers as they came of professional age.

One influence was the public schools begun in the mid-1970s in Manhattan's District 4 (East Harlem) by veteran teacher Deborah Meier and her colleagues and by the district superintendent, an imaginative and risk-taking son of East Harlem named Anthony Alvarado, and his assistant, Sy Fliegel. These schools — there are now over fifty of them, mostly middle schools — were small (two or three could be housed in one standard school building), involved teachers in governance and decision-making, and were open to children outside their neighborhoods, even outside the district. The schools varied in quality and in the degree to which they experimented with curriculum — some were more traditional than others. A number of them were centered on a theme: performing arts, science, journalism, humanities. Among the most experimental and the most nationally visible, were Central Park East Elementary School (the original school) and Central Park East Secondary School (opened in 1985), both of which have been directed by Meier. The faculty in these two small schools have spent an extraordinary amount of time trying to create open, exploratory classrooms that demand a high level of achievement. A complex meld of rigor and play, of traditional and experimental education.

The second influence was the city's alternative high schools, some of which developed from those 1960s' experiments with free schools and street academies. They are considerably smaller than the standard high school and have tended to serve special populations: young people who have been in trouble or are "at risk," immigrant children, creative kids fading in traditional classrooms, students with special interests in performing arts or science or a particular vocation. In 1983, Anthony Alvarado, having risen from the superintendency of District 4 to the chancellorship of the city schools, established a citywide superintendency for alternative high schools, thereby creating a structure for their fuller development, an administrative niche where experiments in secondary education could find a wider public house.

School reform in New York City, then, has a long spiritual and conceptual history, blending both private and public initiatives, but it is significant that the current innovations are playing out almost entirely within the public school establishment. Nearly all of those involved are long-time teachers and administrators. As one put it, "We *are* the school system." And it is hard to imagine a system more imposing — the largest, most complex school system in the United States. It enrolls a million children in a thousand schools spread across thirty-two elementary and junior high school districts (each with a local school board and superintendent), six high school superintendencies (one per borough — Manhattan, Bronx, Queens, Brooklyn, Staten Island — and the sixth for alternative high schools), all connected, by a variety of governance agreements, to a massive centralized bureaucracy (employing, by one count, six thousand people), the central board, and the chancellor, whose job has been called "the toughest in American education." The system employs 125,000 people, has an operating budget of $7.5 billion, is the twelfth largest corporation in the United States. How strange and how fitting that experiments in scale should take place in this city. The experimental high schools I came to study were set to enroll about a hundred students each. The cap on each would be about five hundred kids.

Though several of these schools came about through local initiatives, most were developed by two mechanisms. One was the Center for Collaborative Education, a coalition of New York schools (including the Central Park East schools mentioned earlier) affiliated with a national coalition of over 750, mostly public, reform-minded schools called the Coalition of Essential Schools, founded by Theodore Sizer, former chairman of the Department of Education at Brown University. The second mechanism was a program called New Visions Schools, which sought to enlist organizations outside the school system — labor unions, colleges, community organizations, churches, museums — to sponsor new public schools. The hope was that such partnerships would spark creativity and provide resources and a measure of external support. But, though there were differences, there were two important similarities between Coalition and New Visions schools: a number of private foundations came together to assist with development money, and there was a network of advocates outside the specific Coalition or New Vision school that would — at least some of the time — help the new school navigate the bureaucracy of the New York City school system.

In all, I got to spend time with nine of the new directors. Louis Delgado, Charlene Jordan, Sylvia Rabiner, Bill Ling, and Haven Henderson were part of the Coalition network; Mary Stevens, Mark Weiss, Michael Johnson, and Frances Lucerna were developing New Visions schools. For most, this would be their first time running a school; for a few, their first venture into administration. They had not planned to become principals when they first entered the classroom. Now they were meeting daily with their teachers (and some were still hiring), developing curricula from the ground up, fresh, not without strain; working out different patterns for the day by rethinking the traditional schedule, and thereby rethinking the philosophy of education behind it; getting the word out — by parent and student convocations — to junior high students across the city, bringing their vision to the people of the city who could choose or reject it; chasing down furniture and supplies, haggling over space, troubleshooting a thousand big and little problems.

And there were problems. There were the inevitable complexities of moving from individual vision to group practice and of getting those students who had been ignored and betrayed for so long to trust what they were trying to do. Furthermore, the system itself was still reverberating from the recent stormy dismissal of its dynamic and controversial chancellor, Joseph Fernandez. And, for all the drive of the political moment, the new schools were still embedded within a cumbersome, troubled bureaucracy, a system backlogged, by one estimate, with forty-three thousand work orders. To make matters even worse, as fall got closer, an earlier inspection of asbestos contamination would be declared suspect, possibly fraudulent, and that would delay the opening of all New York schools. This and other logistical and material snafus would send some of the new directors and their teachers shuttling to two, three, and in one case *four* temporary sites, a brutal disruption, trying to create schools out of boxes, on the run. But for all that, the work moved forward, a time of stimulating and anxious possibility. As one director put it, "We might fail. Ten years from now, this might be seen as a dead end. But look at what we're trying to do: change the face of the biggest educational bureaucracy in the country."

I met with the directors whenever they could hold things at bay. I worked from a brief list of questions: What do you hope to accomplish? What are your fears? What makes change so hard? Why is change in public education worth working for? The conversations that followed didn't always stick to the list, took some interesting personal turns, opened up a range of topics. Most discussions of school reform and restructuring, certainly at the legislative and policy level, center on broad performance goals (raising test scores, increasing retention) usually framed in a discourse of institutional participation and economic competitiveness. These concerns were not absent from our conversations, but what emerged revealed more about the human dimension of structural change, the complex blend of motives that would compel someone to work so hard to reimagine public schools. As the new directors spoke — over breakfast, at the end of the day, in the evening as the light softened outside the windows — a rich blend of life history, classroom experience, beliefs, and values came forth, multilayered, unfolding.

Louis Delgado, Vanguard High School

Louis Delgado was about five foot eight or five foot nine, thin mustache, thick dark brown hair, powerfully built — a weightlifter's torso — wore a dress shirt and tie in the 100° heat of a New York summer. He was upbeat, had a full smile and a hearty laugh, and he spoke with a trace of a Brooklyn accent. His articulation was precise — hitting each syllable in words like momentum, political, *stressing the* t *in* respect *— as though the words carried weight, as though each deserved special care.*

It's a remarkable time. We can experiment, really take chances and risks — just like we expect our students to do! How long will it last? I don't know. As the going gets tough, there will be people retreating to the old ways of thinking. There's a mindset, tradition, and everyone carries it: teachers, parents, students. But right now, there's momentum. Look, people are fed up with what's going on; you can see the results of our factory-type education before kids get out of their teens. I don't want to be part of that. I want to be part of the solution. This is a golden opportunity to make change.

I want to create a school in which people respect learning. This isn't just about teachers getting respect; students have to feel respected too. I don't want to get psychoanalytical about this, but I'm sure this is tied to my own experience. It's . . . it's not just about being polite — even the curriculum has to convey respect. The curriculum has to be challenging enough that it's respectful. I want to be accountable for that. Yeah, I do. I want the school to be a place that's welcoming, has a nice tone, a place where you can voice your opinion, where you can make mistakes, where there's constructive criticism. A place safe enough for students to criticize each other, hold debates, argue both sides of an issue.

There's no way in the world this is going to be smooth sailing. It's going to be a struggle. But you pick your struggles, and this is the one I've chosen. My job as director will be to keep us all focused, because when there's a struggle, we all have a tendency to retreat back to tradition. We're going to have to throw ourselves way out there! We can't stay too close to home — it has to be radical. Change will not happen over one graduating class. It may take the rest of my career; it may take a generation to make a dent. I get up in the middle of the night — this has happened a whole bunch of times over the past five or six months — and I write out all these unanswered questions.

I was born and raised in Brooklyn. Went to parochial school through the eighth grade. But when I was thirteen, my father died, so I went to Puerto Rico, to a Catholic boarding school. I must tell you, I was very unhappy. I had lost my dad, and I was sent away. It was a difficult time. Punitive. Condescending. At seventeen I went into the navy. And it was there that I met racism head on. It made me feel like I wasn't an American. In Brooklyn, I was in a primarily Puerto Rican neighborhood. Then I went to Puerto Rico. The navy had a powerful effect on me. I felt powerless, second, third class. I felt humiliated. It was a struggle, a real uphill battle, but [laughs] one I volunteered for!

After the navy, I went home to Brooklyn. I was twenty, unemployed, collecting, I remember, exactly sixty dollars a week. Finally, from the unemployment line one day, they pulled out ten former enlisted men and said, "OK, you ten have jobs. You have to go to this training, and you'll become a security officer in the schools." "A security officer?" I thought. "Well, at least I'll have a job." It was through the CETA program, and when it was over, they sent me to a junior high school in Coney Island, the other side of Brooklyn. A tough place. Little did I know that would be a turning point. I was surrounded by people who were involved with learning.

Let me tell you, I understood the kids. The struggles they were going through were struggles I could relate to. When these teenagers talked to me about their craziness, I had an ear for it. And I began to offer guidance. I got very close to a lot of kids, and their parents started inviting me to dinner. It was a nice relationship. Well, the administration noticed this and asked me if I wanted to become a paraprofessional, a teacher's assistant. They wanted me to work with the special ed students — a very needy bunch. I also started to go to school, to chip away at my college credits. Two years as a security officer, five years as a paraprofessional, I got my B.A. I felt so proud and honored. And that's how I became a teacher.

I went to an alternative high school and helped them develop a program for special ed students to do internships. It's a crime what happens to special ed kids, dead-end, the bottom, in basements — they're exposed to their weaknesses all the time. So here I was, trying to set them up for internships, internships that *they* chose. "You want to be a mechanic, fine. You want to be a lawyer, OK." My job wasn't to question; my job was to set them up so that they'd be working with mechanics or lawyers. And they'd see that in a lawyer's office, for example, not everyone was a lawyer. They'd discover a range of career opportunities — and they were where they wanted to be. That opened up a lot of doors for them. And it was amazing! Parents were calling and telling me about their child's new self-confidence.

What I learned from this was that all children can learn — if you provide the proper setting and tools. Sure, everyone has limits. Everyone has strengths and weaknesses. All of us. But if you can figure out how to help students maximize what they have, there can be a place for everyone. It was so encouraging to recruit those young people and place them and monitor their progress. An incredible experience. And, once again, people noticed the work I was doing and encouraged me to move more into administration. So I became the director of the Internships Department and, later, an assistant principal. And a short while ago, I was selected to direct this new school.

I guess I've really come to believe in the things a school can do. I mean, consider: we're talking with people in the community, trying to set things up so that we can have after-school programs. Going back to the TV, hanging out on the corner — that is not constructive. There are so many obstacles for these students. I want to create a school that's open from eight to eight — no joke — that has art, dance, weightlifting, a place to study, tutoring. A lot of our kids don't have a place to go. I want to provide a place they can stay at, come back to. We'll be getting kids at the age of thirteen or fourteen. They'll be looking for guidance. They have to resolve problems today that adults have trouble resolving.

What I think I want, what keeps me going is that I want to give every student the feeling that they have a chance after high school. Whatever it is they want to do. I want them to have the sense that they can make a difference. I know it can happen because I lived it. I want to give that back. To be able to touch a lot of students — that would mean the world to me. To get these kids graduating with a sense of hope. I have a great staff. We want [laughs], we want to start an *epidemic* of hope.

Charlene Jordan, The Coalition School for Social Change

Charlene Jordan — Charlene Marie Carmella Valicenti Jordan — was forty years old, five foot six inches tall, had brown eyes, brown hair, a smoky voice like one you'd hear on late-night radio, and a quick happy laugh with a little catch at the end. She was outgoing, direct, coming up to you through a full room, hand extended, smiling. "Hi, I'm Charlene Jordan." Talking to a group of parents, she was both informal and respectful, telling a story, laughing at herself, getting serious when a question required it.

Her school would eventually be located in a renovated office building on West Fifty-eighth Street near Broadway, in affluent midtown Manhattan, right below Columbus Circle, close to the Museum of Modern Art and Carnegie Hall. Her first class of students would be primarily Black and Latino, drawn from Central and East Harlem, with a small number of Jews and Italians from midtown. She took a hand in the redesign of the interior, shaping it to suit her vision of the school. The building was still under construction when we met, and was beset with delays. It would not be ready until several months after *school was scheduled to start, so Charlene was spending a lot of time finding temporary quarters. "It's been a hairy summer."*

We met, then, in the recreation room of her house about forty-five minutes north of the city, just beyond Yonkers. There was a still life behind us, bright oil swirls of peaches and apples. The table we sat at was full of papers and food, my tape recorder wedged between plates of cheddar and smoked mozzarella and sliced cantaloupe. As we talked, we could hear her husband fixing something in the kitchen upstairs, and her nine-year-old daughter and a friend playing in the back yard, just beyond the window.

I'm a Bronx girl, born and raised. My grandparents, on both sides, were born in Italy and immigrated here. I grew up in a lower-middle-class Italian and Jewish neighborhood. We lived in attached houses. It was very communal — you know, a communal cement back yard! I was raised with lots of kids. My father worked in the garment industry, and his father was one of the organizers for the union. We didn't have a lot of money, a lot of things. My uncle lived with us, and my grandmother came to live with us, and I had two sisters — so it was a real extended family, and it was, ah, *interesting*. In retrospect, I think it was a wonderful way to grow up, though I didn't always think that then. I can remember sometimes being embarrassed, but now I look back on it and want to be like them. We have big family dinners, and holidays are a big deal for me. I came to appreciate it.

My father really wanted me to go to college. I was a good student, got real good grades, and I would be the first one in my family to go to college. But there was no money to send me any place except City College. So I went to Lehman [of the City University of New York], where tuition was sixty dollars a semester. With books, my entire college education probably cost eight hundred dollars! I think it did a lot for me. It opened up a completely different way of thinking. At first I couldn't handle the freedom; I had always been so restricted. And it showed. I didn't do well the first term; I just wanted to sit around and watch. [Laughs.] But I stayed with it, and I learned a lot about myself.

When I accepted this position to direct the school, my fantasy was that I was going to be able to visit schools all over New York City and have deep philosophical discussions about education. Well, I've had time to visit a few schools and talk to a few people. Not much more. Instead, my staff and I, we've gotten sucked into all kinds of bureaucratic tangles, little — excuse me — bullshit things, which, I suppose, is part and parcel of opening a school. It doesn't have to be that way. It's just that the system is not set up to deal with change; it's hard to get them to change their view of how schools should run.

Having the opportunity to meet the kids and their parents was probably the best part of these last few months. Kids are what ground you; they remind you of what you're supposed to be doing. Going to the meetings and actually sitting with parents and kids and talking about their hopes and dreams, finding out what the kids are looking for in a school.

Kids say they want safe places. They're real concerned about that. They also want — and they're very clear about this — they want teachers who take an interest in them, and get to know them, and who don't judge them too harshly before they find out what they really can do. I remember one group in particular — we were out at this middle school, and a girl stood up and said she doesn't want teachers who will judge her too harshly, and the other kids started nodding, going, "Yeah. Yeah." "What does that mean?" I asked. "Well," she said, "sometimes you really *do* know things, but it takes you a little bit longer to say what you know or do what you know — and we want people who are patient with us and won't rush us."

Parents ask very difficult questions. Right from the beginning they ask, "How are you going to get my kid ready for college? And what does your curriculum do? What are you going to be teaching them? What does the first year look like? What kind of classes?" All the questions I still can't answer! There are also lots of questions about kids who have been classified special ed, and whether these kinds of schools can work for them. The parents want to know how, if the school is so small, you can provide as good an education as a big school with so many different teachers and programs. Well, that's a great question. How *does* a small school compensate? They make us think hard. They also want to know what role there is for them in the school. And I tell them I don't know exactly, because, to be honest, I haven't seen it done well — parental involvement — have *never* seen it done well. You hear school people saying how we're going to "empower" parents by asking them to come in and be part of a committee. But nobody tells them what their role is going to be on this committee, and they've never done this before, and nobody gives them any guidelines. So they walk into a school that they don't really know — and all of a sudden, they're supposed to be "empowered." It's absurd. And disrespectful. But we do have a little core of parents who want to be involved. They're very articulate and a little pushy — and I like that 'cause I'm a little pushy — and I think they're going to do good things. They realize that they're going to have to help define their role. I'm anxious for the parents, the kids, and the teachers to become a community — but that's not so easy to do. Everybody says "a school is a culture," but, you know, you *build* a culture. It doesn't walk in the door with you.

What's exciting to me is that I'm working with people who are saying, "Let's start and see where this goes." The teachers I'm working with left comfortable positions to work in this school. That's what this is for me, a chance to work with a group of people who reject settling, reject complacency, who want to make a place that we can modify from year to year, try things we've never dreamed of. That's what this is for me, a chance to work with people willing to do whatever it takes to educate children.

Look, change is hard. It's not always rewarded. When you do something different — even when it works — people don't always look at it and say, "Wow, that's terrific!" People are afraid of change. Maybe they're afraid they'll have to change, too — and maybe they're afraid they can't. I don't know. Changing a system means you have to change something about yourself. It's not just how you do things, but how you think. And, God, that has to affect other things in your life. If you begin to question the "why" and the "how," well, then, maybe you begin to question other aspects of your life. You change how you think about yourself and your life. Scary [laughs] and fun.

My biggest fear is that we're not going to be able to do the kinds of things for children that we want to do. I worry. We're going to have kids who have done very poorly. And we have all these hopes, these expectations for them: we imagine them — you see it in your head — we imagine all these kids standing and presenting their work at the end of the year. But then you think, "My God, are we going to be able to help this kid do this?" The work we want them to do will be hard. Are *we* going to be able to help them? Maybe not right away, but by year two or year three? Will we be able to keep believing in them? If we lose our belief in them, we're dead. That's my biggest fear. Will we be able to learn from our mistakes? I hope I can provide the leadership to enable this to happen.

I've seen success in public schools. And I've seen a lot of awful things, things that make me angry. It's not just to do this to people. Something has to change. But in the alternative schools I've worked in, when I see kids being successful who were unsuccessful before, when I see them beginning to plan for the future — then I know it can be done. So the question for me becomes "Who's going to do it?" Well, *I* want to do it. I want to be part of the movement. Public education is fundamental to democracy, and I believe it is the place where all people should come together.

Of course it's going to be hard. Of course. But too many in this country have the belief that if it's too hard, we should just stop. That we should throw people away. But you don't throw people away. You throw away ideas, maybe, but you don't just toss out a whole generation of kids. It's a struggle. But it has to be done.

This is the biggest public education system in the nation. It's such a challenge. But if we can make public education work for the people in this city, then people all around the country can look and say, "Well, if *they* can do it, then *we* can do it, too." And that's what I hope for, that it's not just this little piece of West Fifty-eighth Street I'm going to affect. All these people are doing new schools in Brooklyn and the Bronx and Queens, and if we can all make some important differences in kids' lives, differences people can look at, well, that would be something.

Sylvia Rabiner, Landmark High School

Sylvia Rabiner's school, like Charlene Jordan's, would be in that renovated office building in midtown Manhattan. And, like Charlene, she was frazzled by the delays and the search for a temporary site. I met Sylvia at the end of one of her long days in the High School of the Humanities, between Chelsea and Greenwich Village, on West Eighteenth Street. The entrance took me into a huge, high-ceilinged foyer, cathedral-like, dark but for the sunlight from the open door and the broken panes of stained glass. A guard pointed me back through a far hallway, and I found Sylvia in a conference room in the rear of the school. We sat at the corner of an old table, leaning in from each side of the angle. A big fan by the window whirred through our conversation.

In addition to teaching in New York high schools, coordinating staff development and school-based management programs, and teaching English in Turkey and the Philippines, Sylvia has been a freelance writer, publishing in Mademoiselle, Working Mother, *and* The Village Voice. *She had short, dark brown hair, wore glasses, was in her late forties. In the heat of the day, she wore sandals, a willowy skirt, and a blue, sleeveless top. Her voice was melodic, a touch of drama to it, a tendency toward rising intonation at the end of a sentence, questioning, curious, soft and passionate.*

I'll be honest with you. I worry, "Can I do this?" At its worst, at its very worst, the worry is like this: I'll get to our temporary building on the first day of school, and boxes will be arriving, and carpenters will be carpentering, and there will be no procedures in place, and my staff will be immensely anxious. It's sort of this vision [laughs] of *hell!* The fear has to do with the unknown. Will I have the skill to manage the people? Will I be able to handle the irate parent? How about food services, the vendors, the computers for the kids, the school board? Now, of course, if I take it apart piece by piece, I've already done a lot of these things. It's a more general fear: everyone is depending on me. It all comes and stops here. The buck stops here. And I want to take care of everybody, and I want to do it right.

There have been a lot of sleepless nights, let me tell you. A million details to take care of. Weekends, I can't see friends because I need time to sort things out. It's not as if you're starting a school and can just replicate something that exists — no, you're being asked to *create* a place. How do you do this and still remain tied in with the larger system? All the requirements, all the competency exams — they still exist.

Things that are important, that lead to growth, cause pain. But it's time. It's time for me to stretch and test my limits. There was a lot about working in a big system that was horrible: the repressiveness, the control. I used to work in a school of six thousand kids — lots of working-class Italian and Polish kids, some Hispanic kids — and there were times when I felt like I was sitting on something that could explode. It was deadly. I mean, when I was a reading teacher, the kids were required to read out of kits, to read out of *kits*. Now, if there's anything on God's green Earth that's gonna make you hate reading, it's being asked to find the main idea fifty times a day on why insects do some damned thing.

So one day I went to the book room and found some old anthologies that nobody wanted. They had D. H. Lawrence stories and, let's see, E. B White. Traditional stuff. My kids were ranked very low as readers, and people thought, "Well, if they can't read, they can't think." And so we read these stories, and, when necessary, I read them aloud — and the kids got into hot discussions. It wasn't that they couldn't think or couldn't be interested. It enraged me that people had made assumptions about their capacity for an intellectual life. These were imaginative, funny kids. Energetic. Very courageous. I just kept thinking, there's so much talent here that society wastes. Labels and wastes. Doesn't encourage. We don't listen to them.

Maybe I'm going to be very disappointed with this new school of ours. Maybe school, by its very nature, just keeps sliding back into being school. Maybe we can't do it. But I think there are ways to make it much more interesting. My hope is that by gathering together in one small school people who share a vision, we can make a difference.

If these small schools succeed, they could open up possibilities for doing things in a new way. Look at what happens to new teachers. We could affect the way we help new teachers, change what happens to them when they enter their first school. Ask teachers about their first experience. Almost without exception, you'll hear a horror story. It's almost as if everything is done to make their lives as hard as possible, with the idea, I suppose, that the weak will sink, and the strong will stay — like some kind of boot camp. There's a lot about a big school that leaves you completely unsupported. In my first school, we never talked about teaching. My chairperson was selling real estate. Everybody there had a job doing something else. People had Tupperware parties in the cafeteria. One woman [laughs] was selling semiporn underwear. It was a bizarre place. Six thousand kids. Three hundred and fifty adults. So if you're a new, young teacher in a place like that, you're given a schedule of classes — some of which will probably be new to you — and you're told to do a good job, and you're fighting to stay alive. It exhausts you. How do they expect people to survive and thrive?

I have one completely new teacher on my staff. During our meeting this morning, she was saying how glad she was to be here. And another guy, someone who's been teaching for sixteen years, said, "Boy, when I started, nobody talked to me. I haven't talked teaching this much since I began. I'm so lucky to be here with you all." It was a wonderful moment. At times like that, I'm very happy.

You know, we're always speaking about "it," the system, as if the system is some force that existed independently of people. Maybe in a horrible way, that becomes the case. We talk about all these well-meaning people who somehow get *seized* by the system and are corrupted by it. Well, maybe that's what happens. At the end of my first month at that big school, I got my time card back from the assistant principal with four red circles on it — those times when, instead of coming in at 8:35, I had punched in at 8:36 or 8:37. Is that the system? Or is that some awful corruption that happened to this man — something that made him think that it was going to improve me as a human being or improve my teaching to humiliate me by letting me know in *that* way that, over the course of a month, I was eight minutes late? You hear these stories repeated over and over. Is that the system? Or some mindless compliance to it?

Big schools are wonderfully efficient machines for moving paper along. That big high school worked like a charm with six thousand kids. It *functioned* beautifully. It was as if all the procedures were in place to accommodate the system but not the people in it. It was good for the building, I suppose, that all the kids were quiet and facing straight ahead. Not making a peep. But was it good for any of the human beings in the building? Am I making sense? We had lost sight of who we really were, both the staff and the kids. You can't treat people that way. The kids respond by cutting, by hostility, by setting fires in the waste baskets. The staff reacts with anger. They get cynical; they burn out.

In our new school, we'll really need to keep focused on what's important to us, even if it means that we'll bypass or subvert the rules and regs. I think we're on the right track. We're working together as teams. We're building into the schedule time for people to talk to one another. There's lots of participation, and I want to make sure that continues as the school grows. We're paying attention to the students as they come in, really looking at who they are, meeting with their families. Organizations need to be personal. Everybody needs to have the sense that they can be heard. It doesn't take a whole hell of a lot to make people feel delighted. A principal I know said his job is to pay attention to the staff so that they can pay attention to the students. That personalization has to go right across the board, has to encompass the secretaries, the parents, everyone. Everyone in a school should be there to help, and if that atmosphere exists, it's got to be better for the kids. Is it still possible to talk about love?

Mary Stevens, the 1199 School for Social Change

The New Visions school Mary Stevens would be directing was sponsored by New York's Drug, Hospital, and Health Care Union, Local 1199. With a membership of nearly 120,000 — from orderlies and home care workers to nurses and lab techs — 1199 was one of the most powerful unions in the state. I learned about the 1199 School for Social Change by visiting first with Moe Foner, a long-time union activist and current director of the union's Bread and Roses Cultural Project, and Susan Kempler, the coordinator of the 1199 Adult Education Program. We met in the Bread and Roses office on West Forty-second Street. Moe was in his seventies, thin and angular, precise haircut, glasses; Susan was in her early fifties, had a gentle face, blue eyes, salt-and-pepper hair. We sat around Moe's cluttered desk, the phone emitting a frequent oscillating beep. There were books and papers stacked all around us, a VCR and large monitor, boxes of videotapes and audio cassettes ("1199: The History of a Fighting Union," "Not Bread Alone: A Conference on Workers' Culture"), and, along the walls, a series of framed posters called "Images of Labor" that combined reflections on work and society with paintings and sketches of working people.

Moe began with an overview of the union. In addition to contract agreements, what he called the "bread and butter issues," 1199 had developed cultural projects, sponsored child care, a children's camp, scholarship funds, youth mentoring programs, and a series of educational and training programs "to help people move up the ladder from dead-end jobs to more skilled jobs." So, "with that kind of background" and given the political moment, "we felt we should begin thinking about schools."

The school would be located in the Bronx — in temporary quarters for now — open to all children, though special effort would be made to recruit the children of 1199 members. It would begin as a high school, ninth grade through twelfth, but the plan was to eventually make it kindergarten through twelve and offer adult education classes for the parents of its students. There was talk between the state and the federal Department of Housing and Urban Development about building a model housing project in the Bronx, and if that came to pass — "it's a long way off" — it would become an ideal setting for the 1199 school.

Susan explained that the school would focus on the sciences, biology particularly, public policy, public health, and community organiz-

ing — trying to tap the multiple ways health care could play out across a curriculum. And for students not interested in a health care career, there would be a number of other, related pursuits: business, computer science, social science, and the arts, particularly the intersection of art and political activism. The union affiliation — especially a union with the connections of 1199 — would also make possible a range of mentorships and internships.

The affiliation with 1199 was of aid in yet another, more immediate, way, laid out by both Moe and Susan, taking turns, switching back and forth. The school "is operating within the board of education's nest, and that creates all kinds of problems." There were problems with hiring and work rules — whom the school could hire and when and what teachers would be allowed to do. "Virtually every day, new problems arise." It was here — in the political zone "that saps so much energy" — that 1199 was particularly resourceful, the union's "political clout" helping to "overcome what could be insurmountable obstacles." Phone calls, favors called in, pressure applied, compromises struck — "you play every card you can." And so, in fits and starts, the 1199 School for Social Change moved toward realization. "We don't anticipate that we're going to change the map of the world with this one small school," Moe said in closing. "But," Susan added, "every little bit helps."

One week later, I met the school's director, Mary Stevens, in a coffee shop called Socrates, located in the Tribeca (Triangle Below Canal Street) section of Manhattan. Socrates was lined with red Naugahyde booths and Formica tables — mirrors ran alongside, beginning right at your shoulder. I found a booth in the back, the kitchen door flapping open, the dishes clattering beyond. A full breakfast was three or four bucks.

Mary chose it because it was close to one of her morning appointments, but still she rushed in a half-hour late, her clogs tip-tapping rapidly across the linoleum, apologizing for yet another meeting that absorbed more time than anticipated. She wore her hair cut close to rich brown skin, wore wire-rim glasses and simple hoop earrings. She looked to be in her mid-thirties, casual in a T-shirt tucked into dark gray pants. She seemed harried, yet quickly assumed control. Moe had described Mary as someone who "liked kids tremendously and was full of piss and vinegar," and I heard that mix of affection and intensity in her voice. She was a powerful child advocate.

It's been hard. Starting a different school is so hard. I have a dynamite staff, and we have a site now, but there are tentative things about it and many anxieties about space. I don't have a secretary yet, so I have to deal with mounds of stuff. Sometimes I get to the school at seven-thirty in the morning and get home at ten o'clock at night. I don't think that people who aren't educators understand everything that's involved. And that you can't be on the run all the time. You need time to reflect on what you're doing. Otherwise, you just repeat the same old things that don't work. You can have crappy small schools too. My staff and I are at the beginning of things, and we have to move very fast. One of my staff said, "My God, we're doing a week's work in a day!" And she's right. So how can we reflect on things? It's as if we're saying [laughs], "I know you need time, but hurry up and take your time!" It frightens the hell out of me. But calm down, Mary. Calm down.

But look at what's possible! That's what excites me about this. What has happened to many kids, particularly poor kids, particularly children of color — their possibilities have been stunted. We talk about freedom, we talk about having a stake in the society, we talk about educating kids to become positive citizens. But some kids get more of that than others. Whether we do it consciously or not, we educate certain kids to be in power, to be leaders, and other kids to be at the bottom of the heap. It frightens me that we lose so much humanity. It's one thing to say kids don't come to school prepared to learn, but it's quite another to say let's take the child as he is when he walks in the door. It's up to *us* to help the child find out what his strengths are, and help him develop those strengths. Are we willing to do it? A teacher has to say, "If a child is not learning, then I'm not doing my job." A teacher's job is to educate children, and if ten kids aren't learning, then you have to ask yourself, "What is going wrong?" And not say that there's something wrong with this population — as we tend to do — but ask instead, "What aren't we doing right?" Are our egos strong enough to do that?

Some of our kids don't feel their lives are worth living. This is a country with so much wealth, and you mean to tell me we can't feed our kids? We can't put our kids in a bed at night? We can't educate them? There's public outrage when kids shoot each other. But how can you treat kids inhumanely, then turn around and say to them, "Act like a human being!" We devalue kids, ignore them, allow them to grow up in horrendous circumstances — and then when they kill, we're shocked. But they've become exactly what we told them they are. Teachers can't allow this to continue.

I think we need to rethink schools. The world's changed and we're going to have to change with it. Maybe schools should become the hub of the community. Providing health services. Adult education for parents. Day care. School is the one place everyone is still connected to. Churches aren't what they used to be. Families aren't. But all kids *do go to school.* Now, *this* is where social action comes into play. This may be one of the most important ways our connections to 1199 will play out; 1199 lives what they speak. They have significantly bettered the lives of their constituency. And they have definitely made their constituency feel a part of their group. *That's* what I want us to achieve with our kids, to make them feel that they own this place, that they belong in this school.

I've been thinking a lot about people who've had to take their own circumstances into their hands and change them. Nelson Mandela, for example. Or Rigoberta Menchú [the indigenous peoples activist and Nobel Prize winner]. How do you begin again? Some of our kids will be coming from schools where they haven't been successful. So can we look at someone like Nelson Mandela, someone who lived through horrible circumstances, and ask, "How did this man come out whole?" Read about him, talk and write about him. And maybe we then have kids write biographies of their own family members who have made it through tough times. Analyze how they were able to survive, to sustain themselves. And isn't labor history germane here? How people have said, "Enough already!" — and how they changed themselves collectively.

We have to be sure our kids have real skills, that they're well educated, well read, that they know how to communicate, both orally and in writing. Let me be clear about something: though we're trying to develop new curricula and a new kind of school, I don't think all traditional education is bad. My second-grade teacher, Mrs. Perkins — I'll never forget Mrs. Perkins! She had the most exciting classroom I've seen. We sat in those little seats, straight ahead [laughs], and we made those little loops to learn how to write. And nobody's psyche got damaged. And we did all this wonderful stuff. She had kids actively engaged. She brought in interesting things for us to do. She cared about us. She wanted us to learn. Be careful about what you call "traditional." If a child isn't learning to read and write, you may have to sit down and do very step-by-step things. Sometimes kids have to follow routines, do things by rote. We make a big mistake when we categorize whole ways of doing things as "bad." It depends on the interaction between teacher and student, depends on the nature of the relationship. I think it would be interesting to look closely at what *good* traditional teachers did. What did they do that was successful?

My staff and I are right now trying to figure out what kids need to know in order to be powerful, in order to continue to educate themselves, in order to become agents of change. We're struggling with that. Look [laughs], we are not training urban guerrillas. But I think it *is* revolutionary to get kids to believe they are worthy, to think, to understand themselves as learning, growing beings — and to realize that in order to grow, they must continue to change. And how can we help them see that even if you've had a very, very hard life, there have been things that have supported you up to this point. What rituals, what people have sustained you? And how can we create a school that offers something further to sustain these children? A core, some thread that binds us, something that runs through the culture of the school. A respect for all individuals. This is what we have to work out — and figure out how to translate that into a curriculum that says to every child: We believe in you. We believe you have the capacity to change yourself.

I worry that as our children become assured and critical thinkers, the society will not be ready for them. Many of these kids come from populations that have historically been on the bottom, and have not been expected to achieve much. My hope is that if the society isn't ready, the kids will have the tools to change it, to make their voices heard, that they will be astute enough to know the ways to get in there and be heard, that they'll know what collective action can do, what can happen when you join your voice with others — that change may not occur overnight, but if you keep hammering, it will happen. That that fine sand was once a rock. That you don't give up the struggle.

Mark Weiss, The School for the Physical City

The New Visions school Mark Weiss would be directing was the School for the Physical City, and its mission, as the promotional material read, was to "prepare and empower city youth to take care of and take charge of the city." It would combine middle and high school, running from sixth grade to twelfth. Unlike most of the New Visions schools, this one had multiple sponsors: Cooper Union, a private, tuition-free arts, architecture, and engineering college geared toward the children of working people; Outward Bound, which was trying to apply its expeditionary character-building program to educational settings; and the New York City Mission Society, the oldest charitable organization in the city, which was interested in facilitating parent and community involvement in the school. "They all came together separately," Mark explained, "but seemed a natural fit." His hope was that the multiple partners would lead to additional human and fiscal resources: advocacy, technical expertise, links to city planners and architects and college faculty, and, of course, dollars.

Mark Weiss was forty-nine years old and had taught high school, been a principal, worked at the Board of Education, and, most recently, been an assistant to the superintendent of alternative high schools. He had a wealth of administrative experience and connections. We spoke in the kitchen of his house, cast-iron skillets hanging nearby, an old grocery scale, braided garlic, hot red peppers, bunches of thyme and rosemary, and a cluster of dried flowers, silver green and lavender. Newspapers and books were lying on the table and on the preparation area by the sink. He was currently reading Seymour Papert's The Children's Machine, *a book about computer technology and schooling.*

Mark, stocky in red T-shirt and jeans, had gray hair, a beard with a little brown still in it, and a boyish face — a warm, friendly presence. During the time I spent with him in New York, I saw him strike up conversation with a security guard, a cashier in a market, and a park ranger — giving advice and a good repairman's phone number to the ranger. He loved to talk and loved to entertain ideas — and his wide reading in literature and politics gave him an unusual take on things. He punctuated his speech with slang, with questions, with self-interrogation, with stories that drove home a theoretical point, with statistics that girded his dream.

Let me give you some numbers. At the high school level, we have twenty-five thousand kids already in small, alternative, public school choice programs. There are fifty new schools planned for this year and next. So if each school gets started, and each school serves, on the average, five hundred kids, then you have another twenty-five thousand kids served by what we hope will be better places. There are 272,000 kids in the public high schools in New York City, so a total of fifty thousand would bring us up to a fifth of the total. Now, if we can show that this is the right way to go, then we might be able to double the number to a hundred thousand. And that would be a critical mass for big change.

Kids are falling away from school at early ages. As soon as they are capable of leaving or resisting it or rejecting it, that's what they do. By statistics, by data, we know that in large high schools, the percentage of graduates compared to those entering is incredibly small. We've lowered the drop-out rate; kids are staying in school longer — and then not graduating. The statistics have not gotten better. There's a school in the Bronx that has eighteen hundred kids and graduates a hundred a year. That's not unusual. Alternative schools — where I've done my work — do better with graduation rates. But the primary challenge made against us is: Are alternative schools too easy, too loose, not academically rigorous? That's a common thread in the criticism of alternative schools, and those of us who are in them worry about that criticism and want to stretch ourselves to educate kids well. We know we can get kids to come to school, and we know we can educate some kids well. But we don't know if we can educate large numbers well. We need to prove ourselves.

But to tell you the truth, I don't know if we can do it within the budgets we're typically given. Some people would like to believe we can do it for 10 percent more money. But my own sense — and I've been in administration a long time — is that resources are really important, and money drives what you can do in a school. Sure, a heroic principal can take a minute budget and find some great people, and they can bust their chops for five years — and make one great school. But, really, what's so great about that? One great school's not good enough. We can't afford to do that to our kids.

I don't think I've ever thought as clearly about what learning is. The big leap between teachers learning in order to teach and then teachers knowing enough about learning in order to teach what they know. That's fascinating to me. Now, the models we have guide us to learn in big groups, but the best form of education is tutoring. Intimate human relationships. No one at a policy level ever says that, though, because we can't afford it. So we have an approximation of what good education is. See, it's dollars again. I mean, we worked out a space plan for the new school that would allow for lots of individual work, and when we presented it to the central office, the person there said, "That's not efficient." She didn't like the openness of the rooms. And I said, "I don't think we should be interested in efficiency; we should be interested in what's good for kids." Right? Now it'll be my job to keep an eye on this. I need to protect the *idea* of this school.

If I let go of these plans now, who knows what'll happen? I'll need to find out who this plan goes to, who gets it next, and who gets it after that, who monitors the landlord's renovation of the space, how we decide what the design elements are. OK, there's a wall here. Is it a glass wall? Or is it a low wall? Can it open and close? How many doors are there? Who decides all of that? I need to ask enough of those questions to figure out where the possible points of intervention are in this bureaucracy. That's some of the stuff I've learned in twenty-six years. How to intervene. Good timing. Getting to know the people personally. The name of the guy who's going to be working on that wall! Go meet him on the first day. My father was a traveling salesman. He was the mayor of Flatbush Avenue [laughs]; everybody knew Jimmie Weiss. He was a schmoozer. I guess I'm following in his footsteps. We have to know how to do this. We have to be right in there. A lot of people who consider themselves progressive think that if you just have the right ideas, people will come to *you*. They miss the whole human dimension of this work.

I've been thinking a lot lately about change. Been thinking about the difference between form and content. We tend to think that if you change the form of institutions, content's gonna change. So we create new structures or new procedures — and then people take this new form but carry over the same old content. At my previous school, we were given management systems that said you had to list your goals and your objectives and your strategies and then evaluate the whole thing. The *goal* had to be something broad that wasn't quantified, like "improve attendance." The *objective* was something you could quantify, so you would commit yourself — as a principal, say — to raising attendance by 2 percent. Well, it took me some time to figure out that it wasn't the goals and objectives that were the crucial pieces, but the *strategies.* They are what get you to that goal — and they reflect your philosophy. A lot of administrators who want to raise their attendance by 2 percent send out postcards, make telephone calls, give awards for attendance. But you can also raise attendance by having a better school. A place where there's education going on, where kids are engaged and motivated and want to come to school. Making the calls, sending the cards — all that might raise your attendance by 2 percent. You will have met your goal. But kids might be no more engaged, could still hate the place. They just go because you nag them into going, but the quality of the school would be no better.

I'll give you a more complicated example . . . two examples, actually: AIDS and teen pregnancy. There's a lot of teaching about AIDS, but I think we have a lot to learn about AIDS education. First of all, we need to learn how kids see all this. We need to ask students, "So, what are you hearing about this AIDS business? What do you think AIDS is all about?" I don't want us repeating the mistakes we made with education about teenage pregnancy. We'd warn the kids about pregnancy; give a little lesson; then have huge numbers of kids going out and getting pregnant. We've been incredibly unsuccessful. I think we put too much faith in lessons, in the *form*. And we don't connect education about AIDS and pregnancy to the general mission of the school.

Face it, when kids have sex the first time, they don't do it safely. Did you? I don't know a hell of a lot of fourteen- and fifteen-year-olds who, the first or second time, don't do something risky. But if they're hopeful, there can come a time when they'll say, "Uh-oh, I've just done something that could ruin my whole life!" If they're hopeful, they might say, "I'd better look at what I'm doing." Of course we need to provide information. Of course we need to educate people about reproduction and birth control and about the transmission of AIDS. Of course. But the bigger question for me is: How do we set up schooling so that it instills hope? We keep thinking we can take care of problems with rules and prescriptions [dramatic voice]: "These Are the Ten AIDS Lessons." And then the chancellor can say, "Every school gave the ten AIDS lessons." Fine. We need the AIDS lesson, but we need much more.

We need to create schools that give people a substantial sense of the future.

I think a teacher's "presence" counts for a lot in a school. I don't mean inspectorial, supervisory presence, but adults being around, contributing to a community where people take care of each other. See who walks around the halls, who touches people, and who pulls away. Who takes responsibility for the community? Look at any community. Who picks up the litter on the basketball court? Who plants a few flowers? These little things are big things. This sort of everyday concern, attentiveness matters a lot. That's what's going to make a school work. Those who have thought about the mission of the place in the abstract, who have a "form" for it but can't put it into play on a day-to-day basis — they'll be all the weaker for it. What I like about schools is that challenge. Making it work every day.

What do I hope for? When our first class graduates, I hope the kids will be able to say, "Boy, what a rich, incredible experience I had with this group of people who started where I started. And here we are five years later. And remember those early days when we were still in that temporary building, and we got a chance to shape what it looked like? And we all got a chance to talk about what it means to study our city? And I learned the phrase 'public works' and met a guy named Sam Schwartz who really seemed to care about kids and had been the traffic commissioner, the chief engineer for New York City, and he took us into the water tunnels, and we realized how important water is to the life of the city. And then we read poetry together, and I never thought engineering and poetry could be connected." Whew! I think of scenarios like this. Hundreds of scenarios like this. "And then these people from Outward Bound were at our school, and we went on a five-day wilderness trip in the Catskill Mountains, and I didn't think my view of the city would change just from being there, but somehow nature helped me clarify how I thought about the city." And so on and so on. I imagine all these rich tastes of things. And here's where I think *acquired* taste is so important. Somebody saying, "You know, this is an interesting thing; try this; don't back away from this." We want to open kids up to all the possibilities of learning and do it with a variety of people who have widely different perspectives on things.

I deeply believe in a public taking care of itself, supporting itself, promoting itself. A people making a future for themselves. That's what democracy is. And that's why public schools are so important to me — they're a way to help people fully participate in a country that has tremendous resources and potential. I wonder if the word *democracy* is being used more or less in our society over the last twenty to thirty years compared, say, to the last two hundred years. I think we talk about it less, think about it less. I feel like walking around with a button that says "Democracy" and ask people, "What does it mean to you?"

Michael Johnson, The Science Skills Center High School for Science, Technology, and the Creative Arts

A plain, four-page typewritten handout on the Science Skills Center — a nonprofit community educational program — has on its last page a list of "significant achievements." Among them:

In 1989, sixteen fifth- and sixth-graders passed the New York State Biology Regents.

In 1990, sixteen passed the Biology Regents, including the youngest ever to take the exam — nine years old.

In 1991, nine fifth- through eighth-grade students passed the Sequential Math 1 Regents. *One fifth-grader scored a perfect 100, and another fifth-grader scored a 99.*

One hundred former Science Skills Center students are now in college, pursuing careers in physics, premed, chemistry, and biology.

The list continues to the bottom of the page.

Wearing a green T-shirt with "Science Skills Center" printed across the front, Michael Johnson sat across from me in his small office located in a wing of P.S. 9 in the Crown Heights section of Brooklyn. We were almost toe-to-toe, a fan propped up on a desk alongside us cooling us as we spoke. He was a compact, animated African-American man with strong hands that moved quickly as he talked, reinforcing his ideas: fingertips of both hands touching his chest to indicate involvement, a finger to his temple whipped upward toward the ceiling to represent the flash of insight. His speech would take off, then stop abruptly. He would look at me often to maintain contact, and he would comment on the flow of ideas: "That's right . . . that's right," he might say, or "Good question." Then he would move quickly ahead, his voice running the scale, from reflective basso to the soaring pitch of amazement.

I think there's been a great misunderstanding about science. Science and math are always presented as this passionless, abstract stuff — and it's false, it's just not true. If you study the history of science, read the biographies of great scientists, you'll find tremendous passion. And imagination. Many insights came in dreams, not in formulas, in things seemingly unrelated to science, all sorts of things triggering ideas. Take

Newton. I mean, there must have been thousands and thousands of people who saw objects drop [laughs]. You mean nothing ever *fell* until Newton? It's amazing. Some guy finally says, "Wait a minute, things always fall *down!*" I mean, come on . . . This image of the scientist being cold and calculating — the metaphor being the computer — that's just wrong. They were emotional people and were motivated by spiritual concerns as well — again, look at Newton. And if you consider unified field theory — it's an attempt to find out what it is that links up the whole universe. You're searching for God.

You ask me why I'm here — it has to do with love. Education's about getting a kid to love words, love language, to love to be able to manipulate numbers. That's what it's really about. The good teachers I had, I remember — they had a love for the subject, and somehow they transferred that love of the subject to me. Educators have to be motivated by love. I mean, here's this young human being coming to you and saying, "I don't know why if you mix this chemical with that chemical, you get a new chemical." Now, perhaps they could teach themselves that. But you have the experience and you have the opportunity to present them with this information — and to present them with something that I think is even more important. You have the opportunity to present them with a love of learning. The desire to know after you're gone.

The Science Skills Center began about fourteen years ago when a group of us — engineers, scientists — became concerned that many minority students, African American and Latino in particular, were not considering science as a career possibility. Many of them were turned off to science. Many of them were taught poorly and thought science was too hard, or that it was a "White thing." So what we began to do, on Saturdays, very informally, was to have workshops; we'd pull students into these workshops. We did science experiments, science projects, and we found that even those students who didn't like science or were afraid of science were *liking* science. Liking to *do* science.

So we began informally, and then we wrote a proposal, the first proposal I ever wrote in my life. And we won it! It was a community development grant to do an afterschool program, and my thinking was that if you're going to do an afterschool "latchkey" program, let's do it in science and mathematics. Well, it worked! Over time we became incorporated, more formal, and were able to get larger grants. Finally we applied to the National Science Foundation — when we started, I didn't even know what the NSF was — and we got the largest grant ever given to an organization our size. I mean, grants of that amount would usually go to universities. We've just done so much work in the area of science education.

Now we run both afterschool and Saturday programs. And summer programs, too. We'll want to incorporate all this into our new school. For example, at New York City Technical College our kids are doing robotics, and at Downstate Medical Center they're following a rotation through various medical specialties with medical students, working with cadavers, and doing gross anatomy. We'll want to involve universities. We'll want to involve scientists. We're doing exciting things with industries. My hope is — and this is kind of bold — that people will say, "That's *some* high school" — that our students will come out strong and positive. With knowledge and skill. Ethical and moral people. That's my hope.

Now, to be truthful, I was worried about applying to start a school. Many of the things we do here are unorthodox. Teachers don't punch a clock here. They may come in early, stay late. They have meetings all the time. We have a great many teacher-generated projects: the robotics curriculum was written entirely by the teachers. Parents are very actively involved: they can visit classes — we have an open-door policy — they're part of the curriculum committee; they're part of the management committee. Our system is so different from the public school system, I was reluctant to get involved.

Most teachers in the public schools really care about the kids, and many have great ideas. I know. I visit schools all the time. But something happens because of the way the public school is structured. The lack of respect for employees. The constraints of the contracts. All that. But we weighed the pluses and minuses. And our feeling was that we could make a greater impact if we could do the kind of work we do in the Center from nine to three, and could do it in social studies and English and foreign language. Then we'd have a tremendous student at the end of it all.

You've gotta go where the action is. Most kids are in public school. That's where you've got to make the change. The kids hanging out on the corners are not in exclusive academies. You can have wonderful private schools, but if we don't change the public school system, we're going to lose. You can't educate the top 10 percent well and think the country's going to make it. You've got to educate everyone. You can't escape from that.

The whole school culture is something I look at as curriculum. The lunch room. The dismissal. The clubs. We won't have any varsity teams at our school. Too often in our community athletes become heroes, and that's not what I want to promote. Also, varsity teams somehow make kids think that all they need to do is sit in the stands and watch the players; that they don't need to be involved in physical activity. I'd rather see a more focused intramural program. Kids get involved in sports when there's no team for them to sit and watch. I'll be willing to lose whatever happens to "school spirit" in exchange for what might happen in terms of who become the heroes of the school. The people who belong to the debating team. The people who belong to the foreign language club and travel all over the world. *They* become the heroes of the school.

I'm also very interested in language. I have students write narratives in math because it leads to deeper understanding. I'll ask them to explain to me what a decimal is. They'll say, "I'll show you." And I'll say, "No, don't show me. *Explain* to me what a decimal is, what it does." They know that when a certain thing happens, you move the decimal two places to the right. But they don't know why. Getting students to speak. To talk about concepts. One thing we do here is rely on study groups. Each student is linked to a buddy, and those buddies are linked to study groups. We'll take a concept — let's say, reproduction in humans — and the students in the study groups cannot move on until everyone understands that concept. The students are teaching other students and are responsible for each other. You'll see a lot of talking going on.

I want us to be concerned about language. I want an attention to language incorporated into every aspect of the program. How do we speak to each other? What do we call each other? How do males refer to females? Females to males? How do teachers refer to students? How do we talk to parents? All this is important. The interesting thing about our school is that it'll probably be one of the most multicultural schools you'll find. We'll have a large number of Asian students, Russian, White American, African American, Caribbean American. A mix of students. And one of the things we're concerned about is groups learning to live with each other. Education, in a narrow sense, is not our goal. Can you get along with your neighbor? Can you understand that this person has a different life style? This is as important to me as being able to read. We don't want to just educate technocrats, "hired guns," people who can only construct computers and do calculations. We want people who have morals, who can say, "No, you can't do that to people."

I think all educators, by definition, are visionaries. Now some of those visions [laughs] are a little more stunted or callused than others. But, by definition, education is something for the future; it's not something you do for the immediate. Yes, you excite a young mind, and that's an immediate and wonderful thing. But education is a public investment — one that should not make a profit. Education [laughs] should lose money! I mean, what did it cost for a Jonas Salk or a Madame Curie? Those wonderful people. What would be the cost? Or for the person or people who will solve AIDS? You're gonna come up with a *cost* for that? You see what I'm saying?

I have a vision of the kind of country I want. I would like to see a country where young people don't feel they have to destroy themselves on the street. Where they're realizing their dream, their mission in life, their gift to life. Where they have a sense of worthiness. That's the reason I'm in this. These are the people who will take over the planet. We'll be gone. What kinds of decisions are they going to make? Are they going to be informed, ethical decisions? Educational visions are shortsighted when they are concerned only with immediate gains. Educational vision should be about the long term, about the kind of country you want.

Luis Garden Acosta and Frances Lucerna, El Puente Academy for Peace and Justice

The community center known as El Puente (The Bridge) was located in the Williamsburg section of Brooklyn, in an area called the South Side, just across the East River from Manhattan. After a typical bumper-to-bumper cab ride — the Williamsburg Bridge under repair, the honking of horns, the heat and exhaust — I walked from Fourth Street into a brief and simple reception area where two young people politely assisted me into the large main room, three stories high. There was a natural flow from the street into El Puente, people hanging around outside and talking, walking in and out of the building, the reception area very close to the street, a few feet back, a few steps up. But the moment I walked into the main area, I saw that, though the street flowed in and out, there was something extraordinary going on here. The first thing was the hue and vibrancy and the seeming intensity of purpose, and, as I was being awed by that, I simultaneously realized that I was in what used to be a church. Where pews would have been, there were young people at tables, in circled groups, in twos and threes, working on art projects or reading or participating in discussions. The open second story — probably the choir loft — had been refurbished into offices: desks, filing cabinets, book cases, boxes stacked and labeled. In one corner was a glassed-in cubicle that looked like a small videotaping studio, the future home, I later learned, of EPTV, El Puente Television. And back above where the altar used to be, now a stage, was a dome, painted to look like a shining gold heaven. Beautiful stylized angels surrounded Mary, Queen of Heaven, blue, peach, green, and red gowns, pastel wings, white clouds. Inscribed along the outside: Mary of the Angels, Pray for Us.

The walls were covered with bright, striking art, all made by the young people of El Puente. Huge masks of the three kings of the Orient, part of a celebration of Three Kings Day. A cluster of smaller masks of demons and exaggerated animals worn during carnivál. *There were posters, made for Black History Month, celebrating important African Americans, like the Harlem-born painter Jacob Lawrence. There was a mural, painted on a yellow-gold background, showing students watching a video of Martin Luther King, Jr., taking notes, reading Gandhi; surrounding them were images of striking farm workers, civil rights marchers, Rosa Parks on the bus, the flag of the United States, the dove of peace. Six tall panels, extending a good twenty feet, presented young people against a street scene of tenements, billboards, and the Williamsburg Bridge. They moved from isolation and confusion ("Which way to go¿," "Who can I talk to¿," "¿Qué es el SIDA¿" or "What is AIDS¿") through reflection — "Reach out and get involved in positive alternatives" — to mentoring, community work, and the doors of El Puente. Hanging from wires overhead, taking up the entire center of the ceiling, was a giant "incinerator monster": a hideous gray head with skulls for eyes and, where hair should be, a tall smokestack that read, "Death by Smoke, Inc." The monster's body was long and black, funereal, and extending out from it were nine tentacles with gloved hands, the word* blood *scrawled across each open palm.*

On one of the partitions along the walls, I began reading a newspaper article showing a photograph of people marching across the Williamsburg Bridge, carrying the monster in protest against a garbage incinerator being planned for the area. It was then that Luis and Frances found me, with warm greetings, and we went off to a conference room adjacent to the main floor.

Luis Garden Acosta was the founder and Frances Lucerna was the co-founder of El Puente, and now Frances would be principal of the new academy, which would be housed within El Puente itself. The conference room held a large square table, some folding chairs, a portable blackboard with El Puente's four cardinal principles written on it (holism, collective self-help, safety, respect), *a few boxes, and, in the corner, a pail and a mop. As we talked, sounds of young people wafted in from a small courtyard: exclamations, laughter, music. It was at this table, Luis informed me, that representatives of the various constituencies in Williamsburg — Hassidim, Latino (predominantly Puerto Rican and Dominican), African American, Polish American, and Italian American — had been meeting to "create a dialogue to face common problems together." Like the incinerator. This coming together was remarkable, a bridge among hostile factions, for there was a rancorous, at times violent, history among them — between Latinos and Hassidim, particularly.*

Luis was a big man, dressed in a loose linen shirt. He had curly black hair, a broad forehead, and a mustache, and he spoke slowly, precisely, rocking from the waist in rhythm with his long sentences, almost sermonic, full of statistic and achievement and history.

Frances had been a professional dancer before becoming a teacher, and she had a dancer's poise. She was charming and yet charged with can-do. A study in grace and force. She wore her long hair pulled back, spoke with intensity — her words rushing suddenly — and humor and with a tendency toward the aphoristic.

Luis: You're right in the middle of the largest, most concentrated Latino census tract in the city of New York. Williamsburg. The South Side. About half is Puerto Rican. Half, maybe more than half, is Dominican. And there are the beginnings of immigration from El Salvador, from Nicaragua, from Ecuador, from Mexico. Maybe fifty thousand people. This used to be called the teenage gang capital of New York City. Every single week in 1981 we lost one adolescent through violence. We lost forty-eight young people that year. I was the associate executive director of the municipal hospital for this community, and I knew that every week my emergency room was going to be filled with blood. We'd do everything possible, and still lose one child every week — carried out and buried.

What I came to see was that no one institution — as institutions like hospitals or schools are typically organized in communities — no one institution could deal with the overall problems that were taking our children from us. What we had to do was bring everyone together who had any interest in young people and community. So I sponsored a series of meetings at the hospital. The conclusion we came to was that we had to raise our own village — and I'm reworking that African proverb here — in order to raise our children. And the only way to do that was through collective self-help and not through agencies that only served to fragment us further. There was no center or movement, no center for the development of young people in a holistic manner. If you had a problem, you could go to X, Y, or Z problem center, but there was no integration of services. Part of the problem, a big part of the problem, was the treatment itself. There was this cadre of treatment-oriented fixers who continued to inject into our community the feeling that all we were good for was to become better clients.

Frances: You see, we as a people have been almost brainwashed into believing we were beings of need rather than beings of resource. What we had to come to was an understanding that we have in ourselves all the resources we need, individually and collectively, to be successful.

Luis: We realized that we needed to build a movement focused on development — not treatment — on the whole human being and the whole community. One did not exist without the other: body-mind-spirit-community. We realized that to achieve this integration, we had to change the way institutions related to our community. The way the hospital related, the way the school related, the way the church related. We would have to become a bridge to connect all of them — and that's where we got the name El Puente. We saw it as a bridge connecting youth development and community development. Connecting the Puerto Rican and Dominican communities with the White ethnic and Hassidic communities of Williamsburg — for Williamsburg is a place that could dwarf Crown Heights if ignited. And we wanted a bridge, too, for people to return — people like Frances, who was a dancer in a professional company, or for people like me — back into the neighborhood. If the village raised you, then you have a responsibility to raise the village.

So you can see how the school fits in. Not as a place where you go to fix your mind. But a place central to the development of young people, rooted in the neighborhood, and moving outward.

Frances: Learning is a miraculous human process. It's not something that's instituted. It's part of our fundamental human experience, how we relate to each other, how we nurture and sustain our lives. I think we have forgotten this. And so we have arrived at this monstrosity of a bureaucracy that places more value on standards and benchmarks that are outside ourselves, outside of both our individual and collective experience.

Look what's happened to reading, writing, and arithmetic — these "basics." We don't see them any longer as life skills. They're "subjects" to be taken, subjects outside our experience. They're not seen as essential to our understanding of the world, but if young people know that if they can read, if they can write, if they can understand algebraic codes — if they see that they can use those skills, use them to bring about change in their own lives or in the lives of their families or in their communities . . . well, then, there's no stopping them.

A good example is the newspaper here at El Puente. The first day we got these young people together, they said: "For-get it, man! I *hate* to write. Forget it." [Laughs] Two weeks later, they're writing long articles on what they're observing. It was the first time they made a connection between the skill of writing and their desire to express what they see and live every day.

And math. We have a community survey group who are creating maps; they're mapping the whole community. The participants are out talking to people, listing their needs and resources, recording demographics, and charting the terrain. Then they come in and transform all that information into a formal community map. They see that they're doing something that is mathematical and coded, but that has relevance to their lives. And that's the way we're thinking about learning for the new academy.

Luis: Let me tell you about a group here called MASH Ministry, the Medical, Alternative, and Sexual Health Ministry. They won an award from the governor for their measles vaccination program. You see, we had lost about twenty-three people in a terrible epidemic, and the Department of Health was saying, "Well, it's impossible to provide service. Maybe they're undocumented and afraid to come to the clinic." Our young people didn't think so. They surveyed sixty families in the neighborhood, and found that forty-five of them did not have any vaccinations and wanted them immediately. So I said, "Well, let us do it."

Frances: Our survey team went out and did some further work. We looked at all the problems with access to health care. What did families experience when they went to clinics, and what did they feel they needed?

Luis: We decided to set up a vaccination clinic here at El Puente and brought in personnel from the Department of Health. In ten days, these young people got 1207 of their peers inoculated against measles.

Frances: We created a kind of Disneyworld. We showed *Peter Pan.* The kids got their faces painted. We set things up so the parents could talk to each other. An amazing system.

Luis [laughing]: The kids were asking when they could come back to be vaccinated again! You see, young people looked at a need, created an environment to fill that need, and developed skills along the way.

OK, so let's take all this back to the creation of the El Puente Academy for Peace and Justice. Williamsburg is the most toxic neighborhood in New York City, particularly in regard to lead pollution. The *New York Times* reported a finding of 42,500 parts per million of lead in the ground. Right on the corner of a Catholic school. Right across the street from a public school. The Center for Disease Control cites five hundred to one thousand parts per million of lead as being at risk; 42,500 is at the Superfund eligibility level. We have in our community forty-three garbage transfer stations and Radiac, what they call a "temporary" holding facility for nuclear and chemical waste. Then there's Brooklyn's largest bus terminal, the Brooklyn-Queens Expressway, and the Williamsburg Bridge — all of which makes the community nothing but a highway for people coming from Long Island to Manhattan. Add to this the city's proposal to build the first *fifty-five-story* incinerator right in Williamsburg, and you have an urban environmental nightmare. Well, are we going to learn our times tables while young people are literally dying from the environment? We have the highest rate of certain stomach cancers. Or are we going to use this crisis as an activist motivation not only to learn the principles of math and science and politics that are involved, but also to survive? Because it *is* a question of survival.

Let's say that as part of our ninth-grade curriculum, we help young people develop a project around the topic of lead. First of all, they'll have to understand what lead is — which takes them into general chemistry. They've got to understand why lead is where it is in the periodic table, its properties as an element, and why it is found in the ground, in the air, on the walls. And how does the human body work, and why is such a small amount of lead such a problem? They'll have to deal with dissemination rates and dispersal rates in volumes of air. And how lead would be formed in the incinerator, and how it would reach us, and what would happen as we breathed it.

They're going to have to study law and government, and the three branches of government, and the mission of government to protect the well-being of its citizens, and learn how citizens can seek redress from their government in case of a public health disaster. And that, of course, will lead to public health law and the justice system and the ways the courts might intervene. And what one might get from the executive branch, and how, under what conditions, would we solicit legislators? What help can the Clean Air Act provide? How does one attempt to amend such legislation to protect our well-being?

So you see, such a project would involve math, physical science, and social science, and students would be researching and writing and giving expression to what they're learning through their newspaper and in videos they'll make for the community. A liberal education based on the matter of their survival.

Frances: Let's also talk about some other realities. We're starting a public school, part of the New York system. In working with the school development team here at El Puente, I've been very direct about standardized tests like the Regents exams, the SAT's, all that. They're not the measures of success we believe in, but our young people need to know how to deal with them. In the scheme of things, in the way we look at the world, we think they're very inadequate and are just another mechanism for tracking students. But we're going to prepare for them straight on. Until we, all of us, can revamp or abolish them, we'll teach our students how to take them. I think success in being able to take such tests is the ability to put them in context, to put them in perspective. They are not a measure of who you are as a human being. They are not a measure of all the knowledge you've acquired or of your ability to impart knowledge. They are just what they are. A means to an end.

Luis: You know, I think the greatest challenge for us is going to be getting people to appreciate the uniqueness of this venture. The system, in all its forms — from management to union — rarely sees the child or the community or one single school. But we must respond to the unique challenge every child, every school provides and not think of them as abstractions that do or do not fit into an assessment, a budget, a union contract. That's the biggest challenge.

Frances: In the short time we have been dealing with the Board of Education, I must say that we have met individuals who are really good and decent human beings who believe in young people and believe in what we're doing — but who themselves are victims of the bureaucracy.

Luis: Wonderful people who, in a way, are locked up in a prison they helped build themselves.

Frances: And I think it's very important to recognize that, to respect them. To do otherwise wouldn't be right. I come with the point of view that there is the potential to find common ground. So let's do it.

But there is also the tendency in a bureaucracy for people to maintain the little power they have by holding on to little bits of information. So there's the day-in and day-out mundane brokering and negotiating to try to access these bits of information. And then you try to put these bits together to see exactly what it is we're dealing with. There are just so many voices. And this leads to a larger issue that wears me down: the inherent distrust of process. Process is so central to El Puente — the respect for human development that comes with process. Instead, you are overwhelmed with rules, regs, and deadlines.

Luis: That's right. Macro-form instead of individual process.

Frances: I have this recurring nightmare. I'm in this school building, and I'm lost, and I can't find the right room, and the bells are always going off . . . And here I am creating a school! [Laughs] I suppose I'm dealing with some demon within myself. My worst fear is that in creating a school, we'll lose what we have here at El Puente, which is organic and safe and respectful and encourages these young people to realize their potential. I want to hold on to that. I want to keep the humanity of it.

Bill Ling, Manhattan International High School

Bill Ling speaks Mandarin Chinese, Spanish, French, a little Italian, and English — the result, he explained, of the "interesting detour" his "very untraditional, adventurous" parents took when they left Shanghai to travel and study abroad. He arrived in the United States when he was eleven and was fortunate to be admitted to a school for international students at the United Nations. He has led, he said, "a charmed life."

Bill has been a teacher in an elementary school, in a large comprehensive high school, and, for the last eight years, in a small, very successful high school for immigrant students located within La Guardia Community College in Queens. For two years now, he has been the assistant principal, and was preparing to open a similar school in Manhattan, on the Lower East Side, in Chinatown.

We met in Bill's tiny office. It was packed with binders, reports, manila folders in upright files, a big green lamp, books (Leading Constitutional Decisions, Computers in the American History Classroom, Hispanic Biographies, The American Spirit, The History of the Chinese in America, The Working Citizen, A Child of Fortune), *posters stored in tubular containers, cardboard boxes with the flaps hanging open, two sweaters, a phone, a computer and printer, and a stuffed book bag. The edges of the shelves and the sides of the printer were festooned with Post-its and "while you were out" slips, and a "Far Side" cartoon. The walls were covered with student art work, calendars, class schedules, memos, and newspaper articles on immigration.*

Bill swiveled out his chair so that we could talk face to face. He was in his early forties, slim, glasses, black hair combed straight across, but for the few strands falling over his forehead. He wore a thin, light blue shirt — with a single black pen clipped into the pocket —khaki slacks, and white athletic shoes. His conversation was modulated by anecdote, by imitations of imagined others, and by reflective laughter. It was also enhanced by gesture: bringing his index finger to his thumb to make a point, rubbing his chin in mock consternation. And when Louis Delgado, who was also working with his teachers at La Guardia, dropped in to say good-bye, Bill slid into fluent Spanish.

I was an LEP [limited English proficiency] kid when I came to this country. *Extremely* limited [laughs]. I had traveled quite a bit with my parents as a youngster — France, Italy, Uruguay, Argentina — and I knew the difficulties of picking up another language. So when the opportunity came to create another school in the service of such kids, I was very, very interested.

The kids are recent arrivals. We will accept those who have been in this country up to four years, and students have to score at or below the twenty-first percentile on an English language-proficiency test. We hope for some degree of proficiency in the native language, because mastery of one's first language will be a tremendous help in picking up a second language. We believe every kid comes with tremendous strengths: they come with a different culture and with knowledge of another language. There is no insistence that a child leave his past, his language, at the door. We welcome it. Yet we have an obligation to help them adjust. And the first thing, the critical thing, is the language, fluency in the English language. But there's also the culture. What are the expectations here? I mean [laughs], Americans like to talk about themselves quite a bit. In my culture, we don't. [Clears throat, mimicking insult.] "What do you mean, how do *I* feel?" Another characteristic [articulates each word precisely] is stating what is on your mind. "Tell me your opinion." "Well, *my* opinion is ———. *My* view on the matter is ———." Yet another thing is assertiveness. Sometimes I feel this little push in my back: "You must be *assertive*, Bill." It's a whole different thing you're dealing with.

I was a teacher for a long time. Now I have to look at things from an administrative point of view. Sometimes I hear myself say things and stop: Did I really say that? Suddenly, the word *budget* is injected into my conversation. As a teacher, I didn't talk about budget. I don't want to slip into that mindset thoroughly, forgetting what the classroom is all about. I don't want to say "no, it's impossible." It's easy to say: "Ho, those are pipe dreams!" and "You're not living in the real world!" I fear that. I zip that up.

You can get buried in paper. It's easy for that to happen. Totally buried. The reports are incredible. It never ends. And I'm getting a taste of it. It's a treadmill. One principal told me, "Once you decide to go into this, you have to prepare for no closure. Ever." The danger is that you may take the easy way out. You start establishing rules and regulations. "This is how it will be . . ." You try to institute predictable reactions to everything. But you have to see change as part of the organism. People grow. They have different needs at different times. And a school has different needs at different times. The continual struggle with the big issues keeps us alive. Makes us question things. But the pull toward tradition is very strong. The temptation is to say, "This is the schedule. This is the curriculum. Everyone who comes in must adapt to this curriculum, must adapt to this schedule." Teacher as worker.

We're right now trying to design a first-year curriculum on the broad theme of beginnings. The beginnings of this nation, beginnings in biology, beginnings in history, beginning to explore your future in America. Gradually, we'll move on — we're projecting here to the second semester — to the theme of cities and civilizations. What does it mean to live in a city? The science of it, the mathematics. The students, of course, will come in with their own experiences of living in cities or in rural areas, and the curriculum will encourage them to talk about the differences between their backgrounds and New York City. To verbalize the differences, talk to each other about them, draw pictures, make comparisons. In our school, we would like to make the teaching of English omnipresent in the curriculum. We want to connect it in all sorts of ways to the academic work the students are doing. Here's one small example: In science, students learn about "catalysts." Now, this word can be revisited in English: *catalyst* as a stimulus to an idea, or to change. We want to demonstrate relationships like that, so the kids can see how language ties everything together.

The students reflect the immigrant groups currently coming to New York City. The city now has a largely Latino population coming in, mostly from the Dominican Republic. We're also getting more kids from Haiti, kids from Eastern Europe, particularly Poland and the old Soviet Union. And we're getting more and more Chinese kids — and some Koreans, though they're settling more in Queens. What it looks like now is that our first class will be mostly Hispanic, with some Haitians, some students from the Middle East, Yemen particularly, and a few Chinese kids, and a few Polish kids. And I have two students who are Nigerian. Though Nigeria is an English-speaking nation, these students are native speakers of Yoruba and Hausa, and their English is very limited. So I figured we could be of help.

The parents of our students are very practical people. Being in New York City, the uppermost concern on their minds is safety. That their children be in a nurturing environment, a caring environment, with adults who have close supervision of their kids, close knowledge of them. Many of these parents came to join husbands or wives or other relatives. Some were not necessarily comfortable about coming but needed to keep their families together. They are very, very worried about what awaits them here. There may be wonderful opportunities in the future, but, on the other hand, tremendous dangers. And they worry about the schools. The unfortunate thing is that the reputation of our schools is not good — and when they see large schools, they do worry. They sense that a smaller school may be better. And, remember, a lot of these people come from societies in which the schools are small. Immigrant parents also tend to be very motivated to have their kids attend college. So they expect a good English-language program. They want to know: "Will you prepare my child for college, for an American university? Will you do that?"

The students come with varying degrees of proficiency in English, some with zero percent; some have to learn an entirely new writing system, a new alphabet. Some of them — those who have been here two or three years — are very conversant in English. They're American in terms of their personal language; they're quite proficient. But because we want to prepare them for college, we will challenge them to become proficient in academic English.

These students come with extremely different needs. Some come from intact families who have some degree of economic stability. Some come from struggling families, and they need an environment in which they can see the school as a family. Some kids are here living with brothers or sisters. And some are living by themselves. We'll have kids who have experienced tremendous trauma, have witnessed murder, warfare — there's all kinds of tragedies in their lives. If they end up in a big school where these needs cannot be addressed, they will be totally lost, devastated. And the experience of being in America will be a disastrous one rather than a hopeful one.

America has been schizophrenic in its immigration policy. By and large, immigrants have come and been able to flourish. But not always. They've struggled through racism and everything else. America's a racist society, perhaps, but all other races are still coming to this country. I don't see them flowing into any other place in such large numbers. There's something here that beckons people.

I also believe that every immigrant coming to this country has an obligation. You need to see this nation as your adopted land. You have a responsibility to the welfare of this country, just as you have a responsibility to the community you live in — to keep it healthy, to keep it clean, to keep it safe. Your responsibility does not end with being admitted, with pledging allegiance. You need to know what's happening in the country, in its politics, in its economy. I'm not asking anyone to reject their culture. Certainly not. But I am asking whether we don't have a responsibility to give back, to participate.

Now, if we want our immigrants to become an informed populace, then we have to provide a good public education. It's the Jeffersonian principle. Immigrants would never be able to adapt to this society without it. So the country has a responsibility to provide a decent education for them. Our country is not based on the British model, believing some can be educated, some not. It's a very lofty goal, fraught with problems, with funding inequalities. But as a principle, I think it's a beautiful idea: education for all. It's central to the principles our country was founded upon.

Haven Henderson, The Legacy School for Integrated Studies

Washington Heights is a Dominican and African-American neighborhood just north of Harlem: old apartment buildings, restaurants, bodégas, lots of small businesses, music, buses and cabs, the smell of food, bustle on the street. Haven Henderson lived with her teenage son on the fourth floor of a once-luxury apartment building — marble stairs, chipped tile, carved wood in the lobby — on Fort Washington Avenue, right by the Columbia Presbyterian Medical Center. We settled in on two adjoining couches, comfortable, many pillows, papers and books around us: schedules, memos, curriculum materials, scholarly articles, Derrick Bell's And We Are Not Saved, Fidel and Malcolm, *a Mary Renault novel, and* The One Best System, *a historical study of schooling in urban America.*

Haven had worked with Deborah Meier at Central Park East Secondary School for the last five years, teaching and developing programs and curricula, and that work and that relationship have reinforced her long-held beliefs about what's possible in the public schools. Her own school, along with four other small schools, would be temporarily located in the old Stuyvesant High School building in the East Village.

She was a tall African-American woman, early forties, with a deceptively easy manner. She seemed, at times, to toss off a thought, but it was not unusual for an idea to keep her up half the night. She was, then, alternately casual and intense, leaning back at one point in our conversation, her left arm thrown over the couch, almost languid, twirling a tiny dreadlock with her right hand, and, a moment later, leaning forward, chin in hand, stringing concepts together, pursuing an idea. She had an uncompromisingly analytical mind.

Why the Legacy School for Integrated Studies? Well, I've got to say that I was very much influenced by two films I saw. One was called *After the Warming,* which was about human beings' relationship with both the natural world and technology, from prehistory all the way up to projections for 2050. I thought it was phenomenal. The second was the Legacy series, which was a study of six civilizations. I thought, "Boy, if we could achieve teaching at that level — integrating knowledge like that!" That kind of integration provides purpose for understanding knowledge, gets kids to see that there's a relationship between observing and studying and reading and writing and knowledge about themselves. I want children to see the *reason* for knowledge, what it does, why it's important, how we build on knowledge, the way it all fits together, that it's dynamic, connected, purposive.

We want our children to leave our school very well educated, whoever they are, wherever they come from, whatever their skills when they come to us. When they leave, we want them to feel prepared, to feel confident about their knowledge, to feel they can compete in the world, at college, at work. I am very much concerned with what it means for kids to be powerful — people use that rhetoric all the time, but I want to push on it. When you're teaching students who are poor, who are African American, who are Latino, it means looking at racism in society and providing explanations for the racism they live through. That way, they can make some sense out of the world and make decisions about how to live in the world. They need to make their own decisions, but they need to make them with a lot of information.

So the kind of integrated curriculum I'm talking about means you'll have to look very broadly at the world. If you only look at the experience of African Americans, for example, without looking at that experience in relation to world history, you're going to miss a lot. But if you look at it in the context of human behavior and development, historical changes, pendulum swings, then you get to see something much broader. We'd like kids to know that things change, that they can be a part of change, and that they can have some control over events and make some decisions about them. *That's* why I'm so excited about this curriculum. It presents knowledge as something dynamic, something you seek, something that will continue to prepare you for life.

I've taught for sixteen years, prekindergarten to adult high school. I developed after-school programs for kids, adult literacy programs, day care centers. I guess I have a lot of history developing educational programs. I've always liked teaching. I taught elementary school in California for eight years — taught Chicano, Asian, and African-American students — and one of the things I got interested in was English as a second language. So when I got to graduate school, I studied linguistics. And I worked for four years at a junior high school down in Chinatown, teaching ESL. Now at some point in all that, I began to think I'd like to go into administration. You know, when you're in a classroom, you're always wondering what will happen to the kids when they leave you. I wanted to have more influence on what happens to the kids' lives in school. So I began a doctoral program in administration at Columbia Teachers College.

Around that time, I was at a friend's party, and she told me that I should meet Debbie Meier, who was then starting Central Park East Secondary School. We thought very much alike, my friend said, and she suggested I give Debbie a call. So I called her and [pause, lowered voice] . . . we fought immediately [laughs]. When I got off the phone, I thought, "That so-and-so, I don't wanna work with her." And it turned out that when *she* hung up the phone, she thought, "Well, that arrogant so-and-so." But she sent me the information anyway — and when I read it, I got goose bumps. I understood *exactly* what she wanted to do because it was so much what *I* wanted to do. I thought, "My God, I've got to apologize to this woman." So we met again and tried to be nice to each other [laughs]. And I ended up going to work with her.

Several years ago, I did a study of kids who graduated from Central Park East and went on to a college of their choice. I asked them about their achievement. Did *they* think they'd achieved? How did they think they'd achieved? What helped them? How interested were they in the academic work they did? They were all Latino and Black, but otherwise came from a range of backgrounds: upper middle class to poor; parents who had gone to college, and parents who hadn't graduated from high school; also levels of achievement — high achievers to kids labeled learning disabled. Listen to what I found.

They all thought it was important to understand about their history. They all thought it was important to understand themselves as adolescents. They all thought it was important that they have close relationships with teachers, and that they liked where they came to school, and that the kids cared for each other. They thought it was important that they had community service and internship experience — that it helped them interact with adults and be in the world of work. But what they emphasized consistently was the school's *expectations.* That they all knew we expected them to achieve, and that it was our expectations of them that helped them develop expectations for themselves. That really struck me. It wasn't just that the kids had fun learning — a standard progressive notion — or, my big concern, that they were engaged. I mean, sometimes they were engaged and sometimes they thought the work was hokey. But what they said was most important to them was that we believed in them, that we believed they could achieve, that we asked them to do important intellectual work and believed they could do it. That turned out to be the biggest thing. Now, look, for this to hold true, you need to have a lot of the other stuff in place: respect, a sense of community, a good curriculum. But the most important thing I got from them was that we had the right kind of expectations for them.

It wasn't easy. They talked about trying to wear us down or outwit us; figured we'd let up, saying to themselves, "Look, they're not gonna flunk us." And I must tell you, there were nights when the staff would call each other, crying on the phone, "Are we asking too much? Are we being unrealistic?" But we decided to keep the expectations high, and we were going to hold them to the task, at all pains: giving kids low grades, even not graduating kids who weren't ready. Some of these kids just didn't believe they could be successful in school or go to college. They would look at us in disbelief when we told them they were intellectuals. They hadn't had much in their school experience to let them know they could be successful. They didn't have the taste of achievement. But they knew we cared deeply about it, and that we believed they could do it, and they began to sense what it meant to achieve and go on and be powerful.

And, you know, the next two classes that followed saw this. My son was in the second class, and my son was a typical underachiever. I mean, here his mother is an educator, fancies herself an intellectual — man, it was classic. He just wanted to be accepted as OK. You know, he kept giving me this stuff [laughing, voice high] . . . *that's* what he did to me! But when he saw that first class graduate, and they had all these choices of colleges to go to, that made quite a difference. He and the others wanted the possibilities the first class had. The achievement became contagious.

I'm interested in getting parents involved in our new school. There are a number of parents who've already said they'd like to be active in a parents' association. And I'm encouraging them to organize themselves; I'll provide facilities and whatever they need. I want them involved in the building of this community. There are going to be tensions. Of course. At Central Park East we had some conflicts with families, so we started something called Family Forums. We'd have an issue and invite parents in to talk about it. For example, around the AIDS curriculum. When we knew we had to teach an AIDS curriculum, we brought in materials we thought were good, and we invited parents to come in and look at them. We asked, "What do you think of these, and what do you think about us teaching about AIDS?" We had ongoing talks about that. And condoms. The passing out of condoms. "What are you comfortable with? What information might we have as teachers that you don't have, and what information do you have as parents that you think we should know?" When we decided to talk about homosexuality, we wrote some pieces in the school newsletter and sent things home to parents. We said we were going to begin talking about the issue among ourselves as a staff so that, in some way, we could begin to talk about it with kids. What did they think?

We need to have mechanisms in place to help us build consensus. Because, look, if there's tension between school and parents, then we've lost something. School has to be a safe place. And if you agree to that, then you need to think of all the things that would make a child safe. If there's tension between the school and the community, then the child will feel torn. We have to understand families and communities and try to work together.

I'm also interested in what I see as the limits or dilemma of multicultural education. Now, understand, the need for a quote-unquote multicultural curriculum is obvious. Curriculum needs to be more truthful, more inclusive. Kids need to know who they are. But that alone won't get it. What's more interesting to me right now is how do we best *teach* it so that kids learn very well, get a strong education. I'm interested in thinking of ways to change the structure of the school so that *all* kids, regardless of class, regardless of background, will learn as best they can. So it's not enough, say, to have a litany of names of Black inventors — you want to be able to present it in ways that make sense, are compelling. How best do we teach?

Education is political. It's naïve to say it isn't. But I don't think one should politic*ize* teaching. I may have a political point of view, a way of looking at the world, but I'm going to be in a roomful of kids who think in lots of different ways about the world, and so do their parents. To think there's not that range of beliefs is ignorant. So is it fair for me to teach them only from the lens of my perspective? Or should I introduce many lenses? I think that's more powerful. They'll have to interact with all sorts of people in this world. Kids need to form their own opinions, have to define who they are. My lens is one lens. I think it's a good lens and a powerful lens they can use. But it's not the only one. I don't want to restrict the class to my point of view, and I don't want anyone else to do that either. Now that is not easy. I think my staff and I will have to work hard to check ourselves, to keep ourselves from being narrowly ideological — and that's part of what our working together is all about. Just take the issue of racism among the Black intelligentsia. They may all agree that it exists, but there's a wide range of opinion on the causes, the effects — lots of disagreement. Kids should know about that disagreement. It's interesting stuff.

Students need to have experience figuring things out. Why did this person think this way? Why did Booker T. Washington believe people had to stay close to the earth? What was that all about? And why did W.E.B. DuBois believe so strongly in people going to college, becoming intellectuals? Were they both right? Wrong? What was that time period like for them? *That's* what real education is all about. Look, it's no secret that that's how the elite are educated. They're disadvantaged in that the scope of their curriculum is often limited; they're trapped in their own notions of supremacy. They don't fully acknowledge and integrate other cultures. But in terms of structure and process, well, look at it: the small classroom, the seminar approach, the analyses, the intellectual give-and-take, the integration of disciplines, the writing, lots of writing.

What there is for the privileged few, we want to make available for everybody, democratize it, make it available to kids who are in a system burdened with racism. Let's develop a curriculum like one we've never developed before. That's revolutionary. That's truly revolutionary. To have a well-educated American population to challenge, to make democracy real, to teach kids that they can make change happen, that they can be decision-makers, that they can make their communities better. That's our hope.

6

Berea and Wheelwright, Kentucky

I THE LETTER ran to eight pages, eloquent, impassioned, in the ornate script of the last century:

> . . . *God being my helper I shall renew the battle every day. And I trust that ere our tongues shall be palsied in death we shall witness the reign of universal emancipation.*

It was written from Berea, Madison County, Kentucky, on November 5, 1857, signed by John G. Fee, one of the founders of Berea College. The Reverend Fee and a few others had settled in a stretch of half-cleared wilderness — a brush-covered ridge near the foothills of the Cumberland Mountains — in the early 1850s in order to create a community free of slavery, an abolitionist exemplar. (The settlers named Berea after the city in Macedonia where the apostle Paul found a people who were devout and open to scriptural truth — the new Bereans' hope for themselves.) Fee and his companions inaugurated a one-room schoolhouse in 1855; in 1859 they drafted the constitution for a college that would be "under an influence strictly Christian, and as such opposed to sectarianism, slave holding, caste, and every other wrong institution or practice." It was to be a moral place and a place of social change.

Fee was a small man, "sandy complexioned" with a "kindly face," and was a tireless advocate for a radically egalitarian, nondenominational Christianity. Fee was a Kentuckian himself and had been profoundly influenced by the revivalist movements of his time, which, in various ways, advocated emancipation, free speech (his Christianity blended with Enlightenment rationality and the Bill of Rights), feminism, social reform (Berea College would be "Anti-slavery, Anti-caste, Anti-secret societies, Anti-rum, Anti-sin"), moral purity and human perfectibility, and the dignity of labor. From the beginning, students worked at the college to defray expenses — "those who have energy enough to work their way through college will develop energy of character." The Reverend Fee wanted a college that would "not merely . . . make students acquainted with science but also . . . educate their hearts and develop their consciences." For this, for the stand on slavery particularly, he and the other settlers were threatened, mobbed, and, finally, confronted by a band of armed men who exiled them from Kentucky in a drizzling rain. But Fee and his companions persisted. "Do right, trust God, hold on, and you will see the Red Sea divide before you." Berea College opened its doors in 1866, the only biracial educational institution in all the slaveholding states.

I sat, on the second day of my visit to the college, in the basement archive of the library with a box of Fee's documents spread out before me. I read letters to newspaper editors in Kentucky and Ohio defending and clarifying the settlers' motives, letters to missionary organizations and philanthropists requesting assistance, and pamphlets and sermons on topics ranging from the evils of Freemasonry to the evils of alcohol. Fee was a country preacher, a man with an unbending sense of right and wrong. As one modern, and sympathetic, commentator observed of Fee and the other Bereans, if they were to "step out of the pictures" on the walls of the college chapel, we would probably find them to be "too 'religious,' or too dogmatic, too absolutist, too narrow-minded, and too old-fashioned" for contemporary taste. Undoubtedly so. But as I held the yellowed letters to the light, following Fee's faded script and picturing him intent over the page, I found myself moved in ways I wouldn't have predicted by his courage and by the strength with which his memory still animated the college.

Modern-day Berea has become a regional center for Appalachian crafts and folk art. Car loads, bus loads of tourists come in on the weekends for the music and craft fairs, for the museum with its spinning wheels, muzzle-loading rifles, and little dolls and "play pretties," and for the small shops along Main Street: eighty-year-old soft-white wood constructions that sell dulcimers, brooms, quilts, ceramics, and toys made of wood and textile. Berea College sits right across the street — FOR MOUNTAIN YOUTH, a Historical Society sign announces — and tours of the campus are available year round. The campus is lovely. One hundred and forty acres of oak, maple, hickory, and magnolia, flowering shrubbery, clusters of geraniums, petunias, mums, and bluebonnets, endless leaves dappling the wood and red brick of buildings from the turn of the century.

But for some faculty, the college may have become a bit too lovely. They came to Berea to teach because its history had special meaning to them. While a few Berea faculty believe that the institution should be politically neutral and others try to urge Berea in the direction of the elite liberal arts colleges of the East, a number of the professoriate continually try to reclaim the school's origins. There is something unique about the place — the more religious among the activist faculty use the word *prophetic* — and to teach there is to honor the principles of the founders, to articulate those principles daily and to resist the kind of settling, the complacency, that comes with growth and establishment.

One group of such faculty are those in the Department of Education. Berea College has been training teachers for the region from the beginning. As early as 1858, three years after the opening of the elementary school, Fee wrote to a friend that "the interests of truth and humanity now require a school of a higher grade — one that shall prepare young men and young ladies to go out as teachers." In 1867 a "normal course" — that is, a pre-baccalaureate teacher-preparation program — was established. By 1907, the Normal Department had a faculty of its own who would go on to produce books for rural teachers: *Teaching a District School, Rural Arithmetic, Reading and Composition for Rural Schools.* In 1931, in compliance with changing Kentucky law, teacher education was upgraded to a four-year degree program, with the hope that broader coursework in humanities and social sciences would create a teaching force who would, as one trustee put it, feel "less keenly the tinsel of civilization" and be "sustained by real vision." And starting in the 1940s, and continuing to this day, the Education Department has assisted teachers in rural, mostly public, schools with goods, workshops, and supervision — following a much older Berea tradition of sending traveling teachers and libraries by horseback into the hollows of Appalachia. It is a department built on basic commitments, codified in the *Manual of Policies and Procedures,* "to serving promising students who are economically disadvantaged; to education of high quality founded in the liberal arts; to the Christian ethic and to service; to the dignity of labor; to community democracy, interracial education, and gender equality; to simple living and concern for the welfare of others; and to service of the Appalachian region."

I had come to Berea because I wanted to get a sense of how such humanistic and democratic principles would play out in the practice of teacher education. During my stay, I observed one of the faculty work with young people preparing for careers in education and talked at length with some of them. Then, following the trail of so many earlier teachers from Berea, I traveled far into the Appalachian Mountains to visit with people who had been teaching in the local schools for a long time. The journey revealed much about the way tradition and innovation can play off each other and the interrelation of hope, risk, vocation, and faith, many kinds of faith, in good teaching.

The Education Department was in Knapp Hall, an old brick building on the southwest corner of the campus, weatherworn, clean, wood and high windows on the inside. Professor Janet Fortune took the stairs in a quick fluid step that was half-shuffle, half-skip, lightly touching the banister, telling me a story over her shoulder about her grandmother, late of Crooked Creek in the Blue Ridge Mountains: ". . . and as she got sicker, poor soul, she would sing rather than talk — she would sing what she was going to do, you know, like 'I'm go-ing to close the window.'" Janet related the tale in an accent that reached its way back to southeast Mississippi and wound through Alabama and the Carolinas. The stairs, wood covered with tile, creaked under our step. "Well, wouldn't you know, the kids in the family started singing back to her! And pretty soon, the adults would just leave the room, and there they'd be, singing to each other and fussing over imaginary guests, moving a chair, fixing an imaginary hem . . ." She stopped on the landing to the second floor, where the faculty offices were located, and turned quickly to me. "The adults *had* to leave, don't you see" — she laughed, hand to her chest. "The room was getting just too crowded!"

A casual conversation with Janet Fortune slid around in mirth and gravity. She laughed often and fully — head back, eyes closed — the kind of laughter that made you feel part of the story . . . and terrifically funny yourself. But she was possessed of a deep seriousness, a trace melancholic, and at the turn of a phrase you found yourself pondering something that a moment before was flitting about in idle speech — or laughing about something that would normally quiet you down. She was born in Hattiesburg, Mississippi. Her father, who went on to become the chancellor of the University of Mississippi, came from "the hollows of North Carolina," his family "dirt poor, the one that always got the Christmas basket from the neighbors." Somehow that poverty left its mark on Janet's consciousness. She received her B.A. from the University of North Carolina at Chapel Hill, taught for years, fifth grade through high school, from Pascagoula, Mississippi, on the Gulf Coast, to Simsbury, Connecticut. She went back to school at the University of North Carolina at Greensboro for her doctorate, reading widely in philosophy, feminist theology, and education, and when it came time to apply for jobs found Berea College to be the place for her. "The call was really to work with mountain kids." So five years ago she moved to Berea, Kentucky, with her son and bought a house on Cherry Road.

We walked through the double doors from the stairwell onto the second floor: a wave of heat, hardwood, high ceilings, lots of windows, the comfortable smell of old wood. "I'm the luckiest damned person in the world," Janet mused. We were heading toward her office, where she was to meet with several of the student teachers she was supervising.

"Teaching is a wonder — and I get to help people become a part of it." The faculty offices opened out onto a small reception area that held a worn couch and some stuffed chairs. I flopped down in one to wait for Janet while she held her conferences. She would then be teaching a course on language arts for middle school and, later in the day, be observing one of her student teachers. Across the hall, a newer cohort of education students began drifting into a large room for an introductory-level course. Most looked to be in their late teens, though a few were in their thirties or forties. The ratio of women to men was about four to one. I read the jackets and T-shirts: *Kentucky Basketball, Berea College Country Dancers, Guns 'n' Roses, Christ Is My Life, Hard Rock Café, BAMA, Chill Out* — this admonition scripted over two palm trees bent toward a setting sun.

There are about fifteen hundred students at Berea College, 80 percent of them from Kentucky and the southern Appalachian Mountains. So, sitting back and listening, you'd hear a wonderful sampling of midland and Southern speech: Alabama, Georgia, east Tennessee, West Virginia, and the different sounds of Kentucky itself: the Bluegrass, the eastern mountains. What all these students had in common was that they came from families of modest means — the college would, with rare exception, accept no other — and to help with the cost, they worked ten to fifteen hours a week at jobs ranging from janitorial and maintenance, to farming and weaving, to tutoring and community service. One of the most popular majors was education.

Students entering the major had to take a set of introductory courses, and then their record was reviewed by the faculty to determine entrance to the teacher-education program. It is hard to generalize about any group of college students, but my conversations with the education majors at Berea kept revealing a high level of idealism. (As Kristi, a second-year student, put it, "Teaching requires that you go that extra mile; if a teacher doesn't do that, then her dreams are just gone.") And, of course, at a Christian college many students expressed religious values, though within the Christian population here, there was quite a range of beliefs. There were fundamentalist students and students questioning their faith in the most fundamental way. There were those who, as another student, Yolanda, put it, "used religion as a weapon" and others who advocated an inclusive Christianity geared toward social justice. Most of the students could be located on a wide and complex middle ground. What struck me was the way Berea, true to its origins, created a place where both religious commitment and free speech were honored, and that seemed to generate in the students an unusual sweep and reflectiveness. Kristi spoke in the same few sentences about God's blessings, *Moll Flanders,* and Marge Piercy. About three quarters of these students would stay in some part of Kentucky or Appalachia to teach, primarily in public schools.

After students were accepted into the teacher-education program, they took further courses to develop an area of expertise. (Janet taught a number of courses related to middle school.) And as the prospective educators approached their senior year, they applied for student teaching, to be supervised by one of Berea's faculty. Over my stay, I would get the opportunity to talk with these advanced students, about where they came from, what brought them into teaching, what lay ahead — their hopes and fears.

Ashley Isaacs, twenty-three,
Millersburg, Bourbon County, Kentucky

I've always wanted to be a teacher. My aunt's a teacher. I played teacher since I was about seven years old. I've always loved school. My mother always taught us, if you see anybody who's hurting, you help them. You don't just say, "Oh, that's sad" — you go out and do something about it. Mom's always taught me to be a doer.

I'm student teaching now. Kindergarten. I'm just so geared toward kindergarten. It's their first big time in school, and it's wonderful to watch the development. After a week or so, the kids will say, "Oh, that word has two *e*'s in it!" You get to watch this; you have a part in it. You think, "This is so great; this is what I've been going through all these classes for, to get in *this* classroom with *these* kids." You get to help these little people.

I hope I can carry out all my ideas. I hope I won't someday turn around and say [snarling], "Oh, it's all the family's fault!" I hope I won't become that blaming person. Sure, it's hard when you're faced with problems every day. You'll get your heart broken. I hope I'll know how to handle it. Teachers tend to forget that something is *causing* a kid's problems. We don't look behind the behavior. We don't ask ourselves, "Now, why is he doing that?" There's a reason behind everything a child does. It's not about blame. I hope I get very good at understanding that.

Eef Fontanez, twenty-two, Clarksburg, West Virginia

I had one horrible teacher in high school — a journalism teacher — who would give an assignment and then read the newspaper. If we had questions, she'd act as if we were bothering her. And I knew that was wrong; I *knew* that was not how you taught. I was about to go to college and wanted to do something with my life, and teaching just sort of came to me. It wasn't like a vision, or anything [laughs]. I always played school. I always helped my younger brothers and sisters — even when I was in the fourth and fifth grades. But when it came down to my senior year in high school, I was, like, what do I *really* want to do with my life? And it's odd, isn't it, the way that teacher helped me make my decision. Seeing the things she could have done differently made me see that I might have a shot at being a teacher.

While I was in high school, I went to an Upward Bound program at Salem College. That's where underprivileged kids prepare for college. I was in it for three summers, and it helped me a lot, let me tell you. Looking back on it, it's so clear to me. My study skills were poor. I didn't know how to study. But at Upward Bound I learned how. I was taking college classes: a math class, an English class, a history class. Just being in that kind of college atmosphere — you know, with *Doctor* So-and-so — that was amazing for me. Here I was, this Puerto Rican West Virginian [laughs], this Appalachian kid. It really helped me. I wanted to prove I could do it.

During my freshman year at Berea, I took a seminar called Guns or Butter, taught by one of the best professors on this campus. He would sit down with you, no matter how late it was, and help you improve your paper. He wrote notes, individual notes on the computer, and handed them back to you with your paper. And he'd encourage you to rewrite the paper. He helped me so much to see the bigger picture — the class was about Central America and U.S. intervention — and those critical thinking skills have stayed with me. It's not unpatriotic to question your government. In fact, it's very American to say "This is not right." I cannot tell you how it helped me, academically, intellectually, to consider different points of view. I come from a very conservative part of the country, and I'm still trying to resolve the conflict. Granted, Berea has its problems, but it *is* different here. I go home and feel really isolated sometimes. I hear things that are so racist. It saddens me. I haven't resolved it. It's been hard. You hear all this stuff.

Sheila Robinson, twenty-two, Jonesville, Virginia

I was born in Rochester, New York. We lived there until I was fourteen. Then we moved to Jonesville, in the southwestern region of Virginia, and that's where my family is now. Jonesville is all White. My family is the only Black family in the whole town. It's a small town, nice, smaller than Berea. My father is the pastor in a Pentecostal church. His congregation is all White. We moved to Jonesville because my father wanted to get us out of Rochester and come back home — he's from Harlan, Kentucky. We kids were getting to the age where we were very impressionable, and my father didn't want us to turn out bad. He wanted us to be safe. The crime was terrible. I'm glad we moved, though at first I was devastated. The only Black family in a small Southern town? But now I hate to go back to Rochester. Really. It's like there's a cloud over the city, and everyone's in this tight box, and they don't know where to go and don't know what to do. It's hard to go back.

My mom, she told me once, "Sheila, I always knew that whatever you did when you got older, you were going to work with people — you're a people person." I, I don't know. I guess it's just that I care. I would like to work with African-American youngsters and make a difference. I want to go everywhere and help everybody [laughs], but I know that's not possible. So I'll work with those where the need is greatest. Wherever I'm needed most, I'll go. They say teaching is a calling. I really like that. A calling.

In the class where I'm student teaching now, the kids are great. You know that fear I had when we moved to Virginia? It came back when I anticipated my student teaching. The schools in this area are predominantly White, and here I come, I'm going to teach them, and I imagine them thinking, "Humph, this Black lady, how's she think she's going to teach us anything?" But they've been really good, so I'm kind of relaxed now. Janet told me, "You're not going to have any problems." But, still . . . you can say that, but you don't know. It's hard at times. You still get hurt.

Spanish and math are my areas of emphasis. And in the class I'm in now, the kids are so excited. They want to learn Spanish. Most of them never had it before, probably never heard it before, except on TV. When we lived in Rochester, I had a lot of Puerto Rican friends, and I wanted to relate to them better. One day I realized that a lot of prejudices come from not knowing other cultures, and I realized that taking Spanish meant a lot more than learning words. You have to learn about their heritage and their culture. It's not just learning the language itself, but much more. So when my students learn Spanish, I hope it helps get rid of the prejudices they might have, some of the stereotypes they pick up from TV.

I guess I want my students to learn to love something — Spanish, math, whatever — and to be able to use it in their lives, to take it and make their lives better. I want them to have the opportunities I've had because I had an education, to know that they can do what they want to do.

Kathy Walsh, twenty-two, Warsaw, Gallatin County, Kentucky

When I see a teacher who is enthusiastic and excited and loves what she's teaching, that makes me feel excited, too — that it's something important because she feels it's important. I was thinking about this the other day during my student teaching, thinking about Professor Fortune, how her enthusiasm carries over. Sometimes you don't realize how much you're learning. I don't know what it is she does exactly, but she

> can give you a whole new perspective on things. She has helped me see things that were always there that I never noticed. And, you know, I've seen her change *her* whole point of view, right in class. She'll say, "Hmm, I really need to think about that." She listens to what her students say, and I think that's very important. Her classes have helped me grow. I mean it's not just in the classroom that you get more reflective, but in your life, with your family, with your friends. I've just grown so much.
>
> I love children. They're just a joy to be with. And I guess I feel I can give something back; teaching is something worthwhile. I wouldn't be happy doing something that's just for me. I need to give something, to teach, to show, to help guide students. But I worry that I won't know enough. Sometimes I feel I don't know anything. I had a lot of science in high school, and I want to bring that into my classroom. But I don't have a lot of knowledge of history, so during the summer I try to learn as much as I can. People say to me, "Oh, well, you're naïve. You're young. When you've been teaching as long as I have . . ." I'm sure I'll get discouraged. I'll have my bad days. But if that drive to teach ever goes away, well . . . I'd be doing more harm than good. And the kids can tell. They know.
>
> My family and I travel around a lot, and some of the best teachers I have ever seen are here in eastern Kentucky. Some of them are working with *no* materials, and yet they're teaching something worthwhile, something valuable. You hear so much about the kids and poverty — that they're poor and stupid and they can't learn — but I've seen such gifted children. When I go home and I hear people in northern Kentucky — which is wealthier than here — when I hear them complaining because they don't have this or that, I just think, "If you could only see . . ." I want to teach here in eastern Kentucky. The teachers have so much less to work with, but they have so much more inside.

Janet opened her class, Reading and Language Arts for the Middle Grades, by raising some fundamental questions about literacy. She asked her students to "take fifteen or twenty minutes and jot down what comes to your mind when you think about literacy. How would you define it? In our society, who gets to define it? What are your personal associations to literacy?" This wouldn't be evaluated; students could write it any way they wanted. It was a warm-up. Central to Janet's pedagogy was the desire to promote a reflective cast of mind, a willingness to consider the habitual ways we think about curriculum, about learning, about children. "Why am I doing this?" was the basic question she wanted her student teachers to ask. "Why am I thinking this way?" I was sitting on the floor next to a cordial, sandy-haired man named Dwayne Satterfield who let me look over his shoulder as he wrote:

> We are quick to rubber-stamp individuals as illiterate before coming to understand the "why" of this person's present situation. My father was a millwright in a factory for 35 years. He knew his work inside and out; however, with increased technology he became more illiterate year by year. . . .

This was a tiny class, the smallest Janet had ever taught, so she held it in her office. It was all male — another first. Janet sat in a rocking chair by her computer; the rest of us sat around the room, in chairs, cross-legged on rugs, or backs against the wall. A fiddle-leaf philodendron curled close around the old silver radiator; red and brown shawls hung over the backs of gray metal chairs; and a full, hanging fern dropped its leaves on a stack of books on language arts. The books themselves, packed into cases along three of the four walls, looked like a multicolored patchwork: blue spines and yellow, orange and black, tan and white. There were whole sections on the philosophy of language, on feminist theology, on adolescent literature — as well as all the books on education. Looking around the room, I could see Robert Coles's *The Call of Stories* and Sharon Welch's *A Feminist Ethic of Risk,* Roald Dahl's *Charlie and the Great Glass Elevator,* and, over my shoulder, a row of books on phenomenology and critical theory: Heidegger, Merleau-Ponty, and Max Horkheimer. And novels — from *The Idiot* to Gloria Naylor's *Mama Day* — were interspersed everywhere. By the window, a poster for the Children's Defense Fund made its appeal in pastel yellows, blues, and grays. Next to the fern, an advertisement from the Crazy Ladies Bookstore featured a flower erupting in violet and fiery red.

After twenty minutes or so, Janet told the class to wind up what they were doing, but to keep in mind what they wrote as the rest of the day progressed. Janet was a working philosopher, trying continually to convert her academic study of philosophy, theology, and language to the practice of teaching. One way she did this was through the use of art and literature. Last semester, for example, she asked students in an introductory course to represent with construction paper, Magic Markers, scissors, and glue what they thought about when they thought about school. One student made an eye, another made a short row of desks, and Janet urged them to talk out the beliefs that led to these constructions — school was for seeing, school was for order — and the different kinds of classrooms that would emerge from such beliefs. Her hope was that through the use of analogy, through the use of a range of media, she could encourage a shift in perspective, could spark reflection. Today she was going to rely on a story by Tillie Olsen called "I Stand Here Ironing" to forward her discussion of literacy. She reached into her bag and pulled out a book. "I want you to think about school while I read this," Janet said. "See what you think."

"I Stand Here Ironing" is a brief, first-person story, an agitated monologue filled with recollection, directed to a teacher who had phoned asking the narrator to come see her about her daughter. The request has upset the speaker — "what you asked me moves tormented back and forth with the iron" — and triggers a tale of Depression-era poverty. The speaker recounts, with pain, the way she had to let others raise her oldest daughter, Emily — the subject of the phone call — so that she could work, the effect this had on Emily — the vulnerability, the sadness — and the bringing of Emily back into the family, but only after the girl had absorbed the loss, too late to make things whole again. The speaker tells of Emily's uncertain growth in school, but of the strange development of a gift for mimicry, a talent, her mother observes, that leaves her "as imprisoned in her difference as she had been in anonymity." The monologue ends, as it began, with the mother ironing, appealing finally to the teacher to "help [Emily] to know — help make it so there is cause for her to know — that she is more than this dress on the ironing board, helpless before the iron."

As she read the story, Janet let her face register sadness, pleasure, anger, and peace, her cadenced voice transferring the pain and longing from the story's San Francisco setting to the farms and mountains and coalfields her students knew. Dwayne was resting his chin on his folded hands. Larry, a tiny guitar dangling from his neck, was leaning forward, elbows on thighs. Rodney, tall, glasses, black hair parted in the middle, leaned back against a filing cabinet, hugging his knees to his chest. Billy, rangy and powerful, was watching Janet and absentmindedly tapping a pencil on his shoe. "What does this story tell us about school," Janet asked, looking slowly around the room. "They don't understand," Rodney said, under his breath. "Understand?" Janet prompted. "Understand all the girl has gone through," Rodney replied, releasing his knees and bringing his chair forward. There were some leaves and trees sketched, in ballpoint pen, on the legs of his jeans. "Here," said Dwayne — at twenty-nine, the oldest of the lot — "here, I wrote a quote down while you were reading." He flipped back a page in his notebook: "'Running out to that huge school where she was one, she was lost, she was a drop . . .' That describes a lot of kids, I reckon. Big . . . impersonal . . . school just loses them."

The discussion continued; then Janet said, "I want to tie this story back to the writing you did about literacy. What does this story convey — and to whom? Or, let me put it another way: What about this story would make it part of someone's literacy?"

Dwayne scooted around from his position on the rug. "It describes the struggle for existence — and in a language that can be understood by working people." He paused, picking at a piece of lint in the rug. "The experiences speak to me; they surely do. My family's experiences are similar."

"Why are those experiences important?" Janet asked.

"Simple," Dwayne replied. "They're the kinds of experiences a lot of folks have had."

"So?" Janet prodded.

"So," Dwayne answered back, "they're inviting . . . engaging. Something pulls at me."

"Inviting," Janet repeated. "Interesting word, Dwayne." It seems that "invitation" had been the focus of another discussion a few weeks back, Janet framing the word in a theological context as a calling-together, a summoning into the life of the sacred.

"Rodney," she asked, "can you recall our discussion of the word *invitation*?"

Rodney opened the cover of his notebook. "We spoke," he said, "about *invitation* as being summoned, being called."

Janet paused for a moment. "Dwayne said that some of the experiences in 'I Stand Here Ironing' are invitational. Do they call to us? Invite us?"

"They call to me," said Dwayne. "I know those people. They interest me."

"What is the narrator's concern?" asked Janet.

"Providing for her family," said Larry, looking down at the floor.

"How is that presented to us?" Janet asked in return.

Larry looked up, the guitar coming to rest on his breastbone. "Through moving . . . or sad rec . . . recollections."

"Recollections," Janet repeated. "Memory."

Larry, a quiet young man, began talking more fully about some reading he was doing for his psychology class. "A smell or a sound," he explained, "a voice, too. It . . . they can trigger all this memory. And that's what's happening in the story. What the teacher said to the mother stimulated all these memories."

Janet talked a bit about an association of her own, the way the smell of hand lotion still called up a memory of her mother kissing her good night; then she pulled herself up in the rocker and said: "If I'm in your middle-grade classroom, I'll need to hear stories, to read stories that can sit inside me. There needs to be a relationship between what children read and their own life experience." She paused. "I am *not* saying we shouldn't make kids stretch, but there should be a basic connection. You have to figure out what they know — and engage it. Invite it . . . and middle-school kids know a lot, they truly know a lot."

We took a break, and when we returned, Janet had the group do two more activities that would push them to reflect on the connections between literacy and experience. She sat down in the middle of the floor and spread out a boxful of cartoons she had clipped from magazines, newspapers, and calendars: political cartoons, cocktail party cartoons from *The New Yorker,* Gary Larson cartoons with garrulous cows and urbane cockroaches. She asked us to notice which cartoons clicked with us immediately — which ones raised a quick laugh — and which lost us, fell flat, left us with no basis for connection. For about twenty minutes we sat around, sifting through cartoons, chuckling, snorting, wincing at the sick ones — Billy's deep *heh-heh,* Janet's soaring, fingers-to-lips *haw, haw, haw* — the laughter mixing with free-ranging talk about what we found funny and why, probing our own memories for connections.

As a final activity, Janet called up an assignment she had given to the class during their previous meeting: each student had to bring in a piece of writing that was especially meaningful to him. Dwayne, Rodney, and company poked around in their knapsacks, and the final thirty minutes or so of Janet's class was spent listening to and reacting to print that had deep personal value. Larry read some poems written by his sister, Missy, who had graduated from Berea the year before. Billy read from Genesis, which he described as the bedrock of his faith. Rodney read a prose poem he had written about daybreak: "The birds find their voice again . . . the sun floats higher . . . the clouds tumble across the sky." And Dwayne read two things — a section from James Agee's *A Death in the Family* and an elegy he had written for his father:

> "He's gone," Mama had said. Found dead, his purple hand still grasping the ignition switch of his truck. A faint grin, a smirk. "It's natural, I didn't do a thing," said the mortician — as if to say, "I've just done something, you guess what." Now all things are new . . .

The passages held significance for each reader, and Janet closed the class by asking the men to think about what it was that these pieces of writing revealed about their own uses of literacy, what value literacy had in each of their lives.

The class was typical of the way Janet liked to work. She did not tell prospective teachers that they had to be reflective; she created the circumstances that spark reflection. The purpose of the course, as stated in its title, was to provide instruction in reading and language arts for middle-grade students. But before Janet could impart techniques, she believed, she had to get her students to consider the nature and motive of their own use of written language. On the issue of pedagogical technique itself, Janet also believed that instruction in either procedures or the theories behind them would be premature without some sense of what it felt like to engage language fully. So during the first three or four weeks of the class, Janet did not tell her students how to run a classroom, but gave them the experience of writing, reading, speaking, and responding to each other across a range of activities — the kind of rich language use she would eventually help them re-create in their own classrooms.

Later that day, after Janet had finished with her committee meetings and student conferences, she took a break, and we walked down to Brushy Fork, a creek behind Berea's intramural field. We walked under maple trees and oaks, down some old stone steps, shuffling through leaves and acorns, twigs and strips of bark. "I think it's especially important," she said, "that these students have someplace where they can try things out and say what comes to mind. In some of the communities around here, what men can do and women can do is pretty much set in stone. These students are curious and so alive. They have a lot going on inside, but just getting some of the men to talk in class can be a real achievement." When we got to the creek, Janet looked around and saw a felled tree extending along dry ground. We sat down. The sun came in streaks through the trees; there was the smell of leaves matted into earth and water.

"You know," she continued, "I take a lot of chances with this stuff. Many of our students come wanting us to teach them how to teach. Right away. Now, there are places in this state where you can go in and sit with a basal reader or be walked through the social studies manual. But that . . . that's not what we're about." She picked up a stick and started splashing the water lightly. "What I'm going to say is sappy, and I'm sorry, but I don't know how else to talk about it. . . . You can't be around children for long without seeing . . . without figuring out that there's this . . . there's what the Quakers call this light that binds us, person to person . . . and that who you're dealing with are incredible, beautiful human beings." She laughed. "Look, I've had a kid pull a knife on me. I'm not naïve. But no one could have told me what to do in that situation. That's difficult for our students to hear at first. Hell, we could practice, we could role-play, but there's always going to be that instant in which you'll have to respond. And what I want . . ." Janet swished the stick more fully in the water now ". . . what I want is for them to respond from the core of understanding children and from a solid belief as to who we are as human beings. What you do at any given moment in a classroom reveals your basic philosophy about kids. These young teachers need technique, yes, but what counts more is what underlies technique. What counts . . . what really counts is sweeping aside the veils that keep us from seeing kids in all their richness."

Dwayne Satterfield, twenty-nine, Dandridge, Tennessee

It was my mother who encouraged me to think about teaching as a career — she's been a teacher's aide for about fifteen years — so I started taking introductory education classes at the community college I was at in Tennessee. One of those had a practicum in the fourth grade — and I enjoyed being with the kids, enjoyed interacting with them. This gave me a few scares [laughs] but also gave me a way to look at kids and know that I would like to be part of their development. To see a child come to a realization, to work a math problem and feel the excitement of doing it right.

I'm big on motives. Why do we do the things we do? I believe — now, this is a belief, I'm stating beliefs here — I believe we're equipped for things. I've been through certain experiences which have equipped me — not predestined me; I'm not a believer in that — to do some things better than others. And I believe that teaching requires an examination of motives, of our experiences. I'm *not* saying that a person has to be in touch with a deity to be a good teacher, goodness no, but for *me* the way to examine motives is through prayer and study and meditation — they all fit in together for me.

I think religion has to be connected to helping people. That's the heart of the matter. Otherwise, *religion* is an empty word. Faith should be something that urges us forward to give ourselves away. I'm wary of political activists in the religious realm. A guy like Randall Terry scares me. He's a driven man. In the church I attend there's great diversity of ideas. They're mostly country people, and they come together to study the Bible. And they ask questions that you'd never dream could be asked in a setting like that. And the pastor loves it. He's not scared of these questions. And this is what we need more of — to work on the big questions together. The image I have of Christ is of someone who comes to people in need. I want to help people find out who they are and how they can fit into the world. The idea of faith is to reach out to my fellow human beings. Can I be of assistance?

Mindy Botts, twenty-two,
Denniston, Menifee County, Kentucky

My mother is a teacher, and she does such fantastic things. We disagree, but not on the big questions: the *why,* what's exciting about learning, why we need to learn. We agree on these. Still, our discussions get pretty intense. I worry that what I teach is important — and I'm constantly questioning that. "Why am I doing this? What makes it valuable? Will it matter in the scheme of things?" One of my big concerns is being able to look at the big picture. It's easy to lose that perspective.

I went to high school about one and a half hours from here in Menifee County. It was a very small school — there were sixty in my graduating class. I didn't come to Berea for religious reasons. To be honest, I didn't want to go to school *anywhere.* I mean, I wanted to learn, but I was tired of school. I wanted to go into teaching right then. Right then! Let me out now! I figured I would learn along the way. My first two years at Berea, I hated it. I didn't like all the restrictions. I was rebelling against everything. I just didn't want to be here. I was going to go to class. I was going to do a good job. But [laughing] I wasn't going to *like* it.

I remember a Philosophy for Children class. It dealt with questioning and how asking the questions may be more important than getting the right answer. I ended up with half my stuff being questions rather than answers — and that used to be very disturbing to me — but I'm becoming a little more comfortable with it. It's funny, at first I didn't like the class — remember, in those days I was all bristled up — but many of the things I don't like end up teaching me more than the things I do like. And they become a part of me.

Last year, I went to Germany with the Kentucky Institute for International Study. We spent five weeks in Munich, and I was in a classroom that would be the equivalent of our second or third grade. The teacher was remarkable. The children were reading stories together, acting them out, writing — everything was integrated, even dance and math! It was amazing, just amazing. Over the entrance to the school was a motto. It said, "We learn not for the school, but we learn for our life." I don't think I'll ever forget that.

Tracy Payne Williams, twenty-two, Jacksonville, Alabama

I always played teacher when I was young, but what really got me was when I would watch my friends who came from pretty bad homes — it was their teachers who encouraged them; the teachers seemed to be the only route . . . When I entered high school, my best friend and I started taking different courses. I went off into algebra and she took consumer math and such. And from that point, she decided, "Well, I'm not going to college." And I'd always say, "Hey, go to college with me. Let's go to college together!" We were really close. But she'd say, "I can't do it. I just can't do it!" Well, we had this English teacher, and she would say to us, "Anybody can go to college if you just try." So she started encouraging this girl, and, you know, that girl went on to state college back home and became an English major. Yes, she did!

My aunt went to Berea, and she always told me about it. I guess I was interested in Berea because of what it did for people, the way it took in students who came from poor families and had to strive extra hard, who needed an extra push. Just someone to say "you can do it" and build their confidence. And Berea seemed like the place that gave those people a chance, people like me.

I'm a religious person. But, you know, all my beliefs came from other people — family members, preachers, pastors, church — they came from other people, not something I drew for myself. When I came to Berea, I learned there were different perspectives. You meet people with very different beliefs; you can't just say someone's right and someone's wrong. I learned for myself what I believe. It became truly my own . . . I've always been good at biology and math. I love science. I can't wait to teach it. Now, I've had many conversations about this. I believe the Bible and science can go together. Darwin has some interesting theories that seem right on. And I'm fascinated with genetics. But I believe in the Bible too. What the Bible tells us and what science tells us are different kinds of things. I just think they can all connect. I hope I'm open-minded enough to accept both.

My supervising teacher told me something; she said, "Tracy, it's easy to start talking about students and labeling them, so be sure not to listen to everything you hear about a student." When you hear bad things about a kid, you start looking for the bad. You do! There's this one child in class who every teacher has said something bad about. And I never noticed anything about her because, at that point, I didn't know all the students' names. To me, this student was a joy. She was nice and friendly and seemed like she was always paying attention. But they'd all labeled her this way. So the next time I went to class, I tried looking at her *that* way, and I did see those things, I *did,* because I was looking for them. Do you know what I mean? Before, I'd not even noticed. I think we should look for the good in our students. And I just hope I can continue to do that. Try to see the good things about them.

After Brushy Fork, Janet and I rushed to observe Tracy Williams teach a practice lesson in a sixth-grade class at Foley Middle School. Red Foley, the star of "Ozark Jubilee" and "Grand Ole Opry," was a Berea alumnus, and the school named after him was only a mile away from the campus. Though we were there in a few left turns and a straight roadway, we were late, and as we came through the door we almost stepped on the ankle of a boy who was lying on his side. His head was propped on one hand as he and the other students counted what looked like a pile of poker chips. We shifted quickly — a few students looking up at us, Tracy waving "hi" — and high-stepped over bodies to two chairs in the corner. Kids were sitting cross-legged, kneeling butts to heels, or lying belly-down on the linoleum; the desks were pushed back against the walls. Yellow, red, green, and blue bottle caps — we saw finally that they were bottle caps — were spread all across the floor, and students were clustered around game boards in groups of five or six. It took a moment to get a fix on the game. The boards were simple poster board, laminated, lined to make four wide columns, each column identified with a color: red, green, blue, and yellow. The students were animatedly talking and pointing to columns on the boards, and stacking bottle caps in those columns, then, in various negotiated transactions, counting caps of one color and, in some kind of trade, replacing them with a single cap of another color in an adjacent column. "Gosh, almighty!" exclaimed one girl to her colleagues by our chairs, "we've gotta move all these blue chips over!" After the momentary stir of our entrance, Janet and I were forgotten.

Tracy was standing in the front of the room; the problem the students were solving was on the board behind her:

> Imagine you are in Base Four Land, and you have four yellow, six blue, three green, and two red chips on your board. If you traded up, how many red chips would you have?

Tracy was wearing faded overalls and a lace blouse, a full, colorful ribbon — gold flowers on velvet black — in her long brown hair. She was watching the activity closely, a little pensive, and whenever a student looked up with a question or comment, her face broke into a full smile, and she walked quickly to that part of the room, leaning into the group, getting at eye level, complimenting them and thanking them for their diligence. And soon the hands started shooting up. Tracy called on a girl in the back with wildly teased hair. She got up on her knees and said, "You'd end up with three red chips." "All right!" said Tracy. "Very good, Joy. You're absolutely right. Thank you." Joy nodded, very cool, but stayed on her knees a few moments longer. Then she smiled faintly and stretched back out on the floor.

"This is a lesson," Tracy had written in her lesson plan, "to give students an understanding of our base 10 system by working with other base systems." To achieve this, Tracy had the students imagine that they lived in alternate mathematical universes (Base Four Land, Base Six Land) and play that numerical life out on the board games spread around the room. Here's how it worked: Each column on the board represented a power of the base, with the left-most column (red) being the highest, and the right-hand column (yellow) being the lowest. So, for example, if students were in Base Ten Land, and had ten chips in the yellow column, they could "trade up" to a single chip that would go into the next column, the blue one. That would give them 1 chip in the blue column and 0 chips in the yellow column: 1 - 0. 10. Base Ten Land.

Tracy turned back to the board and began writing out another problem, this time placing the students in Base Three Land:

If I have 2 chips in my pocket worth 18 yellow chips, what color are my chips?

And, again, the *tip-tap* of bottle caps, the shifting of positions around the boards, the cooperative haggling — "Hey, you guys, count 'em out." "OK, OK, now trade for blue" — and hands were waving in the air. Tracy called on a group close to the front this time, and a boy whose T-shirt read "Every Knee Shall Bend" stood up and said, "You would have two green chips." "That's great," said Tracy. "You all are just great." Then she paused, looking down as if to collect her thoughts, the students watching her. "You know" — she looked up, serious — "you may think, 'Well, this was fun, but, gee, Mrs. Williams didn't teach us anything about real mathematics — about place value and borrowing and carrying.' Well" — another pause, then a big smile — "Well, I'm fixin' to show you what you learned about those concepts." She was pulling the arithmetical rabbit out of the hat, and seemed to have the students caught up in the show. I couldn't know what each was thinking, but I didn't see one kid looking out the window or doodling or nodding out. Sixth grade. Border territory. Some girls still in ponytails, others with big hair; before long the boys' voices would undergo a major shift in pitch. A time of desire and self-consciousness, of flirtations with rebellion and the first stirring dreams of release. And they watched Tracy as she began explaining how the columns on their game boards were really powers of the base.

"They should have had this long ago," Tracy would tell me later. "They were getting through math by memorizing how to do things, but because they didn't understand what they were doing, none of it would stick. So every year they had to start all over again." The problem became clear to Tracy after a few days of observing from the back of the class; she watched as the students moved into a section of their workbooks where they had to think about what numbers represented, basic number theory. Many of them were soon adrift. "They had no idea," Tracy said, "that .1 was less than 1. They didn't understand how decimals worked, or concepts like place value . . . or equivalence . . . or what it meant to have a base ten system." So Tracy spoke with Janet, and Janet encouraged her to talk to her supervising teacher, to explain that she had had a lot of math (she had taken eight mathematics courses at Berea) and would like to try something different. The teacher was receptive, and Tracy began developing a lesson from some old New Math materials.

And, so, on the day of our visit, Tracy stood before the board, asking the students questions about place value and equivalence and trading up and trading down. And David explained how trading up and down could be done by multiplication and division, and Joy saw equivalence, and Typhanie pointed out a computational error, and Jessica came up to the board, and Amy said that this stuff wasn't so hard after all.

As the final step in the lesson, Tracy passed out a sheet with three questions on it:

1. How would you explain, in your own words, how to play the chip-trading game to someone?
2. What did this game teach you about place value, borrowing, and carrying?
3. Did you come to any understanding of base-number systems? What does it mean to say that someone uses a base 10 number system?

She went through the questions, encouraging the class to do as well as they could, but said it would be OK if the answers were a little messy. The writing would help them further understand the mathematical concepts. Typhanie asked if they could use drawings with their writing, and Tracy said they sure could. "That would be great, Typhanie, writing and illustrations together, you bet." The students got to work, writing, erasing, raising a hand now and then, and Janet sat next to me, writing intently, her forehead cradled in her hand, the pen moving quickly across her ruled notebook.

The bell rang, and the students scribbled some last little something and headed for the door. Tracy came over and dropped into an empty chair. "Was that OK?"

Janet began by asking Tracy what she thought went well. Tracy was pleased with the attention the students gave her and with the way they worked in groups. "They were doing a lot together, taking turns, discovering things on their own." She had the sense that they were learning mathematical concepts — she was excited about that — and as we sat there, she started flipping through their papers, seeing evidence of comprehension. "They say 'I hate writing' but look at this; they seemed to care about this. I wanted a way to get them to write about mathematics. They never get to do that. Oh, I hope this works." There were tiny beads of sweat on her upper lip, and as she read quickly through the sheets, she slid down a little in the chair, relaxing into the success of the lesson. "The math," said Janet, "was beautiful."

Janet gave her a minute or so, watching her, and then began to talk. "Tracy, your students, the girls especially, are very interested in who you are. The little girl in front couldn't take her eyes off you. It's quite a power you have, and you treat it, and them, with respect." Janet's voice was gaining force, quiet and intense. She looked at Tracy or down at her notes. Other people came in and out of the room, an announcement about cheerleading practice was read over the PA system, but Janet's focus didn't break. "When you move around the room, Tracy, that dance you do, you go right to where the children are. You bend down or kneel down. That says to them, 'You are important.'" Again, Janet looked at her notes; Tracy sat, her head down a little, watching Janet. "You have the incredible ability to be right on top of what you say and do. You recall who answered last. You connect one answer to another question. You think ahead to where you're going and formulate questions to get you there. It's just wonderful to watch you teach."

II

WHEELWRIGHT lies about a hundred and fifty miles southeast of Berea, in Floyd County, deep in Kentucky coal country. King Coal. Extending for roughly two miles along a fork of Left Beaver Creek, a tributary of the Big Sandy River, the town was originally a settlement called Otter Creek, had just a few houses, and survived on farming and through participation in Kentucky's once-robust, if ravaging, timber industry: oak, hickory, ash, walnut. As railroads began to open up Floyd County, mining companies moved in, buying mineral rights, and in 1916 the Elkhorn Coal Corporation established a town at Otter Creek and christened it after an executive named Wheelwright. During the early period, Wheelwright was an unruly place — moonshining, gunfights — little more, really, than a mining camp, where the only sidewalk was an uneven stretch of wooden planks extending down the main street. But by the mid-1920s, as coal continued to boom, Elkhorn had built a decent town: row houses, company stores, a recreation hall, and a theater. It was in 1931, though, when the Inland Steel Corporation of Chicago bought Wheelwright, that the town was developed into what most of the old-timers recall as a "real good place to live." Inland refurbished Elkhorn's buildings — supplying Colonial façades to some — added a swimming pool and golf course and built a library. The company store was well stocked, and prices were reasonable. The population grew to three thousand. WHEELWRIGHT, the frame on a license plate read, THE MODERN COAL TOWN.

Coal markets began their decline in the early 1950s, but Wheelwright continued to do well through the decade. Inland started reducing its work force in the early 1960s, and by 1966 was employing half the number of miners it had had on its payroll during the war boom. In 1966, with little public notice, it sold Wheelwright to another company, which continued operating the mines but began selling off houses, supermarket, library, hospital, the theater — even the streetlights and sidewalks. Finally, the town was purchased by the Kentucky Housing

Corporation and homes were sold to individual families. These days, a little coal is still mined, deep-mined and strip-mined, but Wheelwright is an abandoned company town. The two-story Colonial recreation hall is gutted; the library is dismantled and overgrown with kudzu; a brief walk will take you by houses that are empty and store fronts long boarded up. People drive thirty-three miles north to Prestonsburg, the county seat, to see a movie.

Long before my arrival in Berea, Janet had talked about taking me to Wheelwright. Company towns were such an important part of the lives of the people in eastern Kentucky, and Wheelwright, she said, was "a place with real history." Whenever she could, she brought her students there — because of "the sociology, the memory," and because there were some fine teachers working in the local schools. One of these teachers was a man named Bud Reynolds. So on a drizzling Sunday morning, Janet and I headed east on the Daniel Boone Parkway to Floyd County, where Bud had been teaching for twenty years.

It was about a two-and-a-half-hour drive, and it took us along a dramatic change in terrain, from the farmland of the Bluegrass through the dark, chiseled rock of the Daniel Boone National Forest — a roadway blasted through the mountains, sycamore, pine, oak, and elm growing in thick clusters up and back from the traffic — from there onto 80 East and the clear loss of level ground. Ancient streams had cut deep valleys in the land, and all around us were hollows sloping to narrow V bottoms, some with house trailers nestled in the crevices and shrubbery. We passed a series of hamlets with the kinds of names that charmed William Least Heat-Moon's ear as he drove the nation's blue highways: Pigeonroost, Dwarf, Rowdy — this last named for the Rowdy Branch of Troublesome Creek.

Janet recalled her first visit to Wheelwright, the effect the town had on her: standing at the entrance to the closed Inland mine, walking through the remains of the bath house where miners had washed the coal from their skin — the old pipes leaking overhead, the sun shining through broken windows onto bare tile. And she talked about Bud, about the first time she met him. "I had heard about this guy, this social studies teacher in middle school. He was a real character, they said, something special. But sitting in his classroom, I'll tell you . . . Kids were all over the place, talking, working with maps, finding places they were reading about, doing geography, leaving the room to go to the library down the hall, coming back with books. And almost everything in the room, a lot of it anyway, was stuff the kids had made — reports on world events, maps, flags of different nations — all this stuff. And there was Bud, walking around the room, talking, goading, coaching, asking questions, giving advice. The place just felt so damned comfortable."

Bud Reynolds lived in Martin, Kentucky, about a half-hour of winding road from Wheelwright. He usually taught seventh- and eighth-grade social studies, but during the year of my visit was team-teaching an experimental eleventh-grade course at Wheelwright High School with a veteran teacher there named Delores Woody. The Commonwealth of Kentucky had recently passed comprehensive school reform legislation — one of the most ambitious reform bills in the nation — that, among its many mandates, called for a fundamental revision of curriculum to enhance creative, active learning, problem solving and the application of knowledge, and the development of the ability to communicate and collaborate. Bud and Delores were responding to the legislation by combining their specialties — social studies and English — to produce an American Studies curriculum rich in research, writing, and collaborative student projects. Their classroom was also one of the sites in the Kentucky Telecommunications Project, the brainchild of another local teacher, Carol Stumbo, who solicited funding from a foundation in New York to establish a computer network among five classrooms of different grade levels in different regions of the state. Students at each site were to develop projects related to local concerns and, via electronic mail, share questions and findings about their work, shaping their writing to different audiences, ideally developing a network of writers that transcended local boundaries. So fifth-graders in Paducah, in the far west of Kentucky, would pose questions about, say, the environment to the eleventh-graders at Wheelwright, and the students at Wheelwright would explain the economy of the Eastern Coal Field to seniors in Louisville.

Well along Route 80, Janet and I passed an abandoned tipple — a plant where coal was screened and loaded — a sign for Alice Lloyd College, "a light onto the mountains," at Pippa Passes, Kentucky; an occasional house tucked down in the trees and shrubbery, with the sun, fresh from the clouds, glinting sharply off a half-hidden window; the Loose Caboose Café; the Mountain Christian Academy School; a sign announcing Floyd County; then off the highway and a bumpy turn into Martin. PEACE ON EARTH was painted in big red letters on the side of the first building we saw as we entered town.

Martin developed in the first decade of this century as tracks for the Chesapeake and Ohio Railroad were laid through the area, opening a line that would carry tens of millions of tons of coal out of places like Wheelwright. Martin became a hub for the C & O and flourished through the war years, but when both coal and rail power went into decline, Martin did as well. There were lots of retired folks in Martin, and most of the younger people worked in what mining and railroad jobs remained, and in the fast-food chains and mini-marts that have opened on the outskirts of town, by Route 80. Five hundred or so people now live in and around Martin.

Janet drove down Main Street past the hospital — where a marquee announced painting classes — past the five-and-dime, past a hardware store, past some old fellows, whittling, who puzzled at the strange car, and soon we found ourselves on the outskirts of town, looking up at the broadcasting tower of a radio station, WMDJ. We hurried to find it on our dial; the DJ was just introducing "Bubba Shot the Juke Box Last Night." "All right, Bubba," Janet hooted and admitted we were lost. "Just ask for Bud Reynolds's house," Bud's sister, Patty, had told Janet by phone the day before. So we turned around and pulled up to a house where a lady sat rocking on a porch swing. She regarded us. Then we asked for Bud, and her face brightened. "Oh, Bud Reynolds! Why sure . . ." It seemed we had missed the first left by the police station. "Right there, just over the creek."

Bud and Patty's house was a converted general store, about twenty-five feet from the railroad tracks. We knocked and Bud opened the door with a bear hug for Janet and a "Howdy, Mike buddy," for me, though we had never met before. He was a barrel-chested man, about five foot eight, in his mid-forties, Clark Gable handsome, mustache, wavy hair graying at the temples, friendly as a country politician. His family had been in Martin for generations. I would be staying there, at his house. Of course I would. Of course. Bud wouldn't have it any other way.

That night Bud took me to the one place in town where the locals gathered to have a drink and relax and, occasionally, hear music: the AmVets Club. The outside of the building was tan brick; the windows were sealed over with gray wood. DANCE SAT NITE, a sign announced, DJ FREE ADM. Bud led the way, telling me the names of some of the men I'd most likely meet, and the name of the bartender, Tad, a retired miner. "Coal and railroad," Bud said as he closed the door behind us, "that's what's around the bar."

AmVets Post 27 was one large room, dark, spare, with booths along two walls, a linoleum floor, and a large flag of the United States on the wall. In a dim corner to the right of the door, a neon *Bud* sign glowed blue above a simple stage. That, Bud explained, was where the band would set up — when they had one. At the far end of the room, straight ahead of us, was a big oval bar, a few lights hanging overhead, seven or eight men, about three women, a layer of smoke drifting from their heads up into the lights. Behind the bar a wide screen was flashing pictures of Michael Milken, Leona Helmsley, and Jim and Tammy Faye Bakker — the video images of Travis Tritt's "Lord Have Mercy on the Working Man." We pulled out two stools and Bud introduced me to Tad, who set two cans of beer on the bar. *Tink. Tink.* NOTICE, read a sign over his shoulder. AS OF FEB. 20, ALL BEER $1.25.

As the night progressed, the residents of Martin came and went. A few couples took booths and talked. Two miners arrived straight from work "to wash down the coal dust," their faces so covered with grime and soot, I had to strain to see features beyond eyes and teeth. Bud and I spent most of the evening talking with Tad and with two of Bud's high school buddies, Tim Allen and Bobby Sherman Dingas, both of whom worked for CSX, the remaining railroad in Martin. Bud had taught all their kids.

Tad told me about the mines, explaining how you position yourself when you're working in a narrow space, how you lie on your back and pick across your body at the coal seam or settle in low on your haunches, bracing your back against the roof of the mine to keep from tilting over when your shovel is full. A fellow sitting on the other side of me said, "Hell, Tad's worked a twenty-seven-inch seam. Right, Tad?" and Tad nodded. It took me a while to realize what that meant, that Tad had spent days crouched or supine in a space tighter than most adults could crawl through without mishap. The fellow by me repeated the number with clear respect. These were the badges of honor developed deep within the earth.

Bobby Sherman and Tim or Timmy (or, as Bobby Sherman tended to pronounce it, "Shit, Tim" or "Goddammit, Timmy") were combatively tight, the closeness bred of mutual close calls, one a pragmatist, the other philosophical in bent. Our topics of conversation were those I would hear repeatedly during my stay in Floyd County: local politics ("politics is real big around here"), the treatment eastern Kentucky receives from the balance of the commonwealth ("Sometimes I think the rest of the state, the Bluegrass and all, would like to see us disappear, drop off into West Virginia."), and coal — the complicated, bitter, wistful, begrudging, dependent, grateful attitudes the locals have toward coal.

For a while I talked to Bobby Sherman alone — Tim was busy watching Bud lose money at a video slot machine. He told me about his history with Bud (they were third cousins, actually), an upcoming City Council election, the way an English teacher got him to read books "other than sports books" (he read history and politics now), a chemistry teacher "we could never stump" (and whom he still sought out), and his anger about the stereotyped portrayals of eastern Kentucky: "There's some damned intelligent people here." Then Bud and Tim, drained of dollar bills, rejoined us, and the conversation got more raucous. At one point, Bud tossed a match into kindling by asking, "Why don't you boys tell Mike what you think about strip mining?"

Tim shook his head. "I don't like it, but what can we do? It ain't so bad, maybe, if they try to replant . . ."

Bobby Sherman stubbed out his cigarette. "Goddammit, Tim, you know nothing comes back. That shit they plant just goes right into the rock."

Tim took his hands out of his overalls. "Bobby" — he poked the air in front of Bobby Sherman's chest — "do you want coal to leave? Do you? You and me would be out picking up cans to survive."

Bobby Sherman dropped his foot from the rung on his stool. "Timmy, do you think I don't know that? I *know* that, goddammit. But they're still ruining the mountains."

And so the argument went. I would hear variations of it in Wheelwright.

Somewhere around midnight Bud reminded himself that tomorrow was a school day. The miners had left; the couples, too; Bud had given in to the seductions of the video game for the last time; and Timmy and Bobby Sherman were hot at it on another topic — hands waving, upper bodies whipping around in barstool disbelief. Bud managed to excuse us, taking a gracious raincheck on the round Timmy was about to buy. We shook hands all around, again resisting the invitation of that one last beer, and headed out onto Main Street. Empty, now. Quiet. Dim lights in the display windows of a few shops. One window was filled with homecoming memorabilia for the high school reunion, just past. "Welcome Home Purple Flashes." We stopped, and Bud guided me through the faded photographs and open yearbooks; then we walked slowly up one block and over the bridge toward the tracks.

When coal prospered, the trains came through Martin with great frequency, day and night. Now Bud's house shook only once every hour or two. Sometime during the middle of the night, I got up, restless, and heard it: at first, a soft hiss, strange and distant, becoming, quickly, something closer to a rumble, but far off still. The warning bells at the railroad crossing started up, and I threw on some clothes and went outside. The tracks were on a gravel embankment, and I walked up to see the headlight of the engine, a hundred or so yards down the line. A single miner, Tad had told me, could load ten to fifteen tons of coal in a day; one high-volume freight car could carry 125 tons. I couldn't imagine such numbers, but I was beginning to feel the sheer force of them at my feet. I bent over and laid my hand on the ground. Except for the diesel's headlight, everything was dark. I could hear the squeals and clanks of the individual cars now, and, sooner than I expected, the train was right above me, four to five feet up the grade, swift and rhythmic, *clack, clack, clack,* powerful, metal on metal, all compression and force. What promise this once held, spawning communities on hillsides, in valleys. I thought of Tad, shoulders against rock, steadying himself, and began counting the cars. There would be eighty in all. Freight and coal. Coal. Burrowing deep into the mountains of Floyd County, then bulldozing the tops off them. Timmy and Bobby Sherman. Tad shifting his weight, his lamp illuminating the darkness.

Monday morning and off to Wheelwright. The sun, hazy behind the perennial early fog of the area — lifting off the rivers and myriad streams — sat, fat and comfortable, in a crook in the mountains. Route 122 South, passing Drift, Minnie, McDowell, and Hi Hat ("The Church of God the Prophecy Welcomes You to Hi Hat, Kentucky"), passing Ted's Welding (boarded up), passing the Moonlight Bar (closed, boarded up), passing abandoned cars, a rusted school bus (angling up from a ditch), kudzu creeping up over the hoods, the roofs. The road curved and curved, the fog hanging in the air, up through the trees, car lights winding out of the mist on the other side of the road. Bud explained how some of these towns, once developed because of coal or a railroad route or the construction of a highway, grew to local prominence (Hi Hat was named after the top hat on the logo of the Elkhorn Mining Company; Drift once had a semipro baseball team), only to fade, almost away, when a mine went dry or a rail line closed or a new interstate routed traffic away.

We came up behind a coal truck — for some of the remaining mines, Bud said, the highway was the only way left to get coal out — and slowed down to twenty. On the old railroad tracks along the side of the road a dog, in a combination of leap and trot, was shaking the life out of a big piece of butcher paper. LOWER BURTON — COMMUNITY WITH PRIDE a hand-lettered sign announced, and down in a little hollow there was a row of company houses, kept up, painted, some flowers and shrubs around them. Bud started talking about the blessing he felt this assignment at Wheelwright to be. He had been caught up for several years in some enervating union battles — he was past president of the Floyd County chapter — and had done about all he could do with social studies at his school in Martin. "I think I was doing good work, but in some ways I was just going through the motions." He was feeling stale, burned out. "It's so hard to change," he said, "and there is such pressure toward conformity in our schools. You go along to get along. But I had to take a chance, Mike. And I am so glad I did."

It was at the sign for Bypro Junction that we turned off Route 122, over a bridge, past a post office, and down the brief main street of Bypro to the high school, a half mile away, built on the outskirts of Wheelwright fifty-five years ago. It was built, Bud said, on a baseball diamond donated by Inland Steel, outside the town, in a wide field surrounded by trees to give it the feel of a campus. We pulled into the parking lot, a mix of grass and gravel now, and found a space by the gym, the newest of the school's three buildings, built in 1951. I could hear the hard squeak of rubber soles, the excited slap and thump of basketball. "Every boy in eastern Kentucky" — Bud chuckled — "has a hoop on the side of the barn. They listen to the Kentucky games on the radio and fantasize about playing for the Wildcats." Especially in the rural parts of the state, high school basketball was at the center of a town's winter life — scores, predictions, the chatter about the game brought people a little closer. And for those gifted players, the possibility of a state tournament and maybe a college scholarship hung like a dream just above the net.

The main building of the high school was faded red brick, air-conditioning units jutting, almost hanging, from some of the windows, the panes of three or four windows painted over from the inside. "Hey, Bud," I said as we walked toward the entrance, "tell me about this teacher you're working with." "Ho! Delores!" he answered. "She's something else, Mike. She was born here, you know. Just up the way at Weeksbury. Her daddy worked in the mines his whole life. She went to school right here at Wheelwright. Hell, she taught some of the parents of the kids she's teaching now." Bud stopped to hand me some of the books he was carrying. "I am so damned lucky to be with Delores Woody. She's due to retire next year, so there was no reason in the world for her to do something out of the ordinary. But do you know what she said to me? Listen to this, buddy — she said, 'I want to do something exciting. I don't want to go quietly into the sunset.'" Bud laughed. "Isn't that wild?" And he opened the front door and led me up a flight of wooden stairs.

The stairs were worn and sagging in the middle, and they gave a little under my step. The hallways were light blue and decorated with pine trees, butterflies, flowers, and a full sun, but most of the sun had peeled away. Some lockers were punched in, some bent outward, almost torn from the hinges — "Marty loves Missy" was written neatly inside one without any door at all. This was a school with no money for repairs. A musty smell hung in the air, decades of water seeping into plaster, into wood beneath the buckled linoleum. The bell rang harsh and loud — no temper to the metal — and we took a quick turn into Mrs. Woody's classroom.

The students were milling around, talking, returning books to cabinets and bookcases, getting things organized. It was loud but not disorderly. The girls tended toward jeans and blouses or inscribed sweatshirts, make-up and bountiful hair. The boys wore jeans, athletic shoes, and T-shirts. There were lots of University of Kentucky logos. The ratio of girls to boys was about two to one. Delores Woody sat at her desk: bright rose jacket, pearls, glasses, head cocked sideways, going over a paper with a student. The bell rang again, and the class went to their seats. This was the beginning of the fourth week of instruction.

Bud walked over to a student named Sherry — blond, dressed in black skirt and sweater — and asked her to bring in her group's storyboard. Sherry signaled to four other students, and they left for the Computer Lab down the hall, just as the public address system began crackling its announcements. Bud introduced me to Delores, the three of us talking quickly through the morning news. A minute later Sherry and her colleagues rolled and wrestled through the door what looked like a metal clothes rack on wheels, a long bar on which old maps of the United States were fastened with rings, easy to flip over. Across one large map, the students had taped white paper and sketched out a series of frames, each representing a segment of the video about Wheelwright their classmates had elected them to plan and shoot over the next few weeks. The video would be their way of introducing Wheelwright High School to the students at the four other schools involved in the Kentucky Telecommunications Project: a sixth-grade class in Lexington, in the center of the Bluegrass region; an eleventh- and-twelfth-grade class in Louisville, the financial hub of the commonwealth; an eighth-grade class in Covington, way to the north, just this side of Cincinnati; and a fifth-grade class in Paducah, the westernmost node in the electronic mail network.

Sherry said a few words about the group's progress, then turned the floor over to another student, Mary Rose, who took us through the storyboard, frame by frame. "We thought we'd begin by introducing the class" — she pointed to the first frame, labeled *Introduction.* "That's you," she said, extending her hand, palm outward, toward us. "Then we want to explain about how we're learning both social studies and English together," and here she pointed to the next frame, labeled *American Studies.* "You know," she continued, "what it is we're doing in this class — like all our projects and stuff." She paused and looked at Sherry, smiling. "Then comes a commercial break," and the class laughed. Bud waited for a moment to let the group savor the idea, then asked whether anyone had suggestions. Rhonda, poker-faced in the back of the room, recommended "Visit Wheelwright, the Garden Spot of Kentucky." Laughter. Angie, sitting a few desks away from Rhonda, leaned in and suggested that "we show some of us lying on the rocks by the mine, sunning ourselves." Mary Rose continued, pointing to the next frame. "We thought we needed a news center, you know, someplace where a newscaster would give news about Wheelwright — the way it was, and the way it is now." "Mary Rose," Delores said from her desk, "I've got some old photographs that you might be able to use. Remind me to show you when we go to the Computer Lab." "OK," said Mary Rose, "I will," and she took the class through the remaining frames: Wheelwright High School, the closed Inland mine, a view of the town from the top of 79 Hill, and so on.

Bud stepped forward and congratulated the team on their work. "You know, many of the students in the Telecommunications Project will not be familiar with the other sites. For that fact, neither will the teachers — heck, I've never been to Paducah! This video will be a great opportunity to introduce Wheelwright." Bud took a few steps further into the middle of the desks. "You'll be showing people where you live through *your* eyes, showing them how times have changed the town — and, well, what things look like now. This is fantastic. Way to go!" Delores agreed with Bud and raised a question — to him but not really to him. "Mr. Reynolds, let me ask you something. Do you think the fifth- and sixth-graders in the Telecommunications Project would be interested in seeing the same things as the eleventh- and twelfth-graders?" "Well, Mrs. Woody," Bud replied, "I wonder. I hadn't thought about that." He fell silent, letting the question sit.

After about twenty seconds, Terry, the fellow who had been designated the group's cameraman and who, up until then, hadn't said much, started thinking out loud. "Maybe we oughta include the grammar school," he said. "You know, show where the high school students came from. Fifth-graders might want to see that." "Where would that shot go?" asked Bud, rubbing his chin. Terry moved in front of the storyboard and studied it for a moment. "How about here?" He pointed to the space just before the frame of the high school. "How about putting it right before the high school?" "That might work," Mrs. Woody speculated. "That might be nice." She walked over to Terry. "What we're talking about, Terry, is audience, isn't it?" "Yes, ma'am," he said. "Who would want to watch it?" "Yes," she agreed, "who would want to watch it. And why. When you're thinking about your shots, you need to be thinking about your viewers, too." Terry wondered if there might be other places in the video where they could appeal to the fifth- and sixth-graders, and Bud suggested they talk that over the next time they met.

The curriculum Bud and Delores developed — or, more accurately, were developing, for it was very much in process — required a degree of intellectual self-sufficiency that was traditionally not the norm in many Kentucky classsrooms, especially those in poorer districts. This active, problem-solving orientation was central to the Kentucky Education Reform Act, or KERA, as everyone called it, and it drove Bud and Delores's experimental course of study. There were three fundamental components of this curriculum, and during my visit I would get to see the students engage in all three, both effectively and with complications.

There was the American Studies component, an attempt to cross disciplinary lines — fusing social studies and English — to encourage students to think and write about historical and social issues in a more original and creative way than is usually done in the standard curriculum. The general theme Bud and Delores chose for this component was "The Struggle for Freedom," and, over the year, this theme would be further broken out into units on which students would spend four to five weeks. Bud and Delores posed the first unit, "The American Revolution," but the remainder would be determined jointly by the teachers and their students. (They would, for example, eventually work on the civil rights movement and the passing of the cold war.) Students worked in groups on topics related to these units — what were the reasons behind the desire for colonial independence, who were the great civil rights leaders before Martin Luther King, Jr. — deciding, with Bud and Delores's help, how to research a topic, how best to present it, and how to divide labor and schedule time to carry out the work.

The second component emerged from the Kentucky Telecommunications Project. Here, the students, again in groups, were to develop, over the entire year, a community-based project; it was this ongoing project that would provide the foundation for their communication with the students in Lexington, Louisville, Covington, and Paducah. As it would turn out, Bud and Delores's students would develop a recycling project, establish a tutoring service for the students at the elementary school, survey the needs of the local senior citizens, and explore the question: Is there a future in Wheelwright? Such endeavors would require that they use writing in a number of ways, for a number of purposes: field notes, rough, preliminary reports, letters to county, state, and federal agencies (the recycling group, for example, would write to the EPA), letters to the editor, position papers, and so on. The teachers' hope was that the projects would stimulate the development of both a local community of writers — groups of students at Wheelwright using writing around shared concerns — and a community that extended beyond the boundaries of Floyd County. And such broader community-building, in fact, did begin once the students mastered the technology: those students working on the recycling project would ask the students at other sites about recycling efforts in their neighborhoods, and those pondering the future of Wheelwright would gather unemployment statistics from across the commonwealth. Students would do work that was rich in local meaning even as they sought assistance and audience well beyond the local.

The third component involved the development, by each student, of a portfolio of writing reflecting a range of genres: personal narrative, book review, critical analysis, story, poem, and so on. The writing, for the most part, would come from the American Studies curriculum or the Telecommunications Project, and though there would be due dates for the papers, the students could, as their skills improved, revise them throughout the year or substitute a new piece of a particular genre for an old one.

During the week of my visit, the students were working on an editorial for their portfolios and, in groups, researching an issue related to the struggle for freedom in the American Revolution. They had not yet determined their projects for the Telecommunications Project, but were hard at work on their video introducing Wheelwright and were learning the ways and means of electronic mail and FAX machines in the Computer Lab.

After Sherry, Mary Rose, Terry, and the others had presented their video storyboard to the class, Bud and Delores broke the students into groups to pursue their work on the American Revolution. They had been at this for a little over a week and, predictably, were having some trouble striking out on their own. "Remember," Bud told them once they had reconfigured into clusters of four and five, "there are some basic questions you want to keep asking yourselves. What were the economic conditions in the colonies and in England? What were the differences in the colonies themselves — economic differences, political differences, differences in geography? What were the motives driving some Colonists to break away? Can you relate to any of those motives? Put yourselves in their shoes. And how about the Loyalists? Why did they resist revolution? See if you can put yourselves in their shoes, too."

Over the course of my stay, I would come to know two groups. One was trying to compile information on specific Revolutionary War figures — what led each of them to take extraordinary action. The other was struggling to find a way to convey to the class what it felt like to be a Loyalist in the colonies. "You don't want to just stand in front of the class and read a paper," Mr. Reynolds had said. "Make it lively." Bud and Delores had been coaching the groups, sitting with them and playing out options, making suggestions, recommending sources, retrieving materials from places beyond the school's library, which was terribly outdated and understocked. But the students still had to plan and execute academic work in a way that was unfamiliar to them.

There were some things they could do well. Some were pretty resourceful at scouting around for materials. One girl had gone to Morehead State College, three counties away, and checked out from the library a set of slides of posters and broadsides decrying the Stamp Act and the Quartering Act and the other British actions that sparked Colonial outrage. These created a big stir in her group. Most students, from what I could tell, were also willing to help each other out. There were religious and social traditions in eastern Kentucky that probably set the stage for mutual assistance, and Bud and Delores's students took to collaboration. A student in one of the groups had photocopied some pages from a history book and, as she was reading a passage from them to her colleagues, she came across the name Roger Sherman. "Who was he?" she asked. No one knew — nor did I — so she turned to another group and asked them. And a girl in that group said she knew how to find out real quick, went over to the bookcase by the door, and ran her finger through the index of an old edition of Samuel Eliot Morrison's *The History of the American Republic.* "Here," she said coming back with the book open. "He was one of the guys who signed the Constitution," and she handed the book to her classmate.

But, overall, this curriculum was proving to be a significant challenge for them. And for Bud and Delores as well.

For some time, Bud had run a pretty open classroom, rich with student projects — that was what had attracted Janet Fortune to him in the first place. And since the mid-1980s, Delores, along with Carol Stumbo — the creator of the Telecommunications Project — had been supervising a student-produced magazine called *Mantrip,* a compilation of interviews with local people about the economic, cultural, and political history of the region. These teachers believed in the capacities of their students for independent work and also had an experimental bent. But so much was new here: the cross-disciplinary American Studies curriculum; the eschewing of textbook instruction — with very limited materials to put in its place; the number of unknowns in the Telecommunications Project; the first-time use of the portfolio method for compiling and evaluating student writing; the pressures and expectations of the new school-reform legislation. As I got to know Bud and Delores, I became convinced that Carol — on leave herself to help the local schools implement the state's reforms — had recommended them quite deliberately for this experiment. Bud was tapped because of his willingness to try new things, his pedagogical restlessness. He had a high tolerance for ambiguity, could throw himself into the middle of things and ride them out. And Carol knew that he was in desperate need of something fresh. Delores was chosen because she was rock solid, had roots here that went back generations, had taught kids and their kids — yet, as well, possessed a streak of antitraditionalism, valued her students tremendously, and liked to set them loose. Yet, like their students, the teachers were setting forth on new terrain, and they were bound to misstep. How much or how little should they guide the students? What degree of structure was paradoxically necessary to foster self-sufficiency? With so much new going on, some blunders would be inevitable, and how in God's name were successful teachers supposed to get used to failure — and then pick up the pieces, recalibrate, and start again? Was this *really* the way Delores wanted to end a fine career? Between them, Bud and Delores had spent over fifty years in the classroom, and they were launching into a curriculum more complex and uncertain than anything in their experience.

And the students. It was, of course, exciting to be part of something so new. In a town that technology had left behind, the prospect of playing with so much technology — of having your own electronic connection to Lexington and Louisville — well, from the beginning that carried a jolt. But these were also students who had succeeded in the traditional curriculum, who knew how to mine a textbook, take multiple choice tests, and recast a lecture in an essay exam. A lot was riding on those skills. Many of the students hoped to attend a technical school or go to Prestonsburg Community College, at the county seat. Becoming certified in, say, computer or medical technology could mean the difference between a life of hard labor — or, worse, unemployment (Wheelwright's unemployment rate was an unbelievable 70 percent) — and a life of relative choice and possibility. And some of the class hoped to attend a four-year college or university: Morehead State, or Pikeville, a Methodist college in the adjoining county, or Eastern Kentucky University (Bud's alma mater), or Alice Lloyd, a remarkable school where, as with Berea, tuition could be defrayed through work (Delores had gone there), or Berea (Carol Stumbo's alma mater). A handful of students might leave the state: West Virginia, Tennessee. It would be hard to overstate the importance of these hopes to the eleventh-graders at Wheelwright . . . or to their families. Imagine their anxiety when they found that the rules of the game had changed.

The students trusted Bud and Delores — that was clear. They sought their help. But even with their teachers' guidance, they went down blind alleys, felt uncertain, couldn't find sources. Nor were they always sure when they were on beam — all the traditional benchmarks had been removed: textbook units, quiz grades, the reliable daily routines. And the signs of frustration were growing: the week before, a science teacher stopped Bud in the parking lot to tell him that a student they both admired had been complaining about feeling overwhelmed; the parent of another girl had called Delores and asked why they couldn't return to "the old way." "After all," the mother said, "it worked just fine for her brother," who was now off at college. But the frustration hit its peak right at the time of my visit, and I couldn't help being caught up in it.

The first incident arose with the group trying to convey the motives and feelings of the Loyalists. Sherry, who had introduced the Wheelwright video, was in this group, as was Rhonda, a quick-witted girl with curly brown hair, and Angie, a serious student who politely spoke her mind. They had just about had it, trying to figure out a creative way to present the things they were finding — and they were stymied and starting to shut down. Bud was trying to revive their energies, and I was listening in. He suggested they write an editorial, but they rejected that because they were already working on an editorial for their portfolios. He suggested they do something with transparencies, but Angie said that students find them boring. He suggested they do a broadside, something that could be taped to the classroom wall. Naw, nobody would find that interesting. OK, Bud said. How about dressing up as Loyalists and making your case to the class? They looked at him as if he was nuts. "Why, Rhonda here," he said, "could get a red coat and dress up as George the Third." "Oh, Mr. Reynolds," she replied, "you must be kidding! Red's not my color." *Heh, heh.* She curled her lip. As they slumped down in their seats or looked at the tops of their desks, their responses became briefer, softer.

Then Bud went at it another way. "Well," he said, shifting toward Sherry, who hadn't said much, "let me ask you this: Do any Americans today show interest in royalty? Do we feel any connection to it at all?" "Sure," Sherry answered. "Yeah, Lady Di," added Rhonda. "Well," Bud asked, "is there anything we could do with that?" Some stirring then, some changes of posture. "Yeah," Angie joked. "We could bring in *The National Enquirer.*" A bit more exchange, getting more animated, and I looked at Bud, got the OK, and leaned over to Angie and wondered whether the group could do a 1770s version of *The National Enquirer,* focusing on the Loyalists. Rhonda and Sherry laughed and sat up; Angie got excited. She liked the idea a lot, she said, and complimented me. I reminded her that it was her idea—with a twist. All I did was point it out. "Well, thank you," she said, "for bringing my idea forward." Then Bud found a sheet of paper and began jotting down their ideas for producing a Loyalist tabloid.

The second incident, one with a messier trajectory, involved the group investigating the motives of key Revolutionary colonials. This group included Candi, who wrote well, Alena, also a writer with promise, and Krystal, a reflective, strong-willed girl. During the week before my visit they had begun work on an idea that had fizzled out, and they felt it was time wasted. Now, I was sitting in on their group, and as they tried to develop a new project, their discontent surfaced. One complained about the time that was lost. Another said it was hard to figure out what to do next. I asked them what might help. "If they'd give us a schedule," one snapped. "It just seems like we're spending a lot of time getting nowhere," another said. Others added, "All of a sudden, they're throwing all this new stuff at us." "We want to do this right, but how can we when we've never done a presentation before?" Nothing I said did much good; in fact, the more we talked about it, the angrier they got. From class we all went to the Computer Lab, where Carol Stumbo was checking in on the Telecommunications Project. The students knew Carol and told her about their frustrations. Carol pulled Bud and Delores into the conversation and encouraged the students to talk to them directly. By the time the lunch bell rang, a lot of feeling had been expressed, but little was resolved. Learning was shutting down. Krystal, Alena, and company felt adrift and, I thought, in some way betrayed.

Delores, Bud, Carol, and I walked up one brief flight of stairs to the tiny faculty lounge. It was only seven steps above the main hallway, so we talked against the din of slamming lockers, high-decibel greetings and insults, heavy feet stampeding across linoleum and wood. We sat around the corner of the table; birds and flowers and red schoolhouses were printed on the plastic covering.

"This is not good, Delores," Bud said, cradling a Styrofoam cup of the morning's coffee. "Alena is fit to be tied." I told them what had happened in the group, and agreed that things had reached a critical level. It was possible that Bud and Delores would lose the good will of some of their best students. They had misjudged the difficulty of the changes they were making in the curriculum. "We're going to have to give them more help than we have been," Delores said, looking out into the middle of the room. "I didn't know they were so frustrated."

Then Carol spoke up. She was a woman of notable integrity. Glasses, hair in a bun, old wool jacket; when she spoke, she looked right at you with understanding and force. "Well, we need to listen to them . . . carefully. They know what they need. And what they're saying has merit." She reached into her jacket pocket and took out a cigarette, and thought for a moment. "Well, Bud," she said, "can you live with the criticism and still believe in the program?"

Bud bummed a cigarette and sat quietly. This was a Bud I hadn't seen. He was pensive, glum. We sat in silence. Some time passed. Then he stubbed out the cigarette and looked up at us. His face started to relax. Carol had cut into the paralysis. "We're doing the right thing," he said, "we just gotta change how we do it." And the three of them spent the rest of the hour talking about how to provide more structure and guidance without compromising the goals of the curriculum. They would share with the students the material from the commissioner of education's office that spelled out KERA's new performance standards, talk with them about — spark discussion about —these new "learning goals and valued outcomes" so that they could consider, firsthand, the thinking behind this new approach. They would draw up time-management schedules for the students and help them figure out how to allocate their resources to their various projects.

"You people are right," Delores said to the class the next morning. "We made a mistake. Sometimes people need boundaries in order to use their time effectively." She and Bud would keep closer tabs on the students' developing projects, at least for a while, and direct their work a little more than they had up until then.

A few days later Krystal found me in the Computer Lab. She was carrying an open notebook at her side, almost swinging it, pages flapping. She stopped on a squeak, still bouncing on the balls of her feet, and told me that she and Alena and the others had come up with a great idea, a really great idea. They would do a panel. Like on "Nightline." The important Revolutionary War figures would talk among themselves about their reasons for wanting independence. They would take questions from the audience, too. And what did I think about that?

III

THE COMPUTER LAB was right down the hall from Mrs. Woody's classroom, so it was easy for students to go back and forth, splitting their time as they needed to. And though they were scheduled for the lab for one hour a day (the second of their two hours with Bud and Delores), they soon began coming in at lunch and during their free period and after school. The lab was about the size of a classroom, roughly twenty-five by forty feet, and was decorated with a pastiche of textbook publishers' promotional posters — including a brightly illustrated timeline of United States history that covered a large bulletin board — by posters of Gandhi and Martin Luther King, Jr. and the Bill of Rights, and by Native American artifacts. There were prints of old Kentucky over one wall, and the entire wall opposite was covered with a forest scene: trees and fallen logs and leaves and grazing deer. Dictionaries were stacked here and there on ledges by the windows; by the entrance was a desk with a neat row of frayed reference books. In one corner sat the rack on which Sherry and Mary Rose's video storyboard was taped; next to it was an open metal cabinet stocked with computer disks and ribbons and paper. The middle of the room was taken up with two big tables and mismatched chairs, and computer terminals extended along three walls. Carol Stumbo had gotten most of them through grants and cagey deals and her own pocketbook. By the desk with the reference books sat a brand-new FAX machine, and it was beeping, delivering a letter from the sixth-graders in Lexington.

Bud asked Terry, the cameraman for the video project, whether he wanted to respond to the letter, and looked around for someone to be his partner. A fellow with short brown hair and a pleasant face was laying his knapsack down in the corner by the door, and Bud nabbed him. "Have you sent a message on e-mail yet?" He hadn't. "Well, come on, John-boy, let's do it."

John sat at the keyboard of a terminal, Terry on a chair next to him. They began with a greeting to Lexington and a word of thanks for the letter. Terry would try a sentence out loud, John typing it in but raising a question about it, then the two reconsidering what to do. "The eleventh-graders in our class," they wrote, "are making a video about Wheelwright, and we can't wait to show it to you." "Now what?" asked John. Terry sat back and thought for a moment. "How about this? 'As we get further and further into the project, it is becoming more exciting and challenging.'" John typed the sentence in and read it. "Do we say 'further and further,'" he mused, "or 'farther and farther.'" They decided on "farther and farther," and John made the revision. Terry looked at John. "We gotta say something to get their interest. Maybe, uh, 'Throughout the video, we will be showing you how life in the mountains is.'" John typed, but stopped midway. "Maybe we should say 'how we live in the mountains.'" "I like that," said Terry, and John typed it in. John leaned back from the terminal, hands still on the keyboard. "We maybe could say something about sharing information." "Yeah," Terry agreed, "what do we say? Maybe just 'We are looking forward to sharing our information with you.'" Good. OK. And so it went with Terry and John until they were done composing. Then Bud came over and showed them the routine for sending electronic mail.

On this day, rain was splattering against the windows. The heaters were ticking and clanking. It was pleasantly warm, comfortable. Around the room, Rhonda sat on the arm of a chair, showing another girl how to reorganize text on the word processor; Sherry was at the video storyboard, down on her knees, adding some frames along the bottom; Delores sat at the big table in the middle with a girl named Jimmie Lou, offering advice on a piece of writing; Jimmy, a tall, personable boy who was the techno-whiz in the class, was sending a FAX; three girls huddled around a cheerleading sweater, giggling — hearts and boys' names adorning their binders; Candi was helping Mary Rose get the transitions right in her mock editorial about the Boston Massacre; and Krystal was asking me for help in creating "a more snappy opening" for her editorial calling the Colonists to arms, an editorial that, after a little guidance, would begin:

> How would you like to have no control in your own home? How would you like for people to impose laws that you had no say about? And how would you like to pay unreasonable taxes on almost everything? How do you decide when enough is enough?

Krystal's father had been a student of Delores's, and, as Delores euphemistically described him, had been a "rather active" boy. A few of his relatives had moved to California, so when Krystal mentioned to him that a teacher from Los Angeles was in her class, he asked to visit. We picked the lunch period of the next day and sat in the corner of the Computer Lab, talking about local history, the economy, and his hopes for his daughter. He was a slim, angular man, cordial, deeply religious, and his people had been here for generations. His ancestors had sold the mineral rights to their property — as had so many of the early inhabitants — for next to nothing, for just over fifteen cents an acre. The profit, of course, went to companies housed in Illinois or Ohio or Pennsylvania — or in other regions of the state. He himself worked in the mines — and was glad to have the work — but, like so many of the people I met in Floyd County, he brooded over the history of that work. "Sometimes I think it would have been better if the companies had never come in . . . if we could have developed on our own . . . you know, kept the money here." There was a weariness to his voice when he talked about the mines. "It's like always, I suppose; the working man serves the rich man. The working man comes home. He's tired. He goes to bed. He gets up and goes on back to work. He don't have time to create something on his own." But when he talked about Krystal, his spirits lifted. "She's a dandy. Did Mrs. Woody tell you she won a contest last year?" (Krystal wrote a slogan, encouraging people to vote, that was judged best in all of the state's high schools.) "I hope she goes on to college. She's got a good mind and she's real studious. She always does a little extra. She'll have some opportunities."

As Bud and I were driving back to Martin that evening, I asked him whether I could visit the old Inland mine, the source of Wheelwright's past prosperity. Sure, he said, "and let's take a few of the kids along." So the next day he recruited the letter-writers Terry and John — who, it turned out, had a free period right after lunch — to escort us. It was a short drive, across town and up 79 Hill, though we took a few detours: past the dilapidated movie theater ("it's a fresh-air theater now," quipped Terry), the miners' bathhouse that Janet had described to me, and a blighted hollow called Muddy Gut, the focus of a "48 Hours" report back in 1989 that Floyd County residents were still mad about. "It showed only the worst part of life here," Terry said. "I swear, when the producers came to the high school, they asked us to take our shoes off!"

Terry lived with his mother, the third of four children, all boys. His interests ran to the life sciences, anatomy and biology particularly, and he was thinking about going to college, maybe to learn about radiological technology. John, the youngest of three children, thought he might want to go away to college — "to see other places" — but then come back to Floyd County to live. (Terry said he too wanted "to see what the rest of the world is like.") John figured he might major in x-ray technology or pharmacy, work that would be "cool and well paid," not closed in and dangerous. Both John's father and Terry's worked in the deep mines.

The access road to the old Inland mine was brief and bumpy, gravel kicking up under Bud's Toyota, and led to an uneven plateau where we could park. We got out of the car, and behind us were two tunnels into the mountain, closed off with iron gates. SAFETY FIRST was embossed in the concrete face of the mine, but the Inland logo had been blasted off. Someone, in irregular script, had painted MISS BIG over the right tunnel.

"A lot of people used to work here," Terry said. "People still talk about it." I walked up to the entrance and tried to look in, but couldn't see much. Rock and wood and other rubble lay just inside. The darkness began a few feet in, and I could feel, on my cheek, the chill beyond. We walked to the edge of the road, where we could look out over Wheelwright. The town sat at the bottom of a narrow valley, rich green trees rising up all around it. Wheelwright had been carved out of wilderness. "You can see," said Terry, "we got some nice stuff here." "Yep," added John, "but at night it's the deadest place in America."

Bud pointed out across the town to a hill beyond the houses. "That's where the prison's going to be built," he said. "What do you boys think about that?" The conversation that followed reminded me of the one between Tim and Bobby Sherman at the AmVets club in Martin — but without the pyrotechnics. It seemed that a privately operated state prison was to be built in Wheelwright, and it could bring with it up to eighty jobs. Terry and John went back and forth: who wanted a prison in your own back yard? But think of what eighty jobs could mean to Wheelwright. Who wanted a prison? But eighty jobs! Looking down into the town, you could see the stores boarded up and overgrown. Some were old company stores, Terry explained. But you could see the houses, too; most were neat, kept up. A woman stood on her porch, leaning against a post. Shirts fluttered on a clothesline. In a back yard in the distance, a white table sat clean with four empty chairs around it.

When we got back to the high school, I asked Delores if I could see the photographs of old Wheelwright that she had mentioned to Sherry and Mary Rose when they were presenting their storyboard to the class. She took out of the metal cabinets a large, flat box of eight-by-ten and ten-by-fourteen prints and laid them out on the table in the middle of the room, slowly, edge to edge. There were photos of the golf course and a huge public swimming pool; of a community hall — two stories, pillars, a delicate railing along the balcony of the second floor; photos, too, of a bowling alley, a bright soda fountain, and the front of the movie theater the boys, Bud, and I had passed that day — clean brick, neon, at least a hundred people talking, buying tickets, lining up for *Our Hearts Were Growing Up,* a movie about upper-class girls at Princeton. There was a set of photographs showing a union meeting, held on a Sunday morning in the elementary school; a brand-new coal-preparation plant, the sun glinting off a huge vat of water; and the face of the mine we had stood before that morning, men sitting in coal cars, on barrels, talking, laughing, men walking away from the mine, carrying their gear — power packs, canteens — and men walking in twos and threes toward the entrance, clean, their heads cocked in conversation.

One of the striking things about the photographs was how populated they were with young people: outside the theater a few older men were smoking in the background, but most were couples in their twenties and thirties; the miners were in their thirties, forties, maybe. The demographics of Wheelwright have changed considerably. The population these days is about a fourth the size it was right after the war, and the age distribution tends toward the bipolar: children and adolescents on one end, retirees on the other. All those people in the pictures had retired, moved on, or passed away. Many of their children left to find work. The students Bud and Delores taught were, in many cases, the children, or the children of the children, of those who stayed. What I began to understand, though, was the way the history of those times long past, smoothed out by some — the explosions and falling rock and backbreaking work receding in the reminiscence — still held sway in the collective mind of Wheelwright. Kids heard stories of work and promise from their parents and grandparents. And those kids lived in the midst of the decayed monuments of prosperity — "the shell of better times," as Delores said — the overgrown library, the stark bathhouse. They knew, as Terry and John knew, that the empty mines had been a source of prosperity — a prosperity they could only imagine. To attain it, they have little choice but to move, perhaps away from the region itself. The per capita annual income of Floyd County is $10,372.

Some relished flight. "I can't wait to shake the dust from my feet," said one boy — for there were many limits here: isolation and provincial morality and the meanness and violence poverty brings. But others did not want to go; they fretted over it — for there were the mountains and forests and streams, the shared history, the closeness of family. "This is my home," said another boy, "and I love it." But regardless of how Bud and Delores's students felt about their home, there were no jobs. "Many of these young people," Delores observed, "have a difficult time just staying in school." More than half the families of the students at Wheelwright High School were on public assistance. "Mrs. Woody," one girl said wistfully, "we certainly would have liked to live in Wheelwright back then." But today many of them would simply have to leave.

Consider, then. How do you help them come to understand this place where they were born — this poor, difficult, intermittently comforting and brutal, familiar, beautiful place that existed before Inland, before Elkhorn — and the people who have worked so hard during its economic ascent and decline? And how, simultaneously, do you help them prepare for the journey beyond this place, keeping one foot within the circle of their birth, and, with the other, stepping outward, to return possibly, possibly not? The more time I spent with Bud and Delores, the more I came to realize that this was the conceptual tension that enriched the use of the Computer Lab.

One key element in this tension was represented by the magazine *Mantrip*, founded by Carol and Delores in 1985. *Mantrip* was inspired by the *Foxfire* books — the anthologies of Appalachian lore and practice compiled by high school students in Rabun Gap, Georgia — but whereas *Foxfire* tended toward compilation of traditional methods of building, cooking, healing, and crafting, *Mantrip* contained primarily student interviews with locals about their origins, the work they did (a "mantrip" was the car that carried miners underground), and the history of Wheelwright and its surrounding communities. The focus, then, was more on the mines, unions, immigration, politics, race relations, and religion. So, twice a year, Wheelwright students would set out for the kitchens and living rooms of their neighbors and tape-record stories about the old-time good times and the tunnels that wouldn't hold, about ballroom dances and damaged lungs. They learned about Polish and Hungarian and Italian settlers — frightened, hopeful — and about segregated schools and lunch rooms, and, too, about the brotherhood some felt underground. They learned something about how people can make good decisions — as Carol once put it — when their choices are very limited. They talked to preachers — Old Regular Baptists, Freewill Baptists, Charismatics — about the origins of their ministry. They heard powerful affirmations of God's design and family cohesion and awful stories of abuse. They were led to reflect on the security as well as the social control, the prosperity along with the dependency that came with being Inland Steel's company town. They heard contradictions and had to record them. And they heard exciting tales about legendary bad men ("He killed seven men that he counted — but some he didn't count!"), about ways to ward off witches (carving a picture into the bark of a tree), and they heard the old songs, sung in the traditional high-lonesome style. It all provided a chance, as one student editor put it, to create "a testimonial to the life and people we have come to know."

Creating such a testimonial was crucial, for the region had, for generations, been depicted by outsiders in one-dimensional ways, usually as backward and uncivilized. As early as 1826, the traveler Anne Royall wrote that the midland dialect heard in the mountains was a "mangled and mutilated" English. And once "Appalachia" began to be defined as a distinct American region, that definition emphasized Appalachia's isolation and poverty, sometimes in insulting "local color" portraits, sometimes to raise national consciousness and spark reform. (Even William Frost, Berea's third president and a major force in the creation of Appalachia in the public mind, had a tendency to speak of mountain people as though they were the artifacts of another time.) As Bud was fond of pointing out, this general image of eastern Kentucky still had strong currency *within* the commonwealth itself: a past governor of Kentucky, he told me, once quipped that Route 80 — the highway that took Janet and me into Floyd County — was a road that led "from nowhere to nowhere." So from all sorts of sources, and for a very long time, young people in eastern Kentucky have been subjected to a variety of derogatory portraits of themselves.

It was important to Bud and Delores, therefore, that they established the conditions for their students to observe closely the sadness and joy of mountain life, to listen with a clear ear to the stories emerging from the hollows. "I want them to know about their history," Delores had said, "I want them to take pride in the people who settled the area, who worked hard and wanted the most for their children. I suppose I want them to have a sense of place." A significant amount of the writing done in the Computer Lab — some destined for the students' portfolios, a good deal generated by the Telecommunications Project — was writing that encouraged these young people to think about their daily experience and the place where they lived, to render that reality and, in rendering it, define it.

Thus it was that Sheldon sat before the terminal, his long legs curled back around the legs of the chair, composing a piece for his portfolio, intermittently rhapsodic and comic:

> I've lived in the mountains of eastern Kentucky and never once have I wanted any other home. These hills are my protectors. I feel that I am safe and secure from all the troubles the rest of the world holds. These aren't just thoughts that I write on paper; these are feelings straight from my heart.

> I love nothing more than waking up in the morning to the tantalizing smell of bacon and eggs and feeling the morning wind roll off the mountain tops as I take a walk after breakfast.
>
> People my age, in their late teens, are constantly talking about how much they want to "get out of here." This is actually very funny to me because it reminds me of a "getting away from home" story that my Uncle Gayle once told me.
>
> At that time in his life, all my uncle wanted to do was to get out of Kentucky. He wanted to hit the big city of Detroit wide open much the same way the teens today want to try their wings, but he was in for a big surprise.
>
> When he got to Detroit, he worked for about a week in a factory — then he lost his job. It was in December, and he spent Christmas Eve on the floor of his non-furnished apartment eating dry crackers and listening to the "Twelve Days of Christmas" being played from a nearby department store. He was kicked out of his apartment the next week . . . To this day my uncle cringes at the tune of "Twelve Days of Christmas," and I just smile and thank God that I live here.

But economic conditions beyond his control may force Sheldon to leave the security of the mountains — for school, for work. And the pedagogy to contribute to his setting forth on that journey was, paradoxically, also present in the Computer Lab. "These young people," Delores pointed out, "need to learn to live in a world driven by technology. If they can take a sense of identity with them, it will help. They'll know who they are and where they're from. And they'll be secure in that knowledge." A sense of place that can help them move beyond place.

The electronic mail itself, of course, enabled the students to forge connections beyond Wheelwright. It had taken some time to get that system going, debugging it, teaching all the eleventh-graders to use it. Bud, a high-tech impresario, helped the teachers at the other sites to master it, and they, in turn, aided their students. The primary purpose of the network was to get students to interact around their formal projects — at Wheelwright, the projects involving recycling, senior citizen care, tutoring, and an exploration of the economic future of the town. And, as Bud later told me, such interaction did develop. But a less formal series of exchanges developed as well. As students became comfortable with the technology, they started communicating about all sorts of topics — basketball, music, and movies — and Bud quickly set things up so that students could establish electronic mailboxes on any topic they wished and go at it.

By the time Bud and Delores's students were entering their second term, their projects were well under way. The recycling group had gone to the two elementary schools that fed into Wheelwright and put on a skit for the kids, did a lesson for them on the benefits of recycling, and established an environmental-consciousness poster contest. In addition, they prepared an itemized budget for a community-wide recycling project. The group interested in services for the elderly had visited hospitals, nursing homes, and retirement homes in Floyd County (and adjacent counties to make comparisons), and interviewed patients, residents, and staff. Their goal was to write an assessment of the quality of care and produce a pamphlet for senior citizens on the services available to them in the region. "Our seniors," they wrote in their interim report, "are to be treasured, not neglected." Those involved in tutoring elementary school students had been working in the two local schools, recording their experiences in field notes, researching other "cross-age" tutoring programs, and making arrangements to get the fifth-, sixth-, and eighth-graders on-line with their peers in the Telecommunications Project. And the students interested in the economic future of Wheelwright had gone to Prestonsburg to interview the economic director of the county and the owners of local industries — like R & S Truck Body, the site of a hundred and fifty jobs — about the advantages and disadvantages of owning a company in Floyd County, the incentives that might bring in other industry, the opportunities for women, and the outlook for the future. They wanted to prepare a report for other young people on their prospects if they chose to stay close to home.

The Wheelwright students had been reporting on these projects to the students in the electronic network, soliciting information from across the state, and, in turn, learning about and responding to projects originating in the other sites. The eighth-graders in Covington, for example, had gotten involved in the local Habitat for Humanity and were establishing a literacy tutorial for younger children. The projects gave rise to editorials for *The Floyd County Times,* letters to government officials (ranging from county supervisors to state senators to the directors of federal agencies), and reports on findings — all genres that required a recasting of experience and observation into a public voice. *Opening the World Through Writing,* read the logo on the makeshift stationery for the Telecommunications Project. By about the third week of their second term, the students at Wheelwright were preparing interim reports on their projects for the foundation in New York that had been funding them.

Bud was a kind of technological populist, and the power of e-mail, he believed, was that it could, once mastered, lead to spontaneous, unpredictable communication as well as more formal exchange. Students argued back and forth about the Chicago Bulls, trashed or praised current movies, swapped autobiographical portraits, suggested places they might go if and when they visited each other. Some, like Sheldon, the fellow who wrote the paean to mountain life, soon tired of this loose exchange and sent out word that he would like to see other pieces of creative writing. "Is anybody thinking and writing out there?" he asked, and poems and stories started coming back. Candi wanted to know what others thought about Somalia, and a boy in the sixth-grade class in Lexington asked if others had ever been in the hospital, because he was going to be admitted tomorrow. Some students, using only an initial, tentatively brought up alcoholism. One girl asked whether anyone wanted to talk about rape. These private, agonizing topics found an oddly safe space in this electronic forum. "You can't control this kind of technology," Bud mused. "The glory of it is that students will take it in new directions — and surprise us all." "I think our students need to examine everything that happens to them from different viewpoints," Delores said. And the Telecommunications Project encouraged the students to shift about in a network of observation, becoming familiar with it, enhancing their own perspectives, considering in new light some of what they'd come to know about economy and society growing up in Wheelwright, Floyd County, Kentucky.

IV

THERE IS A WEATHERED BRIDGE over the Levisa Fork of the Big Sandy River in Prestonsburg — P-burg — site of the school board, the district office, the local chapter of the Kentucky Association of Teachers. Bud and I leaned against a thick concrete pillar — graffiti, the traces of a poster — watching the water flow northward toward the Ohio River. The engineers who plotted the railroad lines that opened up the Eastern Coal Field followed the course of the Big Sandy's many branching tributaries. In the distance, we could see an old access bridge extending over the water, the water moving with a purl, a ripple, brushing the bottom limbs of the trees on the bank, here and there a log breaking the flow. HELL IS UPON US, the big spray-painted letters read, right at our feet. VICTORY IS BELOW. HEAR THE WIND? The trees angled up from the bank, thick, clustered, deep green, rustling in the light breeze. "I have never felt so free in all my life!" Bud exclaimed, putting one foot on the drain pipe that ran along the walkway and leaning out over the Levisa. "We're really pushing on the envelope, Mike. I have never felt this hopeful."

We unwrapped some sandwiches and opened two sodas. And Bud talked. "I came into teaching with a view about changing kids' lives, but then I got into the routine of schooling. The stereotype of good teaching in this area is when the kids are all in straight rows, listening. Well, you get into a rut. And the kids shut down. They get into *their* rut.

I'd get this very guilty feeling, like I wasn't doing my best. And I'd start to think, 'Good God, if this is all there is . . .' I began changing when I got those kids out of their seats. I think I work twice as hard now, but when I see them respond — well, it hits on what made me go into teaching. You see what school can mean to these kids, and you're part of it. But we have just got to take risks. We've got to take chances. It's the perception that nothing can change that's our biggest impediment."

From Prestonsburg we set out for Berea. It was a long, relaxing drive, Bud and I mulling over the last few days while he intermittently checked in on sports radio, and I watched in wonder the moonlight on rockface and trees, then on rows and rows of tobacco and the gray wood siding of curing barns, then on Bluegrass farmland, the fog, pearlish in the moonlight, hanging just above the fields. Whenever I rolled the window down, there was the smell of pine or tobacco or skunk or wet hay, and the resonance of an occasional car, and the chirping of crickets, loud crickets — "Them's Kentucky crickets, boy" — and, somewhere in the distance, the wail of a train whistle. It was well past ten when we pulled into Janet's driveway.

Janet made coffee for Bud — he was continuing on to Lexington for the U.K. game the next day — and we talked a while longer, and then Bud hit the road, with warm farewells at the screen door. I went to the guest room. About half a block up from Cherry Road, the land dropped off to a deep ravine, and freight trains ran west to east along the narrow bottom. I lay in bed, the moonlight angling across the old quilts, thinking and listening to the whistle through the night.

Since she was a little girl, Janet Fortune had been drawn to Appalachia. Her father's lineage compelled her. Shannon Wilson, the archivist at Berea who had guided me through the Reverend Fee's papers, liked to say that mountain people were a people with memory. Janet was influenced by memory that existed before her birth. Little wonder that she entered the tradition at Berea that confirmed service to the mountains, that celebrated teacher education as noble work, God's work, even — though Janet would probably laugh off the ministerial implications. But not the call to serve, and not, at the least, a hint of the sacred. She wanted to foster in her students a sense of the majesty of teaching, a contemplative cast of mind, an awe of what it meant to learn and grow. And these young teachers, many of them, would find their places in public schools in the Eastern Coal Field, in West Virginia, in Tennessee — Dwayne Satterfield and Mindy Botts and Sheila Robinson and Tracy Payne Williams — wanting to change things, to spark a love of learning, to see the good in students, to be of service.

Bud and Carol and Delores shared a pedagogy driven by a belief in the power of student experience and by a paradoxical urgency to foster both a sense of place and a broadening of horizon. This pedagogy was, of course, enriched by their personal histories and shaped by the demands of their classroom, but it emerged from hopes and values fundamentally similar to those that animated the student teachers: a desire to make a difference, to encourage intellectual excitement and independence, to contribute to social justice and human growth. The fascinating thing was the way the veterans had to continually reconsider old practices, experiment, try new things to realize those values, to reconnect with them. Freedom. The multiple definitions of freedom, the play of freedom through so much of their work: The American Studies curriculum and "The Struggle for Freedom," the freedom provided by the grant from the foundation in New York, the freedom that led, momentarily, to student rebellion — itself, a manifestation of freedom — and then to original, unexpected achievement. As Bud said, they were all pushing on the performance envelope, not to pierce, finally, into some unbounded space, but to re-establish a connection with something deep in the heart.

If the young teachers working with Janet find their way in this profession, their desire to make a contribution will mature, sharpen, will shape the direction of their lives. But as with any value, any article of faith, it will not go unchallenged. I thought of Bud spending himself in union battles, then finding himself — in the middle of this rejuvenating experiment — facing the prospect of failure. "Teaching is fraught with failure," a friend of mine said once. During the ride to Berea, I asked Bud what was going through his mind on that day when everything seemed to be falling in. "All I could think of," he answered, "was 'Am I going to fail? My God, am I going to fail at this?'" What pulled him through, finally, was his long-held belief in what students could do and, I think, his connection to Carol, her ability to reinvigorate his faith. "Can you live with the criticism and still believe in the program?" Those fears the young teachers expressed — Will I know enough? Will I do the right thing? — they will never leave. Good teachers, novice and senior, live their classroom lives, maybe out of necessity, in a domain between principle and uncertainty.

7

Hattiesburg, Tupelo, Jackson, Indianola, Hollandale, and Webb, Mississippi

I IT WAS LATE IN THE EVENING as the small commuter plane, a British Jet Stream 31, left the runway with a grinding ascent in rain and fog toward the Pine Belt Regional Airport, in woody southeastern Mississippi. A forty-five-minute flight. I found the overhead light and nervously browsed through a newspaper: JURY SEATED IN BECKWITH MURDER TRIAL read the headline.

> *A white supremacist's two previous trials in the 1963 killing of civil rights leader Medgar Evers both ended with all-white juries deadlocked. This time, the jury of his peers is mostly black . . .*

The lights on the tips of the wings blinked steadily, the light diffusing in the fog, opalescent, seeming to freeze the rain with each flash, flying back over the curve of the wing. The engines muffled speech. The pilot had left the curtain open. I watched as he and his co-pilot gave occasional signals to each other: thumbs up, a pass of an open hand. They stared ahead into the fog. Then, suddenly, out of my window, through the rain streaming, beading up, I could see the distant lights of gas stations and truckstops, the fog floating behind the trees behind them. It would be a short drive to Hattiesburg.

Hattiesburg, named for the wife of the city's founder, was originally a railroad hub, then a production and distribution center for a booming yellow pine industry, then, during World War II, an army town for nearby Camp Shelby, and, in the last two or three decades, a site of small industry, medical technology, and education. The city's one-time teachers' college became the region's largest postsecondary institution, the University of Southern Mississippi. Hattiesburg — which, at forty-five thousand, is the fourth largest city in Mississippi — was one of a number of sites I would visit, trying to get a sense of good teaching across the state. I was led there by Dixie Goswami, a professor at Clemson who had worked with several Hattiesburg High School teachers. She gave me the phone number of one, Lois Rodgers, and that started me on my way.

Hattiesburg High School was the single public high school in Hattiesburg proper, located in the center of the city, enrolling eleven hundred students, 67 percent Black, 33 percent White. It was built in the early 1960s, laid out like a sideways H. During my stay, I would spend time in four classrooms, all on the south end of that H, three in a converted gymnasium, renovated after desegregation to incorporate students from the formerly Black high school across town. It was an odd building, a big circular structure with a domed roof supported by a series of thin concrete arches. Covered open-air walkways connected the classrooms, and it was a quick shot each to each, a damp breeze catching you at every turn.

"OK," said Susan. "We need the micropipette."

Amy began to read: "Place one small drop of red blood-antigen complex onto the middle of the microscope slide."

"OK, got that," Amanda replied, reaching for the test tube that held the blood-antigen complex. "But, wait, let's move the slide a little closer." The girls bunched in over the slide, and the talk came quickly.

"Let me do the blood, OK?"

"Like that, right?"

"Put a little more."

"Oh, ugh!"

"Did Miss Sullivan say to use it all?"

"Yeah. What comes next?"

Susan, Amy, and Amanda were conducting an experiment in Aleta Sullivan's human anatomy and physiology class. According to the scenario Ms. Sullivan had given them, they were members of a team from the Centers for Disease Control trying to figure out the cause of a violent illness affecting students who had just returned from an archaeological dig. Based on their results, they would have to make suggestions about the various actions the CDC might take. Then they were to write an essay assessing the validity of their procedure and the possible role human error might have played in their results. How do you establish confidence amid uncertainty? A dinosaur skeleton and an inflated shark hung above them; ferns grew moist in glass cases around them; off to the side, a skeleton leaned forward from its post, skull cocked slightly, like a quizzical Mr. Bones.

Amy read further in the instruction booklet. "Place one drop of your 'unknown' serum next to (but not touching) the drop of blood-antigen complex."

Amanda got another micropipette, drew the serum, and carefully, carefully squeezed a drop alongside the little bubble of blood. Susan leaned in from the side, cheek resting against fist, almost right above the slide.

"OK," Amy continued, "now it says, 'Using a toothpick, mix the two drops together . . . Observe whether or not the mixture shows agglutination. Positive agglutination means that the mixture shows definite signs of dark red clumps in a mostly clear liquid. Negative agglutination means that the mixture remains a rather muddy red color.'"

Amanda picked a toothpick off the tray that held the materials for the experiment. "Here goes," she announced. "C'mon, agglutination!"

"Oh," whispered Susan, "It's turning . . ."

"Yeah," Amy said flatly. "Muddy red."

"Aw, shoot," added Amanda. "It didn't do it. It's not positive."

The three looked on, Amanda occasionally poking at the mixture with the toothpick. Then, from the group, a rush of observation:

"Wait! Look there. Something's happening. That didn't just clump up, did it?"

"Well . . ."

"Is that clumpin' or is it just bubbles?"

"I think . . . I think it's just bubbles."

"I think it's muddy."

"Looks like tomato juice, huh?"

Susan straightened up; Amanda tapped her pipette against the tray, disappointed. "Ours was a dud," she announced.

"Should we do it again?" Susan asked.

"Yeah," said Amy, reaching for a clean slide. "Let's do it again just to be on the safe side."

LaFonda's short fingers moved in slow, deliberate motion over the keyboard of the word processor, little finger up as if at tea, the fingers, the thumb moving, finding letters with a soft touch. Touch, then press:

T-h-e n-i-g-h-t t-i-m-e . . .

She was bundled up, the puffy sleeves of her blue ski jacket resting on the arms of the wheelchair, thinking, concentrating, a smile passing as she found the key, completed the line:

i-s e-x-c-i-t-i-n-g a-n-d f-u-n

Mrs. Wynn, her teacher, was working with another student close by. That student couldn't or wouldn't write, and Mrs. Wynn, gentle and persistent, was trying to elicit a few words, coming at it one way, then another, then another — for eventually the student would have to write a short, timed essay to pass the high school equivalency exam, the goal of many in this special education class. That was not LaFonda's goal, however.

She wanted to go to college and become a social worker. She continued to compose her poem, pausing, reading the lines, nodding, then back to the keyboard, pressing softly. Earlier, via a laptop machine called Liberator — a complex keyboard of letters and icons and grammatical functions that produces a mechanical voice — she had read to the class a story about oceans and shorelines and freedom. Mrs. Wynn and another teacher have been trying to get her enrolled in the local community college. The word processor and Liberator have been of great help. LaFonda used to be in a vocational program, her words and desire muffled. But Joann Wynn knew better; she had been pushing on the boundaries of what traditional special education thought was possible. She got up from her reluctant writer, who was composing now, and went over to check on LaFonda.

LaFonda laughed softly at her concluding couplet, enjoying the rhyme, and extended her little finger toward the print key, reaching. And the poem began whirring out of the printer:

The Night Time

The night time is exciting and fun
When everyone can do,
what they want.

The night time is like a hunter's home.
It is spooky, scaring
and soundless.

You can see it black body.
And you can see it
million eyes.

Boo Boo, goes the night child.
You can see its moving and
you can hear its talking.

If you want ugly night monsters to go away,
You better get on your knees and pray.

Bette Ford's twelfth-grade English class was working in groups, trying to decide how to adapt the research they had been doing on Mississippi history to an audience of elementary school children. Over the next two weeks, each group was to decide on a focus, a set of objectives — what they wanted the children to learn — and a means of presentation that would appeal to kids.

Chris, who had prepared for his group meeting by writing a brief paper on his findings, suggested they do something on the picking of cotton.

"Cotton pickin'?" Anthony said incredulously, bristling at that symbol of domination.

Thinking that some sort of performance might be a part of their presentation, Jennifer, comically but with an edge, folded her arms and announced, "You're not gonna see *me* pick any cotton!"

"C'mon," Chris replied. "At one time, Mississippi's economy was dependent on cotton. And, besides, my grandmother and my neighbor told me some interesting things — the older people have a lot of stories about cotton."

That softened the group somewhat, but there was still contention. Bette came by, listened in, and wondered whether it would help the process if Chris read his paper. So Chris slipped the paper out of the pocket in his binder. He had written about people picking three hundred pounds of cotton and receiving four or five dollars for their work. He quoted his grandmother: "You did not spend that money foolishly because you had to buy essentials with it." He quoted another source: "The fields was the only time Whites and Blacks came together." He concluded by reflecting on the injustice of this economy and on the strength of the Black sharecroppers who made his life possible.

Jennifer, whose father was from the Delta town of Indianola, began talking about the scars on her father's hands, the thousand little tears left from the jagged pods of the cotton plant. Tyra wondered whether they could turn Chris's research into a short story, because "kids like stories." "Hey," Anthony suggested, "it might could start something like 'The sun beat down on their backs . . .'" Jennifer reached into her backpack and pulled out an old Mississippi history book she had found — high school level, 1946, the cover worn at the edges, frayed cardboard. "There's some stuff in here on cotton." She flipped through and found a print of sharecroppers arrayed symmetrically in the distance as in a painting of Flemish peasants. But she was skeptical about the information, for the discussion of slavery depicted Blacks as "happy and well-dressed and cared-for." "We'll need," said Tyra, "to be sure to use words little kids know." "But how are we going to talk about the violence?" Jennifer asked, just as the bell rang. "How are we going to write this so that little kids can understand?"

During the final months of 1993, two events brought uncomfortable media attention to Mississippi. Kim Fails, the student body president of Wingfield High School in Jackson, the state capital, read over the public address system a brief prayer asking that God bless "our parents, teachers, and country throughout the day." The principal who had approved the reading, Dr. Bishop Knox, was at first fired by the district superintendent, then suspended with pay, and across the state students staged rallies and walkouts in favor of prayer in the public schools. Outside Ovett, a tiny town about forty-five minutes northeast of Hattiesburg, Brenda and Wanda Henson, a lesbian couple from the Gulf Coast, bought a 120-acre defunct pig farm and established within it a feminist educational retreat called Camp Sister Spirit. Some of the residents of Ovett reacted with calls for their removal, with gunshots and death threats, and with the carcass of a female dog laid across the camp's mailbox, sanitary napkins taped to its belly. "Oprah" came south, as did "20/20," National Public Radio, the *New York Times*, and the *Village Voice*.

Just before these events hit the news, advanced placement English teacher Lois Rodgers — my first contact in Hattiesburg — attended a conference at the North Carolina Center for Teaching, where she saw a videotape of Anna Deavere Smith's *Fires in the Mirror*. Smith, an actress and writer and professor of theater at Stanford, had traveled to Brooklyn to interview residents and public figures about the 1991 racial explosion in Crown Heights, four days of riots and demonstrations sparked when a Hasidic Jew lost control of his car and killed a seven-year-old Black child. She developed from the interviews a one-woman show, assuming the character of a Jewish housewife, an African American street kid, a local rabbi, the Reverend Al Sharpton, relatives of those killed or injured . . . a flow of postures — slumped, poised, rigid with anger — and voices — ingratiating, controlled, thick with pain, sputtering in disbelief — offering many perspectives on "race, power, turf, and tribes." "I really need to show this to my students," Lois decided.

Lois's AP curriculum included a range of themes and styles — from *The Metamorphosis* and *As I Lay Dying* and *The Grapes of Wrath* to Kate Chopin and Toni Morrison to Septima Clark's *Ready from Within* — and required students to write poetry and short stories, research papers, stylistic analyses, argumentative essays, and reflections on their own learning, and to work on projects that mix genres and media, image and print. Running throughout all the books and assignments was a concern about perspective, a continued attempt "to get my students to see that life is not about having one simple answer." *Fires in the Mirror* fit perfectly. And when Lois returned to Hattiesburg, the school prayer and Camp Sister Spirit controversies "fell right into my lap."

After viewing *Fires in the Mirror,* Lois's students began interviewing people in Hattiesburg, Jackson, and Ovett, and sought out previously recorded interviews from TV and local media, editorials, letters to the editor — wherever they could find voice and opinion. The one deviation from Anna Deavere Smith's method of presentation would be that, because of class size and logistics, all characters would not be played by one person; each student was to assume the persona of two or three. They wrote scripts, constructed storyboards, found costumes and locations, rehearsed, taped, and wrote analyses of the entire process. A paper that took a position on school prayer or Camp Sister Spirit was to follow. As it turned out, one of Lois's sections worked with the school prayer controversy, three with the events in Ovett.

HONK 4 PRAYER reads the sign being waved by the two women standing by the school flagpole. They are animated, worked-up; they complete each other's sentences, wave vigorously to supportive passers-by. "Honey," one says straight into the video camera, "they've been honkin' for days, passin' by and honkin'. This fight ain't over. I support them kids . . ." "One hundred percent," the other interjects. "Since when did we need permission to pray to God?" The scene shifts to the front of a synagogue. A girl is dressed in an oversized man's suit jacket and speaks as a local rabbi. "They say this is a Christian country, but that represents confusion of the fact that most of the country's founding fathers were Christian with the nature of the Republic they established. It was our forefathers' intention to maintain the separation of church and state." The scene shifts again to the director of the ACLU in Hattiesburg, sitting at a big desk, talking into the phone. "Ours is not an antireligious stance," she explains, her speech very precise, dwelling on vowels. "On the contrary, it is a stance respectful of different religions." "We need to move ourselves back," a minister says, hands clasped, speaking from a pew, "to being a God-dependent nation. We need a moral absolute to help us discern right and wrong." "Well-meaning people," the editorial page editor of the *Hattiesburg American* begins, "are missing the point by jumping to the defense of prayer and God. Prayer and God are *not* under attack. This is about defending the rights of others." A pause. Music. Kim Fails, the student body president who had read the prayer, appears, holding a Bible with her school binder. "I'm not quite sure what to make of this controversy," she says. "The students voted for the prayer. Ninety-six said no, but 490 said yes. I represent the whole student body. When there's a vote and majority rules, I must act accordingly. This is getting to be more like a dictatorship where they aren't willing to listen to what kids want." An erstwhile youth minister sits on a ledge, hugging his knees. He draws a comparison between these students advocating school prayer and civil rights activists like Rosa Parks. "Sometimes," he says, turning toward the camera, "you have to break laws to change them."

"You've kicked that soapbox under my feet, and I've taken a stand on it," announces Brenda Henson, co-founder of Camp Sister Spirit. "I'm not going to leave this place. I want to make a difference in Mississippi. We want to live our lives and do our work." Her speech fades into brief connecting licks of country guitar; an Ovett attorney, played by a girl, sits at his desk. "This group came in overnight," he says, "and threatens to turn the community into Homosexual Hub Central. You have to understand this community. People don't even mow their *lawns* on Sunday, much less accept homosexuality." Brenda and Wanda Henson now, on a couch, holding hands. Brenda talks, angry, on a roll; Wanda responds with enthusiastic *Amens.* "You don't have to be a lesbian to benefit from a feminist education. Think about it. As women, the way we look is more important than what we think. If we get raped, it's our fault; if we get beaten, we provoked it. If we don't like sex, we're frigid; if we like it, we're nymphos. If we raise our voices, we're considered nagging bitches . . . This is what these men are scared of."

A woman in a carpenter's cap pounds nails into a plank. She looks up, smiles, holds out her hammer. "A month ago I didn't know the front of this thing from the back. Now I can do all kinds of carpentry work. It's helped me to become independent. So what if I'm a lesbian? It's nothing to be ashamed of. I've come out of the closet, and I'm sitting in the living room with my feet propped up. By gosh, I'm feeling kinda proud of myself." Shift again to a kitchen, flowering vines on the wallpaper. An Ovett housewife looks straight into the camera, wide-eyed, scared. "The Bible," she says deliberately, "is very specific. It says the man is head of the household. We are to honor and support our husbands and children. That does not make us slaves." Other residents — from Ovett, from nearby communities — move across the screen, some shaded, for they have asked to remain anonymous. "I believe homosexuality is wrong, but these women are trying to do nothin' but good: clothe the naked, feed the needy." "What people do behind closed doors is nobody else's business. I say, let these women be." "The media has portrayed the lesbians as living in fear, but what about *us* — we're living in fear, too!" "Let he who is without sin cast the first stone." Music. The words *White Sheets* come on the screen. The light changes to dusk. Two guys are sitting on the back of a pickup truck, the gate down. One holds a bolt-action rifle. "We don't want them running around teaching our kids to be lesbians," he drawls. "It ain't what the sweet Lord Jesus wants." He looks into the camera and pumps the rifle. "We're gonna fight for Ovett — it's about all we got left." A boy appears in the next scene; he plays a female guard in Camp Sister Spirit. It is very dark now, the feel of threat deep in the woods, a narrow road, a truck dimming its lights. "The other night, I was shot at," the guard says softly. "We just wanted to create a safe space here, but I don't feel safe. Dead animals and bullet holes . . . I'm scared." Wanda Henson, stocking cap, in close to the camera. "We're not gonna be run outta here. We're not gonna back down."

The characters continued across the flickering monitor throughout the afternoon, linked each to the other with bits of music — from Nirvana to David Allan Coe to "It's a Beautiful Day in the Neighborhood" — and with ironic or evocative words and phrases: "Small Talk", "Love Thy Neighbor," "Heat Zone," "Lack of Communication," "Shades of Blindness," "White Sheets." Like Anna Deavere Smith before them, the students made the most of a single prop: a folder, a pen, a bottle of beer, a telephone, a pair of glasses waved in the air, a rifle. And, like her, they tried to adapt speech and posture to character, appropriating nods and tics and a small wave of the hand, a waver in the voice, an exasperated sigh of indignity, playing characters across gender and race, trying on the physical mannerisms of another, feeling, they said, uncomfortable at times, but trying to assume perspective: the ACLU lawyer, the frightened citizen, the bigot, the women in Camp Sister Spirit, the man or woman on the street, seeking anonymity. "You have to develop that character in your mind," said one girl. "I personally don't believe in lesbianism," said another, "but playing one really made me think." "She had so much character," said one of the girls who assumed the role of Wanda Henson, "that I thought it would be fun to play her." "I don't think you can know," said a girl who played a lawyer, "what it's like to be in the minority. I mean, I cannot really know what it's like to be Black or gay." "I think I came to understand," observed a boy who played a good ol' boy, "something about the fear behind prejudice."

Each of these teachers — Aleta Sullivan, Joann Wynn, Bette Ford, Lois Rodgers — was creating the conditions for students to puzzle over the complex, to work out of discomfort or ambiguity, and, in some instances, to develop a medium to express what they found. And what they found was often surprising, unexpected.

Aleta and the rest taught in an environment of constraint and possibility. Though the last decade has seen significant improvement in its support of public education, Mississippi is still lowest in the nation in per pupil expenditure ($3323) and lowest in average teacher salary ($24,369). This impoverishment has its origins in Mississippi's historic undercutting and underfunding of public education because of the threat it might pose to the social order. The turn-of-the-century ruling elite would have agreed with a Virginia newspaper's editorial on schooling for Blacks, "When they learn to spell dog and cat they throw away the hoe." By 1924 there were in Mississippi 1020 high schools for Whites and only three for Blacks — though there were more Black than White adolescents of eligible age. And with the advent of the Brown decision, in 1954, there were protracted attempts to forestall integration: massive White exodus to private academies and legislative subversion, such as the repeal, in 1957, of the state's compulsory attendance law. Poor, mostly rural, Whites as well as Blacks suffered the consequences.

Public education received a vitalizing jolt in 1982, however, when Governor William Winter, through shrewd negotiation and consensus building, achieved passage of his Education Reform Act, the first in the nation's flurry of 1980s reform legislation. The bill established a state board of education and a state superintendency, instituted a statewide kindergarten program, increased teacher salaries, reduced teacher-student ratios in the primary grades, raised graduation requirements, instituted changes in teacher certification and accountability, and put in place an elaborate set of curriculum guidelines and objectives and a series of tests to assess children's attainment of those objectives. It was an extraordinary political achievement, and it invigorated public interest in public schools. But the curricular guidelines it established and the means of assessment of basic competencies, of often narrowly defined achievement — tended to discourage rather than promote the kind of instruction Aleta, Joann, Bette, and Lois (and the other teachers I visited in Mississippi) believed was central to the growth of their students. So they worked around the mandates, figured out how to incorporate and go beyond them, argued for their revision. Without the Reform Act of 1982, the public schools would have even less support than they do; with it came constraints on the development of what policy analyst Rexford Brown calls a literacy of thoughtfulness.

Teachers, as we have seen, work not only within the boundaries of institutional mandate, but within the context of local history and culture, as well. The teachers I saw in Mississippi, many of whom were either natives or long-time residents, were raised within the knotted memory and codes of the state — repressive and closed and brutal, communitarian and brave and melancholy. This was what they came from and pushed against, in their lives, in their classrooms, creating new possibilities amid the wisps and traces of the past.

I had long conversations with Lois and Bette about their life and work. We sat in classrooms after school or in the teachers' lounge, leaning against an old refrigerator. In Lois's case, since I stayed with her family in the adjoining town of Petal, we also talked in her dining room, the TV announcing a sale to no one in particular, her husband barbecuing some pork chops just outside the door.

Lois was a tall, imposing woman, White, late forties, born in Pascagoula on the Gulf Coast, raised in Petal. She was passionate about teaching, spun a web of story and opinion about pedagogy, social issues, and "red neck" legislators. Though she was a shrewd strategist, there was a fearless quality to her advocacy; as one cautious admirer put it, she didn't care whose ox she gored. But she was warm and generous and fiercely loyal — you wanted her on your side in a fight — and had developed deep friendships among the teachers at Hattiesburg High. Driving home one day, reflecting on some of the women there and on herself, she said: "We were reared in homes where we were taught to be little ladies. That Southern femininity junk. But there are a lot of us who don't want to just be ornaments. It's true, OK, that women down here don't have the top positions, so we've learned to be strong in what we do have. And school has become one place where we can assert ourselves, where we can make a difference in the lives of kids." She has made some enemies and has run afoul of some fundamentalist members of the community — and that has "made me weigh what I say in the classroom." But it was hard to imagine her voice subdued in any significant way, for she seemed driven to think through, to articulate the powerful relation of teaching to human development and the social order. Here she is on race, the topic we discussed most fully.

"I think we Mississippians have come a long way in a short period of time — I mean, what has it been, 1970 since we actually integrated? We go to school together. We work together. But there is still a good deal of social separation. In our society, almost all issues involving both races can quickly polarize and become a Black-White issue. At school we interact, but we don't always sit together. If you go to a faculty meeting, you'll see a couple of us, Black and White, sitting together, but the majority of times all the White teachers who are big buddies will sit together, and all the Black teachers will sit together. It's the same with many of our students. We'll talk, we'll kid, there's lots of interaction — and all that represents huge change — but socially we're still miles away from where we need to be.

"Nobody talks openly about it, but this color business is about power. There's still the stereotypical assumption that if your color is not White, then you're somehow less. I've really tried to work on this in my class. When we read Septima Clark, we have some really down-home discussions, and the students end up talking pretty frankly about race. The reason I do these things is that I want my students to understand that they have to try out more than just their way of looking at things. That's the key to us somehow learning to get along with each other.

"Many of my White students just don't see that they've been the dominant culture; they don't have any idea, say, of what it'd be like to be Black going into a White neighborhood. There were some wonderful articles I brought to class when we were doing the civil rights stuff, articles on how, in Washington, D.C., the nation's capital, for God's sake, if you're a Black man, they frisk you all the time, and you might have all this education, but if your skin is the wrong color, they just assume something's wrong. I was trying to make them aware. I brought in excerpts from Williams's — do you know Patricia Williams's book, *The Alchemy of Race and Rights?* — I brought in excerpts from that book. I also use Toni Morrison's *The Bluest Eye,* since, if you don't live something, literature is just about the only way you can learn it. I had students tell me, 'Mrs. Rogers, I never realized what children like this must go through. I never thought about the idea that if there is a White standard of beauty that everyone has to live up to, then if you're not White, how that could be so harmful.' I think that's significant, don't you? I feel very strongly about this issue of race relations. It's going to destroy our whole nation, not just Mississippi, if we don't address it."

Bette Ford was in her early fifties, born in Coffeeville, Alabama, but raised in Hattiesburg from the age of five, African American, attended segregated schools, worked for the Student Nonviolent Coordinating Committee in the summer of 1963, and has taught for twenty-four years. She was a reflective, soft-spoken woman; a mutual friend described her as "scholarly and elegant." Lois had told me to ask her about a particular incident involving Maya Angelou's *I Know Why the Caged Bird Sings,* and when I did, it became the focus of a long discussion of race, censorship, and growth.

It seemed that a parent called the school complaining about the language in Angelou's novel, vowing that he was going to do whatever he could to get the book banned not only from Bette's classroom, but from the district. It happened that the day after the call, Bette was scheduled to attend a meeting in Jackson, so there was a substitute teacher in her class. It also happened that on that day — coincidentally, Bette believes — someone distributed hate literature on campus, an old letter, probably from desegregation days, complaining about Blacks trying to usurp power. During the day, a few White students were talking on campus about getting the book banned, and a few Black students who worked in the office heard about the parent's complaint and, when they saw the substitute teacher, wondered if Mrs. Ford had been suspended. All this came together and sparked some racial clashes that, fortunately, were brought under control. And the principal stood behind Bette's choice of books. But the incident was deeply troubling to Bette — a weird confluence of events that played off a whole web of tensions in Mississippi history — and she spent some time in her classes having her students talk and write about it.

Lois had said that the horror of censorship is that "it's like this invisible thing that you can't really fight because you're never sure when it might come at you." I asked Bette how she continued to teach with conviction when the threat of censorship was ever-present. She paused a long time. Then . . .

"I pray a lot. I talk to my students about why I make certain choices. And I try, from early in the year, to gain as much rapport with my students' parents as I can. I feel foremost an obligation as a teacher to be sensitive to both the academic and personal needs of all my students — and that involves being sensitive to what would offend them, and being sensitive to who they are and where they come from. I need to respect that. Yet I also believe that, somehow, we need to have conversations in my classroom that will get all of us to thinking about where everybody else is coming from. Does that make sense? I feel a strong sense of responsibility to make a mark in my classroom, to get people thinking about how we arrive at what we think, and whether we are thinking critically, rationally.

"Please understand, I am sensitive to some quote-unquote Bible Belt fears. The mores and standards of this culture helped shape who I am. Now, I'm also African American, and I feel a special commitment to making sure the voices of Black people are heard in classroom conversations and through our literature.

"There are some people who feel we ought to hush, but, I'm sorry, I just don't believe that. I . . . I don't believe we can! Sometimes it may mean that I get myself in fixes that I don't know how to get out of. But I think that social issues, race especially, ought to be raised in the classroom. Cautiously, maybe, gingerly, but if we don't learn to deal with them there, then where *are* we going to learn to deal with them?

"In my early years as a teacher, I'm sure this job was more about me than it was about my students. I felt that I had to prove that I was a good teacher, and at least a part of that had to do with being a Black teacher after the dismantling of segregation. Part of being 'good,' part of proving myself, meant giving in to things in the establishment that I was unsure about. Well, after ten or so years, I was almost burned out, and I talked with several people about changing careers. One man in particular suggested that a good way to start renewing myself would be to get to know my students better. Well, I thought I *knew* my students! But I really didn't. I did not listen well enough to what my students were saying, Black or White. I was so preoccupied.

"I think that what I'm talking about was as much a spiritual evolution as a professional one. There were issues that I would not have dealt with in the classroom because I would not have felt comfortable. I knew I would have been challenging the system. I suppose now I have a deeper sense of commitment to what I feel I need to do, in spite of the consequences — and that brings me back to *I Know Why the Caged Bird Sings.* I am ready to fight, if I have to, to keep that book from being removed from our school. Fortunately, this is a place that trusts teachers to teach according to their knowledge and experience. But I would be willing to defend what I believe. I feel a deep responsibility to both my students and to my own sense of what's right. And I am much more comfortable with that now than I would have been earlier in my life."

II FROM HATTIESBURG, I flew north to the other side of the state, to Tupelo — the name comes from the Creek and refers to a genus of gumtree — a city of thirty-one thousand people in the upper eastern quadrant of Mississippi, about seventy-five miles from the Tennessee border. Originally a railroad and agricultural town, Tupelo has developed over the last two generations into a center of light industry and medical technology; it has the largest hospital complex in Mississippi and, with surrounding Lee County, is the leading producer of upholstered furniture in the world. (And, though the locals don't make much of it, Tupelo is also the birthplace of Elvis Presley, his two-room "shotgun" house drawing sixty thousand visitors a year, myself among them.) In the aftermath of the Brown decision, the city's newspaper editor and key civic leaders developed plans for desegregation, and Lee County became the first county in Mississippi to attempt integration of its schools. Public education in Tupelo has enjoyed a broad base of support ever since, a mix of volunteerism, school-business partnerships, and funding. A few years back, the citizens approved, by 89 percent, a $17 million school bond, one of the largest in Mississippi history, and a local textile millionaire gave $3.5 million to establish an institute for teacher development.

Tupelo High School was located at the southwest edge of town, surrounded by flat, open land, an expansive new construction built on seventy-five acres donated by that same textile magnate. It was the only public high school in Tupelo, with nearly eighteen hundred students, 28 percent African American, 72 percent White. It had a core of seasoned activist teachers who have long campaigned for better schools and salaries. Two of them, Martha Jo Patterson and Jane Talbert, regularly traveled to the state capital in Jackson to, as Martha Jo put it, "sometimes slap those legislators, sometimes beg from them." It was through Jane that I heard about a new science teacher, Sharon Davis. Sharon taught chemistry, advanced physics, and conceptual physics, and, in her first year, was voted by the student body one of the two best teachers at Tupelo High School. I arranged to spend time in conceptual physics, a qualitative more than quantitative study of fundamental physical principles.

If you looked out at Sharon's classroom from the blackboard, you would see an arrangement of school desks, two rows against each wall facing the middle, two rows in the middle facing the board. The chairs were slightly askew, some turned in a little, some turned out. Behind the chairs were six black octagonal lab tables — gas jets, water faucets, narrow troughs for drainage — resting on bases of blond wood. Along the three walls in the back were sinks and cabinets, some open, revealing pulleys, blocks of wood, scales, beakers, flasks, pipettes, graduated cylinders, mortars and pestles. Near the left-hand corner was an emergency shower with a large triangular handle at the end of a pull cord.

Sharon walked over from her desk by the doorway, black slacks, cowboy boots, sweater, a gelled flurry of dark brown curls, delicate glasses. It was her last class of the day. "We're going to talk," she said with a slight dramatic dip of the head, "about speed and velocity." Shannon and Trey watched her from below the windows; Bev in tie-dyed T-shirt and hiking boots sat cross-legged on a lab table; Dale, the big guy from Canada, leaned against a second table; Bryan, another husky kid, stood by him, hands in pockets; Scott and red-headed Heather, as usual, were up front; Millie and Stephanie were along the wall; Paige, Sharon's student teacher, sat chin in hand on the lab table closest to the cabinets, flasks and beakers and scales behind her; Brad, the boy who could distinguish only light and dark, sat to Sharon's right, and she occasionally moved toward him as she spoke. There were about twenty-five students in this section of conceptual physics. They were dressed mostly in jeans, for the rainy winds had been blowing for days, hiking boots and athletic shoes, denim or plaid shirts, sweaters, jackets, and long-sleeved pullovers. Many bore print: *Tupelo High School Homecoming, Tupelo Band, Tupelo High School Theater Company '93 "Murder in the Wings," Wynonna "Girls with Guitars," Ole Miss, Mississippi 4-H Meat-Judging Team, Cross-Country Invitational, Dixie Debs '92.*

Sharon turned to a brief illustration on the board:

Tupelo ——— Fulton
17 miles

"Speed and velocity," Sharon repeated. "I live in Fulton. If I come to school and return, make a round trip, how far have I traveled?"

"Thirty-four miles," offered Heather from the front row.

"OK, correct. Now let me ask you this: Is it possible that the answer to my question could be *zero* miles?"

"Well." Heather paused. "Only if you look at it different."

"Right. Exactly right," Sharon said, raising her hand in a quick wave over her head and turning back to the board. "Perspective is key here." She wrote:

<u>distance</u>: total linear measurement
<u>displacement</u>: change in position of an object from its starting point

From the back of the room, Bryan asked "What about I drive from home to school to work then back home?" As he spoke, Sharon sketched his itinerary on the board.

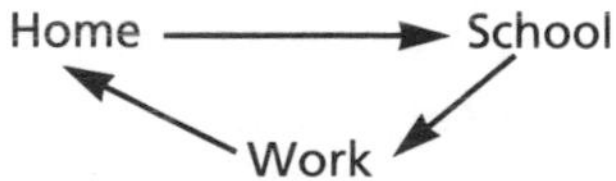

"If displacement is defined as how far you wound up from where you started," she asked, "then what do you think, darlin'? What's the displacement?"

Bryan took his hands out of his pockets and folded his arms across his chest. "Zero," he said.

"Right." Sharon nodded. "Get that in your IBMs." She looked down at her chalk as though she were contemplating it. "Now let me ask you this. Given the speed limit in Mississippi, how fast can Bryan here drive in an hour?"

From the class came a choral "Fifty-five."

"OK, Bryan?"

"Yes, ma'am."

"If I say you drove fifty-five miles per hour north from your house to school, what bit of information have I added?"

"North . . . er, direction."

"All right. If we have speed and direction, then we have velocity." Sharon turned once again to the board. "And to be able to talk about displacement, you'll *have* to know direction. Why?"

As Bev answered that one from atop the lab table, Sharon wrote two properties of motion on the board:

<u>scalar</u>: has magnitude
<u>vector</u>: has magnitude and direction

"Bev," Sharon asked, looking over her shoulder from the board, "is speed scalar or vector and why?"

"It's scalar," answered Bev, "because you only know how fast."

"How about velocity?"

"Uh, vector, you have both speed and direction."

"Okey-dokey," Sharon pronounced with lightness and finality. "Let's look at the side board." And she walked to the chalkboard by the door. A sign in the middle, highlighted with radiating lines, read: *Every Good Scientist Performs an Experiment Thrice.* Written around it in precise script were the following instructions:

PHYSICS: YOU'LL NEED

1. A long piece of string
2. A balloon
3. A piece of tape
4. A straw
5. At least three people
6. A stopwatch
7. A meter stick
8. Plenty of room!

Then an illustration:

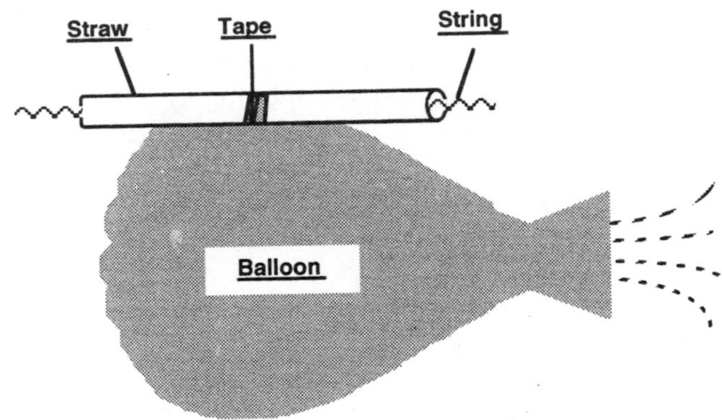

And underneath the illustration:

Purpose: To determine the speed of a balloon

Sharon went over the instructions, holding up the objects she had laid out on her desk before class: balloon, straw, string, stopwatch, and yardstick. Students were to time a balloon propelled by escaping air as it traveled along a string, measure the distance it traveled, and calculate its speed.

"Got it?" she asked. Assent. She clapped her hands. "OK, let's hit it!" And then came the focused chaos of preparation.

Some students went out into the long hallway; some stayed in the lab. One group of boys extended their string from the top of the door frame at the back of the room to the top of the window on the opposite wall. A group of girls ran a line from the two lab faucets that were farthest apart. Outside the room, teams of students, boys and girls, unfurled string up and down the hallway, tested stopwatches, added another layer of tape to affix straw to balloon. Among them walked Sharon, a hand full of meter sticks — Zeus with thunderbolts — passing them out one by one, answering questions, reminding students to keep the string taut, asking why some might want to cut their straws in half ("What's the relation between surface area and friction?"). And the experiments began — the balloons flying down the strings or wobbling, spiraling forward, or, in one case, popping, fragments of red latex clinging to the lockers nearby. ("We broke the sound barrier," Bryan announced.) Then the stopwatches: 1.72 seconds, 1.93 seconds, 2.01 seconds. Then the measurements, students kneeling, scooting, marking off distance in three-meter increments. And then the calculations. "Ms. Davis," Heather announced, "our balloon's speed was 290 centimeters per second." "OK," said Sharon, "let's run it again."

After class, alone in the cafeteria, at a table in a far corner, Sharon and I split a soft drink, and she talked about the interplay of her personal history and her work.

"I was born in September of 1957 in Booneville, about forty-five miles north of here. At the time there were maybe three thousand or so people there. My daddy was a plumber and electrician and an itinerant preacher, Southern Baptist preacher — so I grew up in a very strict environment. When Daddy would preach, I always felt like I was on display as a measurement of his virtue.

"My brother had bronchial asthma when he was little, so I became my dad's 'boy.' I would go on jobs with him during the summers, pulling wires and crawling around under houses. From an early age, I knew things like an electrical current created a magnetic field. I didn't understand exactly what that meant, but I knew that if you put a compass by one of those wires, it would do strange things. It amazed me to watch Daddy. Things that looked complicated to me, he could just sit and figure out. He was a very bright man. He gave me the desire to know how things worked. And the gift to ask a lot of questions.

"He was always asking me questions, questions that would make me think about things, sometimes related to electricity or plumbing, sometimes not. He would say, 'Have you ever wondered why . . . ?' I think it had an effect on how I perceived things. I didn't look at them as a 'woman' would have looked at them. I looked at them with a different eye. He made me reason things out. He . . . he was a paradox, he really was. As a preacher, there were some things he didn't question at all. Women back then, I guess, not many of my friends were encouraged to think for themselves — I mean, we're talking about a small Mississippi town. And when we went to school, the teachers stood in front of us, they gave us information, we memorized it, you know, and if we had a good memory, we made A's. But as far as learning a lot, well . . .

"When I was in about the sixth grade, I started dreaming of being a doctor. I began working toward that goal, and I took all my high school courses with that in mind. When I graduated, I went on to a community college in premed, taking about twenty-one to twenty-two hours every semester. I worked very hard, was kind of a bookworm. The truth is, I was painfully shy. It's still hard for me to look people right in the face — if you notice, I talk, like, to the walls. The only people I can look straight in the eye and be comfortable with are my students.

"My daddy always told me that I could be whatever I wanted to be. But, well, I don't know, somehow, I guess, when it came right down to it, I didn't really believe that. The women I knew, all of them were married and had kids. If they worked, they worked in one of the factories. The only professional women I knew were teachers. At college, I was encouraged to go into the med-tech program, not medical school. Looking back on it, I see that girls were encouraged to become nurses, but not doctors; teachers, but not professors. I don't know, I guess I got a little discouraged, began to think, 'No, I can't do this.' So I quit school and got married. I've been a cashier in a variety store, a bookkeeper, a computer operator, a hostess in a bank, a salesperson in a jewelry store, and an assistant buyer for Pier One. In 1987 I went back to school, and in 1990 I graduated. I started teaching eighth grade in the fall of 1990, and I've been at Tupelo High School for two years now. I love it.

"I think it's real important to have a woman teaching chemistry and physics. I see girls around me in school who look and act the same way I did, and I want to tell them, 'If you want to do something . . .' A few weeks ago at Christmas break, a girl came back to visit me. She had enrolled in my advanced physics course the year before but began to doubt herself. 'I think I've made a mistake,' she said. 'I don't think I should be in this class. I think it's going to be too hard for me.' I told her that if she stuck with me and worked hard and did her best, she'd see she could do it. Now she's in premed at Notre Dame. That made me feel real good. It was almost like I was there with her. It was as though I had a second chance through her.

"Once you lose the wonder, you can't really perceive this stuff," Sharon said of learning physics, and it was a sense of wonder, a fascination with the physics of the everyday, that made her teaching seem, at times, as though she were turning the pages of a marvelous book, telling the story to anyone who would listen. Two days after the balloon experiment, after more coverage of speed and velocity and after introducing acceleration ("the rate of a rate," she explained), as we settled into our desks — complaining about the wind and rain, swapping impressions of the Wynonna Judd concert the night before — as all the between-period dust of schooling settled, Sharon ascended in two loud clacking steps up a chair, then onto her desk, then onto a narrow demonstration table. "A long time ago, a very long time ago," she announced, grabbing us with the spectacle of a grown woman standing on furniture, "in the last quarter of the sixteenth century, a young medical student from Pisa, Italy, named Galileo Galilei decided to eat his lunch at the top of the tallest tower in town. Anyone heard of that tower?" Big response: the Leaning Tower of Pisa! Sharon's head was close to the ceiling, amid fluorescence, student-made molecular models dangling within reach. She tapped her heels twice on the table — like a dancer — and brought up from her side a brown lunch bag with the name *Galileo* written across the front. "That's right. So that afternoon, he climbed the tower with his medical school notes and his lunch — and let's see what his mother had packed." Sharon proceeded with some flourish to pull out a bunch of rubber grapes — the kind you'd find on a coffee table display — a sandwich in a Baggie, a plastic cup, and "a note from his mother, a list of things to pick up at the store." Well, OK, so Galileo did not perform his famous gravitational experiments with plastic grapes, and, no, there wasn't a note from mother, but everybody kind of knew that, watching, giggling, waiting to see Sharon's next move. Sharon laughed herself — a quick descending lilt — at her own fabrication as she plucked with relish a grape from its wire stem and dropped it nonchalantly to the floor.

"The great Greek philosopher Aristotle — y'all heard of him, right?" Sharon intoned. "Well, he believed, guess what, that objects that were more massive would fall faster. 'OK,' thought young Galileo, 'let's see.'" And over the next five or so minutes, Sharon dropped, in tandem, a grape and a sandwich, a sandwich and a plastic cup, even a single grape and the entire bunch, falling with a rubbery *splat.* She asked her students to record what they saw.

"But then," Sharon continued, "Galileo wondered what would happen if he dropped that note from his mother." So Sharon steadied both hands, a grape in one, the note in the other, and released them. The grape plummeted; the note fluttered slowly to the floor. "Oh, oh," Galileo worried, "maybe Aristotle was right." Shaking her head once,

Sharon broke character: "What's going on here, class?" "Resistance!" yelled Heather and Scott and Bev and from the side Shannon and, way in the back, Bryan. "Right, exactly right," Sharon said. "Now watch." And she crumpled the note and, plucking yet another grape from the bunch, dropped both simultaneously — and both hit simultaneously. "What did I just do?" Sharon asked. "You decreased the resistance on the paper," answered Heather. "OK, now think about this," Sharon continued. "What would happen if I dropped the full sheet of paper and the grape in a big vacuum tube?" "They'd fall together," said Brad, from Sharon's right, looking past the experiment at the vague light from the windows, "because there'd be no resistance." "You bet," said Sharon, and, in a quick, turning step, descended from the Leaning Tower of Pisa to the tan linoleum floor.

There was not much room to move on the day the second-graders came to build their rockets. After Sharon had climbed down from that demonstration table, she discussed free fall, the state when no other force except gravity is acting on a falling body, and she discussed as well the shift from potential to kinetic energy, the effect of surface area and resistance, and the difference between how fast and how far an object falls — her chalk *tap, tap, tapping* on the board as she sketched out tables for free fall speed and free fall distance. Then over the following week or so, she covered Newton's three laws of motion, wondered aloud about the kinds of phenomena that could have led Newton to think so systematically about motion, presented everyday examples of the laws at work, and led the class through an application of the laws to rockets and the space shuttle. This culminated in a project that had her students building and launching their own small solid-fuel rockets.

The launch took place by the soccer field on the west side of school, a broad stretch of grass, dry now, with trees in the distance in one direction, a ravine in the other, and beyond it the Natchez Trace, a historic parkway running from Nashville to Natchez. Some of the students used a simplified version of the medieval astrolabe — essentially, a reversed protractor with a plumb line attached — to calculate measures of distance and speed. Sharon had invited Karol Vogue's second-grade class from Pierce Street Elementary School in the center of town to come out and watch the show, and so, as Sharon's students ignited rockets and took measurements, the children were counting down in unison, squealing at blast-off, running to catch the nose cones dancing down the air on small parachutes.

This set the stage for a cross-age collaboration. Sharon's students rewrote the instructions for the rocket kits so that second-graders could read them, and also wrote for the children booklets that explained and illustrated concepts from the study of motion. And then the boys and girls from Pierce Street Elementary came to room B-219 at Tupelo High School.

Sharon drifted among the mixed groups of seniors and second-graders, boys and girls, Black and White, observing, guiding, stopping occasionally to scribble a note to herself. Her seniors were doing most of the work: helping the children follow the directions in careful sequence ("What's it say to do next?"); giving guidance on performing particular tasks ("You'll have to go slow on this part"); or asking questions of the kind Sharon asked, to spark thought ("What do you think you'll have to do next?"). There was encouragement and occasionally direct intervention, embracing the hand of a child and guiding it through a difficult cut or twist. There was chitchat — "What do you wanna be when you grow up?" — and the teasing-out of local connections. And around the room, the children were eyeing the fit of the four-finned base to the main rocket cylinder, twisting the nose cone into its plastic container, leaning over the instructions, reading them word by word. On the walls surrounding the crowded lab tables, Sharon had taped the writing the children had done about the launch a few days before:

> We really enjoyed launching the rockets up in the air.
> The best part was when we did the countdown.
> I can't wait for you to teach us how to do it.

The next phase of the project was the launch itself. The rockets were about two feet long: four narrow fins at the base, which was hot pink, a long silver cylinder, and a black nose cone. The fuel was a mix of sulfur and gunpowder; when ignited, it produced four Newtons — about nine pounds — of force, propelling the rocket over seventy feet per second to a height of about 120 feet. Sharon had said that her primary goal as a teacher was to get students to see that an understanding of physics, the course that strikes fear into the heart of so many, was within the reach of everyone, regardless of background. Her rhapsody over the physical universe was an inclusive one.

The launching device was a small black box, about an eight-inch cube, with long wires that extended to an ignition filament inserted in the base of the rocket. The device had two buttons. When a child pushed the first, an electric current was sent through the system, *beep, beep, beep* emitting from the box. As the current completed its circuit, the beeping progressed to a steady, high-pitched noise, signaling the time to push the second button, which would increase the current, igniting the fuel. Countdown. Five. Four. Three. Two. One. And a fat blast of smoke shot the rocket upward, the smoke thinning to a neat white stream against the blue sky over the Natchez Trace. At the height of the rocket's trajectory, a second small explosion released the cone and its parachute, the little puff of smoke marking the apex for those students taking measurements with the astrolabe. Then the nose cone descending, the children zigzagging on the dry grass, the wonder, the outstretched hands.

III

FROM TUPELO I took a Greyhound to Jackson, just southwest of the center of the state, where I would visit schools that were to implement a supplementary mathematics curriculum called the Algebra Project.

The Algebra Project is both a curriculum and a social movement. It was developed by voter-registration activist Bob Moses, an early SNCC field secretary and organizer of Freedom Summer, who was also a math teacher. It attempts to prepare children, all children, at the sixth-grade level for algebra, the gateway to participation in high school mathematics and science, which, in turn, is necessary for college-level work. Moses draws parallels between mathematical literacy and the earlier political literacy fostered by the civil rights movement: both are necessary for a fuller, more equitable participation in society. And as with the civil rights movement, the curriculum assumes that all people are capable of participation, and, in this case, capable of grasping the conceptual basics of algebra — equivalence, displacement, and so on. The curriculum is built around a sequence of accessible activities: taking bus rides, measuring, rating, comparing objects and events, and playing a range of games. After engaging in one of these activities, children draw or somehow model it, talk and write about it, attempt to translate it into a more formal mathematical language, and develop, through consensus, symbols to represent it. The process aims at making children more adept at and more comfortable with symbolic operations and procedural routines — essential if they are to succeed at algebra when it shows up in the curriculum in grade eight or nine. The Algebra Project is in place in over seventy-five schools across the country. This so-called Southern initiative of the project is a fairly new development, one laden with symbolism for Bob Moses, a return to Mississippi.

After leaving Tupelo, the bus took a wavy route over to the eastern border of the state, close to Alabama, then a long zigzag across to Jackson. It was a six-hour ride, and I filled it by intermittently reading about the Algebra Project and gazing out the big Greyhound window at the long, slow countryside. Bare cypress trees jutted out of muddy swamps, the brown water glittering in the sun. Small houses were scattered across vast fields, and, up close to the road, splintered sheds, their wood worn gray and gray-black, folded in on themselves. There was pasture, fenced in, with cows, cows. And wide pine forests, the trees tall, close together, the sun flickering through as we drove by. We passed a storehouse for butane tanks, silver capsules stacked in neat pyramids, then a cluster of earth movers where a foundation was being laid, a huge crane sitting immobile over a swamp, its line in the water. A sign pointed with a diagonal arrow up an uneven dirt road: *Antioch Baptist Church Welcome.* And suddenly, from behind distant trees, two giant smokestacks sent white smoke billowing straight up out of the dark green pine. A young Black man sat two rows in front of me — there were only six or seven other passengers on the bus — and he looked out the window all the way, barely stirring, his right leg propped up, his elbow resting on his knee, his chin in his hand, watching. Metallic gray clouds, long and irregular, drifted across the sun. In an open field, a basketball backboard and bent hoop rose on a pole among weeds. Then, up ahead, a wreck, the bus slowing. A heavyset man in his sixties walked up the road alongside us — he was holding a bloody handkerchief to his temple. Farther down the road, we passed a small trailer park, far from town. A man in a cap and plaid jacket stood outside, regarding the clouds moving across the sky.

I read. "How can a culture be created in . . . which every child is expected to be as good as possible in his or her mathematical development?"

We drove through Aberdeen, West Point — the names crisp on elevated water towers — Columbus, Starkville, Louisville, Philadelphia, Carthage, and Canton. We passed endless franchises (KFC, McDonald's, Hardees, Waffle House, Popeye's, Burger King, Wendy's), and factory outlets, and video stores: *Hard Target, Last Action Hero.* We drove into old business districts, for the Greyhound depots were usually in the center of the city, taking up half of a small building, the other half a café or dress shop or appliance store or barbecue restaurant, the stove pipe angling skyward with tin elbow-joints, wired to the roof. Some of the businesses were closed down or sparsely decorated, faded cardboard enticements propped up in their windows. Stoplights hung from wires dipping across intersections. There were only a few people on the street, as cash flowed to the malls on the outskirts of town. Some of these places had violent civil rights histories. It was just outside of Philadelphia that James Chaney, Andrew Goodman, and Michael Schwerner were murdered. We drove down Beacon Street past the Mississippi Tarp Company, the Save Inn, WHOC Radio, a Conoco station, the Beacon Street Baptist Church. Along the side streets were nice frame houses and trees. Across from the minimart, where the driver stopped for a soda, Jack's

Car Wash sat, closed. *Try us!* a hand-painted sign beckoned. *Affordable!* As we pulled away, heading out of the city, sun glinted off windshields in a small used-car lot, a single strip of green flags fluttered in the breeze. I wondered if this was the road they were on. Their station wagon run off the highway, burned. Their bodies buried in an earthen dam.

"Students of arithmetic have in their minds one question that they associate with counting numbers: 'how many?' Students of algebra need to have two: 'how many?' and another question, such as 'which way?' . . . Children understand the question, 'which way?' from their early years, but it is not a question they associate with number."

Soon after leaving Canton, exiting under a bridge and onto South 55, we saw signs announcing the Jackson city limit. Billboards loomed quickly at the window, reflecting some of the current contradictions in Mississippi: *Prayer in Our Schools* and, a moment later, *Isle of Capri Casino — Vicksburg.* It was a state of incredible social complexity. During a brief visit with Jacque Rogers, an English teacher at Collins High School — about a third of the way between Hattiesburg and Jackson — I had watched, within the space of a few class periods, a student video memorializing a local recipient of the Purple Heart and listened as a girl sobbed her way through a bitter, despairing poem her father had written about his tour of duty in Vietnam. I heard a smart rap on Septima Clark — ". . . a mother to my nation/She taught my ancestors so they could control their destination" — listened as a girl, in passionate discussion of a Maya Angelou poem, revealed how frequently she still heard the word "nigger," and watched a group of Black and White students energetically rehearse a video script entitled "America: A Cultural Kaleidoscope."

The highway began to widen, and suddenly there was all this concrete, a sweep of freeways — the curving on-ramps, the sleek diagonal overpass. And there was height. The Ramada Plaza Hotel. The tallest building I'd seen yet in the state. With a population of 197,000, Jackson was the largest city in Mississippi — four times larger than the next, Biloxi — and the state's primary center for trade, finance, and capital formation. The next morning I would be visiting a school located in the economically depressed west side of the city, Brinkley Middle School, 630 students, almost all African American. From there, I would travel north through the Delta, a two-hundred-mile stretch of flat, fertile land that begins at the intersection of the Mississippi and Yazoo rivers, west of Jackson, close to Vicksburg, and extends northward to the Tennessee border. Plantation culture flourished in the Delta, and, in some ways, the area still exhibits the social and political hierarchy and the economic stratification of the Old South.

Picture twelve chairs in a circle, each with a number and a sign from the Chinese Zodiac taped to it: the monkey, the rooster, the pig, the dragon. Lynn Moss's sixth-graders in Room 216 at Brinkley Middle School had been discovering some interesting things about the cycles of years connected to each sign — learning that numbers are orderly, patterned, and that therefore you can make generalizations about them. They were now preparing to play a game involving the concept of equivalence that would show them how a physical event can be transformed into an equation, an introduction to the act of symbolic representation.

Here's how the game, called the Winding Game, is played. The monkey chair at the top of the circle is designated *zero.* A walk around the eleven remaining chairs — one complete lap, or "wind" — is the equivalent of twelve chairs or signs. The students work in teams, and take turns selecting a peer to walk the circle, the "winder." The winder picks a number between 0 and 144 and proceeds to walk off that number through a combination of laps and remaining chairs; the additional chairs are called the "residue," and it will be between 0 and 11. The other teams have to determine the original number and represent it with a simple formula. Randolf, for example, chose 54, so, head down, concentrating, a loose shoelace dragging after his deliberate step, he walked off four full laps past the monkey chair (which would be the equivalent of the number 48) and continued to the tiger chair, chair number 6, the residue. The other teams quickly recorded the number of winds and the residue and then formally represented what they saw with the formula W (number of winds) x 12 + Res (residue)=—. As one girl explained to me, "This is like algebra."

The children played the game vigorously, and everyone seemed engaged. Some stood on tiptoe to get a clear look at the winder. Some used the eraser end of their pencils as a pointer, ticking off each rotation in the air. Some bickered among themselves over the accuracy of what they were seeing — and arriving at agreement is central to the Algebra Project, for it illustrates how mathematics is a human enterprise, procedures and symbolic notations emerging out of trial and deliberation and consensus.

The class played four or five rounds in all, the designated winders walking off 50, then 86, then 37. One winder had a big cyst on his neck — and, Lynn later told me, had a police record. Another boy wore a gauze bandage on his forearm; his mother, Lynn said, had been on a gambling tear for three days. A girl with little gold hearts in her braids squinted when she tried to read the numbers. Some children had thick, rasping coughs. On the way to Brinkley the cabbie had driven through blocks where half the houses were boarded up or gutted, the shells of old cars rusting in vacant lots. Some of the boys and girls in Lynn's class looked to be very poor: threadbare pants or dresses, worn shoes, mismatched socks, the elastic gone limp, ashen skin. The class was of "mixed ability," so it included kids who were designated "slow learners," several of whom were being mainstreamed from special ed. Lynn had paired one of the special ed children with a tall, lean boy, one of the children whose shirt and trousers looked worn, off-size. His voice was already changing, and he had a serious, methodical way about him, watching the winders closely, quickly catching on to the use of the formula. Without much fanfare, he led the other boy through the procedure, talking it out with him, then watching as, after one mistrial, he successfully played the Winding Game.

From here, Lynn Moss's class would continue with activities that introduced the concepts of displacement (and eventually learn methods to add displacements), benchmark (and the role of consensus in establishing benchmarks), comparison (particularly the systematic comparison of features or properties), opposites (and the use of positive and negative integers), and location, relation, and positionality ("all position is relative position"). As well, they would continue to create symbolic representations of events and procedures and consider "how mathematicians construct models for physical space."

"The big difference," Lynn explained during her break, "between regular math and the Algebra Project is the level of the kids' involvement. I know in my heart what school reform should look like — and this is as close as I've seen." She leaned on the back of the chair of the dragon. "My hope is that as teachers see what kids can do, it'll change the way they perceive them, change what they think is possible."

A man about five-ten, a little weight on him, salt-and-pepper hair, goatee, glasses, was applying masking tape in precise strips to the linoleum floor of Debbie Murphy's seventh-grade classroom at Lockard Middle School in Indianola, the seat for Sunflower County in the heart of the Mississippi Delta. He bent at the waist, one leg straight back, the other forward about twenty degrees, knee locked, the legs of a caliper, silent, concentrating, laying down another strip of tape, and another, creating what looked like a complex pathway or mathematical tree. There was a triangular hub in the middle with three rays or paths extending outward, then three more paths radiating from the tips of each of these lines, then from the tips of each of those, three more paths again. From above, it resembled an urban planner's sketch of a transportation system.

Bob Moses stood back regarding the tree, then popped the top off a black marker and began labeling each of the elements. He printed "start" on the sides of the triangular hub. He wrote 0, +1, -1 on each of the three paths radiating from it. He straightened up again, looking at the tree, then bent back to it, turning to the next cluster of rays, and the next, labeling each 0, +1, -1, so that, when he was finished, and he could hear the murmur and thump of Debbie's kids coming down the hall . . . by then he was, with hand to lips, regarding a tree with thirty-nine labeled paths radiating from a triangular starting point. He stood over the triangle as the seventh-graders jammed through the door. "Be careful of the flagway," he said softly, looking up with wide, delicate eyes. "Try not to step on the flagway."

The students in Mrs. Murphy's class had gone through the first year of the Algebra Project when they were in the sixth grade, so Bob was coming to them now to field-test a new game, a more advanced activity for the curriculum he was currently developing. Debbie had made arrangements to keep the class for several periods on this day so that there would be adequate time. She was in her late twenties, pulled her blond hair back into a ponytail, wore earrings in the shape of a Celtic cross, a blue denim work shirt, black jeans. She moved easily, warmly among her students — half of them Black, half White, one Latino — chatting, addressing small queries, running a hand over a shoulder, a forearm. Bob would take the class today. Debbie would assist him and orchestrate the schedule, but mostly hang back, observe, assess, and confer with him. Bob, in turn, would check his perceptions with Debbie, for it was teachers like her, skillful practitioners, working day to day, who had enabled him to refine and implement the Algebra Project.

It would be a long morning, for the game, at this stage of development, was elaborate and involved a number of interlinking procedures. The students knew Bob from previous visits. He walked over to Mrs. Murphy's desk, leaned against it, and, in an informal but not chatty voice, asked someone to define the concept of prime number. Different members of the class did it readily: a number that has only two factors, 1 and itself. The class worked in groups, so Bob asked the groups to write down as many prime numbers as they knew. Then they reported in: 3, 5, 7, 11, 13, 17, and so on. When one number appeared that, in fact, was not a prime number, Bob used it as an occasion for discussion, a test case. And the class took a few minutes, argued pro and con, worked out a factor tree, and arrived at an answer. Bob's academic training was in analytic philosophy (he had pursued doctoral studies at Harvard), so he has imbued the Algebra Project with an exploratory, contemplative ethos. An answer is not automatically dismissed as wrong, but is considered by the class, examined, worked through. Then its truth or utility is determined.

Once Bob was assured that all the students had an operational knowledge of prime numbers, he was ready to begin the game. Students were to select any three numbers from an array of numbers he and Debbie provided and determine their prime factors. These prime factors would become the "input" numbers that would generate one of three arbitrary "output" numbers that would move the students through the pathway Bob had taped to the floor. Here's how it worked. If one of the prime factors of a number is repeated (for example, the primes 3, 3, 2 for 18), then the "output" number is 0. If a number has only two prime factors (for example, 51 has 3 and 17), then the output number is +1. If a number has one prime factor (for example, 41), then the output number is -1. Once the groups had worked their factor trees and determined output numbers, they were ready for the pathway — the flagway, as Bob called it. Using tape and toothpicks, they made little flags on which they wrote the three output numbers their original numbers had generated (for example, 0, +1, -1) and walked the paths of the flagway. So the student with the 0, +1, -1 flag — a tall girl wearing an oversized baseball jersey — began at the triangular hub, stepped along the ray marked 0, took a quick turn at +1, squeaked sharply on the linoleum at -1, and ended up at the tip of -1, the "station" where she placed her flag.

For the next phase of the activity, Bob shifted to an object made with small Unifix cubes that mapped the two-dimensional flagway onto a three-dimensional structure. The Unifix construction looked something like the skeleton of a tiered building. There was a tall foundational column, a central spine from which jutted rows or pathways of increasing length. The rows formed with this central column a 90 degree angle. Short pathways further connected the rows, forming other 90 degree intersections. The columns of the structure were red and designated 0; the rows going in one direction were yellow and designated -1; the rows in the other direction were green and designated +1. Bob spent a little time having one student walk a series of output numbers on the flagway while another student traced that series along the three-dimensional structure.

From here the game became more layered with a number of procedures that I won't try to detail. The broad sketch is this. Students continued to factor numbers into their primes and convert those primes into the output numbers 0, +1, -1, but they added in several steps whereby they further translated those output numbers into simple algebraic notation: 0 = a, +1 = b, -1 = c. This introduced the concept of *power*, for a series like 0, 0, +1 would be presented as a^2b, and the students saw that either numerical or algebraic notation brought a flag to the same station. They also, by now, were seeing that a whole array of numbers were yielding a limited number of combinations — as the girl in the baseball jersey put it, "Why are all the flags ending up in just a few places?"

The way teams scored points got a little complicated — Bob was still working all this out — but basically they got points for each of the numbers they could factor into primes, convert into output numbers, and locate on the three-dimensional structure. Debbie's class was at this game for over two hours, and, from start to finish, it involved a number of interlinking operations. There was one time when Bob had to quiet a team of giggling girls and another when Debbie had to urge a boy to concentrate, but otherwise the entire class was focused and energized. Kids rushed to get their numbers, team members urged each other on as they worked out factor trees, students walked the flagway, traced paths on the Unifix cube structure, shifted between symbolic designations (using 0, 0, +1 at one moment, a^2b the next), and began noticing patterns, distributions, combinations.

Bob had been working with pathways for some time. (The trip on the train or bus that opens the first unit of the Algebra Project curriculum is mapped onto a simple pathway.) And he had been puzzling over ways to introduce those aspects of finite mathematics dealing with prime numbers, probabilities, and multinomials. During a recent plane ride, a connection hit him. "We had been doing these other activities with train and bus systems, with pathways and trees, and I saw how we could use that to demonstrate some things about prime numbers and combinatorics." So he began working on the flagwalk game. He tested and retested it — like a playwright going before one audience, then another, to sharpen revision. What struck me as I watched Debbie Murphy's seventh-graders play the game — other than their obvious engagement with the activity — was the number of skills they demonstrated and the number of topics that could be later addressed by Debbie as the class talked over all they had done. They systematically moved through an interlocking set of procedures. They played with representations and models, mapping one onto another. They converted from one notation to another. They determined prime factors and began to see patterns and distributions in numbers.

Math teachers will tell you what a disaster that shift from arithmetic to algebra can be. It is not uncommon to watch half a class drift into failure as they confront a different mode of symbolic notation and operation. Debbie Murphy herself tells a personal tale of failure. "The very first time I encountered algebra, the teacher wrote $2 + 3 = a$ on the board and asked, 'What is *a*?' I had no idea what that meant: *a* is *a*, I thought. She then told us that *a* equaled 5. So I raised my hand and asked if *a* equaled 5, then what would *b* equal? You see, I thought *a* must equal 5 *all* the time. Well, she ridiculed me, made a total idiot out of me. I went home and cried. I'll tell you, that's what brought me into teaching, compelled me, you could say." There was no small irony in the fact that Debbie grew up twenty miles north, in Ruleville, home of the voter-registration activist Fannie Lou Hamer, and was sent to, sheltered in, private schools there. She had limited knowledge of the events that shaped Bob Moses's political life. But these days, unpredictable alliances are possible in Mississippi. "The place is shot through with ambiguities," a native told me. So Debbie Murphy and Bob Moses tried to figure out how to ease that shift from arithmetic to algebra, Debbie working from her skill and commitment and her own knowledge of hurt and confusion. "When I saw the Algebra Project," she said, "I knew exactly what it was trying to do."

Highway 61, the route the old blues musicians used to travel from town to town, snaked back south through the Delta, past harvested soy bean, corn, and wheat fields, past cotton fields, bare but for residual wisps of fiber on the branches, past an occasional tractor and an elevated irrigation device called a center pivot, poised over the bare land like a giant tubular insect. There were endless catfish farms cut into the land, broad levied ponds, almost glasslike in the morning sun, the crisp, still air of winter. "The new plantations," a friend of mine called them. *Farm fresh,* the signs read, *grain fed.*

WELCOME TO HOLLANDALE. At thirty-five hundred, Hollandale was a fair-sized Delta town. It was one of the places those musicians used to play. The highway led onto Old Creek Road, then Old Highway 61, past modest frame houses — white, cream, gray blue, an occasional screened sun porch. A right turn off this road took you through downtown Hollandale, a block of stores with ornate chipped façades, the traces of old signs visible behind fading newer ones: an auto shop, an appliance store, a Radio Shack, a temporary holding facility, the Southern Belle Restaurant. Then another block or so through what used to be the edge of town, a cluster of dilapidated buildings, the one-time Blue Front district of juke joints — echoes of the Mississippi Sheiks, a young Howlin' Wolf — mostly vacant now, waiting for the city to secure the funds to level them. Another couple of hundred yards, just outside town, sits Simmons Elementary School, one of the first schools in the Delta to incorporate the Algebra Project into its mathematics curriculum. I was curious to see how the project fit into the life of a particular school.

Simmons Elementary was 95 percent African American — Hollandale was about 65 to 70 percent Black — for White academies were still prevalent in these Delta towns. The school was simple and clean, with plants, both artificial and real, in the office and teachers' lounge, and paintings, old prints, and children's art work in the hallways. There were moral and inspirational maxims, extending on computer printout: "No one can do everything, but everyone can do something." These were the work of the principal, Robert Woodruff. During my stay at Simmons, I got to talk with Mr. Woodruff, with students, and with a parent, Sandra Howard, who had attended Simmons herself and who, as she baby-sat, gathered kids in her front room to work on Algebra Project assignments. I also talked with the school's curriculum coordinator, a resourceful woman named Margaret Fields, who was born and raised just up Highway 61 in Arcola. And I met the district superintendent, Howard Sanders, a man who blended a full smile with a tough mind and who chaired the Delta advisory board for the Algebra Project. I heard, as one could expect, that the implementation of the project was initially bumpy: integrating it into the existing curriculum took time and retraining, and there were the limitations posed by the state mathematics guidelines, which, though they were about to be revised in a more problem-solving, conceptual direction, were fairly focused on discrete skills and narrow goals. Those implementation problems were working themselves out. I got from the children and from Mrs. Howard various testimonials ("It's fun" "We really learned a lot") and concerns ("It gets difficult" "Sometimes it's too repetitious"). But what most struck me was the way the Algebra Project complemented the school's sense of its own purpose, its place in the community.

The Delta has been a place of profoundly limited opportunity for Black people, and the depth of inequality seems overwhelming. Yet, as has always been the case in the United States, there have been Black-run institutions — public and private — that have stood as a moral and intellectual force against degradation. "You do what you've got to do," Margaret Fields said simply. "We try to develop the belief in this school that while we need to keep the history of the community in mind, and the background of the kids in mind, that's not the *only* thing to keep in mind. What can we do now that the kids are here, with us? How can we make them strong, help them believe that they can make a difference in their community?"

Though some students might be able to continue their schooling successfully and stay in Hollandale — and Superintendent Sanders was seeking ways to link the Algebra Project to local economic development — many young people will have to confront a central tension in rural America and leave home to secure decent employment. In either case, Principal Woodruff saw the mission of his school as developing ability, providing exposure to the new, enhancing choices and options. He and his faculty, for example, tapped a good portion of their resources to arrange field trips to local colleges, to museums, to the municipal airport in Greenville, for some of the children have never seen an airplane. Margaret Fields coordinated a program with a college in New York to improve the school's curriculum. And both Robert Woodruff and Superintendent Sanders have supported faculty development programs and conference participation that fed back into instruction. The methodology and the political and social assumptions of the Algebra Project fit perfectly with the beliefs that drove Simmons Elementary School. This confluence was clear in many of the things the students said about the travel activities connected to the Algebra Project, about their sense of themselves as learners, and about their perception of the future: "We see a lot of things we never saw before." "We make new friends, and they become pen pals." "I like going to the different colleges." "The kids at Arcola ask us what [algebra] is like, what do we learn, where do we go?" "Math'll take you a long way in life." "My mom thinks it's great because it prepares me for the future — she wants me to teach it to her."

There were well over a hundred people in the gymnasium of West Tallahatchie High School: teachers, middle and high school students, little kids, many parents, some civic leaders, including two newly elected county supervisors. It was about six in the evening. Outside, the sun had dipped below the horizon and was suffusing a pink-salmon light over sheds and bare trees and small houses off the road. We sat close to one another at round and rectangular tables clustered along one long wall. In front of us were two small chalkboards on rollers and an easel with a large pad. The school was located in Webb, in Tallahatchie County, about eighty miles northeast of Hollandale. It was a very poor community, Cass Pennington, the district superintendent, told me. One of the poorest in the South. I would hear from others that it was also one of the most economically and politically entrenched. It was not too long ago that the county leadership kept discouraging desperately needed small industry because it might threaten the supply of cheap agricultural labor. The two supervisors — who were now being introduced —were the first Black supervisors to be elected in the history of this predominantly African-American county. The school was virtually all African American. Many of the parents in this room went to schools that were segregated by law; now school was segregated by demographic fact.

Shirley Conner was coordinating this meeting, explaining its purpose, introducing folks around. It was essential to the Algebra Project that parents be pulled into the process to see what was possible and become advocates for it. Shirley, a teacher at Simmons High School, adjacent to Simmons Elementary in Hollandale, was also working for the project as an "implementation specialist," driving the expanse of the Delta to help new teachers integrate the curriculum into their classes. She was a handsome woman in her late thirties, rich brown skin, a keen, direct intelligence. She had been at it all day — her days now ran ten to twelve hours, sometimes longer — and you could see the exhaustion in her graceful delivery. Bob Moses was off in the corner, talking with two co-workers from the early biracial days of the Student Nonviolent Coordinating Committee, Hollis Watkins and Mike Sayer, both of whom were now involved with Southern Echo, a community-leadership development program based in Jackson. They saw the Algebra Project as a continuation, an extension of the work that caught them up so long ago.

"I imagine a lot of you already know Mr. Bob Moses," Shirley said, extending her left hand behind her. Bob walked to the side of the easel. He, too, looked beat. "Hi, everybody," he said softly. "How are you?" People murmured in response and acknowledgment. "I want to start us off tonight with an activity." He gestured to the floor of the gym, where he had laid out with masking tape a flagwalk like the one he had used with Debbie Murphy's seventh graders. "But first, a question." He walked closer to the tables, looking around, a slow gaze. "What is a prime number?" A boy to the far right raised his hand. Bob asked his name: Martin. "OK, Martin, what is a prime number?" "A prime number," Martin replied, a little nervous but intent and well-spoken, "is a number that can only be multiplied by one and itself." Bob thanked him. "Does anyone else have anything to add to what Martin just said?" Tyranda, on the other side of the room, raised her hand. "A prime number," she offered, "is a number that can only be *divided* by one and itself." Bob unfolded his arms, cradling his chin in his right hand: "Why don't you both come on up here." They did, the audience watched, shifting, scraping a few chairs to improve their line of sight.

"Pick a prime number, Tyranda," Bob instructed, and Tyranda wrote 11 on the pad. "Now show me how what you said holds true. But first, repeat what you said, nice and loud." Tyranda did, then, marker in hand, wrote $11 \div 1 = 11$ $11 \div 11 = 1$. "There's no other numbers that'll go into 11," she summarized, putting down the marker. Bob turned to Martin. "Martin?" "Yes sir." "Demonstrate for me what you said." Martin took the marker from Tyranda and talked as he wrote. "You can get 11 if you times it by 1, but there are no other numbers you can multiply to get it." Bob turned to Tyranda. "What do you think of what Martin just said?" Bob's voice, the whole time, remained at the same pitch and volume, steady, curious. It's hard not to lead, not to give away a bias when you question, but Bob came awfully close to sounding neutral. "He's talking about multiplying," Tyranda observed, "but I'm saying you get prime numbers by dividing." Though there were glitches in both Martin's and Tyranda's use of multiplication and division, they clearly knew how prime numbers worked. Bob saw that, didn't want to shut things down, wanted to keep inviting talk.

He turned to the audience, asking for questions and comments. One parent raised her hand. "Are all odd numbers prime numbers?" "Well," Bob replied, "let's see." He asked her to pick an odd number. She picked 9. Bob wrote it on the board and asked her to guide him through a factor tree. As she watched the tree develop she said, "No, no, it ain't a prime number." A woman sitting at our table thanked Bob and the lady, for, she said, she had always confused prime numbers and odd numbers, too. The community was talking about mathematics.

A man from the side of the room stood halfway up and called the group's attention back to Martin and Tyranda. "Isn't the important operation there?" he said, pointing to the work the children had done, "Isn't it division more than multiplication?" Bob turned to Martin. "Martin, did you hear what he said? He didn't like your multiplication idea too much. Can you say why?" Martin stated the man's position but noted that multiplication might still work. Then a parent from the table next to ours, a pencil over his ear, suggested that Martin and company break another number into its prime factors. "It's been a long time," he noted apologetically as he sat down, and a lot of people laughed and assented.

Bob asked the audience for a number. "Eighteen," someone called out. He turned to Martin, and Martin proceeded to work out a factor tree.

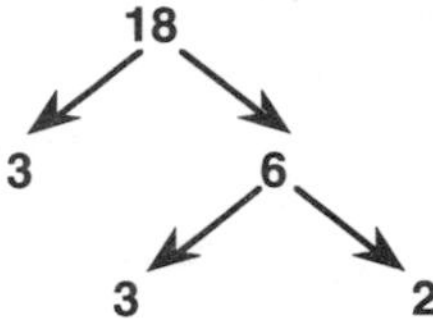

Someone standing along the wall asked if there was another way to do it. Bob handed Tyranda a marker and asked if she saw another way. She thought a moment, then:

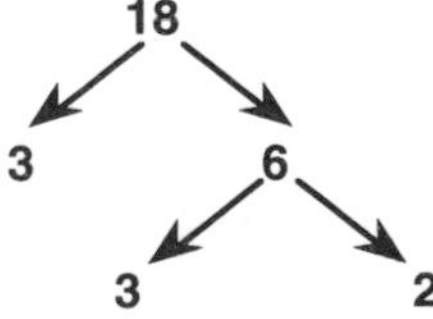

A woman sitting by the easel spoke up. "What's the difference?" she asked. "You still get the same numbers. See what I'm sayin'? You still get two 3s and a 2." A man sitting by her turned and said, "But what I see is that 18 have other factors other than 3 and 2." "OK, the first woman replied. "but you still come out with the same prime numbers . . ."

There was some further discussion; then Bob had each table choose three numbers and calculate factor trees. Then he turned and gestured to the floor. "I put a flagway on the floor up here, and we're going to figure out what it's got to do with your prime numbers."

It was about eight when we broke up. The participants remained in clusters, talking: parents, teachers, students, the county supervisors, the folks from Southern Echo. Bob, head down, listening, was conferring with Shirley Conner. I stood in the doorway, looking out into sweeping darkness, light from a farmhouse or two twinkling in the distance. People were shaking out coats, buttoning up, saying goodbye. "This was wonderful," a woman said, coming up alongside me. "The parents learned something, too. Math is a scary thing, you know. But . . ." And here she turned, her eye catching something, suddenly quizzical. I followed her line of sight to a poster with a funny little cartoon cat peering out of a paper bag. "But now," she said laughing, "the, the cat's out of the bag! It's something we all can do."

8

Polaris and Missoula, Montana

THE TWO-LANE HIGHWAY extended with an intermittent dip and rise as far as I could see, no cars coming or going, a clear band of asphalt running pasture beyond pasture. On either side of State Highway 278 were grasslands and grazing cattle, creeks and ponds, bales of hay and isolated haystacking machines called "beaverslides"; beyond that grew clumps of brush and a little juniper. Then came rolling meadows, then foothills and fir trees, rising in the far distance to snow-covered mountains, crisp and striking. In addition to cattle, there were occasional sheep, deer, magpies with white-tipped wing and tail, coyote, sandhill cranes, and two humpbacked moose making their way into willow.

I was traveling with Claudette Morton, director of the Rural Education Center at Western Montana College in Dillon, the seat of this county called Beaverhead, the largest in Montana, as big as Rhode Island and Connecticut combined, with a population of eighty-four hundred, half of whom lived in Dillon. We were headed northwest to a one-room school near the ghost town of Polaris, in the middle of the Grasshopper Valley, surrounded by the Beaverhead National Forest. There are nearly a hundred single-teacher elementary schools in Montana alone, Claudette told me, and another sixty or so schools with two to four teachers, combining children from more than one grade level in a single classroom. It's the scale, the size of the land, she explained, and the population density. Montana is the fourth largest state in the union, yet has a population of just under 800,000 — and a large proportion reside in and around a dozen or so cities. Vast stretches of the state, especially in the eastern plains, are sparsely populated. By one rough estimate, there is in Montana about one kindergarten-through-twelfth-grade student per square mile. So the single-teacher elementary, the current incarnation of the one-room country school that for a good part of our history defined nonurban public education, is still a necessity. Approximately 830 such schools are to be found in half of the states in the union, Maine to California, the largest numbers in Nebraska, Montana, and South Dakota, states with expansive, sparsely populated rural landscape.

The drive to Polaris out of Dillon was just over thirty-five miles and took about forty-five minutes, though the time varied depending on weather — at about 6500 feet Claudette had to slow to fifteen miles per hour as we passed through clouds that surrounded us in thick whiteness. There were always potential delays, even in good weather. One morning Claudette's husband, George, and I encountered a transfer of cattle from one pasture to another, somewhere between seventy-five and a hundred cows and calves lumbering along the highway, mooing, bleating, breaking into a heavy trot as George tried to inch his way through, an occasional cowboy assisting our passage.

The one-room schoolhouse has been characterized many ways in our history: as a symbol of progress, as the forge of rural culture, as, in Hamlin Garland's words, "a barren temple of the arts," as provincial and backward. It was all these things and more — a complex institution. What is clear, though, is that since before the turn of this century, there has been a systematic attempt to close down these little schools, to consolidate them into larger systems. In 1910 there were 200,000 one-teacher schools in the United States; fifty years later that number dropped to 23,695. The consolidation was driven by shifts in population and the disrepair of older buildings, by unfavorable comparison with the large urban (or suburban) school and its multiple facilities and services, and by the desire of policymakers to concentrate control and to achieve uniformity and efficiency in finance and governance. ("The best," asserted an influential big city superintendent, "is the best everywhere.") Recent analyses of rural education have undermined the assumption that big is necessarily more effective — and, in many quarters, as we have seen, the model of the large urban school is under attack. But the drive for consolidation continues (in Montana there were 820 one-teacher schools recorded in a 1958–59 survey; by 1984 there were 99), held at bay only in those areas where citizens can organize and argue that distance, transportation, weather, and community need make it impossible to close their local school. This battle has been going on across rural America for over a hundred years, and is basically a conflict between local control — governance by a small independent school board that has say over location, hiring, curriculum, resources, and policies — and control by more distant governing bodies and agencies that redistribute (and attempt to equalize) resources, certify and hire teachers, establish curriculum and policy, and determine central, strategic (sometimes equally inconvenient) locations for school buildings. Traveling to Polaris, I began to understand the conflict. At one point, we passed two children waiting at roadside, their house in the distance, off a crooked pathway, no other house in sight. A school bus was coming toward them from the north, red lights flashing.

As Claudette and I ascended into the national forest, it began to snow, flurries coming at the windshield in an upward curl, light powder on the highway, light as confectioner's sugar, blowing in rippling waves across the road. Claudette steadied herself — she knew the snowfall would get heavier — and continued talking about the region and about rural schools. It seemed that people were finally beginning to appreciate the potential of small schools, she said, the possibilities of individualized instruction, independent work, children tutoring other children. And the close attention, the intimate connection of school and community. Nobody gets lost. For a long time, it was just assumed that kids from these rural schools got an inadequate education and did poorly as they moved on. Anything so small and so country had to be inferior. While it is true that the transition to larger town high schools can be a problem, some new studies, and reviews of old ones, suggest that, on average, children from rural schools do as well as everybody else. And in some cases, from some schools or regions, they do better. These little schools have gotten, Claudette believed, a bad rap.

We passed two large ranches, cattle dotting broad snow-covered pastures, and came on the unmarked dirt road, white now, that led to Polaris, veering suddenly off Highway 278. It curved for about four miles through grassland and shrubbery, past old fences and sporadic power poles. Polaris, named after the polestar, or North Star, at the tip of the handle of the Little Dipper, was, in the mid-1880s, a silver-mining town, not too far north of the region being homesteaded by some of the families who, today, hold two or three of the largest ranches in the area. Polaris was now the site of a post office, a house owned by an old cowboy named Walt Melcher, and the Polar Bear, once run by Walt and his wife, closed these days — though Walt would open it for the occasional traveler who needed a drink to cut the chill. Polaris School, about a mile south of the town, was established in 1892 — four and five generations of some local families have attended it — and the first variation of the present schoolhouse was erected in 1925. A teacherage was built onto the side of the school by one Junior Stallings in 1949 — before that, teachers boarded with local families — and a first-year teacher named Andy Bayliss now lived and worked there, finishing up the last month of a one-year contract.

Claudette had hooked me up with Andy because, though he was still finding his way, he was already a knowledgeable and creative teacher who played to the strengths of the one-room school. On Claudette's recommendation, I had read some books and articles — ones sympathetic to rural education — that lamented the unimaginative nature of instruction in some rural classrooms: materials were limited and dated, resources were scarce, teaching practices tended toward recitation and rote learning, without much variability. This was not always the fault of the teachers. Some were isolated, out of contact with other teachers or teacher-education institutions. Publishers produced few materials geared toward rural schools — too diverse and diffused to be a lucrative market. And community norms sometimes constrained experimentation. But Andy was inventive and ambitious, eager to extend what children could do. On this day of my stay with him I was going to try to record the flow of his practice, capture a day in the life of this rural schoolteacher and his students.

Even with the delays, Claudette and I got to Polaris early, pulling in through an open gate, rolling to a stop by the wooden walkway that led to the school. She set the brake, and I opened the door, confirming that I would ride back to Dillon with Andy, who would be needing supplies and a little company. She handed me a package of materials to give to him and pulled away, leaving no other sound but a meadowlark and the soft rippling of Farlin Creek, running amid sedges and willows along the northern border of the school yard. Just beyond the creek, behind a simple fence, cows, powdered with snow, stood quietly, nosing the ground.

Polaris School faced the road. It was a neat frame building, clapboard siding, gray with white trim, with a raised front porch and a dormer jutting out from a pitched roof. There was a large propane tank on the side and, farther back, an old log barn from the days when students rode their horses to school. Behind the school was a swing set and slide, a tool shed, also gray and white, and an abbreviated basketball court. A boy, an early arrival, dressed in a slicker and cowboy hat, was shooting baskets, finding his footing on the slippery concrete, propelling the wet ball in a heavy arc through the air.

Andy Bayliss sat at the table closest to the tall windows in the back wall of the schoolhouse, eating a bowl of cereal, listening to Peanuts Wilson on an old rockabilly tape he had found in the discount bin at the Safeway in Dillon, gazing out beyond the silhouette of Tyler shooting baskets to the sharp, white peak of Bald Mountain. In the midst of this vast expanse of meadow and mountain, Andy lived in tight quarters. The teacherage had a separate entrance, leading to a narrow living room, a desk covered with textbooks and school supplies, a couch, a VCR and stacks of videotapes, six pairs of skis. Off to one side was a bedroom only partly closed off from the classroom, the dividing wall running three quarters of the way to the ceiling. Straight through the living room was a kitchen — skillets, loose dishes, canned goods — that, through a rear door, led to the restrooms Andy shared with his students.

So Andy liked to come into the classroom early, put a cassette into the radio-tape player, and look out at the mountains. Morning light flooded across the counter along the base of the windows: rocks, sprouting geraniums, a microscope and slides, a spider plant sitting on the *New World Dictionary.* Andy Bayliss was the sixty-first teacher to lead instruction at Polaris School. He bobbed his head in time with the slapping bass, the wailing, stuttering saxophone, enjoying the full light, a lick of his brown hair sticking straight up.

His day was about to begin.

Eight-twenty, and Andy saw James and Russell joining Tyler on the basketball court. The three oldest boys in the school, all good athletes. He clicked off the tape and rinsed his bowl and spoon. The troublesome tuft of hair would not lie down. His slacks were already dusty with chalk. He was a meticulous planner, charting curriculum for each of his fifteen students — they ranged from second grade to eighth — and writing on the blackboard daily schedules and lists of assignments for various groups of children. This was the general plan for today:

8:30	Morning Business
9:00	Math 7, Math 3–4
9:30	Habitat Studies, Montana Studies
10:00	Snack, Recess
10:20	Math 5–6, Montana Studies
11:00	Science
11:30	Silent Reading
12:00	Lunch
12:30	Native American Role Play
1:30	Art
2:30	Track
3:15	*Ciao*

In addition, there were recommended readings, due dates, page numbers in textbooks. The class, as Andy conceived it, wouldn't work without such detail, such clarity of expectation.

To successfully teach children from so many grade levels required the ability to manage a classroom efficiently and resourcefully. It was common for Andy to conduct a lesson for one group of children while the remainder worked separately or in pairs on math problems or reading assignments or on an art or science project begun earlier in the week. Andy was fortunate to have a skillful aide, Michele Reynolds, who could assist those children working independently. Or she could tutor Colt, the one second-grader, or James, the sole eighth-grade student. Or she could seclude herself in the tiny library attached to the classroom to prepare materials for children who needed more time with one lesson or were ready to move ahead on another, beyond the assignment, beyond grade level. There were also multiple possibilities for students helping other students, tapping into their own experience and achievement, pairing one of the older kids with one of the younger to listen to a story or review math homework or edit a piece of writing. And Andy and Michele could split the class, Andy explaining a project for Montana Studies to the fifth- through eight-graders while Michele played a math game with the younger children. Sometimes things got a little hectic — I was reminded of a description of a nineteenth-century country school where "the teacher was mending pens for one class . . . hearing another spell . . . [and] calling a covey of small boys to be quiet" — but, overall, there was a good deal of effective individualized instruction as well as movement in and out of groups, a fluid configuration. It is interesting to note that such practice is currently receiving a good deal of attention in teacher education programs; in the good multigrade classroom, it exists of necessity.

At 8:30 sharp, Andy led the class in the Pledge of Allegiance, then asked them to choose a song. This was a morning ritual. On this day, a number of the children wanted to hear country singer Alan Jackson, a favorite in this community, so Dustin, a fourth-grader, clattered through the pile of cassettes by the tape player and selected "Chattahoochee":

> Way down yonder on the Chattahoochee
> It gets hotter than a hootchie-kootchie

Almost everyone knew the words, or at least the driving chorus, so the class, squeezed into a soft couch facing the blackboard or sitting on the floor with backs against it, sang about a wild Friday night all the way across the United States. When the song was over, Andy reached up for a map over the blackboard, pulled it down with a *flap*, and traced the Chattahoochee River, running his finger along the Alabama-Georgia border. "See? That's the river he's singing about. It forms a natural boundary." Then Andy chose a song, a traditional one, from a loose cluster of lyric sheets he had hanging by the piano and asked Melissa to put another cassette in the player. A scratchy piano came on, and a woman's voice announced "The Little Black Bull." Andy stood by the lyrics, hand under the first line, and the class began:

> Oooooh, the little black bull
> came down the meadow . . .
> a long time ago . . .

Andy followed the lyrics with his right hand, pumping his left arm, bending at the knees. The class sang over the piano, some voices off key, some too loud, lively: *a long time agoooo . . .*

At 8:45 it was on to the business of the day. Andy briefly reviewed another list on the board. There was the matter of the spelling folders, each student's personal "dictionary" of misspelled words, culled from various projects and essays. These had to be shown to Mrs. Reynolds today or tomorrow. There was the reminder to include all drafts of a paper when it's turned in. And there was lost and found: a sparkling blue pencil, a chisel, *To Kill A Mockingbird.* Then a quick survey of who owed work in mathematics, in Montana Studies, in science. The children listened, asked a question or two, affirmed or disputed or negotiated their assignments and due dates.

It was not uncommon in rural schools like Polaris for children to miss days during county fair or hunting season or branding or vacations that couldn't be planned around the school calendar. School (and this has always been true of schooling in rural America) had to adjust to the rhythms and demands of the region. Normally, Andy had a class of fifteen, but this week Crystal, a talented sixth-grader with a sweet disposition ("a real gift to this valley," Andy called her), was away with her family visiting relatives in western Washington. That left Andy with fourteen.

Of the fourteen, all but one, Colt, the second-grader, had one or more siblings in the room. Tyler, the basketball enthusiast, was a seventh-grader. His strong-willed sister Rossy was in the fourth. His little brother, Leo, with whom he occasionally scrapped, was in the third. Their family had lived in the area for five generations; their mother was head of the three-member school board to which Andy directly reported. Russell, already skilled in rodeo, was in the seventh grade, and his gregarious sister Melissa was in the fourth. Their ancestors also came to the region in the late nineteenth century; the herd of cattle that surrounded Claudette's husband and me belonged to their family. Erica, an avid reader, was in the seventh grade, and her rambunctious brother Dustin in the third; when Erica was absent one morning, Dustin told Andy with barely contained excitement that "she's sicker than heck." James, about to graduate from Polaris School, was a skilled athlete but inconsistent with his studies; his fourth-grade sister Rebecca, or Reba, was a model scholar. Sixth-grader Charlie, a clever writer, was brother to third-grader Clarissa, who was just coming into her own. And Heather, a diligent seventh-grade student, was the polar opposite of her casual, at times testy, fifth-grade brother Stephen.

Most of these children grew up with one another, so familiarity combined with blood to create interpersonal dynamics that were, at times, cooperative and communal. As one local explained, "Cooperation is a necessity in ranch life; everyone has a job, everyone contributes. You can't do it without everybody's help." Thus mutual assistance and cross-age tutoring came almost naturally. When the children were singing "Little Black Bull," Tyler steadied Colt, who was balanced on the arm of the couch, his shadow falling across the older boy; during morning business, Rossy guided Melissa through the textbook to the set of math problems Andy had assigned to her. This sort of thing went on throughout the day. But at other times, a family-style bickering dominated the room: pissy complaints about who was sitting in a particular chair or using a book or tool or simply crossing someone's space. Another rural teacher I met said she had a firm rule: keep brother-and-sister things at home. But the tension was not always between siblings. It was, frankly, hard to fathom or predict — a disruptive spasm in the rhythm of the day — and, for Andy, was "the part of the job that wears you down."

Eight fifty-five and time for the fluoride rinse. Andy walked quickly to his desk and grabbed a plastic bottle of pink liquid. He shook it vigorously. The class moaned. This signaled another routine, a weekly one mandated by the County Health Department for rural schools, so Andy's students knew what to do. There was a rush for coats and sweaters, and a burst out the door to the perimeter of the school yard, behind the old horse barn. Andy distributed little paper cups, poured fluoride all around, asked Russell to keep time, sixty seconds, and everyone swished the fluoride in mock torture, jumping around in the snow, the snow squeaking and crunching, as if something underneath was giving way. The fluoride tingled. Russell eyed his watch. People did the Saint Vitus dance. Rossy chased Leo, Dustin taunted Clarissa, James dusted the snow off a basketball and, cheeks working the vibrant liquid, sank a fifteen-foot set shot. Russell raised five fingers, four, three, two — *spitooie* over the fence, in the snow. Mouths open to the cold air. Tongues wagging. The drama complete. As they were walking back inside, Russell and Tyler each scooped a handful of snow from the base of the slide and sucked on it. Then a stomping of feet, the hanging of coats, and the business for the morning was over.

Seventh-grade math students went to the couch. Third- and fourth-graders went to the back of the room with Michele to play a math game. Colt, whose industry was legend in this room, checked the wall charts for his assignment. Stephen and James worked on their science projects, though Michele had to call them back to the task once or twice. And since, as Andy put it, no resource goes unused out here, I was asked to talk with Charlie about his writing.

The classroom at Polaris School was about twenty-eight by thirty-five feet. If you began at the front of the room, you would have before you the black chalkboard and maps, a rack of books and handouts, and the old piano. Toward the corner there were cupboards and a large heater, run on propane, with a tall silver stovepipe. The intersection of piano and cupboard formed a kind of cubbyhole, and in it was a pile of worn, fluffy pillows where, occasionally, you would find Erica curled up reading a novel. She loved this school, she would tell you if asked. Everyone knows you, and you aren't made to feel stupid, and it's safe. She had a friend near Denver, and that girl talked a lot about kids who already had problems with drugs. At thirteen, Erica's age. But it did get lonely out here. So she studied Spanish by audiotape at night and wrote stories and read.

Continuing along the west wall, you entered the library, an eight-by-twelve-foot room with crammed shelves along three walls: children's and adolescent literature, six different encyclopedias, *National Geographic,* reference books on subjects ranging from plants and rocks and grains to Indians, oceans, music, and light. Back out to the classroom, continuing along the wall through a long anarchy of shelves, both metal and wooden, and tables, card and kitchen, on which you would find glue, scissors, files for rock sculpture, tape, athletic trophies, a poinsettia, rulers, yarn, a three-hole punch, piles of books on Montana, displays of books the students had made, and, finally, a computer in a wooden console.

Turning the next corner, against the south wall, beyond which the teacherage lay, there were blue-green plastic tubs stacked on metal shelves, each tub with a student's name affixed, filled with tools and art supplies. Then a small table with cups full of brushes and a cardboard box of crayons, peeled and broken; the microwave (the school's hot lunch program, Andy joked); and the restrooms and rear entrance to the teacherage. At the southeast corner was a noisy wall heater and a large piece of corkboard on a stand, like a movable blackboard. The corkboard became a flimsy partition, forming another cubby of sorts, and sometimes Russell or Tyler or James or Stephen went there to read under an old parlor lamp. Then came the long counter under the full windows that looked out onto Bald Mountain, the counter rich with plants and field guides and sparkling rocks. Then Andy's desk, the light from the last of the windows slanting over half of it, a bright, warm triangle. Turn around in the desk's swivel chair, the one Andy was now retrieving, and you're facing the blackboard at the front of the room.

Before the blackboard was that fat couch into which the children crammed to sing, and throughout the rest of the room were folding chairs and dark Formica tables. Andy's students moved often from couch to table to rug to nook — the floor creaking beneath their step — or to the library, or outdoors, leaving a trail of paper and pencil and crayon behind them. During the first month or so of the term, some parents and board members visited the room, and, as one put it to me, wondered, "What in God's name was going on here?" Andy had found those tables and chairs in the storeroom — they were used for civic functions — and had replaced the old school desks with them, and there was all this activity. The board was not heavy-handed — Andy enjoyed good relations with them — but that was not a comfortable position for a first-year teacher to be in. Over time, Andy was able to explain in detail and with polite assurance his methods and goals to individual parents and to the board. And after a while, the district came to see that something interesting was going on here.

Student work was on bold display. Along the top third of the west wall, from the jamb of the library door nearly to the computer console, extended a hand-drawn map of the region, embellished in greens and blues and browns. Mountain ranges and rivers were marked, as were roadways, forests, Polaris School, the post office, and each of the children's homes. Over the microwave was a large bar chart depicting the results of six hundred coin tosses, a lesson in probability. There were paper constructions and crayon mosaics, dense and bright, over shelves, by the bathrooms, in small free spaces. There were data sheets on science experiments, and illustrated summaries of novels and short stories, and large interpretive maps drawn up during geography and social studies — like the one of Alaska pinned to the corkboard partition. And above the door of the girls' bathroom was Leo's science lesson *cum* personal narrative, printed on a large piece of brown wrapping paper cut into an irregular circle:

> 1) I am the sun. 2) All of the planets orbit around me. 3) I am the only star you can see in the daytime. 4) I am the hottest object in the solar system. 5) I produce energy.

Student writing was everywhere, like Erica's reminiscence of ice fishing with her father, placed amid paper mosaics:

> I went ice fishing with Dad . . . There was a small fire, and my ears were kept warm by a hat pulled tight over my head. Dad, who is always trying to do the strangest things, put bait in two different places on my pole. I put it in the water . . . The only clouds I remember were white, pure; they looked like cotton in the sky. I was so happy, my cheeks rosy, and having Dad there beside me waiting in silence was such an awesome

> comfort. It wasn't until Dad pulled out my pole that I had the most incredible feeling. I was awed at the sight — two different fish on my pole. I felt a gratitude for Dad, a feeling for him that had never been quite as strong as it was then . . .

And Charlie's story "Mean Miss Gorf," bound into a cloth-covered book, shown to me within ten minutes of my arrival by an admiring Reba and Melissa. It began:

> Once there was a mean teacher at Polaris school. Her name was Miss Gorf. She was skinny as a rail and mean as a rattlesnake. She had the power to turn a kid into a shiny red apple. First she would wiggle her right ear, then her left ear, and then she'd stick out her tongue.
>
> One day Miss Gorf was teaching arithmetic, and the problem was 6,503,526,679 divided by 6. After three minutes she yelled, "Time's up," and we turned in our answers.
>
> She looked them over and said, "Good job Charlie, James, Crystal, Russell, Tyler, but I am disappointed in you Erica. Sorry." She wiggled her left ear, then her right ear, then stuck out her tongue, and there was a nice shiny red apple where Erica once was standing.

And the collaborative poem composed by the class on a long sheet of butcher paper — what you do when you don't have an overhead projector, Andy explained — hanging in the nook by the piano:

My Surroundings

In fall it's colorful, bright.
Foxes hide fast in the red,
dead trees.

Moose covered with frost.
As we climb we look and see
white on the top of the mountains.

Great blocks of rock are
wintery white, rough on my hands.

Eagle fly on wind, black
above me.

Then we see a mountain cat
battling a rat.

Picturesque sunsets.

"What you're doing down there is different," one parent told Andy after a few months had passed, "but I think it's beneficial." "The kids seem interested," said another, "in going to school." The combination of Andy's congeniality, the rationale for his practice and the specificity of his goals, and, pure and simple, the quality of the work the class was producing — it all became persuasive.

Andy was sitting in his swivel chair facing the couch, where seventh-graders Heather, Russell, Erica, and Tyler were working in teams of two, studying patterns and number theory and making their way through story problems like the following:

> Loren was studying the meaning of new words. After the first day he had 15 words left to learn. After the second day he had 12 words left to learn. The next day he had 9 words left. At that rate, how many days will it take him to learn all the words?

Heather suggested to Russell that the two of them count down on their collective fingers. They quickly did so, then she ventured, "It'll take a total of six days." Erica and Tyler were solving the problem with a factor tree, arriving at multiples of 5 and 3. The answer, they said in disagreement with Heather and Russell, was five. Andy pointed out the different strategies they were using, then asked each team to justify their answers. "It's going in a number pattern," Heather said, leaning over Russell to Erica and Tyler, "and they're losing three words a day." Erica agreed that there was a pattern, but pointed to the factor tree she and Tyler had calculated, arguing that the answer had to lie in the multiples. Andy urged more cross-talk, which led, within the next two minutes or so, to Tyler asking Heather to review her procedure; Erica defending her answer; Russell wondering if, after all, he might be swayed by Erica, for "maybe the problem doesn't give us enough information"; and Erica lighting up suddenly and saying, "Oh, it *is* six!" In a recent rural math contest, students from Polaris won an award for group problem-solving, and this exchange demonstrated why. Andy encouraged students to work together, articulate strategies, consider alternatives, and come to consensus.

Across the room, Michele sat cross-legged on the floor between two teams of third- and fourth-graders playing a math game. The school board wanted students to develop facility with estimating and rapid calculation, necessary in ranch life. Historically, rural boards were responsible for curriculum, and some still exercise control over what gets taught. That was not so at Polaris, but the board did want there to be some "basic skills" work combined with Andy's more reflective, conceptual approach. Andy agreed that such skills were necessary, so he and Michele worked up activities like this.

The students had their multiplication tables in front of them: Leo, Dustin, and Rossy on one side, Melissa, Reba, and Clarissa on the other. Michele had fashioned two oversized cardboard dice, one displaying the numbers 1 through 6, the other 7 through 12. Each team would throw a die and create a division problem that had, as its remainder, the number that came up on the roll. So when Rossy threw a 4, her team hurriedly consulted the multiplication table to figure out that if, say, 21 divided by 7 equals 3, then, well, 25 divided by 7 would leave a remainder of 4 — the number Rossy threw. *See you add a four to it. Put the four there. We've gotta get a remainder of four. That'll do it. The four'll do it. Oh, oh, I see. Yes. Yessss.* The team that created the most division problems at the end of the period would win, gaining familiarity with the multiplication table and some arithmetic flexibility along the way.

During this period, Sheryl, the itinerant speech therapist, had quietly entered the room and taken second-grader Colt to the library. One way that small independent rural districts like Polaris try to meet the special needs of their students is by joining a cooperative to get services like those Sheryl provided. This co-op included ten schools in two counties, so sometimes Sheryl covered 120 miles in a day, spending anywhere from a half-hour to two hours at each site, depending on need. On this day, she worked with Colt on *l* blends (*gl, pl*) and digraphs (*sh, ch*). Then, when Andy had a moment, she conferred with him on strategies to address these in the more natural language flow of the classroom — she was especially concerned with the "l" sound — and I would see Andy play out her suggestions throughout the day.

At nine-thirty, Michele went into the library to review with the older students their works-in-progress on Montana Studies. One segment of their research required them to plan for a visiting historian or geographer a road tour that would cover at least three hundred miles and include sites important in Native American history, early trapping and mining, homesteading, agriculture, and the like. The assignment involved maps, written text, and an oral report, and Andy asked Michele to check in on Tyler, Russell, Erica, Heather, and James. Were the maps developing? Was the accompanying text more than just a bare-bones sketch?

Meanwhile, Andy convened the younger students at the couch to make sure they understood a new science assignment on habitat and adaptation. Each was to select a grassland animal, a forest animal, and an animal from a habitat of their own choosing and describe how body and behavior were adapted to environment, how various adaptations help the animal to eat, move, regulate temperature, and avoid enemies. "Let's say my forest animal is a squirrel," Andy speculated. "Think of what it eats and how its body has adapted to that." "A squirrel eats nuts," said Clarissa, her arms resting on her knees. "Yeah," added Rossy, thrusting herself out of the cushioned recesses of the couch, "so he'd have to have strong jaw muscles." "Good," said Andy. "Anything else?" "Mr. Bayliss" — Melissa waved her hand — "he'd have *sharp* teeth." "Yes, he would, Melissa. Thank you." Andy wanted the students to "think about animals in a new way, as beings adapted over time to their environments," and that was beginning to happen.

The discussion continued, and later that day Andy picked up the subject again when he tutored Colt.

Colt was a very good student, but, still, the adaptation assignment would be a challenge for a second-grader. Many traditional one-room schools had children follow lessons in textbooks for their grade level, but, whenever possible, Andy liked to give the same assignment to a range of kids, encouraging them to engage it as best they could. This was one of the things, he believed, that made the multigrade classroom an exciting place. It could be especially rich for younger children, for it gave them opportunity to stretch beyond grade level. So he clicked on the computer and pulled Colt in beside him.

"What grassland animal did you choose, Colt?" "The antelope," Colt replied. "Great," said Andy, "let's get that in a sentence." "My grassland animal," Colt began, leaning in on his forearm to watch the screen as Andy typed, "is an antelope." "Good," said Andy. "Now how about adaptation? What about the antelope helps it live in its environment?" Colt ran the fingers of his left hand over his short bristly hair, thought a moment, and began: "It kind of has flat teeth and they eat grass." Andy typed and Colt watched. Then, appropriating the recommendations of the speech therapist, Andy had Colt read the text he had generated so far, paying special attention to the *l* sound in *land, animal, antelope,* and *flat.* Colt's pronunciation sounded good, and Andy had him read one more time.

"OK, Colt, what else do they have that helps them live?" "I know that they have legbones . . ." Colt checked himself. "I think that their hip," he revised, "is how they walk . . . because, uh, because if they didn't have a hip, they couldn't walk." Andy typed, then had Colt read. This wasn't particularly an example of adaptation — though with elaboration it might be — but Colt was on a roll, and Andy knew he could return to this hip business later in the week. "What about temperature, Colt? Like with the lambs you're raising, how do antelope keep warm or cool?" "Antelope have fur," Colt said, leaning in closer to the screen as his words appeared letter by quick letter. "It makes them warm."

"Great!" said Andy, "and protection, avoiding enemies?" Colt let out a mild sigh of exasperation and rubbed his blond stubble again. "Mr. Bayliss . . ." "C'mon Colt, one more line." Colt looked back at the screen. "They put their horns down." Andy typed, Colt watching. "You know, Colt," Andy prodded, "it wouldn't be a complete report, would it, if we didn't say *why* the antelope does that." Colt said, "No, it wouldn't," and added "to protect themselves."

Once the students completed their individual projects — another week or so down the line — Andy would push their thinking by having them create "imaginary animals with weird adaptations and strange habitats." Melissa would write about the porcupine-octopus that lives at the edge of the ocean and protects itself from other animals with its quills; and Colt would draw a fierce baboon-lion, a monkeylike creature with big claws, able to leap about the savanna to both hunt prey and avoid danger.

Ten o'clock, and it was time for a snack and recess. Michele and Andy took turns supervising the children during these breaks, and on this day Andy watched over them while Michele checked their "dictionaries," the lists of words they had misspelled in their writing. She was particularly concerned about James, handsome, laconic James, whom they were trying to prepare for ninth grade at the high school in Dillon. "He has the intelligence," she said to me, rubbing her temple, "but he just hasn't done the work he's capable of doing." She opened his folder, running her finger down a list of words: *historical, museum, process.* Earlier in the month, in quick script in his journal, he had written lyrically about a trip to nearby Black Mountain:

> All I hear is the gentle whisper of the creek and the wind blowing through the willows . . . I see a beautiful green valley and creeks and a big mountain with a little snow on it. The sun is hidden behind a cloud. I see baby horses, baby elk and baby antelope . . . curious about life and how God made the earth. I feel a crisp and cool mountain breeze; then the sun pokes out and warms everything up. Touching each and every soul. I love this earth.

There were many sides to this boy. And much promise. Michele closed his folder, turned and looked out the window.

Melissa stayed inside to practice her piano, and the empty classroom and the library — where Michele was fretting over James —filled with a hesitant but melodic rendition of "Pony Ride." Melissa guided herself with a whispered *one-two-three, one-two-three-four,* the keys yielding an almost muted tinkle, like the sound of an old recording, *one-two-*

three, played in this room so many times before, Melissa beginning again.

On the top shelf of the library, above *Huckleberry Finn, Wind in the Willows,* and the like, was a pile of old documents and record books. At various times during my stay I would page through them, uncovering a copy of the original petition from Polaris to the county superintendent of public schools announcing that "[m]oney has been raised by public subscription for the purpose of building a schoolhouse." I found the dusty forms that guided the governance and management of a school on the frontier, announcing that "the Public Free Schools of the State shall be open to all children and youths between the ages of six and twenty-one years." I read the minutes of board meetings: a resolution to "levy extra 3 mill tax to cover debt;" a contract sent to a Miss Emma Bartels, who, the board determined, "was best qualified to teach;" a vote "to ask people of the district to furnish wood for the year as we're short of funds." I found various school census reports and teacher's reports dating back to 1894, some attached to others with straight pins, the paper rusted slightly at the point of piercing. They recorded enrollment, attendance, visits by trustees and parents, number of books in the library (forty-two in 1919), teachers' salaries ($85 per month in 1919), whether Arbor Day was observed "in accordance with the law," and whether instruction was given on "the effects of alcoholic drinks and narcotics" and on "the prevention of communicable diseases." I found, as well, student registries, written in the neat and ornate hand of various district clerks. As I turned the pages, the same names appeared year after year — Tash, Harrison, Marchesseau — the children seeming to grow up before me as I ran my finger down the lists of names, the names of the families migrating from Canada, from the Midwest, from Kentucky, who settled this valley. Those names were now represented on the school board that hired Andy, now appeared on the Polaris School registry. How many sat at that piano? Listening to Melissa play "Pony Ride," I wondered about the harsh journey, the solitude, and the powerful sense of continuity that some in the Grasshopper Valley must feel.

And outside, the class ran an energetic game of tag while the snow fell in gently manic flurries, flowing sideways, kicking up, up, down, riding the erratic breeze.

Ten-twenty. Erica, Russell, Tyler, Heather, and James, the seventh- and eighth-graders, crammed themselves around the small table in the library, preparing for another phase of Montana Studies. This was the delivery of basic geographical, historical, and civic facts about the state, the story the state tells itself about itself and expects its students to know. Andy gave it his own twist, however. Knowing that once these young people begin high school, they would have to be able to take efficient notes, he decided to simulate for them the academic lecture. The transition to town high schools was a big concern for rural educators, and it was that concern Andy was playing out here.

He reviewed somc basic note-taking techniques and explained the setting the students could expect in the typical science or history or social studies classroom. Then, using the materials provided to rural teachers by the county, he surveyed the official Montana symbols: bitterroot, the state flower; ponderosa pine, the state tree; black spotted cutthroat trout, the state fish; grizzly bear, the state animal. The basic geography of Montana: the western mountains and the continental divide — directing the flow of rivers to opposite sides of the Rockies — and the vast eastern plains, part of the Great Plains. And Montana's primary sources of revenue: agriculture, ranching, mining, tourism. Then came a quick historical sketch: from the indigenous peoples, to the French explorers and trappers, to the Louisiana Purchase, to the gold and silver rush (Polaris figured here), to the Indian wars, to copper. Montana was organized as a territory in 1864 and became a state in 1889. Its motto: *Oro y plata,* gold and silver.

When he finished, Andy walked around the table, asking to see people's notes, pointing out different methods — Heather's outline format, Russell's list — and making suggestions for improvement. He paid special attention to James who, come fall, would be facing the real thing. Because of the possibility of stretching beyond grade level and because of the presence of older role models, Andy believed that the multigrade classroom was a stimulating place for younger students, but he worried that it was not as rich for the older ones. James. Was he doing all he could do for James?

Michele thought Rossy was "incredible in math" and wanted to "keep pushing her." So while Andy lectured on Montana Studies, and the younger children worked independently in the larger room, Michele slid in alongside Rossy with a sheet of new math problems. She had copied these from a more advanced textbook and wanted to see how Rossy would do with them.

Though the school board was able to buy into the co-op that provided itinerant teachers for some enrichment and certain special needs — like the speech therapist for Colt — a district with one school and fifteen kids clearly cannot mount a gifted-and-talented program or hire a special education resource teacher. Rural children miss out on some of the services that are a part of urban schooling; historically, that has been one of the arguments for consolidation. But it is also true that, in the hands of good teachers, the small multigrade classroom gives rise to the possibility of dealing with special needs directly and within the flow of daily instruction. There would be multiple opportunities for Rossy to work beyond the confines of her mathematics textbook.

Difficulties can be addressed in similar fashion. Andy told me about one of the girls who, during the previous two years of schooling, displayed the kinds of problems with reading that could have gotten her diagnosed as learning disabled. By the time Andy arrived at Polaris, she was doing better but was still reading below grade level. So he worked out a plan with her parents whereby she continued to read the books her peers were reading, but received extra help in the classroom, and read at least a half-hour a night under her parents' supervision. And Andy saw her parents frequently, after school, at local events, so there was a steady exchange of information. "Little schools should not try to act like big schools," Claudette said to me on our way to Polaris. "They need to take advantage of their smallness." "This classroom is a full-inclusion classroom," Andy quipped when I quoted Claudette to him. "It has to be."

When I was getting out of Claudette's car in the school yard that morning, I noticed some plastic ribbons tied to the pussy willows growing along Farlin Creek, a pink flutter among the thin, dense branches. It turned out that these were identifying markers that Andy's students had tied around the clusters of buds they were studying.

Eleven o'clock and time for science. Andy tried as much as possible to make his curriculum "continuous with experiences outside school." The class had been keeping a naturalist's journal, a detailed account of the growth of a bud on the willows, and, on this day, Andy wanted them to go out and make further observations. The naturalist's journal has a long and venerable history, and the way Andy used it, it involved close observation, description, drawing, and notions of scale and context.

The students had to note day, time, weather, direction of wind, and, using all their senses, had to write a narrative account: "smell the buds and the ground; listen and look for birds or other wildlife; feel the bark or the buds." As well, they were to attempt scale drawings of the bud and its surrounding leaves and branches. The younger students needed help with this, but they were able to approximate most of the tasks.

On this day, I stayed with Tyler. He had watched his bud grow from 1/2 cm to 2 1/2 cm, into the silky flower that gives the pussy willow its name. "This is a harsh place," Andy told him. "How has the willow adapted to it?" Tyler measured the bud, recorded the weather, checked the wind, a gentle breeze from the northeast, and sketched what he would need to complete his scale drawing. Andy had asked why the willow grows in this dense, clustered way, rather than, say, long and snaky up a phone pole. Tyler assumed that the plant was able to protect itself and make the most of available water. When he finally completed his series of observations and sketches, he would be required to draw a map of the surrounding area and the location of the plant within it, and, using his data, write a paragraph on the way the willow has adapted to the type of land and climate in which it lives. "Tyler's fished in creeks like that for years," Andy later told me. "I just wanted him to take a little closer look, maybe a little different look, at what he already knows."

Eleven-thirty and time for silent reading. Clarissa, Dustin, Tyler, and Reba sat on the couch. Erica was deep in pillows alongside the piano. James and Leo sat at opposite sides of one of the tables by the windows, bending over their books, their heads in alignment, a foot apart. Rossy, Heather, and Charlie sat at separate tables. Russell and Stephen slid down against the back wall by the restrooms, their feet, big in high-top athletic shoes, sticking out into the room from under the corkboard partition. Occasionally a thump and rustle would send Michelle back there to investigate. ("Boys, I've had enough!") Andy was in the library with Colt, working on that story about the adaptation of the antelope. Most of the children were reading mysteries or horror stories — *The Curse of the Mummy's Tomb, The Headless Cupid* — though Heather was leaning back in her chair with *To Kill a Mockingbird,* and James was engrossed in his favorite author, Louis L'Amour.

The books were of the children's own choosing, though Andy required that they keep a journal in which they responded to one of a list of questions: "What is the setting?" "Why did the author include minor characters?" "Why do you think the book ended as it did?" And so on. Toward the end of the half-hour period — or at some other time in the day when people were working independently — students would be pulling out notebooks and steno pads and writing about their reading.

Reading is, of course, central to the elementary school curriculum, and Andy found multiple ways for students to use it and enjoy it. He had Colt dictate texts that became his reader. He encouraged students to consult the library's reference books on projects ranging from the Montana Studies map to the adaptation-habitat assignment to the dimensions and characteristics of objects appearing in their artwork. (For example, I saw Rossy retrieve for Melissa a book on bats for one of her drawings.) He had teams of children select a poem, decide how it should be read, and read it aloud to the class — Edgar Allan Poe to Shel Silverstein. He was vigilant for the quick lesson, like the time he zeroed in on the lyric sheet to "America the Beautiful" — sung so often, so mechanically — asking the class the meaning of "amber waves of grain" and "purple mountain majesties," and asking someone to please look up "grace" in the dictionary, leading to a discussion of the phrase "shed His grace on thee." And he usually read a story or part of a novel to the class just for fun before or after lunch or at the end of the day. Once when I was in the library with Erica helping her revise a story, I could hear him reading from *Scary Stories* in a Peter Lorre voice.

Twelve noon. Lunch. Those who brought mini-pizzas or containers of cooked food lined up in front of the microwave; the others unwrapped sandwiches, opened bags of chips, peeled oranges and bananas. Since there were no vending or ice machines here, most children brought their lunches in small portable coolers, the modern version of the lunch pail. Lunch was a quick affair, a little chatter inflected with sports and mainstream popular culture — Heather and Tyler talking to each other in the voice of Pauly Shore. It was not long before someone yelled, "Last one out is *it*," and there was a scramble for jackets and the door. Andy followed outside holding at chest-level a Tupperware container of left-over spaghetti, scooping a forkful toward his open mouth.

Andy Bayliss was thirty-four, five-eleven, thin, brown hair, boyish. He grew up in Marshall, Missouri, went to grade school and high school there, worked for a few years after graduation. When his parents moved to Oregon, he enrolled at Southern Oregon State College, where he took a bachelor of science degree in geography and biology. He worked six years as a biology technician for the Forest Service — "running around streams, counting fish" — and, during the winters, was a ski instructor. He used his athletic skill as a passport, and skied in the Italian Alps, in Argentina and Chile, and in Alaska. He was in his early thirties when he began to think that the work he was doing "had no effect on the flow of events," and wondered about teaching as a way to make a difference, to help young people "develop informed opinions and think for themselves." So he enrolled in a teacher-education program at the University of Alaska Southeast at Juneau and did his student teaching in Anchorage. He became intrigued by the possibilities of the multigrade classroom, and craved a place where he could settle in and ski and canoe and hike. So he followed a path that began somewhere back in the recesses of the Republic, following hundreds of thousands before him, mostly women, mostly young, often inexperienced, working under term-to-term contracts, staying half a year, a year, maybe two or three, living at home, if local, or boarding, often in tight quarters (bathing, as one woman put it, "with a teacup and handkerchief"), or, as time progressed and conditions improved, living in a teacherage like Andy's. It was, for many, lonely work, and, for women especially, terribly underpaid. Much has changed for teachers in small rural districts, but it is still common for them to be employed, as Andy was, from year to year, with minimal possibility for tenure, and they still got paid less than their larger-district counterparts. In Montana some country teachers are paid in the $11,000-to-$13,000 range. Andy's starting salary, and this was somewhere close to average in rural Montana, was $15,500. But add the teacherage. And the multigrade experience. And the landscape. From the front door of the school, Andy showed me the slopes he skied when the snow was fresh.

It did, however, get lonely. Andy's weekdays, of course, were filled with activity, and on weekend days, weather permitting, he was out on the land. Occasionally after school there were board meetings or other civic events, but for the most part evenings were solitary. Hospitable as the residents of the Grasshopper Valley were, they were spread out, and for someone like Andy, who came to Polaris without a family, there was minimal opportunity for companionship. As for having a woman visitor to the teacherage, well, that would be, to the community's way of thinking, a delicate proposition. There were definite strictures on behavior. Andy felt the isolation in another way. Like all new teachers, even ones with a feel for the classroom, Andy was wrestling with the question of authority. How to "be myself" yet do something about the bickering, and how to pull in those students who had a tendency to withdraw or rebel. At heart, he was trying to figure out how to *be* in his classroom, and he had to come to an answer pretty much on his own. There was an experienced and talented teacher named Linda Hicks at a small school in Glen who had befriended Andy, and she provided good counsel, but Glen was on the other side of the Pioneer mountain range, on the eastern edge of the county, so it was difficult to meet with her — particularly during school hours, when Andy could watch her teach. Laments about such isolation, both social and professional, are scattered through the letters and diaries of rural teachers; Andy's questions and conflicts echo across the history of the one-room school.

But for now, Andy was *it*, standing in the middle of the dirt driveway, the children on either side of him. One, then another tried to sprint around him to get to the other side. Dustin or Reba or Russell, his long legs pumping, would take off, running through the grass, jutting hips forward or to the side to elude Andy's tag. And Andy, with a big grin and a grunt of exertion, accelerated across the dirt, the grass, down an incline by the propane tank, striding out, catching the curve of a shoulder with his fingertips.

Twelve-thirty-five, and the students were settling back into the classroom. In a packet of materials provided by the county, Andy found a role-playing activity that caught his fancy. It was a council between Nez Perce leader Chief Joseph and General Oliver Otis Howard, who had traveled west to force the Nez Perce onto a reservation. (This figured in Montana history for, in their subsequent attempts to elude containment, the Nez Perce would travel across southwestern Montana — engaging the U.S. Army in a bloody battle at Big Hole, about 60 miles from Polaris — and up the middle of the state, through the plains toward Canada.) In addition to the general and Chief Joseph, there were roles for eight other students — from a Nez Perce warrior to a railroad executive to a rancher — so, with a little doctoring, adding a few warriors and aides, Andy was able to fit the assignment to his class.

The curricular materials gave paragraph-long descriptions of each character, but Andy felt they didn't offer an adequate account of the history surrounding the council, nor did they convey Chief Joseph's eloquence on the injustice of the government's treatment of the Nez Perce. So he found a brief history in the school's library and read it by way of introduction. "As I read this," he said, "be thinking of the role you might want to play." "This'll be interesting," I heard Heather whisper to Erica. When he asked the students to choose roles, to his relief there were no major disputes. Only James chose not to participate. Andy had the class spend about ten minutes working up their roles, and he and Michele moved among them, asking questions, providing direction.

The event itself lasted about twenty minutes. Andy had rearranged the tables into a square, and the children seemed to get carried away with the drama. The younger children had to lean into things to be heard, but they made themselves known. Some children, both younger and older, tended to follow the descriptions in the materials, the line of argument, the phrasing, but some truly assumed the role and generated passionate language and real exchange.

Erica played an Indian warrior, one of the younger Nez Perce who could no longer tolerate the dislocation and slaughter of his people. She argued fiercely, articulately, the role seeming to touch some personal understanding of injustice. Taking on Tyler, who chose the role of a rancher, and Stephen, who played General Howard, she proclaimed in various retorts: "I'm a warrior . . . The more land we give you, the more you want . . . You ask us to move to a reservation. Why don't *your* people move to a reservation? . . . There are White men killing Indians, but it is only against the law when an Indian kills a White."

Heather was the other vocal spokesperson for the Nez Perce, assuming the role of Chief Joseph, gaining from Andy's reading a sense of the chief's eloquence, trying to match it as she played off Erica's spirited defense. "How can we make peace?" she asked toward the end of the council, "when you kill our people and our livestock? You say you need protection, but you would not need protection if Whites weren't killing our women and children. This land is our father and mother, and it is being taken from us."

And fifth-grader Stephen, who wasn't particularly engaged by school and made that known in his daily interactions with Andy, took on the role of General Howard with vigor. Stephen had Russell roll up and tape the right arm of his jean jacket — the general had lost an arm in the Civil War — and using his left fist as a gavel, called the council to order. In line with the historical account, he played the general as insistent and uncompromising — "I give you three days to make a decision to move" — and as an impatient emissary dead-set on a resolution favorable to the U.S. government. During one of Heather's impassioned declarations, he stood up and interrupted: "I say we should have peace here. Let's get to the point."

When Stephen called the council to a close, Andy directed the class to think about what they had heard and to ask themselves what might have gone differently and how that would have affected the course of history. They would write on this later in the week.

One day, after the class had sung a few traditional songs like "Little Black Bull," Andy held out to me a dog-eared set of lyric sheets and the accompanying audio cassette. "This is my music program." He laughed apologetically. It was a typical act of self-deprecation, but Andy's remark underscored the fact that multigrade rural schools, usually the only schools in their respective districts, work with limited resources. The good rural teacher, therefore, is always improvising, making do, keeping an eye and ear open for opportunities to enrich the curriculum. So, at ten after two, Andy was introducing Mrs. Sally Park and her daughter Jenny — they had slipped in during the role play — and preparing the class for a lesson in the techniques of watercoloring.

During the summer, between terms in Andy's teacher-education program in Juneau, he ran a day camp with Jenny Park. She had since moved to a ranch near Salmon, Idaho, just west over the Beaverhead Mountains. Her mother, an artist who lived in Denver, was visiting, and since she liked to volunteer in schools, Jenny and Andy made arrangements for this afternoon art lesson. Andy introduced Mrs. Park just as something was flaring between Rossy and Stephen. "Hey, everyone," reprimanded Tyler, "listen to Mrs. Park!"

Sally Park began the lesson by holding up a picture book, open to a panoramic Western scene: soft mountains in the background, grassland in the middle, a cowboy on his horse in the left foreground. Using her finger as a pointer, she talked briefly about the way the painting was composed, the arrangement of the shapes within it — the movement from the hazy background to the detailed foreground. "As you move forward, the colors and shapes become sharper, more distinct." She showed the students how the artist used color to contribute to the illusion of perspective: the soft blue sky in the distance, the contrasting of darks and lights to make an object stand out. Then she returned to the issue of definition: "Notice, then, how the edges of things up close will be highly defined, and look how soft the edges are on those faraway mountains."

The students each had a watercolor kit before them, a thin tray with eight bright but eroded cakes of color, the paints bleeding each into the other at the borders: orange into purple, red into brown. Andy laid brushes on the tables. Jenny filled cups and little pie tins with water. (And Melissa, giggling, flicked a brushful of water at Reba.) Mrs. Park demonstrated a technique, then gave the children a chance to try it as Jenny moved among them, assisting the younger children. And some students helped each other. "Here," Russell said as Jenny was leaning over Leo, "I can show him how to do it."

Over the hour Andy's students learned how to do a wash, "loading" a brush with water and paint, sweeping it across the paper with broad strokes of color. They learned how to bleed colors one into the other, and how to make shadows, and how to use particular brushes for specific effects: the thin grass-like streaks you can get from a big dry brush, the way you can wet and shape the tip of a fine sable brush for dots and precise lines. Mrs. Park showed them the crisp, dark speckles that appear when salt is sprinkled on damp watercolor, and the rivulet effects you get by blowing across wet paper. And she demonstrated the way you can draw the outline of a petal or a leaf just with water, then float a color in, the paint following the wet tracing, fading and light.

The students were ready to turn this range of techniques toward the production of watercolors of their own. They would continue over the next few days. The light blue washes, the mauve circles of bleeding purple and red, the waves and dots and fine green lines of grass, all used in service of an original work. With pencil and fine brush, James would render the tree-covered face of a mountain. Rossy would paint a stark, creviced Bald Mountain against a blue and yellow sky. Erica, a rose-colored barn. Dustin, a purple-finned Cadillac. Russell, a field of haystacks, light brown and orange.

While the class was busy creating their watercolors, about two-fifteen or so, I looked out the window to see a pickup truck and horse trailer pull into the yard and around the swings. A tall woman got out — she was wearing a jacket, gloves, and a stocking cap — took a shovel from inside the trailer, and began breaking up the soil along the south boundary of the school yard. I soon found out that this was Cathy Tash, head of the school board. Many of the tasks that in large districts would be divided among units in a bureaucracy are in small independent districts taken on by the school board and community: from purchasing school supplies to stockpiling wood to painting the classroom. It was one more indicator of the degree to which the school was a focus of community activity. Cathy leaned into the shovel. She was digging out the long-jump pit, hard and crusted from winter.

This was the first day of practice for the coming rural schools track meet, a big event in this region, one with history. Looking through those old record books, I found faded clippings from the Dillon newspaper describing the "fierce competition" among schools in the sprints, hurdles, and field events. Now the students in Andy Bayliss's class would be preparing for the standing long jump, the running long jump, the shot put, the high jump. Erica's mother Delores came into the room as Sally and Jenny Park were packing up for the drive back to Salmon. She wore sweats and had a stopwatch hanging around her neck. She and Cathy were the volunteer track coaches.

By two-forty, Tyler, Russell, and James had joined Cathy and were filling the long-jump pit with the fresh sand she had in her trailer. Andy, Melissa, and Erica had gone into the barn where the crossbar for the high jump lay bent in hay, and were setting up the stands and thumping out the padding for the first trials at four feet. And Erica's mother had marked off a corner of the concrete basketball court and was showing Rossy and Heather how to execute the little backward hop and turn of the shot put.

Snow fell in the lightest flurries. The day had warmed considerably. Leo and Russell were in T-shirts; most of the other children in pullovers and sweatshirts. All of them, second grade through eighth, were practicing some event, many moving from one to the other. One of the benefits of small schools like Polaris is that students get to participate in so many activities, to play so many roles. Rossy, Heather, and Leo marked the length of their puts with pencils stuck in the ground. Dustin, Tyler, Melissa, and Erica ran at the crossbar in a focused, striding curve across the grass, right leg and arm over the bar, shoulders, butt, sometimes clearing it, sometimes catching it with a heel, sending it clattering to the ground. Erica matched Tyler jump for jump. At the long-jump pit, fresh now, Colt was sprinting down the runway, his face twisted with effort. Cathy stood by with a garden rake, preparing the surface between jumps with its flat end. James would come next, then Russell. Both would register impressive distances. Their strong takeoff, the fluid lift of their legs, their extension at the end.

Practice lasted well into the afternoon; some children left as their parents arrived, some stayed longer, some lingered. As I walked back inside the school, I saw Erica lying on the padding of the high-jump pit, legs crossed, a book open on her chest, looking off toward the northern mountains. James was drifting back and farther back off the court, onto the grass, finding his spot, setting, releasing the basketball with a little jump and a twisting thrust off his right side, the ball arcing through the air, swishing through the net.

II THE INTERMOUNTAIN COACH to Missoula and the Co-Teach program took about five-and-half hours, north out of Dillon on the first leg to Butte, a gray, chilly day, the bus close to empty, the long wipers flapping across the windshield, one then the other, in loose counterpoint. We passed Apex, Glen (where Andy's friend Linda Hicks taught), the Humbug Spires Primitive Area, the road to the Big Hole Battlefield (of Nez Perce fame), Divide (near the Continental Divide), Wisdom (just beneath Divide on the road sign, reading "divide wisdom"), Feely, Rocker, then Butte, the site of the biggest copper boom in the nation's history. Giant A-frame mining hoists rose on hills throughout the city. Old brick buildings, like those you'd find in the Rust Belt — Cleveland or Pittsburgh — lined the wet, clear streets downtown: the Bronx Lounge, the *fireproof* Leggat Hotel. A two-hour layover, hanging around the depot. A blond teenager, guitar and knapsack slung over his shoulder, piloted an F-14 Tomcat on a video game. Jehovah's Witnesses distributed *Awake!* "Loneliness," the cover read, "what you can do about it."

Out of Butte in light rain, headed northwest through Anaconda (once called Copperopolis, this was the site of the smelter for Butte's ore), we drove on ascending narrow roads through the Deer Lodge National Forest, passing Georgetown Lake, frozen still, opaque, a dull, dead gray. Clouds settled over the tops of pines like wisps of torn cotton. Someone had sprayed on rock face RED LOVE KILLS DEAD LOVE KILLS above a crude heart, ripped down the middle. Descending from the forest, past Porter's Corner, through Philipsburg, an old mining town, seventy-eight miles from Missoula: houses spread over foothills; a historic downtown, street names etched into wooden street signs; clusters of house trailers, big satellite dishes curved in the space of their brief front yards. Onto Interstate 90, through Drummond ("The Bullship Capital of The World") where a young woman watched our bus from the window of the Frosty Freeze attached to the depot. Then past Bearmouth, the northern edge of the Lolo National Forest, Bonner, Milltown, and the outskirts of Missoula at dusk, car lights, city lights twinkling in the distance, stars fallen to the ground.

Pre-school teacher Shelley Neilsen sat on the vivid alphabet rug of the Co-Teach classroom — bright red and yellow and orange and blue letters and numbers, too — with the blond boy settled calmly between her outstretched legs. Jonathan had stopped making the groaning, grunting noise he had been making before she slid in behind him. There was a puzzle in front of them: five pieces, two of which, the two largest pieces, fit snugly within the square border. Placed one way, the two pieces presented a night scene — a black sky and two white stars — placed the other way and you had blue sky and puffy clouds. The middle of these pieces was cut out, leaving an empty circle into which you would lay the three remaining segments. Placed one way, they complemented the blue sky with a radiant gold-orange sun; placed another and there was a smiling ivory man-in-the-moon.

Jonathan had dumped the puzzle on the floor, holding the square base in both hands — arms rigid, straight out — and turning it rapidly back and forth in front of his eyes. Then he picked up the two larger pieces that fit within the base, repeating the motion — *night, day, night, day* — and, suddenly, plopped one down into the base. That was when Shelley slid in quickly behind him. She was talking softly to him and trying to guide him to put another piece in place.

Around them played ten other children, for this was the "free play" time at the beginning of the day. Zachary and Brandon were strategically locating Ninja Turtles amid an assortment of blocks and were spinning an excited tale about some kind of Ninja rescue. Michael stood close by, watching, close enough to be within the two boys' social space, but keeping some distance. He watched placidly, holding a little brown bear.

At the small chalkboard bolted onto the easel, Stacia Butterfield, the other teacher in the room, made an A for Kimberlie to copy. She handed Kimberlie the chalk, and Kimberlie took it, but wheeled around to Stacia to kiss her. Stacia embraced Kimberlie, then moved her back to the board, where Kimberlie drew one wobbly diagonal line, one leg of the A. Kimberlie turned and looked out at the other children. Stacia reached for Kimberlie's hand and gently directed the chalk over the A. Kimberlie giggled. Then she traced an irregular A over Stacia's A.

Dusty was being held by Ginny MacDonald, the paraprofessional assistant in the Co-Teach Program. He was humming, a steady vibration, and was vigorously shaking his legs. He rolled his head back, arching, and tossed with a sideways pitch a little blue truck he was holding. Charles walked over. "Hi, Dusty," he said, picking up the truck and honking a bulb sticking out of the top of the cab. He sat down next to Dusty and kissed him on his forehead. Mariah, who had brought from home two cloth bunnies for show and tell, came over, one bunny in each hand, nodding them in the air as though they were conversing. "Dusty," she said, "and Charles."

Robby was stacking Unifix cubes high, then higher, eyeballing his construction from base to tip. "Boy, that's a tall tower, Robby," Stacia said, looking over from the chalkboard where she was working with Kimberlie on that A. "Yeah," he said, "I'm trying to see how tall I can make it go."

Rochelle, a student intern gaining practicum credit for a psychology class, sat with Tom in the corner by the entrance. She held him around the waist with one hand, and with the other was turning the pages of a picture book propped open on her lap. Tom wore a helmet, and, occasionally his head flew back and turned uncontrollably, grazing Rochelle on the chin. She rolled with it. "What is this, Tom?" she asked. Tom squirmed and looked away. "What do you call this?" she said, pointing to the book. Tom focused. "Dog," he said softly, the word muffled. "What color is the dog, Tom?" she continued. "White," he answered, touching the page of the book.

Edie put down the plastic fish she was playing with and ran over to Tom's walker, sitting at the entry to the play area. She got inside it and tried walking around in it, grasping the handles as she had seen Tom do.

Co-Teach was a half-day, eight-month preschool program located on the campus of the University of Montana, in a long room in the basement of McGill Hall, home of the university's early-childhood programs. It was a collaborative venture of the university, the Missoula Public School District, and the Missoula Area Special Education Cooperative that sought to integrate — as soon in their school lives as possible — children with disabilities and children who had no special educational needs. Such collaborations between public education and other public (or private) institutions are developing around the country, and this one yielded many things: a convergence of services and expertise; an inquiring, analytical ethos mixed with care and play; multiple sources of funding; and a wealth of student interns. But the heart of the collaboration was the desire to create optimal conditions for children with very different physical and mental abilities to learn from one another. Thus: Co-Teach.

Like many preschools, Co-Teach sought to help children develop the social and academic skills they would need when they entered kindergarten. The school day included a time for children to play alone or with each other; several structured activities in which they sat in a circle, discussed upcoming plans, and participated in show and tell; and a series of learning centers and small group activities that involved a number of academic concepts and skills. And there was recess and snack time and field trips. So, on any given day, there were multiple opportunities to participate in group activities and play cooperatively, to express needs and feelings, to make decisions and solve problems, and to learn basic concepts like color and shape and the rudiments of literacy and numeracy. All this was given definition and variety by themes that changed every week or two and included All About Me, Our Favorite Nursery Rhymes, Music Around the World, Friends and Mail, and Earth, Stars, and Environment, the theme addressed during my visit.

Of the eleven children in Co-Teach, ten were White and one was Native American, reflecting the demographics of the area. (Montana's significant Native American population is located more to the north and along the Canadian border, the "high line," and through the eastern plains.) The children ranged in age from four to seven years, and most of them came from two-parent families, lower middle class to middle class. Seven of the children had disabilities; four did not. The disabilities, sometimes in combination, included autism, visual and auditory impairment, epilepsy, hydrocephalus, fetal alcohol syndrome, and significant speech and language delays. The eligibility for special education services was determined by the school district, and appropriate funds for those children were routed to Co-Teach. The parents of the other students paid a fee based on local child care rates — a fee one parent characterized to me as being less expensive than that charged by other preschools, "and for a program that's so much better." These parents also expressed in various ways their desire for their children to, as one put it, "learn to relate to all sorts of kids."

You entered Co-Teach from the parking lot behind McGill, down a ramp or a flight of stairs to Room 015, at adult-eye level with the playground shared by Co-Teach and other School of Education early-childhood programs. Because there was a gymnasium on the floor directly above, Co-Teach usually proceeded amid the muffled rumbling of gymnastics and basketball. Newcomers like me couldn't help but look toward the ceiling, wondering. But the room was spacious and rich in colors, shapes, letters, numbers, and words, books, toys, games, art supplies, and manipulatives. And people. In addition to the staff, there were always in the room three to five of the twenty practicum students whom Shelley supervised. A remarkable ratio of children to adults.

As with many preschools and kindergartens, this was a room where just about everything served multiple purposes. The rug in the free play area was also an alphabet chart. The children's three wooden coat closets were painted, in turn, red, yellow, and blue — a quick lesson in color. The stairs to the bathroom were used to develop strength and coordination. Everything gave rise to learning — one of the joys of working with children of this age — and it all created the opportunity for expression, with words, with gestures. What made Co-Teach a bit different was the number of structures in place, sometimes subtle, to enhance learning, to enable children of varied abilities to participate in the curriculum — for example, the transition from free play to circle time.

Preparation for changes in routine is a part of most preschool environments. But such preparation was especially important in Co-Teach, some of whose students could be painfully unsettled by sudden shifts in activity. There were, therefore, carefully orchestrated transitions between each of the segments of the day.

About three or four minutes before circle time, one of the staff would announce that "it's almost time to go to circle," and they and the practicum students would follow up by preparing those children who might have a particularly hard time: by talking, by assisting in putting toys away. All this led to a further step in transition. The child designated for the day as room helper — each child's turn came up about once every two weeks — would ring, with assistance if necessary, a triangle. It was a big-deal, clangorous event, and the children would finish cleaning up and move out beyond the counter that separated the free play area. The counter, about three feet high, served as a guide, and the class lined up alongside it, a loose line, some kids receiving assistance, but in a casual, encouraging way, for fun lay ahead. In front of the children, extending to the circle area, were multicolored footprints, numbered one to twenty. When everyone seemed more or less ready, Shelley or Stacia or Ginny would begin a song they sang every day, using the familiar music as a further bridge between activities. *"If you're ready to go to circle, clap your hands . . ."* or stamp your feet, or touch your head, or whatever. One of the children was the designated line leader — again, each child got a turn about every two weeks — and chose how the class would actually get to circle: walk, wobble, fly, swim, hop . . . And off they'd go, in a march or bounce or waddle — everyone moving as best they could — arms pumping or waving or flapping with enthusiasm, ceremony.

Circle time was a series of activities, repeated daily: singing, previewing the day or week or special events (a speaker, a field trip), show and tell, using the calendar, describing the weather. The activities became familiar — especially by the end of the school year, the time of my visit — and the familiarity enabled children, to varying degrees, to know the cognitive and motor procedures, anticipate them, execute them to the best of their ability. But within the familiar, there was space for choice and for the new. Co-Teach children chose two or three songs from a repertoire of six. Each week's news, each day's news, had something original to it. Even show and tell, one of the most standard of primary grade routines, took a twist as the things kids brought in changed.

Robby's truck, Kimberlie's mittens, Mariah's rabbits (named Alex and Flowers — "because I like flowers"), Zachary's sunglasses ("I picked them myself") all gave rise to different perceptions, different questions. And there was the calendar, which changes, though in a systematic way, and the assessment of the weather, which, in Montana, as a waitress told me, changes every fifteen minutes.

Depending on the day, circle time would be followed by three small-group activities, through which all children would rotate, or a variety of learning centers from which children could choose. During Earth, Stars, and Environment week, children could, with glue, beans, and popcorn, make floral designs on art paper; plant seeds in Styrofoam cups that they filled with potting soil; create on paper-plate planets their own worlds with stones, twigs, flowers, leaves, wood chips, and pine cones ("I like," observed the student intern Dakota, "how each of you has your own idea of your world."); play with plastic fish and eels at the water table (a table waist-high to kids, with a deep central trough); sort objects into living and nonliving categories; make rockets out of construction paper and invent stories about them; and trace out constellations on a black-paper sky.

Recess took place in the enclosed playground right outside — and just above — the Co-Teach classroom. There were small tables and benches, a grassy area, sand, wood chips, a swing set, a small track, and a miniature jungle gym, yellow and blue, with a modest slide attached. There was no fixed routine for this time; kids played as they wished. But it did provide opportunities for individualized work with some of the children: to encourage Tom, for example, to walk without the aid of his walker, to get Jonathan — who loved to swing — to say "swing." It was a time to be alert to possibility. Shelley was sitting on the grass with Dusty cradled in her lap; she was trying to guide his right hand, which held a gum wrapper found on the ground, into a paper bag. Suddenly, he put his hands on the outside of Shelley's hands and brought them together, as in a clap. She silently let him guide her hands in a soft clap. Several days later, while Charles was giving Dusty a hug, Dusty took Charles's hands and guided them in a clapping motion.

Recess was followed by snack time, with its motor routines — the use of a spoon, pouring from a pitcher — and its continually unfolding opportunity for expression. The children sat at two tables by the kitchen and the low sink. An adult led each table, and those children who needed assistance had one of the teachers or practicum students sitting alongside or behind. When possible, the snacks reflected the theme of the week. While children were learning about the earth, the stars, and the environment, for example, they ate "ants on a log," raisins in peanut butter on a celery stick; on another day, two student interns brought in "dirt cake," mixed from the crushed dark cookies of Oreos, and presented it in little buckets with plastic shovels for serving spoons.

The setting gave rise to requests ("Can I have some more milk," Kimberlie asked in her tiny voice) and to expressions of preference — Brandon, for example, asking that the raisins be removed from his celery sticks. Those children who could not talk were encouraged to point or somehow gesture as items were laid out before them. Furthermore, as the children ate, there were multiple opportunities to label and distinguish. When Edie was selecting carrots from a vegetable tray, Shelley casually asked her which of the vegetables was orange, was red, was green. And there were opportunities to make connections. Once when the children were eating granola, Stacia noted that the class had made their own granola a few weeks back, and asked if anyone could remember what they had put in it, thus encouraging a brief moment of recall and summary.

There was, as well, a wealth of spontaneous, student-generated talk. Students had a choice of crackers with peanut butter or "ants on a log." Stacia had placed plates of both before Jonathan, asking him to touch the one he wanted. Zachary turned to him and said, "You should try the ants on a log, Jonathan; they're good, really they are." On the occasion of dirt cake, Zachary looked down the table to catch Mariah's eye. "Hey, Mariah, it's cake that looks like dirt. But, you know, it's just Oreo cookies that are crushed up to make it look like mud." A moment later, after explaining the ingredients, he commented on the presentation: "See, they put it in a bucket, and then stick a shovel in it, and it makes it look like dirt." And some talk was not food-related but simply came forth, as good talk often will, over a meal. "When you really talk to kids," Stacia observed one morning, "instructional opportunities arise all the time." Edie was sitting next to Dakota, eating carrot sticks and looking at one of the many displays of student work. "When did they put that up?" she asked. "Yesterday," Dakota answered. "And what do those letters say?" Edie continued. "What are those letters?" Dakota slid back in her chair and began talking with Edie about the display and the words, letting Edie's questions direct the conversation.

One of the things that most struck me about Co-Teach was the way the staff and student interns rarely missed a chance to extend, no matter how slightly, what a student could do, always alert to the instructional potential of the moment, the "teachable moment." When Brandon asked Rochelle to remove the raisins from his ants on a log, he mentioned offhandedly that he used to like them. "Gee," she mused as she picked the raisins off the peanut butter, "what do you suppose happened between then and now to make you change?"

After snack time came the final activity of the day, usually something involving language: watching a video tape that the students would then discuss, or dictating thank-you notes to guests, or, most often, listening to a story. During the reading of a story, the teachers or interns explained how books work: how they're made, how you know who wrote them, how illustrations complement text. And they asked for observations or for predictions: "What do you think is going to happen? OK, let's see."

And then departure. Putting on sweaters and coats, saying good-bye, the arrival of parents, the walk to the bus, waiting in the parking lot behind McGill. The walk, sometimes assisted, provided one more opportunity to work on strength and coordination, to experience, again, the continuity of leave-taking and the promise of returning, and to talk. As the intern Kevin was slowly walking Tom up the ramp to the bus, Tom, who had difficulty articulating, turned to him and uttered a phonetic mouthful: "Rush Limbaugh." "What?" Kevin asked, for Tom spoke softly. "Rush Limbaugh," he repeated, a grin taking shape on his face.

III

THE FOREGOING SKETCH of a typical day in Co-Teach offers one point of entry to the program; focusing on a single child can provide another.

Michael was almost six years old and had been in Co-Teach for two years, a longer-than-usual stay. According to his mother, he was an "easy baby" who "didn't cry a lot or seem to demand much." However, "past age two, normal development seemed to taper off." When he was three years, ten months, his autism was diagnosed, and a month later his parents enrolled him in Co-Teach, the kind of early intervention that can make a profound difference in the way his life develops. Michael was a sweet-tempered boy with Paul McCartney good looks — a sweep of brown hair, doe eyes. Here is a series of observations of Michael, gained over the week of my visit. Among other things, they illustrate some of the ways teaching and learning unfold when a child with a disability is educated in an adequately staffed, integrated setting.

> Michael was watching Zachary and Brandon execute a Ninja turtle rescue, and then moved alongside them to the counter that separated the entrance from the free play area. Alongside, but down a ways. He was holding a little brown bear upright on the counter, rocking it slightly, left paw, right paw. Dakota, who had been sitting on the floor in the midst of the children, playing, observing, got to her knees and inched over to Michael. "Is the bear dancing, Michael?" she asked. Michael smiled a little and increased the rhythm of the rocking. "Dance," said Dakota.

"Make the bear dance." "Dance," said Michael, smiling now. "Good job!" affirmed Dakota. "You made the bear dance."

After exhibiting a truck during show and tell and answering a few questions about it ("How much did it cost?" "What's it do?" "Can I play with it?"), Robby passed it along for each child to hold and examine. Michael took it from Mariah as it came around the circle, turned it slowly one way, then another, and, when Shelley said it was time to pass it on, he looked over toward Tom and held it out to him.

Zachary was holding a strand of Unifix cubes. "Look at this," he said to Michael, standing nearby. "Look at this," Michael repeated. A minute or so later, Debbie, another student intern, came into the classroom, walking by Michael. "Hi, Michael," she said. "How are you?" "How are you," Michael said softly, without raising his voice at the end of the question.

It was time to go from free play to circle time. The children began lining up. Today, Michael was line leader. Stacia guided him to the front of the line. "Michael," she asked, "how do you want us to go to circle?" He started moving his arms, smiling. "Ah," Stacia continued, "do you want us to swim or march?" "Maesh," Michael replied, smiling more broadly now, pumping his arms, marching in place, looking back over his shoulder to see the class lined up behind him.

Michael was paging through a book called *Numbers* when Shelley moved over from Charles to ask him to count the chickens on the page open before him. He kept looking at the page. She lightly placed the tip of her finger under one chicken, then another. "One," she said in a soft voice. "Two." Michael's face got tight, and he made a low groaning noise. Then he began screaming, shaking his hands and slapping his thighs. Shelley remained calm. "Do you want me to leave you alone, Michael?" He continued. "Would you like me to leave?" He started to calm down — then he nodded. "OK," Shelley said, and went back to Charles. A few minutes later, Charles came over to Michael, who had gone back to looking at *Numbers*. Charles knelt beside him, watching him turn the pages.

The class was sitting in a circle, listening to Dakota read a story. Dusty, who could now sit through much of a story with minimal assistance, was, on this day, especially active, making his humming sound, bucking his legs. Ginny sat behind him, her legs out along his legs and her arms bracing his chair. Michael leaned forward in his chair, looking past several students, to watch him.

Michael was at a learning center with a pile of Unifix cubes in front of him, snapping one onto the other, forming a long single strand.

It was circle time. The class was gleefully singing "Boa Constrictor," a song about a hapless youth being devoured body part by body part: *"I'm being eaten by a boa constrictor, and I don't like it one bit . . ."* As the snake gulped ankles to head, the children placed their hands on their knees, hips, bellies, necks, singing out the names for each along the way. Smiling, Michael touched his knees, belly, and neck, mouthing some of the lyrics.

Edie walked over and gave me a hug. Michael, who was standing nearby, turned and pointed to the book she was carrying. "Book," I said. He looked at me. "Book," I said again. The next day, as the class was lining up for recess, Michael came up to me and looked at my notebook. "Book," I said. "Book," he repeated and reached for my hand, holding it as we prepared to go outside.

On this day, Michael's father brought him to school. As his father started to leave, Michael screamed and shook, slapping his hands against the window from which he was watching the departure. Shelley snagged three paper plates from a shelf and came to Michael, putting her hand against the small of his back. Softly, softly, she spoke to him, laying the three plates on the counter before him. One had a happy face, one an angry face, one a sad face. "What are you feeling, Michael?" she asked. "Show me." Michael calmed down and touched the plate with the sad face on it.

Circle time, and the class was singing a song about six little ducks who quack and wobble. The children accompanied the song with motions of their hands and bodies. Stacia took Michael's hands in hers and opened and closed fingers against thumbs: *quack, quack, quack.*

The next day when someone again selected the duck song, Michael grinned and opened and closed his fingers and thumbs like a bill. *Quack, quack, quack,* he sang, his bills flapping.

Michael and Mariah were at a learning center with Stacia. The task was to cut three pieces of construction paper and build a rocket: a rectangular strip rolled into a tube became the body; another smaller rectangle, once trimmed, became the wings; a square curved and stapled became the nose cone — which would be glued to the tip of the body. A model that Stacia had made sat before them. Mariah, the youngest child in Co-Teach, had some difficulty manipulating the scissors but was able to construct a passable rocket. Michael watched Mariah. It was a hard task for him. But Stacia talked him through the steps he could do and guided his hand as he used the scissors and stapler. His nose cone was jagged, but stapled properly and glued to a cylindrical body. The wings were irregular, and time ran out before they could be affixed.

There was a little track on the playground outside the Co-Teach classroom. During recess, Kimberlie would mount a tricycle and round the track for the period, saying "hi" as she approached you and "bye" as she peddled past. Michael was the other child who, every day, took to the track. He jogged its circumference, either ahead of or behind Kimberlie. He looked straight ahead or at the immediate stretch of track in front of him, moving his arms with a light thrust, a steady step, unwavering pace, no variation.

Michael was standing at the counter by the toys. He had before him a house with a red plunger coming out the top of the roof. He pushed it. It played "This Old House." When the song was over, Michael pressed the plunger again.

Then he went to the book rack and brought two books back to the counter. Shelley was standing nearby, conferring with one of the practicum students. She knelt down next to him, looking at the pages as he turned them. "What's that, Michael?" she asked when a rabbit appeared. "Bun . . ," he said softly. "Good!" she said. "Bunny." "Bunny," Michael repeated.

Michael walked up to Jeff, one of the student interns, a big jovial guy, and motioned with his arms. "Up?" Jeff asked. "You want me to lift you up?" Michael nodded. "Well, let's see you count to five, Michael. How about it?" A hail-fellow-well-met demeanor. Michael smiled and with his fingers ticked off *one-two-three-four-five.* "All right!" Jeff applauded and hoisted Michael into the air. A high, sweeping lift. Michael laughing and laughing.

The class was in the gym above the Co-Teach classroom. Some college students were finishing a game of basketball. Michael walked to the boundary of the court and watched. The dribbling of the ball. The abrupt turns and pivots, the bursts of speed. His mother said he watched games on television for long stretches of time. He watched the young men play.

Shelley, Stacia, Rochelle, Dakota, and the rest organized a game of kickball. The children who needed assistance had an adult alongside them. The game was loose, but it worked. When it was his turn, Michael gave the ball a solid kick and, with Stacia by his side, ran to first base.

When Zachary connected, Michael ran with Stacia to the next base, stamping on it, laughing. Stacia moved away. Michael stayed on base alone. Stacia walked to home plate. When Edie kicked the ball, Stacia called to Michael from home, coaching him, and he took off, arms pumping, and crossed the base, grinning.

Michael was finishing his snack at a table with five other children. It was a little hectic. The children were handing in their plates, and two of them had food on their faces and needed to be cleaned up. The student intern at the table missed Michael's gesture: holding his plastic glass out to be refilled. Michael started screaming. Stacia, who was at the next table, moved alongside him, calming him. "What do you want, Michael?" she asked. "Tell me what you want. Use your words." After a few moments he pointed to the pitcher at the other end of the table and said, "Water."

It was Michael's turn for show and tell. He sat in the chair at the head of the circle, Shelley beside him. He looked calm and held his toy lightly on his lap. Shelley began the questioning. "Michael, are those elves?" "Elves," he said. Zachary raised his hand. "Call on Zachary," Shelley prompted. Michael looked at Zachary. "Zaschary," he said. "Are they on a log?" Zachary asked. "Log," Michael said. Mariah raised her hand. Shelley pointed over Michael's shoulder. "Call on Mariah," she said, "Maimia," Michael said, following Shelley's line of sight. "Can I play with it?" she asked. Yes, Michael nodded. One or two questions followed in similar fashion. Then, when it was time to pass the toy around the circle, Michael, without prompting, handed it to Brandon, sitting to his immediate right.

IV ASKED WHAT IN EDUCATION she would change if she could, Michele, the talented prekindergarten teacher in William Ayers's *The Good Preschool Teacher,* answered. "Numbers and money. There's always too many kids and always too few resources." Clearly, it is numbers that enable Co-Teach to be as good as it is. When I asked her about it, Shelley spoke at length on this point. "There's no way we could do what we do without having a lot of skilled adults in the room. That's why the university collaboration is so valuable to us. There are some days when we don't have as many practicum students or one of us is sick, and it becomes a much different day. You spend your time making sure the kids are safe." She paused. "You know, it's interesting; I find especially with kids with disabilities, you *have* to have that time to spend with them. If I'm able to sit down with a child and develop that rapport *every day,* then they respond, and I can get a sense of what they're really capable of doing."

It is important to point out, though, that in the case of Co-Teach, it was not just numbers: the practicum students I observed struck me as a group of special sensibilities. In addition, they were the recipients of expert supervision, something that did not go unnoticed by one of the parents, who praised Shelley's ability to "oversee everything." Many times I saw Shelley or Stacia give a quick lesson on how to hold or guide a child: how to balance yourself or use your legs as a brace or direct without forcing the movement of a child's hand. And when an intern led circle time or a small-group activity, there was a casual suggestion, a piece of advice in the flow of classroom talk. During the beginning-of-the-week introduction to the theme of Earth, Stars and Environment, Dakota was explaining the concept of "world," for the children would soon be going to learning centers to create their own paper-plate worlds. She spoke well, but her explanation was too abstract, and kids were drifting. "What are some of the things we might find in the world, Dakota?" Shelley asked from the side of the circle, and Dakota picked up the cue and began grounding her discussion. And the children started asking questions. Rochelle commented favorably on this style of supervision, comparing it to another practicum she had where student interns felt "jumped on." In Co-Teach, suggestions were made in more collegial fashion as the day unfolded. And the quality of supervision contributed to an atmosphere in Co-Teach that was unmistakable. Michael's mother referred to the program as an "oasis" where the teachers "set a tone" that influenced everyone who spent time in the room.

All the parents I spoke with commented on the feel of Co-Teach. As Brandon's mother succinctly put it, "I just like what I saw here." How, then, was that "tone," that "feel" created?

To begin with, there was affection, pure and simple. Lots of touch, embrace, a demonstration that kids were genuinely welcome and appreciated: a practicum student rubbing the back of Dusty's head; another student reaching out and tweaking Edie's sneakered foot; Shelley slipping on a purple hand-puppet snake and gobbling on Jonathan's neck. And caring was related to a sense of security, safety, something Shelley commented on when she talked about the ratio of adults to students in Co-Teach. From what I could tell, children felt safe here: safe to explore, safe to try things out, and safe from threat — both from others and from their own impulses. When an outburst or tantrum erupted, the staff was quick to respond. They were adept at determining the cause of distress. As Stacia put it, "there's a reason why a child acts as she does, and you have to be creative in figuring that out." They would, when necessary, restrain the child, holding him or her in a protective embrace, a "time out" until the fury or frustration subsided. And just in the daily flow of things, the staff intervened to teach the children how to resolve problems peacefully. Robby's father thought his son's "social skills have improved one hundred percent. They teach kids how to deal with situations rather than fighting over them." The way Brandon's mother saw it, "The kids don't have to defend themselves; they learn to use words instead." It is important to remember that this developing civility was being fostered in a program that contained a marked percentage of children who, in many settings, would be seen as a source of trouble and discord. It is equally important to note that this safe community could be built because of the number of teachers and interns in the room. Conservative critics have a point when they say you can't simply throw money at schools. But a thoughtful response to potentially difficult situations often requires resources: people, money, physical setting. The development of decent civil space requires the means to cultivate, guide, and support. The economics of civility.

Considerations of civil behavior in Co-Teach were linked to considerations of difference. This was, after all, a shared environment where there were, in some cases, profound differences in what children were able to do, and some children did what they did in unusual ways. The staff addressed these issues on several levels.

One was the curriculum itself, particularly the first four or five weeks of the program. A typical activity was this: Shelley put up a large piece of paper and solicited from the class ways we're alike (e.g., we all like to play outside and swing on the swings) and ways we're different (e.g., we have different ways of playing and different ways of asking for a push on the swings). Such activities gave rise to discussions of identity, difference, similarity, relatedness, and the sharing of common space.

Then there was the day-to-day encounter with behavior. In the beginning, some children would ask why a particular child was making humming or groaning noises while the teacher was reading a story. Shelley or Stacia would explain that that was the child's way of listening or joining in or singing along. And as time went on, the unusual behavior subsided — or became less intense — and everybody grew familiar with it, treated it as less of a big deal. And something else happened. Some children began trying out the unusual behavior for a few days, for a week. Shelley saw this "as an attempt to try to understand the other child." I thought of Edie during free play slipping into Tom's walker and seeing what it was like to move around in it.

I don't want to overstate the degree to which the children in Co-Teach lived and played together. The three boys without disabilities spent a good deal of time with each other, playing games, concocting stories. And some children were able only occasionally to move into the world of others. But there was, overall, a significant amount of interaction and cross-talk and willingness to share. The staff worked hard to achieve common affirmation, a sense of decency and acceptance. During my stay, I never saw a child shun another, and I did see a fair number of attempts to connect and include.

The creation of community — in a region or in a classroom — must include concerns about civic space and rights and the social bond, but it also has to include the acknowledgment of human growth and potential. Another aspect of the effectiveness of Co-Teach was the staff's keen eye for signs of growth, no matter how small, and a willingness to stay with a child through a mess, through seemingly botched attempts to do things, through normally irritating behavior. For it was over the long haul that tiny changes could lead to measurable gains. There was a wooden telephone in the play area, the receiver of which was attached to its base with a cord made of thick yarn. Jonathan was knocking the base on the counter, and the receiver was flopping over the side, slapping hard. The noise didn't seem to bother the other kids, absorbed in their own play, but it certainly wore on my ear. Shelley came over and began talking to Jonathan about the telephone. As he momentarily steadied it, looking off but seeming to attend to her voice, as he held the base flat on the counter, Shelley said, "Look, Jonathan," and touched the buttons. "Beep, beep, beep . . . oh, hello? Hey, Jonathan, it's for you!" She handed him the receiver. He looked at it briefly, then looked away. The next day during free play, Jonathan was back at that phone. *Slap, slap, slap.* Shelley came over, again talking to Jonathan about the phone and demonstrating its use. Jonathan took the receiver from her hand and held it. Through the rest of the week, Jonathan would find the phone during free play, mashing his palm against the key pad, slamming the base but occasionally looking at the receiver, shaking it, holding it. And when she could, Shelley came over and picked up where she'd left off, calming the slamming behavior, talking in an easy voice about that incoming call for Jonathan. Shelley could see possibility, tiny approximations in the children's behavior. She possessed a mix of perceptual acuity and patience that enabled her to foster growth in situations where many of us would see only deficiency and chaos.

This tolerant and keen vision was related to a fundamental belief in human potential, a belief inclusive of those with physical or cognitive disabilities. Thus, the staff of Co-Teach continually challenged children, extending expectations just beyond the present. Commenting on her son's progress, Michael's mother put it this way: "You guys never let him slack off. You keep things challenging for him." The staff of Co-Teach not only seized the teachable moment; they leaned into it. We were all going across campus to the Star Lab — a dome onto which the constellations are projected — when Shelley noticed Jonathan veer from the group toward a sign in front of one of the buildings. It was a fancy plate mounted on granite that gave the name of the building, its history, and the departments in it. Jonathan ran his hands over the words. Shelley knelt beside him, one hand on the small of his back, and read the sign, pointing to the words with him. Later, I asked her about the episode. "When Jonathan saw that big sign," she said, "he really got excited. He was looking at the words, touching them. Just because language isn't yet efficient for him doesn't mean he's not clicking, that he doesn't have some interest in words." (I thought, here, of something Michael's mother said to me. "All too often people think of nonverbal persons as voids, that their world must surely be flat.") Shelley swept her hands in front of her, as though clearing a space, and extended that moment with Jonathan into broader contexts. "People ask, 'Oh, what's wrong with that child? What's his disability? What does he have?' But once you know the label, it can lower expectations. 'Oh, he has autism, he's never gonna talk.' Or, 'She has Down syndrome, she's never gonna be able to read.' I think it's important to keep in mind that the label is part of the machinery of eligibility for services, and once we do what we need to do with it, we turn back to the child, to his strengths, his behaviors. Sure, some of these children have big problems, but you have to try to see what the kids *can* do, what they like to do, what they enjoy, what draws them. That, not the labels, will tell you something about what they can become."

I want to close this visit with some observations on Co-Teach and institutional structure. To orient us, three vignettes.

> Michael's mother, Judi, was the guest at the weekly Co-Teach staff meeting. About ten practicum students were present, Shelley and Stacia, and Rick van den Pol, a professor of education at the university and director of Educational Research and Service, the division that oversees Co-Teach. Judi was describing the process of getting Michael into kindergarten — "mainstreaming" him into a regular public school. She had talked to a number of teachers and administrators along the way, visited a number of schools, and was describing what she and other parents of children with disabilities often encounter. "Frankly," she said, "you're made to feel that the kids are a kind of human debris." Rick asked her what parents might want. "Respect," she said. "And an attempt to put yourself in the parents' shoes."

> Shelley and Stacia were having one of their weekly meetings with the occupational therapist, the speech and language therapist, and the physical therapist from the Missoula Public School District. They had these joint

meetings for two reasons. One was to assess the progress of the children in Co-Teach receiving special education services. Federal law requires that for each child a precisely specified program of instruction and set of goals (known as an IEP–Individualized Educational Plan or Program) be developed and the child's progress be systematically monitored. The other reason was to incorporate the goals of the three therapists into the ongoing events of the classroom day. During this meeting, they discussed ways to make snack time even more rich in language, the possibility of having some children use tools in dirt rather than sand — a more strenuous activity — and some physical activities that could be incorporated into the field trip to the Star Lab.

Woven throughout the meeting was reference to mainstreaming, so afterward I asked Shelley about the mechanics of inclusion. "Inclusion is one of those ideas," she replied, "that educators are still striving to realize." I clicked on my tape recorder. "It's powerful and beneficial to have kids with disabilities educated with their normally developing, same-age peers — especially at such a young age. But the unfortunate thing is that the process isn't always thought out clearly and isn't always successful. It's like: Here's a kid, he's in first grade, he has a disability, inclusion's the thing right now, so let's put him in this classroom. That's a real disservice to the child, to the teacher, and to the concept of inclusion. For inclusion to be successful, people have to work together — and that runs against the tradition of a teacher having her own classroom, her own domain. There has to be a collaborative effort. I think a lot of efforts at mainstreaming have failed on this level."

In the very back of the Co-Teach classroom, out of the way of the children's activities, was a work and storage area. There was a desk for the practicum students, shelves packed with manipulatives and games, rubber mats and medicine balls. Rick van den Pol and I found two chairs and began our interview. One of the questions I asked was how he would characterize the conceptual foundation of Co-Teach. His response:

"I think the whole notion of interdisciplinary service has really become important to us. Historically, we've worked with the occupational therapists and the physical therapists and the special education teachers. And as we've developed, we've had more exchanges with the early-childhood people here at the university. The interdisciplinary model feels right to me now. If you look around, you'll find materials that are influenced by Montessori, and you'll also see people recording frequency counts of behavior. By and large, the people who work here rarely get into abstract arguments about which philosophy is correct — no one's keeping score, you know: 'Chalk one up for Skinner. Chalk one up for Piaget.' We try to base our questions on what seems to be useful to a particular child. Does what we're doing seem helpful? It keeps us open to changing what we do."

Co-Teach sat at the intersection of multiple institutions. Its connection to the University of Montana afforded the program a research orientation, access to a range of disciplinary specialists, and a cadre of capable students, who themselves brought the influence of their training and, in some cases, experience as parents or teachers. The relationship with the school district provided resources for those children deemed eligible for special education services. It brought, as well, a degree of material and logistical support, such as the bus that enabled some children to attend Co-Teach. And it incorporated into Co-Teach the skills of an occupational therapist, a speech and language therapist, and a physical therapist, contributing to the services the children received and enhancing the Co-Teach brain trust.

Co-Teach sought to establish links with families, incorporating them into the process of educating their children. Robby's father praised Shelley and company for being "very open to parents' input," for soliciting assistance in developing goals and pedagogical strategies. I saw Shelley and Stacia conferring with parents daily as they dropped off or picked up their children, talk to them at length on the phone in the back of the classroom, or write in what they called home-school notebooks that would travel back and forth in a child's backpack. These relationships signified a simple but important truth about experimental educational programs: parents will stay and will spread the word if they perceive the program to be a hospitable place that does well by their kids. But there was another level of parental involvement, as represented by Michael's mother's guest appearance at the staff meeting. Some parents moved beyond the institutional boundary of Co-Teach, contributing to its operation as a preschool and as an educational setting for practicum students. This was especially important, considering that there has been, among some professionals in education and psychology, a tendency to define as pathological the families of children with disabilities, to see them as part of the problem. The staff at Co-Teach saw parents as potential contributors to the program's intellectual life.

The interdisciplinary orientation described by Rick van den Pol widened the conceptual territory within which Co-Teach functioned. He mentioned two professional fields: special education and early childhood education. No discipline is conceptually monolithic. In fact, some of the issues raised in this chapter — mainstreaming or inclusion, the usefulness of diagnostic categories, the treatment of autism — are at the center of huge debates within the special education community. But generally speaking, special education has been influenced by behaviorist psychology, so it tends to focus, in a very precise way, on behavior and its reinforcers, on exact measures of what students do over time. Thus, as Rick noted, the staff took frequency counts of kinds of behavior to assess student progress and program effectiveness. (And this orientation has been strengthened by the legal mandates that have come to surround the special education enterprise.) One of the benefits of the special education perspective is that it encourages precision, analytical rigor, careful description and discussion of instruction and objectives. The downside is that the precision itself can lead to reductive curricula — breaking tasks down to meaningless micro-units of activity — and to stunted expectations. Influenced by Dewey and Piaget, rather than behaviorist psychology, the early-childhood perspective affirms the inclination of all children to learn, explore, construct meaning out of experience, and attain mastery. It asserts that these inclinations will thrive in caring environments rich in toys and materials, numbers and print. This perspective leads to stimulating, student-centered classrooms, but it can overstate the degree to which kids will automatically and naturally learn from play and diminish the role that structure and direction can have in that learning.

Early-childhood and special education are fields that give rise to strongly held beliefs among their respective constituencies. Rick told me of being assailed at one professional conference because children in Co-Teach were made to line up, a task thought to be "developmentally inappropriate" for preschoolers — so the bringing together of these perspectives could be volatile. But from what I could tell, it was a generative fusion; the integrated population served by Co-Teach virtually demanded such an unsettling of received perspectives and methods. All the parents I spoke with commented favorably on the blend of structure and exploration. They liked what it did for their children.

Co-Teach was made possible by the realignment of a number of institutional borders, by a collaborative, multiperspectival orientation, and by the interchange of many kinds of knowledge. Though one might take issue with some aspect of the program's philosophy or methods, these characteristics can be powerful guides in helping us imagine different kinds of classrooms. They contributed to the development of a particular kind of public educational space that fostered the growth of children with a wide range of ability and need — a democratic ideal. A small experiment in social change.

Both Co-Teach and Polaris School were public responses to the needs of a diverse citizenry, and their organizational and administrative structures mirrored that diversity. The one-room school and its independent district — though greatly reduced in number and linked more closely now to county superintendencies and state agencies — still shared many of the characteristics of its nineteenth-century ancestors: individualistic and self-reliant, governed through hands-on participatory democracy, community-run. A school like Polaris, with few intervening institutional layers between parents, school board, and instruction, had more local control than any urban neighborhood school could ever have. Co-Teach, on the other hand, as small as it was, was collaborative and complex, nested in agencies and regulations at every level, from federal to local school district to university department. It would take an elaborate chart to sketch all the lines of influence and authority. Polaris and Co-Teach reflected two historical strains in our nation's thinking about institutions and governance.

Yet, in some compelling ways, the educational settings that were created within these two institutional structures shared a great deal. One of the readers of this chapter observed that Co-Teach was like a one-room school. The comparison was instructive: a range of ages, a cross-section of ability, a mix of shared assignments and individualized instruction, the encouragement of peer learning. Educational planning and governance in the twentieth century have been characterized by a move toward consolidation, division of labor, bureaucratization — and excellence has been determined by the degree of fit to this "one best system" model. These attempts at standardization have been responsible for a number of improvements in the quality of schooling — more than critics of bureaucracies like to admit — but the passion for the systematic has blinded many to a basic truth. Local history, community need, the political moment, broad social trends and forces can come together in powerful configurations to create a range of educational settings of quality. Structurally, anatomically, they can be quite different. The irony is that once we get in close, assessing the feel of the room, the intellectual atmosphere, the social dynamics, we find they may well share as much as they differ, reflecting educational needs both diverse and common.

9

Tucson, Arizona

I "SHE'S A WEAVER, she's a creator, this Spider Woman, and she creates the web of life. It's ephemeral, but enduring . . ." I shifted my weight against the door on the passenger's side of the old pickup — aware of its rattling, I reached around and locked it — and looked more fully at Michelle as she explained this spirit being to me. "All these contradictions . . ." She drove with a slight lean toward the windshield, both hands on the wheel, but concentrating, too, on what she was saying, turning her head slightly toward me, her eyes still on the road, negotiating bumps while trying to help me see. "But for the students you'll be meeting, contradictions are less of a problem; they're in the weave of things."

I moved again, stretching my legs down to the floorboard, looking out the window at the pine trees — they were stirring a little in the warm morning breeze — and at the cactuses, those big cactuses called *saguaros*. We fell momentarily silent, and I allowed my gaze to wander across the faded dashboard, the mesquite leaves and Dentine wrappers on the floor, two feathers, tied at the quills, lying in the space where a radio would go. Michelle glanced over and saw me looking at the feathers. "Indians usually hang them from the rearview mirror," she explained, "but the string broke, so" — she shrugged — "so now they're here." She made a wide right turn, then a left over gravel and asphalt, reached up to the visor for a card key, and we entered the parking structure closest to the Modern Languages Building of the University of Arizona. She maneuvered the truck into a space with one hand, replacing the card key with the other, and, finally, reached for the ignition. A green disk dangled from a little key chain; TUBA CITY was printed in white letters around the circumference.

Tuba City, population seventy-three hundred, is in northeastern

Arizona, just inside the Navajo Reservation — which contains within it the smaller territory of the Hopi — the largest reservation in the United States. For the past three summers, some students from Tuba City High School, a public high school within the reservation, have traveled south to the university to participate in a four-and-a-half-week intensive English program. The program was the brainchild of two high school teachers, one of whom, Manny Begay, told me about its origins.

Manny had been teaching math at Tuba City since 1973, and after some years became aware of "the amount of talent I saw that wasn't going anywhere. Students were continually seeing high school as an end in itself, not as a steppingstone." So, with the aid of some foundation money, he and several other teachers developed a strong math-science curriculum oriented toward college work. The program grew, but it became obvious that, though "the kids were doing well in calculus and physics, they were still struggling with language arts." Around the same time — this would have been the mid-1980s — the community expressed the desire to see more representation of Native American history and literature in the curriculum. Manny saw this convergence of need and desire as an opportunity. Back, then, to the foundation, followed by a series of negotiations with the University of Arizona, and the summer program was born. It was to provide an opportunity for students to develop their English skills and to become familiar with a college campus. Manny became the coordinator. Michelle Taigue, a faculty member at the university and my partner in the bouncing truck, was chosen to develop the curriculum and teach the first class. The program grew —there were now three classes, two of sophomores and Michelle's section of juniors and seniors — and Michelle was still in the thick of it, revising it continually.

Such summer programs are a common feature of the college-bound student's life in the United States. Every summer, hundreds of programs, sometimes two or three to a campus, provide instruction that is in some cases preparatory (study skills, introduction to writing for college, basic math), in some cases an enrichment (courses in literature, science, engineering), and these are mounted for students as young as middle-schoolers, though, more frequently, for students who will be entering college in the fall. State colleges in the Midwest offer them, open access colleges on the East Coast, Stanford, Berkeley, and the Ivy League. An educational system that defines itself as democratic and open needs such programs. They are an important link between the usually segmented domains of secondary and postsecondary education, an institutional mechanism to assist in the difficult transition from high school to college. As well, they make available the considerable resources of colleges and universities to the project of public education. And, as was true of the Arizona program, they can be the site of experiments with curriculum, experiments that can feed back into the schools.

"I was sick of hearing what Indian kids couldn't do," Michelle told me. "'They can't read the classics. They can't write well because they come from an oral culture.' All that stuff. I was sick, too," she continued, "of watching, again and again, their own rich traditions being kept out of the English classroom." So she set out to compose a curriculum that combined novels and Native American stories, Greek tragedies and ceremonial songs. "They're all of a piece if you teach them right."

The syllabus for Michelle's course moved from "ancient and contemporary mythologies" to "explore the relationship between the self and imagination." "What is our connection to ancient and contemporary mythologies?" the syllabus asked. "How are we shaped by ancestors and family?" "What are the connections among remembering, writing, reading?" "How can we create ourselves through writing? Speaking? Dreaming? Storytelling?" Students explored these questions by reading Scott Momaday's *The Way to Rainy Mountain*; *Oedipus the King*; Navajo poet Luci Tapahonso's *A Breeze Swept Through*; a selection of coyote tales; a homemade anthology of stories and reflections by Leslie Marmon Silko, Momaday, Tapahonso, and others; Arizona novelist Barbara Kingsolver's *Animal Dreams*; Carson McCullers's *The Ballad of the Sad Café*; and David Seals's gonzo vision quest, *The Powwow Highway*. In addition, students wrote almost every day: entries in journals, personal narratives, commentaries on the books. There were guest speakers and opportunities for all three classes — sophomores, juniors, and seniors — to come together to share their work and ideas. My visit to the program came right at its midpoint, so the students were immersed in their studies. A lot of college courses don't require as much in so short a time.

We made our way out of the parking structure into the dry Arizona heat — blinking in the sudden blast of light — and walked a short diagonal line to the Modern Languages Building. Michelle told me about the students. There was Jarvis, who won the state high school chess championship. There were two girls who went by the names of their spirit animals, Fish and Frog, and Frog had had her share of sorrow. There was Bert, Bertha, who wanted to be a writer. And there was Edwin, also known as Lizard. Michelle guided me toward an entrance, down some stairs, then into a cool, well-lit classroom. "Hi," she said, loud and bright, as though we were walking into a back yard picnic. "Hi . . . hi . . . hello . . . hi," said the Red Sox cap and the soccer T-shirt and all kinds of jeans and shorts and sneakers. The desks were arranged in a circle. Michelle sidled through an opening, lifting her bookbag, and I followed, lifting mine. There were thirteen students, mostly girls, a tutor named Patricia, and a woman from the reservation named Percy who lived in the dorms with the students and watched over them. Michelle introduced me, and we all talked a bit. Some of the students were quiet, a few were forthcoming, and once the exchange between us loosened up, Michelle settled in to work on *Animal Dreams,* the reading for that day.

The novel is set in a small town in New Mexico and has two narrators: Doc Homer, the town's physician, and Codi, his mordant, rootless daughter, who has dropped out of medical school and, with great uncertainty, returned home to care for her father. Most of the narration is Codi's, and her conflict and enlightenment come from the failing Doc Homer, an old high school flame named Loyd, and the letters of her sister Hali, who has found her own difficult peace on the farming cooperatives in Nicaragua. It is a bittersweet novel, moving and surprisingly comic, thanks to Codi's take on things, but it is not an easy one: there is the alternation of speakers, it is fairly long, and Kingsolver's style, though warm and grounded in the particulars of place and conversation, is, at times, elaborate and highly metaphoric.

Michelle told us that Kingsolver thought one of her audiences for this book might be high school students — Codi takes a temporary job teaching biology in the local high school — and "if Barbara were in town, she would be very interested in what you think of her book." Edwin sat up. "Then why don't we write to her?" "No! Could we?" another student asked. "Well, sure," said Michelle, leaning forward, holding *Animal Dreams* in both hands, kind of waving it and bending it as she talked. "What would you want to say to Barbara? What do you think of this book?"

Silence.

Then Frog said faintly, "I like the way Codi talks." "Yeah," added Edwin, "I like the way she tells her story." "How would you describe the way she talks?" asked Michelle. "Sarcastic," Frog said, a little more assured. Another student observed that "the book read like a movie," and then someone else raised a hand and added that "the book jumps around too much for me." Michelle listened, sometimes repeating all or part of what a student said, looking around the room, inviting further response. "It seems," said Hana, "that there's death on every other page." "Is it a morbid book?" Michelle asked. "Well, not the way it's presented," Hana replied. Then Fish came in: "Poor Codi" — she tapped the book — "she seems like she doesn't have any place that's home." "I like her sister's letters," said the girl next to me, Dawn Manygoats. "But, you know, the letters are not happy. I just know something bad is going to happen . . ."

Michelle started nudging them toward fuller responses. She had a way of shaping space for ideas to develop, guiding but pulling back, casually, associatively, letting students take their time, say the obvious, fall silent, be uncertain. So an ordinary exchange could suddenly lead to an inspired moment. At one point, Frog called attention to a description of the river behind Doc Homer's house, and Michelle asked her how water figures in the book.

"Life," said Frog.

"It brings life and takes life," added Edwin.

There was a pause. Then Jill — tall, lean, slumped down in her desk, her long legs straight out — Jill said, "Doesn't she talk a lot about memory when she talks about the river?"

"Whew! Water and memory. Do you see a connection?" Michelle asked.

"Both run deep," replied Jill.

"It's like there's no ending to either of them," added Frog.

The class moved on this way through the late morning. Some of the students had a keen eye for Kingsolver's details: a crescent on the belly of a coyote pup, marigold petals on a gravesite. And most of the girls responded to the main character, Codi. The class was about halfway through the book, and, except for one or two students, were liking it. Michelle again brought up the letter to Kingsolver. "I think it'd be wonderful to write it," she urged. "Do you mean a critique?" Dawn Manygoats asked. Michelle said it could be whatever they wanted it to be. "How about a letter to *Codi?*" someone else inquired. "Great idea!" said Michelle. "But whatever you make them, make them due tomorrow."

Michelle's classroom style was a mix of openness and intensity. The way she saw it, the program itself, the whole four-and-a-half weeks, was an evolving story, a narrative that everyone created, so it was crucial that she pick up on whatever emerged in the classroom, to follow leads, to work all students into the ongoing conversation. Yet stories have structures, narratives aren't shapeless, so she tried to provide focus and organization by making connections among the things the students said, by returning to a previous exchange or pointing out a recurring theme. And sometimes she'd directly intervene. A kind of systematic spontaneity, she called it, laughing at the oxymoron.

There's a fair-sized literature that suggests a mismatch between the communication styles of various groups of Native Americans and the styles that tend to lead to success in mainstream, predominantly White, classrooms. One must be cautious about such generalizations — they can veer toward stereotype — but it does seem that the reserve of some Indian people is misread in school as a sign of intellectual inadequacy. Now, the students Michelle was working with had been successful in school — and some, I would come to find out, were anything but "reserved." Still, there were brief responses, stretches of silence, signs of reticence. Michelle had a way of honoring all this by working within it, with gentle prodding or humor or by giving a little assistance and elaboration or by just letting someone be. She never assumed that not talking meant that people didn't know things. Narratives have moments of silence too. But the narrative that was developing in this class was a complex one — being formed at the intersection of cultures — so Michelle tried to push at the boundaries of silence as well. A mix of styles. "Structured spontaneity." You needed an oxymoronic language here, the language of a culture broker.

The program was set up so that the juniors and seniors and the sophomores could occasionally meet together around a topic of common interest. That afternoon, all three classes met for a session on dreams. There were about fifty students in all, Michelle's thirteen and a lot of sophomores. Chit-chat, laughter, and the scraping of chairs. There are historical frictions between the Navajo and the Hopi, but I would see little evidence of discord among these students, who, for the most part, had grown up together in Tuba City. I took a seat in the back of the class. Next to me, a sophomore girl had a little white monkey sitting on her desk, about eight inches tall, plastic hands extended toward her. She stroked it while silently watching the goings-on in the rest of the room. Beth Alvarado and Pat Baliani, the teachers of the sophomore sections, moved to the front of the blackboard; they ah-hemmed a little, then AH-HEM, and the students began turning forward and settling down. The girl next to me handed the monkey to the girl next to her, who dropped it into a bookbag by her desk. The top of its fuzzy head peered out. Beth walked casually to the front of a small table in front of the blackboard, her brown hair curling to her shoulders.

The book the students were to read after *Animal Dreams* was *Oedipus the King,* and because of variability in scheduling, some of the sophomores had already started it. Beth wanted to make a link between the two works, and did so through the topics of dreams and prophecies. "In *Oedipus,*" she said, leaning back on the table, her palms on the edge, her legs crossed at the ankles, "in this play, there are no dreams, but there are prophecies." She explained how the two can forward dramatic action, with illustrations from Kingsolver and from Sophocles. Then she observed that "in literature today we tend to use dreams in the way we used to use prophecies," and that led her to a discussion of dreams and prophecies as dramatic devices.

Beth then turned the floor over to Pat Baliani, whose job was to prime the students to write their own dream dramas. Pat came to the table and assumed virtually the same position Beth had, except he leaned on one hand only, the other holding a sheaf of yellow papers in front of him. Pat was a playwright, and he looked to be in his mid-thirties. He started talking about the ways he used dreams in his writing. "They help me a lot. In fact, I keep two big black binders, you know, the thick ones, full of them." As he said this, he laid the papers on the desk and made a two-inch bracket in the air with thumb and forefinger. "Thick ones!" He picked up the papers and read a few selections from his dream-binders. The students got very quiet; the ones in the back leaned forward.

"I'm sitting with the other four Stones" — and there was laughter. "Everything is really cool. They're old and smiley and I'm young. We're posing for an album cover. Then I realize I'm naked!" Big hoots — this *was* high school — and Pat had the room. He read a few more. "I'm a cornerback for Dallas . . ." and "I've planted a bomb in an Italian bike shop . . ." And then there were questions. "How do you turn those dreams into longer writing?" "Can you fly in your dreams?" And one of the sophomores, a guy named Spencer, wanted to know if Pat's been naked in other dreams too. More guffaws. And Pat, who had a disarming classroom presence, said sure and asked if any of the students dreamed about being naked in embarrassing situations. No one admitted to this. "Funny," he said. "My friends have these dreams all the time." He told them about a recurring dream in which he's teaching in his underwear. "Nah," Edwin said from the middle of the room. "Honest," Pat answered. "Teaching makes us all very self-conscious sometimes. I'm nervous right now," he revealed. I wondered if these young people believed him. I did. Almost every teacher I know has had some version of that underwear dream.

More questions. Then Beth, who had been enjoying the show from the corner by the door, walked slowly out to join Pat. She proceeded to give the assignment. "We want you to write a dream in which there's dramatic action," she said and took a few steps back toward the door, to the edge of the blackboard. She had been jotting in chalk some of the qualities of dreams, abstracting them from Pat's presentation and the ensuing questions: "time and space distorted," "bizarre events" — that sort of thing. These two worked together nicely; though it seemed casual, you could tell the lesson took some planning. Beth went over the dream qualities, asking a few questions, drawing examples from the readings and from Pat's vignettes. Then she added the semantic zinger. "In this dream, we want you to incorporate any eight of the following ten words . . . in any way you want." And she listed them:

serpent
lemon
skateboard
footsteps
mesa
feather
horse
rose
cinnamon
sirens

I heard a student close to me say to herself, "*Those* words? Are you kidding?" There was some rustle and mumbling. Beth asked that the class "break into groups of four or five" and start in. I looked for a cluster of Michelle's students, found one in the center of the room, and asked if I could join them. "Yeah." "Sure." Edwin reached behind and pulled up a chair.

At first we all looked at each other, uncertain. Shuffling of feet. Doodling. "Do you wanna do it?" Frog asked me, looking up from a cartoon figure she was sketching. I begged off. Another pause, then Jill said, "The serpent skateboarded with a feather on the mesa . . ." "Hey," someone else said, "write that down!" Frog asked, "What's next?" and everyone started looking at everyone else again. Jill had long wavy hair, and a girl behind her reached for a thin strand and started braiding it. "Come on, you guys," Jill finally declared. "Let's go. I'm not doing this alone." And Jarvis, the fellow who won the state chess championship, suggested that we set the dream in Las Vegas. "Oh, yeah," several said and started suggesting place names: Circus Circus, the Pink Flamingo. They'd been there, and this got them going:

> Eating a cinnamon roll in Las Vegas at the Pink Flamingo,
> we all sit and wait for action, while across the room a
> Chippendales dancer is on a horse passing out roses to all
> the girls. But then the room spins and we all turn into a
> feathered serpent . . .

There was some give-and-take at this point, and the group decided that each of us would be a part of the serpent. "Well, then," someone asked, "who'll be the butt?" Jill flatly stated that she was going to be the head, since, after all, she was transcribing this silly thing. She then turned to me and asked what part I'd like to be. Earlier, during the morning class, Michelle made a crack about my socks — multicolored argyles, definitely city-boy issue — so I ventured, "Socks. Can this serpent have legs?" "Oh, yeah," said Jill. "Per-fect," added Edwin, "and Jarvis can be the foot deodorant!" Someone became the body, someone became the legs, someone delicately transformed "butt" to "tail." And we were done.

Beth and Pat asked the class to read their dream dramas. In the momentary reluctance that followed, the members of one group were eagerly waving their hands. "I had this bad dream," their spokesman began, "I was in this weird class, and I had to write a dream using words like *serpent, lemon, skateboard.*" Big laughs. A few more got read, and they were more dreamlike than ours, eerie and dissociated. Then Spencer, the sophomore who asked Pat Baliani if he'd been naked in other dreams, stood to read the dream drama he and his partner had created. Spencer was wearing baggy shorts, sneakers, and a hugely oversized T-shirt. His baseball cap was turned around backward. He looked like an extra from *Bill and Ted's Excellent Adventure.* He began to read, and the writing was invitingly clever. In one segment, a snake went up alongside the main character, who was dreaming within his dream. "'I turned to my right and there it was, mouth open, rattle rattling, and it crawled in to my mouth.'" (*Ooooaaa* from the class.) "'That's funny,' I said to myself, 'it tastes like *cinnamon.*'" The students applauded. Spencer looked up from the paper, a smile that was at once devilish and grateful on his round, boyish face.

I'm not sure what I expected on that first day of my visit, but I don't think I expected such energetic thinking, and such a nice combination of the serious and the wacky. Part of the richness was that what I'd seen was unclassifiable in any easy way. There was reserve and invitation, respect and adolescent irreverence, snakes and feathers and skateboards and a Chippendales dancer. These may not have been the contradictions Michelle was talking about earlier, but they were the ones I appreciated now as I sat with Edwin and Jarvis and Jill and Frog and the rest, enjoying Spencer's performance.

II THE NEXT MORNING Michelle started her work with *Oedipus the King* by taking the class to the Center for Creative Photography, a photographic archive and gallery at the university. It was a sleek, modern building with prints and posters and other displays along its cool and spacious walls: Edward Weston landscapes, portraits from Richard Avedon's *American West,* Hopi dancers. Michelle, the students, and I gawked our way up a winding staircase to the viewing rooms, where we were met by a friendly man named Victor. Michelle introduced everyone — and Victor repeated each person's name. Then he guided us into a narrow room, almost chilly, with wooden and Plexiglas cases along both walls. At the end of the room was a cabinet with many thin drawers. That was where they kept the photographs.

Victor asked that we stand along the cases on one side, or, if we'd like, sit on the rug. We settled in — some standing, some sitting, one or two half-curled against the cases — and Victor began. He must have worked with students a lot, for he was able to say relatively high-brow things in a casual way. He explained how photographs are stored and displayed, and that "here at the Center we consider photographs to be art, just as painting is art." The photographs we would be seeing were of ancient Greek temples. The man who made them was a prominent American photographer named Richard Misrach. Victor walked over to the cabinet. A pair of white gloves was sitting on top. He put them on, hand in air, tugging finger by finger. There was a hole in the right glove, so a thumb poked out a little. The students watched, intent on this glove business. He opened the top drawer of the cabinet, wide and quite thin, picked up a print along the edges, and slowly took it to the illuminated wooden tray of a display case. "We look at things all the time," he said, "but do we *see* them?" More prints to more cases. "Seeing, really *seeing,* calls for active concentration." Then, *flap, flap, flap,* he brought the Plexiglas covers, which were hinged at the top, down onto the borders of the trays, and we were free to touch, point, lean, do anything as we tried to see, really see, the inscribed floors, the cracked walls, the Doric columns smashed and jutting into the dark sky.

Misrach, Victor explained, shot in the evening, firing hand-held flashes off a pillar or a wall — and the effect was striking. The blue-black space beyond the ruins, the brightened walls and pillars, the empty floors. Illuminated emptiness. A supplicant or demigod could appear, but doesn't. One photograph, though, had a faint silhouette on the corner of a wall. We clustered around this one, tapping on the Plexiglas. Victor explained that Misrach leaves his shutter open, situates himself between camera and wall, and fires a flash. A shadow signature. This could be enchanted territory after all.

We spent an hour with the photographs; then Michelle walked to the center of the floor. We moved back farther toward the wall, giving her room. She slowly passed her hand over the photographs of the temples and started talking about myth and the presence of the spiritual. She asked how the Greeks in *Oedipus the King* divined the meaning of events, and the students volunteered: "From the blind guy" and "that place, the o-oracle?" and "from birds — like my grandmother does." And she developed this into a discussion of the power of the spiritual and drew some specific comparisons between Greek mythology, her native Yaqui, and the students' Navajo and Hopi traditions. She paced back and forth, the hem of her maroon dress flipping around her ankles, and as she told these tales she assumed a range of storyteller's voices: old, cracking voices, children's voices, voices mixing Yaqui and Spanish, even animal clicks and trills.

One of the stories she told was of Arachne, the proud Greek maiden whom Athena turned into a spider. Both the Navajo and the Hopi have spider women in their lore — though each is a very different kind of figure from Arachne — and Michelle used this link to set out on the story. "Arachne was a maiden, beautiful, young, just about your age . . ." And she stopped and turned, feigning mild puzzlement. She reached out to the girl closest to her. "Uh, Hana, how old are you?" "Sixteen," Hana said. "Ah, sixteen," repeated Michelle, not missing a beat. "That was *ex-actly* her age. So, anyway, here's the lovely Arachne at her loom . . ."

And having drawn Hana — and, through Hana, all the girls — into the story, she continued telling us of Arachne's pride in her tapestries and her bold challenge to Athena, the best of the weavers among the goddesses. "So, of course, they had a contest," she exclaimed, her fingers picking at the air as though she were weaving the figures herself. "They spun and spun, and these beautiful gods and goddesses appeared in the fabric. Why, Hana, you could even see the expressions on the faces of the gods! And they spun and spun. And when they were done, whose tapestry do you think was better?" Murmurs here: Athena's . . . no, Arachne's . . . Whose? "It was hard to tell," said Michelle, dropping her hands to her side. But Athena, indignant, shredded Arachne's tapestry (Michelle slashed the air) and turned her into a spider. "She shriveled up and her arms got skinny and crooked, like this." The storyteller hooked her right arm and let it quiver. "And today this spider woman continues to weave her web. We see her all over . . . everywhere . . . all around us." The students were smiling; a few applauded. Michelle turned her head slightly, closing her eyes momentarily, dramatically, and raised a hand. She had more to say.

She talked about the spider woman in Leslie Silko's *Ceremony* and about Navajo tales in which pride and retribution are the central themes. She shifted between the ancient Greek and the Native American, not looking for neat parallels, but suggesting correspondences. The myths and tales, she said, were "compelling and beautiful because they're so invested with power." But, though powerful, they were also present, kind of everyday. They were real for Michelle, not an artifact, not sealed away. I had read *Oedipus* a number of times in the past — had taught it, in fact — and had never understood, no, *felt*, the spiritual dimension of the play as I did sitting in that little room. I was suddenly curious to reread a classic that I figured I knew, that I had wrapped up in its historical gloss, nicely under control. But looking at Misrach's photographs and listening to Michelle made the world of the Greeks real and disturbing.

The students had been reading *Oedipus the King* for the last few days — overlapping with *Animal Dreams* — and Michelle had us scheduled to read the play aloud in the afternoon. The seniors were to have a go at dramalogue. The sophomores were already working with *Oedipus*, and the dormitory buzz on Sophocles was favorable. In fact, Spencer was so taken with the play — which, in tribute to the king's arrogance, he renamed *Oeddie with Attitude* — that he was already halfway through *Oedipus at Colonus*, the unassigned second play in the Theban trilogy.

When Michelle's class reconvened after lunch, she formed us into a circle, and each student selected a character. Some read for two — a queen's attendant, say, and a messenger from Corinth — and all of us, at

Michelle's suggestion, ended up being the chorus. Darold, a rangy, six-foot Hopi boy, was Oedipus, and as he read he curled his foot back alongside his desk, bouncing it. Jill was a feisty Tiresias; she was a little sweet on Darold and had a good time taunting him. Some of the words in the play were tough — proper names like Labdacus and unusual nouns like *suppliant* and *perquisite* — and when Suzy Worker, who was doing a serious Creon, stumbled on one of them, she jerked her head a little and, under her breath, said, *"Ach."* Antina, a tall, beautiful girl who had married young, read both the priest and the messenger with a gentle cadence. Certain lines in the play raised an *"ooooo"* from the class, for they were so harsh: Oedipus' taunt of Tiresias — "You are blind in mind and ears as well as in your eyes." Or Tiresias' indictment of Oedipus: "You are the land's pollution." And the two halves of the circle, split into alternating parts of the choral ode, read with a slight rise and fall, little glitches in their timing and pronunciation fading into the communal voice grieving for its blighted city.

The class read the play straight through, stopping only once in a while to comment or ask a question. Several students called attention to those places where Oedipus unknowingly threatened himself — the moments of sharpest irony. In their eyes, it seemed weird to be so blind to one's place in the scheme of things.

The students finished reading the play just before four o'clock, quitting time, but Michelle leaned on the clock a little to get a few quick reactions. The class thought *Oedipus the King* was "sad" or "tragic." It gave one girl "the chills," and to another it read "like a mystery." Some students were taken with particular characters — Tiresias was a favorite, possibly because of Jill's enthusiastic rendering. Edwin was bemused by Oedipus' bluster. And Suzy Worker made a nice comparison with *Animal Dreams,* observing that the central character, Codi, wandered rootless and finally found a home while Oedipus found a home, only to be "banished to wander."

Michelle Taigue grew up on the border of South Tucson. Historically, a large percentage of the population has been Mexican, and as you entered the community — "Welcome to South Tucson," the sign read — you passed the El Minuto Café and the Mi Carita Tortilla Factory, a school with the proud banner "We Are An 'A' School," and billboards announcing a norteña music festival. Other billboards reminded the locals that "Tourism Creates Jobs." Parts of South Tucson were very poor: on some streets there were collapsing tin shacks in back yards, and empty lots, and an occasional tossed mattress or abandoned car. But other streets, many of them, displayed houses that were holding their own: stucco or wood, well kept, built in the 1930s. Their yards were rich with prickly pear cactus, pines, palo verde trees, big gray bushes known as

Texas rangers, clusters of desert verbena, pink and violet, and long delicate orange flowers known as Mexican birds of paradise. The streets were tranquil in the tempered heat of late afternoon.

Michelle carried a lot of memories of her old neighborhood, and as we got to know each other — driving to and from school, talking about her students and the curriculum, running errands — she talked about growing up, and about her family, and the families before them. She reminisced about the gardens and the cooking, about her father, who was a butcher, and his friends who came up from Mexico along a road they called Camino de la Muerte, because so many people had died on it. She told me about the books she read — novels of all kinds, and poems — and about sitting in her back yard listening to her father and his friends tell stories. Michelle later gave me some accounts she had written about the telling of these tales, and they helped me appreciate the origins of her own storyteller's gift: the way she pulls in her listeners and adapts a tale to the particulars of place. Here's her rendering of a story told by Mosco, a friend of her father's, to the young Michelle:

> "You know, little Micaela, [your] dog here used to be the son of San Lazaro," Mosco said as he gently patted Tiger's head. We all had gathered on the lawn in my grandfather's front yard, enjoying the warm evening and cool breeze coming up from the arroyo that runs east of his garden. "San Lazaro lived over on 24th Street," said Mosco, pointing with his chin and gesturing with his lips the way all my dad's friends did when they were really into the story. "You know, over there by Chevela's place. Well, he had a lovely little house there with San Miguelito growing all the way up the side of his ramada like your Tia Betina's. And since San Lazaro kept such a nice house and garden, Jesucristo himself came over for dinner. Hay, Micaela, what a dinner San Lazaro's wife made! She picked fresh chilies and green corn from the garden, and tomatoes, muy rojos, bigger and juicier than even your grandpapa's . . ."

The story continued: All day long they cooked — "the air was dancing with food" — and when the dishes were finally brought out, San Lazaro's son went and plopped himself right at the table and began gobbling the wonderful fare. His parents were "hot with shame," and Jesus, shocked at the boy's bad manners, said, "As you act like a dog, so shall you be one." And immediately the boy started barking and running around in little circles. And that is the story of San Lazaro y Los Perros.

There was joy in the stories, and surprise, and a kind of peace. But as Michelle told the tales and commented on them, she sometimes became somber and pensive, for Michelle's own heritage reflected the Southwest's broader history of loss and violation. Michelle Taigue, neé Grijalva, was of Yaqui, Mexican, and Welsh descent. Her great-grandfather, the Welshman, was a fierce Indian fighter. ("The only good Indian is a dead Indian," he wrote — echoing General Sheridan — in his diary, which Michelle, through a twist of history, now has.) Her father's people, the Yaqui, had been uprooted and dispersed by the Mexican government. (Her father passed as Mexican to escape the suffering, "wearing a mask," as Michelle put it, to survive.) And her mother, who was Mexican and Welsh, faced the censure of her own people for marrying Michelle's father, and also knew intimately the corrosive American prejudice toward the Mexican.

These multiple layers of violation are reflected in the languages Michelle acquired as a child. Though she has used all three in her personal life and in her teaching — "They're all resources," she said — they carry with them a complex history. Spanish, the language her father used to tell her the Yaqui tales, was the language of the decrees that justified the scattering of his people. And English, the language she now was using to tell me her father's stories, was, in her earlier years, a source of pain. "I would listen to my father and his drinking buddies," she said, "and they were articulate and dynamic in Spanish or Yaqui. But with English, they stumbled and felt ignorant. They were ridiculed." And when the young Michelle carried those Yaqui tales to school, she encountered another version of linguistic and cultural degradation.

It seems that when she told one of her teachers that she came from the talking tree — an old Yaqui creation story — the teacher thought something might be wrong with her and recommended placement in a special education class. That recommendation, fortunately, never came to pass. Some time after, Michelle was poking around in the school's little library and came upon a copy of *Bulfinch's Mythology* that had been adapted for children. She read. She read about gods and goddesses intervening in the lives of mortals. She read about magical birds and powerful snakes and bones being turned into rocks, about Prometheus bringing fire to earth, about flowers growing from the blood of Adonis. She couldn't believe it! Here was a world similar to the world overheard in her back yard. Excited, she took the book to her teacher. Her teacher complimented her on her reading and explained that these myths came from one of the great periods of our civilization. Yes, Michelle said, they're just like me, just like the stories I told you. "No," the teacher replied — as Michelle remembers it, the teacher had an odd expression on her face — "no, that's very different."

But Michelle Taigue refused to accept that judgment — and that refusal was at the core of the curriculum she was fashioning for the students from Tuba City. She knew, in a very personal way, how languages and traditions could limit and oppress, but she knew as well what was possible. It was that possibility that drew her now, using words like *tapestry* and *weave* when she talked about her teaching.

III IT WAS HARD to ignore the weather in Tucson. People talked about it all the time: the heat (dry heat, they kept telling me) and the monsoons — the sudden, wild afternoon downpour — and the feel of the air, the color of the sky. The morning after Michelle told me the story of San Lazaro y Los Perros, the sky was filled with full, dark clouds, and they were diffusing the emerging light into grays, blues, and creamy yellow. They looked puffy and ribbed, stretching back over the jagged tops of the mountains. I imagined the underbelly of some great desert beast, lumbering away from the heat, over the hills, looking for water. And I thought of something Michelle had written: "Everything had a voice in the desert, so everything had a story."

A breeze came up and died down — big news here because a certain kind of breeze, it was said, could signal rain. For the past few days there had been hopeful forecasts but no showers, and rain was on everyone's mind. (Yesterday a guy passing me on the street looked skyward and laughed. "Boy, for once I wish the weatherman was right!") The dry leaves on the trees started rustling. The boughs of a huge pine across the road swayed in all directions, off phase, but rhythmic somehow, like a fat, happy goddess having a good shimmy. Maybe she would bring rain. The sky was getting brighter, though the clouds still muted the sun. Cactus, tumbleweed, ocotillo — a landscape lush and spare and alive.

Over the next few days, the students would write stories set against this kind of terrain. During the first two weeks of the program, the classes had been taught how to construct a story, use descriptive detail, and manipulate point of view. It was their teachers' hope that they would see how the detail of their own lives — their historical particulars, the smell and touch of immediate landscape, the tales told in Tuba City — how all this could become the stuff of a literature they would create. To this end, the students had spent a morning with Luci Tapahonso, a Navajo poet whom Michelle brought in from the University of Kansas.

The students had read Luci's book, *A Breeze Swept Through*, and a brief narrative taken from *Sonora Review* titled "What I Am." The narrative guides the reader through sketches of the three generations of women who make the speaker the person she is today. "Your mother is your home," one of the women says. "Remember who you are," says another. And the poems are close to home: poems about lightning and trees along the river and a daughter, "first born of dawn woman"; there are poems about car wrecks and country music and hot coffee and

Navajo cowboys "with raisin eyes . . . (who are) just bad news"; and there are poems for grandmothers and for daughters — at Christmastime, at spring, entering school.

Luci talked to the students about her early work as a telephone operator, about having a baby very young, but getting along, persisting, about writing and writing — taking a poem through seven, eight, nine revisions. They liked her very much. "She made the kids feel good about themselves," Percy, the dorm supervisor, told me. And Edwin wrote after her visit that she "read with such grace and meaning." It was the reading of the work that seemed to move them powerfully. Luci read in a conversational way and with a touch of reservation dialect. Also, she occasionally worked Navajo into her English line, so that, for example, in her comic poem about a no-good husband, "Yáadí Lá" (roughly, "not again!" or "here we go again"), we have this scene:

> later her sister came over, she said,   he's gone, huh?
> mą'ii' ałt'ąą dishį́į́   honey, i won't do it again   'aach' ééh
> noo dah diil whod.   (old coyote was probably saying
> in vain: honey, i won't do it again.)
> they just laughed and drank diet pepsi at the kitchen table.

"It was neat," said Edwin, "the way she wove the Navajo language into her poems." Here was a writer who talked the talk the students heard on the streets of Tuba City, but could take that talk and shape it, make poetry out of it, and who encouraged them to do the same.

On the first day the students read their stories, all sections met together — Michelle's, Beth's, and Pat's — so that the seniors could hear the work being produced by the sophomores. I sat in the back of the room with Percy and Patricia Youngdahl, the tutor assigned to Michelle's class. Patricia was a Presbyterian minister who, in her mid-thirties, decided to pursue a doctorate in rhetoric and composition. She had a slim face with big eyes, and when she laughed — a quick, bright laugh — she pulled her head back a little, looking at you, bringing you in. The students were always talking to her, easy chatter, and called her the "pastor in the grass," toying with her self-description as an environmentalist. Percy — actually Prescilla Piestewa — was a Mexican-American woman who married into the Hopi and became a respected member of the community. Michelle worked Percy fully into the class — referred to her as her co-teacher — and Percy, an avid reader, commented on the books the students were reading, reminded them about homework and due dates, asked to see papers in progress, and orchestrated activities in the dorms, from volleyball games to homesickness intervention. She wore her long black hair pulled back and spoke in an even, contemplative way. ("But when she gives you that Percy-look," Jill told me, "you listen!") The students respected her, and her presence in the program signified the support of the reservation.

Beth and Michelle called the combined classes to attention. We all settled in, and Beth asked for volunteers. Nothing, then titters, then a raised hand or two: the boy in front of us cradling his right arm at the triceps with a free hand, a girl across the room wiggling the fingers of a hand held at half mast, looking over her shoulder and grinning at Percy. Beth called on the girl. Then the boy. Then came a flow of stories that took us through the day. Story after story, loosely linked by common geography and event, playing off each other, counterpointing, unfolding. A documentary of life in Tuba City.

There was a wealth of local detail, insider's terrain — from the deserted Rattle and Hum Road to Butthole Rock to the Pueblo Cafeteria and its "bouncing fish sticks"; from radio station KTNN to the homeless man who "smells like flowers." One rich piece of local lore, a collaborative poem, celebrated the Indian cowboy Jim Chee and his affair with a girl from Lukachukai, whose "voice belongs on the radio." Another took us to a powwow where the women were covered with "colored stardust": beads woven through shawls, leggings, and barrettes. There were witch and ghost stories: a man who could turn himself into a wolf; bones in a cave that rearranged themselves; the dead walking around during full moon, close to an open window where the young storyteller lay. And there was all the proud and goofy drama of being a teenager: sabotaging a sister's Marie Osmond doll, mock-heroic basketball games, two girls waddling around in a single stretchy nightgown. There were send-ups and put-downs — in awkward romances, in school politics, in athletic rivalries — kids posturing and preening and "acting all bad."

And, in the turn of a page, there was tragedy. On the rocky dirt near Rattle and Hum Road, a boy was thrown to death from his rolling truck. In another painful story, a young girl realized that the town saw her father as a hopeless drunk. "What idiot invented alcohol?" she asked. "Did his children get confused as we did?" Confusion. One student wrote candidly about her struggles with drugs — "I didn't care about anything" — and another worried about her family "falling apart." "I try," she finally said, "I try to understand this complicated place."

The death and sadness momentarily overwhelmed the hijinks and local victories. But there was a powerful drive on these students' parts to come to terms with the pain in their lives, to absorb it and move beyond. The optimism of youth, perhaps, or a psychological benefit of being in special programs like this one. But there was something else, too. Many of the students seemed to live with a sense of legacy. One dimension of that legacy involved family history: a history of hard work and struggle, extending way into the past, generations past, but somehow present — a recognition of what others had done to make the present possible. (In one paper, a girl tried to honor "what our mother had to go through in the beginning to get where she is now.") And another dimension was cultural. There were many references to tribal stories and prayers, to ceremonies, and to the land, which was never inert — and all this became powerfully motivational. "You are Navajo," a teacher said in one of the stories, "and because of this, it's important to know who you are." Identity, achievement, and tradition were inseparable. During an initiation ceremony, a medicine man prayed that a girl "will do good in school and in your homework." What weight that must have carried.

There was conflict, of course, and insecurity. Can I live up to this, some must have wondered. One paper captured the tension. The writer began with the resolve to be a pediatrician and the recognition that this "will be a difficult journey." She then moved back and forth, as if on a winding journey, between dreams of success — which she characterized as "the freshness of the future" — and fears about her ability, which, significantly, she defined in terms of tribal relation: "failure is like being alone." It was a painful paper to hear, for the writer was so forthcoming about her internal struggle: "I know it's going to be hard, and there's no easy way around it."

The next day, all the classes met separately, and Michelle's class shared the papers they had been writing. Percy asked Suzy Worker to start us off with "those nice descriptions of Tuba City." Suzy tended to look at you with a sidelong glance, a slight dip of the head. "OK," she said quickly.

"Tuba City. Tuba City. If I say it a thousand times more, will it still be Tuba City?" Her voice was rhythmic, a trace of singsong to it, and the opening repetition of Tuba City caught the students' attention. Darold listened with his eyes closed. Bert, who wanted to be a writer, had her chin cupped in the palm of her hand. Suzy continued, taking us "up the curve of the canyon" and down the main street, stopping at the new stop light, pointing out the McDonald's, the site of the old Wagon Wheel, the movie theater, and "the police station on your left." There's the Trading Post, where all the tourists buy their trinkets, and *there* . . . there's the motel where they stay. She described the trees, and the look of the city after it rains, and "in the distance, some Hopi houses."

Then she read her description of the city for insiders — experimenting with point of view.

In this piece, the paragraphs were short and abrupt, each opening with a "clump, clump," the sound of the hoofbeats of the horse Suzy was riding through the town, looking, musing, remembering:

Clump, clump.
Starting from Kerley Valley, you see your neighbor's pit bulls.
Stupid dogs!
Always wanting to eat you . . .

Clump, clump.
Rodeo queen making a truck full of guys whistle . . .

Clump, clump.
Your grandma sitting in a hogan making frybread . . .

Clump, clump.
Your essay for English due the next day!

Clump, clump — clump, clump?
And now your horse is tired and ready to rest.

Michelle asked Edwin to read next, and he said "Sure," sitting up, holding his paper about a foot in front of his face. Edwin was quick-witted and liked to tease and spar. He would occasionally take a verbal jab at a classmate, and was not afraid to make bold suggestions and challenge Michelle. But he was thoughtful, too, serious, actually — and when he engaged you, you knew the conversation was not taken lightly.

Edwin's essay took us back in time to his deceased grandfather's cornfields, where the young Edwin and his cousin learned about farming, responsibility, and the Hopi religious tradition. The writing was replete with detail: a freezer "filled with stored corn and meats"; "old irons, garden tools, axes with no handles" sitting outside the house; precise instructions on the proper way to hoe ("dig into the ground a little in front of the weed and pull toward yourself"); and, alongside Edwin and his cousin, demonstrating, guiding, was Grandfather Lorenzo: "powerful hands with strong, stubby fingers . . . black hair with white strands here and there . . . a left eye one-third closed." In an aside within the essay, Edwin explained that it is the Hopi belief that some things in their religion — some of the things he learned from his grandfather — cannot be made available to the uninitiated. "Sorry to say, they cannot be mentioned here." But what did come through as Edwin learned to till the soil and protect the crops from "rabbits, coyotes, and crows" was his love for Lorenzo Phillips and the heritage the old man embodied — "the things he taught us we'll never forget" — and the connection to the land that developed under his tutelage: "When you look from our village down to our fields, you see life in everything growing down there."

The third reader of the day was Bertha Benally. Bert had almond eyes and high cheekbones, brown hair and rich brown skin. She dressed in shorts, blouses or T-shirts, and white tennis shoes, looking as if she might hold student office, a little on the preppie side. Her writing seemed much older than her years. It was sober and cosmic in its sweep — responsibility to the past, the cycles of life and death — and quite formal, almost incantational, in its phrasing. The piece she read, like Edwin's, dealt with grandparents, the land, and tradition, but it was more philosophical and read like a ceremonial prayer:

> This is my home, where my grandparents on my father's side have always lived. This is a home where my father and his sisters and brothers were raised to be what they are today. This mountain, Black Mesa, represents the culture of my native home, where once the elders sat beneath the sparkling stars and only wondered about the future of tomorrow, which I live in now . . .
>
> My grandparents know very little English; I know very little of my native language. Since I was young my mother had always told me I spoke very good Navajo. And she could never understand why I stopped speaking it. Maybe I was more involved in modern society, listening to Michael Jackson. Or maybe I thought that knowing about my native tradition wasn't important to me. And for sure, I was definitely wrong about that. Because these days everyone is trying to learn about their culture. And those who don't care will soon learn the consequences about that which will be lost.

Bert's was the first paper that gave such direct expression to the conflict between Native tradition and mainstream popular culture. It was clear that many of these students, along with tens of millions of other American adolescents, had incorporated teen fashion, movies, music and MTV into their lives. But it was also clear that celluloid romance and heavy metal somehow coexisted with Native American custom and history. Negotiating such a bicultural life cannot be easy, and I wondered whether the tension increased as they entered their last year of high school and realized that they might soon leave the communal source of their beliefs.

Bert's narrative shifted to particular memories of life at her grandparents' house: the branding of cattle — the wild struggle of the roping and, afterward, the peace of work accomplished — and her grandfather's secret forays into town to buy children the candy her grandmother had forbidden them. And as Bert brought her paper to a close, she gave us her grandfather reflecting on his tradition and the responsibility that lives within it:

> "My grandchildren [he said], look into my eyes and see the darkness of fear brought upon your people. Your grandmother and I are so old. We see the selfishness of the people losing their tradition. Is this the way we all should live? You are the leaders of tomorrow, and you should do something about it, now. We are old and you are young. This is the beginning, where you should be an adult and teach yourself and others to know who you are, a Native Indian. You are the shadows of your ancestors . . ."

After Bert came several students who dwelled on the weather in Tuba City. Hana wrote that "the sand storms feel like needles" and warned "If there's a dust storm, don't smile!" But "after a rain, it smells fresh, like Tuba City after a shower." Another student described the city in the desert as "an oasis — there's trees and springs." And yet another thought that "the clouds overhead make you feel clean and safe." Sand and clouds and rain. Darold closed the day with a poem about the rain:

Last night,
I heard the raindrops falling
from way up high in the sky
falling to dry parched land.
I felt the raindrops hit
the top of my head.
Listening
to the thousands of little water drops
hitting a hard surface.
Feeling
the slushy water soaking through the
tennis shoes on my feet.
The rain has stopped,
only seeing what is left
of the clouds,
the pigeons have started
their cooing.
Everything is back to normal again.

Many of the students made covers for the pieces they were writing. And many of the covers displayed the land. Bert's, for example, was a dark pencil sketch on gray paper, a rockface, steep and fissured, wide at the base, narrowing at the top, as though you were looking upward.

Black Mesa, perhaps. Edwin's cover was a bright paste-up of the cornfield described in the reminiscence of his grandfather. On gold paper he had placed three green cornstalks with small multicolored circles pasted on the leaves: blue, yellow, and violet corn. Behind the stalks was a jagged, brown mountain with a large sun at the ridge. And the whole gold landscape was further pasted on black paper — night bordering the day — and in the top left corner sat a white crescent moon amid a cluster of tiny stars, triangular in shape to convey their twinkling.

IV

THE PAGES OF THE LITTLE BOOK folded out, making it stand upright, a white dove on the black cover, pictures and neat print bending at the angles inside. Librarians call these toy books — this type, an accordion book — and it is an old art, going back at least to the eighteenth century. Beth had demonstrated how to hinge pages together with strips of construction paper and paste so that they folded out in a series of panels. She showed everyone how to make covers from cardboard and old fabric. The class had been working on their accordion books for a while, and we spent the morning reading from them and passing them around. Two that got a lot of attention were by Hana and Frog.

Rain figured prominently in Hana's description of Tuba City, and in this work she used rain and water to metaphorically celebrate her English class. Hana's book offered a poem, the lines of which flowed across unfolding yellow pages like little streams of water. The poem incorporated a phrase from Leslie Silko's "Indian Song: Survival" into Hana's own writing, and incorporated, as well, a reference to the tutor, Patricia, as "the pastor in the grass" — all leading to the lovely lines "These two [Michelle and Patricia] are the rain that brings rainbows./We, the class, are the rainbows."

Frog adopted the persona of a child to write a book for children. The book was about her family, and introduced to us various members and memorable scenes in a series of small panels with drawings and explanatory text. Frog signaled the child persona by writing in simple sentences, and by writing with her left hand and using stick figures. The references to her father and to her older brother — clearly a favorite of hers — were all in past tense. She later explained, in a moving essay, that, within a few years of each other, her father had died and her brother had been killed in an automobile accident. "I'm doing pretty good now," Frog told us, "but sometimes I get awfully sad." It was as if the child's script and the childlike drawings were calling back a simpler time. Perhaps Frog was trying to make the family whole again, using language, as Scott Momaday once put it, to ward off disorder.

In the discussion of one of the accordion books, a reference came up to "talking Johnny." Michelle asked if anybody wanted to explain to Patricia and Mike what talking Johnny meant. Maybe even a demonstration, huh? "Real-ly?" asked Bert, who was sitting close to Michelle. "It's sorta the way they speak English on the rez," ventured Darold. "Do you guys know what it means to be talkin' Johnny?" Michelle asked, suddenly turning to us. "No, nope, uh-unh," we said, stonefaced. "Well, then . . ." She turned back to the class. The students were looking at each other, a few were laughing, aware that Michelle was goading them, but not quite ready to move, not just yet. "Tell you what," Michelle conceded. "During lunch come up with something, anything, to help Patricia and Mike better understand what it sounds like to be talking Johnny. Consider them your audience." We broke for lunch and were heading out the door when I asked Percy where the "Johnny" came from. She motioned my head down a little. "John" is slang for a Navajo. Like, hey, look at those two Johns. It's not complimentary.

When we returned to the classroom, the students were all afire. Even Michelle was surprised at the excitement. They had spent their break with Percy drawing up the outlines for two skits. And as the skits were played out before us, it became clear that, though Patricia and I were the audience that brought them into being, we quickly receded. These were for an audience of peers, marked by spontaneous local gesture.

The first of the two plays was set in an Indian boarding school and involved five of the girls, with Hana, Jill, and Bert doing most of the improvising. It was lunch time, and they were gossiping in dialect about boys. One girl would say something racy, and the next would give her a shove and say, "Nooooo, that's not true." A third girl would lose her cue and start laughing, and the next would blurt out something rude about a boy's hair or muscles or manners, that, in turn, would spark the first speaker to some outrageous quip that erupted the whole loose-limbed giggling machine all over again.

It's hard for me to capture in print the sound of talking Johnny. It is cadenced speech with little delays — some words are accented at the beginning more than in standard English speech, or are elongated, and the letters at the end of some words are dropped; "don't," for example, becomes "don'". The English is influenced, I imagine, by the rhythms of Navajo. Michelle later explained that talking Johnny is stigmatized speech on the reservation, a mark of the less formally educated, a kind of speech that has been ridiculed by dominant Whites — and that judgment, in classic sociolinguistic fashion, has worked its way into the judgment of those within the community who aspire to the mainstream middle-class. She had hoped that her on-the-spot assignment would encourage the students to think of the reservation dialect as yet another linguistic resource, full of creative possibility. This was probably the first time, I thought, that students were encouraged to speak that dialect in school — in a university, no less. No wonder the titters. This was taboo speech.

The second skit had Edwin and Jarvis buying moonshine whiskey — "quarts" in Tuba City idiom — from Darold, who played the bootlegger, and then going on to visit Antina, to drink and play cards. As in the first skit, there were funny exchanges. The students in the audience laughed and gave knowing looks and seemed to treat this as a slice of familiar life. I didn't get a sense of ridicule or censure, though, as Edwin and Jarvis mock-stumbled into Antina's imaginary apartment, it was clear that there wasn't much illusion here either. It was simply a depiction of what is. It was hard to know what impelled Edwin and his colleagues to stage this skit or what private twinges may have registered with the students in the audience — though some of these students had lost loved ones to alcohol and some were deeply troubled by stereotypes and assumptions about Indians and alcohol, by the sheer weight of the history connecting the two. But what did seem clear was that Michelle, in a relatively short time, had created a classroom into which these students could comfortably bring a range of their experience. They could tap that experience to analyze a contemporary novel or a classical play, to write a surreal tale or a reflective autobiographical essay, to produce a skit on a local social problem — and they could do it with a sweep of language: from academic English to Indian poetry to the dialect spoken in a house trailer in Tuba City. Considering the history of Indian education in the United States, such a mix of language and experience was remarkable.

From colonial days until very recently, and with the exception of a brief period during the New Deal, the general trend in our nation's educational policy for Native Americans has been systematically to undercut their experience, their linguistic and cultural heritage, and their religious traditions. Usually driven by a combination of greed, political opportunism, religious evangelism, and humanitarian impulse — some weird amalgam of racism, nationalism, and Christian good works — educational policymakers at times argued that, through schooling, the Indian could be sped along the evolutionary fast-track from "childish ignorance" and a "nearly subhuman" stage of development toward "civilization," "enlightenment," and "prosperity and happiness." At other times, policymakers argued just as vigorously that quick progress was impossible for such "utterly depraved races," as Teddy Roosevelt once put it. And, so, depending on the era and the prevailing mood, children were enrolled in missionary schools to Christianize them, or were taken away to boarding schools to separate them from tribal life, or were taught in reservation schools where the use of Indian language was punished, or were tracked into surrounding White schools, where their customs were ridiculed and their intelligence devalued. What they got in return was usually a curriculum geared toward basic skills and vocational training. As one influential commissioner of Indian Affairs explained, "The Indian takes to beet farming as naturally as the Italian takes to art or the German to science," and, therefore, to quote another expert, to expose Indians to literature or to the arts was to "sow seeds on stony ground."

That moment when the young Michelle Grijalva was told that her stories were inferior to the myths she found in Bulfinch was embedded in a long and shameful history. And though the rapacious political oratory has faded and the theories about evolution, race, and cognition have been dismantled, there's a voice of diminishment that still echoes down the scholastic corridors of Native America: it says "leave your Indian at home!" No wonder Michelle worked so hard to create a space where all Indian experience, venal and lofty, could be played with or analyzed, where everything was useful, where all languages contributed to the creation of classroom stories.

The class talked a while longer about rez dialect, Michelle asking the students questions about pronunciation and usage, reinforcing their role as linguistic experts. Then she demonstrated her own Yaqui border patois: a blend of English and Spanish — Spanglish — and Tex-Mex constructions and occasional Yaqui words and phrases. The class got a big kick out of this, and Michelle had fun getting her tongue going on all those old rhythms. She and the students made some comparisons between the two dialects, and then she veered off in another direction. "You know," she said, "you did so much with these skits in so little time, maybe you would want to write a play, maybe set it on the reservation. And we could see if we could videotape it." Whoa, yeah! Edwin had shot video plays at school, as had a Navajo girl named Cindy, who, it turned out, wanted to be a photographer.

"What should it be about?" Michelle asked. "Let's call it *Boyz in the Hood,*" said Edwin. Others piped up, adapting titles from other films about minority youth: "How 'bout *Straight Out of the Hogan*?" "Yeah, *Homies Off the Rez*!" "OK, OK," said Jill, putting her hand halfway out in front of her, as if to slow the momentum. "But if it's *Homies Off the Rez,* then *who* can Patricia and Mike play?" The class laughed, then began deliberating. Edwin speculated aloud, "We could be coming home after college, bringing some new friends with us, and, you know, it could be . . . awkward." "You mean," I asked him, "Patricia and I would be stuffy, out of place?" "Yeah," he said, "but, uh, us too. Sorta out of place." "You could be real nosy," said Jill, "like tourists." "What are the kinds of things tourists do?" Michelle queried. This really opened things up. Students reeled off the questions they're asked that make them feel like curios:

> Do you live in tepees?
> Do you wear loincloths?
> Do you eat berries?
> Do you smoke peace pipes?
> Do you carry tomahawks?

"They're surprised that we have toilets," said Jill. "And they never say 'restrooms.' It's always 'toilets'. 'Oh, you have toy-lets!' *Sheeee,* what do they think we *do*?"

Michelle set a time line. The class would have a week to write and revise the play. She'd help them, or they could see Patricia or me, or they could work with Percy up in the dorms. "Seven days from now, we shoot." A group of about six students took on the project, and, during the last few days before taping, exhausted themselves with all-nighters, filling in gaps in dialogue and revising. Michelle, Percy, Patricia, and I watched the play evolve and helped out a little, but mostly the students did it on their own.

The play those exhausted but eager actors put on had a straightforward dramatic line. After four years at Harvard, Edwin returns to the reservation to find that one of his old classmates has had a child out of wedlock and that another, having lost his college scholarship, is bootlegging. After encounters with each old friend that are both comic and soul-searching, Edwin and some others successfully convince both to return to school. Patricia and I played minor characters, two of Edwin's Harvard classmates, served up as comic relief, who return with him to do "a research paper about the reservation lifestyle for an anthropology class." We took pictures; we asked everyone if they lived in tepees; we fretted that we wouldn't be able to understand "the natives" because "they use a form of language called Johnny talk." And as Edwin surveyed the region for us, his tongue was stiff with high-brow diction. "There is where my friends and I used to *collaborate,*" he said somberly. And there, he pointed out, there "is where I kissed my first *companion* with warmth and compassion." He called his friend's child a *cherub* and suggested that, while we waited for a ride, we could *ruminate.* The rest of the class had a good laugh.

But there was serious stuff going on here. About halfway through the play, the two rude anthropologists have a conversion experience and apologize for not seeing "how sacred the Navajo religion is to the people," and, in fact, become part of the group urging the bootlegger to go back to school. And two of the major social problems on the reservation, alcoholism and teenage pregnancy, were brought to some kind of resolution — though the way the resolution played itself out revealed both ambivalence about and faith in the power of schooling.

School.

The big action in the play had to do with the straightening out of the lives of Edwin's old classmates, but a locus of tension — the most immediate tension in the play — involved schooling, and it came up during the first encounter between Edwin and his bootlegging buddy. Edwin was talking in polysyllables, the comically exaggerated language of the university. "You don't have to use all those fancy words," Edwin's pal reprimanded. "Just talk the way we used to. Or did you forget?" "No," Edwin replied defensively, "I didn't forget. I just lived in the city too long." "You're back on the rez, dude," the partner shot back. "Forget that city shit."

There was some complex resalvaging going on between Edwin and his buddy. Edwin reclaimed his friend's potential and connected him again with school. Yet, to reach out to his friend, Edwin eventually had to shed the very language associated with school and talk from the heart: "You should go back to school. I know you can do it. You still have your whole life ahead of you . . . Get your ass in gear. Please. Before your life gets any worse." For his part, Edwin's buddy reaffirmed communal solidarity — reminding Edwin of who he was and where he came from. Yet his friend spoke from despair; he had drifted to the underside of reservation life. Nonetheless, he was able to deliver a warning about the dangers of an educational system that historically has done much harm to Indian youth, yet could also help both of them better their lives.

As Edwin and Darold and Bert and the others enter their last year at Tuba City High School, as they begin filling out application forms for the University of Arizona, for Stanford, Berkeley, or UCLA, for MIT or Harvard, as they read catalogues and look at publicity stills of smiling students and ivy-covered halls — as they do all this, what will they feel? The "freshness of the future"? The excitement of new places and new challenges? An even keener awareness of the possibility lacking for so many of their peers on the reservation? "I'm really ready to leave Tuba City for a while," one girl told me. But they also know that some who leave change in disturbing ways. What will they lose? How will they fit in at Stanford? And after Stanford, how will they fit in at home? Will they talk different? Act funny? What will happen to them? One of the things most vexing the superintendent of the Tuba City schools is the early return to the reservation of some very promising students. They leave elite universities because they feel miserably out of place. They come back "just for a year." But they stay for more than a year. Some enroll in a college closer to home: a community college or state university. Some don't. Edwin and company know all this, of course. What, then, will happen to them? Will they be able to make it? Or will they become a kind of curiosity? Michelle told me that Edwin wanted "to live in both worlds." There must have been times when he and the others wondered whether they could do it without losing their souls.

V

"IT'S A WEIRD LOVE STORY."

"It's a tragedy; they just linger on."

"It's sad, the way nobody can be made happy by their love."

It was Monday morning of the fourth week of the program, and all three classes were together, clustered around actress Cindy Meier, who, leaning forward, elbow on knee, was encouraging general reactions to Carson McCullers's *The Ballad of the Sad Café.* The students had read the book over the weekend, moving back to the reading list after spending time with their own writing, ready now to pick up the ideas about the tragedy they had discussed while reading *Oedipus the King.* Cindy was blond, in her late thirties, her voice melodious and trained, her questions and responses filled with reflective pauses. As she worked the room, it became clear that many of the students liked *The Ballad of the Sad Café;* they found the characters compelling and were moved by their misery.

The short novel is an unsettling meditation, in the Southern Gothic vein, on a small town that holds a few buildings, a few peach trees, and "a miserable main street only a hundred yards long." The largest building on this street is the house of Amelia Evans, now boarded up and dilapidated, but, at one time, the site of a café that stood brightly against the town's dreary boredom. Miss Amelia had lived in town all her life and was its most prosperous citizen; she was, as well, solitary, tough, and adept at bootlegging, doctoring, and any kind of repair. Her solitude and self-reliance were broken, however, by the appearance of a strange little man named Cousin Lyman, who became the object of her desire and for whom she opened the café. The café prospered, and the townspeople, both decent and small-minded, enjoyed its warmth until Marvin Macy — a ne'er-do-well who was married to Miss Amelia for ten grotesque days — got released from jail and returned to town with blood in his eye. In a weird twist, Cousin Lyman began longing for Marvin Macy, followed him everywhere, eventually invited him to move into Miss Amelia's house, and watched gleefully as the inevitable showdown between Amelia and Macy developed. And when it did, he attacked Miss Amelia himself, and, after destroying the café, ran off with Marvin Macy, leaving Amelia Evans to her haunting grief.

Cindy had become familiar with that pain, had been trying to live it for the past two months with her fellow actors at a local theater company called *a.k.a.*, which was about to produce Edward Albee's dramatic adaptation of the novel. Pat Baliani knew the people at *a.k.a.* — they had put on a piece of his the year before — so he made arrangements for all three classes to attend the full dress rehearsal of the McCullers-Albee play, planned for that evening. Cindy was here to prime the students and help them get a sense of how theater works; this was also a unique opportunity for them to make some comparisons between the techniques of drama and fiction. Cindy talked a bit about the theater company, its history, the actors, the time they'd spent on *The Ballad of the Sad Café*. Then, in an almost folksy gesture, she slowly swept her right hand across the air as though pointing at something way over at the side wall: "So . . . so," she said, "let's go back to the book. If you were going to turn it into a play, what kinds of things would you include? I mean, Amelia has about twenty lines in the novel. Marvin Macy grunts. Cousin Lyman . . . well, McCullers says he chatters a lot, but he doesn't have too many lines either." Here Cindy opened both palms up and out to the students, shrugged, and, with a quizzical look, repeated, "What would you include?"

"The town," said a sophomore girl named Joni. "You'd need to show the audience what life is like there." "You'd need more dialogue," another student suggested. Then a string of suggestions came from various points in the room: "the café," "the fight," "when Cousin Lyman first comes to town," "the marriage of Marvin and Amelia."

"Would you use flashbacks?" Cindy asked next. The students thought about this. Then a sophomore named Ty, who, Pat told me, wanted to be a film director, said yes, yes, you'd need to. "How about a narrator? Would you need a narrator?" "Yes," responded Ty, "in order to create the mood." "That's a good point," Cindy observed, then looked out at the class, catching Edwin's waving hand. "Like in the play *Our Town*," he said, "the narrator gives the audience insight into what's happening." "Yes," Cindy said, "this play is a little like *Our Town*. In fact, Albee did create a narrator — that's the part I play." Some "ah's" and "oh's" here.

"Did you like the narrator in the novel?" Cindy continued. "Yes," said Frog. "When Miss Amelia and Marvin Macy got married, they didn't talk much, so you need the narrator." Cindy built on Frog's observation and noted how unspoken the feelings are in *The Ballad of the Sad Café*. She talked a bit more about the way Albee used the narrator in the play, and pointed out that he took a number of the narrator's observations in the novel and converted them into lines of dialogue. "You'll find that the townspeople are much more vivid in the play than in the story."

This exchange went on for most of the morning as Cindy held a conversation with fifty students, carried along by the students' responses, but guiding, adjusting here and there. At one point, soon after the discussion of the narrator's role in articulating the muted feelings of the townspeople, she asked the class to join her in an exercise, the kind an actor might attempt. Cindy had the students close their eyes "and imagine a place, a place that means something to you, go back to that place, back in memory, back . . ." More of this, then, just as gently: "But realize, too, that you're not there now. How does this make you feel?" The students, many of whom grew up with a strong sense of place, seemed to take to this exercise. There was a range of stilled forms: chin in palm of hand; head resting on arms; torso low in desk, head back, arms folded. Then Cindy had the students open their eyes, come to, and write. Describe the place and the feelings surrounding it — and the feelings of not being there now. A number of students remembered a grandmother's house or a patch of landscape. Warmth, security, connection — and a wistful feeling, even sadness, at their separation from it.

"All right," said Cindy, "let's talk about acting. A lot of people think acting is pretending you're somebody you're not. You know, like putting on a mask. But, actually" — the students were attentive to this — "acting is remembering." She explained how an actor tries to find some experience in his or her own life that connects with a character's experience, how, in fact, the actors at *a.k.a.* went through the very exercise the students had just done, went through it to tap the joy and loss the townspeople must feel about Miss Amelia's café. "When you come to the theater tonight, bring these memories and feelings about your special place with you."

Then Ty, the sophomore who wanted to make movies, raised his hand and asked, "Can we convince you to do a scene?" The students broke into applause. Cindy seemed surprised and a little shy. She chattered for a moment and ran her hands over her thighs, smoothing her dress. "OK. Sure . . . As I told you, I'm the narrator. So, uh, why don't I give you my favorite speech? It's the part where the narrator comments on love. Remember it?" Cindy lowered her head, looked up, and in an easy Southern accent began:

> The time has come to speak about love . . . But what sort of thing is love? . . . Often the beloved is only a stimulus for all the stored-up love which has lain quiet within the lover for a long time hitherto. And somehow every lover knows this. He feels in his soul that his love is a solitary thing. He comes to know a new, strange loneliness . . .

It was a very hot evening. Two noisy air conditioners close to the lighting booth were doing their best, but they could do little more than stir up the heat. The theater was small. A rectangular space of about thirty feet by twenty feet served as the stage, and about four rows of tiered seats extended along two sides. When we filed in, the actors were already on stage. Some were resting against the back wall by an old Coke machine, some were gossiping, two were sparring. There was chatter and laziness and laughter and, in the corner, a guy strumming a guitar. We had walked into the life of the town. Stumpy MacPhail, Merlie Ryan, the Rainey twins — they were all doing just fine without us. There was a potbelly stove by the Coke machine, a rifle in a wooden box, a few tables, and the backdrop of a two-story house. Up on a ladder, by the front second-story window, sat Miss Amelia, severe, still, looking down on the street.

The students knocked their shins against the seats, hushed each other, looking and looking again at the actors, who were no more than eight to ten feet beyond their reach. Then Cindy stepped forward from the crowd, broke character just long enough to give the students a little wave, and began musing about the town and Miss Amelia's house and the café:

> The town is lonesome — sad — like a place that is far off and estranged from all other places in the world . . . But once . . . once, this building — this boarded-up house — was a café. Oh, there were tables with paper napkins, colored streamers hanging from the lamps, and great gatherings on Saturday nights . . .

At this point, the guitar player broke into "Rolling in My Sweet Baby's Arms," and the melancholy of the town and its lost café began to weigh on us. Miss Amelia, stirred by the memory, came alive and slowly descended the ladder.

Even in the heat — the heat of a Georgia summer? — the students got caught up in the play: fanning themselves with their programs, craning their necks to see movement over by the Coke machine, shifting in their seats, and falling silent. They laughed at the actors' bickering and scuffling — and the actors later said how much they liked that response. The students got a big kick, for example, out of exchanges like this one between Cousin Lyman and Marvin Macy's brother.

> I'm just tryin' to be helpful.
> You be more help you go hide under a log!

They enjoyed, as well, the physical theatrics: Miss Amelia grabbing the busybody Emma Hale by the dress stretched across her full rump and giving it an energetic tug, Emma shocked, her arms flailing.

Cousin Lyman turned out to be a favorite. The actor who played him cranked it up and gave us a wanderer full of smarmy longing. His eyes glittered; his sweaty hair stuck to the side of his face; he sniggered and snorted and wanted desperately to be loved. *"Eeech,"* one of the sophomore girls cried when he shuffled near. And when he betrayed Miss Amelia, we hated him, riveted by his simpering treachery. "You really did a great job," a student later wrote in a letter to him.

But the central moment in the play — the one that had Edwin and the others in the back row up on their feet — was the fight between Marvin Macy and Miss Amelia. Both actors were lean and strong, barefooted, pants legs rolled up. They stalked each other, seething with hatred, grabbing an arm, lunging for a leg. Then they'd slap to the floor, hard, grappling for advantage — their faces right on each other, close enough to kiss, trying to get a thumb on a windpipe. And when Cousin Lyman, who had been perched on the ladder in front of Miss Amelia's house, finally propelled himself through the air onto Amelia's shoulders, and when Marvin Macy took the advantage and locked her beneath him, and when Amelia went limp as the two men destroyed the café — as these things quickly passed, the audience fell silent, stilled by the presence of evil.

The next day all three classes met to talk about the play. Pat Baliani led the discussion. Like Michelle, he created a lot of conversational space — encouraging comment, following leads, looping back to link one point to another. And as the morning unfolded, he pursued three general topics: the nature of dramatic conflict; the difference between dramatic action and narrative action; and the definition of tragedy and the determination of whether *Oedipus the King* and *The Ballad of the Sad Café* were tragedies.

"How would you characterize the dramatic conflict in *Oedipus*," asked Pat, looking over his shoulder from the blackboard, chalk ready. Someone said that there was a conflict between Oedipus and his brother-in-law, Creon. Ty then asked if there wasn't also a conflict between Oedipus and the state, and Pat added that to the board. Spencer suggested that Oedipus was in conflict with himself, and that prompted Suzy Worker to wonder if the real conflict in the play wasn't between Oedipus and his fate. Pat finished the list and turned back around to the class, smiling. "Boy," he said, "some of you were telling me that *Oedipus* was a complex play. No wonder!"

In trying to distinguish between narrative action and dramatic action, Pat asked if someone could sum up the action of either the novelistic or dramatic version of *The Ballad of the Sad Café.* There was silence; then Suzy Worker tentatively said, "Love?" And what followed was a good example of the benefits of Pat's teaching style. Suzy's one-word answer could hardly qualify as a summary of action, and in many classrooms such an answer would either be negatively evaluated or politely sidestepped. But Pat touched his fingers to his chin and said, "Love, hmmm, that's interesting. Tell me more, Suzy." Suzy hesitated for a moment, then proceeded to give a summary that, in effect, combined narrative and dramatic action. "Well," she began, "Amelia loved her father, right? . . . but, but he died. So, she loved Cousin Lyman." Her voice was tentative, then, suddenly, got more assured. "And Marvin Macy loved Amelia, but she didn't love him. And, uh, Lyman loved Marvin Macy." Pause. "And everybody loved the café." Pat reached back and dropped his chalk into the tray, taken with the symmetry of Suzy's response.

Pat was pursuing the possibility that *The Ballad of the Sad Café* was a tragedy. "What about catharsis . . . pity and fear. Is fear aroused in you as you watch this play?" He looked around. Sitting, almost slumping, against the back wall of the classroom was Camille, a sophomore in a black T-shirt, wearing a black visor. She looked disengaged. Pat asked her what she thought. She nodded slightly to acknowledge the question. "I guess I got a fear," she said, "because everyone in the play who falls in love ends up getting hurt. It makes me afraid of love." Pat acknowledged the answer and solicited other responses. Frog read from the novel to support Camille's observation: "The lover craves any possible relation with the beloved, even if this experience can cause him only great pain."

"But," came the voice of Beth, the teacher of the other sophomore section, "what about the comedy? You all laughed a lot last night. Can a tragedy have comedy in it?" This led to some deliberation, then Frog suggested that the funny parts were not the most important parts of the play. This helped move things along, and a few others spoke up. But it was, again, Camille, speaking cautiously from that far corner, who caught us with her insight into the dynamics of the play. "Maybe you have to enjoy something," she said, pulling herself up in the chair as she got going. "You know, laugh with it, enjoy it . . . otherwise, you won't . . ." Here she stopped, needing to come at her idea a different way. "When you go into the theater, you don't know anything about the characters, but once you start laughing, only then can you feel bad for them." Pat turned to Beth, once again backed onto the pedagogical ropes.

It was interesting to reflect on why *The Ballad of the Sad Café,* not an easy book for high-schoolers, was so successful with the reservation students. Certainly, the production and the opportunity to talk to the actors were important. And there was the enigmatic nature of the characters, the small town feel, the novel-drama comparison. But Michelle and Manny Begay, the teacher from Tuba City, saw more.

The way Michelle put it, the students knew about the evil people can inflict on each other or have heard tales of such things. Call it witchery or dark medicine, summoning forces to overwhelm another. Various tribal cultures had languages all their own for these forces. The inexplicable, terribly destructive power that flows among Amelia, Marvin Macy, and Cousin Lyman does not gain its force from the supernatural, but its manifestation is not all that different from, say, the bad medicine depicted in books like Louise Erdrich's *Tracks* or Leslie Silko's *Ceremony.* Desire gone bad; ill will that twists reason from its moorings.

And these students knew about hardship and pain. Manny speculated that perhaps it was because they had seen so much — the poverty and despair, the alcoholism, the families strained and threatened —that they could respond in so profound a way to the loss of the café and to Miss Amelia's anguish. The successes these students had experienced in their school and community had, in some ways, shielded them from the despair that reservation poverty can bring, but that didn't mean they were unacquainted with sorrow or loss or a boredom that threatens to flatten out all hope. There was plenty of reason for them to respond as they did to *The Ballad of the Sad Café.*

The beauty of Michelle's curriculum was that it honored the rich particulars of Navajo and Hopi life while assuming a broad range of human experience. Some curricula that try to reflect the backgrounds of "nonmainstream" students define culture and experience narrowly. Rather than building from students' experience, they, in effect, trap the students within the confines of their past. Michelle's approach revealed deep respect for her students' lives, and a source of its power was the way she used Native American language and lore to inspire student writing and, for that fact, to enhance non-Indian literature. Would *Oedipus the King* have been as successful if it had come first rather than as part of the unfolding story spun by Michelle? But hers was also an approach that resisted limits, that sought ways to stretch beyond itself, presenting the opportunity, for example, for these Tuba City youngsters to move about in the seemingly foreign social and psychological terrain of a tiny Georgia town, only to find intriguing connection there.

VI

THE LAST FEW DAYS of the program alternated between a sprint to complete assignments and the bittersweet calm that comes with closure. Michelle, Beth, and Pat had compiled such an ambitious reading list that, try as they might, they couldn't do it justice. Too many projects proved too interesting to cut short, and other projects — like the students' video play about life on the reservation — sprang from the daily life of the classroom, and their fresh energy couldn't be denied. Still, the students were willing to work like crazy to honor the original list and finish all the assignments. "I just never knew English could be this much fun," one girl told me. So they revised papers during lunch, and read late into the night, and stayed after school for last-minute tutoring. Fortunately, they were required to read some of the books on the list before arriving at the program, so while Michelle and company had to make some abrupt adjustments, they didn't have to perform radical curricular surgery.

David Seals's *The Powwow Highway* was one of the books the students read before starting the program; it was chosen, in part, because a movie had been made of it. The two media would provide students with the opportunity to compare novelistic and cinematic technique, a nice follow-up to the novelistic-dramatic comparison afforded by *The Ballad of the Sad Café.* But as things worked out, the students were able to have only about an hour's discussion. Beth's tutor, Ann Brigham, added a saving touch by taping a huge piece of butcher paper around the walls of Beth's classroom. As students had a free moment during the day, they came by to write or paint a reaction, or to express one through collage, or to write out a favorite quotation from *The Powwow Highway.* On the desk by the podium sat paints, pens, brushes, magazines, scissors, tape, glue.

The Powwow Highway is a wild blend of Native American history and lore, radical politics, and 1970s' dope-smoking, anarchic hijinks. Starting at the Northern Cheyenne Reservation in Montana, Buddy Red Wing and Philbert Bono rumble southward in a junkyard Buick to rescue Buddy's sister — busted on phony possession charges in New Mexico. Along the way, there are fistfights, spiritual, material, and sexual adventures, bittersweet reminiscences, and lots of beer, marijuana, and hamburgers. But also along the way, Philbert, whom Seals initially presents as a lumbering buffoon, "the laughingstock of the tribe," connects with his native traditions, has visionary recognitions, and, by the novel's end, becomes heroic. For his part, Buddy, who was a member of the American Indian Movement (as was Seals), sees traditional Indian beliefs as "fairy tales" and "soap operas," and hammers hard for militant political action, not spiritual regeneration, as a solution to Native America's oppression. The book is irreverent and cleverly written and dated in its embrace of marijuana economics, but it leaves the reader with a serious and, I think, intentionally unresolved dilemma: Does the redemption of Native America lie in political militancy or in a reclamation of religious and social traditions? Michelle's take on the book was that Buddy and Philbert, in their exaggerated and comic ways — the exaggeration of trickster tales, perhaps — represented the two halves of a once-whole Indian identity, warrior and ceremonial priest, before the decimation of Native America.

The book sparked a wide range of opinion among the students. The language is hip and cynical and X-rated, and while some students got a big kick out of it, there was a more substantial reaction to the book's antiestablishment tone and social critique. There was, as well, Buddy's in-your-face bravura. At one point in the movie, a stereo salesman addressed Buddy as "Chief" and told him with a sneer that there'd be "no ghetto deals" on the merchandise. A cheer went up in the darkened auditorium when Buddy nailed the guy. Macho theatrics, but how often in popular media did these students get to see an Indian as the righteous, and victorious, hero? When Buddy caught up with Philbert, grinning after a mad sprint from the stereo store, a girl leaned over to another in front of me and whispered, "He's cute!" The students enjoyed seeing Indians on the screen, in the center of attention, tough and funny and defiant. Someone in small, neat script wrote in the center of the mural: "Buddy wants freedom from the white man."

But the most sympathetic response was toward Philbert and his vision quest; in fact, many of the quotations that found their way from book to mural referred to Philbert. One of the biggest complaints about the movie, therefore, was that it left out so much of the history and lore that swirled around Philbert as he progressed along his journey. Bert thought the movie was "simplistic." It was "cheap and thin," said one of the sophomore boys, and Hana noted that "it was the same with *The Ballad of the Sad Café;* the play had less in it, the book had more background." And Edwin thought that "the book was better — it blended in the thoughts the characters are having."

Some of the strongest negative feelings toward *The Powwow Highway,* interestingly, came from a few sophomore boys who arrived at the program with the most militant politics. They liked the tenor of Seals's criticism of White America. And they certainly responded to Buddy's don't-mess-with-me demeanor; Buddy was "cool." But they took strong issue with some of his characterizations of the reservation. In bold red letters, someone — I believe it was Ty, the fledgling director — scrawled across a far corner of the mural: "The reservation is *not* the Third World." For these students, Buddy's analogy demeaned a world they lived in and were trying to advance; the analogy was too sweeping, too dismissive, in their eyes. They were equally upset with the ever-presence of alcohol and drugs. ALL INDIANS DO NOT DRINK flashed across the middle of the mural in the same red scrawl.

There was, I think, a clash here between two generations' visions of Indian activism. The students could identify with Buddy's anger and defiance, but not with his alienation, and not with his particular blend of nationalism, neo-Marxism, and anarchy. They were young and were trying to shape a life on the reservation, finding meaning in the tradition that Buddy dismissed while struggling to create a future that appropriated the White man's technology. They were angry, all right, but it was still a hopeful anger — and they resisted its potential devolution into bitterness. In their way, they were trying to form, in a late-twentieth-century context, an Indian identity that once again brought together what Buddy and Philbert individually represented: warrior and celebrant.

> You know, everything had to begin, and this was how it was: the Kiowas came one by one into the world through a hollow log. They were many more than now, but not all of them got out. There was a woman whose body was swollen up with child, and she got stuck in the log. After that, no one could get through, and that is why the Kiowas are a small tribe in number. They looked all around and saw the world. It made them glad to see so many things. They called themselves KWUDA, "coming out."

Darold read slowly, a tale of birth and promise, the opening of Scott Momaday's *The Way to Rainy Mountain.* Michelle had asked the students to begin this last day of class with a kind of ceremony, a reading of their favorite passages from Momaday, an author they had read when the class began. "Man tells stories in order to understand his experience," he had written in his essay "The Man Made of Words," and such ideas had guided the course. Now the students were returning to Momaday, ending with his retelling of the journey of the Kiowa people, "a going forth upon the way to Rainy Mountain." They were subdued. Things were a little flat. Walking to class, even Michelle was down, exhausted, ready to send them forth but sad to see them go. There would be a breakfast and a reception and dance — but Michelle's work was almost over.

Jill came next, then Jarvis, then Frog, then Suzy Worker:

> While the child was in the tree, a redbird came among the branches. It was not like any bird that you have seen; it was very beautiful, and it did not fly away. It kept still upon a limb, close to the child. After a while the child got out of its cradle and began to climb after the redbird. And at the same time the tree began to grow taller, and the child was borne up into the sky.

Others read too — Hana, Edwin — and the mood slowly lifted. Things were coming to their proper end.

After the last student finished reading, Michelle got up and walked slowly to the board. She started erasing it. Everything was quiet for a moment. Then: "Thinking back over the past four-and-a-half weeks," she said, talking to the board, moving the eraser in broad arcs, "thinking back . . . what are some of the themes . . . the ideas . . . the powerful words we've been working with?"

"Identity," said Jill. And Michelle wrote it on the top of the board.

"Tradition," said Dawn Manygoats.

"Dreams," said Edwin.

And the words grew in number, Michelle placing them all across the board — high, low, middle, edge — leaving space between them:

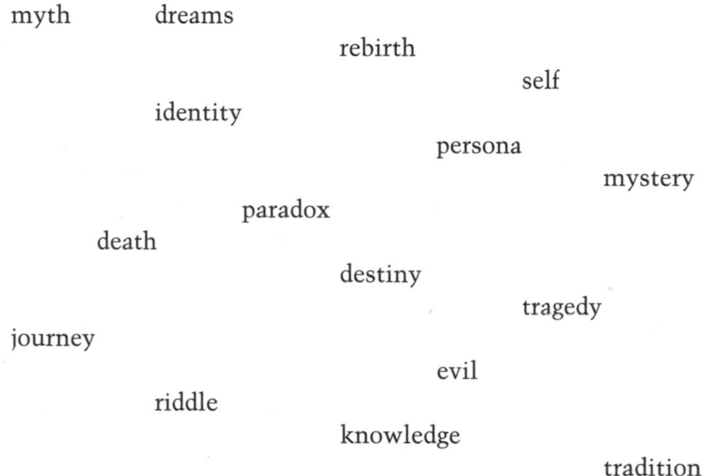

Occasionally, she prodded: "What about the Center for Creative Photography? What words would you associate with that?" "Image," someone said. "Illusion," said another.

After filling the board with theme words, Michelle asked the students where they'd place the material they had read, the places they visited, the people who visited them. Bert suggested that *Oedipus the King* be placed under "paradox." Darold thought *The Powwow Highway* belonged with "journey." "Can something go in two places?" Antina asked. Sure. She wondered, then, if *Oedipus* shouldn't also go under "destiny." "Luci," said Frog, "she oughta be put by 'tradition.'" "OK," said Michelle, and dutifully wrote Tapahonso's *A Breeze Swept Through* in the appropriate place on the board. At some point in the free-flowing but methodical development of this array of key words and works, Michelle started to draw lines connecting themes and books and people. So, for example, following Bert's and Antina's contributions, she connected *Oedipus the King* with "paradox" and "destiny." Now and then she asked for other connections — what was interrelated? "Come on, any thoughts?" And "tradition" got linked to "identity," as did "journey." "Death" was associated with "rebirth"; "dreams" with "knowledge." This continued until the board was filled with ideas, books, poems, visitors, places — a thick conceptual map of the four-and-a-half weeks together. Michelle stepped back and looked at it — quizzical, appreciative — and asked the class what they had here. "A web," said Jill. "Yeah," said Michelle. She chuckled. "The Web of Life."

She held out a fresh piece of chalk — her piece was worn to a stub — and said, "Place yourself in this web. Where would you place yourself? Draw yourself into it." She looked at Edwin, a certain volunteer. "*Sheeeee,*" he said, sliding out of his desk — and as he approached the board, he held out his arms and cried, "I'm lost in the web of life!" The class had moved beyond the sadness of the morning. He looked at the web for a long time, hip cocked, arms limp at his side, then carefully drew himself between "riddle" and "knowledge." The figure was huge and musclebound — Edwin Schwarzenegger — and that prompted Jill to suggest, "Maybe that should be under 'dreams.'"

One by one the students went to the board, issuing disclaimers, teasing each other, but, finally, placing themselves in the web. Dawn, who was interested in her people's religious ceremonies, drew a skirted stick figure under "tradition." Jill, whose "What I Am" essay had revealed a struggle to shape herself ("My story of how I came to be does not have to do with . . . religion, but with creation of mind"), Jill placed her wavy-haired portrait carefully between "self" and "identity." And so it went. The students, in one of their last academic activities in the program, situating themselves in the conceptual web that Michelle had helped them create.

About thirteen years ago, Michelle and her husband, Johnny, began building a house way up in the Rincon Mountains, on the eastern boundary of Tucson. It was made of stone, and every stone came from the surrounding desert. They built a little pond and an outdoor bath the same way. They brought in electricity and telephone lines — and they bought an answering machine. Michelle had to laugh at that. After class, the blues slipping back, Michelle and I went shopping for the week's supplies and for a cake for her husband, whose birthday we were going to celebrate that night. Then we set off in the rattling truck, toward the mountains.

It was a long drive, about an hour or so, and we spent some of it talking about the students, and more of it lost in our own thoughts. It was nice to sit back, the sun warming our seats, and drift in and out of conversation, quiet, reflective, the cactus and brush and surrounding foothills moving by in rocking, continuous peace.

Long drives encourage long views, and I found myself thinking about Michelle's class against the backdrop of a broader history. During my visit, I read everything I could on Indian education, and what struck me, as we put some miles between us and the city, was how little that reading could have prepared me for what I saw during my stay. By and large, what I read was a catalogue of failure, failure measured every way you could imagine. In tests of vocabulary, reading comprehension, and language usage, Indian students did poorly — as they did in assessments of self-concept, self-esteem, self-image, and locus of control. They were lower than White students in the grades they got in English, math, science, and social studies. They were tardy and absent more, and dropped out with greater frequency. And all of these measures were further broken down to show more specific liabilities: in mathematical reasoning and reading readiness and geographical knowledge. How do you summon hope in the face of such measures, I wondered. What knowledge can help you create a vision of the possible?

The students Michelle worked with were clear exceptions to this dreary profile; they had benefited from a strong academic program and the efforts of individual teachers like Manny Begay. But even they had troubles with standardized tests, their abilities fading behind the scores. Test scores were one of the district's biggest worries. Michelle said that she avoided the literature on Indian educational performance because she was afraid it would blinker her sense of what could be done. The way she said this caught me: it wasn't arrogant; it was cautious. She was still shaping an approach and didn't want to spook it, and she drew her inspiration from sources with less institutional clout than performance assessments: from her own experience, from a firm belief in what young people could accomplish, and from an extensive knowledge of the Native American rhetorical tradition.

In her teaching, she tapped a long, rich history of storytelling: stories to pass on cultural ideals, to serve as moral exemplars and cautionary tales, to maintain a history of family and place. She tapped a familiarity with songs and chants: songs of love and purification, chants for birth, for hunting, for harvest. She tapped an appreciation of humor — parody, caricature, irony — for various tribes made keen distinctions between kinds of humorous speech and granted status to those who displayed skill with them. Michelle cherished that heritage, intellectually and personally, and the fact that it was primarily an oral heritage, and a multilingual one, did not create barriers for her. She believed in a generative interplay between the spoken and the written word and operated with a definition of English broad enough to embrace it — an English that adapted to the telling of ceremonial stories, that appreciated the cadence of talking Johnny, that wasn't threatened by the Navajo line. An American English.

There were still bugs in the way these beliefs worked themselves out in Michelle's classroom. The sweep of the curriculum and Michelle's openness to possibilities — the spontaneity of the storyteller's give-and-take — sometimes worked against a sustained focus on the students' writing. Michelle was aware of this and tried to correct for it through tutoring; still, she felt that she hadn't yet got the balance right. But this complication was offset by the benefits of her approach: it fostered self-direction and achievement, cultural pride as well as cultural experimentation, serious play, and a kind of linguistic good will.

Michelle scooted up in the seat a little, for the tumbleweed was stirring, rolling across the desert in gusty fits. She looked back and forth, from the desert to the road, humming to herself. Just as we turned onto Old Spanish Trail, the last road we'd be on that had a name, the thunder started cracking above us. "My God, wouldn't you know it!" Michelle cried. We had an open truckbed full of groceries, all in paper sacks: vegetables, meats, chips, flour, napkins — bags and bags. Everybody had been praying for rain, taunting the weatherman for weeks. Michelle exhorted the truck to get a move on, patting the faded dash. The sky got darker, the tumbleweed blowing out onto the road, and the rain's sharp *rat-a-tat* began on the roof. Michelle leaned into the windshield, the wipers hardly making a difference, and told me to brace myself as we turned up a pitted dirt road. The truck bounced wildly and the rain came harder — downpour, deluge, cats and dogs — as Michelle and I cursed and laughed nervously and held on up the road, which was flooding fast. Johnny had left the gate open, so we went straight through to the front of the house, up onto a small rise. Then Johnny, who had been waiting by the kitchen window, ran out to meet us — tall and rangy, shorts and jackboots, big knees pumping in the rain — and the three of us darted back and forth from house to truckbed, grabbing things out of pulpy bags, boxes of pasta and detergent unfolding in our hands.

Johnny and I were close to the same size, so I dried off and changed into some clothes of his. Percy had come up earlier and brought her twelve-year-old son, Adam. We all sat by an open window, watching the rain hit the parched desert, the smell of sage moist and rich in the air. The house had a big central room with thick wood beams, a fireplace, stained glass, and rugs on the walls. It still wasn't finished — you had to walk across a plank to get to the bathroom — but it was comfortable, warm stone, and you could feel yourself relaxing into its permanence.

The rain let up as quickly as it had come, and the water, everywhere a few minutes ago, seeped into the desert. I walked outside. The air was a little damp, and there was a stray puddle or two on flat rock. I sat down on a big metal box under the kitchen window and felt the vibration of some sort of generator. Everything was quiet but for crickets and a few birds chirping and cawing. The sky was a vast, clear blue; in the distance, to the west, a jet trail was forming. Suddenly a bird streaked across my field of vision, squawking, a sharp tracery, and dipped quickly toward a big cluster of rocks and bushes. Then silence. I remembered a line I had copied from Michelle's work: "Everything had a voice in thc desert . . ." I got up and went to the truck to find my notebook. The ground was completely dry, the door handle warm to the touch. It was back about a week before, scribbled out of some writing Michelle had given me. I flipped back, a slip of paper falling out, a leaf . . . There it was:

> Everything had a voice in the desert, so everything had a story. And the voices blended, sometimes in harmony, sometimes in cacophony, but difference disappeared as we listened to the stories. In this way I came to understand Yaqui *etehoim* [stories], but they were never separated from people or places, and Spanish, English, and Yaqui and the rest blended together in a rich tapestry where each colored the other and no strand could be pulled without the whole thing unweaving.

Michelle was not naïve about the ways these voices, these languages could supersede and silence each other — her own history provided a harsh reminder — but she was dogged in her pursuit of dynamic interaction. It was a linguistic article of faith.

A lizard scurried up on a rock by my foot, turning his head in fits and starts, then scampered off. I could hear Michelle's and Johnny's voices coming from inside the house — they must have moved into the kitchen — talking back and forth about preparing food, oven temperatures, soggy chips, ice chests, cilantro. The interplay of languages was at the very heart of Michelle's classroom. There were many languages in the desert, and in the street, and in the library — and they all sang of possibility. They all had promise if you didn't use them to narrow ends, to constrain and subject. Michelle was encouraging her students to give expression to their history in new ways and to use the language of the old ways to consider new experience, believing that they were capable of navigating complex linguistic terrain and accomplishing wonderful things as they took up the journey.

The door cracked open and Adam walked out, asking if I wanted to go exploring. I pulled myself back in, a little lost in thought, and set the notebook down. Yeah . . . sure . . . that sounded good. There was a simple trail around the property, starting about ten yards from where I was sitting, looping around an incline through some brush, and back around, eventually, to the other side of the house. A post marked that place where the trail began, and a few rocks kicked to the side here and there gave us the hint of a pathway. Off we went.

Adam walked slowly, steadily in front of me, pointing things out as we made our way. Percy had told me that Adam was a nature buff, and, in fact, when school started up again, he was slated to enter an accelerated program in biological science. Usually Adam was pretty quiet, played it close to the vest, but out here he was a walking guidebook. Bola cactus, barrel cactus, cat's claw acacia. He pinched off a little piece of creosote and had me rub it between my fingers — it smelled like oil. Funny thing, a plant that smells like oil. We came upon a decomposing cluster of prickly pear cactus. Then another. "Was it the drought that killed these things?" I asked him. "Maybe," he said, "or it could be pack rats, too. They make their home in prickly pears. Then they eat their home!" Adam hunkered down by a boulder to point out velvet ants in the crevices, big desert ants with white, furry backs. He shook a long pole coming out of a cactus, and the pods on top rattled. "Like a rattlesnake, huh?" I shook it myself. Like a rattling snake.

We were circling back toward Michelle and Johnny's when Adam stopped suddenly, without a sound, and reached back to stop me. "Oooo, there's a rabbit," he said, nodding toward a clump of cactus and shrubbery, not taking his eyes off it. "Where?" I asked. "There," he said, gesturing again, speaking softly. "Right in the mesquite." He moved a few quiet steps, his hand behind him, guiding me. "See it now?" I hunched down, scanning the area, squinting. I couldn't see a thing. For a second, I figured I'd better lie and say yes, but then I felt even more stupid. "Uh, no Adam, your eyes are better than mine." There. The truth. I was off the hook. But Adam wouldn't buy it. He took two methodical steps, very close to the bush, and gestured for me again. "There," he said. "You can't miss it." And he was right. There was this figure-ground reversal, or some damned thing — and there it was. A small brown rabbit, plain as day, watching us, ears erect. I felt simultaneously accomplished and silly. But mostly I felt relief that I hadn't lied to Adam.

Later in the day, after more guests arrived, I stood outside with Terry Piestewa, Adam's father, who had driven in from Tuba City to join his wife and son. I told him the story about the rabbit — to honor Adam's keen eye and to have a laugh at my urban ineptitude. Terry, who was full-blood Hopi, folded his arms across his barrel chest and laughed. Then he told me a story about a cousin who was also at a loss in the desert. "We'd point things out to him, and he'd go, 'Oh, yeah, I see,' but really, he was looking like this." And here Terry squinted and looked uncertainly back and forth, a groping scan, clueless. I told him that I'd almost said "I see" to Adam too — and we really laughed at that.

"Thanks for the story," I said, appreciating his generosity. "I don't feel so bad." "No," he said in return. "Why should you? You learn these things." Yes, of course you do, I thought. Traditionally, you learned them through apprenticeship, observation, close human contact: the way Edwin described learning about farming in his tribute to his Grandfather Lorenzo. And in Adam's case that traditional learning was blended with the academic training he was receiving in school. You learn these things. Adam, the tracker-scientist.

Terry and I talked more about Adam, about his skill in the natural world and his success in school. Terry was proud of Adam's accomplishments. He had initiated his son into tribal custom, into the bear clan and the badger clan, and, as well, had thrown his support behind Adam's work in the classroom. The intersection of these worlds is, of course, a potential source of conflict, but because the community was involved in the Tuba City schools, at least some of this conflict was open to negotiation. Manny Begay had told me a story about one of the biology classes in the high school. At some point, the students were going to have to dissect frogs. Now, to the Navajo, the frog is a powerful figure, so a medicine man was invited in to assess the situation. He thought it over and performed a ceremony and explained to the Navajo students that, for the purposes of learning biology, they could dissect the frog, but that otherwise they were to continue to honor their beliefs. I told Terry this story. "Sure," he said, "as long as the parents know these things. Some of the grandparents don't approve, but the elders know we need the technology. This is a good school. In the old days, schools didn't ask us anything. The BIA used to come and take our kids away to boarding school. The parents wouldn't see them for years. Sometimes they died there."

One of the superintendents of Indian schools at the turn of the century detailed how, in order to "humanize, christianize, and educate" the Indian, teachers had "to divorce him from his primitive habits and customs . . . We want the power of the Latin," the superintendent enthusiastically explained, "as well as the intellectuality of the Saxon. [We] must recreate him, make him a new personality." Is it any wonder that historically there has been so much ambivalence, if not resistance, on the part of Indian parents toward White society's schooling? Standing outside Michelle's house with Terry, watching the sun move slowly toward the jagged ridge of the mountains, I understood, more fully than before, how important it was to have Percy involved in Michelle's classroom. And for Manny to be walking the halls, visiting classes, settling down in the dorms. And for Manny's wife to visit, and for their small daughter and Percy's kids to be around the place, drawing, writing stories themselves, playing with the students. There are compelling ways to make available the power of the Latin and the intellectuality of the Saxon, but such work has to be based on a respect for Indian society, not on contempt or a desire to erase. Only then can mainstream education provide a resource for creating what one pair of Indian activists calls "a contemporary expression of tribal identity."

The sun was behind the mountains when Johnny came to the door to retrieve Terry and me. The sky was deep blue and way off, toward Mexico, the lightning was starting up again, muted somewhat by low clouds, soft forked light flashing over Sonora. "Let's go inside," Terry said, and about halfway there, the aroma caught us, and we walked faster. The large wooden table in the corner of the house was covered with an old lace tablecloth, cream-colored webbing over mahogany. Big pots, burned along the sides, sat on decorated cutting boards. Carne seca, beans and peppers, stacks of tortillas that you could stretch your hand across. Ceviche, enchiladas, pine boughs crisscrossed on the middle of the table. Feathers and ornamental corn in a bowl to the side.

While Terry and I were outside, other guests had arrived. The teachers Beth and Pat, Terry's oldest son and his wife and baby, Patricia the tutor and a few other people from school, some friends of Johnny's. We gathered around the table, lifting lids and inhaling deeply and complimenting the cooks, wrapping carne seca in the huge tortillas, scooping beans, dropping some, pouring drinks, fingering ice. We reached arm over arm to get to this or that, teased each other about the size of portions, anticipated the meal.

Terry, Michelle, and I sat on a ledge by an open window, talking about the students, many of whom Terry knew. They were the future, Terry said. Creating themselves out of past and present, I thought. In that web Michelle drew, everything was linked: tradition and identity, self and dreams. Someone proposed a toast, and we raised our cans, clinking them. In the distance, over Michelle's shoulder, I could see the lightning coming toward the earth, sharp now in the night sky, erratic and fresh.

10

Possible Lives

I was riding with Percy and Terry Piestewa through Kerley Valley, following the route Suzy Worker had sketched when she took us, both as outsiders and insiders, shifting point of view, down the main street of Tuba City. Clump clump. Manny Begay had invited me to Tuba City to visit the high school Michelle's students attended and to see the places they had written about. The Tuba Trading Post, the motel where the tourists stay, McDonald's, the police station . . . A correspondence of landscape and language.

Terry turned south, crossing the highway, and drove a mile or two to Moenkopi, the farthest west of the Hopi villages that originate deep in the spare and beautiful center of the reservation. Brick and stone dwellings, a few newer wood constructions, some cars, trucks, a tractor, limited electricity, the hum of generators. We walked to the edge of the mesa. Below, out on the open floor of the valley, were neat rows of cornstalks, the fields Edwin had described in the essay honoring his grandfather.

It was fall, and school was in session. I visited some of the classes of the sort Suzy, Edwin, and the others had taken before coming to the summer program. In Effie Hyden's course in anatomy and physiology, a bespectacled girl in overalls was explaining the procedure for coronary bypass surgery, sketching a shunt into the aorta of a heart she had drawn on the board. In physics-math down the hall, Mani Roi was reviewing the concepts of distance and displacement, drawing, as I had seen Sharon Davis do in Tupelo, a quick schematic of local geography:

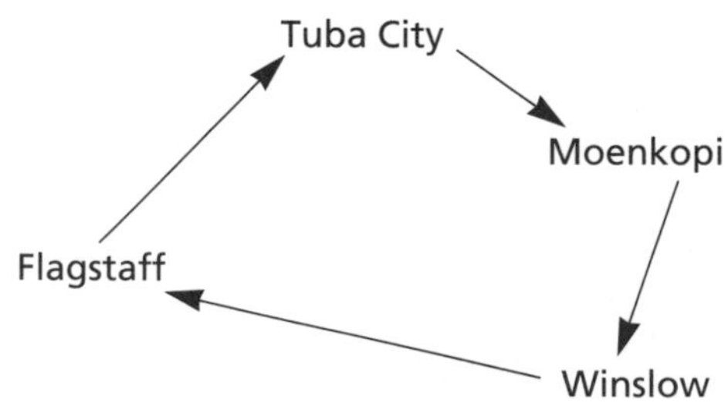

Winslow, seventy miles south as the crow flies, was the location of the school's football rival, and that night the Tuba City Warriors were hosting the Winslow Bulldogs. Terry said, Let's go. The stands were about three-quarters full when we arrived. There were families, many greetings, little kids playing in the aisles, old men in cowboy hats, a few Navajo policemen. As we made our way up the stairs, I heard English, Spanish, Navajo, and Hopi, and the dialects and accents Darold, Bertha, and the rest had played with in their sketches of life in Tuba City. The sky was brushed with feathery clouds, the air warm and gentle. First and ten. Ball on the eleven-yard line. The band played "Achy-Breaky Heart" with a deep, rolling beat. People yelled at the Warrior quarterback. Bud Reynolds, the teacher from Kentucky, had talked about the way high school athletics bring a small town together. Next to me, Percy was furiously rattling an old cow bell. The crowd began stamping on the metal bleachers, a wave of noise meant to intimidate and inspire. And off in the distance, atop one of the hills beyond the border of the school, a lone figure sat on a horse, watching the game.

I THE EXIT from the Warriors' stadium led back through Tuba City, car light, lights from trucks, streetlights, moonlight over the roads that continued a journey I had begun three-and-a-half years before, trying to fashion a response to the loss of faith in our public schools. I was looking for a language of possibility, an imagery to spark our imagination. It was a wonderful trip, one many could take, full of revealing conversation and the pleasure of the land — Happy Jack Road, Holy Moses Wash — a journey of surprise and resonance.

The search led outward, across landscapes — urban and rural — that were new to me, across the immensity of this country and its remarkable particularity: snow falling on a creek, a pasture, a frame schoolhouse; a block of brick storefronts — its mix of dry goods, melons, language, fish on ice, apples, information, opportunity; billowing smokestacks jutting out of pine; the desert after rainfall; empty mills where rivers cross, thick with pain and goldenrod; a train whistle through the hollows; cornfields symmetrical on a page and in the clear air below.

And, as is the case with so many journeys, this one led inward as well. I had been studying schools for much of my adult life, had been trying to understand how they enhanced the lives of students or diminished them. Most of that work was located in and around the LA Basin. For all its bewildering complication, Los Angeles was familiar territory, home. These trips to Calexico, to Baltimore, to Eastern Kentucky, to a nation within a nation in northern Arizona brought forth new cultural practices, new languages, new gestures. I was fortunate to have been escorted into so many classrooms, so many homes, to have been guided into the everyday events of the communities I visited, for the invitation eased the unfamiliarity and discomfort that could have been present on all sides. What I experienced was a kind of awe at our variety, yet an intimate regard, a handshake on the corner, a sense of shared humanity. The complex interplay of difference and commonality. What began as a search for a fresh language of educational critique and invention became, as well, a search for what is best in this country — realized infrequently, threatened at every turn — but there to be summoned, possible in the public domain, there to instruct a traveler settling into a seat in the corner of a classroom.

It was, in many ways, an odd time to be on such a journey. The country was in the grip of a nasty reactive politics, a volatile mix of anger and anxiety. And people of all political persuasions were withdrawing from engagement with the public sphere. It was time of economic and moral cocooning. The question for me — framed in terms of public schools, our pre-eminent public institution — was how to generate a hopeful vision in a time of bitterness and lost faith, and, further, how to do that in a way that holds simultaneously to what educational philosopher David Purpel calls "the interlocking and interdependent hinges" of criticism and creativity. How to sharpen awareness of injustice and incompetence, how to maintain the skeptic's acuity, yet nurture the ability to imagine the possible and act from hope.

The journey was odd for me in another way, considering my own teaching history. My work in the classroom has mostly been with people whom our schools, public and private, have failed: working-class and immigrant students, students from nonmainstream linguistic and cultural backgrounds, students of all backgrounds who didn't fit a curriculum or timetable or definition of achievement and were thereby categorized in some way as different or deficient. There are, as we have seen along this journey, long-standing social and cultural reasons for this failure of our schools, tangled, disturbing histories of discrimination, skewed perception, and protection of privilege.

And yet there were these rooms. Vital, varied, they were providing a powerful education for the children in them, many of whom were members of the very groups defined as inferior in times past and, not infrequently, in our ungenerous present. What I began to see — and it took the accumulation of diverse classrooms to help me see it — was that these classrooms, in addition to whatever else we may understand about them, represented a dynamic, at times compromised and contested, strain in American educational history: a faith in the capacity of a people, a drive toward equality and opportunity, a belief in the intimate link between mass education and a free society. These rooms were embodiments of the democratic ideal. To be sure, this democratic impulse has been undercut and violated virtually since its first articulation. Thomas Jefferson's proposal to the Virginia legislature for three years of free public schooling, for example, excluded the commonwealth's significant number of enslaved Black children. But it has been advanced, realized in daily classroom life by a long history of educators working both within the mainstream and outside it, challenging it through workingmen's organizations, women's groups, Black schools, appropriating the ideal, often against political and economic resistance, to their own emancipatory ends.

The teachers I visited were working within that rich tradition. They provided example after different example of people doing public intellectual work in institutional settings, using the power of the institution to realize democratic goals for the children in their charge, and finessing, negotiating, subverting institutional power when it blocked the realization of those goals. At a time of profound disillusionment with public institutional life, these people were, in their distinct ways, creating the conditions for children to develop lives of possibility.

My hope is that these classrooms will help us imagine — and, in imagining, struggle to achieve — what schools in the public domain, and perhaps a range of public institutions, can be.

Whether or not an institution is democratic is often determined by procedural criteria. Do members have a vote, input into policy, a place at the table? These concerns are important, of course, but considered alone, or primarily, can lead to reductive definitions of democracy, democracy as procedure, as a set of rules. My visits led me to be more interested in the *experience* of democracy, the phenomenology of it. What did it feel like to be in those classrooms in Watts, on the South Side, in the Eastern Coal Field, in Hattiesburg and Missoula, in Calexico and Tucson? If we can situate ourselves within that experience, we may come to understand on many levels, not just the definitional and formal, what schooling for all in a democratic society can be and how we can meaningfully talk about it.

The first thing to say about the rooms I visited is that they created a sense of safety. There was physical safety, which for some children in some environments is a real consideration. But there was also safety from insult and diminishment: "They don't make fun of you if you mess up," said the middle school student in Chicago. And there was safety to take risks, to push beyond what you can comfortably do at present, "coaxing our thinking along," as one of Steve Gilbert's students put it, "bringing out our best interpretive abilities."

Intimately related to safety is respect, a word I heard frequently during my travels. From what I could tell, it meant many things, operated on many levels: fair treatment, decency, an absence of intimidation, and, beyond the realm of individual civility, a respect for the history, the language and culture of the peoples represented in the classroom. Surveying the images of Mexican and Mexican-American history on Carlos Jimenez's walls and bulletin boards, a Chicano student exclaimed, "This room is something *positive.* As you walk around, you say, 'Hey, we're somebody!'" Respect also has an intellectual dimension. As New York principal Louis Delgado put it, "It's not just about being polite — even the curriculum has to convey respect. [It] has to be challenging enough that it's respectful." It is interesting that virtually all of our current discussions of academic standards are framed either in the quasi-technical language of assessment and accountability or as a lament for diminished performance. There could be a whole other discussion of standards in a language of expectation, respect, and democratic theory.

Talking about safety and respect leads to a consideration of authority. Most discussions of authority in the classroom involve either a teacher's "management" style (one common treatment, for example, contrasts an authoritarian with a democratic style) or the degree to which a teacher involves students in making decisions about what will be taught and how the class will be run. While none of the teachers I observed could be categorized as authoritarian, I did see a range of classroom management styles, and while some teachers involved students in determining the rules of classroom conduct and gave them significant responsibility to provide the class its direction, others came with curriculum and codes of conduct fairly well in place.

But two things seemed to hold across classrooms. First, a teacher's authority came from multiple sources — knowledge, care, the construction of safe and respectful space, solidarity with students' background — rather than solely from age or role. Though there were times when our teachers asserted authority in a direct and unilateral way, in general, authority was not expressed or experienced as a blunt exercise of power. As one of Stephanie Terry's first-graders put it, "She doesn't fuss a lot."

The second thing to note was that even in classrooms that were run in a relatively traditional manner, authority was distributed. In various ways, students contributed to the flow of events, shaped the direction of discussion, became authorities on their own experience and on the work they were doing. Think of Stephanie Terry's students reporting on their observations of the tree frog and hermit crab and Michelle Taigue's Navajo and Hopi students explaining slang and dialect on the reservation. There were multiple pathways of authority, multiple opportunities for members of the class to assume authority. And since authority and the generation of knowledge are intimately connected — those who can speak affect what is known — there were multiple opportunities to shape the knowledge emerging in the classroom.

These classrooms, then, were places of expectation and responsibility. Teachers took students seriously as intellectual and social beings. Young people had to work hard, think things through, come to terms with each other — and there were times when such effort took a student to his or her limits. "They looked at us in disbelief," said New York principal Haven Henderson, "when we told them they were intellectuals." The teachers we met assumed that a small society of achievement and civic behavior could flourish. "All children," said Evangelina Jones in Calexico, "have minds and souls and have the ability to participate fully in society." It is important to note that such assumptions were realized through a range of supports, guides, and structures: from the way teachers organized curriculum and invited and answered questions, to the means of assistance they and their aides provided (tutoring, conferences, written and oral feedback), to the various ways they encouraged peer support and assistance, to the atmosphere they created in the room — which takes us back to considerations of safety and respect. These classrooms required thought, participation, effort — they were places where you did things — but not without mechanisms to aid involvement and achievement. Such aid to participation should be a defining quality of public institutions in a democracy.

This mix of expectation, responsibility, and assistance established the conditions for students like the young woman in Mark Hall's Graphic Arts Lab in Pasadena to say, "I'm just learning all this. I can't wait to get really proficient at it." Or for the child in Calexico, engaged with an exercise on the telling of time, to implore Elena Castro to "make [the problems] harder." Earlier, I suggested that there could be in our country an alternative discussion of standards, one that involved expectation, respect, and democratic theory. Yvonne Hutchinson, the middle school teacher from Watts, offered one direction such a discussion might take:

> Teachers will say either "we can't lower our standards" or "this poor child is reading below grade level, so I'll need a third- or fourth-grade book." But what you need to do is find a way to make that eighth-grade book *accessible.* You have to respect the child . . . We get so busy looking at children in terms of labels that we fail to look for the *potential* — and to demand that kids live up to that potential. Children can tell right off those people who believe in them and those who patronize them. . . . They rise to whatever expectations are set. They rise or fail to rise. And when they rise, they can sometimes rise to great heights.

The students I talked to, from primary-grade children to graduating seniors, each in their own way, had the sense that these classrooms were salutary places, places that felt good to be in, places that honored their best interests. "They really care about you," that student in Mark Hall's lab said of the Graphic Arts Academy. "It's like we're a family." Discussing difficult times in making their video, two students recalled Bell High School teacher Larry Stone's encouragement: "Girls, you have to do this . . . It'll work out. I believe in you." Calling Michelle Smith, of the COMETS program in Chicago, a "good teacher," a student explained that "she's teaching us how to do things we couldn't do before." "Math'll take you a long way in life," said an Algebra Project student in Hollandale, Mississippi. There was variation in the way it was experienced and expressed — nurturance, social cohesion, the fostering of competence, a sense of growth, a feeling of opportunity, futurity — but there was among the students I met a common recognition of concern and benefit.

The foregoing characteristics combined to create vital public space. The rooms I visited felt alive. People were learning things, both cognitive and social, and doing things, individually and collectively, making contributions, connecting ideas, generating knowledge. To be sure, not everyone was engaged. And everyone, students and teachers, had bad days. But overall these classrooms were exciting places to be, places of reflection and challenge, of deliberation and expression, of quiet work and public presentation. People were encouraged to be smart. "I wanted to feel the challenge of the tough courses," said Carlos Jimenez's student about electives like Mexican-American history. "I think I came to understand," said Lois Rodgers's student after completing a video project on Camp Sister Spirit, "something about the fear behind prejudice." "[Rick Takagaki's] classes made me realize I needed to go experience things," observed a University High student in Los Angeles. These young people were acting as agents in their own development. And that agency became an essential force in sustaining the classroom. The work they were doing had an effect beyond itself.

In an important post-revolutionary essay on education, the eighteenth-century journalist Samuel Harrison Smith wrote that the free play of intelligence was central to a democracy, and that individual intellectual growth was intimately connected to broad-scale intellectual development, to the "general diffusion of knowledge." To a significant degree, the occasion and energy for intellectual growth in these classrooms came from engagement with others, often over a common problem. Consider Aleta Sullivan's human anatomy and physiology students trying to find a solution to their blood-antigen experiment, or Bette Ford's students, also at Hattiesburg High, struggling to convey to an audience of children the complex legacy of sharecropping, or Michelle Taigue's students in Tucson trying to render in a videoplay the tension between White, urban education and the social fabric of reservation life.

Smith celebrated "the improvement of the mind and the collision of mind with mind." As a number of contemporary critics of our public schools and of the larger public sphere have noted, what Smith referred to as "the general diffusion of knowledge" has been restricted in our country, and many voices remain silent. If we consider these rooms to be miniature public spheres or preparatory arenas for civic life, then it is essential to note how the formation of intellectually safe and respectful space, the distribution of authority and responsibility, the maintenance of high expectations and the means to attain them — how all this is essential to the development of the intelligence of a people.

II

THE CLASSROOMS we visited were created spaces. Other public institutions — or other classrooms in other schools — could provide a very different experience. What accounted for those rooms in Los Angeles, Chicago, Wheelwright, Jackson, Polaris, and the balance of our towns and cities? How did they come to be?

One way to answer that question is to recall the conversation with Emily Palacio, the director of curriculum development for the Calexico Unified School District. Talking about the classrooms I was observing at Dool Elementary School, she said, "You have to understand the number of things that had to be put in place so that those teachers you saw could flourish." Schools, classrooms exist in elaborate social cultural, political, economic contexts. The work of Elena Castro and her talented colleagues at Dool was made possible by federal affirmative action policies that encouraged people like her to enter the teaching force, by the Bilingual Education Act and other federal and state legislation that affected the ways we think about language, culture, and pedagogy, by a shift in the local Calexico demographic and power base. You'd also have to consider the way the foregoing changes affected teacher education; in fact, you'd have to factor in the very existence of the San Diego satellite campus — a source of local teachers, the majority of those I visited. Also of importance is the current district administration, people like Emily Palacio who encourage individual teacher initiative and — no small matter — are skilled in ways to find money to fund good ideas. There is an activist and supportive school board and productive relations between the board and the administration. And there is the Calexico community's belief in the schools, a willingness to support them, fiscally and socially, to trust children to them, to become involved in them. This is a partial list, but it underscores Emily's point: good schools and classrooms do not exist in a vacuum.

I'll return to this idea later, for I want to consider it from a different perspective: What are the forces beyond the schoolhouse that threaten good work in the classroom? But for now, I'd like to bring my question about the creation of the classrooms we saw in to the level of the teacher, for the teacher has been so much the focus of this journey. As I hope the visits have shown, any meaningful discussion of schooling and school reform must have the instructional encounter at its center. Furthermore, the teacher, as political philosopher Amy Gutmann points out, is positioned dynamically between state and community and, of all those involved with schooling, holds the potential for most immediately "cultivating the capacity for democratic deliberation." What did these teachers know how to do and what assumptions did they share that made their classrooms possible?

The first thing to remember in posing such a question is that there was a great deal of variation in what these teachers did and how they did it. Region, demographics, grade level, subject matter, all these shaped and differentiated good work in eleventh-grade American studies in eastern Kentucky, in math and algebra courses in the Mississippi Delta, in a one-room schoolhouse in western Montana. There were, as well, a range of individual styles and preferences. Elena Castro in Calexico developed an abundant curriculum around learning stations; Stephanie Terry in Baltimore thought learning stations would sabotage her curriculum. Ed Murphy's video-production class at Bell High School was a fairly unstructured affair, organized around student-generated projects; Steve Gilbert's advanced placement English class in Chicago proceeded in close analytic connection to specific literary texts. This variability enlivened the journey.

With this understanding of differences, let me attempt some generalizations, knowing that they are not meant to be tight categories and don't apply equally to everyone.

To begin, the teachers we spent time with were knowledgeable. They knew subject matter or languages or technologies, which they acquired in a variety of ways: from formal schooling to curriculum-development projects to individual practice and study. In most cases, this acquisition of knowledge was ongoing, developing; they were still learning, and their pursuits were a source of excitement and renewal.

But, of course, good teachers not only know things, but are also adept at conveying what they know: presenting it, clarifying it, sparking interest in it, using it to generate thought and action. Part of the pleasure of this journey for me was being guided through books I hadn't read before, working, with a fresh take, calculations I had long since forgotten, considering a historical or current event in an unexpected context. Teaching, then, involves additional knowledge and skill, applied knowledge, craft, what educational psychologist Lee Shulman calls "the wisdom of practice." Some of this knowledge is fairly specific to subject matter: familiarity with the materials of one's field, a ready stock of illustrations and analogies, a grasp of the ways particular concepts and operations are typically misunderstood and a repertoire of responses to facilitate understanding. And some aspects of pedagogical craft are more general: from structuring and pacing a lesson to conducting a discussion and responding to questions. One of the many reductive debates within educational circles sets those who define and study teaching primarily in terms of process and technique against those who insist on the centrality of subject matter knowledge. Good teaching is a dynamic of both knowledge and technique. John Dewey, so often misunderstood on issues like this, is instructive here. "The more the educator knows of music," he writes, using one area of study as an example, "the more he can perceive the possibilities of the inchoate musical impulses of a child . . . [T]he various studies represent working resources, available capital . . . [yet] the teacher should be occupied not with subject matter in itself but in its interaction with the pupils' present needs and capacities."

As one teaches, one's knowledge plays out in social space, and this is one of the things that makes teaching such a complex activity. As studies of teacher cognition have shown, and as we saw in the classrooms we visited, teaching well means knowing one's students well and being able to read them quickly and, in turn, making decisions to slow down or speed up, to stay with a point or return to it later, to underscore certain connections, to use or forgo a particular illustration. This decision-making operates as much by feel as by reason: it involves hunch, intuition, a best, quick guess.

There is another dimension to the ability to make judgments about instruction. The teachers we observed operate with a knowledge of individual student's lives, of local history and economy, and of social-cultural traditions and practices. They gain this knowledge in any number of ways: living in the communities in which they work; getting involved in local institutions and projects; drawing on personal and cultural histories that resemble the histories of the children they teach; educating themselves about the communities and cultures of the students before them; connecting with parents and involving parents in schooling; seeing students as resources and learning from them.

This is a difficult and delicate issue. We often in America, and teachers are no exception, judge people harshly by their origins ("trailer trash," I overheard in one lunchroom; "scummy parents," in another), or, less maliciously, we pity or patronize or pigeonhole them. (Recall here Yvonne Hutchinson's litany: "slow," "poor," "impoverished," "deprived," "oppressed.") And because our social history is so confused and blighted, we easily slip into stereotype when we consider ethnicity or race or gender. Educational literature has been complicit here, offering thumbnail sketches of populations as a guide to instruction. Recall, for example, Michelle Taigue's complaint about characterizing Native American children as having difficulty with writing "because they come from an oral culture." Yet look at the way the teachers we met used knowledge from beyond the classroom to enhance their ability to counsel and to teach. I suspect that if we were to study that knowledge, we would find it structured in ways that work against reductive perception. For one thing, it is acquired from multiple sources. It is, from all I could tell, rich knowledge, grounded in particular people's lives, balancing strengths and liabilities, reflecting variability within groups. I think it contributed to the ability of many of these teachers both to understand, at times celebrate, where their students came from and to envision for them other domains of actions and influence — to, as a friend of mine put it, help them develop both roots and wings.

As one spends more time in a classroom, one's subject matter knowledge is influenced by, even transformed by these human connections. I think here of feminist educator and ethicist Nel Noddings's call to consider subject matter in terms of what she calls an ethic of care. "Our guiding principles for teaching arithmetic, or any other subject, are derived from our primary concern for the persons whom we teach." This way of talking about teaching and learning, observes Noddings, this "language of relation" has "almost disappeared from formal educational discourse." Yet many of the teachers we came to know spoke about what they taught in ways that intersected cognition and relation, subject matter and students' lives. Here's Sharon Davis, the physics teacher from Tupelo, reflecting on her curriculum. "One reason physics is so scary is that students have not been shown that a significant part of physics involves taking a different perspective on the everyday flow of events around them. For example, could they come to think about the bending of the elbow to eat as a response to electrical impulses from the brain? If kids look at life from one perspective only, then much of life will remain baffling. They will be limited in how they function, in what they can do." There's an interest here in the formation of experience, a connection in Sharon's mind between physics, perception, and human growth.

A teacher must use these various kinds of knowledge — knowledge of subject matter, of practice, of one's students, of relation — within the institutional confines of mass education. The teachers I visited had, over time, developed ways to act with some effectiveness within these constraints — though not without times of confusion and defeat — and they had determined ways of organizing their classrooms that enabled them to honor their beliefs about teaching and learning. We saw a good deal of variation here; there is no one best way: lecture-discussion, Socratic dialogue, laboratory demonstration, learning centers, small-group collaborative learning, a kind of artisans' workshop where students pursue independent projects. Not infrequently, these approaches existed in combination in the same classroom. In a number of cases, the current organization evolved. Teachers experimented with ways to create a common space where meaningful work could be done. This quality of reflective experimentation, of trying new things, of tinkering and adjusting, sometimes with uneven results, sometimes failing, was part of the history of many of the classrooms in *Possible Lives.*

The ability of many of these teachers to work effectively within their schools and districts was strengthened by the way they pulled others into their professional lives. You won't find this discussed very much in teacher-education literature, and, I must admit, it was so obvious that it took me a while to appreciate its full significance. Now I find myself talking about it to new teachers all the time. With the autonomy of the classroom comes the potential for isolation and loneliness — something many beginning teachers feel acutely. Evangelina Jones in Calexico, recalling her own first difficult year, said simply, "If you don't get support, you die a little very day." This isolation, for beginning and continuing teachers alike, is complicated and mystified by what Deborah Britzman, who studies the socialization of teachers, identifies as common myths about teaching: that the effective teacher is a rugged individualist, the source and center of authority and control; that the teacher is expert; and that the teacher is self-made, is a "natural" — "pedagogy becomes a product of one's personality." "These myths," Britzman observes, "valorize the individual and make inconsequential the institutional constraints which frame the teacher's work." The situation is further complicated for women (who make up 80 percent of the elementary and about half of the secondary teaching force) by the play of cultural expectations — shaped in the mid-nineteenth century, but in some ways still with us — about the way women should act in the classroom: good-girl forbearance, silent sacrifice, submission to institutional regulation.

Given this complex social-cultural backdrop, it is telling how many of the teachers I visited developed formal or informal social arrangements that enriched their teaching, gained them emotional and intellectual support, and shored up their ability to temper or challenge the constraints of their position. A significant number of them team-taught or established other kinds of collaborative relationships. Some were engaged with school reform, within their school — as were the three COMETS teachers on Chicago's South Side — or at the district, regional, or state level, like several of the teachers from Mississippi. Some fulfilled personal and professional needs through study and advocacy groups — I think here of Stephanie Terry and her colleagues who worked in and studied urban schools — or through less organized arrangements, like the lunch-time gatherings of the Calexico teachers in Elena Castro's classroom. A fair number were involved in their local unions and, in some cases, became advocates for teachers in larger national and state arenas. And some teachers developed networks with parents and others in the community that provided knowledge, resources, and support.

These relationships and professional networks reinforced, at times revitalized, a belief held in some way by all the teachers I met: a belief in the value of their work, even as they voiced with clarity its limits and contradictions. "Women down here don't have the top positions," said Lois Rodgers of Hattiesburg High School, "so we've learned to be strong in what we do have." Teaching provided for them a sphere of influence, a source of identity and meaning. Reflecting on his career of twenty-six years, Chicago's Steve Gilbert said that "if at the end of my life, there are five hundred people who see the world differently because of the work I've done, well, I would be very happy about that." It was this sense of value that guided and sustained these teachers in their classroom work and that, in many ways, accounted for their persistence, the long hours, the extra push. There were times of doubt and ambiguity, of deep frustration, and, in several cases, of burn-out. And there were pedagogical dark nights of the soul: I picture Stephanie Terry in Baltimore struggling with the decision of whether or not to refer a child to special education or Bud Reynolds in Wheelwright confronting the possibility of his own failure. But their relationships and commitments and the children themselves pulled them back, rekindling their belief that they could, again to quote Lois Rodgers, "make a difference in the lives of kids."

At heart, the teachers in *Possible Lives* were able to affirm in a deep and comprehensive way the capability of the students in their classrooms. Thus the high expectations they held for what their students could accomplish. As with other characteristics we've considered, there was considerable variation in the origins and architecture of this affirmation: It emerged from and was shaped by one's family or church or from the early experience of being valued and affirmed by a teacher; from the experience of race or class or gender or sexual orientation; from spiritual sources or an intellectual populism. It came from love or anger, from a sense of injustice or a sense of abundance and hope. In any one teacher's history there was usually a complex intersection of such sources. But what was common was a belief in the worth and potential of the children, all the children, who came under their charge.

Such affirmation of intellectual and civic potential, particularly within populations that have been historically devalued in our society, gives to these teachers' work a dimension of advocacy, a moral and political purpose. "Teaching children to read is, after all, an egalitarian business," writes Michael Walzer in *Spheres of Justice.* "Like the democratic theorist," he continues, the reading teacher "assumes that all her students have an interest and are able to learn." We tend to forget what a radical idea this is in the history of Western political thought — this belief that *all* members of the state have an intellectual and civic contribution to make, have the potential for full participation in society. The shame of our schools is that, over time, we have denied such merit to so many. "I do think it is revolutionary," said New York principal Mary Stevens, "to get kids to believe they are worthy . . . to understand themselves as learning, growing beings." Given the populations with whom many of our teachers choose to work, the enactment of egalitarian beliefs in their classrooms becomes a vehicle for social change, a realization of the democratic ideal in real time.

III

WE HAVE CONSIDERED the classrooms in *Possible Lives* as democratic spaces, tried to get a sense of the experience of being in them, and detailed what it was that teachers did to help create them. I would now like to consider what it is that threatens them. What did we encounter along the journey that menaces achievement, that limits the development of broad-scale intellectual and civic excellence? This question takes us to the heart of school reform, though offers a somewhat different way to think and talk about it.

The majority of national-level reports and addresses on reform over the past decade and a half have tended to represent school failure — which is usually characterized as being of crisis proportions — in one of two ways. The first asserts that there has been a significant decline in standards, as determined by national and cross-national test scores, and that the remedy lies in more rigorous curriculum and instruction, higher and more precisely articulated standards and goals, and more testing. The cause of this decline, if I accurately read the rhetoric of the discussion, is essentially a failure of will — students don't work hard enough, teachers don't demand enough, parents aren't involved enough — and we will be able to gauge a stiffening of will through a rise in scores on standardized tests. The second cause of school failure is found in the way schools are organized and governed. The solution lies in a restructuring of school management and decision-making processes, bringing more responsibility for the way a school is run closer to the school site itself. There is a belief at work here, understandable in a technological-managerial society, that a change in institutional structure — rather than, say, a rethinking of state and national funding priorities or a re-evaluation of basic assumptions about teaching and learning — will necessarily lead to fundamental changes in behavior and, thus, in educational outcomes.

Each of these calls to reform could lead to public discussions of some merit. One discussion, for example, would call attention to the significant numbers of children — often poor, immigrant, or minority —who routinely face unchallenging, demeaning curricula, curricula that, as Bob Moses of the Algebra Project would argue, locks them out of fuller intellectual and sociopolitical involvement in civic and institutional life. And, as those New York principals made clear, the way most urban schools are organized and situated within their district bureaucracies stifles inventive and comprehensive work with young people. These issues came to the fore at many points in the trip across country.

Yet the national discussion of the problems in our schools, as ever-present and sweeping as it is, seems, much of the time, to be incomplete, narrow, somehow lacking: failure of will, declining standards, bureaucracy. Perhaps its limitations are to be found in the crisis rhetoric itself, a rhetoric that levels nuance and variation, and leads readily to a stark and simplified model of cause and effect — with overtones of a fall from pre-crisis grace and the promise of a post-reform redemption. And perhaps the difficulty lies in the measures of achievement and the models of effectiveness that are at the center of many reform proposals: standardized tests, reductive comparison designs that ignore social and cultural variables, ways of analyzing institutions that focus on function and structure. Whatever the case, the solutions offered in our reform literature seem one-dimensional, at times utopian ("By the year 2000, all children will be ready to learn," reads the first of our National Education Goals), and the analysis of problems in the schools seems thin and acontextual and, well, bloodless. As Calexico's Emily Palacio explained near the beginning of this journey, schools and classrooms, teachers and students, exist in a complex axis of history, politics, economics, and culture. While some of what ails our schools surely does lie in curriculum and school structure, there is much more to our failure to teach our children well.

Life in schools and classrooms is vulnerable to the disruptions in the communities around them: unemployment, crime, substance abuse, violence, sudden wrenching shifts in demographics — all of which, themselves, are causally linked to broader social and economic transformations. You could measure the decline of King Coal in eastern Kentucky by the buckle in the stairs at Wheelwright High School, by the angle of the lockers torn from the wall. You could chart Janeane Vigliotti's course across campus at Monterey Park High School, seeking to diffuse tensions between Latino and Asian students, you could chart that course and the lines of force affecting it throughout the LA Basin and beyond, to Mexico, El Salvador, and the Pacific Rim. Any comprehensive program of reform would have to view school problems in these larger contexts. There is a popular conservative line of thought that plays down the effect of such environmental variables on behavior and achievement, that argues that the reason for violence and failure is a collapse of values. To be sure, there are moral and ethical dimensions to the problems in our schools — we saw that along the way — and the classrooms we visited encouraged ethical behavior and moral reflection. But to deny the complex ways a disrupted or devastated material reality diminishes hope, engenders rage, and shrivels our sense of who we are — and the relation of all that to behavior and achievement — seems naïve, sociologically and morally.

There *is* a significant moral dimension to school failure, but it is not much discussed in the reform literature. It involves the political history of towns and cities, the decisions, deals, and enactment into policy of prejudice and privilege that have had direct and long-standing effect on school funding, equity, and autonomy. When that *Chicago Tribune* editor observed that "it took an extraordinary combination of greed, racism, political cowardice, and public apathy" to bring the Chicago schools to their current state, he could have been describing any number of other districts in our country. I think the thing that most struck me as I read the histories of the troubled districts in this journey was how far back their current problems extended. We saw, in Chicago, a legacy of corruption and disregard that began in the mid-nineteenth century with the building of the first schoolhouse and the selling of the first school lands. The immensely complicated political and economic situation in New York City was duly noted by a journalist in 1903: "[The city] has the most difficult educational problem in the country." Schools in Mississippi are still recovering financially from apartheid and from a systematic underfunding of public education that began in the post-Reconstruction state house. Public schools are, in many ways, powerful cultural institutions, and we tend to focus on that power both in our criticism of their failings and in our expression of hope for what they might achieve for our children and what social ills they might correct. But it is important to keep in mind that in terms of the sheer blunt power of political and economic interests and the way that power plays out in city, state, and national life, schools are relatively weak institutions, compromised and undercut continually in our history. The students in Bonnie Tarta's U.S. history class in Chicago had a sense of this; thus one of them recommended "amend[ing] the Constitution to assure education for everyone." She was calling for some mechanism to guarantee not just the right but the practice of equitable universal schooling.

Life in the classroom is vulnerable not only to political and economic forces, but also to the inhumane and anti-egalitarian beliefs and biases in the culture at large. Schools are open systems, permeable institutions: beliefs about race and gender, about class and language, about intelligence, ability, and achievement emerge in the classroom; the appeals of commercial culture, the imagery of power and glamor play across the school yard.

Some of the teachers we visited developed ways to subject these beliefs and practices to scrutiny. Rick Takagaki, the economics teacher in West Los Angeles, role-played his students into discussions of economy and social structure. Lois Rodgers set the stage at Hattiesburg High for reflection on sexism and homophobia. A number of those New York principals were constructing curricula that would lead to the study of race and class. Shelley Neilsen and her colleagues in Co-Teach created the conditions for Missoula preschoolers to have a different experience of ability.

But once the lesson is over, once the alternative social arrangements disperse at the end of the hour, children move back into a world that is less generous to contemplation and growth. When those Monterey Park students leave the stage of *Womanspeak,* exhale the last powerful breaths of Susan B. Anthony and Emma Goldman, they must make their way across the complex social landscape of old-country gender expectations, commodified sexuality, a job structure that is still unfair to women. To be sure, these young women learn from *Womanspeak,* are emboldened by the dialogue — they are not without agency and imagination — but the limits they will encounter because of their gender can compromise what their education yields and what they envision for themselves. I think here of Sharon Davis, the physics teacher from Tupelo. In spite of her hard work and achievement in high school, she still observed a social structure around her that reflected back no images of women in science, and she began to doubt her ability to become a physician. The possible life she created for herself in the classroom seemed less and less likely as she surveyed the streets and offices of her small Mississippi town.

And the schools themselves can diminish hope and ability. As Sharon Davis pursued her studies in college, she encountered a sex-typed division of intellectual labor that intensified her doubts about being a doctor. "I was encouraged to go into the med-tech program, not medical school . . . Girls were encouraged to become nurses, but not doctors; teachers, but not professors." Michelle Taigue, telling her Yaqui creation stories in school, was thought to be in need of remediation. Elena Castro went to school at a time — and this was not so long ago — when the use of Spanish was forbidden, and as a result, she was judged to be either intransigent or inept. The public school, that institution Horace Mann thought would be the "great equalizer" of American society, has in many ways compromised the democratic ideal. Bias and ignorance have been institutionalized in curriculum and instruction, counseling and assessment, in the thousands of small interactions between teachers and students in the school day.

It is instructive to keep in mind, however, that in some cases these violations did not evolve entirely from bigotry. The prohibition of Spanish, for example, while surely reflecting racist attitudes, was constructed, as well, from prevailing notions about assimilation and the process of forming national identity. The model of assimilation at work was sociologically and historically flawed — a careful reading of the immigrant experience reveals that people, even so-called model assimilationists, create complex mechanisms for maintaining and integrating old-country culture while coming to terms with the new — but at the time the linguistic prohibition seemed to some practitioners to be educationally sound. There is an important cautionary tale here. Many educational practices that we recognize in hindsight to be at best misguided were justified by prevailing belief and theory — were, in some cases, even seen as the forward-looking thing to do. To be sure, some of the awful things done to students in our classrooms, though shaped by broader social forces, must be understood as individual acts of cruelty. What is more disturbing is the way damage is done through standard wisdom, sanctioned practice.

We got a sense of some troubling traditional practices as we watched the teachers on this journey push against the status quo and listened to their reasoning. A number of the children in the COMETS program in Chicago were significantly limited in their knowledge of academic subjects, but rather than relying on standard approaches to remediation, their teachers tried creating for them a rich, multidisciplinary curriculum. "Even a kid who can't use a ruler," Michelle Smith observed, "can do some mathematical things." Joanne Wynn, the special education teacher at Hattiesburg High, knew that though her student La Fonda had a great deal of trouble speaking, she could move beyond low-level vocational training and, with technological assistance, use language in sophisticated ways: "The night time is like a hunter's home./You can see it black body./And you can see it million eyes."

For some time it has been accepted practice to respond to children who are having trouble with school tasks — or who, based on some assessment, are predicted to have trouble — by providing assistance through a curriculum that isolates for mastery disparate elements of discrete skills, that relies on drill and memory, that lowers expectations so as not to discourage, that limits the scope of assignments, that narrows rather than expands the focus of study. A lot of people in and outside school view these practices as sensible and humane. They mark traditional method in remedial and compensatory reading, writing, and math instruction, in English-as-a-second-language instruction and in some bilingual education programs, in special education, and in many of the courses students encounter in nonacademic tracks in high school. There has been educational theory to support such practices, instruction in teacher-education programs and commercially produced materials to promulgate them, legally mandated accountability measures to enforce a number of them, and in some cases professional and parental organizations developed around them. Such practices, and the theories driving them, shape the way we think and what we see. I remember a group of teachers from a neighboring district visiting Elena Castro's bilingual third-grade classroom in Calexico. Walking amid the dazzling student work, squeezing by kids clustered around a table, one turned to her colleague and whispered, "This is too much stimulation. Our students couldn't handle it." A number of the classrooms we visited developed in resistance to such beliefs.

In the beginning of the chapter on Los Angeles, I said that I've come to believe that a defining characteristic of good teaching is a tendency to push on the existing order of things. This is not simply rebelliousness; the teachers we visited are institutional beings. Rather, it's an ability to live one's working life with what philosopher Maxine Greene calls a "consciousness of possibility," an ability to imagine a better state of things, to, in Greene's language, "possibilize." Consider: Stephanie Terry asked herself why her inner-city Baltimore kids shouldn't be doing the kind of work she saw in elite schools. Carlos Jimenez wrote a history of Mexican Americans in order to teach what hadn't been taught before. Bud Reynolds envisioned students in economically devastated Wheelwright connected through electronic mail to young people across the Commonwealth of Kentucky. Bob Moses thought of the teaching of algebra in terms of the civil rights movement. Andy Bayliss stood in his classroom before school began in Polaris, Montana, and imagined how the space would change if he replaced those old desks with tables and chairs. The teachers in the Graphic Arts Academy in Pasadena decided to blur the boundaries that keep "academic" and "vocational" study separate, that split hand from brain. Michelle Taigue resisted the message of failure in the literature on Indian education and formulated a curriculum that invited achievement. Shelley Neilsen tried to see through the categories of disability to "what the kids *can* do." The New York principals were creating schools where a range of children could study and work together, schools without rigid curricular tracks and disciplinary borders. You can read their interviews as a series of meditations on ability, achievement, and the social order.

There has developed over the last thirty years a critical literature, written both by educators and outside observers, that investigates the ways school has enacted bias and fostered inequality. Some of my own work falls within this tradition. These studies have helped us focus on the kinds of limiting beliefs and practices I have been discussing and have encouraged change in the way we teach and counsel children. The theoretical framework of some of the studies, however, or the generalizations that have been drawn from them, suggest a one-dimensional relationship between educational institutions and the social order, lead to a vision of schools as being, in some necessary and unitary way, the reproductive mechanisms of an unjust society. This perspective misses the history of work for social change in and around the classroom, the effects of so many to create democratic public space, the kind of teaching that is possible today, that waits to be done.

Many representations of school in our reform literature — and, for that fact, in the various forums of our culture wars — are static ideological abstractions. And teachers are either the focus of blame or, despite all the current talk about "teacher empowerment," are impotent shadow figures. We lack adequately complex models of schools as institutions in which both limiting and liberating forces contend. We rarely hear discussion, for example, of the ways bad ideas get converted into standard practices and the complex process by which teachers grow uncomfortable with them and begin to change them. To weigh common practice in the balance of your own beliefs and experience, your knowledge, your sense of the possible, is a dynamic and powerful act. It is also discomforting, often unpleasant — for you're straining in the web of the accepted. It can produce doubt, uncertainty, and, chances are, will result in blunders, even failure as you try new things. This mix of agency and unease is rarely addressed in teacher education and is not part of our usual definitions and measures of good teaching, yet it is central to the realization of more humane institutional space.

Most discussions of change in schools revolve around major reform efforts or, on a different plane, around community action, legislation, or the courts. We saw the effects of such change especially as we traveled through Chicago, New York, Kentucky, and Mississippi. But perhaps because we tend to imagine social change in terms of major shifts and transformations, and perhaps because we are so cynical about our public institutions, we play down or miss entirely the significance of the everyday acts of courage and insight, the little breakthroughs, the mundane reimagining of the possible. These are the particular human moments of institutional self-criticism and renewal. John Dewey suggested that "mind" is a verb; "[d]emocracy knows no final closure," notes social theorist Peter McLaren. How does the mind reflect back on itself and its attendant social structures in ways that foster democracy in the ongoing flow of classroom life?

IV

IN *Tinkering Toward Utopia,* an analysis of the last hundred years of school reform in America, historians David Tyack and Larry Cuban note a common pattern in our nation's reform efforts: they come "from the top down or the outside in." That is, they are commonly conceived and advanced by people at a far remove from the place where any reform effort is targeted, where it would finally have its effect: the classroom, the immediate lives of teachers and students. This distance cannot help but influence the way problems are framed and the kinds of solutions that are formulated. The vantage point from which you consider schools — your location physically and experientially — will affect what you see and what you can imagine.

Many of the proposals to reform our schools — their modes of inquiry, their language, their recommendations — emanate from the office of the legislative analyst, from the corporate or foundation or university president's conference room, from policy panels and roundtables. Though some of these reformers solicit the views of administrators, teachers, and others close to the school, their analytic process tends to work at a high level of generality, with data on demographics, the economy, test scores, and the like; their focus tends to be on systems, structures, and broad social trends. This macro-level perspective is an important one. It places education in large social and economic contexts and encourages us to think of our schools in systemic ways. It is, to use examples of our time, legitimate to discuss the relation between education and the economy, work and school. Government and business concern about the preparation of the work force is not, of necessity, crass or malevolent, and the hope for a better material life for one's children has throughout this century driven participation in our nation's public educational experiment. And state and national goals, frameworks, and standards can play a role in improving the quality of schooling — though, as we saw when we got close to classrooms, they can have contradictory effects. Bud Reynolds and Delores Woody in Kentucky were emboldened by their state's reform guidelines; the teachers we visited in Mississippi felt constrained and undercut by the performance goals in the Mississippi Education Reform Act.

And that seeming contradiction is a case in point.

If we situate ourselves in classrooms like those on this journey, find a seat and settle in, what might happen to the way we hear current debates and proposals about education, to the way we understand the issues and talk about schools? What kinds of questions would we ask, what kind of discussion might we desire? My hope is that we would begin to feel uncomfortable with, limited by, the rhetoric of decline and despair that characterizes so much of our public talk about the schools. What also might happen is that we would see current remedies in a different, or at least more nuanced way. We might ask ourselves how a particular proposal would advance or constrain the work we saw in a classroom that had special meaning for us, that caught us up in its intelligence and decency. Would that proposal create or restrict the conditions for other such classrooms to flourish? We might well continue to raise questions about school-work relationships or about standards, achievement, and accountability, but such questions would come from a broader network of experience, imagery, observation, and expression. What we imagine for our public schools would itself change.

Our talk about schools would include concerns about emotional as well as physical safety. It would consider the matter of respect — and we desperately need a national conversation about the ways, intellectual as well as social, by which respect for young people is conveyed. This talk would be rich with imagery, from all sorts of classrooms, in a range of communities, reflecting a wide sweep of histories, cultural practices, languages and dialects, classrooms vibrant with achievement and thoughtfulness, play and hard work, characterized by what developmental psychologist Eleanor Duckworth nicely calls the having of wonderful ideas.

This revitalized talk would build from and contribute to an expansive definition of intelligence — one befitting an egalitarian society — that resists single measures and the segmentation of hand and brain. We would consider, too, the way achievement includes deliberation, risk, unease, and the creative possibilities of failure. Our discussion would intersect themes too often split in debates about school but that blend continually in the kinds of classrooms we visited: authority, expectation, care, well-being, cognition, futurity, love. ("Is it still possible," New York principal Sylvia Rabiner asks, "to talk about love?") We might consider the connection between authority — who speaks and how — and the construction of knowledge. The way care enhances what you see and what you think is possible. The relation between care and standards, how expectation is not just a measure of achievement but an invitation to achieve. The way love and intelligence together create civic space and a sense of the future.

There would be talk of principles, of decency and right and wrong, of commitment and connection. The classrooms we visited promoted the conditions for young people to act as moral beings and to engage in ethical deliberation. "We don't want to just educate technocrats," said Michael Johnson of New York's Science Skills Center. "We want people who have morals, who can say, 'No, you can't do that to people.'" Moral discourse has currently been appropriated by conservative writers and by the religious right and is either a lament for lost values or a call for sectarian belief. There is another moral discourse — powerful at times in our past but faint now — that needs to ring out across the Republic, a language that celebrates human worth and decries all that diminishes it.

Our fresh public talk would also include frank and angry appraisal of the way social and economic forces undercut our schools, continually threaten the kinds of classrooms represented in these pages. Such talk would, I hope, help us sharpen our critique of public education. Rather than sweeping condemnation, we would aim specific fury at damaging legislation and policy, at particular cases of corruption and ineptitude, at those who compromise safety, respect, and the potential of all young people to have wonderful ideas.

"The child of three who discovers what can be done with blocks," writes John Dewey, "or of six who finds out what he can make by putting five cents and five cents together, is really a discoverer, even though everybody else in the world knows it." "The experience of learning is itself democratic," says Michael Walzer, "bringing its own rewards of mutuality and camaraderie as well as of individual achievement." To imagine a vibrant democratic state, you must have a deep belief in the majesty of common intelligence, in its distribution through the population, and in the resultant ability of the population to become participatory civic beings. For all their contradictory fears and biases, our early advocates of public education — from Thomas Jefferson to Horace Mann — held that faith. It is striking, then, to behold the image of our young people that emerges in public discussion about the schools. Their ignorance is calibrated and broadcasted; they drift across charts, inarticulate. They are a threat to the present and future of the nation.

It is as if we have projected onto the next generation all the deficits of our own economic and political imagination. To be sure, there are things they don't know, can't do well, and, historically, our schools have failed many among them. But when we construct our nation's intellectual merit and our sense of the future from broad and aggregated test scores, we reduce teaching and learning to a few coordinates of achievement. Such measures are not adequate to define our collective intelligence or the meaning and purpose of our schools. Septima Clark, a teacher for most of her life, encouraged us to "think of the lives that can be developed into Americans who will redeem the soul of America." A short list of test scores cannot spark such thought. The rhetoric of decline that appropriates these measures limits our imagination as well. It is a strange kind of critical language, presents itself as tough-minded, clear-headed, but is, in fact, weary, cynical, dismissive of so many kinds of achievement. It flattens perception, functions more as a bludgeon than an analytical tool.

Our national discussion of public schools is terribly thin of the specific moments of intellectual and social achievement that engender faith in democracy. We miss in our public talk the power of the block placed upon the block, of the sum of the coins. We miss the moments of possibility that distinguish the classrooms of this book, that emerge daily as we move back out into the schools, finding them in a middle school in Wapato, Washington, its community disrupted by poverty and violence, a school in which counselors, teachers, and students are working to create a safe space — "We're a work in progress," says the principal — where Yakima, Mexican, Asian, and Anglo students can learn and live together. Finding possibility after hours in the library of a high school in Lincoln, Nebraska, where a group of students have been reading the educational reform literature, trying to use it to heal their school's curricular and social divides. Sitting with teachers in Providence, Rhode Island, who are writing about their work as a way to influence school reform: "How do we make positive change sustainable?" asks one. "How do we create a rigorous curriculum that does not lose people?" asks another. "I want to both celebrate and investigate my school," says a third.

When a local public school is lost to incompetence, indifference, or despair, it should be an occasion for mourning, for it is a loss of a particular site of possibility. When public education itself is threatened, as it seems to be threatened now — by cynicism and retreat, by the cold rapture of the market, by thin measure and the loss of civic imagination — when this happens, we need to assemble what the classroom can teach us, articulate what we come to know, speak it loudly, hold it fast to the heart.

A Note on Method

I sought many kinds of information to write this book.

When I was in a classroom, I took notes on both teacher and student activity, and occasionally, when it would not disrupt things, I was able to audio-record discussion. Several times, class was scheduled to be videotaped for other purposes, and I was provided with copies of those tapes. I collected instructional materials and selections from textbooks, and teachers allowed me to see notes, lesson plans, or whatever kind of written or graphic aids they used. It was usually possible to talk with teachers right after a lesson or a class or at the end of the day, asking them about what I wrote or recorded, recounting for them a particular moment, trying to cue their recall of what they were thinking during some stretch of classroom talk, as some event unfolded. This helped me understand the decisions they were making, their planned or spontaneous activity, the strategy, intuition, feeling, and doubt that constitute any few minutes of a teacher's life in the classroom. I was further able to audio-record lengthy interviews with teachers and administrators, asking about life history, philosophy of education, and opinion on local political and social issues.

Students often shared their work with me, and, with permission, I copied by hand or photocopied a full sample of it. Particularly in those places where I spent more than a day or two, students talked about a wide range of topics, some of it focused and fairly formal, some casual, as we walked across campus, ate lunch, worked together on an assignment.

I met many parents at school, at community functions, in the neighborhood. Sometimes we were able to sit in a classroom or living room or kitchen and have a long conversation; sometimes our exchanges were quick, on the fly, as they were picking up kids, as we bumped into each other in the supermarket or at a coffee shop.

To understand the place of a particular classroom in broader institutional contexts, I reviewed policy documents and, when possible, interviewed administrators at the district, city, or county level. As well, I read historical accounts and other archival materials (in libraries or historical societies) to enhance my understanding of the surrounding community. Interviews with long-time residents — the stuff of oral histories — were invaluable here. As was the case in the other settings, I let the place and the participants determine whether I would audio-record or take notes or whether I would wait until later to write down my recollection of the exchange. *Possible Lives* was enriched by all this talk: interview, conversation, query, explanation, musing, gossip, banter.

As prod for my memory, I took a number of photographs of classrooms, schools, and neighborhoods, or I made sketches and diagrams of them.

I was fortunate to have these multiple sources of information and be afforded multiple perspectives. They did not lead to neat resolution. They suggested complexity, even contradiction, and, therefore, were immensely valuable. All too often, classrooms and schools and the neighborhoods surrounding them — especially in poorer urban and rural areas — are depicted in simplified, stereotypic ways.

In studying classrooms, there is always a conflict between collecting information and interfering with the instructional lives of teachers and students. My presence altered things in ways I will never fully understand. Typically, the teacher would have discussed my visit before my arrival and, on the first day, I would introduce myself to students and briefly explain my project: basically, that I teach at UCLA and write about education, and that I was traveling around the country to find out more about good work in public schools. Then I would take an empty desk or chair along the wall or in the back of the room and watch and write. But it usually didn't take long to be beckoned away from the notebook — at least momentarily — into the flow of classroom life. I would follow the teacher's lead and the dynamics of the classroom in determining how little or how much to participate. In some cases, I took part in discussion groups, tutored students, read drafts of papers, spent time shooting baskets or walking around the yard with a kid who was having a bad day. Occasionally, I found myself incorporated into the classroom work itself: becoming a character in a play or appearing as a figure in a butcher-paper triptych. Some traditions in social research would hold that such engagement compromises inquiry. But if detachment can sharpen vision, it can also limit what is seen and felt. If it was the messy, complex life of classrooms I wanted to understand, then it was precisely these various forms of participation that could help me see and feel.

Though I may have, to some degree, become a part of things, what I saw and heard was influenced by my personal and professional history, by my beliefs about teaching and learning, and by my hopes for public education. And the very act of writing influenced the depiction of the classrooms in these pages. Narrative and vignette demand a selecting and ordering of events, and the particulars of style, word choice, and turns of phrase involve judgment and interpretation. This is an unavoidable aspect of the act of writing: the rhetoric of depiction. So, though I do think the reader gets in closer to the classroom than in many discussions of education today, it is, of course, my close account. An account by the teacher or an aide or a student would differ, perhaps considerably.

During the writing of a particular chapter, I would confer by phone with the teachers or administrators I was writing about: checking details, getting updates, reading to them passages from what I was writing. This led to further elaboration and revision. When I had a draft, I sent it to them for comment. They, in turn, would often share it with their students and with others in their communities. Was I getting it, I wanted to know. Did the writing honor their work? Did I do right by the students?

Clearly, *Possible Lives* is the product of my values, my perception, and my pen, but there has been a good deal of collaboration along the way that has taught me an immense amount about teaching and about public education, and has significantly influenced the language and direction of this book. I hope that the teachers I visited will see in my attempt to render their classroom lives some degree of match with their perception and, within the constraints of my ability, a fair and honorable representation of their work, the difficult moments, and the promise.

Notes

Page

Introduction

1 Reports from Rand and Sandia: David W. Grissmer, Sheila Nataraj Kirby, Mark Berends, and Stephanie Williamson, *Student Achievement and the Changing American Family* (Santa Monica: Rand, 1994); Charles C. Carson, Robert M. Huelskamp, and Thomas D. Woodall, *Perspectives on Education in America* (Albuquerque: Sandia National Laboratories, 1991).

2 "America's schools are the least successful": Marvin Cetron and Owen Davies, *Crystal Globe,* quoted in Bruce W. Nelan, "How the World Will Look in 50 Years," *Time* magazine, Fall 1992, p. 38.

3 "Americans have translated": David Tyack and Larry Cuban, *Tinkering Toward Utopia: A Century of Public School Reform,* (Cambridge: Harvard University Press, in press), p. 1.

3 "our very future": National Commission on Excellence in Education, "A Nation at Risk," in Beatrice and Ronald Gross, eds., *The Great School Debate: Which Way for American Education* (New York: Simon and Schuster, 1985), pp. 23–49.

3 "everyday cognition": The phrase, used in a slightly different way here is from Barbara Rogoff and Jean Lave, eds., *Everyday Cognition: Its Development in Social Context* (Cambridge: Harvard University Press, 1984), p. 4.

7 The Walter Lippmann quotation is from Robert N. Bellah, Richard Madsen, William M. Sullivan, Ann Swidler, and Steven M. Tipton, *The Good Society* (New York: Random House–Vintage, 1992), p. 298.

10 The Walt Whitman line is quoted in Isaac B. Berkson, *Theories of Americanization: A Critical Study.* (New York: Teachers College, Columbia University, 1920), p. 8.

1. Los Angeles and the LA Basin

11 Mike Davis, *City of Quartz: Excavating the Future in Los Angeles* (New York: Vintage, 1992), p. 104.

11 "room for millions": promotional poster on display in the Ellis Island Museum, New York City.

11 George Joseph Sánchez, *Becoming Mexican American: Ethnicity and Acculturation in Chicano L.A. 1900–1943*, Stanford, unpublished doctoral dissertation, June 1989, p. 123.

11 Carey McWilliams, *Southern California: An Island on the Land*, 1946, (Salt Lake City: Gibbs M. Smith Inc., Peregrine Smith Books, 1973), p. 328.

12 over ninety languages: Zena Pearlstone, *Ethnic L.A.* (Beverly Hills: Hillcrest Press, 1990), p. 33.

12 722 miles of freeway: *Moving People: A Layman's Handbook for Improving Public Transportation*, Board of Supervisors, County of Los Angeles, nd, p. 5.

12 statistics on Los Angeles Unified School District: Henry Chu and Jean Merl, "The Great School District — Is Smaller Better?" *Los Angeles Times*, May 19, 1993, pp. A1, A12, A13.

13 "conflictual and kaleidoscopic": *Los Angeles: Through the Kaleidoscope of Urban Restructuring*, Edward W. Soja, Allan D. Heskin, and Marco Cenzatti. UCLA Graduate School of Architecture and Urban Planning, 1985, p. 2.

13 "Gatsby": Kevin Starr, "An Epilogue: Making Dreams Come True," *L.A. 2000 — A City for the Future*, Los Angeles, 1988, p. 84.

13 "mediated town": Michael Sorkin, "Explaining Los Angeles," in *California Counterpoint: New West Coast Architecture 1982*, San Francisco Art Institute, 1982, p. 8.

13 Information on Watts: "Watts Next: The Challenge of Change," A Los Angeles Design Action Planning Team Report, June 9–12, 1989. Cosponsored: Los Angeles City Planning Department and Urban Design Advisory Coalition; Watts Redevelopment Project Biennial Report, Nov. 14, 1991, Community Redevelopment Agency of the City of Los Angeles; Melvin L. Oliver and James H. Johnson, Jr., "Inter-ethnic Conflict in an Urban Ghetto: The Case of Blacks and Latinos in Los Angeles," *Research in Social Movements, Conflict and Change*, vol. 6, 1994, pp. 57–94; David Grant, Center for the Study of Urban Poverty UCLA, personal communication, June 1993.

17 Maya Angelou, "On the Pulse of Morning" (New York: Random House, 1993), lines 24–26, 44–45, 75–76.

19 Information on Bell: "Economic Market Profile," City of Bell, 1990; Ed Murphy, personal communication, May 1993.

24 Information on Garfield High School: Carlos Jiménez, personal communication, June 1993; Ricardo Romo, *East Los Angeles: History of a*

Barrio (Austin: University of Texas Press, 1983); Rodolfo F. Acuña, *A Community Under Siege: A Chronicle of Chicanos East of the Los Angeles River 1945–1975*, Chicano Studies Research Center Publications, monograph no. 11, UCLA 1984.

29 *Womanspeak*, Gloria Goldsmith (Denver: Pioneer Drama Service, 1976).

32 Information on Monterey Park: "City History and Local Government," Monterey Park Chamber of Commerce, nd; "City of Monterey Park Population and Housing Profile," City of Monterey Park Community Development Department, Sept. 1987; Tom Waldman, "Monterey Park: The Rise and Fall of an All-American City," *California Journal*, vol. 20, no. 5, May 1989, pp. 203–208; Timothy Patrick Fong, *The Unique Convergence: A Community Study of Monterey Park, California*, unpublished doctoral dissertation, Dept. of Ethnic Studies, Berkeley: University of California Press, 1992; Janeane Vigliotti, personal communication, May 1993.

35 Information on Pasadena: Ann Scheid, *Pasadena: Crown of the Valley* (Chatsworth, CA: Windsor Publications, 1986); "City of Pasadena General Plan Revision," September 1991, June 1992, August 1992; Charles Wollenberg, *All Deliberate Speed: Segregation and Exclusion in California Schools, 1855–1975* (Berkeley: University of California Press, 1976); Zena Pearlstone, *Ethnic L.A.*; Judy Codding, personal communication, May 1993.

37 "Graphic Arts Academy," Pasadena High School, nd, no page numbers.

41 John Dewey, *Democracy and Education* (New York: Free Press, 1916 and 1966) p. 250.

42 Sandra Cisneros, *The House on Mango Street* (New York: Vintage, 1989).

42 Information on Santa Monica: Fred E. Basten, *Santa Monica Bay: The First 100 Years*. (Los Angeles: Douglas-West Publishers, 1974).

46 Information on University High School: "History of University High School" nd, no author; "University High School — How It Happened," A. L. Cavanagh, June 10, 1945; Jack Moscowitz and Rick Takagaki, personal communication, May 1993.

52 Jonathan Kozol, *Savage Inequalities: Children in America's Schools*, (New York: Harper Perennial, 1992).

52 LAUSD breakup conference: Forum on Children's Issues, May 5, 1993, sponsored by Norton Family Foundation.

52 Information on LAUSD: Sandy Banks, "Dissatisfaction Fuels Drive to Dismantle L.A. Unified" *Los Angeles Times*, May 17, 1993, pp. A1, A18; Paul Butler, "LEARNing the Hard Way," *LA Village View*, May 14–20, 1993, pp. 4, 8; Henry Chu and Jean Merl, "The Great School District — Is Smaller Better?"

In this and subsequent chapters, I let local custom and individual preference determine the use of terms for ethnic or racial identity: Black or African American, White or Anglo, Native American or Indian, Latino-Latina, Hispanic, or Mexican American or Chicano-Chicana. These terms have specific social and political meaning in different contexts, though they are sometimes used interchangeably. I also let local custom and individual preference determine the use of Ms. or Mrs. I use teachers' and administrators' real names, and students often requested that I use theirs as well. Occasionally, because of the sensitive or legally protected nature of some material, I rely on pseudonyms.

2. Calexico, California

60 On the history of Calexico and the Imperial Valley: Tracey Henderson, *Imperial Valley* (San Diego: Neyenesch Printers, 1968); Otis B. Tout, *The First Thirty Years: Being an Account of the Principal Events in the History of Imperial Valley Southern California, U.S.A.* (San Diego: Arts and Crafts Press, 1931; reprinted, Imperial County Historical Society, 1990).

61 School statistics: Emily Palacio, personal communication, August 1994; Ernesto Portillo, Jr., "In Calexico Schools, a Major Turnaround" *San Diego Union Tribune,* Aug. 9, 1992, pp. B1, B2.

64 "An increasing number of teacher educators": See, for example, John I. Goodland, *Teachers for Our Nation's Schools* (San Francisco: Jossey-Bass, 1990).

72 "A sketch of Calexico's history": see note for p. 60. Also see Albert Camarillo, *Chicanos in California: A History of Mexican Americans in California* (San Francisco: Boyd and Fraser Publishing, 1984).

73 "God and civilization": quoted in Héctor Calderón, "Reinventing the Border," in Barbara Roche Rico and Sandra Mano, *American Mosaic: Multicultural Readings in Context,* (Boston: Houghton Mifflin, 1991, pp. 554–562).

76 On bilingual education: Kenji Hakuta, *Mirror of Language: The Debate on Bilingualism* (New York: Basic Books, 1986); François Grosjean, *Life with Two Languages: An Introduction to Bilingualism* (Cambridge: Harvard University Press, 1982); Heinz Kloss, *The American Bilingual Tradition* (Rowley, MA: Newbury House, 1977); James Crawford, *Bilingual Education: History, Politics, Theory, and Practice* (Trenton, NJ: Crane, 1989); Harvey A. Daniels, ed., *Not only English: Affirming America's Multilingual Heritage* (Urbana, IL: NCTE, 1990); Ira Katznelson and Margaret Weir, *Schooling for All: Class, Race, and the Decline of the Democratic Ideal* (New York: Basic Books, 1985).

83 "The World Is a Rainbow": Little House Music (ASCAP), 1978. Youngheart Music Education Service, Los Angeles. Written by Greg Scelsa.

88 "primarily interested in action": quoted in Charles Wollenberg, *All Deliberate Speed: Segregation and Exclusion in California Schools, 1855–1975*, p. 113.

3. Baltimore, Maryland

101 "New Friends for Catfish," in *Taking Time*, Senior authors Virginia A. Arnold and Carl B. Smith. (New York: Macmillan, 1987, pp. 48–57).
102 *The Magic Fish*, Freya Littledale, illus. Winslow Pinney Pels, (New York: Scholastic Text, 1966).
103 History of the Old West Side: Elizabeth Fee, Linda Shopes, Linda Zeidman (eds.), *The Baltimore Book* (Philadelphia: Temple University Press, 1991).
104 *The Yucky Reptile Alphabet Book*, Jerry Pallotta, illus. Ralph Masiello (Watertown, MA: Charlesbridge Publishing, 1989).
104 *The Calypso Alphabet*, John Agard, illus. Jennifer Bent (New York: Holt, nd).
106 *Amazing Grace*, Mary Hoffman, illus. Caroline Binch (New York: Dial, 1991).
120 Margaret Musgrove, *Ashanti to Zulu: African Traditions*, illus. Leo and Diane Dillon (New York: Dial Press, 1976).
120 Dr. Seuss, *Green Eggs and Ham* (New York: Beginner Books, 1960).
123 *The True Story of the Three Little Pigs*, Jon Scieszka, illus. Lane Smith (New York: Viking, 1989).
125 learning disability and African American boys: see, e.g., Gerald Coles, *The Learning Mystique: A Critical Look At Learning Disabilities* (New York: Pantheon, 1987); National Coalition of Advocates for Students, *Barriers to Excellence: Our Children at Risk* (Boston: National Coalition of Advocates for Students, 1985).
128 "a third of the kids": Mike Bowler, *The Lessons of Change: Baltimore Schools in the Modern Era.* (Baltimore: Fund for Educational Excellence, 1991), p. 34.
129 Christina Rossetti: the poem is from a collection called *Sing-Song* (1872).
130 school funding statistics: Elizabeth Fee, et al., *The Baltimore Book*, p. 67; Mike Bowler, *The Lessons of Change*, p. 18.

4. Chicago, Illinois

135 Studs Terkel, *Division Street: America* (New York: New Press, 1993), p. xxviii.
138 State Representative: Michael L. Weaver, "Chicago Schools' Mess Cheating Kids," *Champaigne-Urbana News-Gazette* (Oct. 31, 1993), p. B3.
138 letter-writer: *Chicago Tribune* (Oct. 12, 1993), p. 18.

139 Information on Advanced Placement: The College Board, *A Guide to the Advanced Placement Program, May, 1994* (New York: nd); David A. Dudley, "The Beginnings of the Advanced Placement Program," manuscript, Dec. 1963; The College Board, "An Informal History of the AP Readings: 1956–76" nd; William H. Cornog, "The Advanced Placement Program: Reflections on Its Origins," *The College Board Review* (n. 115, Spring 1980) 14–17; Daniel Mahala and Michael Vivion, "The Role of AP and the Composition Program," *Writing Program Administration* v. 17 n. 1–2 (Fall-Winter 1993), pp. 43–53; James Crouse and Dale Trusheim. *The Case Against the SAT* (Chicago: University of Chicago Press, 1988).

140 All references to William Faulkner, *As I Lay Dying* (New York: Vintage, 1990).

141 "My Mother is a fish": p. 84.

149 "There is more surface . . .": p. 82.

149 "It makes a neater job": p. 83.

149 "don't bother none": p. 195.

149 "Folks seems . . .": p. 234.

149 "ain't so sho": p. 238.

151 "ain't nothing justifies": p. 238.

152 "sweet, hot blast": p. 61.

154 statistics on Chicago schools: William Ayers, "Reforming Schools and Rethinking Classrooms: A Chicago Chronicle," *Rethinking Schools,* Oct.–Nov. 1989, pp. 6–7; Don Moore, personal communication, February 1995.

155 Michael B. Katz, *Improving Poor People: The Welfare State, The "Underclass," and Urban Schools as History* (Princeton: Princeton University Press, in press), p. 1 of ch. 3, "Urban Schools."

155 William Ayers, "Reforming Schools and Rethinking Classrooms," p. 7.

155 Jeannie Oakes, personal communication, December 1993.

156 "Great Migration," see James R. Grossman, *Land of Hope: Chicago, Black Southerners, and the Great Migration* (Chicago: University of Chicago Press, 1989).

164 "The reason for living": Faulkner, p. 169.

164 "When the switch fell": Faulkner, p. 170.

164 Addie's individual words and phrases: Faulkner, pp. 169–176.

164 "coming swift": Faulkner, p. 175.

165 "I could get ready to die": Faulkner, p. 176.

170 Alice Walker, "Everyday Use," *In Love and Trouble: Stories of Black Women* (New York: Harcourt Brace Jovanovich, 1973), pp. 47–59.

171 "backward enough": Walker, p. 57.

172 Cavazos quotation: cited in Jonathan Kozol, *Savage Inequalities,* p. 227.

176 Department of Justice, Office of Juvenile Justice and Delinquency Prevention, Fact Sheet #17, June 1994.
177 "be aware of me!": Faulkner, p. 170.
185 On English departments: see Mike Rose, "The Language of Exclusion: Writing Instruction at the University," *College English* 47 (April 1985) pp. 341–355.
187 The scene with Mr. Antolini is in chap. 24, J. D. Salinger, *The Catcher in the Rye* (New York: New American Library Signet: 1953), pp. 163–174.
189 William Bennett: Casey Banas and Devonda Byers, "Chicago's Schools Hit as Worst," *Chicago Tribune*, November 7, 1987, p. 1.
189 Information on corruption: Mary J. Herrick, *The Chicago Schools: A Social and Political History* (Beverly Hills: Sage, 1971), pp. 142, 219.
190 recent study cited in NTanya Lee, "New Study Assesses Chicago Reform," *School Voices* (Fall 1993), v. IV, n. 1, pp. 5, 8.
190 some observers of urban school reform: see, for example, John Smyth (ed.), *A Socially Critical View of the Self-Managing School* (London: Falmer Press, 1993).
191 Asa Hilliard, "Do We Have the Will to Educate All Children?" *Educational Leadership* (Sept. 1991), pp. 31–36.
192 Editor *Chicago Tribune:* quoted in Jonathan Kozol, *Savage Inequalities*, p. 72.
192 Deborah Meier: "America's Education Reform," PBS, April 23, 1993.

5. New York, New York

193 Franklin K. Lane High School: Architectural League of New York and the Public Education Association, *New Schools for New York: Plans and Precedents for Small Schools* (New York: Princeton Architectural Press, 1992), pp. 174–176.
193 "school planner": David Tyack and Larry Cuban, *Tinkering Toward Utopia: Reflections on a Century of Public School Reform* (Cambridge: Harvard University Press, in press), p. 16.
194 History of New York City education reform: Tyack and Cuban, *Tinkering Toward Utopia*, pp. 76–78; *New Schools for New York*, pp. 152–193; Colin Greer, *The Great School Legend: A Revisionist Interpretation of Public Education* (New York: Viking Press, 1973), pp. 105–129.
194 On recent history: Deborah Meier, "Success in East Harlem," *American Educator*, Fall 1987, pp. 34–39; Susan Chira, "Is Smaller Better? Educators Now Say Yes for High School," *New York Times*, Wed., July 14, 1993, A–1, B–8; David L. Kirp, "What School Choice Really Means," *The Atlantic Monthly*, Nov. 1992, pp. 119–132.

195 Statistics and information on the New York City district: Joseph A. Fernandez with John Underwood, *Tales Out of School: Joseph Fernandez's Crusade to Rescue American Education* (Boston: Little, Brown, 1993); Susan Chira, "Is Smaller Better?"; Norm Fruchter, "Asbestos Crisis and Education Crisis," *School Voices* (Fall 1993), v. IV, n. 1, pp. 1, 4; personal communications, Norm Fruchter, Heather Lewis, Deborah Meier, Mark Weiss, September 1993.

6. Berea and Wheelwright, Kentucky

236 Letter, John G. Fee, Nov. 5, 1857, Berea College Archives.

236 "under an influence": quoted in Louis Smith, "Berea's Great Commitments" (Berea, Kentucky: Berea College Press, nd), p. 9.

236 description of Fee: Elisabeth S. Peck and Emily Ann Smith, *Berea's First 125 Years: 1855–1980,* (Lexington: University of Kentucky Press, 1982), p. 41.

236 "Anti-slavery": quoted in Brown, "Berea College," p. 29.

236 "those who have energy": pp. 2–3, Letter, John G. Fee, Oct. 16, 1869, Berea College Archives.

237 "not merely": quoted in Brown, pp. 22–23.

237 "Do Right": quoted in Jerome Hughes, "The Distinctive Role of Berea College" (Berea: Berea College, nd) p. 3.

237 "step out of the pictures": Brown, p. 33.

237 "But for some faculty": see, for example, D. Michael Rivage-Seul, "Berea at the Crossroads", *CROSS Currents,* Spring 1992, pp. 65–74.

238 "the interests of truth": Peck and Smith, *Berea's First 125 Years,* p. 82.

238 feel "less keenly": Peck and Smith, *Berea's First 125 Years,* p. 100.

238 History of teacher education: Peck and Smith, *Berea's First 125 Years,* pp. 89–109; J.A.R. Rogers, *Birth of Berea College: A Story of Providence,* 1902, Berea College Archives; E. H. Fairchild, *Berea College, Kentucky: An Interesting History,* 1883, Berea College Archives.

238 *Manual of Policies and Procedures,* Teacher Education Program, Education Department, Berea College, revised 1992, pp. 5–6.

240 current statistics: Janet Fortune, personal communication, Oct. 1992.

246 Tillie Olsen, "I Stand Here Ironing," in *Tell Me a Riddle* (New York: Dell, 1976), pp. 9–21.

256 History of Wheelwright: "Wheelwright: Modern Coal Town" *Mantrip* #6 (Fall 1988), pp. 34–39; Amy Allen and Brad Compton, "When a Coal Town Dies", *Mantrip* #9 (Spring 1990) pp. 34–37; Robert M. Rennick, *Kentucky Place Names,* (Lexington: University of Kentucky Press, 1984); John E. Kleber (ed. in chief) *The Kentucky Encyclopedia,* (Lexington: University of Kentucky Press, 1992).

258 History of Martin: Robert M. Rennick, *Kentucky Place Names;* Alton Crisp, "The Early History of Martin, KY," nd ms.

265 KERA: "Kentucky's Learning Goals and Valued Outcomes: Report Summary," The Council on School Performance Standards, Sept. 1991.

269 Wheelwright unemployment rate: John Voskuhl, "Wheelwright" *The Courier-Journal,* Louisville, Dec. 21, 1992, B1.

276 Per capita income: John Voskuhl, "Wheelwright."

277 *The Foxfire Book* (Garden City, NY: Doubleday, 1972).

277 *Mantrip:* The material is drawn from *Mantrip,* v. 2, n. 1 (Spring 1987) through v. 7, n. 1 and 2 (Spring 1992).

278 Anne Royall in David Hackett Fischer, *Albion's Seed: Four British Folkways in America.* (New York: Oxford University Press, 1989), p. 652.

278 On President Frost: Shannon Wilson, personal communication, Oct. 1992.

7. Hattlesburg, Tupelo, Jackson, Indianola, Hollandale, and Webb, Mississippi

284 "Jury Seated": *Northeast Mississippi Daily Journal,* Jan. 27, 1994, p. B1.

284 Information on Hattiesburg: *Hattiesburg: A Pictoral History,* (Jackson: University of Mississippi Press, 1982); Hattiesburg School statistics, Lois Rodgers, personal communication, January 1994.

285 directions for experiment: student packet for "Warlord's Revenge — Can You Dig It" (St. Louis: American Association of Immunologists, nd) p. 7.

289 Anna Deavere Smith, *Fires in the Mirror,* (Alexandria, VA: PBS Video, 1993).

292 statistics on funding: John Wright, ed., *The Universal Almanac,* 1994, (Kansas City: Andrews and McMeel), p. 236.

293 Virginia newspaper editorial and high school statistics for 1924: James D. Anderson, *The Education of Blacks in the South, 1860–1935.* (Chapel Hill: University of North Carolina Press, 1988), pp. 97, 188, 204.

293 Education Reform Act: Andrew P. Mullins, Jr., *A History of the Education Reform Act of 1982,* unpublished doctoral dissertation, University of Mississippi, 1992.

293 Rexford G. Brown, *Schools of Thought* (San Francisco: Jossey-Bass, 1991).

297 Information on Tupelo: "Tupelo, Mississippi: Community Profile" (Tupelo: Community Development Foundation, nd); "An Inside Look: Tupelo/Lee County" (Tupelo: Community Development Foundation, nd); Helene Cooper, "Tupelo, Miss., Concocts an Effective Recipe for Economic Health," *Wall Street Journal,* Thursday, March 3, 1994, pp. A1, A5; Ben McClelland, personal communication, January 1994.

297 school statistics for Tupelo: Sharon Davis, personal communication, January 1994.

306 Algebra Project. "Report: Southern Initiative of the Algebra Project" (Jackson: Positive Innovations, Inc., 1993); Alexis Jetter, "Mississippi Learning," *New York Times Magazine*, Feb. 21, 1993; Robert P. Moses, Mieko Kamii, Susan McAllister Swap, Jeffrey Howard, "The Algebra Project: Organizing in the Spirit of Ella," *Harvard Educational Review* (November 1989), vol. 59, no. 4, pp. 423–443.

308 Quotations: Robert P. Moses, et al. "The Algebra Project," pp. 428, 432–433.

308 On Jackson and the Delta: Peggy W. Prenshaw and Jesse O. McKee, eds., *Sense of Place: Mississippi*, (Jackson: University Press of Mississippi, 1979); Kay Mills, *This Little Light of Mine: The Life of Fannie Lou Hamer* (New York: Plume, 1993).

310 Algebra Project curriculum: Robert P. Moses, *Algebra in the Mississippi Delta*, fourth edition, 1991.

8. Polaris and Missoula, Montana

320 Information on Montana: "Beaverhead County, Montana" (Dillon, MT: Beaverhead Chamber of Commerce, nd); Claudette Morton, "The Rural Teacher, Alive and Well?" (Dillon, MT: Western Montana College Rural Education Center, 1992–93); George Miller, personal communication, April 1994.

321 Hamlin Garland, *A Son of the Middle Border* (New York: Macmillan, 1925), p. 95.

321 Small schools statistics: Ivan Muse and Ralph B. Smith with Bruce Barker, *The One-Teacher School in the 1980's* OERI, ERIC 1987, pp. XV–XVII; Paul Nachtigal, "Rural School Improvement Efforts: An Interpretive History," in *Rural Education: In Search of a Better Way*, Paul Nachtigal, ed. (Boulder, CO: Westview Press, 1982), p. 16.

321 "The best": Boston superintendent John D. Philbrick quoted in David Tyack and Elisabeth Hansot, *Learning Together: A History of Coeducation in American Public Schools* (New York: Russell Sage, 1992), p. 79.

322 On the performance of rural students: See Muse and Smith, *The One Teacher School in the 1980's*; Wayne W. Welch, "Academic Performance of Rural Students," in *The Condition of Rural Education*, Department of Education, in press.

322 History of Polaris: Roberta Carkeek Cheney, *Names of the Face of Montana: The Story of Montana's Place Names* (Missoula: University of Montana Publications in History, 1971), p. 176; documents on file at Polaris School.

322 "unimaginative nature of instruction": see, for example, Richard A. Schmuck and Patricia A. Schmuck, *Small Districts, Big Problems:*

Making School Everybody's House (Newbury Park, CA: Corwin Press, 1992).

325 nineteenth-century teacher: from Theodore Dwight's *Things as They Are: or, Notes of a Traveler Through Some of the Middle and Northern States,* quoted in Carl F. Kaestle, *Pillars of the Republic: Common Schools and American Society* 1780–1860 (New York: Hill and Wang, 1983), p. 17.

331 The math problem is from Alan R. Hoffer, et al. *Mathematics in Action* (New York: Macmillan–McGraw-Hill, 1991), p. 235.

335 old documents and record books on file at Polaris School.

339 "teacup & handkerchief": quoted in Wayne E. Fuller, *The Old Country School: The Story of Rural Education in the Middle West* (Chicago: University of Chicago Press, 1982), p. 208. Also, on women teachers: Polly Welts Kaufman, *Women Teachers on the Frontier* (New Haven: Yale University Press, 1984).

356 William Ayers, *The Good Preschool Teacher.* (New York: Teachers College Press, Columbia University, 1989), p. 94.

364 "one best system": The phrase is David Tyack's, *The One Best System: A History of American Urban Education* (Cambridge: Harvard University Press, 1974).

9. Tucson, Arizona

365 Navajo Reservation: After my first visit, the political leadership of the Navajo nation moved to officially abandon the name *Navajo* — which came from the Spanish invaders — and adopt the group's traditional name, *Diné*, or "the people." *Navajo* was the name in use during my observation of Michelle Taigue's class, so I use it here.

367 Barbara Kingsolver, *Animal Dreams* (New York: Harper Collins, 1990).

369 Literature on Native American communication style: See, for example, Susan U. Philips, *The Invisible Culture: Communication in Classroom and Community on the Warm Springs Indian Reservation* (New York: Longman, 1983).

375 Leslie Marmon Silko, *Ceremony,* (New York: Viking Penquin, 1977).

375 Sophocles, *Oedipus the King, Oedipus at Colonus, Antigone,* (New York: Washington Square Press, 1967).

376 "you are blind in mind and ears": p. 27.

376 "you are the land's pollution": p. 25.

377 *Mosco's* story from Michelle Taigue, *Never Again I: Death and Beauty in Yaqui Stories,* unpublished doctoral dissertation, Department of English, University of Arizona, 1990, pp. 127–129.

379 Luci Tapahonso, "What I Am," *Sonora Review* vol. 14–15 (Spring 1988), pp. 55–58.

379 Luci Tapahonso, *A Breeze Swept Through* (Albuquerque: West End Press, 1987).
379 "first born of dawn woman" is from *A Breeze Swept Through,* p. 2.
380 "with raisin eyes" is from "Raisin Eyes," pp. 38–39.
380 "Yáadí Lá," p. 30.
386 "to ward off disorder": a paraphrase of ". . . a warding off, an exertion of language upon ignorance and disorder", N. Scott Momaday, *The Way to Rainy Mountain,* (Albuquerque: University of New Mexico Press, 1976), p. 33.
388 Historical quotations about Indian education: from Frederick E. Hoxie, *A Final Promise: The Campaign to Assimilate the Indians, 1880– 1920* (New York: Cambridge University Press, 1989), pp. 92, 106, 168, 194.
389 "Leave your Indian at home": Joe Suina, "And Then I Went to School: Memories of a Pueblo Childhood," *Rethinking Schools* May–June 1991, p. 11.
392 "Miserable Main St.": Carson McCullers, *The Ballad of The Sad Café and Other Stories* (New York: Bantam, 1991), p. 3.
393 Edward Albee, *The Ballad of the Sad Café* (Boston: Houghton Mifflin; New York: Atheneum, 1963).
394 "The time has come": p. 116.
395 "The town is lonesome": pp. 3–4.
395 "I'm just tryin'": Albee, p. 143.
397 "The lover craves": McCullers, p. 27.
399 David Seals, *The Powwow Highway* (New York: New American Library–Plume 1990).
399 "the laughingstock": p. 133.
399 "fairy tales": p. 202.
401 "You know": Momaday, *The Way to Rainy Mountain,* p. 16.
401 "The Man Made of Words": in *Literature of the American Indians: Views and Interpretations,* Abraham Chapman, ed. (New York: New American Library, 1975) pp. 96–110.
401 "a going forth": *Rainy Mountain:* p. 88.
401 "While the child": *Rainy Mountain:* p. 22.
406 "Everything had a voice . . .": Michelle Taigue, *Never Again I,* p. 156.
408 "humanize, christianize": quoted in Margaret Connell Szasz, *Education and the American Indian: The Road to Self-Determination Since 1928* (2nd edition) (Albuquerque: University of New Mexico Press, 1977), p. 45.
409 "a contemporary expression": Vine Deloria, Jr., and Clifford Lytle, *The Nations Within: The Past and Future of American Indian Sovereignty* (New York: Pantheon, 1984), p. 254.

10. Possible Lives

412 David E. Purpel, *The Moral and Spiritual Crisis in Education: A Curriculum for Justice and Compassion in Education* (Granby, Mass: Bergin and Garvey, 1989), p. 137.

413 "Thomas Jefferson's proposal": see James D. Anderson, *The Education of Blacks in the South, 1860–1935* (Chapel Hill, NC: University of North Carolina Press, 1988), p. 1.

414 Most discussions of authority: see, for example, George H. Wood, *Schools That Work: America's Most Innovative Public Education Programs* (New York: Dutton, 1992).

416 Samuel Harrison Smith, "Remarks on Education" in Frederick Rudolph, ed., *Essays on Education in the Early Republic* (Cambridge, MA, 1965), pp. 188–189.

417 Critics of our public schools and the larger public sphere: See, for example, Michelle Fine, *Framing Dropouts: Notes on the Politics of an Urban Public High School* (New York: SUNY Press, 1991) and Nancy Fraser, "Rethinking the Public Sphere: A Contribution to the Critique of Actually Existing Democracy" (Milwaukee: University of Wisconsin-Milwaukee Center for Twentieth Century Studies, Working Paper no. 10, 1990–91.)

417 "intelligence of a people": The phrase is Daniel Calhoun's, *The Intelligence of a People* (Princeton: Princeton University Press, 1973).

418 Amy Gutmann, *Democratic Education* (Princeton: Princeton University Press, 1987), p. 76.

419 Lee Shulman, "Knowledge and Teaching: Foundations of the New Reform", *Harvard Educational Review* (February 1987), v. 57, n. 1, pp. 1–22.

419 John Dewey, *Democracy and Education* (1916) (New York: The Free Press, 1966), pp. 182–183.

419 Studies of teacher cognition: See, for example, Christopher M. Clark and Penelope L. Peterson, "Teachers' Thought Processes" in *Research in Teaching and Learning,* v. 3. (New York: Macmillan, 1990).

420 Nel Noddings, "Fidelity in Teaching, Teacher Education, and Research for Teaching", *Harvard Educational Review,* v. 56, n. 4 (Nov. 1986), p. 499.

421 Deborah P. Britzman, "Cultural Myths in the Making of a Teacher: Biography and Social Structure in Teacher Education", *Harvard Educational Review,* v. 56, n. 4 (Nov. 1986), pp. 442–456.

421 Statistics on women teachers. See Nancy Hoffman, "'Inquiring after the Schoolmarm': Problems of Historical Research on Female Teachers," *Women's Studies Quarterly 1994:* 1 and 2, p. 104.

423 Michael Walzer, *Spheres of Justice: A Defense of Pluralism and Equality.* (New York: Basic Books, 1983), pp. 203–204.

424 "By the year 2000": "Goals 2000: Community Update", n. 21 (Feb. 1995) Washington, D.C.: U.S. Department of Education.

425 *Chicago Tribune* editor, quoted in Jonathan Kozol, *Savage Inequalities,* p. 72.

425 New York journalist: in Nancy Hoffman, *Woman's "True" Profession: Voices from the History of Teaching* (New York: The Feminist Press, 1981), p. 232.

427 "great equalizer": Horace Mann, *The Republic and the School,* Lawrence C. Cremin, ed. (New York: Teachers College Press, Columbia University, 1957), p. 87.

428 Maxine Greene, *The Dialectic of Freedom* (New York: Teachers College Press, 1988), p. 23. The term "possibilize" is from Greene's *Landscapes of Learning* and is quoted in David E. Purpel, *The Moral and Spiritual Crisis in Education,* p. 135.

430 John Dewey, "mind" is a verb is from *Art as Experience* and is quoted in Maxine Greene, *The Dialectic of Freedom,* p. 6.

430 Peter McLaren, "An Exchange with Eugene E. García, Director of the Office of Bilingual Education and Minority Language Affairs, U.S. Department of Education," *International Journal of Educational Reform,* v. 3 n. 1 (Jan. 1994), pp. 74–80, p. 77.

430 David Tyack and Larry Cuban, *Tinkering Toward Utopia,* p. 139.

432 John Dewey, *Democracy and Education,* p. 159.

432 Michael Walzer, *Spheres of Justice,* p. 206.

433 Septima Clark, *Ready from Within,* Cynthia Stokes Brown, ed. (Trenton, NJ: Africa World Press, 1990), p. 121.

Acknowledgments

I begin with the deepest thanks to John Wright, my agent, for the many years of friendship and advice; to my editor, Dawn Seferian, for believing in the work; to Kathryn Court, Barbara Grossman, and John Sterling for their decency; and to Joyce Seltzer, the editor of *Lives on the Boundary,* for all she taught me. I hope it carried over.

This book is what it is because of those good friends and meticulous critics who read most or all of the manuscript, often through multiple drafts, providing ongoing conceptual and stylistic advice: Bill Ayers, Ellen Cushman, Kevin Fitzsimmons, Linda Flower, Tim Flower, Ruth Glendinning, Kris Gutierrez, Glynda Hull, Rebecca Humenuk, Amy Kantrowitz, Michael Katz, Ken Lincoln, Jonathan Losk, Susan Lytle, Deborah Meier, Carmel Myers, Ron Padgett, Ted Sizer, David Tyack, Samuel Wineberg, Stephen Witte.

Also of great help on particular sections, in reading, in talking through, early in the project and late in the day: Paula Gunn Allen, Susan Anker, Alfredo Artiles, Ben Bagdikian, Lynn Beck, David Bensman, Jane Betz, Sandy Bodner, Deborah Britzman, Linda Brodkey, Rex Brown, John Bruer, Judi Campbell, Jamie Candelaria, Beverly Chin, Dave Cohen, Nick Coles, John Connor, Jim Daniels, Ellen Darion, Gina DeBlanc, Lisa Delpit, Micaela di Leonardo, Joe Dominic, Faith Dunne, Lester Faigley, Michelle Fine, Jennifer Flach, Debbie Fox, Sarah Freedman, Jan Frodesen, Norm Fruchter, Dixie Goswami, Sandra Graham, Marlene Griffith, Mike Gustin, Nancy Hoffman, Andy Hrycyna, Jacqueline Irvine, Russell Jacoby, Harold Levine, George Lipsitz, Bonnie Lisle, Nancy Manzanares, Margaret Marshall, Jan Matesa, Peter McLaren, Bud Mehan, Charles Muscatine, Jeannie Oakes, Mel Oliver, Faye Peitzman, Adolph Reed, Ray Reisler, Sheri Repp, Len Rieser, Renato Rosaldo, Lillian Roybal-Rose, Jacqueline Jones Royster, Mariolina

Salvatori, Cassie Schwerner, Mike Seltzer, Nancy Shapiro, Richard Shavelson, Elaine Simon, Nancy Sizer, Frank Sullivan, Bruce Thomas, John Trimbur, Abby Van Pelt, Victor Walker, John Warnock, Tillie Warnock, Noreen Webb, Amy Stuart Wells, Rae Jean Williams. And thanks to David Bartholomae and the English Department at the University of Pittsburgh and Susan Lytle and the Philadelphia Schools Collaborative for arranging discussion of sections of the manuscript.

Many of the people who helped with local knowledge and local kindness during my visits are mentioned in the pages of this book, but a number are not. I'd like to thank them now. *Los Angeles:* Victor Becerra, Edmundo Cardenas, Ed Frankel, Mili Frankel, David Grant, Aki Handa, Michele Proia, Janet Thornber, Mary Valentine, Irene Viramontes. Gratitude especially to Faye Peitzman and Rae Jean Williams. *Calexico:* Pam Balch, David Ballesteros, Gerald Dadey, Barbara Flores, Leslie Garrison, Diana Harvey, Lilia Sanchez-Moreno, Harry Polkinhorn, Gloria Rodriguez, Olivia Romero, Mickey Western. Dana Murphy set this trip in motion. *Baltimore:* Mike Bowler, Laura Desmond, Tyree Thornton. *Chicago:* Ruby Davis, Ann Feldman, Anne Hallett, Edie Heinemann, Larry Heinemann, David Jolliffe, Sokoni Karanja, Rashid and Muna Khalidi, Mike Klonsky, Don Moore. *New York:* John Garvey, Heather Lewis, Iris Lopez. *Kentucky:* Kathryn Akural, Jacki Betts, Don Bowling, Mabel Hall, Shirley Hall, Stephanie Henry, Adam Howard, Libby Jones, Peggy Rivage-Seul. *Mississippi:* Ken Acton, Constance Bland, Jonie Davis, Carolyn and Dave Dennis, Matt Hammer, Carolyn Hardy, Michael Marks, Ben McClelland, Susan McClelland, Tim Murphy, H. B. Overby, Anthony Petrosky, Jimmy Pierce, Roger and Jill Phillips, Linda Walters. Special thanks to my traveling companions through the Delta: Courtney Cazden, Lisa Delpit, Jacqueline Irvine, and Mary Maxwell West. *Montana:* Glenn Allinger, Joyce Antonioli, Angela Branz-Spall, Dottie Donovan, Pam Gohn, B. J. Granbery, Jan Hahn, Rob and Melissa Henthorn, Roy Herweck, Barry Hicks, Rhonda Honzel, Johnny Lott, Michael Lundin, Gary Lundy, Bill Matthes, Donna Miller, George Miller, Mimi Mitz, Sheryl Noethe, Janice Nugent, Bob Rajala, Cathy Rase, Wendy Rigoni, Connie Sillars, Tim Sullivan, Frank Truax, Wayne Welch, Shannon Williams. Beverly Chin arranged many of these contacts. *Tucson:* Marvin Diogenes, Theresa Enos, Virginia Griffiths, Susan Roberts, Vicki Stein, Hector Tahu. And thanks to John Warnock for maps and streets. *Chapter Ten:* John Appleby, Wendy Aronoff, Jim Barstow, Loretta Brady, Jean Carr, Joseph Check, Kathy Cocetti, Neil Cross, Kathleen Cushman, Dottie Davis, Alyne Decoteau, Susan Dreyer, Pat Farrell, Steve Ferris, Lisa Fishburn, Diane Fitzhugh, Edorah Frazer, Mark Friend, Erik German, Robert Glaser, Dick Hansen, Omar and Emma Hazel, Simon Hole, Lisa Herndon, Emma Kettenring, Joan

Kluck, Judy Kurtz, Chris Louth, Laura Laughlin, Diana Marino, Hilary Masters, Laura Maxwell, Anne McShane, Paula Milano, Rosemarie Montgomery, Peggy Moore, Leah Rugen, Elaina Satti, Fred Schwarzbach, Peggy Silva, Elaine Simon, Kris Stanley, Leatha Swinehart, Sarah Thompson, Arlyn Uhrmacher, Pete VanderWegen, Nate Walcott, Katy Williams, Randy Wisehart. In Wapato, Lincoln, and Providence, particular acknowledgment to Beverly Chin, Scott Dolquist, and Sue Rigdon; Jessie Cherry and Don Ernst; and Grace McEntee and Sara Tortora. Ellen Cushman was a great help throughout this chapter.

For gas, food, lodging: Bill Ayers, Norm Bergman, John and Judy Connor, Matt, Madeline, Robby, and Elise Contreras, Jim Daniels and Kristin Kovacic, Theresa Enos, Janet Fortune, Michael and Edda Katz, Ken Lincoln, Deborah Meier, Terry and Percy Piestewa, Bud Reynolds, Patty Reynolds, Bruce Rodgers, Lois Rodgers, Jacque and Neil Rogers, Mark and Jane Weiss, Stephen Witte. Thanks for the warm meals, the good talk, the comfort of someone's home.

Ruth Glendinning prepared the manuscript, commenting, praising, criticizing. She gave considerable intelligence and care to *Possible Lives.* Kelly Besser, Lora Cowan, Karen Reed, and Amanda Walzer provided valuable research assistance, and Carol Allan assisted with typing. Thanks, too, for last-minute help to Brenda Thomas and the good people at the Communications Processing Center at UCLA and to Frances Ng for making sense of the end notes. At the final stage, Chris Coffin, Bob Overholtzer, Dorothy Henderson, Becky Saikia-Wilson, and Lori Galvin saw the book through production, gracefully under pressure.

During the early phases of this work, I was involved in another project with Glynda Hull, sponsored by the Spencer Foundation. The book that would become *Possible Lives* benefited in multiple ways from that support and conversation. During the last year of travel and writing, I received generous, encouraging support from the Research Foundation of The National Council of Teachers of English and from the John Simon Guggenheim Memorial Foundation.

There is, in our time, a body of hopeful work that gives testament to what schools can do. The briefest sketch would include the "effective schools" research of Ronald Edmonds, Wilbur Brookover, and others, the efforts of James Comer in New Haven and beyond, Henry Levin's "accelerated schools," and Theodore Sizer and the Coalition of Essential Schools. There are Vivian Paley's wonderful books, Maxine Greene's moral vision, Sara Lawrence Lightfoot's *The Good High School,* and George Wood's *Schools That Work.* This book benefits from that tradition.

In writing *Possible Lives,* I found myself at various junctures in composing being drawn to certain books, some about schools, some not, books that helped me think about public education and democratic life. Sometimes they lent specific material — of the sort acknowledged in the end notes — but sometimes they influenced more by their mood and spirit, sitting on the night stand, kept close by on my writing desk. I'm sure I'm forgetting some, but as I look back, I honor: Ira Katznelson and Margaret Weir's *Schooling for All: Class, Race, and the Decline of the Democratic Ideal,* Michael B. Katz's *The Undeserving Poor: From the War on Poverty to the War on Welfare,* David Tyack and Larry Cuban's *Tinkering Toward Utopia: A Century of Public School Reform,* William Least Heat-Moon's *Blue Highways: A Journey into America,* John Dewey's *Experience and Education,* and Maxine Greene's *The Dialectic of Freedom.* I am thankful for the Catholic bishop's pastoral letter *Economic Justice For All,* for Nancy Hoffman's *Woman's "True" Profession: Voices from the History of Teaching,* Septima Clark's *Ready from Within,* Myles Horton's *The Long Haul,* and Leonard Covello's *The Heart Is the Teacher.* And, toward the end, there was Patricia Williams's *The Alchemy of Race and Rights,* Jane Jacobs's *The Death and Life of Great American Cities,* Robert D. Putnam's *Making Democracy Work: Civic Traditions in Modern Italy,* and Anne Whiston Spirn's, *The Granite Garden: Urban Nature and Human Design.* It is my good fortune that these people thought and wrote so well.

41 - Importance of interdisciplinarity

53 Reason for crisis in our schools

56 - Importance of teaching

77 Saving an academic life

79 - Power of participation

81 - Importance of uni

86 - Ideal training for elementary school teachers

87 - Nature of caring in a teacher

88 - Teaching as a means of effecting social change

90 - Value of belief in potential

91 -